CW01209011

Deborah and the War of the Tanks, 1917

To my wife Kim

Who joined me on this journey

Deborah and the War of the Tanks, 1917

John A. Taylor

CAMBRESIS 14-18
www.tank-cambrai.com

Pen & Sword
MILITARY

First published in Great Britain in 2016 by
Pen & Sword Military
an imprint of
Pen & Sword Books Ltd
47 Church Street
Barnsley
South Yorkshire
S70 2AS

Copyright © John A. Taylor 2016

ISBN 978 1 47384 834 4

The right of John A. Taylor to be identified as the Author of this Work has been asserted by him in accordance with the Copyright, Designs and Patents Act 1988.

A CIP catalogue record for this book is available from the British Library

All rights reserved. No part of this book may be reproduced or transmitted in any form or by any means, electronic or mechanical including photocopying, recording or by any information storage and retrieval system, without permission from the Publisher in writing.

Typeset in Ehrhardt by
Mac Style Ltd, Bridlington, East Yorkshire
Printed and bound in the UK by CPI Group (UK) Ltd,
Croydon, CR0 4YY

Pen & Sword Books Ltd incorporates the imprints of Pen & Sword Archaeology, Atlas, Aviation, Battleground, Discovery, Family History, History, Maritime, Military, Naval, Politics, Railways, Select, Transport, True Crime, and Fiction, Frontline Books, Leo Cooper, Praetorian Press, Seaforth Publishing and Wharncliffe.

For a complete list of Pen & Sword titles please contact
PEN & SWORD BOOKS LIMITED
47 Church Street, Barnsley, South Yorkshire, S70 2AS, England
E-mail: enquiries@pen-and-sword.co.uk
Website: www.pen-and-sword.co.uk

Contents

List of Plates vii
List of Maps viii
Acknowledgments x
Foreword xii
Author's Notes xvi

PART I: INTO THE SALIENT 1

Chapter 1	A Vision of the World's End	3
Chapter 2	Temporary Gentlemen	12
Chapter 3	A Very Fine Lot Indeed	19
Chapter 4	*Dracula*'s Fate	25
Chapter 5	Of Knaves and Jokers	29
Chapter 6	The Sword of Deborah	35
Chapter 7	In Honour Bound	40

PART II: THE BATTLE OF PASSCHENDAELE 47

Chapter 8	Ray of Sunshine	49
Chapter 9	Crossing the Canal	56
Chapter 10	Into the Pillar of Fire	62
Chapter 11	*Deborah*, the Dead Man and the Drummer	72
Chapter 12	Failure is an Orphan	80
Chapter 13	The Dead Never Stirred	85
Chapter 14	The Bogs of Passchendaele	90

PART III: GATHERING FORCES 97

Chapter 15	The Coming of Frank Heap	98
Chapter 16	Heap's Progress	104
Chapter 17	'The Best Company of the Best Battalion'	111
Chapter 18	Redundant Oddments	116
Chapter 19	Out of the Salient	122
Chapter 20	High Days and Highlanders	126

PART IV: THE BATTLE OF CAMBRAI		131
Chapter 21	Into Hiding	133
Chapter 22	On the Silent Front	138
Chapter 23	'Things Fall Apart'	145
Chapter 24	To Shake Mightily the Earth	154
Chapter 25	'Now For It!'	163
Chapter 26	Till the Last Man	169
PART V: BEYOND THE GRAND RAVINE		179
Chapter 27	A Mountain to Climb	180
Chapter 28	The Crack of Doom	185
Chapter 29	Into the Hurricane	190
Chapter 30	Green Fields Beyond	198
Chapter 31	Like a Boar at Bay	208
Chapter 32	A Bitter Evening	217
Chapter 33	The Chance Was Gone	223
PART VI: ACROSS THE THRESHOLD		233
Chapter 34	Sticking to their Guns	234
Chapter 35	'The Fates Fought Against Us'	241
Chapter 36	A Peaceful, Unexceptional Place	247
Chapter 37	Varied Fortunes	254
Chapter 38	Rosemary for Remembrance	260
Chapter 39	Weapon of Friendship	266

Appendix A: Order of Battle of D Battalion Tank Corps, and associated infantry and tank units, at Battle of Passchendaele (22 August 1917)   275

Appendix B: Order of Battle of British and German units at Flesquières in Battle of Cambrai (20 November 1917)   276

Appendix C: Order of Battle of D Battalion Tank Corps at Battle of Cambrai (20 November 1917)   277

Notes   278
Sources   297
Index   299

List of Plates

Deborah in German hands in April 1918. *Photograph from Jean Luc Caudron*
Germans inspecting the wreckage of *Deborah*. *Photograph from Philippe Gorczynski*
Willie Anthony and friends at Flesquières, 16 March 1919. *Photograph from the Anthony family*
The same view today.
'Uriah's bus'. *Photograph from the Heap family*
'Burying of a tank'. *Photograph from Tank Museum*
Second Lieutenant George Macdonald and brother officers. *Photograph from Catherine Piper*
Aerial photo of battlefield after the attack of 22 August 1917. *Photographs © Royal Museum of the Army and of Military History (Nr Inv KLM-MRA 201530003 & 20608-sint-juliaan)*
Second Lieutenant Frank Heap. *Photograph from the Heap family*
Boy soldiers. *Photograph from the Heap family*
Gunner George Foot. *Photograph from Charles Foot*
Gunner Fred Tipping. *Photograph from Mike Tipping*
Gunner William Galway. *Photograph from the Galway family*
Gunner Joseph Cheverton. *Photograph from the Summers family*
Cheverton's fiancée Florrie Coote. *Photograph from Derek Leland*
Lance-Corporal David 'Bert' Marsden. *Photograph from David Melliar-Smith*
Colonel Christopher Baker-Carr. *Photograph from Sue Peck*
Lieutenant-Colonel William Kyngdon. *Photograph from* Pemba, The Spice Island of Zanzibar, *by Captain John Craster*
Major R.O.C. Ward. *Photograph from Simon Ward*
Captain Graeme Nixon and Lieutenant Alfred Enoch. *Photograph from Russell Enoch*
Lieutenant Enoch outside a captured German dugout. *Photograph from Russell Enoch*
Officers from No. 12 Company. *Photograph from Russell Enoch*
James Macintosh. *Photograph from John Macintosh*
Major William Watson. *Photograph from William Watson*
Major Watson's officers at La Lovie. *Photograph from Imperial War Museum (Q 2898)*
Aerial photo of Flesquières. *Photograph from National Archives*
Prisoners taken before Cambrai.
Tanks from D and C Battalions on trains. *Photograph from Imperial War Museum (detail from Q 46940)*
Painting by Sergeant Claude Rowberry. *Photograph from Royal Tank Regiment*
A German's soldier's view of the fighting at Flesquières.
Postcard of the legendary lone gunner.
German artist's impression of the battle at Flesquières.
Deborah emerges from the ground in November 1998. *Photograph from Philippe Gorczynski*
Descendants of Deborah's crew meet in 2009. *Photograph from Press Association*
Deborah today. Photograph from *Nord Tourisme*

List of Maps

1. British sectors of the Western Front	ix
2. Into the Salient	2
3. Attack by D Battalion on 22 August 1917	48
4. Actions by D Battalion in the Ypres Salient 1917	122
5. Into Hiding	132
6. The start of the attack on Flesquières, 20 November 1917	155
(a) Relief map with height in metres	156
(b) German units, showing sector held by 84th Infantry Regiment	156
(c) Artillery barrage	157
(d) Overview of attack on the Hindenburg Line at Cambrai	157
7. Flesquières on the evening of 20 November 1917	210
(a) Situation on the evening of 20 November 1917	211
8. Situation at the end of the Battle of Cambrai	230

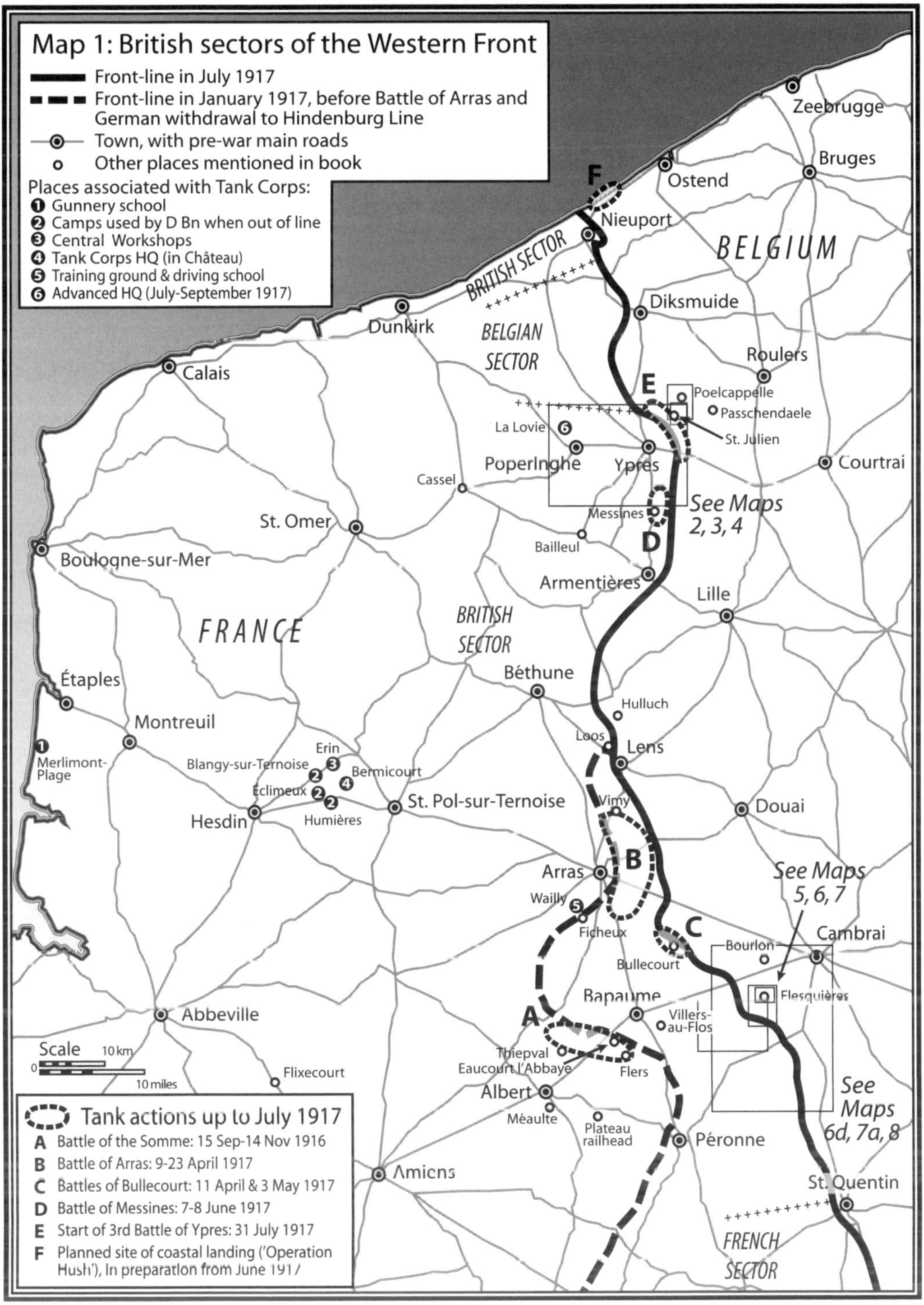

Map 1: British sectors of the Western Front
Front-line in July 1917
Front-line in January 1917, before Battle of Arras and German withdrawal to Hindenburg Line
Town, with pre-war main roads
Other places mentioned in book
Places associated with Tank Corps:
1 Gunnery school
2 Camps used by D Bn when out of line
3 Central Workshops
4 Tank Corps HQ (in Château)
5 Training ground & driving school
6 Advanced HQ (July-September 1917)
Zeebrugge
Bruges
Ostend
Nieuport
BELGIUM
BRITISH SECTOR
Diksmuide
Dunkirk
BELGIAN SECTOR
Roulers
Calais
Poelcappelle
Passchendaele
St. Julien
La Lovie
Poperinghe
Ypres
Courtrai
Cassel
Messines
See Maps 2, 3, 4
St. Omer
Bailleul
Boulogne-sur-Mer
Armentières
Lille
FRANCE
BRITISH SECTOR
Béthune
Étaples
Hulluch
Montreuil
Loos
Lens
Erin
Merlimont-Plage
Blangy-sur-Ternoise
Bermicourt
Eclimeux
Humières
St. Pol-sur-Ternoise
Hesdin
Vimy
Douai
Arras
See Maps 5, 6, 7
Wailly
Ficheux
Cambrai
Bourlon
Bullecourt
Bapaume
Flesquières
Abbeville
Villers-au-Flos
Thiepval
Eaucourt l'Abbaye
Flers
Scale
10 km
10 miles
Flixecourt
Albert
See Maps 6d, 7a, 8
Méaulte
Plateau railhead
Péronne
Amiens
St. Quentin
FRENCH SECTOR
Tank actions up to July 1917
A Battle of the Somme: 15 Sep-14 Nov 1916
B Battle of Arras: 9-23 April 1917
C Battles of Bullecourt: 11 April & 3 May 1917
D Battle of Messines: 7-8 June 1917
E Start of 3rd Battle of Ypres: 31 July 1917
F Planned site of coastal landing ('Operation Hush'), In preparation from June 1917

Acknowledgments

This book tells the story of D51 *Deborah*, a First World War tank which returned from the grave and is now preserved in France as a memorial to the men who fought in her. The task of discovering and preserving *Deborah* was led by Philippe Gorczynski, an authority on the Battle of Cambrai who combines his passion for history with the business of running a hotel in the town. In the subsequent project to unearth her human and military history, he has been supported by a small and equally passionate group of enthusiasts based in the UK.

This book therefore represents the fruits of nine years' research by a dedicated team that includes Vince McGarry, a tireless investigator whose journalistic skills have enabled us to track down a large number of families connected with D and E Battalions of the Tank Corps, and who provided invaluable support in the preparation of this book; Rob Kirk, another ex-journalist who originally brought the team together and has acted as co-ordinator and 'master of ceremonies' for the project; and Alan Hawkins, a genealogist whose expertise at untangling family trees has proved crucial in our research. Their wives Sandrine Gorczynski, Karen McGarry, Elaine Kirk and Margaret Hawkins, and my own wife Kim Badland, have also been active and enthusiastic supporters of the project from the start.

As well as these core members of 'Team Deborah', many others have provided support, notably David Fletcher, Stuart Wheeler, Janice Tait and their colleagues at the Tank Museum in Bovington; Geoffrey Vesey Holt, the historian of the Royal Tank Regiment; and Johan and Luc Vanbeselaere, Dirk Vinck and their friends based in Poelkapelle in Belgium. Special thanks are also due to Lieutenant-Colonel Stephen May and Colonel John Longman for permission to reproduce a painting by Sergeant Claude Rowberry owned by the Royal Tank Regiment; to Dan Snow for his great support; to Jean Luc Caudron for permission to include his photograph of *Deborah* in German hands; to Iona Murray, an archaeologist at Historic Scotland who passed on vital eyewitness evidence from her great-grandfather; to Rosemary O'Neill at Christchurch City Libraries; to historians Gareth Davies, Gwyn Evans, Jean-Luc Gibot, Nigel Henderson, Nigel Jones and Stephen Pope who have generously shared their advice and research; and to Heidi Adler-Schrade, Norbert Schnitzler and Carina Syring for their help with the German translations.

In addition, we have relied on the information and support provided by members of more than 100 families whose ancestors fought in the tanks of D and E Battalions, or were otherwise involved in the Battles of Passchendaele and Cambrai, notably Mary Baker-Carr and Tony Rundell; Julian and Nicola Bion; Roderick and David Bullock; Jim Christie; Paddy Clark; Dr Mary Coghlan and Noel Coghlan; Canon Ian Cohen; Sylvia and Stephanie Collinson-Cooper; Jenny and John Dodd; Brigadier Ben Edwards OBE; Russell and Etheline Enoch; Charles Foot; Stewart Galway; Chris and Mike Head; Will, Peter, Tim, Paul and John Heap; Rob and Sue Henshall; Deborah Howard; Derek Leland; Charles and Ken Macdonald; John Macintosh; Ian MacNiven and Peggy L. Fox; David Melliar-Smith and Deborah Palmer; Sue Peck; Anna Petrou; Alison and Catherine Piper; Corinna Robertson; Joyce and Bob Robinson; Paul Russell; Jean Smith; Doris and John Summers; Mike Tipping; Peggie Trei; Basil Vose; Simon Ward; William and Helena Watson; Ted Wenger; Derek White; Jim Yates; and others too numerous to thank by name.

Despite the involvement and support of so many people, the opinions and interpretations in this book are mine alone, and I take full responsibility for them, and for any errors that may have occurred.

In terms of written records, we have drawn on the rich resources of the National Archives in Kew, and many other collections including the Tank Museum, the Imperial War Museum, the National Army Museum, the Liddell Hart Centre for Military Archives, the Liddle Collection, the London Library and the British Library, as well as the archives of various regiments, sports clubs, schools and colleges. In France we have drawn on the collection of Philippe Gorczynski, the archives of the Historial de la Grande Guerre at Péronne, and the letters owned by Mme Bacquet in Cambrai; and in Germany, on the official holdings of the Militärarchiv at Freiburg im Breisgau and the Hauptstaatsarchiv in Stuttgart. The Great War Forum and Landships Forum have provided a constant source of knowledge and expertise.

The final key component in our research has been the largest, but largely hidden, archive of Great War material, namely the documents, photographs, artefacts and memories preserved by the many families who we have contacted, and which they have shared freely and selflessly with us.

This book is therefore a testament to the knowledge and skills of a large number of people, and to the enduring power of *Deborah* as a unique relic of a war that continues to haunt our memories and imaginations.

Foreword

Tank commander's impressions of the attack at Cambrai, 20 November 1917

Action stations. Everyone inside – driver and officer side by side, front flaps half open – four gunners standing by, closed down – infantry runner sitting on oil container with back to officer – [carrier] pigeons in basket stowed under one sponson [i.e. gun housing on side of tank].

Engine hot, probably been running for some hours; most engines run better once they have boiled, very difficult to guarantee engine would restart if stopped. Not advisable to throttle down too much as sheets of red flame crack out of exhaust pipe or through joints in pipe on roof. If engine kept running too fast exhaust pipes glow red.

Once doors closed tank almost in darkness – similar to overhead yellow London fog – four festoon lamps illuminate interior dimly – used sparingly as visible from outside. Rear door left ajar as long as possible.

Zero hour: comparative silence broken quite suddenly by crash of guns fired simultaneously, whistle and whine of shells overhead, a pause – whole of far side of No Man's Land lit up in dawn light – smoke everywhere – company commander comes to front and shouts signal to start.

Driver hammers one side of engine casing, holds up one finger, gearsman gets first gear, officer hammers other side, same procedure, tank lurches forward.

Other tanks dimly seen on left and right – going good – occasional shell-hole has to be crossed, each time tank's nose dips ammunition boxes, odd tools, etc. slide forward and then backwards with metallic crashes. Gearsmen and gunners hang on. Inside of tank getting hotter. Harsh tapping outside tank indicates hostile M.G. [i.e. machine-gun] fire.

Black mass three feet high and as far as the eye can see appears in growing light – German wire. Tank goes up to it – looks terribly formidable – will it catch in tracks and wind round and round tank turning it into a cocoon, or will it spring up behind again and prevent infantry following? Glance through back shows broad lane through wire along which packets of infantry are following. Second belt rather less thick – front flaps opened to facilitate driving.

Sudden tapping on port side of tank – gunner holds hand up, cut in many places with splash and flake [i.e. flying fragments of metal caused by bullets hitting tank]. Burst of M.G. fire had hit tank at spot where sponson turret joins tank and had ripped away felt packing, hitting gunner in hand – tank swung 10 degrees – all ports closed down.

Vision of crew now restricted to: –

    Driver – a restricted view to the front through eight small holes drilled close together. A glance at the ground under the front horns of the tank through the front flap which has been left ajar.

Officer – as for driver, in addition a thin periscope has been pushed through the top which does give an all-round view.

Gunners – glass prisms. A glance through them gives a view to the immediate front only of a few yards of strange, green-coloured stygian gloom. An occasional spurt of earth indicates a shell burst.

Gearsmen – nothing.

The bell in the tank clangs, having been pulled by infantry N.C.O. at rear who indicates position of German post. Quickest method of directing fire: swing tank to bring two side guns onto target and indicate to gunners by putting burst from front gun near hostile post.

Infantry advancing very slowly – difficult to see what is holding them up.

Fire becoming intense. Tank on right flank stops and black smoke comes out.

Same gunner hit again with splash. All vizors worn – these are steel masks with slits for eyes and chain [mail] attached covering mouth and throat – whole fixed by tape round back of head.

Sweat causes tapes to slip, completely blinding crew – vizors abandoned.

Bullet enters tank like angry bee. No damage.

Hostile fire intense – splash flying all round – cannot be heard in noise, but suddenly dents appear in ammunition boxes – pieces of exhaust flake off as if torn off by invisible hand. Port unditching rail is hanging down in front of tank, cut through by M.G. fire.

Cannot locate M.G's – only just possible to see gearsman inside through smoke and fumes.

Snipers in long grass cannot be seen – firing at loopholes – two gunners hit in hand through gun port, one whilst firing and the other trying to change [ammunition] drum. Tank turned in attempt to locate enemy. Only one M.G. seen and put out of action.

Front gun [of tank] out of action – unable to withdraw it – subsequently found M.G. fire had split casing and splayed the end of Lewis gun like discarded cigarette end.

M.G. fire intensive – driver's flap partially cut through and hanging at an angle of 20 degrees. Front plates of tank hot. Petrol getting short, no other tanks near – impossible to report except by pigeon. Infantry in shell holes unable to advance.[1]

* * *

These were the vivid recollections of Second Lieutenant Horace Birks as he took his tank into action on 20 November 1917, in what would be one of the defining battles of the First World War, and perhaps of any modern war. During the attack Birks was only dimly aware of the other tanks advancing around him, but among them he could easily have caught a glimpse of D51 *Deborah*, the principal subject of this story. If so there would have been little to distinguish her, for *Deborah* was in a sense ordinary – just one of nearly 380 British fighting tanks that attacked the strongly-held German positions before the French town of Cambrai a century ago. In another sense, though, she is unique: for *Deborah* is thought to be the only one of those tanks still in existence, having been buried on the battlefield through a quirk of fate, and reclaimed through a miracle of archaeology.

This book therefore tells the story of a machine, or rather of two machines, since a previous tank bore the same crew number D51, and is therefore likely (since this was the normal practice) to have had the same name. But it is also predominantly a human story, of the men who fought inside both tanks, of the men who fought alongside them, and the men who fought against them. The intention here is not to give a detailed account of the development of the tank, nor of the great battles of Passchendaele in which the first D51 took part, or Cambrai in which the second played a heroic role. Instead this is unashamedly a work of micro-history, written in the belief that by studying the individual and the particular, one can come to a more complete understanding of the whole.

Of course there are enormous challenges in this approach, in seeking to unravel a single thread from the tapestry of the past. Sometimes we catch only brief glimpses of *Deborah* through a dim and distorted prism, like those used by the gunners in Birks' tank. But there are other occasions when the searchlight is turned on her, and we can pick her out clearly amid the smoke and din of battle. And at the end of the story there is always the mute hulk of *Deborah* herself, preserved for decades in the mud of the battlefield, and now on display as a permanent memorial to the Battle of Cambrai.

In a sense, this is a story that subverts much of what we know, or think we know, about the First World War, with its inexorable tide of tragedy sweeping the British people from Sarajevo to the Cenotaph by way of the Somme, from the glorious patriotism of Rupert Brooke to the war-weariness of Wilfred Owen. We often think of the Germans as fighting a 'cleverer' war – an attitude identified by one future tank officer, William Watson, while home after being wounded in 1915: 'In our suburb it is firmly believed that the Germans can detach a million from one front, throw it against another, wipe up the Serbians, land in Syria, and return before the absence has been noticed. Everything English is good, but silly: everything German is wicked, but wise.'[2]

Yet despite this, the much-derided 'donkeys' of the British General Staff – led by Sir Douglas Haig, who was an enthusiastic advocate of tanks from the start – somehow managed to foster the creation, development and increasingly effective use of a revolutionary weapon that has played a decisive role in every conventional war since, from the Blitzkrieg to Desert Storm. It is true that the Germans, who had settled into a generally defensive war on the Western Front, had a less obvious need to develop tanks than the British and French, but by the time they recognized their potential and produced their own clumsy counterpart, they had fallen so far behind in the race that they were unable to catch up, while the British Mark V tank powered ahead to make a crucial contribution to victory in the battles of 1918.

Even the Germans admitted the enormity of the coup that was delivered at Cambrai. In the words of one officer who was captured in the battle: 'Here [our High Command] suffered a terrible shock, just like the one experienced by the Romans when Hannibal and his elephants appeared in Italy after going through Spain and Gaul and across the Alps. What the elephants of Carthage were to the legions of Rome, so to a devastating degree were the English tank squadrons to the German troops – a *tour de force* of English military engineering.'[3]

On a darker note, this book also describes two exceptional cases in which details of planned tank attacks were given away to the enemy by British prisoners. The intention here is not to condemn, but rather to explore the moral complexities of war and the personal dilemmas faced by ordinary soldiers, and the potentially deadly consequences of their actions.

Above all, therefore, it is important to approach this story with an open mind, to set aside our preconceptions about the Great War, and to experience it as the men themselves did – not with hindsight and a sense of inevitability, but as a series of incidents and events that contributed to their own unfolding experience, and enabled them, and us, finally, to achieve a kind of understanding.

In the words of the author Henry Williamson, recalling his own military service fifty years later: 'The war was not all evil. We learned something in those days, although things went wrong later on. We just hadn't the wider vision then that we have now, I suppose.'[4]

Author's Notes

In many cases, passages quoted from books and other documents have been edited to substitute lower case for upper case letters (e.g. the word 'tank' was commonly written 'Tank'), and to simplify or clarify punctuation. Tank names have been italicised.

The village of Flesquières was frequently misspelled at the time (the accent proving a particular bugbear), and in general I have replicated the spelling used in the original documents. See also the note below on the spelling of Belgian place-names.

As far as possible, an individual's rank is shown at the time of the events in question, or at the time he wrote a book or article (which may result in different ranks being shown for the same person).

In general, the quotes from German books have been quite freely translated to give a sense of the original meaning. The writers were frequently imprecise about the nationality of their enemies (they often used 'English' to mean 'British', and described Scottish troops as 'English' or even 'Canadian'). In these cases, the original terms have been followed in the translation.

In some cases, longer extracts and copies of original documents are shown on the website supporting this book: www.deborah-tank.co.uk

Every effort has been made to contact copyright holders for permission to use material, and anyone with a potential concern about this is requested to contact the publisher.

Abbreviations

Bn	Battalion
CWGC	Commonwealth War Graves Commission
HQ	Headquarters
ICRC	International Committee of the Red Cross
IWM	Imperial War Museum
NA	National Archives

PART I
INTO THE SALIENT

Map 2: Into the Salient

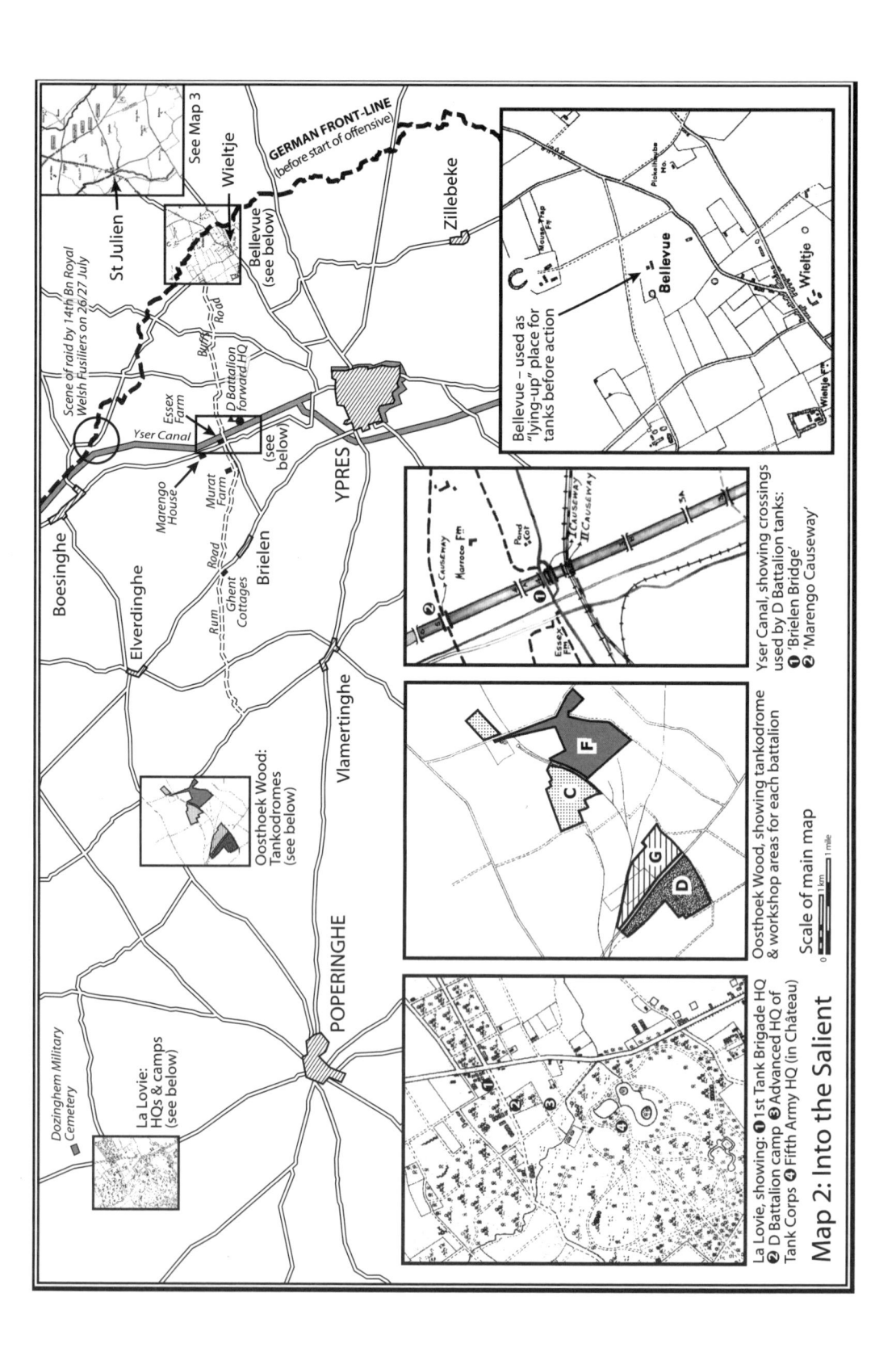

CHAPTER 1

A Vision of the World's End

Through the windows of Johan's car, the road north of Poperinge[1] unfolds, flat and featureless, through a drab Belgian landscape of muddy fields and dank woods. It is only when he switches on his laptop computer, linked to a GPS satellite tracking system and loaded with the meticulous trench maps of the First World War, that the area suddenly springs into long-forgotten life. As we gaze out of the car through the drizzle, each empty field is filled with the ghostly outlines of huts, sheds and hangars – an extraordinary profusion of camps, hospitals, gun emplacements and supply dumps, now swept away like the remains of an ancient civilisation.

But history pressed hard when it wrote on these pages, and although the words have long been erased, their imprint still remains. Down a muddy track, swallowed up by woods, lies the site of the enormous Dozinghem dressing station, named in faux-Flemish style like its fellows, Bandaghem and Mendinghem (this was to have been called Endinghem, but officialdom felt that was going beyond a joke).[2] Here at least there is a tangible reminder of the past, for although the wards and operating theatres are long gone with their reek of anaesthetic and disinfectant, some of the patients and staff remain – more than 3,000 men whose white headstones fill the cemetery beneath the Cross of Sacrifice.

Standing there in the silence, it seems incredible that this whole region once teemed with activity. Very little actual fighting took place here, but for four years this was the rear area and support zone which provided for the needs of the British and allied armies during some of the greatest battles in their history. Here were the camps where the troops rested before going up the line and recovered on their return; the workshops and dumps where their food and ammunition were stored; the hospitals where their wounds were treated; and for some, the cemeteries where their bodies were buried.

Opposite: Map 2 shows places associated with D Battalion during the Third Battle of Ypres (July–October 1917). French place-names are shown, as these were generally used by the British Army at the time.

To the left is the town of Poperinghe, with La Lovie Château to the north and the camp which was home to D Battalion throughout the campaign. The tankodrome and workshops were in Oosthoek Wood, and the areas allocated to four tank battalions are shown (E Battalion also subsequently moved into the wood).

The crew of D51 left here for their first action on 19 August, moving along a supply route called Rum Road to spend the night at Murat Farm before reaching the Yser Canal north of Ypres. A number of crossing-points were used by tanks, including Bridge 4 ('Brielen Bridge') beside Essex Farm and 'Marengo Causeway' to the north. This brought them into the Ypres Salient, indicated by a thick dotted line showing the German positions in July 1917 (i.e. before the start of the offensive). By August the Germans had been driven back beyond St Julien, and after crossing the canal, the tanks moved along a supply route called Buffs Road to reach the former farm of Bellevue near the original German front-line. Here they prepared for their attack.

Although it lay well behind the front line, the area was not entirely safe, for aerodromes and gun batteries were located here and the area offered many targets for German artillery and bomber aircraft; but the destruction was sporadic rather than systematic, and was no more than an irritation for anyone who had been to the front itself.

One Tank Corps officer who arrived here in the summer of 1917 likened the area to 'a disturbed ant-heap ... The countryside was "stiff" with light railways, enormous dumps, fresh sidings, innumerable gun-pits, new roads, enlarged camps.'[3] Now a curving hedge across a field of maize is all that remains to mark the line of a railway that once transported the tanks into the battle zone, and their destination, Oosthoek Wood, where hundreds of tanks were hidden in preparation for the offensive, is a nature reserve called Galgebossen and stands, dripping and deserted, in the autumn rain. A couple of miles away, the woodland at De Lovie, where the tank crews were encamped throughout the summer and autumn of 1917, provides the setting for a smart residential centre for children with special needs, but at the time of our visit, the imposing château at its heart stood grey and empty, awaiting restoration and brooding on its glorious past.

Leaving Dozinghem Military Cemetery, my guide, Johan Vanbeselaere – who was born in the area and is an expert on its tank battles – turns his car eastwards, and before long our way is blocked by a dark expanse of water. This is the Ieper-Ijzer (or Ypres-Yser) Canal, now an idle waterway lined with industrial estates and frequented by joggers and ducks; but for the British troops it was a kind of River Styx, a symbolic barrier that separated a reasonable chance of life from an unreasonable risk of death. A rum ration was issued before the men went into action, and one tank commander recalled: 'The mess had already dubbed rum as "canal-crosser", because it was supposed to give you sufficient courage to cross the Ypres Canal! The name stuck to it ever afterwards.'[4] Despite this, he added sixty years later: 'Even now the menacing streets of Ypres and this nightmare Canal can return to me and leave a stain of foreboding on the brightest day.'[5]

There is nothing but the hum of traffic to be heard here now, but for years this place was rarely free from the distant rumble of gunfire, and crossing the canal represented the rite of passage into the Ypres Salient, a killing field where the British and French trenches bulged outwards into the German lines, and where the armies were engaged in a protracted struggle over a few square miles of sodden farmland.

It was here that the opposing front lines became fixed after the thrust and parry of the first months of the war evolved into a 'race to the sea', in which the great columns of marching men and horse-drawn transport sought to outflank each other, before digging in to create the trench systems that famously stretched from Switzerland to the sea, and would become their home for the next four years. The British recognized Ypres as a vital hub for communications throughout Belgium and northern France, and were determined to hold it at all costs. It was here, in late 1914, that one of the first great set-piece battles of the war was fought, the cloth-capped boys of the old brigade and their French and Belgian allies against the pickelhaubed flower of German youth, musketry against machine guns, until the First Battle of Ypres drew to an inconclusive end and the trench-lines stagnated with the coming of winter. To the British, the battle represented the death of the BEF, because so many men were killed from the small standing army that originally made up the British Expeditionary Force. To the Germans, the deaths of so many of their young recruits meant the battle became known as 'Kindermord', the massacre of the innocents.

The Allied armies found themselves holding a low-lying position surrounded on three sides by hills that were so low as to be almost indiscernible, but which nevertheless gave the enemy a natural vantage-point which they exploited to the full. In April 1915 the Germans launched a fresh offensive in the Salient which became known as the Second Battle of Ypres, and this time the full ghastliness of industrial warfare was unleashed, including the first use of poison gas. But even this failed to break the stalemate, and although the allies were pushed back, the Salient held and the trench-lines atrophied again as the fighting spiralled away to fresh vortices at Verdun and the Somme.

And so it remained until 1917, with the two opposing sides clinging to their positions while Ypres itself, the once prosperous medieval township at the heart of the Salient, was shelled so relentlessly that it became, in the words of one journalist, 'like a ghost city in a vision of the world's end'.[6] Plans for a major Allied offensive here began to coalesce early in that year, spurred on by the prospect of sweeping the Germans out of the Channel ports which provided a base for their increasingly effective U-boat attacks on shipping. The British commander-in-chief, Sir Douglas Haig, also believed that the German army had been dangerously weakened, and that a successful push in Flanders could trigger its collapse; while there was an urgent need to relieve pressure on the French armies, whose morale had been shattered by the disastrous Nivelle offensive in April.

Hopes of a breakthrough were encouraged by a successful attack at Messines in June 1917, in which British, Australian and New Zealand troops swept the Germans from a ridge south of Ypres that had given them a crucial position overlooking the Salient. This had been achieved with the aid of nineteen enormous mines buried under the German positions, whose simultaneous detonation dealt a shattering blow to the defenders, and by a creeping artillery barrage that sheltered the attackers as they advanced across No Man's Land.

Tanks, which had first gone into action only nine months before, were now being used in increasing numbers, and a total of seventy-two were allocated to the attack at Messines where they made a useful, though hardly decisive, contribution to victory. As planning went ahead for the much larger offensive in the Salient, there were some who argued that the time had come to apply an entirely new doctrine of warfare, using tanks in place of the protracted artillery barrage that had become the accepted precursor of an attack.

Lieutenant-Colonel Giffard Martel, then a staff officer at Tank Corps headquarters, was one of those who believed this approach might have worked:

> Before the eight days' preliminary bombardment for the battle had started the ground was comparatively dry, and although this low-lying land was not the most suitable for tanks, yet it is reasonably certain that a surprise attack could have been launched with only a very short preliminary bombardment of a few minutes, and that the tanks would have led the infantry successfully on to the Passchendaele ridge on the first day of the attack. This proposal was made by the Tank Corps ...; but against this was set the great success of Messines as an artillery battle. Those responsible for the third battle of Ypres argued that while they had the recent example of a great success at Messines by making full use of our superior artillery, why should they risk a novel method of attack involving considerable risk. The answer to this (though it is being wise after the event) is that an enemy is rarely caught napping twice running by the same trick, and that surprise is essential in war.[7]

With so much at stake, it would have taken a bold act of faith by the British General Staff to dispense with a prolonged bombardment and gamble on tanks to carry the day. All the evidence suggested that if things went well, tanks could provide valuable support for the infantry, but they were an unreliable weapon which might just as easily contribute nothing.

The tone had been set by the first-ever tank action on 15 September 1916, when a handful of machines crawled towards the German lines near the villages of Flers and Courcelette on the Somme. Despite the initial terror these monsters induced among the Germans, and the euphoria of a British media desperate for something to celebrate, the tanks had failed to achieve much of real military consequence. Although they were sometimes useful in subduing defenders and helping the infantry to gain their objectives, tanks also proved all too vulnerable to mechanical failure, to direct hits by artillery and sometimes even small-arms fire, and above all to sodden and uneven ground which tended to leave them either ditched in impassable obstacles, or 'bellied' and unable to move in the mud.

Although the tank commanders believed they could play a decisive role in the Third Battle of Ypres if they were allowed to lead the attack across unbroken terrain, it was also clear they would face an insuperable challenge if the low-lying ground had first been churned up by artillery fire. Brigadier-General Hugh Elles, the Tank Corps commander, warned that the chances of success for the tanks fell with every shell fired, and since more than four-and-a-quarter million of them were used in the preparatory and opening phases of the battle,[8] those chances now looked very slim indeed.

The challenge was spelled out dramatically by Colonel Christopher Baker-Carr, commander of 1st Tank Brigade which included D Battalion:

> If a careful search had been made from the English Channel to Switzerland, no more unsuitable spot could have been discovered ... Ypres itself at one time had been a seaport, and the drainage system, which had been instituted in order to render the land in the vicinity cultivable, had to be regulated with the utmost care ... For over two years this drainage system had, of necessity, been untended and, in addition to natural decay, had been largely destroyed by shell fire. The result was that many square miles of land consisted merely of a thin crust of soil, beneath which lay a bottomless sea of mud and water. Bad as it was in ordinary times, we knew that it would be a thousand-fold worse after the terrible preliminary bombardment which was now regarded as the indispensable forerunner of an attack.[9]

Nevertheless, such concerns were dismissed by General Headquarters (GHQ), which had incorporated tanks into its plans for the offensive. More than 130 machines were to be used in the initial push, which was eventually scheduled for 31 July 1917. This would make it the largest tank attack in British history, though the French had unleashed a similar number of tanks in their ill-fated assault on the Chemin des Dames ridge in April 1917. The results were hardly encouraging: their vehicles, smaller and lighter than the British equivalent, were devastated by German artillery fire and no fewer than seventy-six were put out of action without any gain whatsoever.

The foreboding felt by the tank crews as they prepared for their journey into the Salient was all the greater because they were clearly being tested not just by the enemy, but also by their own side. Many in the higher echelons of the British army were beginning to question whether tanks could ever live up to expectations, and the new Tank Corps found itself trapped in a situation that we have since come to characterize by the phrase Catch-22: if the tanks took no part in the coming battle they would be seen as superfluous and were likely to be done away with; but if they did take part, they were almost certain to fail.

* * *

As the dog days of July drew on, and whatever the uncertainty about their future, the men of D Battalion were swept up in the mounting frenzy of preparations for the big push, as they began the process of moving their great machines into position ready for the start of the battle.

The epicentre of this activity was Oosthoek Wood, a straggling expanse of trees covering several hundred acres which was to provide shelter for a number of tank battalions and their crews. Among them were D, E and G Battalions, constituting the 1st Brigade of a unit that was still known as the Machine Gun Corps (Heavy Branch) – a title that originally disguised its secret purpose, but was about to be replaced by a more transparent one. On 27 July, just before the battle began, the name was changed by Royal Warrant to the Tank Corps.

Since the end of June, men from the Royal Engineers' 184th Tunnelling Company had been at work in and around the wood, preparing a network of tracks, river crossings, shelters and encampments in readiness for the arrival of the tanks.[10] The complex was known as a 'tankodrome' – a coinage of the Great War that has not stood the test of time, unlike its counterpart, the aerodrome. Oosthoek Wood had been selected for this purpose because it lay more than three miles (or five kilometres) behind the front line, offering a compromise between access to the battlefront and protection from German artillery. It was served by a railway line which enabled the tanks to be brought in by train, with ramps for them to drive down from the flatbed rolling stock on which they travelled. The challenge of detraining an enormous tank with a few inches of clearance on either side was a daunting one for the drivers, the more so because they would have to be unloaded in darkness and camouflaged by daybreak to avoid the risk of observation by enemy aircraft.

The Royal Engineers had been harassed by shellfire almost since their arrival,[11] and Major William Watson, one of the company commanders in D Battalion of the Tank Corps, realized the danger when he reached Oosthoek Wood after a hot and dusty ride in early July to join his reconnaissance officer, Second Lieutenant Frederick King, known for obscure reasons as 'Jumbo'. Watson described the situation with characteristic wry humour: 'It was a part of the world which the German gunner found interesting. Jumbo was quite clear on the point, though Jumbo himself, revelling in the cool and shade of the woods after hot days forward on reconnaissance, did not turn a hair. The ramp and the northern edge of Oosthoek Wood were shelled nightly. There were two painfully fresh shell-holes in the middle of the area allotted to us, and "G" Battalion across the road were not sleeping at all ... Before I left I was told that a shell had dropped into "C" Battalion lines and nearly wiped out Battalion Headquarters.'[12] In fact the wood had been heavily shelled for several hours on 4 July, resulting in the deaths of six men from C Battalion and damaging three of their tanks. Their commander reported that 'owing to this contretemps, which it was thought likely might be frequently repeated during the next three weeks, it was decided to move the majority of the personnel of the camp to a more salubrious situation.'[13]

Meanwhile the rail timetable was fixed, and every evening trains pulled into the sidings at Oosthoek, each bearing an entire company of twelve fighting tanks and their crews. The trains were scheduled to arrive around 9.30 p.m., leaving a short summer's night for the tanks to be unloaded, driven into the shelter of the woods, and camouflaged before dawn. The first contingent from D Battalion arrived on 9 July,[14] and this included a Mark IV tank with the number D51, and probably the name *Deborah*: the new tank and her crew were on their way to war.

As they arrived in the so-called concentration area the men were acutely aware of the need for secrecy, and the orders signed by the adjutant Captain Fred Cozens stressed that 'companies will take great care in camouflaging the tanks <u>and covering up the tracks</u> made by the tanks when moving from the ramp to the tankodrome.'[15] The orders made it sound straightforward, but this was far from the case, as explained by Second Lieutenant Douglas Browne of G Battalion, who had arrived at Oosthoek Wood the day before:

> Parking tanks … among timber at night is always a noisy and trying operation, resembling in sound and destructiveness the gambols of a herd of inebriated elephants. The tank-driver, unaided, can see nothing whatever, and has to be guided by the flashings of an electric torch, with which refinements of signalling are difficult and generally misunderstood. The trees, which appeared to be harmless and nicely spaced in the daytime, become endued [*sic*] with a malignant spirit and (apparently) have changed their positions since last seen. It was as black as a coal-pocket in Oosthoek Wood that night; and for an hour or so it rang with curses and exhortations and the crash and rending of ill-treated timber as tank after tank tried to swing this way or that and pushed down a young tree or two in the act. However, soon after one o'clock we had them all in, herded together more or less in sections, and the first arrivals were already camouflaged. Although the foliage was fairly thick, and probably would have formed an adequate screen, we were running no risks. The camouflage nets were suspended from the trees a few feet above the tanks, the sides being drawn down at a slant and pegged to the ground. All this was exhausting work in the pitchy darkness, and very trying to the temper. At the same time a party was obliterating the tracks we had made between the ramp and the wood. By three o'clock the work was done, and we lay down in and under the tanks to sleep for a few hours.[16]

D Battalion's arrival was no less fraught, as described by Major Watson:

> At dusk we drove down to the ramp at Oosthoek Wood. The train backed in after dark. We brought off our tanks in great style, under the eye of the Brigade Commander, who was always present at these ceremonies. The enemy was not unkind. He threw over a few shells, but one only disturbed our operations by bursting on the farther side of the ramp and so frightening our company dog that we never saw her again. There was no moon, and we found it difficult to drive our tanks into the wood without knocking down trees that made valuable cover. It was none too easy without lights, which we did not wish to use, to fasten the camouflage nets above the tanks on to the branches. The track of the tanks from the ramp to the wood was strewn with branches and straw.[17]

Despite the secrecy, the shelling suggested the Germans had somehow detected the growing threat within Oosthoek Wood. Soon after overseeing the arrival of his tanks, Colonel Christopher Baker-Carr, commander of 1st Tank Brigade, also concluded that the risk of keeping his crews there was too great: 'Some peculiarly well-directed shelling appeared to indicate that the Germans had gleaned information that the wood was harbouring something worthy of their attention. At nights, also, a large number of bombs were dropped in the vicinity, with the result that the crews, who were busy all day in getting their machines into the highest state of efficiency, were deprived of their much-needed rest. I, therefore, withdrew the personnel and installed them in a camp within a few hundred yards of my own headquarters near Lovie Château.'[18]

The sappers of 184th Tunnelling Company were now put to work building alternative accommodation for the tank crews in the woodland around La Lovie, the château that was already home to the commander and staff of Fifth Army. Although this could still be reached by long-range artillery fire, it was three-and-a-half miles (or nearly six kilometres) further back and felt correspondingly safer. The tanks themselves remained in Oosthoek Wood with a small overnight guard. In the words of Captain Edward Glanville Smith of D Battalion:

> This had the disadvantage of adding a five miles' march each way on to our daily programme, since the necessary work entailed visiting the Tankodromes every day of the week, but a good service of [Army Service Corps] lorries, both ways, used to lighten the burden to no small extent ... An honest day's work could be done there, trudging about in the mud and slush (natural adjuncts to any Tankodrome) carrying oil, grease, petrol or unditching rails from the ramp to the company Tankodromes, or trundling worn out sprockets in the opposite direction ... Haversack rations were consumed daily between 12.30 and 1.30, and coffee and omelettes could be obtained by a fortunate few from one or two Belgian farmhouses lying round the edge of the wood. Hordes of small children also used to sell chocolate at huge profits. Camp would be reached about 4.30, and after a good meal we would retire early to bed – the only dry spot in Belgium. A visit to Poperinghe formed an alternative evening's amusement, but a two mile uphill walk back, about 10 at night, after an excellent dinner, was too much of a strain to be repeated often.[19]

As they settled into this schedule, the tank crews were still mystified as to how the Germans had discovered their location with such apparent ease. Shortly afterwards, once the British offensive was under way, they were shocked to learn that their whereabouts had been betrayed to the enemy. But for the time being they could do nothing but prepare their tanks for action, make themselves as comfortable as possible, and hope for the best.

* * *

On 31 July 1917, the long-awaited offensive finally broke over the Germans like a storm, driving the defenders back along a broad front to a distance of more than one-and-a-half miles (or two-and-a-half kilometres).

This time there was no repeat of the first day's fighting on the Somme nearly a year before, when the British had suffered tremendous losses and the survivors often ended up in the same trenches from which they had set out. The success of the initial advance in the Third Battle of Ypres was partly thanks to the growing power of the British artillery, but it was also something of an illusion. On the Somme the German positions were dug deep into the chalky downland and were all but impregnable. A different defensive approach was called for in Flanders where the boggy terrain made it impossible to construct a conventional trench system, and the Germans had adapted their strategy to take account of this. Since they could afford to give ground, their front line was thinly held and rapidly caved in before the British advance, but most of their forces were held further back beyond the range of the main artillery bombardment, and were poised to counter-attack and catch the attackers off-balance.

During the afternoon German artillery began to pound the advancing troops, and in the wake of this came waves of enemy infantry. The attackers suddenly found the tables turned, and in many cases were forced to give up at least some of their newly-won ground, though at the cost of heavy losses to the Germans. Finally the drizzle that had set in during the day turned into a sustained downpour which continued for the next three days and nights, effectively blocking further operations by both sides, who were left to reinforce their new positions as best they could. British casualties in the first three days' fighting came to 31,850 (including nearly 4,500 dead);[20] this was significantly lower than on the first day of the Somme when nearly 20,000 died, though even the British high command struggled to present this in a positive light.

As for the tanks, the statistics told their own story. On the first day 133 tanks went into action, including those used for signalling and supply. Of these just over fifty gave some assistance to the infantry, but the vast majority became stuck in the soft ground or were hit by shells, and only thirty-three made it back to their rallying-points.[21] The losses were severe, but the view within the Tank Corps was that they could have been a lot worse: 'Considering the great difficulties of the ground the result is not unsatisfactory.'[22] Their report pointed out that the terrain 'was very sodden by recent heavy rains and had been heavily bombarded since the 7th July and was covered by many hundreds of thousands of shell holes old and new, many of which had been filled by the rain.'[23]

The casualty lists named forty-four officers and men dead, nine missing and 222 wounded, but the Tank Corps regarded this as 'insignificant' compared to the damage done by the tanks and the lives they had saved among the infantry.[24]

As soon as the battle was under way, the staff officers in La Lovie Château began reviewing the tanks' performance. After mulling over feedback from the infantry, the commander of Fifth Army, General Sir Hubert Gough, sent his findings to Tank Corps headquarters in their camp beneath his windows. The conclusions were balanced, but they must have added to the general air of gloom. General Gough admitted that in many cases tanks had given 'considerable assistance' to the infantry, and improved their morale, but from then on it was all downhill.[25]

His view was that tanks were 'slow, vulnerable, and very susceptible to bad "going". The "going" on a battlefield will always be bad ... From prisoners' statements it would appear that the moral effect of their appearance is diminishing rapidly, except in the case of very young soldiers.' He concluded that tanks had 'considerable possibilities, but also great limitations ... Large forces are out of place unless very great mechanical improvements can be effected. Even so they will always be very vulnerable.'[26]

In reply, Brigadier-General Elles could only repeat that he was well aware of the limitations of tanks, and reassert their potential if used in the right way: 'Tanks offer the only possibility of surprise against entrenched infantry that we have in prospect. Vulnerability will decrease with surprise, good counter-battery work [i.e. destruction of enemy artillery] and superior mobility.' However, he repeated that they were being asked to do the impossible, and added what should have been obvious to anyone: 'Swamp fighting is no part of the function of a tank.'[27]

Following the initial advance there were no further attacks in the Salient for more than two weeks, as the British sought to consolidate their gains and re-establish artillery superiority ready for the next phase. The dreadful weather showed no signs of letting up, and the area pulverized by the bombardment now formed an impassable barrier that left the front-line troops effectively cut off from their support areas. The prospect of getting tanks across this morass were limited, and it was agreed that they would not be called on until after the next spell of dry weather.

It was now clear to the Tank Corps top brass that there was no future in fighting other people's battles, and if they wanted to have any future at all, they would have to find one of their own to fight. On 3 August, a crucial meeting took place at La Lovie between Brigadier-General Elles, his staff officer Lieutenant-Colonel John Fuller, and Colonel John Hardress-Lloyd, latterly commander of D Battalion and now heading 3rd Tank Brigade. They were all men of vision, and the outcome was summarized in the War Diary: 'Discussion … on the advisability from a tank point of view of switching off the present operations and initiating a tank attack on some other part of the line in conjunction with cavalry and the [Royal Flying Corps].' The next day Elles shared the idea with a general at GHQ and reported that he 'does not altogether reject it and asks for certain proposals to be submitted.'[28]

However, 'switching off' the present attack was hardly viable bearing in mind the expectations of Sir Douglas Haig and GHQ. For the foreseeable future, the tank crews would have to grit their teeth and struggle on through the swamp.

CHAPTER 2

Temporary Gentlemen

The men of D Battalion were largely unaware of these machinations, though the rumour mill was grinding away as usual. Since they were in reserve they had taken no part in the fighting, but it could only be a matter of time. Meanwhile there was plenty of scope for speculation about the future as they settled into their makeshift camp in the woods at La Lovie, near the château that accommodated the headquarters of Fifth Army – in the hands of whose commander, General Sir Hubert Gough, their fate now lay.

Along with Second Army to the south and the French First Army to the north, Fifth Army was one of three formations with overall responsibility for the offensive, and the nineteenth-century château provided its staff officers with suitably imposing accommodation. General Gough described it as 'a large, pretentious, ugly square building, with a lake in front of it, which must have made it an easy mark for hostile aeroplanes or long-range guns. A Belgian Count and his family were still in residence … There were sinister stories of their secret influence with the Germans, which was supposed to account for the château having been spared from all bombardments when every building in its vicinity had been pretty well knocked about; I do not believe there was a word of truth in these stories, though it remained a mystery to me why and how the château escaped destruction.'[1]

The chateau may have lacked architectural merit, but at least it was dry. It was a different story for the tank crews, who were living in the woods nearby in what one officer likened to a 'gipsy encampment',[2] initially under tarpaulins slung from the trees. Captain Edward Glanville Smith of D Battalion agreed that 'the La Lovie camp had the advantage of safety; but it could not be described as comfortable. At the best of times Belgium was never dry and a wet summer turned the camp into a quagmire within a week of occupation.'[3] The discomforts of camp life also flooded back into the memory of Second Lieutenant Douglas Browne of G Battalion: 'The camp at Lovie, its leaky tents immersed in dripping shrubs and undergrowth, and surrounded by sodden parapets of sandbags as a protection against the persistent bombing raids, grew always more evil-smelling, steamy, and unhealthy, and those of us who had little to do became more melancholy every day. There was a time, some four days after the battle, when the reaction was at its worst, and when, personally, I felt I could cut my throat for twopence.'[4]

Conditions were no better in the area allocated to the headquarters of the Tank Corps. Captain Evan Charteris, a well-bred aesthete now serving as a staff officer, recalled the camp was in

> a bit of very low ground where the water soon accumulated and the floors of our tents became small areas of mud … Our camp consisted of some thirty tents, a mess hut, and a wooden building for office – all connected by duck boards which ran like viaducts about the swamp in which the camp was pitched. Not two hundred yards away the ground sloped upwards and broke into woodland, scattered over which and hidden as much as possible by the foliage, were encamped

under tents or improvisations of canvas, battalion after battalion right away to the north, where the line was carried on by the French.[5]

In addition, he did not share General Gough's confidence in the safety of La Lovie.

> An aerodrome lay on the other side of the road which ran near our camp, some three-quarters of a mile to the south, near Poperinghe. This was one of the targets for enemy aeroplanes, which on fine nights would visit the neighbourhood two or three times during the dark hours. Lovie Château was twice hit, but while I was there no bomb fell sufficiently near to cause trouble. It was disturbing enough, however, because though a tent is no worse for protection than other covering, yet it seemed to give one a sense of nudity and exposure when that mischievous droning was going on overhead, and at the same time the dangers were enormously increased by the anti-aircraft guns which caused a downpour of missiles.[6]

Despite the hazards and uncertainty, when darkness fell the camp could take on a curious beauty, as Charteris recalled:

> At night all sounds died down very early, lights were few, stars were many, and a clear sky of delicate darkness spread in a vast expanse above us. On this would be reflected the gun-flashes, and against this the fingers of the searchlights would creep and spread like silver feathers in the rare hope of detecting aircraft. Now and then a shell would pitch and burst in Poperinghe. The nights otherwise were intensely still, and voices would carry to us from camps far removed. During one of the air attacks a flame broke out in the sky and a rumour ran that a German machine had been hit; in a moment the night was alive with cheers, which had an impressive effect as they spread and revealed that the whole earth was seething with men.[7]

But there were other sights and sounds that were less reassuring to the tank crews as they prepared to test their courage a few miles away in the Salient. Another young tank officer at La Lovie, Second Lieutenant Wilfred Bion of E Battalion, recalled an incident during a night-time route march near the camp:

> It was wet, cheerless and dark. The vitality of the desolation broke out of black night, mud and abandoned gear like the bubbles in a cauldron. As we stood 'fallen out' in one of our regular halts, the horizon changed from uniform black to dazzling, shimmering white. We stood, stupefied. Then on the breeze came 'drum fire' in which no individual gun could be heard any more than the individual flashes could be seen. The white was now penetrated by the red of bursting shells, the enemy's return fire. I heard a man mutter, 'struth' as we stared at this terrifying spectacle. It seemed the only comment possible as the sight struck chill in one's heart. The order to 'fall in' came down the line and we continued our aimless march. The raid, for that was all it was, was not even mentioned in *Comic Cuts*, the army paper, and since we were not marching in that direction we could ignore it. There must have been few who did not, like me, wonder how anyone survived exposure to such hell.[8]

* * *

This is a good time for us to go in search of D51 *Deborah* and her crew, and the best chance of finding them together is to leave La Lovie – where the officers, NCOs and men inhabit separate areas of the camp, according to military practice – and head over to the tankodrome in Oosthoek Wood, where they are thrown together in the task of preparing their tanks for action. It should be possible to hitch a ride in one of the lorries that shuttle backwards and forwards between the two camps; and although this avoids a five-mile walk, we will be glad enough when the journey is over, since the lorry's suspension is hard, the roads are bumpy and busy with transport and columns of troops, and the soldiers who are cheerfully crammed into the back of the lorry have been wearing their damp woollen uniforms for longer than anyone would wish, and are all to a man smoking heavily.

Our fellow passengers mostly have light blue flashes on their shoulder-straps indicating they belong to D Battalion, so after jumping down from the lorry (with some relief) into the fresh air, the best way to find *Deborah* is to tag along as they make their way down a broad track into Oosthoek Wood, dodging the deep ruts and puddles with their filmy sheen of oil which are a sure sign that the tanks are close at hand. As we plunge deeper into the wood we pass through a gate in the barbed-wire fences that seal off the tankodrome, and soon come across piles of drums containing petrol, oil and grease, with heavy machinery and spare parts stacked nearby under camouflage nets to conceal them from enemy aircraft. The tanks themselves are surprisingly hard to spot among the trees, and are somehow smaller than expected, each dark bulk with its familiar lozenge profile lurking beneath a canopy of camouflage netting. Some stand empty and deserted, but in most cases the crews are already working on them, and in a few the engine has been started and is idling with a throaty, chugging roar while the tank itself is shrouded in a cloud of choking smoke.

Despite the men's relaxed demeanour, you cannot help noticing freshly-broken craters in the ground confirming we are within range of the German artillery, who hurl high-explosive shells into the wood from time to time without pattern or warning. It is strange to think that death might descend so randomly at any moment, but there is some security in the knowledge that the odds of being hit are small, and the men around us are so familiar with the danger that they seem completely oblivious to it. This is a relief since it will take some time to locate the object of our search, guided by the advice of Second Lieutenant James Macintosh, one of the battalion's officers: 'A tank possesses two numbers, a manufacturer's number and a battalion number. The former is branded upon its hindquarters at birth, and remains until dissolution; the latter varies from time to time according to which crew are inhabiting the beast at the moment, and is intended to facilitate identification at a distance. As regards names, the choice, alas, is no longer left to the youthful and revue-full fancy of the young tank pilot; names are passed down from tank to tank, and indicate the battalion, and occasionally the company, to which the bus belongs.'[9]

The slang seems quaint, with its talk of pilots and buses, but the message is clear: we need to keep our eyes open for a tank bearing the large battalion number D51, and the smaller manufacturer's number 2740 on its steel flanks. The document that lists these details does not record a name, but we can also hope to find '*DEBORAH*' painted on her, since that name was later associated with the number D51. Eventually, after stumbling around the rutted woodland for what seems an age, we strike lucky, and are doubly fortunate because there are signs of life, and we can hear a metallic clanging and hammering which shows at least some of the crew are present and working within. Apart from the painted numbers there is little to distinguish D51 from the other tanks we have seen on our search; painted a drab khaki, she looks squat and lethal, and much larger when seen close to, with a length of around eight metres and a height of nearly two-and-a-half. As with the other tanks, the main armament protrudes from box-shaped housings on either side called sponsons, and we have already learned to distinguish between the two basic patterns of tank: the so-called males, with larger sponsons each containing a 6-pounder cannon as well as a light machine gun; and the females, such as D51, which have no cannon but two light machine guns on either side.[10]

The male variety has the advantage of a small door in the back of the sponson which offers an obvious way into and out of the tank, but in the case of a female, the sponsons are too small for this, and instead there is an open oblong hatch in the side of the tank, beneath the sponson and a metre or so above the ground. Suddenly a figure appears inside this hatch and rolls out lengthways, lowering himself down as he does so, and is followed by one man after another. They are all clad in drab overalls apart from one, evidently the officer, who is marginally smarter in tunic and breeches, though these are also greasy and well-worn. If we get close enough to catch a snatch of conversation we can be sure we are in the right place, for his New Zealand accent confirms this is Second Lieutenant George Ranald Macdonald, the first commander of D51, who has travelled from his home in Christchurch to fight for the mother country.

He seems young, although war and the weight of responsibility make him look older than his twenty-five years, and he comes across as intense, intellectual, and rather solemn – though to those who know him, he possesses 'a quiet, incisive wit'.[11] His slightly owlish appearance is not helped by the spectacles that nearly ended his military career before it even began. These are the reason why George Macdonald had to go half way round the world to join up, and then faced another battle to get into a fighting arm, which was always his ambition; for despite his mild-mannered appearance, he once wrote home to his family: 'I rather enjoy shells and bullets and wish my sight wasn't so bad; I should love to stick a German in the gizzard.'[12]

With hindsight, it is hard to decide which is more surprising: that anyone should have been so keen to get into the front line, or that the army should have made it so hard for them to get there. But young men like George Macdonald have always sought to make their stamp on the world, and the outbreak of war in 1914 was too big an adventure to ignore. In Macdonald's case, sibling rivalry may have been a factor in his eagerness for action. He was the youngest of five children, the family of a prosperous engineer and entrepreneur with a passion for traction engines, who ran businesses that supplied farm machinery and operated tramways in the expanding city of Christchurch. George had shown early academic prowess, and after attending one of the country's top schools, he gained a place to study history at another Christchurch – the Oxford college which shared a name, but little else, with his hometown. He graduated from there in 1912, and then joined the Inner Temple, one of London's old-established legal societies, where he qualified as a barrister at the start of 1914, before returning to New Zealand to find work in a law firm.[13] But the prospect was far from enthralling, and the coming of war offered a heaven-sent opportunity for a few months' excitement before he settled down to the responsibilities of career and family.

His first instinct was to join the New Zealand Expeditionary Force, but as he feared, he was rejected on the grounds of short-sightedness. Fortunately he had a fall-back plan, as he explained to his uncle: 'I felt that I was wasting time here in a lawyer's office having no real intention of sticking to law. Dad and Mother were very good and made no difficulties about letting me go though Lord knows they have got enough to worry them. I shall go home [i.e. back to England] armed with a letter from Heaton Rhodes [a prominent New Zealand politician and army officer]. I am counting on my knowledge of French and of motor bicycles and first aid work (signalling is to be learnt on the way …) to counteract my goggles. I think I am sure to get into something.'[14]

Adding to his frustration was the news that his brother Ian had been accepted at Sandhurst, the prestigious training college for army officers, while Guyon had also been commissioned into an infantry regiment. The pressure was on, and George based himself at a gentlemen's club in London and secured a testimonial from the High Commissioner for New Zealand, who pointed out that 'unfortunately young New Zealand men applying here for commissions are at a disadvantage in not being able to get into immediate touch with those familiar with their career, and I think this fact should be taken into consideration when they apply, especially if, so far as is known, they come of good stock and are well-conducted, capable men.'[15]

But the real problem was not George's lack of connections or capability, it was perched on the bridge of his nose. In May 1915 he was recommended for a commission in the infantry, the medical officer merely commenting: 'sight somewhat defective without glasses but quite normal with glasses.' However, his service record shows he also attended a War Office medical board which found him unfit, presumably because of poor eyesight.[16]

George was left seething in his club while the authorities mulled over the conflicting medical reports. Eventually he wrote to Major Arthur Farquharson, who had been Dean of an Oxford college before joining the War Office to help recruit young officers. The frustration was evident in George's letter: 'I have already called on you and pestered you four times. It is now exactly three weeks since you received my application. The last time I called – a week ago – you promised me I should receive my orders within a week. Unfortunately I am not a person of unlimited means and cannot afford to idle in London indefinitely. I shall be extremely grateful if you can give me any definite information about my application. Perhaps it has again been lost.'[17] Major Farquharson was not the sort of person to be swayed by snippy letters from myopic young colonials, and he responded with some information that was definite, though hardly what George wanted to hear: 'As you were rejected by the Headquarters Medical Board … as physically unfit for military service, it is regretted that your application cannot be entertained.'[18]

Shortly after this, however, an opening presented itself, though again it was hardly what George had hoped for. The Army Service Corps fulfilled a vital but inglorious role supplying the food, clothing and equipment for Britain's expanding military forces. The initials ASC were commonly held to stand for 'Ally Sloper's Cavalry', a reference to the red-nosed, work-shy and generally ludicrous anti-hero of a long-running series of comic books. As the nickname implied, the corps still relied heavily on horse-drawn transport, but motor vehicles were being used to carry out more and more of the (as it were) donkey-work. At the beginning of the war, the army had commandeered a recently-built workhouse in south London, and once the elderly occupants were moved out, this became the ASC's main Mechanical Transport depot. It was here that Second Lieutenant Macdonald was ordered to report for training in June 1915, his family background in trams and traction engines clearly outweighing any concerns about his eyesight or attitude. Two months later, he was in France.

For reasons that are unclear, he spent the first few weeks working at a base hospital, where he told his family he 'helped to cut off arms and legs and did all the X ray work; it was very interesting'.[19] After this he took on a more conventional ASC role in transporting the massive 6in naval guns and ammunition used by an artillery battery. George described his command as 'quite a big affair for a humble individual like myself',[20] consisting of fifty-five men, eighteen lorries, nine motorcycles and two cars. Most important of all were five American-built Holt tractors that were used to tow the guns and were propelled by caterpillar tracks, giving them unparalleled power and mobility; looking at these sturdy little vehicles, originally developed for agricultural use, George could never have guessed that they had already helped to inspire a more aggressive machine that would one day play a pivotal role in the war, and in his own life.

Meanwhile George was still thirsting for action, and in early 1916 he applied to join the artillery so that he could at least fire the guns instead of just towing them around. He was probably not surprised by the reply, which said, without giving a reason: 'Your application for transfer to the Royal Garrison Artillery cannot be entertained.' So he returned to France and resumed his duties, evidently with such ability that he became the ammunition officer for heavy artillery in a corps headquarters.[21]

Although out of the front line, George was not out of danger, and in August 1916 he was injured near Albert by a shell which left him, in his own words, with 'about fifteen wounds in both legs and one arm'.[22] The wound was a 'Blighty one', and he was soon back on familiar territory in Oxford, but now as a hospital patient. Soon afterwards, news came through that his brother Guyon, who had been attached to the Royal Flying Corps, was also in hospital in England having cheated death by the narrowest of margins. The newspaper account could have come straight from the *Boy's Own Paper*: 'While flying behind the German lines he was attacked by a Fokker and shot through the right knee. Unfortunately the pressure petrol tank was perforated, as well as the small gravity tank, while another bullet pierced the induction pipe. The machine fell into a cloud, and as soon as Lieutenant Macdonald recovered himself he righted it and started home for his aerodrome, a distance of 25 miles. There was a dressing station quite close, and, although he is suffering from loss of blood and strain, it is hoped that he will save his leg.'[23]

This thrilling escapade must have made George's war seem even more pedestrian, but while he was recuperating in England, word came through that a new and secret unit was seeking volunteers – and it seemed at last to offer the opportunity, metaphorically at least, to stick a German in the gizzard. The humble Holt tractor that had been hauling howitzers across France had spawned a larger and deadlier offspring: an armed and armoured fortress whose caterpillar tracks could cross broken ground and crush barbed wire, and whose guns would bring death to a defenceless enemy as they cowered in their trenches. That at least was the prospect, and it was enough to prompt George to apply to join the Heavy Branch of the Machine Gun Corps in October 1916, soon after the first tanks had gone into action on the Somme. For once his application fell on fertile ground, helped by the close links that the tank pioneers had fostered with the Army Service Corps, whose officers and men possessed the necessary skills in mechanical transport.

The question about George's vision never came up again: faced with such a keen and well-qualified candidate, it seems the authorities decided not to look a gift-horse in the eye. Instead, having had so many battles with the authorities, it would have amused George to know that two splendidly-named grandees were now fighting over him. The opening salvo was fired by Lieutenant-Colonel Charles Ernest Alfred French Somerset Butler, 7th Earl of Carrick, who held a senior role in the Machine Gun Corps and noted that the commanding officer of the Heavy Branch was 'anxious to obtain the services of Lt. G. R. Macdonald', and asked: 'Can he be spared?' Colonel Jacynth d'Ewes FitzErcald Coke, who was a big wheel in army transportation, replied there was 'no objection' to him being sent as a mechanical transport (or M.T.) officer, and accordingly George was ordered to report to Bovington Camp in Dorset, which had become – and remains to this day – the British Army's tank headquarters. At this point Colonel Coke realized the ASC was about to lose him and fired off his own salvo: 'I thought I had made it clear that this [officer] was only being sent to carry out ordinary M.T. duties – we cannot agree to his being transferred.'[24]

But the tanks had claimed their man, and George had found his destiny. The dispute was somehow resolved and he settled into the training programme that had been developed for aspiring tank commanders at Bovington. By April 1917 he was back in France, and the following month he was posted to D Battalion, which had been withdrawn following a series of frustrating and bloody encounters in the Battles of Arras and Bullecourt to an impromptu camp behind the lines at Wailly, later an important base for training but then 'nothing but a broken down, war-scarred village'. The description comes from Captain Edward Glanville Smith, who had won the Military Cross when his tank was knocked out at Bullecourt, and noted that their losses were now being made up: 'Three more reinforcement officers joined 12 Company at Wailly, viz. "Mac" "Vosges" and "Mactosh".'[25]

The nicknames, like George's ('Mac'), give a clue to the public school ethos that prevailed in the officers' mess. The other new officers included 'Mactosh' (though he preferred the shorter 'Tosh'), or Second Lieutenant James Cheyne Macintosh, a nineteen-year-old graduate from South Africa whose advice has already come in useful when we were searching for *Deborah* in Oosthoek Wood. His experience of joining up had in some ways echoed George's, though as the son of a South African MP he was able to pull some strings, and submitted a glowing reference from William Schreiner, the former prime minister of Cape Colony who was now South Africa's High Commissioner in London, and a letter of introduction from General Louis Botha himself. Despite this he was turned down by the Royal Flying Corps on the familiar grounds of short-sightedness, though his vision was felt to be good enough for the Tank Corps.[26]

'Vosges' was the nickname of Second Lieutenant James Vose, so-called because his name sounded like that of a mountain range in Alsace which was the scene of fierce fighting early in the war. Macintosh used an even more convoluted nickname: he called him 'Herr Von' 'because of a close resemblance his real name bore to that of a famous Boche air-fighter'[27] (this was Werner Voss, a friend and rival of the even more famous Baron von Richthofen). Vose had followed a slightly more conventional route into the Tank Corps: a twenty-five year-old native of Bolton, he had studied at Manchester Grammar School before becoming a mechanical engineer, and in 1913 joined the Territorial Army as a private in an ambulance unit. Although they had only signed up for home defence, with the coming of war the men were asked to volunteer for service overseas and Vose found himself in Egypt, helping to defend the Suez Canal against Turkish attacks. From there they were plunged into the ill-fated expedition to Gallipoli, where Vose was wounded, and he was back at home when the call came for volunteers to join a mysterious new unit.[28] The move to the Tank Corps (as it became) played to his strengths as an engineer, and also enabled him to cross a social divide: he became an officer, and in the process what was patronisingly referred to as a 'temporary gentleman', like many others in the Tank Corps – in other words an officer who had no conventional military background, but whose commission was a reflection of the losses and demands of war, and, it must be said, of ability rather than any inherited connections or wealth.

Now, like George Macdonald, he found himself in Oosthoek Wood, preparing himself, his tank and his crew for their first action, while all the time the horizon thudded with gunfire and the rain intermittently sluiced down, turning their camp and the distant battlefield into a quagmire, and filling the men with a strange mixture of anticipation and foreboding.

CHAPTER 3

A Very Fine Lot Indeed

So much for George Macdonald and his fellow officers, but what of the men who made up the other seven-eighths of each tank crew? These were the so-called 'other ranks', the private soldiers (often referred to as 'gunners' in the Tank Corps, though it came to the same thing), and non-commissioned officers such as sergeants, corporals and lance-corporals who were – and remain – the backbone of the British Army.

This is a frustrating area, since there are very few records listing the crew of an individual tank, apart from in the very first actions of September 1916 when the adjutant of D Company jotted their names down in his notebook. Other than this, a combination of chance and careful research sometimes enables us to link a man to a particular tank, and in this way we can name with certainty four members of *Deborah*'s crew in November 1917. While we cannot be sure they were the same men who fought with D51 in the Third Battle of Ypres in August 1917, this is entirely plausible, bearing in mind that strenuous efforts were made to keep the same crews together so they could become an efficient fighting unit.

In the words of Colonel Baker-Carr, commander of 1st Tank Brigade which included D Battalion:

> The members of a tank crew were the most highly and most widely trained men in the British Army. Every man was a skilled machine-gunner; most of them were trained six-pounder gunners; most were fully competent drivers; most, if not all, were able to read a map and steer by compass; every single man was, to a greater or lesser degree, a mechanic.
>
> It took many, many months to train a man to be a competent member of a crew, even from the theoretical standpoint. Actual experience in battle was further needed before he could be regarded as a real, reliable tank man.
>
> Each tank crew was a definite, permanent entity and was encouraged to regard itself as such. Tremendous rivalry existed between crews, with the happiest results to efficiency. If, through casualties in action, sickness, promotion, or any other cause, a tank crew lost one or more of its members, some little time elapsed before that crew regained its previous standard of efficiency and the mutual confidence which was essential for its welfare.[1]

One driver experienced this when he joined the Tank Corps: 'Each tank crew had become one of many little families; they ate, drank, worked, and slept together around their armoured steed, the absolute product of this great mechanical War. Under the conditions which existed, the family-like character of these crews, as regarded their everyday relationships, had no parallel in the whole British Army.'[2]

So where were these men from, and how did they come to be thrown together in this extraordinary new force? The answer, as with the officers, was that they were from all over Britain and Ireland, and sometimes from further afield, and had previously served with a wide range of units, and in the early days (at least) they had volunteered to join the tanks out of a varied mixture of ambition, curiosity, disillusionment and hope.

The so-called Heavy Branch of the Machine Gun Corps had lofty principles for recruitment, as set out in an early report: 'The physical and educational qualifications for the Heavy Branch were to comprise good muscular development, a high standard of intelligence and good eyesight as essentials, but short stature and such defects as flat foot or varicose veins were not of themselves to [be] a bar of selection. Mechanical knowledge or aptitude was desirable, but not indispensable.'[3] However, the expansion of the unit meant a more rough-and-ready approach was often taken, and men were drafted in from other units without much choice in the matter. One of D Battalion's gunners, Private Jason Addy, told how he was undergoing infantry training when the smallest men in his unit were selected, the only additional criterion being whether they knew anything about motorbikes.[4]

Major William Watson, who we met when his tanks were being unloaded in Oosthoek Wood, described the situation when he took command of No. 11 Company:

> The men were of three classes. First came the "Old Tankers," those who had been trained with the original companies. They had been drawn for the most part from the A.S.C.: M.T. [this was the Mechanical Transport section of the Army Service Corps, to which George Macdonald had belonged]. Some had been once or twice in action; some had not. They were excellent tank mechanics. Then came the motor machine gunners – smart fellows, without much experience of active operations. The vast majority of officers and men were volunteers from the infantry – disciplined fighting men.[5]

A more personal perspective was given by Sergeant Harold Aylmer Littledale, who was a tank driver in E Battalion, the sister unit of D Battalion:

> We came from the infantry, from the cavalry, from the artillery, from the Machine-Gun Corps, the Motor-Machine guns, the Flying Corps, the Army Service Corps, and even from the navy ... The spirit of adventure called most of us to the Tanks. This was not because we were any braver than our comrades-in-arms, but because our natures demanded a change to new conditions; for we were of that kind whose natures always demanded a change. And so the call for volunteers found us ready, and when the word of acceptance came, our hearts beat quickly and our hopes rose high; for we were tired of the monotony of the trenches and the monotony of the guns.[6]

As his literary style suggests, Sergeant Littledale's own background was more varied than most, having been born in India where his father – who was a professor of English Literature – helped to establish the system of primary education. The family returned to South Wales, but Harold's own demand for change soon manifested itself, and at the age of seventeen he headed to Canada and then the USA where he became a journalist. While working for the *New York Evening Post* he had himself imprisoned to investigate the state of New Jersey's gaols – a story for which he became one of the first recipients of the Pulitzer Prize. He returned from the USA to fight, serving in the infantry before transferring to the Tank Corps in September 1917.[7]

Winning the Pulitzer Prize was hardly a standard qualification for a tank driver, but although Sergeant Littledale's background was unusual by any standards, it does illustrate the tremendous range of experience found among the crews. It is noteworthy that Second Lieutenant Wilfred Bion, who was critical of many of the officers in E Battalion (including himself), was full of admiration for his men. He wrote of the unit before it left England: 'The officers were, I thought, patchy. There were good ones there, and more came out to the front when we got to France. The others were largely men who had seen a good deal of fighting and had gone into tanks to avoid it. Later, when the tanks got into action, their low morale etc. let them down, and they were gradually weeded out ... The men were a very fine lot indeed. We got a lot of training, and a good deal was expected of us.'[8] (However, he later withdrew the comment that some officers wanted to avoid fighting: 'I am ashamed and would like to cross it out.'[9])

The fact was that the inside of a tank was a democratic place, and the discomforts and dangers were the same for the officer in command – who had often originally served in the ranks – and for his crewmen, a number of whom went on to be commissioned as officers. The crew had to operate as a close-knit team, with the survival of each depending on the courage and vigilance of his comrades, or to quote Second Lieutenant Horace Birks: 'The crews fought each action as a separate entity, relying on the mechanical efficiency of the machine and their own ready wits and stout hearts.'[10] It was an overwhelming responsibility, and not everyone was capable of it; but for those who were, the experience of going into action together had an intensity that nothing in their lives would ever equal again.

* * *

So, what can we learn about the individual crewmen who we glimpsed at work on their tank, D51, during our clandestine visit to Oosthoek Wood? Firstly, we should expect to find among them a young man with a clear, radiant face whose tunic (assuming he was not wearing overalls) bore the blue and crimson ribbon of the Distinguished Conduct Medal, showing that despite his air of angelic innocence, he had already been decorated for bravery in battle. This was Gunner George Charles Foot, and although he was not yet twenty, he was a veteran of the very first tank action and therefore one of the 'Old Tankers' referred to by Major Watson.

George Foot had been born in the thriving North London suburb of Camden, which happened to be the world centre of piano-making, and grew up surrounded by music, for his father was a clerk and then commercial traveller with a firm of musical instrument makers, and later commercial manager of Hawkes & Son, one of the precursors of Boosey & Hawkes.[11] This was an era when a hardworking family could rise up the social scale through thrift and enterprise, and George's parents were soon living in a more salubrious North London suburb, with a second home, idyllically called 'The Roses', in the Buckinghamshire village of Great Missenden – which was connected to the capital by the Metropolitan Railway, and becoming increasingly popular with Londoners seeking to escape the cacophony of city life.

All the signs were that George would follow his father into the music business, as his younger brother did later, but the harmony of their pre-war existence was about to be shattered, and instead he travelled to the nearby town of Aylesbury to enlist in February 1916. A number of army documents indicate he used the surname 'Foote', a slightly more refined spelling which hints at some social aspirations. He was posted initially to the Welsh Regiment, which may seem strange given his background, but most units were now searching far and wide for recruits, and the so-called 'Pals' Battalions consisting of men who had grown up and joined up together were both a rare breed and an endangered species. Like a number of his future comrades in the Tank Corps,

George got his first taste of military life as a despatch-rider, carrying messages from one headquarters to another by motorcycle. It was a responsible and initially exciting role that gave an insight into the world of command, and a knowledge of the internal combustion engine that would stand him in good stead when he made his next move. Young men and motorcycles are often a dangerous combination, and George's family recall he had a wild streak, apparently earning the nickname 'the mad bugger of the Welsh Regiment'.[12] Perhaps this explains why, in May 1916, he answered the call for volunteers to join a new and secret unit that promised even greater excitement, and so became one of the first members of the Heavy Branch of the Machine Gun Corps.[13]

George was with the unit at the very start, before they had even seen a tank or knew very clearly what it was, and then when the first prototype reached them in June. He shared the glorious days when consignments of Mark I machines, shrouded in secrecy, were delivered by rail from factories in Lincoln and Oldbury (in the West Midlands) to the country estate near Thetford, on the Norfolk/Suffolk border, which had been sealed off for their training.

Finally, the time came for the new arm to receive its baptism of fire, and George's D Company was one of the first units to cross to France in August and early September 1916. The Allied push on the Somme, which had begun with such high hopes on 1 July, had ground to a halt, and Sir Douglas Haig believed his new secret weapon could prove a decisive factor in the latest phase of the offensive, known as the Battle of Flers-Courcelette. There was an argument that the British should not show their hand until more tanks were available, but such was the urgency of the hour that the first twenty-five tanks from C and D Companies made their way into action on 15 September 1916.

The story of that battle has been told many times, but suffice to say that it demonstrated both the potential and the limitations of the new weapon, and although it delivered a formidable propaganda coup, the physical gains that resulted were disappointing. Too many of the tanks suffered from mechanical failure, or became inextricably bogged down, or were knocked out by artillery fire, to provide much more than a moral benefit to the attacking infantry, though in a few cases they were able to provide valuable support and even terrify the defenders into submission.

For George Foot, after so much preparation and anticipation, the day ended in anti-climax. The trepidation of his tank commander before the attack was recorded by the war correspondent Philip Gibbs, who did not name him but recalled meeting 'a tiny fellow like a jockey who took me on one side and said, "I want you to do me a favour," and then scribbled down his mother's address and asked me to write to her if "anything" happened to him.' Gibbs continued: 'He and other tank officers were anxious. They had not complete confidence in the steering and control of their engines. It was a difficult and clumsy kind of gear which was apt to break down at a critical moment, as I saw when I rode in one on their field of manoeuvre. These first tanks were only experimental, and the tail arrangement was very weak.'[14]

George's tank – the commander of which was just over five feet tall – was ordered to advance through what had once been High Wood, now devastated after months of fighting, but in the event they only managed a few hundred yards before becoming trapped among the 'broken tree-stumps and deeply-pitted ground'.[15] This was well short of the British front line, let alone the German trenches they were supposed to attack. A letter written in 1971 by the grandson of another officer contains a shocking claim about the commander of George's tank, which had become 'stuck ... at the start': 'Everyone believed he had ditched his tank by putting cotton wool in the oil – pieces of string being found in the oil-feed.' As a parting shot, the writer added: 'After the war [my grandfather] had to go from Ahmednuggar to Poona where he was introduced to [him] as having commanded a tank battalion – having never commanded a section!'[16]

There is no way of establishing the facts about this alleged sabotage, but the human frailties of certain officers were recognized by Second Lieutenant Horace Birks, who joined D Battalion nearly a year later and whose vivid recollections opened this book. 'There were people who were sort of keen on getting there, and people who were not so keen. And the not so keen had all sorts of mechanical failures and so on. The people who were keen managed to get there. Of course, there were people who were so frightened, like myself, one didn't know what to do.'[17]

It is worth noting that the tank accompanying George's managed to go only a few hundred yards further before it also became stuck in a British trench, the disorientated crew then opening fire in the belief that they had reached the German lines, killing a number of British soldiers.[18] Despite this the tank commander, Lieutenant Frederick Robinson, was awarded the Military Cross for having 'fought his tank with great gallantry' and then working for fourteen hours to dig it out under heavy fire.[19]

The fact was that all too many tanks became ditched on that first day of battle, and on the days that followed. Two other men who would play a prominent role in the story of *Deborah* also went into action on 15 September, only to meet similar setbacks. Lieutenant Alfred Enoch was in command of D7, one of ten tanks that set out to attack the strongly-held German positions around the ruined village of Flers. No fewer than half of the group foundered early on, including D7 which became ditched before it had even reached the start-line. As frantic efforts were made to extricate the tank, its engine developed 'a bad knock' and eventually had to be recovered by the ASC.[20]

The experience was a frustrating one for Lieutenant Enoch, a twenty-five year-old Midlander whose war had so far been confined to defending Tyneside against possible invasion as a member of a reserve infantry battalion. He now took charge of another tank which had been hit by a shell and whose commander was suffering from shell shock. All that remained was to bring it back safely, but at least Alfred Enoch had emerged unscathed, and even gained confidence from his initial experience of combat. He had previously been self-conscious about his humble origins compared to other officers he encountered, but his son Russell described how 'there was a very heavy bombardment, and one of these young men broke down and started to scream and scream. My father suddenly realized "I'm as good as any of them", and that gave him some encouragement.'[21]

Enoch's section commander was his friend Captain Graeme Nixon, who was only twenty-one but had already survived several months as an infantry officer in Gallipoli. Four of the six tanks in his section were to attack to the west of Flers, including D12 which he commanded, supporting infantry from New Zealand who had also been blooded at Gallipoli.[22] On this front the tanks were relatively effective, particularly D11 *Die Hard* commanded by Second Lieutenant Herbert Pearsall, and the New Zealanders recorded that two of them 'did excellent work and were a great help to the infantry and had a very demoralising effect upon the enemy who in several cases ran like sheep before them.'[23]

Graeme Nixon was less personally successful, since D12 reached the village but was then hit by a shell which disabled the twin-wheeled steering mechanism at the rear, identified as a source of potential weakness by George Foot's commander, among others. As the tank withdrew it became ditched, before being hit again and set on fire while the crew were trying to dig it out. Nixon returned minus his tank, and minus one crewman who they lost trace of while escaping over the devastated battlefield.[24]

It was left to another tank on the same front – D17 *Dinnaken*, commanded by Lieutenant Stuart Hastie – to penetrate the village, observed by an airman whose report was seized on by an ecstatic press: 'A Tank is walking up the High Street of Flers with the British Army cheering behind.'[25] The reports did not mention that *Dinnaken* was later hit by a shell and had to be abandoned, though fortunately without serious injury to the crew. In fact, as the day drew to a close, there were few who could have foretold that tanks would one day become a decisive weapon of war. Although we have focused on their role here, they made a relatively small contribution to the battle and the official verdict was that they had achieved 'very limited success' in their first action.[26]

Despite their impregnable appearance, their many vulnerabilities had also been exposed. Chief among these was the hazard of ditching or bellying in the broken ground, which left the infantry unsupported and the crewmen in mortal danger as they tried to dig out their machines, or abandoned them and fled on foot. Not far behind came the risk of a direct hit by an artillery shell, whether deliberately aimed or falling by chance, against which their steel walls gave little protection – a danger that was driven home the next day when three surviving tanks pressed forward their attack on the far side of Flers, or what remained of it. All of them were knocked out, with the worst fate reserved for the tank commanded by Second Lieutenant Gordon Court which was 'absolutely blown to bits', killing the entire crew of eight.[27] Even if they avoided disaster on this scale, the tank crews were still vulnerable to injury from shell splinters or bullets that penetrated cracks or loopholes in the armour, or temporarily blinded them by shattering the glass prisms that gave limited visibility, while one man was even injured by a German soldier who crept up and shot him through a loophole.[28] The infantry had also discovered that a tank was at best an unreliable friend, and could turn out to be a veritable enemy since it attracted artillery and small-arms fire from all over the battlefield.

No-one could tell at this stage whether tanks would turn out to be a daring but unsuccessful experiment, though some who recognized their potential were already beginning the gradual learning process that would lead to improvements in their design and performance, and to more effective tactics for co-operation with infantry and artillery. The Germans, after the initial shock of their first encounter, were also learning, and would soon possess more effective anti-tank weapons, although it would take two decades to demonstrate that they had absorbed the most fundamental lesson of all: that the tank, if used appropriately, had the potential to win wars.

Meanwhile, for men such as George Foot, Alfred Enoch and Graeme Nixon, their fate was now tied to the tanks for good or ill, and they were numbered among the 'Old Tankers' even though none of them was older than twenty-five. During the years to come they would face even greater dangers, and as we shall see, their lives would eventually be bound together through a tank called *Deborah*.

CHAPTER 4

Dracula's Fate

Whatever his alleged failings, George Foot's tank commander recommended two of his crew for gallantry awards following the first day's attack, one of them being 'Gunner Foote'. The adjutant of D Company recorded this in his notebook, but it is hard to predict what the official response might have been, since they had never really got into action.[1] However, just a fortnight later George committed an act of such undisputed bravery that it was even reported in *The Times*.

The occasion for this was an attack on Eaucourt l'Abbaye, where a complex of farm buildings on the site of a medieval monastery had been fortified by the Germans, and now that Flers had fallen, this was the next significant obstacle to the Allied advance on the Somme. An attack was planned for 1 October 1916, supported by the only two tanks from D Company that were still serviceable. One of them was D16 which bore the slightly surprising name of *Dracula*, in tribute to Bram Stoker's novel which had appeared less than twenty years before. *Dracula* had been relatively successful on the first day, entering Flers before being been driven back by artillery fire. During the return journey its commander, Lieutenant Arthur Arnold, was shot in the knee when he left the tank to save a wounded soldier from being crushed under the tracks, and D16 made it home under the command of one of the gunners, Jacob Glaister.[2] Both men later received gallantry medals for this, but Arnold was now in hospital in England – though he would return to play a further part in the story of *Deborah*.

With Arnold gone, *Dracula* was now under the command of a dashing twenty-two year-old officer called William Jefferson Wakley who was definitely, to use Birks' phrase, 'keen to get there'. The son of an engineer, Wakley had finished his apprenticeship as a draughtsman and was studying in London when war broke out. Within six weeks he had enlisted in the infantry as a private, and was commissioned a few months later.[3] With his engineering background the tanks had an obvious appeal and he was one of the first to volunteer, but he had not yet commanded a tank in action, having previously been responsible for transporting the machines across the Channel and up to the front line.[4] Events show that Gunner Jacob Glaister was still with D16 on 1 October, and that the crew now included George Foot, whose first tank had been incapacitated in High Wood.

The attack on Eaucourt l'Abbaye involved a number of infantry units including 47th (2nd London) Division and the New Zealand Division. It opened with a fiendish twist that was worthy of a horror film: dozens of oil-drums were hurled out of projectors one minute before the infantry went over the top. According to the New Zealand official history, '30 projectiles were seen to reach their objective satisfactorily, bursting about 1 second after landing and covering the German trenches with lurid flame and great rings of black smoke'. The troops went in against this hellish backdrop, and despite heavy losses they seized a network of trenches known as the Circus near the abbey itself. 'The trenches were found packed with corpses, piled in many places one over the other. One or two loathsome groups in the centre of the position lay burned and half eaten away by the oil ... Their physique ... was strikingly poor, and many of them were mere boys.'[5]

The Londoners of 47th Division attacked to their left, supported by the two tanks which moved along a parallel system of German trenches, firing as they went. With their assistance, two of the three battalions were able to gain their objectives, but although they passed through the ruins of Eaucourt l'Abbaye, they did not clear the enemy from the tunnels and cellars beneath. The third attacking battalion had been held up by uncut barbed wire, and was now driven back by machine-gun fire from the ruins, leaving some pockets of men behind. Exploiting this setback, German troops now began to infiltrate back into the area.

To make matters worse for the attackers, both tanks became ditched in the churned-up ground and were unable to fight their way forward or to withdraw. Wakley and his crew now faced a dilemma, for although the attacking troops were cut off and desperately needed their support, it was also vital to stop their new weapon falling into enemy hands. The drama was described in a newspaper report by an anonymous correspondent, probably Philip Gibbs, the erstwhile confidant of George Foot's tank commander. *The Times* said that 'the part played by the "Tanks" in the operation was picturesque and gave opportunity for the display of great gallantry. One of them, finding herself unable to proceed, continued for a while to operate as a stationary fortress.'[6] The *Official History* described what happened next: 'When the Germans counter-attacked south-eastward down the trenches, the tanks being immovable and unsupported, were set on fire and the crews withdrawn.'[7]

Having abandoned their blazing machines, the crews had to get back across No Man's Land with the battle still raging around them, and it was not long before the inevitable happened. In the words of a medical report, Second Lieutenant Wakley 'was struck by some shrapnel casing a handsbreadth above the knee. The casing lodged fracturing the femur obliquely'.[8] Anyone who has explored the battlefields of the First World War will have come across jagged shards of metal littering the fields, their edges still sharp after a century in the earth. For all its dispassionate language, the doctor's report tells us that one such fragment from a shell-case, which would have been red-hot from the explosion, had been driven into Wakley's leg above the knee, smashing the thigh-bone, and was now embedded in his flesh.

This could easily have been fatal, but Wakley was not going to get off that easily. Two or three of his crewmen, including George Foot, pulled him into a shell crater and stayed with him, but it would have been certain death to try to move him by daylight. When night fell the unwounded men could have slipped back to the British lines, but even if they could have carried their officer, it was doubtful if he would have survived being dragged across the uneven ground. They could simply have abandoned him and saved themselves, rationalizing this on the grounds that he would probably have died anyway, but if this thought occurred to them, they dismissed it. Instead, they must have crept out of their shell crater under cover of darkness, dodging the sweeping machine guns and freezing like statues to avoid being picked out under the sickly light of the flares, to gather water-bottles and (one hopes) ampoules of morphine from the dead infantrymen, and to compete with the rats for the food in their haversacks.

The next day a rescue mission was mounted involving some of the crewmen who had made it back to the British lines, including Gunner Jacob Glaister, the hero of *Dracula*'s first action. Another officer noted that 'several men [lost] their lives trying to rescue [Wakley]',[9] and it was a miracle Glaister was not among them, for his medal citation says he was 'very severely wounded in trying to rescue a wounded officer'.[10] According to a doctor's report he was shot 'through the body, bullet entering right side, leaving left side just under ribs', but incredibly enough, the bullet passed right through his chest without hitting any vital organs. Having himself been rescued, Glaister was taken to a casualty clearing station and then to hospital in Rouen.[11]

Meanwhile the situation around the ruins of Eaucourt l'Abbaye remained dangerously confused, and George Foot and the others could only huddle together in the blood-soaked mud of their crater, occasionally loosening the tourniquet which formed a slender lifeline for William Wakley, and praying the Germans did not launch a counter-attack which would result in their capture – or worse. As if this was not enough, the *Official History* records that 'Rain set in about 11 A.M. on the 2nd October and continued to fall with little intermission throughout the two following days.'[12] Gibbs added a further twist to Wakley's story: 'A day later he was wounded again by a bomb, which – amazing as it seems – did not burst, but injured him badly in the ribs, so that he had to endure great suffering out there in the crater.'[13] The medical reports make no mention of this further injury, but no-one could argue with the conclusion.

Wakley and Foot remained in No Man's Land for three days and nights, until on 4 October the adjutant of D Company noted 'Wakley brought in'.[14] George Foot's local paper said he 'eventually [got] his officer back into the British lines',[15] but in reality it seems the Germans simply decided they had exacted a high enough price for Eaucourt l'Abbaye and pulled back to their next defensive position, allowing the attackers to move forward and occupy the devastated area. The *Times* report, sent from headquarters on 4 October, said 'it was impossible to get [the officer] away until this morning's attack had succeeded'.[16]

So their dreadful vigil came to an end, and George Foot's courage was rewarded with a Distinguished Conduct Medal, the highest award for so-called 'other ranks' apart from the Victoria Cross (which was reserved for the greatest acts of bravery). The citation stated: 'For conspicuous gallantry in action. He displayed great courage and determination fighting with his tank. Later, he remained for 30 hours with a wounded officer under very heavy fire.'[17]

For Glaister and Wakley, an even bigger battle was now beginning as they struggled to recover from their injuries. Glaister was evacuated to hospital in Dublin where he remained for nine weeks, making a good recovery and bathing in the best wishes of his comrades.[18] Among them was his first commander, Lieutenant Arthur Arnold, who wrote from his own hospital bed: '"Too bad that "Dracula" had to be fired in the end. It seems to be the ultimate end of a good many of the Tanks. I am still in bed & my knee is proving a very tedious job. However I believe it will get all right & I hope we may eventually have another dust-up together with the Bosche [sic].'[19]

Glaister, who had been a builder before the war, also received a message of congratulations and a gold watch from Whitehaven Town Council, of which his father was a member. His reply indicates that what we would now regard as public-school values were not restricted to the officer class: 'It is very difficult to give you any idea as to our experiences, but with regard to Myself I only did my duty and what is expected of every man, viz., to play the game straight. I still have trouble with my wounds, but hope to be strong and well again in a month or two.'[20]

Another letter arrived from Major Frank Summers, the commanding officer of D Company, who wrote: 'You must try & get posted back to this Company – as we shall all be pleased & proud to have you back with us.'[21] But when Jacob Glaister returned to duty in December 1916 he went to G Battalion and was based in the depot at Bovington, and although he remained in the Tank Corps for the rest of the war, he never had the chance of another dust-up with the Boche.[22]

For Wakley, the situation was far more grave. Following his rescue he immediately underwent an operation to remove the shrapnel from his leg at a field hospital behind the lines, and from there he was taken to a base hospital in Le Havre. By 18 October he was back in London, at an officers' hospital in Mayfair, but not surprisingly his shattered leg had become infected in the filthy conditions of the battlefield, and a medical report noted 'the wound is freely suppurating' (in other words, inflamed and oozing pus), while Wakley himself had a high temperature and was 'much run down'. The fracture was wired in an attempt to reunite the smashed bone, but by now Wakley had contracted septicaemia, a severe blood infection which was untreatable without antibiotics, and for several weeks his life hung in the balance. By the New Year, doctors realized they had no choice but to amputate his left leg at the hip joint.[23]

This drastic remedy proved surprisingly effective, and in April 1917 the hospital's medical director reported that 'the stump is now quite ready for the artificial limb which Mr Wakley is anxious to obtain as quickly as possible as he is very desirous of again undertaking duty. Mr Wakley was most severely wounded ... He made an outstanding recovery. He has been a most courageous patient and is altogether a very deserving case.' This letter helped persuade the government to pay for the artificial limb, and by August Wakley was back at work, using his skills as a draughtsman to prepare technical drawings at the War Office.[24] He remained there until the end of the war, when he complained that 'even the light duty I am now employed on is a severe strain', and was placed on the retired list with an annual pension.[25]

There we must leave him, except to note that his disability did not dampen his energies in other respects, for in 1921 the High Court granted a decree nisi to Major Cecil Huntingdon Digges La Touche of the Indian Army, divorcing his wife Evelyn on the grounds of adultery with Captain Wakley.[26] The court heard that Major La Touche had 'received a letter from her in which she said that she had been unfaithful to him, and that she had stayed at an hotel in Notting-hill-gate under the name of Wakley. Evidence was given by the manager of the hotel that a Captain and Mrs. Wakley had stayed there together as man and wife.'[27] The divorce left the couple free to marry, and their union was both productive and long-lasting, though the unhappy major – who had previously been invalided home from the fighting in Mesopotamia – died the following year in Lahore, in what is now Pakistan.[28]

It was not an era that paid much attention to the mental suffering of those traumatized by war, unless it manifested itself in the syndrome known as shell shock, and Wakley, Glaister and Foot were left to come to terms as best they could with their ordeal in No Man's Land. Being physically unhurt, George Foot would have simply returned to his unit, to take his place in another crew when a vacancy occurred. His combination of intelligence, dependability and courage marked him out as officer material, but he does not even seem to have been promoted even to NCO; one document lists him as a lance-corporal, but the Tank Corps invariably referred to him by the basic rank of gunner. His family wonder if this was related to his disciplinary record, but the authorities probably felt he needed to gain greater maturity and authority before joining the ranks of the 'temporary gentlemen'. However, he was not yet twenty years old, and as we would say nowadays without thinking, he had time on his side.

CHAPTER 5

Of Knaves and Jokers

If George Foot had the face of angel, no-one would have said the same of his fellow crew member Joseph Cheverton, least of all himself. A battered family photograph shows a stocky, cocky young man with a hint of a grin and his cap at a jaunty angle. On the back he has jotted a pencil note to his parents:

> From your ever loving son J
> what do you think of it
> bit of a knave[1]

Gunner Cheverton may have given that impression, but he also looks like a good person to have on your side, and his sleeve bears an inverted chevron marking two years' good conduct – showing that like Gunner Foot, he was already a veteran at the age of nineteen. Both had started out as private soldiers in the infantry, and now held the same rank in the Tank Corps, but whereas George Foot's family was aspirational and upwardly mobile, Joseph William Cheverton was the son of a tin- and coppersmith and resolutely working class. Joseph had been born in Coventry, where his father had moved to find work in the city's manufacturing industries, but the family soon returned to his parents' hometown of Cambridge, and it was there that Joseph and his three sisters were brought up.[2]

Although Cambridge University was as celebrated then as now, the town where Joseph lived might have been a million miles away from the ancient courtyards and riverside lawns where young men of a similar age but a different class spent three years in a whirl of punting, parties and privilege. For families like the Chevertons, the colleges were no more than a distant glimpse of pinnacles on the skyline beyond the railway tracks, while the students themselves were a source of amusement, annoyance and income. The mistrust was mutual, with Rupert Brooke, who represented the golden archetype of academe until his death from septicaemia in 1915, famously describing the town's residents as 'urban, squat and packed with guile'.[3] It was meant as a jibe, but Joe and his friends might have recognized something of themselves in that description.

By 1914, the Cheverton family was crammed into a tiny terraced house in one of the new roads built for the shopkeepers, college servants and other tradespeople who provided for the needs of the busy town and its transient scholastic population. Joseph's occupation is not recorded, but he probably followed in his father's footsteps by training as a fitter or mechanic. His family recall that he was idolized by his sisters, and he became involved with the local amateur football team, Romsey Town. One of the players was a slightly older man called George Coote, an apprentice house-painter from another large family which included four sisters. Joseph was a good-looking, confident lad, and was soon stepping out with Florence Coote, known as Florrie, who was a year younger. A photograph shows her looking most fetching in a striped Romsey Town football jersey and shorts, probably her brother's, though football was also a surprisingly popular game among women. Joseph's photograph shows him wearing a ring on his third finger, indicating that they were betrothed to be married as soon as the time was right.[4]

And so they might have jogged along, if it had not been for the tide of change sweeping across Europe that would soon empty the students from their college halls, and the young men from the football terraces and public bars. The coming of war found Cambridgeshire without its own regular army regiment, but with a Territorial battalion made up of volunteers who trained in their spare time, which was immediately mobilized as the 1st Battalion Cambridgeshire Regiment. Like other Territorials they had only signed up for home service, and when they were asked to volunteer for service overseas, those who were unable or unwilling to go formed the basis of a reserve battalion, and recruitment later began for a further reserve unit to be called the 3/1st Battalion.[5]

Joseph Cheverton had so far resisted the frenzy of war fever, but in April 1915 the 3/1st Battalion began a recruiting drive, and for two weeks the quiet streets of Cambridge and the sleepy Fenland towns reverberated to the tramp of marching feet and the thud of the bass drum. The local paper listed the names of those who signed up, including Joseph Cheverton.[6] His sweetheart's brother George Coote had already gone overseas with the regiment, but Joseph had slightly longer to wait and formed part of a reinforcement draft that crossed to France at the end of September.[7] Strangely enough, this was probably the first time he had really got to know anyone from the other side of the gulf that divided his town, since almost all the regiment's officers, and a fair sprinkling of other ranks, had been at the university before the war.

Joseph's arrival at the front may not have lived up to expectations, as the regiment had been allocated to a quiet sector near the banks of the river Somme, which at that time was not much livelier than the river Cam. In fact, the General Staff initially seem to have had little faith in the fighting qualities of the Cambridgeshires – probably because they were mere Territorials, with no corresponding regular unit to pass on its skills. So far their war had been distinctly low-key, and although they played a supporting role in the Second Battle of Ypres, they had never taken part in a major attack and spent most of their time holding the line in areas where nothing much happened. Despite this the trenches were never an entirely safe place, and they had lost around eighty men, mostly from sniping and shelling.[8]

If things had been relatively quiet for the Cambridgeshires, they were about to get even quieter. In October 1915 they were detached from their division, which was sent to Salonika (now Thessaloniki) in northern Greece to join a gruelling campaign against the German-backed forces of Bulgaria. The Cambridgeshires were sent in the opposite direction to become the training battalion at Third Army School in the town of Flixecourt. The regimental historian's view was that they had 'fallen on their feet', but the posting was a strenuous one since it involved much digging of practice trenches, frequent drills and parades, and 'all sorts of fancy attacks' for the benefit of senior officers studying at the school.[9] For the next five months the battalion therefore found itself conducting mock battles with a simulated enemy, while the real thing was being enacted with deadly purpose just a few miles away. We do not know what Joseph Cheverton made of this, but it must have been frustrating for anyone who had joined up to fight. One of the company commanders – an intensely intellectual young man called Captain Arthur Adam, known to his men as 'Parson Snowy' on account of his fair hair and evangelical manner – summed it up in a letter home: 'This is indeed a funny war; that is, I suppose it is war; but it isn't like any other I ever came across.'[10]

This period of duty came to an end in April 1916, when the battalion marched back into the line to occupy yet another uneventful sector. A number of the officers were being replaced by regulars, among them Brigadier-General Edward Riddell who took over as commanding officer, only to be warned that he was 'in for a stiff job'.[11] The singular nature of his new command was brought home one night as he watched his men filing down a trench in the rain: 'One of the officers was reciting a few lines from the classics. Probably his memory failed him; anyway he stopped. Whereupon the third man behind him continued the quotation. I pushed into the trench to find out what manner of man this private soldier was; for [he] must be a man of education and imagination. Fate ruled that I should not speak to him. A stray bullet, probably from a fixed rifle two thousand yards away, hit him in the back of the neck. He was dead when we lifted him out of the mud. "Bad luck", said the adjutant. "He might have made a name for himself after the war. He was hopeless as a soldier."'[12]

As the summer wore on, the Cambridgeshires were sucked into the vortex of the Somme, no longer a sleepy sector but now the setting for one of the greatest battles in history. At least there was now the prospect of some real fighting, but the battalion was once again given one of the quieter sections of the line, north of the ruined village of Hamel with the marshy valley of the River Ancre to its right. This was one of the areas where the great offensive launched on 1 July had foundered at the start, and although they arrived at the end of August, the Cambridgeshires took over the same trenches from which the 36th (Ulster) Division had advanced with such high hopes nearly two months before.

Their trenches gave a grandstand view of the one of the strongest German positions on the Somme, the Schwaben Redoubt, which occupied the high ground towards Thiepval, only 500 metres to their right across the Ancre valley, and was still holding out against repeated attacks. Witnessing the bombardment that preceded one assault, 'Parson Snowy' turned to his commanding officer and shouted above the din: 'Nothing on earth can withstand that. Will this mean the end of the war?'[13] It was a naive question, for the Germans in their well-built positions could withstand that, and plenty more, and shortly afterwards even launched a counter-attack which the Cambridgeshires helped to repulse.

Once again the men found themselves exposed to the constant dangers of trench warfare, including a series of poison gas bombardments intended to disrupt the Allied advance. One of these was described by Brigadier-General Riddell: 'From 11 p.m. until dawn the German artillery saturated the valley in which the Cambridgeshires were with gas shells. Those who have worn the old grey flannel gas-mask for five or six hours continuously will know what that means. All night the fluttering sound of those shells as they fell amongst us made rest impossible. Those who removed their masks were immediately incapacitated.' There was no response from the British artillery, who were unable to bring shells up to their guns, and he added: 'Had the Germans only known our plight – blinded, coughing, exhausted infantry, and ammunitionless guns!!'[14]

The frustration was shared by 'Parson Snowy', who had managed to disguise his own short-sightedness from the military authorities. 'There is a serious drawback to me as a soldier which has only just transpired, to wit, that spectacles under an anti-gas apparatus become so misty that I can't see a yard. So I was rendered entirely incapable for 3 hours the other night, when our delightful enemy gave us a few thousand of his more poisonous forms of gas shell. That proceeding made me really angry, because, though it did no real harm, it made us feel very uncomfortable, and prevented sleep at a time it was badly wanted.'[15]

But these proceedings could do real harm, and a number of men were gassed, including Joseph Cheverton who was sent back to England as a casualty in September 1916.[16] This probably happened on 23 September, when the War Diary recorded that 'A large number of gas shells dropped on our frontage and around Hamel during the night, making things very uncomfortable. Casualties 1 officer … & 20 [other ranks] one of whom later on died. In a large number of cases effects were not felt until 12 hours later. There were 3 different kinds of gas used.'[17]

Nearly a month later, the Cambridgeshires finally got their chance. For once they were to lead an attack, and their task was no less than to drive the Germans out of their last foothold in the Schwaben Redoubt, which had maintained its defiance ever since 36th (Ulster) Division had seized it for a few glorious hours on 1 July. As he watched his men going over the top, Brigadier-General Riddell never doubted that they would succeed: 'Shells sizzled overhead like rain. A second later they burst on the rising ground two hundred yards to the north, throwing up fountains of earth mingled with the debris of a battlefield; and although we could not discriminate between one clod of something in the air and another, we knew that men, too, were being blown to pieces. Silhouetted against this cloud of spurting earth and smoke were my Cambridgeshires advancing to victory … I stood up in the open, spell-bound with admiration for the men who were steadily advancing into that upheaval of earth, with the sunlight gleaming on their bayonets.'[18] The regiment had finally proved itself, but it came too late for Joseph Cheverton, who was already back in England – and too late for Captain Arthur Adam, who had been wounded and captured while leading a disastrous raid in the Ancre valley on the night of 16/17 September. No word was ever received of 'Parson Snowy's' fate, but the discovery of a grave several years after the war confirmed that he had died in German hands.[19]

Following Joseph Cheverton's recovery, it may come as no surprise that he was among a draft of eight men from the Cambridgeshire Regiment who transferred to the Heavy Branch of the Machine Gun Corps.[20] His family background in metal-working would have made him especially suitable for the new role, though the unventilated interior of a tank, choking with exhaust fumes and thick with gunsmoke, was hardly the place for someone whose lungs had been damaged by poison gas. However, the newspapers were full of the exploits of the new machines, and although there were many question-marks about them, they must have seemed a better bet than huddling in a trench with only a steel helmet and flannel gas mask for protection, or running around conducting mock attacks for the edification of elderly staff officers.

It may also have occurred to him that Florrie was likely to be impressed by his involvement with the army's newest secret weapon. If so he would hardly be the first young man to think in this way, or the last, and surely none of us would begrudge him this fickle glory.

* * *

It often happens that the people with the best sense of humour are those with the least to laugh about, and this seems to have been the case with the third member of *Deborah*'s crew, a twenty-five year-old Ulsterman called William Galway. The son of a labourer who had no fewer than nine children,[21] he had worked for the local council before being wounded on the most disastrous day in the history of the British Army, and was now on the brink of a battle that had the potential to be even worse. It was not very promising material, but Gunner Galway was described by his commander as 'a true Irish gentleman' who 'kept us in shrieks of laughter' and was 'the life and soul of my crew, doing two men's work and cheering us all up'.[22] No-one has recorded exactly what he managed to find funny in all this, but one imagines that the foibles of the officers, the idiocy of the General Staff, and the incompetence of their allies would have provided a rich comic vein, as in most wars.

William Galway was born and raised in Holywood, a pleasant little town in County Down on the shores of Belfast Lough that was linked to the city by rail, and now boasted a number of large houses belonging to wealthy industrialists. It was a very different story for William, whose parents must have struggled to cope with such a large family, but his personality suggests that it was a happy household. In 1911 his parents and their seven surviving children, aged from three to twenty-two, were all living in the same house with only three incomes to support them – from their father, who was a labourer, his oldest daughter who worked in a tobacco factory, and his oldest son William who was then a grocer's vanman, but later went to work for Belfast Corporation.[23]

Tensions in Ireland had been growing in the years before the war, with the Protestant community becoming increasingly isolated not just from the majority Catholic population, but also from the British government as it made repeated attempts to introduce home rule in the yet unpartitioned island. The Unionists, fearing their interests were being ignored, had formed a militia called the Ulster Volunteer Force to resist home rule, but with the coming of war they agreed to set their grievances aside, and the UVF became a ready-trained unit of the British army known as 36th (Ulster) Division.

As a member of the local Presbyterian church, William Galway's allegiances were clear, and in September 1914 he and his younger cousin enlisted together in 13th (Service) Battalion of the Royal Irish Rifles, newly formed from the County Down Volunteers. The fact that both men had the same name and were in the same company might have caused confusion, but the younger William Galway failed to thrive in the army and suffered from a series of ailments during training, until he was finally discharged in May 1915 complaining of knee pain.[24]

For all his flippancy, the older William was made of sterner stuff, and after training in Ireland and England he travelled to France with his battalion in October 1915.[25] Unlike Territorial units from sleepy English shires, the army's high command had no doubts about the fighting qualities of the Ulstermen, who came from what we would now call a tough neighbourhood, and were united by a common faith, a shared political ideology, and a fierce sense of pride. After a period of familiarization they were sent to hold a key sector of the line near the enemy stronghold of Thiepval, and remained there as preparations got under way for the enormous Allied push on the Somme in the summer of 1916.

The opening of that offensive is generally regarded as the blackest day in the history of the British Army, but the heroic part played in it by 36th (Ulster) Division has entered the realms of military mythology. Rifleman William Galway's unit, A Company of 13th Bn Royal Irish Rifles, found itself in the first wave of the attack against German positions on the gently rising ground north of Thiepval.

Following a five-day bombardment, zero hour was fixed for 7.30 a.m. on 1 July – a propitious day for the Ulstermen, as it was the anniversary of the Battle of the Boyne which had brought triumph for the Protestant King William. At 7.15 a.m., the men of the Royal Irish Rifles filed out of their trenches in Thiepval Wood and formed up in No Man's Land. At zero the thunder of shelling was replaced by the rattle of small-arms fire and cries of 'No Surrender' as the attackers surged forward. The first two platoons of A Company reached the German front line with few casualties, overwhelmed the defenders, and moved on to seize the support trench behind. But the Germans were now emerging from their deep dugouts, and the second wave from A Company was caught in the open as it crossed No Man's Land, losing a large number of men from machine-gun fire. The survivors then moved forward to the second-line trench, clearing the way with hand grenades. According to the battalion's commanding officer, Colonel William Savage: 'This trench was held for a considerable time, but owing to our bombs giving out & not getting any reinforcements we were ordered to retire back.'[26]

To their right, the Ulstermen swept even further forward to occupy the complex of trenches known as the Schwaben Redoubt, but soon found themselves far ahead of their neighbouring units. Isolated and exposed to fire from both flanks, and in the face of determined German counter-attacks, they were eventually forced back to their starting positions leaving only a tenuous hold on a stretch of the German front line. The Schwaben Redoubt would remain in enemy hands for more than two months, until it was finally retaken by the Cambridgeshire Regiment, among others.

For all their heroism, the Ulstermen had suffered a terrible defeat, though a glorious one. A message from Major-General Oliver Nugent, commander of 36th Division, was relayed to 13th Bn Royal Irish Rifles: 'Ulster has every reason to be proud of the men she has given to the service of our country. Though many of our best men have gone the spirit which animated them remains in the Division and will never die.'[27] The cost was summarized by the divisional historian: 'Its casualties in the two days amounted to five thousand five hundred officers and other ranks killed, wounded, and missing. The whole Province was thrown into mourning for its sons.'[28]

In William Galway's company alone, the casualty return shows thirteen men were killed, thirty-four missing, and fifty-four wounded (including ten with shell shock).[29] When the missing were accounted for, it turned out at least thirty-six men from A Company were dead.[30] Among the wounded who made their way back to Thiepval Wood was Rifleman Galway,[31] though the nature of his injuries is unknown. It was probably while he was recovering that the appeal came through for volunteers to join the Heavy Branch of the Machine Gun Corps. Perhaps even his irrepressible sense of humour had been strained by the slaughter on the Somme, but whatever the reason, he transferred to the new unit on 19 October 1916, just over a month after the tanks had first gone into action.[32]

From then on William Galway was separated from most of his fellow Ulstermen, and found himself in a very different unit dedicated to a new kind of warfare. It was not the last time he would come across 36th (Ulster) Division, though strangely enough, on the next occasion he would find his own life and those of his comrades were endangered by the actions of a small number of its men, who took a very different view of their obligations to the British Crown.

CHAPTER 6

The Sword of Deborah

If the other crewmen had all the energy and some of the wildness of youth, the final member of *Deborah*'s crew who can be identified with certainty was a very different stamp of man. At thirty-six, Frederick William Tipping was considerably older than his comrades, not to mention many of their officers, and was the only crew member who was married with a family and an established position in life. The photographs show a lean, dapper figure in his clerk's three-piece suit and collar and tie, complete with ornate watch-chain, or wearing a smart dress-coat; he looks as sober and serious as a Sunday sermon, apart from the cigarette or small cigar poised casually in his hand.[1]

Fred Tipping's life, and that of almost his entire family, revolved around the textile industry in the East Midlands city of Nottingham, and he seems to embody the prosperity and self-confidence of the workers who had seen their industry grow steadily during the previous century of peace. His father was a framework knitter, one of the hardy independent breed who had plied their trade in the region ever since the invention of a hand-operated machine that revolutionized the production of garments such as stockings, and who had woven the wealth of their city, row by row, on the clattering apparatus in the corner of their parlours. While hosiery remained a small-scale trade, the stocking frame used by the knitters had been developed into a machine for mass-producing lace and this was now the main local industry, satisfying the enormous demand from dressmakers and furnishers worldwide, and employing thousands of people – including Fred's mother, who worked as a lace finisher or mender. Fred was brought up in the gritty suburb of Sneinton, where almost everyone worked in either mining or textiles, and it was not surprising that he found employment in the industry as a warehouseman, though his older half-brother Harry bucked the trend by training as a gas fitter.[2]

In the summer of 1904, at the age of twenty-three, Fred married a local girl called Florrie, who worked – not surprisingly – as a lace finisher, and their first son was born before the year was out, followed at two-year intervals by two more sons. Fortunately, as his family grew, Fred seems to have gone up in the world, and by 1911 he had moved away from Sneinton towards the suburb of Carlton, and made the transition out of the warehouse and into the office to become a shipping clerk.[3] Not only that, but he secured a post with one of Nottingham's most prestigious firms, founded by the lace merchant Thomas Adams who combined business acumen with a philanthropic concern for his workers.[4] Although Thomas was now dead, the company of Adams, Page and Co. had maintained his reputation and traditions, and continued to operate from the magnificent warehouse, complete with its own chapel, that he had built in the centre of Nottingham.

With the coming of war, Fred Tipping does not seem to have been in any great hurry to enlist, which is understandable in view of his age and family responsibilities. We know little of his early military career, but when the war ended he was not entitled to receive the 1914–15 Star, the campaign medal awarded to those such as William

Galway, Joseph Cheverton and George Macdonald who had served overseas in the first two years of the war. When he did enlist it was in the Royal Artillery, and a photograph shows him lounging cross-legged against a wall of sandbags, looking relaxed in his gunner's uniform with spurs on his boots and a leather bandolier over his shoulder – both standard accoutrements for mounted troops.[5]

The service cap at his feet displays the badge of the Royal Artillery with its battle honour 'Ubique', or 'Everywhere', reflecting the regiment's participation in every major engagement involving the British Army. This was also the case in the First World War, so without knowing his battery or brigade number it is impossible to find out where he served. All we can say is he probably belonged to the crew of an 18-pounder, the quick-firing horse-drawn field gun that was the mainstay of his branch of the artillery, and at some point he transferred to the Tank Corps where his gunnery skills – and his maturity – would have been greatly valued. The photograph also shows him looking fuller in the face, reminding us that army life with its solid rations, fresh air and exercise brought unexpected health benefits for many who had been brought up in Britain's industrial cities.

However, it goes without saying that this was not always the case. Fred's half-brother Harry enlisted in March 1916, and spent the summer in France with the King's Own (Royal Lancaster Regiment). By the end of the year they were holding the line before Thiepval, the blasted hill that had been the crux of the fighting on the Somme earlier that year, and there he was killed a fortnight before Christmas, probably during routine shelling by artillery or trench mortars.[6] For Fred Tipping, the war now had a very personal significance, and if the desire for revenge was in his heart, he was well-placed to exact it in his new role as a gunner in the Tank Corps.

* * *

We can name with certainty the commander and four crewmen of D51 *Deborah*, leaving a question-mark about three more crew members – including the driver, who was normally a sergeant or other senior NCO. Intriguingly, one man can be identified who took part in both the actions that involved D51, though there is no way of knowing whether he was in the crew of *Deborah* or another of No. 12 Company's tanks. This was David Bertram Marsden, known as Bert, who had been born in West Yorkshire and spent his earliest years in a pit village where his parents ran a pub, before crossing the Pennines to settle on Merseyside. There he became a pork butcher, a trade that was dominated by émigrés from Germany, where the pig was devoured with gusto. Prominent among them was a dynasty called Dimler who ran a chain of shops across Liverpool and Bootle, and in 1911 Bert was working and boarding with the German-born Frederick Dimler and his wife at their establishment in the suburb of Walton.[7]

Perhaps city life did not suit him, or perhaps he spotted a new opening, but after that Bert left Liverpool and moved north to a small town in Cumbria, where he set up as a pork butcher and began courting a local girl called Effie Grave. His family recall he was a keen motorcyclist,[8] and this made him an ideal recruit when a new unit was formed called the Motor Machine Gun Service (MMGS) which operated motorbikes and sidecars armed with Vickers machine guns – a deadly combination under the right circumstances, but not under those now prevailing on the Western Front. Bert joined up in March 1915, and two months later he arrived in France with No. 9 Battery of the MMGS.[9]

By coincidence, the same month saw a turning-point in the war with the sinking of the liner *Lusitania* by a U-boat with the loss of nearly 1,200 lives. The deaths of so many civilians triggered a wave of anti-German outrage in many British cities, not least Liverpool which had been *Lusitania*'s destination. The obvious targets for revenge were the German pork butchers whose shops and homes were systematically ransacked, including Bert Marsden's former workplace, after which the mob turned its wrath on other businesses with foreign-sounding names, and finally on butchers' shops in general to ensure no Germans had been missed. An unsuccessful attempt was made to burn down the residence of the Dimler family's patriarch, and shortly after this two of his relatives enlisted in the Royal Artillery and served abroad before being discharged, almost certainly because they were regarded as enemy aliens.[10]

Meanwhile the riots were brought under control after around 200 shops had been looted, and many people of German extraction were interned, partly for their own protection. There must have been plenty of opportunities for enterprising Britons to step in and replace them, but many – including Bert Marsden – were now preoccupied with a higher form of butchery.

As for the MMGS, by the time it reached the front line it had been made virtually redundant by the stagnation of trench warfare, and instead of speeding round the battlefield on motorbikes the men found themselves in static emplacements, providing anti-aircraft defence or long-range overhead fire. As they struggled to establish a role for themselves, the battery's War Diary often descended into chit-chat: 'Men all comfortable. Played rounders in evening. Held an impromptu concert', reads one entry. There are updates on people's health and activities: 'Lieut Croxford very seedy'; 'Went up to trenches and got very wet'; 'Men helped farmer to cut wild oats in fields but did more damage than work'. There was also a visit from two nurses which ended with a 'very jolly tea'.[11]

And so it dragged on, the most common entry being 'Nothing to report'. On 1 July 1916, that day of catastrophe for the British Army, No. 9 Battery remained in camp, building a road and playing cricket. It was clear this could not go on for ever, and the diary concludes with a curt entry at the end of 1916: 'Battery disbanded on Nov 14th.'[12] The MMGS had run out of road, or rather had not found enough roads to run on, but at least it provided a trained cadre of men who were transferred more or less wholesale to another unit with an equally uncertain future, namely the Heavy Branch of the Machine Gun Corps. These were the motor machine-gunners who Major Watson described as 'smart fellows, without much experience of active operations',[13] and among them was Lance-Corporal Bert Marsden. He was married to Effie Grave while home on leave, and the wedding photograph shows he lost none of his smartness once he was in the uniform of the Tank Corps.[14] At the same time, his new posting would bring far more experience of active operations than he would have imagined, and his new bride would have wished.

* * *

We have had an instructive afternoon in Oosthoek Wood, and it is fascinating to see the crewmen and to watch them at work, though frustrating that we cannot speak to them – since they are merely ghosts, or to use a less emotive term, projections of the past, and if we were to approach them they would vanish for ever, and we would be left alone among the dripping trees.

Suddenly, interrupting our reverie, there is a loud, resounding thump in the woodland a few hundred yards away, followed by a long drawn-out crashing and splintering as shrapnel and clumps of earth strike the surrounding trees, bringing down some large branches. The noise of a shell exploding is familiar from countless war films, but nothing prepares us for this, which is deeper and more visceral than we would expect – as much a physical sensation as a sound, and filled with menace. We expect to see people running for cover, but none of the crewmen appears to take the slightest notice, either out of familiarity or bravado, and we are left wondering if this was also a product of our imagination, until a plume of dirty smoke slowly unfurls above the trees.

It seems the German gunners have woken up and decided it is time for a fresh attempt to destroy whatever is concealed in the woods. Sure enough, the first explosion is followed by two more, though they are thankfully further off and more muffled, and this suddenly seems like a good time to break off our research and return to La Lovie to digest what we have learned.

It is only when we are back on board the lorry and heading away from the tankodrome that we realise with a jolt that in our haste to leave we completely forgot to look at the front of the tank to see if it did indeed bear the name *Deborah*. Despite racking our brains, we cannot be sure, though it seems more than likely that this tank had the same name as the later D51, since the name and crew number normally went together. Sadly there is no way to confirm this when we get back to camp, since the only document that records the tank's details does not mention her name.[15]

In fact, the practice of naming tanks had begun with their first appearance in battle, sometimes preceded by 'H.M.L.S.' ('His Majesty's Landship') to emphasize the nautical conceit, and this was gradually formalized with every tank christened according to the letter of its battalion. The source of the name *Deborah* is unknown: the obvious assumption is that the tank was named after someone's wife or girlfriend, but this is unlikely since the name was relatively uncommon, and in 1900, for example, it was given to fewer than 100 baby girls.[16]

The most likely explanation is that the name was inspired by the Bible, where Deborah was a warrior prophetess who led the Israelites to victory over the Canaanites with their 900 chariots of iron, and whose song of battle is recorded in the Book of Judges: 'So let all thine enemies perish, O Lord: but let them that love him be as the sun when he goeth forth in his might.'[17] For Shakespeare, the name encapsulated feminine power: 'Thou art an Amazon, and fightest with the sword of Deborah'.[18]

This was especially appropriate for a female tank, and if it all sounds rather high-flown, one should remember that the Bible and classics were a shared idiom among the officers who were mainly the product of grammar or public schools. Many tanks were named after figures from mythology or ancient history, such as *Damocles*, *Darius* and *Diogenes*, while *Dusky Dis* was an obscure synonym for the god Pluto taken from Shakespeare's *The Tempest*. Other literary allusions included the Walter Scott character *Dandy* [sic] *Dinmont*, *Drake's Drum*, and, as we have seen, *Dracula*.[19]

Not all the names were so arcane, and many were intended to inspire or terrify, such as *Dreadnought*, *Death's Head*, *Devil-May-Care* and *Dakoit* (an armed robber in India or Burma). *Dashing Dragoon* was probably a tribute to one of the section commanders, Captain Frederick Talbot, who had served in 4th Dragoon Guards during the Boer War.[20] There were also some concessions to popular culture – *Dollar Princess*, for example, was named after a musical, while *Dop Doctor* was a novel about a physician in South Africa with a penchant for the local brandy known as 'dop'.[21]

Some junior officers tried to take things even further downmarket, hence Second Lieutenant Macintosh's comment that the choice of names was 'no longer left to the youthful and revue-full fancy of the young tank pilot'.[22] The rationale for this was spelled out by one such 'pilot', Lieutenant John Coghlan, known to all as Jack: 'I recall one shrewd officer calling his tank "Johnny Walker" [*sic*], with the motto "Still going strong." He informed the well-known firm of his intention, hoping it had no objection, and duly received a case of Black Label for his consideration. My own youthful ardours strayed to the stars on the London stage. I named my tank "Teddy Gerard" [*sic*] after a lady who was then delighting Town, and hoped to pursue the opening move. Alas, an unromantic High Command issued the order that "His Majesty's Land Ships should not be named after stars on the light variety stage" and directed that my tank should be named "Damon". To this day I am hazy about Damon and his fame. I believe he had one friend.'[23] The Johnnie Walker story seems apocryphal, since there is no record of a tank with that name, but the one about Teddie Gerard rings true. Coghlan's final aside shows he recognized Damon as yet another figure from mythology, whose self-sacrificing relationship with Pythias made them an enduring symbol of friendship.

But others, who took the trouble to come up with a variety star whose name began with 'D', managed to get away with it. Private Jason Addy, a member of Lieutenant Alfred Enoch's crew, recalled they named their tank *Delysia* 'after the famous dancer at the time'. This was Alice Delysia, the stage-name of a glamorous and slightly risqué French actress and singer. Addy wrote that 'Corporal Carr obtained an autographed photo from her. We mounted it near the front driving seat during our actions at Ypres and Cambrai.'[24]

Perhaps thankfully, there was nothing to equal the black humour of F Battalion, who named one of their tanks *Fray Bentos* – then, as now, a popular brand of canned chopped meat, reflecting the crew's view of their likely fate – and another *Fritz Phlattner*, to understand which it is necessary to know that 'Fritz' was a common name for a German soldier, and then to say the name out loud.

CHAPTER 7

In Honour Bound

As they made the best of life in their makeshift camp, the tank crews were still mystified as to how the Germans had discovered their hiding-place in Oosthoek Wood with such apparent ease. Then, a week after the start of the British offensive, the bombshell dropped: they had been deliberately betrayed.

The first mention of this came in an intelligence summary from Tank Corps headquarters on 5 August 1917. This stated that during the British advance, an enemy report had been captured which showed there had been a disastrous breach of security about the tanks and their preparations for the attack. The British intelligence summary contained a lengthy translation from the captured German report:

> According to the statement of two prisoners ... a large number of tanks are packed in the wood south of Oosthoek ... Presumably the newly laid out roads already noticed on aeroplane photographs through this wood to Vlamertinghe and from there to the Canal are to serve as approach roads for these tanks ... A tracing showing the assembly place and roads of approach is handed to divisions. Prisoners also state that fascines and bridge building material have been prepared for crossing the Canal by tanks.[1]

The German report revealed that the prisoners had given away more than just the location of the tanks, and the corridors of La Lovie Château were soon in turmoil. On 8 August, the intelligence officer of Fifth Army reported: 'A captured document shows that the enemy was able to establish our order of battle and became acquainted with several salient features of our attack on July 31st by the statements of two of our men who were captured in a raid about 28th July.'[2]

As inquiries continued, the authorities were able to narrow down the source of the leak and soon came up with a name for the informant. This was revealed at an infantry brigade conference on 10 August, when commanders 'were asked to enquire as to whether any N.C.O., who might turn out to be Sergeant Phillips, was made a prisoner before "Z" Day [i.e. 31 July].'[3] The question must have come as a blow to Major Wynn Powell Wheldon, who had just taken over as commander of 14th (Service) Battalion Royal Welsh Fusiliers, for one of his first duties had been to investigate a failed raid on the German lines that resulted in the capture of several men – including Sergeant Phillips.

* * *

The raid on the night of 26/27 July was one of a series carried out ahead of the coming offensive to determine the strength of German positions and the effect of the British bombardment. The officer selected to lead the raid, Second Lieutenant Joseph Brommage, was typical of the 'temporary gentlemen' who were being commissioned into the new battalions of Kitchener's army. Just twenty years old and the Catholic son of a brewery director, he had been brought up in Mid-Glamorgan where he attended the local grammar school before training as a schoolmaster. His teaching career was cut short by the war, and he enlisted in an officers' training corps before joining the newly-formed 14th Battalion of the Royal Welsh Fusiliers in January 1917, shortly after they arrived on the Western Front.[4]

He told a subsequent court of enquiry into the raid how he had led his party of twenty-four men, with two Lewis light machine guns to provide covering fire, into No Man's Land just before midnight while a preparatory barrage pounded the German positions. 'I went forward with the party up to the German parapet and I then dropped back pursuant to my orders to my Lewis Guns in support about 12 yards back. Sergeant Phillips was in charge of the forward raiding party.' The raiders would be given nine minutes to search the German trenches, and Second Lieutenant Brommage would then fire two Very lights (or flares) as the signal to retire.[5]

Corporal Frank Philpotts, the leader of one of the parties of bombers who were sent forward, described how they entered the German front line as soon as the barrage lifted. 'It was difficult to find, it was so broken up. I could only find a thin scoop between shell holes. I found a dugout but it was knocked in and the entrance filled with earth. I could not get in or hear anything, but I fired into it on chance.' One of his men, Private William Sandiford, added: 'It was like a ploughed field and I could not recognise it as a trench except for the broken timber lying about. I saw no Germans.' He glimpsed two of their party dropping into a trench away to the left, before the signal to retire lit up the sky and Corporal Philpotts told him: 'Look slippy and get back.'[6]

Private Sandiford located a tape that had been laid to guide them back across No Man's Land, but lost both the tape and his sense of direction after falling into a shell-hole. 'I wandered back to the German trench and was for a time lost but a good flare showed me the Canal Bank trees and I made for those and got in about post 45.' On his way back to the British lines bordering the Yser Canal, he heard grenade explosions and machine-gun fire. Meanwhile Second Lieutenant Brommage saw about nine of his men returning in the darkness, before he also made his way back to the British lines. But on returning to headquarters there was a sickening discovery: 'I could not find that Sergeant Phillips, Corporal John and 8 other men had returned to our trench … I then returned to the front lines with Corporal Philpot [sic] and I went out at 4 a.m. as far as the German wire to search for the missing men but could not see them.' The tapes were still in place and he added: 'I do not understand how this party lost direction.'[7]

At the end of the inquiry, Lieutenant-Colonel Evelyn Uniacke, who was about to hand over command of the battalion, issued his verdict: 'I am of opinion that these men missed the tape line on retiring & making too much north, struck the enemy lines & were probably made prisoner. I do not attach blame to either of the officers present. 2/Lieut Brommage appears to have done all that was possible after discovering the loss.'[8]

Two of the missing men were later found wounded in No Man's Land,[9] but of the others there was no trace. They had indeed been captured by the Germans, and the original interrogation report on the two captured NCOs has recently been discovered in a German military archive. This contains the men's account of their capture, as recorded by the Germans:

> The patrol consisted of 22 men and one officer. The officer did not leave the trench, so the sergeant who was captured had to lead the raid. The objective of the raid was to penetrate the German second line to establish whether our first and

second trenches were occupied, to take prisoners, and to investigate our system of light signals, if possible by capturing flares and documents. The operation failed because the period of four minutes allowed to cross the area between the positions turned out to be too short, the ground being more badly churned up than expected. The patrol came under its own fire, became disorientated, and some men ran into the German trenches.[10]

The German report, prepared on 29 July, does not name the informants, but gives some background about them. 'One of the prisoners is a farm-worker by occupation, but was a serving soldier for seven years, then a farm-worker for four years until joining the army in September 1915. The other prisoner has had numerous jobs. At the beginning of the war he travelled between England and France as a stoker on a troopship-steamer, likewise joining up as a Kitchener man in September 1915 when the battalion was raised. Both are 32-33 years old and sturdy fellows. They describe the reinforcements arriving now as very inferior, both physically and mentally.'[11]

As well as information about the tanks, the report shows the men divulged a largely accurate summary of plans for the British attack, including the sectors held by different units, details of the artillery barrage, and what they knew of times, dates and code-words. In some cases the prisoners passed on rumours or embroidered the facts, perhaps to curry favour or impress their captors. For example, they claimed the attack would begin with the detonation of two mines, and gave details of their location. This was an obvious concern for the Germans, who had been blasted off Messines ridge a few weeks before by nineteen mines buried under their trenches, though in this case the story was untrue.

The prisoners also claimed a French attack would follow the British one, and would be reinforced by around 6,000 American troops. This must have come as a shock to the Germans, since America had declared war in April 1917 but had not so far joined in the fighting. Recognizing its significance, the German intelligence officer added: 'The prisoner who made this statement is a sergeant, was a serving soldier for seven years, and gave the impression of being completely credible.' Nevertheless, whoever reviewed the report now in the German archives added a large question-mark in the margin.[12] His scepticism was well-founded: although American 'doughboys' had begun landing in France, they would not participate in the fighting until later in the year.

The prisoners also exaggerated the effects of a German poison gas bombardment on the night of 23/24 July, which they said had caused twenty-six deaths in their company alone, and 400–500 casualties in the battalion as a whole. British records confirm the shelling caused 'a large number of casualties'[13] but only a small number were fatal, and records show that fewer than ten men from 14th Bn Royal Welsh Fusiliers died on those dates.[14]

* * *

With exemplary thoroughness, the prisoners' information was communicated to German front-line units, with the result that a copy of the report soon fell into the hands of the advancing British. By then it was too late to do more than issue a warning, which was done by the commander of Fifth Army, Sir Hubert Gough. His routine orders on 16 August contained one item which made a lasting impression on its audience:

> The summary of the examination of Sergt. Phillips, Royal Welsh Fusiliers, extracted from a German Intelligence Summary, and attached, shows that the

N.C.O. in question imparted information of considerable value to the enemy. The Army Commander desires to bring this case to the notice of all ranks, and to point out that the statements made by Sergt. Phillips undoubtedly assisted the enemy in preparing to meet our attack, and were consequently largely responsible for the casualties inflicted on his comrades. All men who are unfortunate enough to be taken prisoner by the enemy must realize that they are in honour bound not to furnish information which can only result in endangering both the lives of their own comrades and the success of the British arms.[15]

To drive the point home, the routine orders included a page summarizing the information disclosed by Sergeant Phillips, including some relating to the Tank Corps: 'The attacks will probably begin in the early morning hours and will be opened by a frontal attack of the tanks. For the crossing of the canal by the tanks and the troops, fascines and bridging material are held in readiness ... The number of tanks available is estimated to be 200. The prisoner himself saw a large number of these on July 24th, in the small wood South of Oosthoek, *i.e.*, in the South-West corner of the rectangular cleared area inside this wood. The crews were billeted in a camp to the North of it.'[16] For some reason the Fifth Army communiqué made no mention of Corporal John, who had been captured at the same time as Sergeant Phillips and was presumably the other NCO referred to in the German interrogation report. It also omitted the claim that American troops would take part in the attack.

When news of this betrayal reached the tank crews they reacted with anger and consternation, coupled with some relief that at last they could explain the German shelling that had harassed them since their arrival in Oosthoek Wood. In his official history of the Tank Corps, Major Clough Williams-Ellis summarized their feelings:

The enemy had obtained information of our tankodrome in Oosthoek Wood from a British prisoner, who was either a garrulous fool or a very treacherous knave. A soldier ... had betrayed every detail of the whereabouts of the tanks of the 1st Brigade, and of the programme of their movements. A German document was captured setting forth the whole of this creature's evidence and explaining its value and significance. The official account of this murderous piece of treachery was periodically read out on parade to all tank units, and formed the text of many discourses on the vital importance of strict secrecy and high *moral* [*sic*]. The name of this man will for ever have a sinister sound for all who served in the Tank Corps.'[17]

Later Second Lieutenant Douglas Browne of G Battalion, who had been on the receiving end of the shelling in Oosthoek Wood, recalled:

We used to debit this unpleasantness to the growing account of Sergeant Phillips. This gentleman, having been captured in a raid, proceeded to give to the enemy every atom of information in his possession. Most of it was fairly accurate ... This piece of treachery having come to the knowledge of our Intelligence Corps, a summary of the disclosures, together with a prophecy as to the offender's probable destiny if ever he returned to England, was ordered to be read out every week on parade throughout the Army. Now that the war is over, and the prisoners are returned, I have often wondered what really has happened to Sergeant Phillips. As he appeared to be a man of some intelligence, he probably has remained in Germany.[18]

The commander of 1st Tank Brigade, Colonel Baker-Carr, went even further in threatening revenge: 'The name of the betrayer and his regiment became a byword in the First Brigade, and a large number of men proposed to call on him after the War was over and explain to him, with vigorous action, exactly what they thought of him.'[19] Second Lieutenant Frank Mitchell of A Battalion even heard a suggestion that 'when Sergeant Phillips returned to England after the war he would be tried and punished in the only way suitable for traitors'.[20]

Meanwhile, the report of the court of enquiry into the raid made its slow progress up the chain of command. From 14th Bn Royal Welsh Fusiliers it was passed up to 113th Infantry Brigade, who passed it up to 38th (Welsh) Division, who passed it up to Fifth Army, and by September it had reached the Adjutant and Quartermaster General at GHQ, after which it seems to have disappeared into a filing cabinet. Along the way a question was asked about why the men's absence had not been reported earlier, but Second Lieutenant Brommage, who led the raid, was in no position to answer. On 1 August he had been shot through the thigh and was now in hospital in England. While there he applied for a transfer to the Indian Army, and never returned to the Royal Welsh Fusiliers or to the Western Front.[21]

As the battle wore on, the story of Sergeant Phillips acquired the status of myth as it spread far and wide. For Lieutenant George Mackenzie of the Royal Artillery, it explained the 'unparalleled readiness' of the enemy gunners to respond to an attack on 16 August. He learned that 'a sergeant of the Welsh Fusiliers who had been employed as [a] clerk at GHQ, and had been returned to the line for disciplinary purposes, had treacherously deserted to the enemy, taking with him not only intimation of tomorrow's attack, but also a copy of a map on which was indicated the position of every battery on that sector of the British front'.[22]

It is true that Fifth Army issued its warning about Sergeant Phillips on 16 August, but this made it clear he had been captured three weeks before, so he could not possibly have been responsible, while the story about him being dismissed from GHQ also seems fanciful. Another survivor of the attack, Private William Groom of 5th Bn London Regiment, heard the same story in an officer's pep-talk: 'At first we thought it was just a yarn to excuse our costly defeat but then we remembered the shells that dropped amongst us, and slaughtered the reserves behind us, at the very moment our barrage opened.'[23]

A version of the story reached 51st (Highland) Division, with some gruesome embroidery: 'The location of our tanks in a wood was said to have been ... given away, with resulting destructive attention from bombers; and it was also said that the spy, caught later *in flagrante delicto*, was obliterated in the mud by an appropriate and lucky tank accident.'[24]

* * *

Now that the facts have finally been uncovered, it is possible to disentangle the mixture of truth, speculation and rumour which make up the story of Sergeant Phillips. It is clear the Tank Corps were mistaken in one important respect: the Germans already knew there were tanks in Oosthoek Wood before Sergeant Phillips and Corporal John were captured on 26/27 July. They had been shelling Oosthoek Wood since the beginning of the month, with the bombardment that killed the tankmen from C Battalion, for instance, taking place on 4 July.[25] The fact was that despite the attempts at camouflage, German aircraft had spotted tell-tale signs almost as soon as the tanks moved in, and the intelligence officer who interrogated Sergeant Phillips added a significant note to his report: 'Confirmed by aerial photographs.'[26]

In one important respect Sergeant Phillips and Corporal John probably did increase to the enemy's knowledge. The aerial photographs had only revealed a small number of tanks in the wood, and the news that there were hundreds must have come as a shock. This may help to answer another question that perplexed the tank crews: if the Germans knew where the tanks were hidden, why did they not dedicate more effort to destroying them? It was true that the massive build-up of British forces in the Salient had created a profusion of targets, but it still seemed surprising that the shelling and bombing of Oosthoek Wood were, in the words of one officer, 'rather desultory'.[27] Or as Major Watson put it: 'Knowing what they did, it is a little astonishing that the German gunners did not increase their nightly ration of shells, which merely disturbed the guard, who slept under the tanks when not on duty, and did not damage a tank.'[28]

This would make sense if the Germans had only spotted a few tanks in the wood. In addition, Major Clough Williams-Ellis offered another more depressing possibility: the tanks may not have been seen as much of a threat. 'Perhaps the Germans, having no illusions as to what fighting in Flanders meant, and being reasonably alive to the natural limitations of tanks, scouted [i e dismissed] the idea of a tank attack being possible or being even seriously contemplated. Be that as it may, they certainly failed to act on the very valuable information given them in anything like an adequate way.'[29]

However, by the time the Germans learned the true scale of the tank preparations at Oosthoek, they may have thought it was too late. The interrogation report was prepared on 29 July, and it was reasonable to assume that by then the tanks would have moved into their forward positions ready for the attack, which was clearly imminent. However, if the Germans did think this they were mistaken. G Battalion had indeed left for the front line, but they were replaced by E Battalion, whose tanks began arriving in the wood on 29 July, while D Battalion had been designated as corps reserve and its tanks (including D51) would remain there until required.

Whatever the practical effect of the prisoners' revelations, the fact remains that they did pass on information of potential value to the enemy, and it seems baffling that they should have done so. Sergeant Phillips, especially, was a seasoned soldier and held a trusted position as a senior NCO. He must have been familiar with the spirit, if not the letter, of the army's standing orders: 'If a man has the misfortune to be taken prisoner, he is not to give any information beyond his own name and rank. The enemy cannot and will not compel him to say more – though he may threaten to do so – on the contrary he will respect a man whose courage and patriotism do not fail even though wounded or a prisoner. Prisoners should be on their guard against Germans dressed as British officers who are employed by the enemy to extract information.'[30] Perhaps some trickery was involved, while Major Watson thought the information was given 'probably under pressure'.[31] At the same time, Sergeant Phillips' account of the raid suggests he felt some resentment towards the officer in charge, and no doubt the Germans played on this, as well as exploiting the confusion, fear and desire for self-preservation that might be found in any prisoner.

Strange to say, despite the curiosity that the story has aroused, no-one has ever identified Sergeant Phillips (or Corporal John), or found out what happened to them after the war. This turns out be harder than it sounds, since both names were relatively common in a Welsh regiment, and the military records give no further details about them.

The crucial clues are to be found in the German interrogation report, which identifies their battalion, and in an 'embarkation roll' which lists 1,000 officers and men who went to France with 14th Bn Royal Welsh Fusiliers in December 1915. This includes the name of 21158 Corporal S. Phillips,[32] and the medal records show this number belonged to Samuel Phillips and confirm that he was promoted to sergeant.[33] Finally, the records kept by the International Committee of the Red Cross show that he was indeed captured near Ypres on 26 July.[34]

* * *

In the late summer of 1917, a letter arrived at the terraced cottage of Mrs Phillips containing the information she had been praying for: her husband was safe and well, though a prisoner-of-war in Germany. The good news appeared in the local Welsh language newspaper: 'The wife of Sergeant Sam Phillips … has received a letter from him saying he is a prisoner of the Germans in Lemberg [this should be Limburg], along with three others.'[35]

A few days later another local paper carried details of a letter sent from another camp in which he described his capture: 'I was sent out one night and was in charge of a patrol when in the dark we went a little too far and got into a German trench. We put up a good fight before we were taken. Send me something to sweeten my coffee as we don't get any sugar or milk and no tea, butter, or jam. I am only allowed to write one letter every fortnight.'[36]

Not surprisingly there was no mention of his interrogation, and Mrs Phillips was no doubt unaware of the furore this had caused. She had married Sam, who was a miner's son, in 1911 when they were both aged twenty-three and he was working as a bricklayer, while his bride worked as a servant on a farm. After the wedding they went to live with her parents in their little cottage, though it must have been a tight fit as their first child was born soon afterwards. Other children followed, including a son born in 1916 who was obviously a parting gift before Sergeant Phillips went off to war.[37]

There was nothing in his past to indicate why he might have given away information, though we should not rush to judgment against him unless we have endured a similar situation ourselves. One searches his photograph for any clue, but the open face seems guileless and there is no obvious sign of malice or calculation. His family, not surprisingly, were aware he had served in the First World War but knew nothing more, not even that he had been taken prisoner, and do not believe that he might have been responsible for any breach of security. There is therefore no clue as to what might have motivated him.

Sergeant Phillips remained in captivity for the rest of the war, and we should leave him there to ponder what the future might hold; but the story has a strange and tragic sequel, and as we shall see, he would later repay any debt of honour that he might owe to his country.

PART II

THE BATTLE OF PASSCHENDAELE

Map 3: Attack by D Battalion on 22 August 1917

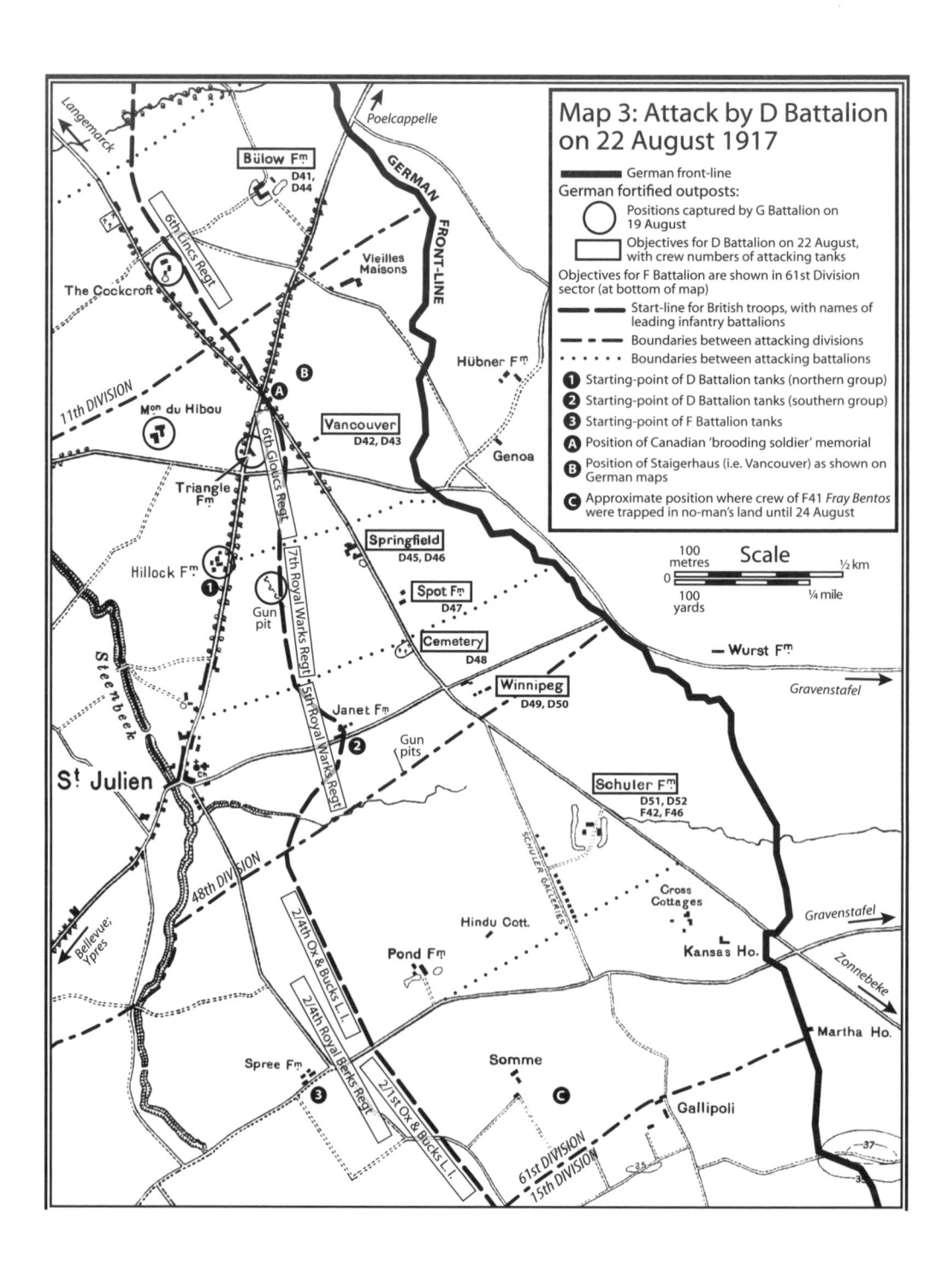

▬▬▬ German front-line
German fortified outposts:
○ Positions captured by G Battalion on 19 August
▢ Objectives for D Battalion on 22 August, with crew numbers of attacking tanks
Objectives for F Battalion are shown in 61st Division sector (at bottom of map)
– – – Start-line for British troops, with names of leading infantry battalions
–·–·– Boundaries between attacking divisions
······ Boundaries between attacking battalions
❶ Starting-point of D Battalion tanks (northern group)
❷ Starting-point of D Battalion tanks (southern group)
❸ Starting-point of F Battalion tanks
Ⓐ Position of Canadian 'brooding soldier' memorial
Ⓑ Position of Staigerhaus (i.e. Vancouver) as shown on German maps
Ⓒ Approximate position where crew of F41 *Fray Bentos* were trapped in no-man's land until 24 August

CHAPTER 8

Ray of Sunshine

In mid-August the British finally began the next phase of their great offensive in the Ypres Salient, now generally referred to as the Battle of Passchendaele, and the full brilliance of the German defensive strategy was revealed. Unable to construct a conventional trench system in the swampy terrain, they had opted for a flexible system of defence in depth, with the front positions held by isolated units whose job was to disrupt the advance, and their main forces further back, beyond the range of most artillery fire and ready to counter-attack when the time was right. To create a series of forward outposts, they had transformed the farmhouses that dotted the area into a network of concrete bunkers which were the only truly solid features in this liquid landscape. Since these seemed all but indestructible, even by artillery, their machine guns now held fearful dominion over the blasted plain across which the British had to advance.

Three-and-a-half miles (or five-and a half kilometres) north-east of Ypres, near the central axis of their offensive, the British had seized what had once been a village called St Julien,[1] through which flowed what had once been a stream called the Steenbeek. The village had been more or less blown off the face of the earth, and the Steenbeek had disappeared just as completely, though its filthy waters still skulked through an ever-shifting morass of shell craters. Half a mile east of St Julien, what had once been a road traversed the quagmire between the devastated villages of Langemarck (to the north-west) and Zonnebeke (to the south-east), and the farmhouses lining this road

Opposite: Map 3 shows plans for the first action involving tanks from D Battalion during the Battle of Passchendaele. At lower left is the village of St Julien, though this had been all but obliterated, along with the river Steenbeek.

The approximate German front line is indicated, though the swampy ground prevented the creation of a continuous trench system. In front were a series of concrete strongpoints, and the objective on 22 August was to seize a number of these in preparation for an attack on the main front line.

The seven outposts to be taken by D Battalion are shown in boxes, with the crew numbers of the tanks that were to attack each one (though a number of crews were now using G Battalion tanks).

To their right, the tanks of F Battalion attacked a further series of strongpoints which are shown in the sector allocated to 61st Division, and to their right again tanks from C Battalion attacked with men from 15th Division. Two F Battalion tanks were to tackle Schuler Farm, which was also the ultimate objective of D51.

The approximate starting positions of the attacking infantry battalions are shown by a thick dashed line, though again this was not a continuous line of trenches. The British start-line incorporated a number of German outposts captured by G Battalion on 19 August, as described in Chapter 8. A description of the attack on 22 August is given in Chapters 10–12, with a full order of battle in Appendix A.

On 27 August, D Battalion launched a fresh attack on Springfield and Vancouver, as well as Genoa, Hübner and Stroppe Farms. This is described in Chapter 13.

had been converted into a chain of bunkers and pillboxes which formed the first bastion of the German defences.

Ironically, the British had seized a number of these strongpoints at the high point of their surge forward on 31 July, before the German counter-attacks swept them back and left them clinging, like drowning men, to the wreckage of St Julien. Now the same positions would have to be taken all over again, and it was clear this was going to be a bloody and protracted business.

In theory tanks offered an ideal solution, since they were largely immune to machine-gun fire and could manoeuvre round to fire on the blockhouses from the rear, demoralising the defenders and forcing them to surrender or withdraw. But this was to ignore the appalling nature of the ground, which severely limited the tanks' powers of movement and left them ditched, and sometimes half-submerged, the moment they strayed off the shattered roads.

These difficulties were exposed when the offensive finally resumed on 16 August. Twelve tanks from G Battalion left their forward positions to support the attack, but as they travelled towards the start-line they became repeatedly bogged down despite heroic efforts by the crews with their unditching gear, and by the tanks which towed each other free, and by the Royal Engineers who laboured to dig them out. Not one arrived in time and the infantry were left to advance unsupported. Not surprisingly they made limited progress, leading even the normally upbeat Colonel Baker-Carr to dismiss it as a 'ghastly failure'.[2]

For those who had doubts about tanks, this fiasco added to the sense that they would never be a viable weapon of war. The Tank Corps was increasingly seen as a costly luxury which tied up thousands of men and drained resources from factories that were straining to feed the guns with ammunition. The products of all this ingenuity and expense now lay scattered across the Salient for anyone to see, in varying states of destruction and often sinking up to their sponsons in mud.

And then, on 19 August, as if the sun had broken out over the battlefield, the whole prospect suddenly changed.

* * *

The occasion for this transformation was a small-scale operation against a cluster of strongpoints to the north of St Julien. Rather than repeat their previous mistake of travelling cross-country, the tanks of G Battalion were ordered to keep to the roads, or what was left of them. Furthermore, they were given a leading role in the operation and the infantry were ordered not to move forward until the positions had been taken.[3]

Eight tanks took part in the attack against a series of positions known as the Cockcroft, Maison du Hibou, Triangle Farm, Hillock Farm and the Gun Pit. The attack was originally conceived on a much larger scale, and the orders issued only two days beforehand included the capture of a further series of strongpoints stretching away to the south called Vancouver, Springfield and Winnipeg – recalling the presence of Canadian troops who had borne the brunt of the first poison gas attack here in April 1915. Tanks had reached some of these positions on the opening day of the offensive, only to be driven back by the German counter-attack. It is not clear why the latest operation was scaled back, though perhaps the available resources were felt to be inadequate against so many objectives.[4] As it was, the plan revolved around surprise, with the tanks advancing along the roads under cover of a sudden barrage, and smoke shells saturating any higher ground from which they could be observed. Once the tanks had subdued the strongpoints, the infantry would then move forward to occupy them.

To the delight, and it must be said astonishment, of the attackers, the Germans fell back almost immediately when the tanks approached, abandoning their positions and leaving the infantry to move in unopposed. This was achieved at a cost to the Tank Corps of two men killed and sixteen wounded, as well as the loss of three tanks which became ditched and had to be abandoned by their crews.[5] A report in the files of Lieutenant-General Sir Ivor Maxse, the commander of XVIII Corps which conducted the operation, summarized the results: ' …our line was carried forward on a front of one mile and to a depth of 400 yards. We had captured five strong points and inflicted on the Germans a loss of seventy-five casualties. <u>The total casualties to our infantry were only fifteen instead of 600 as estimated.</u> Thus it will be seen the tanks on this occasion won a battle and saved British lives.'[6]

A wise person has remarked that success has many parents, and among those who sought to take the credit was Lieutenant-Colonel John Fuller, a staff officer at Tank Corps headquarters, who described how he had devised the method of attack based, apparently, on one used by the ancient Greeks. He told how 'the Fifth Army, which detested tanks and seldom had a good word for them, accepted my tactics'.[7] Fuller's Napoleonic aspirations meant he was widely known as 'Boney', and it was not surprising that the man he liked to call 'the Murat of the Corps'[8] should also seek to take the victor's laurels. The commander of 1st Tank Brigade, Colonel Christopher Baker-Carr – who shared a certain flamboyance with the erstwhile Marshal of France, Joachim Murat – left no doubt in his memoirs that he was the real driving-force behind the attack. At the same time, he was careful to acknowledge the support of Maxse, who he described as 'a kind of god-father to the tanks'.[9] He told how Maxse had ignored the 'contemptuous silence' of the divisional commanders and informed them that 'this was "Baker-Carr's battle" and that any demands I made were to be met'.[10]

Maxse was also no slouch when it came to taking credit for the success, as he showed in a letter to his wife, an equally formidable figure who he addressed as 'Tiny':

> This last little operation was run on a new plan invented, partially, by myself. At any rate, if it was not invented by me it was carried out for the first time by this corps at my instigation … I need scarcely tell you who know me too well that my plan was simplicity itself and was just obviously the thing to be done, in fact mere common-or-garden reasoning … When the results became known yesterday my Corps [Headquarters] became a centre of interest, from G.H.Q down to the humblest platoon commander!! Kig. [i.e. Sir Douglas Haig's Chief of General Staff, Lieutenant-General Launcelot Kiggell] for the first time in the war phoned to ask 'how it was done'? as if one could explain common-sense down a telephone to some one who has never commanded even a humble company!'[11]

Maxse was so much the model of a modern general that he even had a 'spin doctor' back home in the form of his brother Leo, whose father had bought him an ailing periodical called the *National Review* to run. Against the odds, Leo Maxse had turned this into a highly influential journal, and was therefore well placed to keep his brother updated on political developments at home. One of Leo's contacts was the industrialist Frank Dudley Docker, chairman of the Metropolitan Carriage, Wagon and Finance Company which was a leading producer of tanks, and after a visit to their factory in the West Midlands, Leo told his brother how he had extolled the 'recent brilliant little operation in your Corps when the tanks showed their marvellous life-preserving effectiveness'. Leo proposed using this to motivate the workers: 'I could not help wishing that an account of it might be posted up all through the Works for the benefit of the employees, whose co-operation is just as essential to beat the Boche as that of the fighting men.'[12]

The media also did their bit, and back at La Lovie the officers of G Battalion had a visit from the correspondent William Beach Thomas, who filed a jubilant account for the newspapers: 'Yesterday's operation was practically a trial of strength between our movable landships and the stationary concrete forts, and the latter were hopelessly outmatched ... In several of the forts the tank crews found the Germans just about to begin breakfast, and our men sat down and ate the meals gratefully.'[13]

After so many setbacks, the tank crews finally had something to celebrate; indeed Major Clough Williams-Ellis, who had played his part as reconnaissance officer of 1st Tank Brigade, implied that this 'brilliant little exploit' had helped to assure the future of the Tank Corps.[14] But for those involved in the operation, there was a frustrating sense that much more could have been achieved. One of the tank commanders, Second Lieutenant Douglas Browne, felt there had been nothing to stop them taking Vancouver, Springfield and Winnipeg as originally planned. 'The Germans were then completely surprised, in ignorance of what actually was happening (on account of the very effective smoke barrage), and, for the time being, thoroughly demoralised ... The task, however, had been left unfinished.'[15] Confirming the low state of German morale, the advancing troops reportedly found a German officer hanged inside one of the captured strongpoints,[16] though it was unclear whether he could not stand any more of the bombardment and did away with himself, or whether his men could not stand any more of their officer, and did away with him.

Either way, there was further promising evidence in a report from Haig's intelligence chief, Brigadier-General John Charteris, containing comments from a captured member of 125th Infantry Regiment. The prisoner criticized the training of officers, and claimed they sometimes took command after only four weeks' military training: 'A large proportion of the present officers are university students and young business men who know little or nothing about methods of warfare. He has known instances of officers receiving orders to have a trench dug or to fortify a position and they have had no idea how to commence the work. The men are very well trained ... but they are badly led.'[17] Perhaps the prisoner was simply telling his audience what they wanted to hear, and if so there were many who felt the same could be said of Charteris.

However, the attack showed that the Tank Corps had come up with a winning formula that could be repeated to capture more of the enemy strongholds, including those that were in the original attack plan for 19 August. But this would not be a job for G Battalion, who were now withdrawn to rest and regroup. Instead it was time for the more experienced men of D Battalion – including the crew of D51 – to come out of reserve, since in the words of Second Lieutenant Browne: 'D Battalion, one of the old originals, as it never failed to remind us by word and behaviour, had not yet been into action at all.'[18]

* * *

Before following their progress it will be instructive to do what they could not, and pick our way across No Man's Land to see the day's events from the viewpoint of the German 125th Infantry Regiment, which was holding the line opposite. Whatever the British intelligence reports implied, it was a regiment with a long and proud history which had fought against the French in the Napoleonic Wars and again in 1870, then against the Russians on the Eastern Front in 1914, and then against the British on the Somme and at Arras. The regiment was named in honour of Kaiser Friedrich, King of Prussia, but formed part of the army of Württemberg, the smallest of the four kingdoms whose armies had been united following the creation of a unified German state in 1871.

The 125th had previously been resting in a number of quiet sectors – one near the French town of Cambrai, where the defences were so impregnable that a peaceful tour of duty was guaranteed – before being plunged into the 'Flandernschlacht', or Flanders battle. The men moved into the front line on the night of 17/18 August, and their commanding officer, Oberst (i.e. Colonel) Reinhold Stühmke, immediately realized the rules had changed:

> The very manner in which the regiment had to be deployed here indicated that this was not about trench warfare in the hitherto accepted sense of the word, but rather – for the time being, at least – a continuous battle across open country which could bring many surprises. Behind a thin outpost line (or forward position), small detachments maintained a foothold in order to take the initial impact and repel weaker attacks. Behind them lay the attack companies, and even further back, widely and deeply distributed, the attack battalion. In this haphazard position there was no question of a continuously held line, or a clear parade-ground formation. The forward soldiers were posted in shell-holes, all the rest were swallowed up by folds in the ground or clung to the hedgerows, wherever they thought they could best hide from the eyes of the enemy, also in the busy skies, and thus be exposed as little as possible to the enemy's artillery fire.[19]

The majority of German military records were destroyed in the Second World War, but those from the army of Württemberg have survived and provide a revealing picture of their day-to-day activities. Whereas British War Diaries often give the impression of being scribbled in a dugout with a stub of pencil, their German counterparts – true to stereotype – are detailed, methodical and often neatly typewritten. Each has its volume of appendices containing maps, orders and sketches. Professional and precise, they give no clue that they were written in hell.

For despite the British perception that their enemies were all safely ensconced in concrete bunkers, the truth was very different. While the pillboxes provided the lynchpin of the German defences, most of their men were simply huddled in shell-holes with no defence against the devastating power of the British artillery, or the often appalling weather. Even the bunkers themselves were more vulnerable to shelling than is often supposed, and could easily prove a death trap for the defenders as well as the attackers.

Little more than a day after the Württembergers had taken over the sector, they faced the first of the surprises that their commanding officer had referred to. Early on 19 August the bombardment increased to fresh intensity, cutting the telephone wires, and at 6 a.m. (i.e. 5 a.m. UK time) the regimental headquarters received a message by flashlight from the front line: 'Feindlicher Angriff' ('Enemy attack'). Further details followed: 'The enemy has broken through between 1st and 2nd Battalions of the 125th with a tank, of which eight are reported to be on their way.'[20]

The obvious assumption was that a full-scale infantry attack would follow, and when this failed to materialize, the Germans could only conclude that it had been stamped out by their artillery fire. The headquarters of 51st Infantry Brigade, which included 125th Infantry Regiment, tried to make sense of events as they unfolded:

As far as the situation can be assessed from the currently available reports, the enemy planned an advance against 125th Infantry Regiment ... during the morning in conjunction with their heavy artillery barrage and the use of tanks. This attack, being identified in good time by our infantry in the foremost line, was nipped in the bud by the requested curtain barrage and annihilating fire. The tanks definitely came forward but the enemy infantry did not follow, probably caught by our artillery fire while assembling, or prevented by it from advancing. From the behaviour of the tanks, it was supposed they were cruising aimlessly round the countryside in expectation that the infantry would follow them.[21]

Colonel Baker-Carr would no doubt have been annoyed, or possibly amused, to see the British tactics dismissed in this way.

As they advanced, the tanks were exposed to fire from a concrete bunker that controlled the crossing of the Langemarck-Zonnebeke and St Julien-Poelcappelle roads. This position was known to the British as Vancouver, and was one of those that had been removed at the last minute from G Battalion's objectives for the day. The Germans did not normally name their blockhouses, which were simply referred to by the nearest code-number (or 'red-point') marked on their trench-maps – in this case, red-point 325.[22] However, this one was about to earn a name for itself. The bunker was under the command of Leutnant Staiger, a company commander in 125th Infantry Regiment. He described events on the morning of 19 August, soon after they had moved in:

> It was high time. Outbreaks of fire barking out over the foremost positions did not bode well. At 6 in the morning [i.e. 5 a.m. UK time] a heavy bombardment, red flares, smoke shells. 'The enemy are attacking!' Already cut off by tanks, the foremost outpost line under Leutnant Wender fights its way through to our building. Tanks! We're a little unfamiliar with them; they're a new acquaintance. Everything is got ready for the defence, two machine guns under Vizefeldwebel [i.e. company sergeant-major] Auwärter, and two infantry sections. Right! Here they come, creeping up the road, and there they stay; on this occasion the terrain of Flanders is our ally. Now the infantry are coming as well, but our machine guns stop them in their tracks. But the tanks! Two come ever further forward, one behind the other, and so into our flank. A few metres more and they'll be firing directly in the door. Already a shot from the revolver cannon [i.e. the tank's 6-pounder gun] whistles past our heads, machine gun bullets smack into the walls. With so few rounds of armour-piercing ammunition we're relatively defenceless. Hold on, what's that? One of the tanks is sinking into a large shell-hole. It struggles visibly to get out again. It doesn't succeed; the other turns tail and heads off. Now it's easier for us; the attack has been beaten off. We have held onto our building. A minor skirmish goes on between the grey monster and our machine guns. As soon as it opens its peepholes, a few shots go whistling over. As soon as we make a move, they come rattling back. The whole day is spent squabbling like this. Night falls and passes peacefully. We're ready for anything.[23]

From then on, the bunker was known as the 'Staigerhaus' in honour of its commander's staunch defence.

For anyone familiar with the British accounts and their jubilation over the seizure of various strongholds, the main response to the German war diaries is to wonder if they can be talking about the same battle. There are some references to the British infantry working their way forward, and a map shows the enemy front line now incorporating red-point 320 (in other words, the Cockcroft), but there is no mention of the loss of any key positions, and no sense of suppressed catastrophe. In fact, it is hard to avoid the conclusion that the captured ground was simply not that important to the Germans. This was consistent with their doctrine of flexible defence, under which the forward outposts were thinly manned and not intended to be held at all costs. Of course, they could still cause heavy losses to the attackers, so it remained a major achievement for the British to have taken them with so few casualties.

Overall, the Germans felt the day had gone well. A bulletin was issued by 26th Infantry Division, to which all the units belonged: 'The enemy did not achieve any success. The division is fully in possession of the positions it held this morning. Strong enemy infantry, who were ready to attack 125th Infantry Regiment between the Steenbeck and the Langemark-Zonnebeke road at midday, were caught by our frontal and flanking annihilation fire. They did not attack. Only weak elements of the enemy are to be found east of the Langemarck-Zonnebeke road. Red-point 325 is in our hands.'[24]

Despite this, it was clear the defenders were coming under increasing pressure – but from the British artillery, rather than infantry or tanks. In total the 125th lost twenty officers and men killed, ninety wounded and one missing during the day, which they considered heavy casualties.[25] Needless to say there is no mention of any officers hanging themselves, or being hanged.

The next day, however, following further relentless bombardment, 51st Infantry Brigade made a significant comment which partly bears out the British intelligence reports: 'Heavy losses were incurred again today by the fighting battalions. The sustained enemy fire and high casualties are having a demoralising effect on the troops. In many places sections of men had to move around, hunted by enemy artillery fire, to seek shelter in shell craters in the less badly bombarded areas.'[26] Above all, the Germans were under no illusions that they had only won a temporary reprieve, and 26th Division's orders stated that 'a continuation of the enemy attacks is to be expected in the near future.'[27]

As they waited for the next throw of the dice, both sides could draw some encouragement from the events of 19 August. The British concluded that tanks could outflank and overpower the German strongpoints, enabling the infantry to occupy them with little loss of life. The Germans concluded that tanks were being used to compensate for the weakness of the infantry, and the concrete blockhouses could defy them if their defenders were determined enough, especially as the terrain was so obviously unsuitable for tanks. The time had come for D Battalion, including the crew of D51, to prove that the British interpretation was the correct one.

CHAPTER 9

Crossing the Canal

On the same day that G Battalion's tanks were apparently sweeping all before them, Second Lieutenant George Macdonald and his crew climbed aboard D51 and steered their way slowly out of Oosthoek Wood to begin the next phase of the attack.[1] It was the first time D Battalion had gone into action for more than three months, the first time they had used the latest Mark IV tanks, and their first excursion into the dreaded Ypres Salient. For George, it would also be the first time he had come face-to-face with the enemy in any battle, let alone one in which he was commanding a tank.

Furthermore, it was the first attack since Lieutenant-Colonel William Kyngdon had taken over as commander of D Battalion in May, so all in all a great deal was riding on the result. It comes as no surprise that for such a high-profile operation, of the three companies that made up his battalion he selected No. 12, which was led by his most experienced and aggressive commander. Major Robert Ward was often referred to by his initials R.O.C., which provided an appropriate acronym for this glamorous pre-war star of the rugby field and boxing ring, whose military career had been even more daring, though so far less successful, than his sporting one.

One of his section commanders, Captain Edward Glanville Smith, described the first stage of their journey to the front: 'About three weeks after the original attack of July 31st it was learnt that 12 Company were to do the first "show" and in the afternoon of the 19th three fighting sections ... moved out of Oosthoek Wood for the first stage of the journey forward ... The four-and-a-half miles to Murat Farm, via Brielen, over beaten paths, were covered at an easy pace, and the company arrived and camouflaged up at dusk. Murat was a farm in name only, but had once existed 500 yards west of the Yser Canal; it afforded no cover to the crews, who consequently passed the night under tarpaulins.'[2] The men of G Battalion had passed through Murat Farm a few days before, and Second Lieutenant Douglas Browne found it similarly uncongenial: 'I never saw any vestige of a farm at this place; but there was a row of tall splintered trees hung with camouflage netting, a few muddy enclosures bounded by overgrown hedgerows, and the usual squalid dug-outs and elephant-iron shelters.'[3]

Late the next evening, the fateful moment came when the convoy of twelve tanks reached what Captain Smith called a 'shaky wooden bridge' over the Yser Canal.[4] This was the Brielen Bridge, its superstructure supported on two sunken barges, which provided one of several makeshift crossings that were maintained by the Royal Engineers under persistent shellfire, and for which they paid a heavy toll. As the tank crews coaxed their massive vehicles across the creaking causeway, the dark waters of the canal below them and the dark skies of the Salient before them, it must have been hard not to wonder how many of them would return.

The slow pace of the journey reflected the challenges of moving their unwieldy machines along slippery, shell-scarred roadways that were also crammed with troops, mule trains and horse-drawn guns. Captain Smith noted that 'a further two-and-a-half miles via Buffs Road brought the company at dusk to Bellevue, one-and-a-half miles behind the line. Bellevue Farm consisted of a straggly one-time hedge and a pond, and the tanks were camouflaged in the best possible manner, left in charge of a guard, and the crews withdrawn to Murat.'[5] Again, Second Lieutenant Browne recorded his impressions:

> I do not know the cynic who named the spot Bellevue, but no doubt he had his reasons. It was the site, apparently of a small farm – a building, at least, was marked on the map, although long since invisible to the naked eye; and it was happily situated in the original No Man's Land, close to the German front line, the remains of whose first trench ... bounded this desirable property to the east. For the rest, there was a square of bedraggled hedge, entirely imaginary in places, behind parts of which the tanks, like so many ostriches, believed themselves to be concealed: the usual ground surface of mud, wire, and shell-holes; and in one corner a patch of unmitigated bog where a pond had been.[6]

After the crews had left their tanks and made their way back to Murat Farm, they received their orders for the coming operation.

Their objectives were a series of strongpoints strung out along the Langemarck-Zonnebeke road east of St Julien, immediately to the right of the group that had been seized with such *éclat* by G Battalion the day before. Other attacks would be conducted at the same time along a longer stretch of the British line, with the tanks of F Battalion attacking to the right of D, and those of C Battalion to their right again. The purpose in each case was to roll up any German outposts that might hinder the next stage of the British advance; or as the *Official History* put it, 'local attacks were to be made on the 22nd to establish a starting-line for the 25th'.[7]

In the case of D Battalion, the tanks were to set out from St Julien in two separate contingents. The so-called 'northern group' would advance more or less northwards on the road towards Poelcappelle that G Battalion had used before, while the 'southern group' – including D51 – would head eastwards on another road towards a crossroads controlled by the enemy strongpoint known as Winnipeg. On reaching the intersection with the Langemarck-Zonnebeke road, each group would split up and turn along it to left or right to reach their objectives, while the infantry advanced cross-country to reach the same destinations. Having driven out the defenders, the tanks would leave the infantry in charge and return to St Julien using the same routes by which they came.

The plan was designed to replicate the success achieved by G Battalion. In his brigade orders, Colonel Baker-Carr stressed that 'definite, distinct and complete units of infantry are being detailed against each strong point and will operate in conjunction with the tank which is attacking it'.[8] This was reiterated by Lieutenant-Colonel Kyngdon in his orders to D Battalion: 'It will be a tank attack, supported by parties of infantry who will assist the tanks in capturing, and mopping up the line, and the infantry will then consolidate and hold the line.'[9]

Most of D Battalion's tanks would be working with infantry from 48th (South Midland) Division, whose orders were consistent with the Tank Corps tactics: 'Rear platoons [i.e. of infantry] will be prepared to move forward as soon as the tanks are reaching their objectives and to consolidate the Winnipeg-Springfield line as soon as the tanks have dealt with the enemy's positions.'[10] However, two of the tanks would be working with infantry from 11th (Northern) Division, whose orders contained an important qualification: 'Infantry will not wait for tanks should the latter be delayed by bad ground, but will push on as close to the barrage as possible.'[11] This could be seen as a sign of bad faith, but even the most enthusiastic tank advocate would have to admit they had a point. Although the tanks were to move across the battlefield by road, this was far from straightforward, as Major Watson explained: 'A civilian could search for a road in the forward area and not recognise it when he came to it. The roads had been shelled to destruction, like everything else in that ghastly, shattered country, but they possessed at least some sort of foundation which prevented the tanks from sinking into the mud.'[12]

The difficulties had been experienced at first hand by G Battalion, as described by Second Lieutenant Browne:

> The Poelcapelle road ... had been shelled now very heavily for over a month by one army or the other, or both at once; and its condition was this. The central strip of *pavé* [i.e. paving stones] had withstood the shell-fire moderately well, but was badly broken in places by jagged holes. It was covered by a thick greasy scum, and as it was cambered, careful driving was needed if one wished to avoid slipping off. And to avoid this was essential, for the macadamised portions on either side had, for all practical purposes, vanished. They were blown away and merged in the ditches, forming deep gulfs a yard or two wide, out of which the stouter *pavé* stood up like a causeway. Of the double line of trees, half were down, and a large proportion of these victims lay across the road at all angles. Beyond the trees the country was quite impassable for tanks, and on the east side of the road ... was simply a swamp.[13]

The fallen tree trunks provided a major obstacle for the tanks, and to make matters even worse the German artillery had the positions of the roads precisely mapped, and the tanks using them were therefore exposed to constant pounding by shells.

The way to Poelcappelle came to epitomise the horror of war for many in D Battalion, among them Second Lieutenant Horace Birks: 'The road itself was a *pavé* causeway slightly wider than a tank, broken in places with shell holes, winding dark and bleakly towards a hopeless horizon. It ran through a sea of mud reminiscent of a picture of the Abomination of Desolation, cratered inconceivably, littered with the debris of battle and stinking of death.'[14] Under these circumstances, it was hardly surprising that some infantry units had a fall-back plan should the tanks fail to get through.

When the orders were issued, it became clear that George Macdonald in D51, and another tank, D52 *Despot*, had an especially challenging task. After heading east on the road out of St Julien, they would have to run the gauntlet from the strongpoint at Winnipeg, before turning right onto the Langemarck-Zonnebeke road to reach their main objective some way beyond – a formidable blockhouse called Schuler Farm, which was guarded by a system of smaller bunkers called Schuler Galleries. On turning right at Winnipeg, D51 would cross an invisible boundary into a zone that was being attacked by a completely different formation. When they started out, they would be working with infantry from the 5th Bn Royal Warwickshire Regiment, which formed part of 143rd Brigade, which formed part of 48th Division, which formed part of XVIII Corps (commanded by Lieutenant-General Sir Ivor Maxse). As they approached Schuler Farm, they would move into the sector being attacked by 2/4th Bn Oxfordshire & Buckinghamshire Light Infantry, which formed part of 184th Brigade, which formed part of 61st Division, which formed part of XIX Corps. To add to the complexity, two tanks from F Battalion had also been detailed to attack Schuler Farm from the opposite direction.

It looks a tactical nightmare on paper, but it would be infinitely worse on a shell-ravaged battlefield. No-one seems to have told any of the infantry or artillery in XIX Corps, or the crews of F Battalion, that two tanks from D Battalion would be appearing from the left to join their attack on Schuler Farm. Perhaps they thought the knowledge would not make much difference, and they may have been right; but it contradicted the claims of close co-operation with specific units of infantry.

As it happened, one of the section commanders leading the F Battalion attack on Schuler Farm was Captain Arthur Arnold, who had commanded *Dracula* in the first day's action on 15 September 1916. He had recovered after being shot when he left his tank to rescue a wounded soldier, and was now ready for another dust-up with the Boche.

* * *

The men of D Battalion were expecting a tough time when they went into battle, but what happened next nearly stopped their attack before it had even begun.

As we have seen, the twelve tanks were parked up at the bleak spot known as Bellevue, but it was impossible to conceal them in such featureless terrain. The Germans must have seen something that made them suspicious, and Lieutenant Colonel Kyngdon described the outcome: 'During the morning and early afternoon of the 21st August, the enemy artillery was particularly active. As a result 4 tanks at Belle Vue received direct hits and were put out of action.'[15] Major Watson used more evocative language: 'On the day before the action the enemy had spotted [Major Ward's] tanks, which were "lying up" on the western slope of the Pilkem Ridge, and had attempted to destroy them with a hurricane bombardment of 5.9's; but a tank has as many lives as a cat, and only three or four were knocked out, though the flanks of the remainder were scarred and dented with splinters.'[16] Sad to relate, one of those hit was D51, believed to be the first *Deborah*, which was therefore put out of action before it had fired a shot in anger.

The destruction of the tanks was a serious blow, but as Captain Smith pointed out, it could have been far worse were it not for the 'wise precaution' of moving the crews back to Murat Farm: 'Had the crews remained with the tanks the casualties would have undoubtedly been heavy. The guard N.C.O., Sergt. Brown, acted with great resource and promptitude, and quelled fires which broke out on several tanks by skilful use of pyrenes [i.e. fire extinguishers]. Unfortunately one of the guard was killed.'[17]

The loss of a third of their tanks was a serious threat to the operation but a solution was rapidly found, as explained by Lieutenant-Colonel Kyngdon: 'These were replaced by 4 tanks of "G" Battalion from Murat Farm, and manned by the original crews of the shelled tanks.'[18] Their cars ringing with the news of G Battalion's triumph on 19 August, it must have been galling for D Battalion to have to appeal to them for help, but there was no alternative if the attack was to go ahead.

After the weeks they had spent fine-tuning D51 in Oosthoek Wood, George Macdonald and his crew now had only a few hours to transfer their equipment and familiarize themselves with their new tank, G22 *Grasshopper*. At the same time the German gunners continued to torment them, as described by Captain Smith: 'Sunset of [21 August] saw all the crews at Bellevue. The Germans, ever suspicious, gas-shelled heavily from 8 p.m. to 2 a.m., and we spent this period choking in gas-masks, every fresh shell increasing our hatred of the Hun, specially when a few 5.9's were indiscriminately thrown in.'[19] The only compensation was that instead of a female tank, the crew of D51 now had the ultimate killing machine: *Grasshopper* was a male tank whose 6-pounder guns would have far more effect on a concrete pillbox than the Lewis guns of the wrecked D51. As the frantic preparations went ahead, the new D Battalion numbers may have been painted onto the replacement tanks to help the infantry units identify them, so *Grasshopper* became in effect the new D51.[20]

* * *

While the tank crews were making their frantic preparations, the infantry units that would support them were also moving into their forward positions ready for the attack. Among them were 2/4th Bn Oxfordshire and Buckinghamshire Light Infantry, who would work with the tanks of F Battalion to take Schuler Farm – also the ultimate objective for D51's crew. Before getting there, however, they would have to capture a strongly-held blockhouse called Pond Farm, and then the series of smaller bunkers called Schuler Galleries. Private Arthur Judd, a member of the 'Ox and Bucks', described the scene as they took over the front line:

> Trenches here were built up, one couldn't dig down here as in the Somme country. Very flat country, this; in some directions we had an uninterrupted view for miles. Looking across this country, we once had the inspiring sight of a group of our tanks slowly crawling forward to the assembly positions for the attack in which they are shortly to assist us.
>
> Midnight; the relief is complete. We stare into No Man's Land and gaze at the weird array of coloured lights that rise and fall all round in one huge semi-circle ... Jerry is very much alive in his pillboxes out in front, we have constantly to duck our heads as the streams of machine-gun bullets knock up the weeds or shave our parapets. We fear we have no easy task to take that ground where that pillbox stands a little way away to our left front, 'Pond Farm,' they call it. Now and then an appalling crash of shells around us gives rise to the fearful thought that Jerry knows what is coming off ...
>
> August 21st was a bright summer's day. It passed off comparatively quiet. We studied the ground in front as far as we could see – ground we were to attack over on the morrow – we could see those ugly, formidable-looking pillboxes from where the Germans watched, and held on so tenaciously, could see derelict tanks and much rubbish – the result of the earlier stages of this battle – and amid the innumerable shell-holes the dead of other regiments.
>
> Huge pools of water lay about – the result of the previous heavy rains, coupled with the effect of the heavy shelling on the drainage system of the country. 'Looks as though we shall have to swim for it to-morrow!' remarked one.
>
> To-morrow would prove another crisis in our young lives – a day we should always remember, no doubt, if we survived. Oxford will have some lengthy casualty-lists to study after to-morrow; several more heroes of the war. We know it! ...
>
> Yet withal we experienced a certain thrill. These big attacks against Jerry we are called on to make from time to time, this going over the top to meet him always holds the 'unexpected'; the unknown quantity. Despite all our plans, tactical talks, and rehearsals, we feel that right from the start the unexpected will happen.
>
> We hope it may be as 'cushy' as it is intended to be ... If only our tanks can get in amongst his pillboxes – a difficult task we fear over this ground, then we think our job will be easy enough ...

Half an hour after zero we hope to be digging in 700 yards in front of where we are now. That will be a big step forward in the direction of the Passchendaele Ridge, which rises in the distance before us.[21]

* * *

While the British forces were moving laboriously into position, the Germans used this respite to improve their makeshift defences in preparation for the next anticipated attack. There was also time to investigate the abandoned hulk of G29 *Gorgonzola*, which lay ditched before the bunker now known as the Staigerhaus. Leutnant Staiger described events on 20 August:

> As day slowly breaks, our grey enemy is still there, but it appears lifeless. Now the patrol squad under Vizefeldwebel Mösch gets busy. They have to take a look from inside as well, there will probably be something worth taking, and perhaps for our hunger too. The Tommies are better off than us in that respect. Off they stalk! They disappear inside and bring out four Lewis guns and other things; even our hunger is taken care of. And all that with hardly any bother from the previous occupants.
>
> But the sequel is not far off. Already a few shells and pieces of shrapnel are whistling round the building. Still, if that's all that happens then it's not too bad. Already they have claimed a victim: Leutnant Sigel, commander of 2nd Battalion, who was already wounded, suffers a fatal shot on the way back. In any case we are unable to recover his body. It isn't just the light stuff any more. More are coming over, 15 cm, apparently high-trajectory fire [i.e. from 6in howitzers]. 'They're obviously after us.' Now the morning will soon be over; that could be a good thing. How much can the roof withstand? The first shot, possibly. Not a second hit – then our home would become our grave. There's no chance of pulling back. Then comes explosion after explosion, always accompanied by the light stuff, so no-one can escape during the intervals. So we wait – for death! If only evening would come. The explosions are getting closer. A man is screaming: shell shock. As night falls, they again launch a concentrated onslaught against us. Then it gets quieter. We step outside to take a look around. Where there was solid ground this morning, now little lakes are glistening; on all sides the soil has been torn away from the concrete, which stands bare and exposed. One corner has received a hit, the machine guns in the position are buried under bricks. We're all nearly exhausted after the day's tension. The reliefs will be welcomed gratefully. Then back through the poison gas fumes to stand by in some hedgerow, where we still get no peace from the enemy's shells. Such was Flanders in August 1917.[22]

CHAPTER 10

Into the Pillar of Fire

Finally, in the small hours of 22 August, the waiting was over. The tanks moved off from Bellevue during the night and began the slow approach to their starting positions. In the words of Captain Edward Glanville Smith: 'At last we set off up an adjoining wooden road, silently praying that the Boche would not hear the combined noises of twelve ... Daimler engines. Then down the Wieltje-St. Julien Road ... and across the narrow bridge over the Steenbeek (a terrible place in daylight, littered with dead mules and shattered limbers).'[1]

Parties of Royal Engineers had begun work here the day before, repairing the shell-battered bridge in St Julien and building a new crossing nearby so that D Battalion's tanks could negotiate the swamp where the stream had once flowed. The operation was fraught with hazard, but 184th Tunnelling Company reported: 'The first tank crossed the road bridge at 4.am. and the 12th and last went over at 4.20.am. The bridge was satisfactory and where it gave way we filled with bricks. The area around was shelled throughout the night and the behaviour of the men was in every way excellent.'[2] Once through St Julien, the tanks split into two groups as planned and crawled along the approach routes to their respective starting points ready for zero hour at 4.45 a.m., when a hurricane bombardment would mark the start of the attack.

In the hours before dawn, the British front was alive with furtive movement as infantry and tanks moved into position. Just to the right of D51, Private Arthur Judd and his comrades had moved out of the front line into No Man's Land, where positions had been taped out for them. As he explained, 'the old idea of crowding the trenches with men before an attack is finished with – there is more room "outside," besides, "Jerry" has these trenches registered to a nicety'.

> Darkness has fallen, the stars gleam in the sky. Everything seems to be going well. With hushed movements we left our trenches some while ago and got into our positions on the tapes without mishap. In the weird glow of the Verey [*sic*] lights that illumined the scene we were fearful at first of being discovered, and every coloured rocket that went up elicited the whispered enquiry from someone: 'What's that for?' or some gloomy individual would remark: 'He's rumbled us!'
>
> But we are settled down now, we have had our rum issue and feel secure in the knowledge that 'Jerry' cannot know.
>
> The night is quiet, occasionally I fall into a doze; finally must have fallen asleep.
>
> I opened my eyes and seemed to think it looked a little lighter towards the east; had a vague notion of someone saying: 'Another minute!' But in the next instant the sky in the direction I was looking suddenly threw up a stab of flame.
>
> A roll of thunder opened with a single deep boom; then steadied into a throbbing war. The shells screamed overhead so thick and fast they seemed verily to obscure the sky itself, rumbling like earthquakes behind, crashing like a thousand cymbals before us, a pillar of fire against the dark sky, a pillar of cloud against the dawn – leading us on.

It is zero hour and our barrage has fallen, blotting out the enemy bombardment with a drum-fire that makes his counter-barrage seem insignificant, there is no more fear or doubt, only an endless blast of sound, a flicker of flame in the sky, a roaring and howling of shells overhead, and a smoky pall of shrapnel. And as if clamouring to obtain a hearing in all this inferno, the machine-guns clatter with the sound as of a thousand explosive typewriters.

Our first wave of attackers drifts forward silhouetted against that pillar of fire and looking like so many marionettes worked on a string. We of the second wave must follow almost immediately. We must follow hard on the barrage and be on the enemy before he has recovered from the first shock of it.

A pause, hardly perceptible, and with marvellous precision the pillar of fire has "jumped" eighty yards ahead. I plunge forward from shell-hole to shell-hole towards that cauldron of fire, now through the fumes of burnt powder, cordite, steaming earth and falling clods, feeling uplifted with the very might our barrage, appalled at the awe-inspiring spectacle of it. How *could* any poor devil of a German live in it?

Yet I marvelled with every forward movement I made – 'I am still unharmed, alive!'[3]

* * *

Five minutes after zero, divisional headquarters received a message from Major R.O.C. Ward: 'All twelve tanks left starting point at zero, going well.'[1] They were on their way, and now he could do nothing but wait and hope.

The tanks in the northern group made rapid progress along the road towards their objectives – the enemy positions at Bülow Farm, Vancouver and Springfield. Among them was D43 *Delysia* commanded by Lieutenant Enoch, its signed pin-up photograph of Alice Delysia in pride of place beside the driver's seat.

Private Jason Addy described the journey: 'When you're enclosed in a tank and there's so much racket, you don't know whether it's the shells hitting you or what you're doing. The noise of the engine is tremendous, and we had to stand by with pyrenes [i.e. fire extinguishers] sometimes to get ready to shoot the engine if it got too hot. As we had two 20-gallon tanks of petrol in the rear, and all around the sides there was racks of ammunition, if you had a direct hit in a tank you hadn't an earthly. Jerry was shelling back and you could feel the blast of the shells as you were looking through the gun slits ...'[5]

The sensation of coming under fire in a tank was a disturbing one, but Second Lieutenant Horace Birks found it in some ways reassuring: 'You started off cock a hoop until you started hearing these machine guns rattling on the outside and a sort of glow coming from the plate, you got less confident ... One hated hearing these sort of red hot peas hitting on the outside of the tank ... but shell bursts quite close, you didn't feel any effect of them at all. I felt they rather boosted one's morale ... I think one felt fairly well protected ... One felt very sorry for the infantry who were out in the open.'[6]

But Second Lieutenant Wilfred Bion of E Battalion found it more disconcerting when he went into action for the first time in the Salient – particularly in the silence before starting his engine:

> The shelling was simply one continual roar. Your own guns sounded a sharp crack behind. You could, of course, distinguish nothing. You simply had the deep roar of the guns, which was continuous, and imposed on that was the shrill whistle

of the shells passing overhead – just as if it was the wind whistling in a gigantic keyhole. One very big German shell that burst near us could be distinguished above the rest. It sounded like an express train coming through a tunnel – a gradually increasing roar as it came nearer. Then a deafening crash. As the nearer shells burst, the tank used to sway a little and shudder. This was very beastly, as one had previously felt that a tank was the sort of pinnacle of solidity. It seemed as if you were all alone in a huge passage with great doors slamming all around. I can think of no way of describing it.[7]

Along the front to be attacked on 22 August, the position furthest to the left was known to the British as Bülow Farm, presumably in reference to Field Marshal Karl von Bülow, who was widely held responsible for the Germans' failure to take Paris in 1914.

This position was to be assaulted by 6th Bn Lincolnshire Regiment, supporting two tanks – one of which was D44 *Dracula*, whose name we last heard when it was abandoned and set ablaze by William Wakley and George Foot at the start of their three-day ordeal at Eaucourt l'Abbaye. The name, though not the tank, had risen from the grave, and its latest incarnation was commanded by Second Lieutenant Charles Symonds, in his first tank action.

The other crew attacking Bülow Farm was that of D41 *Devil* under Lieutenant Andrew Lawrie, who was just twenty-one years old and had been a medical student at Glasgow University before joining up. He had previously commanded a tank at the Battle of Bullecourt on 3 May 1917, when it was destroyed by five direct hits after being riddled by armour-piercing bullets which injured most of the crew, including himself.[8] The driver of D41 had also fought at Bullecourt and won the Military Medal for his courage: this was Sergeant Joshua Weeks from Glamorgan in South Wales, who was the same age as Lieutenant Lawrie but had been working down the pits when he was only fifteen.[9]

Two hours after zero, the headquarters of 33rd Infantry Brigade received the message they had been praying for: '6.45 A.M. left [company] of Lincs. report to have gained objective including Bulow Fm. & to be consolidating.' But soon afterwards came a bitter blow: '7.30 A.M. Tanks reported held up on Poelcapelle road a direct hit being scored by the artillery on the female tank Devil killing 2/Lt. Lawrie the commander and his Sergeant.'[10]

Half-an-hour later a message from the other tank, *Dracula*, confirmed both the good and bad news: 'Symonds D44 wires our infantry digging in ... Enemy infantry not in sight. Enemy artillery have disabled D41 (Lt. [Lawrie] and Sgt. Weeks killed). Tanks visible abandoned and blocking all round. My tank O.K. Ground bad.'[11]

Colonel Baker-Carr was determined that his tanks should take some credit for the success, and his report told how 'the 2 told off for Bulow Farm ... got sufficiently near to their objectives to bring fire to bear upon them ... The second Tank fired several shots from 6 pdr., at Bulow Farm and the Infantry came up and captured it.'[12]

However, the Lincolnshires told a different story, and a message said that 'infantry reached objectives long before tanks'.[13] They reported that the two tanks had been held up on the road, and rather than wait for them, the infantry followed orders and advanced 'close under the barrage'. As they approached Bülow Farm around fourteen Germans ran out, eight of whom were captured, though half of them were killed by their own artillery and snipers as they made their way back across No Man's Land.[14]

This was also the version accepted by Fifth Army, whose summary of operations said 'the 11th Division on the left ... encountered little resistance, and took Bulow Farm ... before tanks arrived.'[15]

The infantry supported their account with a more detailed description of what happened to the two tanks:

> By zero Dracula, which was leading, had reached the junction of the St. Julien-Poelcappelle and Winnipeg-Langemarck roads, with Devil close behind. They advanced with the infantry, but on getting to within 150 yards of the track leaving Poelcappelle road for Bulow Farm ..., found the road blocked by fallen trees and were unable to proceed any further. They were then about level with Vieilles Maisons upon which they opened fire for a short time [this was another blockhouse to the right]. They then came back towards home. During their homeward journey, a direct hit was observed on Devil ... Nothing further was seen of the tank Dracula until the evening when it was located on the west side of the Poelcappelle road.[16]

Captain Edward Glanville Smith also described what had happened to his section: 'Lieuts. Lawrie and Symonds reached Bulow Farm, but the former, together with his N.C.O., Sergt. Weeks, was killed almost immediately by an unlucky direct hit which completely disabled the tank.'[17] Although Smith did not mention it, the surviving members of the crew then became locked in a desperate battle for survival.

Meanwhile, despite their early success against Bülow Farm, the Lincolnshires were now coming under severe pressure from their right flank, where the enemy were said to be 'very active and aggressive';[18] this was because they were now approaching the main German defensive positions, having moved through the outpost line which was merely designed to disrupt their advance. As they struggled to consolidate, there was no suggestion that they received any support from *Dracula*, which eventually returned to St Julien. Major Ward expected his tanks to fight with more aggression, and whatever he said to Second Lieutenant Symonds, the next time he went into action, things were to end very differently.

Despite the loss of a tank, the attack on Bülow Farm had at least produced the desired outcome. The key question now was whether the garrison of the Staigerhaus would also cut and run.

* * *

The two tank crews that were detailed to attack Vancouver, namely those of D42 *Daphne* and D43 *Delysia*, also formed part of the northern group which moved off at zero hour along the blasted road towards Poelcappelle. Their objective lay near the crossing with the Langemarck-Zonnebeke road, a spot now marked by the sombre and imposing memorial to the Canadian troops who had fought here more than a year before, topped by the carved head of a brooding soldier. There is nothing to recall the tanks that came this way, and no trace of the concrete bulk of the Staigerhaus which stood in the fields beyond.

The support of D Battalion was vital to the men of 6th Bn Gloucestershire Regiment, whose orders stated: 'Tanks will take Vancouver which will be included in our line. If tanks do not arrive no infantry attack will be made on Vancouver.'[19]

The enemy did not flee immediately, but an update at 6.30 a.m. sounded promising: '6/Gloucs report within 50 yards of Springfield road on right ... Tank dealing with

Vancouver, which was still strongly held with machine guns. Tank however cannot leave the road.'[20] An hour-and-a-half later, a message from *Delysia* also suggested the attack was still going well against Vancouver, which stood at the apex of a distinctive triangle of roads: 'A. J. Enoch (D43) wires our infantry in strength on east side of Triangle. Enemy infantry seem to be a minus quantity … My tank going strong on east side of Triangle.'[21]

Therefore, the blow must have been all the greater when divisional headquarters learned just forty minutes later that the attack had broken down: '1/6th Glos now reports left company drove Boche from road, but right [company] not up and they were enfiladed and driven out. Tank engaged Vancouver from road but could not silence M.G's. Left post report battalion on left retiring and right company commander reports 143 [Brigade, i.e. to the right] retiring.'[22]

To appreciate what was going on, we will have to leave the attacking tanks and infantry and make the hazardous journey across No Man's Land towards the squat, battered bulk of the Staigerhaus. Ducking our heads we slip through a low entrance in the massive concrete walls, pass down a short corridor and find ourselves inside one of the cramped chambers of the bunker. At first we can see nothing in the dim interior, filled as it is with smoke from the rifles and machine guns, but after a while we can make out a number of helmeted figures, peering intently through the slits which provide the only source of light. These are the men of 3rd Battalion, 125th Infantry Regiment, and they are fighting for their lives. At first they remain frozen like statues, until someone gives a shout and the machine-gunner adjusts his aim and fires a burst, the noise reverberating inside the chamber with a brittle, ear-shattering din. Only when it dies away do we become aware of a constant rumbling in the background, like distant thunder, and we realise this is the 'drum-fire' of which the Germans often speak.

Suddenly there is a shattering impact as a shell drops close to the bunker: even through the tiny slit windows the shockwave makes us feel as if we have been punched on the nose and leaves our ears singing, and as we instinctively throw ourselves to the ground, we notice that the floor which had seemed so rock-solid is trembling like jelly. The officer shouts something we cannot understand, and there is some forced laughter from the men who remain crouched at their posts. But now we can think only of what would happen if the concrete roof were to come crashing down, crushing our limbs under its massive blocks, or burying us in the shattered ruins, alone and unable to escape. Now we would do anything to be out in the open, taking our chance against artillery and the elements, where we could at least breathe fresh air and see the sky, and be free from this fearful claustrophobia and choking smoke.

One of the men steps down, fumbling with his rifle, and we catch a glimpse of his face, which is gaunt and lined, with reddened eyes from the fumes and lack of sleep. We take the opportunity to creep up and peer cautiously through the slit window he has vacated. It is good to see the daylight and smell the cool air, but the view is limited and disappointing: a grey blur of horizon, a foreground of flooded shell craters, and no sign of life or movement anywhere. The prospect triggers a surge of panic: perhaps the attackers have already swept past on either side of our fortress, and are preparing even now to storm its walls with hand grenades and phosphorous bombs? Is it time to run, and if so, what are the chances of being able to surrender? Despite everything we have heard about the Battle of Passchendaele, for some reason we had not expected the reality to be so ugly and desperate. Then we recall the words of one British officer who described the German pillboxes 'all smelling after capture of rotten eggs (phosgene), stale cigars, sweat and putredinous scatter of blood and brains and hair on bomb-pocked floors and walls'.[23] Before we know it, we have ducked back out of the door and are stumbling across the muddy moonscape, panting with effort as we climb the lip of one crater and slide into the next while our feet turn into slippery balls of mud, until the Staigerhaus is swallowed up in the morass behind.

But the tiny garrison under Leutnant Dürr stood their ground, and the Lewis guns of *Delysia* were powerless to inflict any real damage on them unless the tanks left the road, which would inevitably lead to their ditching and destruction. The commander of 125th Infantry Regiment, Oberst Reinhold Stühmke, summarized the morning's events:

> Through accurate small arms and machine-gun fire using armour-piercing bullets, Leutnant Dürr succeeded in knocking out three tanks that were advancing against the Staigerhaus along the St Julien-Poelcappelle road, under cover of mist and gunsmoke, and were peppering us with cannon and machine-gun fire. The crew from one tank were wounded and it stayed put, another burst into flames, and the third turned tail ...
>
> Between 8 and 9 o'clock a second English attack began, after the Staigerhaus – which obviously caused the enemy a lot of problems – had been vigorously bombarded with large calibre shells, but they got nowhere. In front of the Staigerhaus the enemy formed up in ranks to right and left and started a double flanking manoeuvre. Two machine guns, which were brought into position with great courage, provided frontal support against the attempt to seize the flanks of the stoutly defended fortress. Fire from Dürr's platoon radiated out on three sides. Musketier [i.e. Private] Fahrbach stood up and fired at will; anything that came into his sights was brought down. At 8.35 a.m. Leutnant Dürr reported: 'Enemy trying to approach from the front, left and right, but forced to retreat every time by redeployment of my magnificent men. Crew of one machine gun already wiped out, packing up and heading back with only one man. Hurrah!'[24]

The outcome of the tank attack was summarized by the section commander, Captain Smith: 'Lieuts. Enoch and Sherwood reached the area of their objective, Vancouver, only to find it impossible to cover the ground from the road to the concrete fort, and although they helped the infantry by bombarding it from the road, the place was bullet-proof in front and remained uncaptured.'[25]

Such was the ferocity of the fire directed at *Delysia* that shell splinters penetrated the tank's steel hull.[26] No-one suggested they could have done any more, but the infantry's verdict was brief and resigned: 'As before, the infantry were to wait until the tanks had captured the positions, but the operation failed, as the tanks could not leave the road to locate them.'[27]

* * *

As the crew of D43 *Delysia* headed back towards St Julien from their unsuccessful attack on Vancouver, they passed the wreckage of D41 *Devil* and were confronted by an extraordinary sight. In the words of Private Jason Addy:

> Suddenly somebody shouted out: 'There's Jagger', and on the side of the road –
> Jagger was the corporal that had been in the tank that had been knocked out with

> Lieutenant [Lawrie]. Unfortunately Lieutenant [Lawrie] had been killed and we could see that, as the tank was tipped off the roadside, we could see his arm sticking out of the gun slit and his hand all twisted. But Jagger was standing there on the roadside waving us to stop. We opened the door and he shouted to us: 'I've got two wounded chaps here, can you take them back with you?' He had four wounded actually, but we could only carry two so we pulled in these wounded chaps and laid them down on the floor on either side of the driver's seat and left Jagger to look after the other two.[28]

The full story of Lance-Corporal Ernest Jagger's heroism was recounted by another tank commander, Second Lieutenant Frank Mitchell, though he did not name the protagonists:

> After managing to get into action at St. Julien, a tank was hit by a shell which crashed through the top, killing the officer and sergeant, and wounding three men severely. The senior man left was a lance-corporal, who immediately tackled the problem of getting the wounded back. Fearlessly he got out and, splashing through the mud, hailed another tank. By this time the enemy machine gunners had spotted him, and when he attempted to carry a wounded comrade to the safety of the second tank he was fired at heavily, but he stuck to his task and saw his patient safely on board. He could easily have climbed in as well, but tank men are taught never to desert their comrades. So back through the slush he trudged, the bullets whistling around his ears. With great difficulty he managed to pull the other two wounded from the battered derelict, and, after attending to their wounds, placed them gently in the driest shell hole he could find.
>
> Now the next part of a tank crew's duty is to assist the infantry by forming strong points with Lewis guns. The earnest lance-corporal was rather puzzled. His officer and sergeant were dead, and he could hardly form a strong point with two badly wounded men. Still he decided that he would do the next best thing, so he got into touch with the nearest infantry and handed over the Lewis guns to them. On returning, he could find no trace of his two wounded comrades. It was impossible for them to have even crawled away, and yet they had completely disappeared.
>
> With shells falling all round he scrambled from one crater to another, searching in despair. Suddenly, in the spot where he thought he had placed them, he saw something white moving. He crawled nearer, and stared horrified. It was a human hand. The wounded men had actually been buried in the mud by shell fire!
>
> Frantically he tore at the dirt and slime with his hands; but thank God it was not too late, they still breathed faintly. He worked hard to revive them, and then, by a tremendous effort, he succeeded in getting them to a dressing station.
>
> Thus did a lance-corporal do his duty.[29]

Meanwhile the ordeal was far from over for the wounded men inside D43, as the tank lurched its way over a series of felled tree-trunks, as Private Addy recalled:

> Every time we banged down, those poor chaps, you could see in their faces, were in agony. I'll never forget the look on their faces, and it wasn't only the tree trunks, for by now the road was a shambles of cartwheels, bodies, and everything you could think of that was in battle. We had to go over a lot of them, you hoped they were dead but you had to go over them just the same as you daren't get off the

road. Sometimes you'd see the wounded lying there, you can see them there alive and you can see by the expressions on the men's faces that they thought we were going to go over them. Well we do go over them, but we went over them and got them in the centre, and we'd manoeuvre the tank so that the tracks would go on either side. There was plenty of clearance underneath the tank, and they was terrified just the same. We got back to St Julien and lifted the two boys off and laid them behind a wall and went up to look for the stretcher-bearers. When we'd handed them over we camouflaged the two tanks in their parking places and got on the lorries that were waiting to take us back to La Lovie.[30]

Lance-Corporal Jagger had already won the Military Medal at Bullecourt, for continuing to drive his tank even though partially blinded and then bringing back a severely wounded man under heavy machine-gun fire. For his latest act of bravery, he now also received the Distinguished Conduct Medal and Croix de Guerre.[31]

His dedication earned an even greater reward, and in October 1917 Lance-Corporal Jagger arrived in New York as one of the crew of a tank called *Britannia* commanded by Captain Richard Haigh, who had previously served as Major Watson's deputy in No. 11 Company. They took *Britannia* on a fund-raising and morale-building tour of American cities, and after that Ernest Jagger was posted back to the depot in England, and was never again required to prove his courage on the Western Front.[32]

* * *

Although the garrison of the Staigerhaus were clearly determined to put up a fight, there was still a chance this could be knocked out of them if the attack succeeded against Springfield, which was the next position to the right (from the British perspective). If the Germans could be driven back here, the men in the Staigerhaus would find their flank exposed and might decide to cut and run. Therefore a lot depended on the final two tanks in the northern group, namely D45 *Destroyer* and D46 *Dragon*. They successfully negotiated the long approach, and just over an hour after zero, a pilot swooped overhead and reported 'Tank in action seen at Springfield at 5.50. Barrage good.'[33]

The commander of D46 was Lieutenant David Lewis, a twenty-five year-old bank clerk from Merseyside who had considerable military experience, having enlisted in the Territorials as early as 1909 and served on the Western Front with the King's (Liverpool) Regiment before being commissioned.[34] After transferring to the MGC (Heavy Branch) he was lucky to survive his first attack in the Battle of Arras, when his tank became stuck while crossing a trench and then suffered a direct hit which left it burned out.[35]

Events now seemed to be repeating themselves, as described by Captain Edward Glanville Smith: 'Lieut. Lewis ... reached Springfield Farm which was captured, but in endeavouring to advance further he was ditched.'[36] But this time it was far worse, as the Germans realized *Dragon* was stuck and moved forward to reoccupy their former positions. Lieutenant Lewis and his crew now found themselves cut off and surrounded by the enemy. The other tank, D45 *Destroyer*, was powerless to assist and eventually returned to St Julien, its sponson punctured by shellfire.[37]

This failure had predictable consequences for the infantry from 7th Bn Royal Warwickshire Regiment: 'The tanks moved forward and were to signal the infantry to rush the concrete blockhouses when the tanks had dealt with them. Owing to the bad state of the ground the tanks got ditched. The delay gave the enemy time to recover and our attack was not able to take its two objectives. A series of posts was established in shell holes near up to the block houses.'[38]

With the infantry driven back, the last hope of rescue was gone for Lieutenant Lewis and his men, who could only stay locked inside their suffocating steel fortress and pray for a miracle. They sent off a message by carrier pigeon to outline their plight, and at 11.45 a.m. Lieutenant-Colonel Henry Howard at 48th Division headquarters took a phone call from Major R.O.C. Ward: '[Officer Commanding] No. 12 Coy, Tanks rang up and said that he had received ... a pigeon message from a tank at Springfield, who said that he was surrounded by Germans and still holding out in Springfield.'[39]

Knowing what we do of Major Ward, we can be sure he put his case forcefully, and Lieutenant-Colonel Howard discussed the situation with his commander, Major-General Sir Robert Fanshawe. Three-quarters of an hour later Howard phoned Brigadier-General Gerald Sladen, commander of 143rd Brigade, and 'told him that the Divisional Commander ... wished Genl. Sladen to take steps to rush Springfield and capture it.'[40]

Brigadier-General Sladen has been described as having 'an incisive manner ..., a clear head for an emergency ... [and] the soldier's gift, "an eye for country".'[41] He needed to draw on all those qualities in framing a response, which was tactful but firm: 'He did not think that any movement in daylight up to Springfield is now possible owing to German M.Gs, and even if the tank was still holding out in Springfield this would not prevent the Germans from firing out of their emplacements.' In the end he was ordered to seize any ground that was needed to link up with neighbouring units, but there was no specific instruction about Springfield.[42]

Another pigeon message arrived that evening bearing a final desperate message from *Dragon*, though it had been sent at 7 a.m., more than thirteen hours earlier: 'Am ditched at Springfield. Unditching gear cannot be fixed. Springfield not captured.'[43] But Ward and Sladen were powerless to help, and in his subsequent report Colonel Kyngdon admitted they still had no idea what had become of *Dragon*: 'No further news of the crew was forthcoming up to mid-day on 25th August.'[44] The next day, Colonel Baker-Carr was also none the wiser: 'One tank became ditched and is still there with the crew, as far as is known. The other after remaining sometime returned.'[45]

For Major Watson, the fate of *Dragon*'s crew remained an unsolved mystery: 'One gallant tank drew up alongside a "pillbox," stuck, and fought it out. We never quite knew what happened, but at last the tank caught fire. The crew never returned.'[46] To find out what became of them, we must travel to Germany, where the archives contain an interrogation report which states triumphantly:

> The entire crew of tank 2048 is in our hands. They did not gain their objective, which they did not know, or rather refused to tell us, as they previously became stuck in the mud. They remained lying up all day on 22 August and were continually fired at by the Germans with machine guns and pelted with hand grenades, without suffering any casualties. They sent off a carrier pigeon to their own division, to stop the English artillery destroying the tank to prevent it from falling into our hands. During the night of 22-23 August the Germans threw hand grenades through the slits, so the crew had to abandon the tank and give themselves up.[47]

A more detailed account, tinged with derision, was given by Unteroffizier (i.e. Corporal) Theodor Öchsler of 23rd Reserve Infantry Regiment:

My experiences in the previous three years of war were surpassed by the fighting on 22 August. A hellish bombardment started at 6 a.m. [i.e. 5 a.m. UK time], so we could hardly see what was happening a few metres from our holes through the smoke. However we were all waiting for the expected attack. At last the English launched their assault, to which we gave such a response with our rifle-fire that those who weren't killed flooded back again. Hardly was that business settled when we saw a tank coming along the road in our rear. Threatened by this, we left our holes and found a suitable position behind the road. All of a sudden, what joy as the tank remained stuck in a hole and could not go any further. I launched myself at the monster, along with Leutnant Schulz and Musketier [i.e. Private] Krügel from the same company. All in vain! Hand grenades, rifles, we tried everything, but there were no gaps. The crew were also firing continuously with the guns that were available. A demolition charge of six hand grenades, which I set off under the [tank] cannon, did not help either. Leutnant Schulz damaged the cannon with his rifle, also to no effect. Hand grenades were thrown up on top, but there were no gaps! Still we could take comfort that the tank could not go any further.

In the evening we moved into our usual holes. Leutnant Schulz, Leutnant Henkel ... and I had another go at the tank. With egg grenades, which we put into a small opening, we frightened the crew so much that they immediately began begging for mercy. We shouted: 'Come out of your box, or we'll blow it sky-high', and the little door on the side opened and eight strapping Englishmen were standing there in front of us with their hands up. It was hilarious! After searching them I took them to the battalion, the regiment, and then the 12th Reserve Division. I recounted my experiences of capturing the tank crew to the commander of Fourth Army, His Excellency General Sixt von Armin. He shook me by the hand and congratulated me.[48]

The Germans had captured individual tanks and tankmen in the past, but they had never got their hands on an entire crew. Following their ordeal inside *Dragon*, Lieutenant Lewis and his men now faced interrogation, and it remained to be seen how much they would reveal about their machine, and about the plans for the battle.

CHAPTER 11

Deborah, the Dead Man and the Drummer

At zero hour, as the northern group began to move forward, the six tanks in the southern group – including the crew of D51 in their replacement machine – were assembled near the site of Janet Farm, ready to advance along the road towards Winnipeg and points beyond. The officer in charge was Captain Graeme Nixon, who had commanded a section in the first attack on 15 September 1916. Unlike the varied fortunes of the northern group, their fate is more easily summarized. In the words of Captain Edward Glanville Smith: 'Disaster early overtook this detachment. The road along which they worked ended abruptly by disappearing into a complete swamp. The first tank picked its way along till it finally half submerged, and ditched badly. The unditching beam was brought into action, but the mud defied all efforts of the crew. The following five tanks in succession endeavoured to work round it, but only succeeded in getting off the road and becoming more badly ditched and remained so, despite the gallant efforts of the crews under heavy fire.'[1] Another account says the first tank in the column broke down, another says it was hit by a shell, but whatever the details, the outcome was the same.[2]

At 9.10 a.m., the headquarters of 48th Division received a message by carrier pigeon from Second Lieutenant James Clark in D48 *Diablo*. The tiny slip of paper conveyed a vivid picture of the chaos around him: 'Have not yet established contact with infantry … Heavy fire on bend of Winnipeg-St. Julien Road. On the whole heavy retaliation. Tanks visible D50, knocked out: D47 ditched: Mr. Macdonald's ditched: [Mr] Shaw's ditched: my tank held up by ditched tanks in front and by impassable ground.'[3] He could therefore see virtually every tank in the southern group, trapped in the mud and lashed by a ferocious German counter-bombardment. D50 *Dandy Dinmont* had been knocked out by a direct hit from a shell which wounded its commander, Second Lieutenant Harold Dobinson. D47 *Demon*, commanded by Second Lieutenant James Vose, had been ditched four times and was now half-submerged with water over its carburettor. Clark himself had become ditched three times and his tank was finally put out of action when a shell splinter punctured its petrol tank. The only tank he could not see, D49 *Dollar Princess*, had been ditched twice and its massive unditching beam was smashed during attempts to free it.[4]

Somewhere in this doomed convoy were George Macdonald and the crew of D51. They had ditched twice on their way along the road, but their journey was finally ended by mechanical trouble, with the right track of their substitute tank out of action. D52 *Despot*, the other tank that was detailed to attack Schuler Farm, was also ditched but the crew managed to extricate it, though not before its commander, Second Lieutenant Harry Shaw, had been wounded in the head and shoulder.[5] Despite this he was the only member of the group that made it home, according to a report on the debacle: 'This was the last tank on the road, and was prevented in any case from going forward owing to the impossibility of passing the ditched tanks in front of it.'[6]

An aerial photograph shows a mottled moonscape of shell craters traversed by the thin streak of the road from St Julien to Winnipeg, and beside it a string of stranded hulks marked 'Abandoned tanks'.[7] This bleak picture shows the remains of the southern group, but the prospect was far bleaker for the infantry who now had to attack across this pockmarked ground without the promised tank support.

The 5th Bn Royal Warwickshire Regiment were to capture Winnipeg and a nearby German cemetery, as well as some abandoned gunpits to the right of the road, and their War Diary describes what happened: 'Owing to the tanks being unable to get on, the main objective was not attained. About 9AM the enemy counterattacked strongly and drove us back to our original position.'[8] The records show that thirty men from the battalion were killed.

A fuller account was given by Lieutenant Charles Carrington, who fortunately missed the attack as he was away on a training course. Had he taken part, he might not have lived to write his acclaimed memoirs, *A Subaltern's War* and *Soldier from the Wars Returning*. Carrington pieced together what happened from survivors:

> The day was disastrous. C Company on the right captured the gunpits, but not a tank reached its objective, so impassable was the mud. The leading platoons of D Company went on alone into a withering fire, and were destroyed – to a man. Six weeks later some of their bodies were found, where they had fallen, far up the slope before the Langemarck line. In accordance with orders no more waves went forward, and many more casualties were caused by the German barrage on the men crouching in shell holes waiting for instructions. A heavy counter-attack drove back C Company for a short time, but they rallied and captured the gunpits a second time ... It was found impossible to extend the positions further.[9]

All that the crews of the ditched tanks could do was dismount their Lewis guns and provide fire support to the infantry from their shell-holes,[10] but they were shooting at long range over the heads of the infantry, so it is doubtful if this was of much benefit. However, it was the only contribution to the battle by any of the tanks in the southern group.

This meant the crews were now out in the open and exposed to the full force of the German counter-bombardment, and during the course of this Second Lieutenant George Macdonald, the commander of D51, suffered a wound which finally ended any hopes he may have had of sticking a German in the gizzard. In his own words: 'I was wounded on Aug 22nd a piece of shell penetrating the lung.' A medical report makes it clear he had had a narrow escape: 'He was hit by a fragment of [high explosive] shell which entered his chest below lower angle of left scapula [i.e. shoulder blade] & lodged near front wall of chest as shown by X Rays. There was no haemoptysis [i.e. coughing up of blood], no haemothorax [i.e. collection of blood in the chest cavity], nor any lung symptoms.' It was his second 'Blighty' wound, and from the casualty clearing station he was taken to hospital in Camiers, and from there to England.[11]

Captain Edward Glanville Smith summed up the overall results of D Battalion's efforts on 22 August: 'The net gain on the front during the day was some 200 to 300 yards and, in proportion to this small advance, the casualties were large, especially as regards the crews of Lieuts. Lewis and Lawrie. The crews of the ditched tanks, who had assisted the infantry by forming M.G. posts, were eventually withdrawn to camp – begrimed and "done up" – together with the few surviving tanks. Two valuable lessons had been learnt, (1) the strength of the concreted strong-points of the enemy, and (2) the impossibility of 30 tons of tank to leave the roads and go across the sponge-like shelled marshland.'[12]

It goes without saying that both these facts should have been obvious beforehand, and they hardly justified the loss of seven of the company's tanks (not to mention the four damaged at Bellevue), nor the deaths of six men including Lieutenant Lawrie and Sergeant Weeks, nor the capture of the entire crew of D46 *Dragon*. Three of the six tank commanders in the southern group had been wounded, including Second Lieutenant Macdonald, as well as sixteen other men in the battalion – among them Lance-Corporal Bert Marsden, who may have been in the crew of D51.

The company's reconnaissance officer, Second Lieutenant Horace Furminger – known as 'Contours' because of his pre-war occupation as a map engraver with the Ordnance Survey – was also wounded, and by now he had reached the end of the line. Four days after the attack he applied for a transfer to the Indian Army, but he would have to survive several more battles before he could leave for his new posting with the 26th Punjabis.[13]

* * *

Although the southern group of D Battalion tanks was out of action, there was still a chance that Schuler Farm could be taken by the tanks of F Battalion and the men of 61st (2nd South Midland) Division. Three battalions of infantry were taking part in this attack: in the first wave was 2/4th Bn Oxfordshire and Buckinghamshire Light Infantry (known as the 'Ox and Bucks'), followed by 2/4th Bn Royal Berkshire Regiment and then 2/5th Bn Gloucestershire Regiment in support.

We have already heard from Private Arthur Judd of 2/4th Ox and Bucks, and now it is time to find out what happened as he advanced across No Man's Land, keeping as close as possible to the creeping artillery barrage:

> Looking about me, I can see one or two others, that's all. In and out of shell-holes, over rough ground, through smoke and in uncertain light we soon lose all sense of touch and order.
>
> The barrage lifts again. Still forward. Suddenly between the rolling clouds of smoke a little to my right and so near that I could cast a stone into it, is the German pillbox 'Pond Farm.' It almost takes me by surprise. I had forgotten about it.
>
> Yet in our rehearsals back behind we had practised passing it dozens of times in the same relative position as it is to me now. But astonishing sight. Three or four Boches are walking leisurely about on the top of it! Huge men. Do they want to give themselves up? No, they have rifles in their hands.
>
> I am already in the nearest shell-hole, another fellow plunges down beside me. I point hastily to the pillbox. He has already seen.
>
> Our rifles are at the aim, we cannot miss. I take the first pressure on the trigger and squeeze – nothing happens. Damn!
>
> Force of habit, or was it the Providence to which we all trusted made me drop under cover to see what was wrong? The safety-catch of my rifle was back. Even as I pushed it forward, and all in the space of a second, I felt an ominous 'crack' beside me, a barely perceptible 'Uh!' and the man sharing my shell-hole slithers down on top of me.
>
> A bullet has hit him straight between the eyes, smashing his forehead into a ghastly hole. My left trousered leg is soaked in blood. I am dumbfounded; for the time being unnerved. I shudder to think what may have been my fate.

But what shall I do now? Other bullets strike viciously into the earth with resounding smacks, or whine overhead, apparently in scores. That sniper from inside that pillbox is probably waiting for me to show my head. I think of that old ruse I had seen 'worked' on the pictures – a hat placed on the end of something, and cautiously raised above cover – result, smack, smack, ping. I immediately decide that I shall have to lie low for a space.

So here I am in the midst of a great battle, alone in a shell-hole, with a dead man for company, powerless to move a yard – held fast, and fatal event: the barrage has passed far ahead. I wonder if there can be other of our men nearby, as I can certainly neither see nor hear anyone here.

With all the hundreds taking part in this battle I have not seen more than twenty. I imagine there must be several of our men around this spot, judging by the volume of fire coming from that pillbox. Since our barrage has passed beyond it again, leaving it unharmed, 'Jerry' is probably dealing out terrible execution from the security of its concreted interior.

To add to the unpleasantness of the situation, enemy shells now begin to fall perilously near. All around I see huge fountains of earth thrown up by the explosions and hear the whizz of flying bits of metal. I crouch down in my hole listening, waiting and hoping for a break when I can perchance take a peep out over the top.

I look at my poor dead comrade. I have no idea who he is. I have never seen him before to-day. He belongs to the Royal Berks – whose men are going over with us as 'moppers up.' Quite a young fellow – probably in the early twenties I decide – and unmarried I should say; but I think of the distress the news of his death will cause in some home in England.

I feel I should like to write to his people. It might help to lighten their sorrow to know that his death was mercifully instantaneous. None of his associates know of his end. He will probably be reported 'missing'; his body will perhaps never be recovered.

Bodies of men of several Irish regiments who attacked over this ground three weeks ago are lying about here now, and, of course, several more will have been smashed or buried by the shell-fire – the usual fate of the 'missing.' But it is now quite light, and our final objectives should have been reached. Attacks have to be pushed forward quickly; delays are fatal to success.

One of our 'planes appears, flying low overhead. I can see the occupant as he passes directly over me; he is evidently 'spotting' for our artillery and seems to be signalling. Yes! It seems a little quieter too. I decide to have a peep over the top.

Just as I imagined. Churned up mounds of earth like the rugged surface of the moon. A region apparently deserted, but no! I can see one man wriggling forward very slowly a little way behind me nursing a Lewis gun.

Cautiously, I raise myself a little higher. Who is that? Someone else still farther back seems to be beckoning to me and anyone else to get back to where he is.

He keeps hastily motioning with his arm, as if to say, Here! Here! Why, there are one or two already doubling back in crouched positions and I cannot see that they are even shot at. I am perilously near the pillbox, but the man who is waving must surely be seen by the garrison too, unless – cheerful thought – the pillbox is now in our hands.

I decide to make a dash, I want company, and news of some sort, so running, ducking and dodging in approved rugby style, I join a party of about a dozen of our men – my platoon officer among them, in the shelter of an old German gun-pit.

'The "heavies" are going to have another "crack" at "Pond Farm,"' they say, hence the anxiety to withdraw anyone around it.

According to scraps of news gathered here and there, this is the only 'thorn' still left in our side, so to speak. The biggest part of our company had been held up by this formidable stronghold, but it is *believed* that the rest of our battalion has reached its objective, and if 'Pond Farm' can be reduced we shall link up with the other companies later.

But definite news is scarce, the general situation obscure. Of one thing we are certain. Our company's numbers have been so sadly reduced that we are no longer an effective fighting force ...

We bunch together in the shelter of the gun-pit all day, the sun pouring down from above, our nerves continually on edge from the nearby crashes of the 5.9's. It almost seems that 'Jerry' knows we are here; he certainly does know of the existence and whereabouts of the gun-pit of course. The whole area is being carefully and methodically raked from time to time.

One of our 'refugees' is killed. He had just ventured outside for a while, when the scream of a shell was heard, an appalling crash, and when the smoke cleared – there he lay an awful mess. He was buried on the spot.

There are times during the day when our own bombardment rises into a positive frenzy, smashing up all enemy attempts to concentrate for counter-attack on the positions taken from him, and the rattle of machine-guns, with occasional bursts of rifle-fire from isolated groups continue all day.

Darkness at last. We creep forward and occupy a line of shell-holes and link up with our other companies. 'Pond Farm' is now in our hands.[14]

Throughout this ordeal, Private Judd makes no mention of the tanks from F Battalion that were supposed to work with them. Like those of D Battalion to their left, they had struggled to make any headway against the treacherous ground conditions and enemy shellfire.

The tank that was to spearhead the attack on Pond Farm and Schuler Farm was F42 *Faun*, but it suffered a direct hit at the starting point and then became ditched after only 200 yards. The commander and entire crew were wounded as they struggled to put on the unditching gear, and although a fresh crew were sent up, they were unable to free the tank under heavy fire.[15]

The best chance of seizing the two objectives now lay with the supporting tank, F46 *Fay* commanded by Second Lieutenant Gerald Brooks. The already cramped interior held an additional passenger in the form of his section commander, Captain Arthur Arnold, who had formerly commanded *Dracula*. He described what happened after they moved off at zero hour:

> Progress was very difficult owing to the very boggy condition of the ground and the tank was unable to keep pace with the time-table. The tank commander eventually succeeded in penetrating the German system but it was impossible from the tank to locate the machine guns to whose fire we had been continuously subjected for about an hour. The tank commander was endeavouring to locate

a machine gun by moving in the direction from which its fire appeared to be directed when the tank subsided in the mud. By this time the time-table of the attack had elapsed, including our protective barrage and it was evident that the infantry had failed to reach their objectives.

The tank was in full view of the enemy and still under heavy M.G. fire and within about a minute of stranding was ranged upon by enemy artillery. The projecting Lewis-guns, being un-armoured, were all damaged and, several of the men being already wounded, in my opinion it was useless to keep the crew in the tank until it received a direct hit. I therefore ordered the tank commander to evacuate it. This was done, the men bringing their guns with them. About a minute after leaving the tank I was struck by a M.G. bullet in the left arm and chest and lay in a shell hole. The next thing I knew was that I was being menaced by some five or six Germans who took me prisoner.[16]

The commander of *Fay* was lucky to evade capture, as described in the War Diary: 'The officers and crew crawled in the direction taken by the infantry, who had retired in the meantime. The enemy overtook the officers and crew and 2/Lt. Brooks was spoken to by a German, and waved back to the enemy lines – He got into a shell-hole where he remained till dark, and came into our lines.'[17] One of the crew was killed, both officers and two crewmen were wounded, and three others were captured along with Captain Arnold, who was now taken for interrogation with the crew of *Dragon*.

The final resting-place of *Fay* was several hundred metres short of Schuler Farm, which therefore remained unmolested by the tanks of either D or F Battalion. Desperate, confused fighting continued throughout the day with the British struggling forward to Schuler Galleries, the network of bunkers that guarded Schuler Farm, only to find that Pond Farm to their rear had been reoccupied by the enemy.

In summary, the *Official History* said that 'the 61st Division advanced its line about six hundred yards ... on the whole, little was gained by the XIX Corps.'[18] A report by 61st Division concluded: 'The tanks during the whole operation fought as well as could be expected, but the ground was all against them. They were of service in the early stages of the fight, but the majority quickly became ditched.'[19]

The most celebrated exploit involved F41 *Fray Bentos*, whose name must have seemed grimly appropriate when she became ditched and the infantry supporting her pulled back, leaving her trapped in No Man's Land. The crew stayed there under siege for 48 hours, beating off groups of Germans who made determined efforts to blast their way inside, until finally abandoning their tank on 24 August. Unlike *Dragon*, which was stuck behind German lines with no hope of escape, the crew of *Fray Bentos* had some respite during the daytime, but it was still a harrowing ordeal which left one crew member dead and all the rest wounded, and for which every one of the survivors received a gallantry award.[20]

* * *

On 26 August, an intelligence officer at the German Fourth Army completed his interrogation report on the twelve prisoners from D and F Battalions.[21] There was much the Germans did not know about tanks, and they were keen to extract as much information as possible. However, the men were clearly mindful of the dreadful warnings about Sergeant Phillips that had been issued only a few days previously, and the interrogators were in for a frustrating time.

Captain Arthur Arnold's refusal to talk was all the more impressive since he had been hit by a bullet which he said 'entered the upper portion of my left arm, passed through the left lung and emerged about half-way down my back close to the spine. I was spitting up blood for some eight or nine days after this.'[22] Despite this, the report on his interrogation said that 'Objectives are not revealed, nor which infantry units they were attached to at the time ... He sets great store by the tanks and puts the failure of 31 July and 22 August 1917 down to the unsuitable terrain. The prisoner refused to answer any question that seemed to him of military importance, but answered other questions willingly and with apparent honesty. He seemed to attach particular importance to us not knowing anything about the construction of the propulsion motor.'[23]

They did not get any more out of Lieutenant David Lewis: 'He does not have very high expectations of the tanks, as the losses are out of all proportion to their achievements. His conduct with regard to military questions was the same as the above.' According to the report, the officers 'said they were very appreciative of their treatment since being captured'.[24] That may have been true at the time, but by the end of the war Captain Arnold would have many complaints about the medical treatment he received from the Germans, and almost as many about the way his own government handled his case.[25]

In the meantime, the interrogators might have hoped to get more out of the crewmen, who were 'mostly transferred without being asked beforehand. Of the ten men taken prisoner, only one had joined the Tank Corps voluntarily ... The average age of the prisoners is twenty-seven, only one is over forty, but they are to some extent badly shocked from their experiences and exertions. The driver was still completely deaf on the morning of the 23rd, his hearing returned slowly during the course of the day.'[26] One cannot help wondering if the driver's deafness was a ploy to avoid giving away even the most basic information: 'Propulsion is effected by a six-cylinder Daimler engine, further details of horsepower, cylinder diameter and piston stroke are unobtainable, also the driver did not know the weight of the tank, while the officer refused to give any information on technical matters.'[27]

The crew members did a good job of playing down their extensive knowledge and training, and some of what they told their interrogators was little short of ludicrous: 'The men never got into a tank before it set off for an attack. More than half of the prisoners had been in a tank for the first time early on the morning of 22 August 1917. The officers selected men for their crew who had been into action in a tank a few times, but not too often.'[28]

They also did their best to avoid revealing where the tanks were hidden beforehand, though the Germans knew enough to make an inspired guess: 'For more than a month, the camp of 12 Company has been situated in close proximity to Poperinghe, while the tanks were in a large wood between Ypres and Poperinghe (Oosthoek?) The prisoners did not express any knowledge of other camps. They left their camp shut up on the afternoon of the 21st, and met the tanks at a place they could no longer recall.'[29]

Lacking any concrete information, the interrogators had to make do with some predictable grumbling: 'The crew nearly all have a very low opinion of tanks, they would rather still be in the infantry. Their stay in the machine was portrayed as a veritable hell of heat, noise and terrifying experiences. One of the prisoners asserted that he prayed continuously, and attributed his preservation from danger to this measure. The officers admitted that conditions inside the machine were very unpleasant ... The officers thought enough volunteers would always be found to replace them, whereas the crew stated it would be very hard to find people to serve in the tanks.'[30]

The men now began their long journey to prisoner-of-war camps in Germany, but at least they could take pride that they had revealed nothing that would be of use to the enemy in their future encounters with tanks.

* * *

After the British attack had drawn to a close on the evening of 22 August, the commander of the Staigerhaus, Leutnant Dürr, crept out to examine the remains of D41 *Devil* with its dead commander and driver still on board. Despite the grim situation, the raid ended on a note of slapstick thanks to the travails of a tubby drummer:

> At 7 o'clock in the evening a counter-attack got under way on our left, where the enemy seemed to have had more success. We could clearly see the waves of attackers setting out. Leutnant Dürr used this moment, while the English on our front were distracted, to clear out the destroyed tanks; with him were Unteroffizier [i.e. Corporal] Sontheimer, Musketier [i.e. Private] Rock and Tambour [i.e. Drummer] Hag. Already the gallant men are coming under fire from the infantry. The tank crew think they're still the owners of their vehicle. The Württembergers have to go across at all costs. They creep up like Indians. They're soon there. Leutnant Dürr stands guard with his pistol poised, the others climb inside the steel carriage. They find two dead men, one of them still sitting at his place beside the revolver cannon, with eight bullets in his head and neck. The sharpshooter Günther has certainly found his mark. Three machine guns are twisted out of their housings, ammunition drums, provisions and revolvers seized, and then they form up for the return journey.
>
> The English are firing after them viciously. Leutnant Dürr brings up the rear. In front of him, Tambour Hag, who is somewhat corpulent, is getting weaker. He can't go on. Although Leutnant Dürr is lacking strength due to a serious arm wound he suffered earlier, he takes Hag's captured machine gun on his back and walks slowly behind the deadbeat Hag. Suddenly and silently, Hag falls head-first into a large, water-filled hole and disappears. Leutnant Dürr jumps into the water up to his chest and searches for the missing man. He manages to hold Hag's head out of the water. He is not strong enough to do any more. However, it's enough. His men have been watching from the Staigerhaus and rush to help. The heavy, lifeless man is carried to safety, along with the machine gun. The English are firing after them. Hag has a small gunshot wound to the nape of his neck, he is bandaged, opens his eyes, and is saved.[31]

Since D41 *Devil* was hit by a shell, it is hard to explain the bullet-riddled corpse, unless the 'sharpshooter' Gefreiter (i.e. Lance-Corporal) Günther had fired into the body after it was exposed by damage to the armour plating – which would also explain the arm that Private Addy saw protruding from the wreckage. Similarly it is unclear why one body was found beside a gun, since those who died were the commander and driver.

Neither side had an opportunity to bury Lieutenant Lawrie and Sergeant Weeks, and they are now commemorated on the memorial to the missing at Tyne Cot Cemetery, along with nearly 35,000 other men whose bodies were lost for ever in the mud of the Salient.

CHAPTER 12

Failure is an Orphan

Though painful to admit, the men of D Battalion had achieved virtually nothing that day for all their struggle and sacrifice. It is true that Bülow Farm was taken on the left, but it seems likely that this happened before the arrival of *Devil* and *Dracula*. On the rest of D Battalion's front, the British had edged their positions forward but failed to capture any of the enemy strongholds. In the words of Fifth Army's brief summary: '48th Division on the right encountered bad ground which prevented tanks reaching their objectives, and were held up by machine-gun fire approximately 150 to 200 yards short of their objective.'[1]

Tank Corps headquarters had to admit that operations across the entire front were 'not very successful', but they had warned repeatedly that tanks could not achieve the impossible. Nor did they feel they were the only ones to blame: 'The want of success was chiefly due to the inability of tanks to gain their objectives on account of bad going and the incapacity of the infantry to co-operate with them when they did.'[2]

Even the successes at Bülow Farm, and before that the Cockcroft, were called into question by the staff of 11th Division. As they looked back over recent operations, they came up with an important insight: 'It is true, that the enemy gave up the Cockcroft and Bulow practically without a fight, but any points which he considers valuable … he fights for stubbornly.'[3] In other words, the much-vaunted battle of the Cockcroft had been a success not because of the brilliant tank tactics, but rather because the Germans did not see these positions as strategically important.

Not only that, but there were claims that the tanks might actually have made the situation worse on 22 August. As soon as the action was over D Battalion came under fire again, this time from Major-General Sir Robert Fanshawe, commander of 48th Division whose troops had tried to take Vancouver, Springfield and Winnipeg. He sent an aggrieved memo to his superiors at XVIII Corps:

> In my opinion, the Germans knew that we were going to attack to-day. They bombarded our artillery heavily yesterday and also with gas during last night. This morning, just before zero hour, our assembly positions were heavily shelled. There are various reasons which may account for this. Firstly, some tanks moving at about 7.30 a.m. yesterday near Bellevue Farm, which the enemy may have seen; or the capture of a signalling officer yesterday evening. The enemy did not display any of the signs of surprise this morning as he did on the morning of the 19th; there were no rockets or lights sent up along this division's part of the front.[4]

There is no recorded response from the commander of XVIII Corps, Lieutenant-General Sir Ivor Maxse, who must have been as frustrated as anyone else by the failure and had scant regard for Major-General Fanshawe, who he damned with faint praise as 'a good average divisional commander and trainer'.[5] In fact, the biggest surprise is that anyone could have expected the Germans to be surprised by the second attack. The sudden arrival of tanks on 19 August came out of the blue, but after that the enemy

Failure is an Orphan 81

knew a further push was only a matter of time. This was obvious even to a junior officer like Second Lieutenant Douglas Browne: 'The Germans this time were wide awake, and the stratagems which had proved so successful in effecting a surprise on the 19th could hardly be expected to deceive again so soon after.'[6] One recalls the words of Lieutenant-Colonel Giffard Martel: 'An enemy is rarely caught napping twice running by the same trick.'[7]

Just as the success of 19 August had many parents, so the failure of 22 August found itself an orphan. Colonel Baker-Carr made no mention of it in his memoirs, perhaps recognizing that the tactics which proved so effective at the Cockcroft had not worked second time round, and may even have made things worse for the infantry, who were left to attack unsupported when the tanks failed to deliver.

Lieutenant-General Maxse also made no mention of the operation in his letters home to Tiny, and the debacle was played down in a report from his headquarters: 'The assaulting troops had received definite instructions to await the arrival of the tanks before they started, and as the tanks did not arrive no attack started. Later an advance was made but only little ground was captured. Our casualties for the operation were very slight.'[8]

Maxse was nothing like the popular image of a blinkered Great War general (a biography of him is appropriately entitled *Far From a Donkey*),[9] but the deaths of more than 130 men in the infantry units under his command do not strike one as 'very slight'. However, this was regrettably true by the standards of the time, and also in comparison to neighbouring units such as 61st Division which lost more than 320 men. When all the British and Imperial armed services are taken into account across all fronts, a total of 1,650 people died on that single day, even though no major offensive took place.[10]

The biggest frustration was that there was still no effective way of tackling the concrete bunkers that blocked the advance. An officer from the brigade which attacked with F Battalion invoked the language of the apocalypse: 'Every kind of mechanical means of destruction must be brought to bear against strong points. It is not likely that Stokes [i.e. trench mortars] can be got up with our barrage. This points to a use of tanks – gas – boiling oil – liquid fire – burning phosphorous – smoke etc. The condition of the ground will not always allow of tanks being used. They failed in the late attack on this account.'[11]

* * *

While the British regarded 19 August as a success and 22 August as a failure, the Germans were more consistent: they regarded them both as minor triumphs.

They had beaten off two concentrated attacks without giving any ground from their main defensive position. It is true that their losses were judged to be heavy, with 125th Infantry Regiment alone losing thirty-two officers and men killed, eighty-six wounded and eleven missing,[12] while casualties were probably even higher in 23rd Reserve Infantry Regiment manning the line to their right (from the British perspective). These losses were primarily the result of artillery fire, as described by one infantry officer: 'The English artillery are exceptionally agile and flexible ... They systematically destroy one concrete bunker after another. In comparison with the defensive battle at Arras, it is striking that the enemy uses almost exclusively large calibres.' The report confirms the efficacy of these heavy munitions against the supposedly impregnable blockhouses, of which 'many ... were destroyed by the first shot'.[13]

On the other hand, the Germans saw the enemy infantry as lacking in determination, and the use of tanks as an attempt to compensate for this. The same report continues:

'The English infantry attacked better at Arras. They are no longer so spirited, nor do they come in such compact groups. First of all, it seems that tanks and raiding parties equipped with machine guns have to reach and hold a secure line before the English infantry form up to attack ... The failure of the tank attacks is primarily due to the difficult terrain and machine-gun fire. The machines remain stuck in the mud in the deep shell-holes. The anti-tank batteries fired around 100 shells, which landed close to the tanks. One tank was completely destroyed.'[14]

Their pride at holding the British at bay was sealed two days later, when a message arrived for the 125th from Kaiser Wilhelm II himself: 'For the recent glorious achievements of the regiment, which repulsed two heavy English attacks without giving the least ground, I offer my warmest congratulations, and wish to convey to the regiment, which has always proved itself so magnificently, my deepest appreciation and sincere gratitude.'[15]

* * *

The attack of 22 August was hardly a decisive encounter, but we have considered it so closely not just because it was the first battle involving *Deborah*'s crew, but also because, in the words of Major William Watson, it was 'typical of many a tank action in the Salient'.[16]

The various British units produced various reports on the operation, but there was no real soul-searching about its failure, and no sign that any major lessons had been learned; in fact, the main response was more or less to forget about it. The entire day's fighting by XVIII Corps and D Battalion merited a bare five lines (plus footnote) in the official account of the battle.[17] Major Clough Williams-Ellis, in his history of the Tank Corps, devoted two whole pages to the action of 19 August, but merely mentioned 22 August among a number of what he called 'depressing little engagements'.[18] Lieutenant-Colonel John Fuller later compiled a list of every action fought by the Tank Corps during the Great War, but one searches in vain for any mention of D Battalion on 22 August. It seems that he, too, had simply forgotten about it.[19]

But the soil of Flanders could not forget so easily, at least for the time being. A month after the attack, Private Frank Cunnington walked across the former battlefield, near what had been the boundary between D and F Battalions.

At and beyond Schuler Galleries it was like picking a way through hell itself, no chamber of horrors could be like it. From out of what had once been the earth protruded arms, legs, dead faces, riven bodies which swelled till they burst, and over all clouds of flies. One arm pointed upwards, on its sleeve the red square, symbol of the [Staffordshires]. The shells had killed them, buried them, and churned them up again out of the depths of this horrible, bloody porridge, over which hung the awful stench of the dead and shell fumes, the earth is soaked with it and the hot sunlight over all. We hurried on and were soon on cleaner ground. On ahead we now saw [our observation post] at Kansas House ... About 10 yards in front lay one of our dead on his back, arms flung wide just as he had fallen, eyes open and lips parted in a smile. You had to look twice to realise he was dead, his whole expression was that of surprised pleasure, as if meeting a long lost friend.[20]

On his return journey, Private Cunnington and a colleague came across another reminder of the battle – an abandoned tank with a shell hole in the front. They decided to investigate:

Tom said, 'She's been hit by a dud and the crew's cleared off for the present. Now's the chance to see what the inside of a tank's like.' A narrow door, placed low down, was open, so Tom got head and shoulders inside, looked up for a moment, gasped and hurriedly withdrew. 'Lord, what an awful sight. I wouldn't go in there for a pension!' I looked in and up, and I don't think I shall ever forget it. There on the machinery hung the remains of the lookout man [sic]. The shell had hit him direct, he was smashed to pulp except for the left arm and hand which hung stripped bare of any sign of sleeve. And shocked as I was, I noticed a gold ring on one of the fingers. Perhaps the rest of the crew lay inside, I don't know, we didn't go in to find out. Poor devil, but he couldn't have felt anything, and Tom said how glad he was not to be in the Tank Corps.

Even worse was to come when they passed by again the next day: 'A few chaps are round the tank, [an officer's] servant among them. He wanted the gold ring on the dead man's hand and because he couldn't remove it, he hacked off the finger and secured it by brute force, the callous swine. I loathed the sight of him ever afterwards.'[21]

Just six weeks later, with the British offensive in the Salient nearing its close, Lieutenant-General Maxse gained a very different impression as he toured the same area with his brother-in-law. Their walk from St Julien to Wurst Farm took them along the road where D51 and the southern group had met their fate, and over the crossroads at Winnipeg. He told Tiny they had been 'amongst scenes which were of intense interest to me during August and Sept. last! Now they are in our possession they become less interesting day by day, and are losing their battle characteristics so rapidly that I quite understand why no historian ever can reproduce any accurate description of anything but the broad lines of any battle.'[22]

It was as though the landscape itself was moving on. An even bigger surprise was in store for Arthur Judd, who had narrowly escaped death in the attack near Pond Farm: 'Our battalion never went back to Ypres, but I revisited it – a new clean city – just ten years later. I was amazed at the change, not so much with the re-built city itself, but the transformation of the countryside – a beautiful rich fertile land, fields of flax and wheat waving in the sun, freshly-planted trees, dear little churches set in a wonderland of model villages; children playing gaily in the streets, and above all, peace.'[23]

Nothing much has happened since to change that description, apart from the present-day hazard from cars speeding along the straight rural roads. Most of the concrete pillboxes have been removed, though it is fortunate that at Pond Farm, the farmer's son Stijn Butaye has a rare affinity with the past and part of a waterlogged bunker has survived there, its concrete bulk so battered that it resembles a granite crag or the remains of a coral reef. One of the farm outbuildings is packed with the relics of war that are still turned up by the plough – twisted rifles and bayonets, a shattered fragment of armour plate from a tank, and the fuse-caps of shells, their corroded brass dials still set by the gunner's careful hand to determine the moment of impact. Outside, locked in a wire cage, a few of those that failed to detonate are lurking, scabrous and lethal, packed with explosives or poison gas and awaiting their final appointment with the Belgian bomb disposal squad.[24]

The contrast between memory and forgetting was brought home to the author Henry Williamson when he returned to the battlefield in 1964, and went in search of the Canadian 'brooding soldier' memorial at the Vancouver crossroads, which he had visited soon after it was built:

Where were the crossroads? Where am I? Could the war ever have been here – those four years. For this country today looks like a great English estate during the Edwardian heyday. We stop. Drive on. I am nervous.

'I swear it was at the muddy cross-roads. Is that it, among those trees?'

'Good God! What a difference ...'

For this place was once called Vancouver, a featureless waste of dead men, mules, tanks and shell-holes linked together with five feet of water in each. Triangle farm stood, solid with concrete and steel, like a tooth decayed to its root, with other German pillboxes in line.

The sun of high summer is shining, leaves move to the breeze, all is quiet, a dream of summer. We cross a fine new motor road.

This, rising above lawns and flowers, is the Canadian Memorial, surely *the* memorial for all the soldiers of all wars? For the bowed head and shoulders with reversed arms emerging from the top of the tall stone column has the gravity and strength of grief coming from the full knowledge of old wrongs done to men by men ...

The genius of Man rises out of the stone, and once again our tears fall upon the battlefield.[25]

Like the frozen grief of the brooding soldier, the wrongs that were done on that day could never be erased from the memories of those who were involved. Andrew Lawrie's parents would never forget the telegram telling of his death, and Jason Addy would never forget the twisted arm protruding from their son's tank, and George Macdonald would never forget the day when he had hoped, and failed, to finally come face-to-face with the enemy.

In the mental hospital where he remained until his death, a former private in 2/5th Bn Gloucestershire Regiment was also unable to forget. Ivor Gurney, now regarded as one of the finest poets of the First World War, had been attached to his brigade's machine-gun unit and was held back as a relief during the attack in which so many of his comrades died. Ten days later he was gassed and repatriated, triggering a physical and mental collapse from which he never fully recovered.[26] Decades afterwards, he was still struggling to process the disjointed images that haunted his fractured mind:

> ... Having seen a Passchendaele lit with a flare of fire
> And Ypres a dawn light ruddy and golden of desire,
> The stuck tanks – and shook at our guns going in
> As my body would not stay still at such Hell of din;
> Worse than any of theirs – and seen Gloucesters going over;
> Many for the last time – by accident gone further.
> Dwelt in two pillboxes, had open station –
> And lost of geography any the least notion,
> Seeing Verey lights going up from all quarters,
> And all German, and yet to go onwards where the
> Tangle of time and space might be somehow dissolved,
> Mixed with Londoners, Northerners and strange Gloucesters
> Whom I knew not – and seen shattered Ypres by canal waters.

His poem drifts to a close with a line that provides an epitaph for everyone who fought there:

> Ypres, they that knew you are of a Company through you.[27]

CHAPTER 13

The Dead Never Stirred

For George Macdonald, as he returned to England for the second time on a stretcher, there must have been a frustrating sense that his life was not going to plan. He had commanded two tanks in twenty-four hours, neither of which had got anywhere near the enemy, and after two years of trying to reach the front line, neither had he. George had now been wounded twice, both times in August, and he could only wonder what another summer would bring, assuming both he and the war lasted that long. In the meantime he made a good physical recovery: within a month, a doctor's report said he was 'now convalescent, but somewhat debilitated. Wound healed.' After treatment at an officers' hospital in Knightsbridge, London, he was sent to recuperate at a luxury seafront hotel now serving as a convalescent centre.[1] This was in Lytham St Anne's on the north-west coast of England, a couple of miles from Blackpool which, by a strange coincidence, was the home of D51's next commander.

As for George Macdonald, he would eventually return to the Tank Corps and to the Western Front, though not to a fighting role, and sure enough the following August would bring a final bloody encounter with the Germans. But his association with D Battalion was at an end, and we should leave him to bask in the blustery sea air, and to ponder for a few short weeks the battle he had just survived, and the others yet to come.

There would be no such respite for his former comrades in D Battalion, who made their way disconsolately back to the camp at La Lovie. No war correspondents came to disturb them, and the next day's newspapers made vague reference to 'successful operations' against positions that were held with 'great stubbornness'. The report continued: 'The tanks again took part in the operation. It was not on such a scale as in the affair of August 19, but they seem to have done excellent service.'[2] In fact this attack had been on a much larger scale, but had achieved considerably less.

For the officers, there was the usual round of paperwork to be completed, as described by Second Lieutenant James Macintosh: 'Every subaltern in the Tank Corps enjoys after action the doubtful privilege of writing a detailed history of his performance, together with any suggestions he may wish to make regarding future shows. This Battle History Sheet is forwarded to Corps H.Q., and in some cases to G.H.Q. itself. Its composition frequently causes more misgivings than the action it is intended to describe.'[3] Captain Edward Glanville Smith called these documents 'self-recommendations for a decoration',[4] and it is unfortunate that so few of them have survived, and none at all from D Battalion during this period.

There were also letters of condolence to be written to the relatives of those who died, and these must have caused their authors even more misgivings than the Battle History Sheet. One, probably written by Captain Graeme Nixon, was received by the parents of twenty-one year-old Private Alfred Preston. Relatives were often told their loved ones had died instantly and painlessly, so one can only imagine the suffering that was suppressed in his letter:

I know that anything I may say here will be but slight comfort to you in your great trouble, but I can assure you how we all miss him here. He was most popular with all of us, and his ability had enabled him to become First Driver of his Tank. I have known him personally since June, 1916, and realise how little we can afford to lose such men as him. His death was the result of a direct hit on his Tank with a shell on the 22nd of August last, and although he lived for a few minutes after being hit he suffered little pain. I fully realise what a terrible blow it must be for you, and once again extend the deepest sympathy of all of us out here.[5]

A letter also arrived from the Chaplain of 1st Tank Brigade, Captain the Reverend Arthur Huxtable: 'It is one of the saddest tasks we Chaplains have, sending home the sad news to parents and wives. You must try to find consolation that your son died a hero's death. I saw him just before he started off into action, and he was wonderfully brave and cheerful. You may well feel proud of him, and happy about him too.'[6]

In addition to these duties, the tank commanders normally went through a debriefing, though few can have been as bizarre as that undergone by Second Lieutenant Wilfred Bion at the hands of Clough Williams-Ellis, then a captain and reconnaissance officer of 1st Tank Brigade, following a subsequent attack. Bion had abandoned his tank after it literally sank into the mud a mile-and-a-half from Schuler Farm, and struggled back across No Man's Land; the problem was, he had no idea where they had been in the featureless swamp and was baffled by Williams-Ellis's questions.

'Can you show me whereabouts your tank got stuck?' It sounded simple, but ... I seemed incapable of thought. I said it was a bit to the right of Hill 40, that is, east of it – or was it west? It could be ...

He waited patiently, 'Here, show me on the map.'

Obviously it could not be west – it would be in the German lines. Nor east, because we would not have got into action. But, come to think of it, I was not sure we *had* got into action. I kept thinking of my shell-hole which I shared with a corpse from a previous engagement.

'Here', I said with a wobbly finger.

'Or', he said with scarcely concealed sarcasm, 'possibly here ... perhaps?'

I agreed that it was very likely. The corpse was lying andrews-cross-wise. It was thin, dessicated, not blown-up, and the green skin was stretched tight like parchment over the bones of the face.

'Sir?' He was asking me something.

'I said, did you notice when the alluvial changed to the cretaceous?'

I could hardly believe my ears. 'I didn't notice any change', I said truthfully.

'There seems to be general agreement about *that*.'[7]

Before the war Clough Williams-Ellis was already making his name as an architect, and no doubt he was interested in the subtleties of the underlying geology, but most of the tank commanders like Bion were simply glad to have escaped from it.

* * *

For the men of D Battalion, there was also a nagging awareness that almost every position they had attacked was still in the enemy's hands, and it was only a matter of time before they would have to try to capture them again. Sure enough, a further attack was planned five days later, on 27 August, and this time the challenge of taking Vancouver and Springfield went to No. 11 Company whose commander, Major William

Watson, was a more cerebral and less martial figure than his counterpart in No. 12 Company, Major R.O.C. Ward. Indeed, Watson's greatest claim to fame was that he had published a book describing his adventures as a motorcycle despatch-rider in the early months of the war, and then a series of magazine articles about his experiences in charge of a group of army cyclists. This provoked concern from the military authorities who eventually stifled his literary outpourings, but many must have suspected that he was simply awaiting an opportunity to document the activities of D Battalion, and so it turned out.

Rather than risk another overnight halt at Bellevue, Major Watson's tanks spent the night before the battle hidden in the devastated village of St Julien. He admitted this was a bold move but 'we had realised by then that the nearer we were to the enemy the less likely we were to be shelled.' As before, the Chaplain, Captain the Reverend Arthur Huxtable, was on hand and 'before dawn ... walked from ruin to ruin, where the crews had taken shelter from shells and the weather, and administered the Sacrament to all who desired to partake of it.'[8]

This time only four tanks took part, and any idea that they would lead the attack was ditched as thoroughly as most of their predecessors had been. The new tactics were spelled out by Major Watson: 'The general principle ... will be that tanks will assist the infantry at points where the infantry are held up ... Tank objectives thus depend on the success or failure of the infantry attack.'[9] Or in the words of the infantry orders: 'It is to be clearly understood that these tanks are entirely subsidiary to the operations and in no case are the infantry to await their arrival.'[10]

This turned out to be a wise move, as the weather on the day was described by Fifth Army as 'exceedingly unfavourable',[11] and more frankly by XVIII Corps as 'wretched'. Their report added: 'Rain fell in torrents the previous night and continued to fall on the day of the operations after zero hour. The ground was in such a state that it was almost impossible for the attacking troops to advance. They were literally stuck in the mud.'[12]

The road eastwards from St Julien was still blocked by the derelict hulks of the southern group, so No. 11 Company followed in the tracks of the northern group and advanced up the road towards Poelcappelle. One machine slid off the road early on, but the others engaged their targets before each in succession became bogged down on the flooded battlefield. After hours of desperate fighting the strongpoints at Vancouver and Springfield were finally taken, though the Germans remained in possession of Winnipeg and Schuler Farm to the south.

Under the conditions the infantry do not seem to have expected much from the tanks, or to have paid them much attention, but decades later evidence emerged that one had played a crucial role in the capture of Springfield. This came with the discovery of a diary kept by Edwin Campion Vaughan, a nineteen-year-old lieutenant in 8th Bn Royal Warwickshire Regiment, which was published in 1981 under the title *Some Desperate Glory* and is now acclaimed as a classic memoir of the war.

As he waited with his men under a furious barrage on the outskirts of St Julien on the afternoon of 27 August, Lieutenant Vaughan saw D Battalion's machines heading into action: 'With a laboured groaning and clanking, four tanks churned past us to the Triangle.'[13]

Eventually he led his men forward through appalling scenes of destruction: 'Up the road we staggered, shells bursting around us. A man stopped dead in front of me, and exasperated I cursed him and butted him with my knee. Very gently he said "I'm blind,

Sir," and turned to show me his eyes and nose torn away by a piece of shell. "Oh God! I'm sorry, sonny," I said. "Keep going on the hard part," and left him staggering back in his darkness.'[14]

With his surviving men, Lieutenant Vaughan reached the bunker at Springfield as it was being stormed by another battalion: 'It was now almost dark and there was no firing from the enemy; ploughing across the final stretch of mud, I saw grenades bursting around the pillbox and a party of British rushed in from the other side. As we all closed in, the Boche garrison ran out with their hands up … We sent the 16 prisoners back across the open but they had only gone a hundred yards when a German machine gun mowed them down.' Further horrors awaited inside:

> It was a strongly-built pillbox, almost undamaged; the three defence walls were about ten feet thick, each with a machine gun position, while the fourth wall, which faced our new line, had one small doorway – about three feet square. Crawling through this I found the interior in a horrible condition; water in which floated indescribable filth reached our knees; two dead Boche sprawled face downwards and another lay across a wire bed. Everywhere was dirt and rubbish and the stench was nauseating.
>
> On one of the machine gun niches lay an unconscious German officer, wearing two black and white medal ribbons; his left leg was torn away, the bone shattered and only a few shreds of flesh and muscle held it on. A tourniquet had been applied, but had slipped and the blood was pouring out. I commenced at once to readjust this and had just stopped the bleeding when he came round and gazed in bewilderment at my British uniform. He tried to struggle up, but was unable to do so and, reassuring him, I made him comfortable, arranging a pillow out of a Boche pack. He asked me faintly what had happened, and in troops' German I told him "Drei caput – others Kamerad," [i.e. three men were dead and the rest had surrendered] at which he dropped back his head with a pitiful air of resignation.

Later the wounded officer became 'quite talkative':

> He told me how he had kept his garrison fighting on, and would never have allowed them to surrender. He had seen us advancing and was getting his guns onto us when a shell from the tank behind had come through the doorway, killed two men and blown his leg off. His voice trailed off and he relapsed into a stupor.[15]

The tank that delivered this blow was D26 *Don Quixote*, commanded by Second Lieutenant Harold Puttock, which had fought its way round to Springfield despite ditching twice on the way. This was the spot where Lieutenant David Lewis and the crew of *Dragon* had been captured five days before, but Puttock 'saw no signs of tank reported to have been surrounded at Springfield'.[16] The subsequent reports by D Battalion and 1st Tank Brigade made no mention of the crucial role played by D26, merely noting that the crew abandoned their flooded tank by which time the infantry had advanced 'well beyond' Springfield. Even worse, General Gough's Fifth Army stated: 'Communication in forward areas very difficult owing to weather conditions. No tanks were able to be used.'[17]

It seems unfair that the contribution of *Don Quixote* received no credit, especially in view of the crew's personal sacrifice. Three men were wounded, one of whom was somehow carried back across the waterlogged battlefield to the casualty clearing station at Dozinghem, only to die there later the same day. Private Harry Vaughan, aged twenty, took his place in the growing cemetery nearby, where the headstone bears a message from his family:

> Forget him, no we never will
> We miss him most
> But love him still[18]

For others who had been wounded in the attack, there was no chance of rescue. Another tank, D27 *Double Dee*, had advanced even further before its way was blocked and its petrol tank pierced by a shell splinter. The crew abandoned their stricken machine, dragging with them a severely wounded crewman, twenty-year-old Private Sydney Twigg, on a stretcher improvised from a greatcoat. But he slipped from their grasp somewhere in the flooded expanse of No Man's Land, and was officially listed as missing, believed killed.[19]

There were countless others in a similar plight. In his diary, Lieutenant Edwin Vaughan described the final horror as night fell over Springfield: 'From the darkness on all sides came the groans and wails of wounded men; faint, long, sobbing moans of agony, and despairing shrieks. It was too horribly obvious that dozens of men with serious wounds must have crawled for safety into new shell-holes, and now the water was rising about them and, powerless to move, they were slowly drowning ... And we could do nothing to help them; Dunham [his servant] was crying quietly beside me, and all the men were affected by the piteous cries.'[20] Later that night they made their way to the rear: 'The cries of the wounded had much diminished now, and as we staggered down the road, the reason was only too apparent, for the water was right over the tops of the shell-holes.'[21]

In military terms, the actions of 27 August were considered 'minor affairs', with the *Official History* acknowledging that 'they resulted in considerable further casualties and very little gain of ground'.[22] Major Clough Williams-Ellis did not mention the attack at all in the history of the Tank Corps, even in his catalogue of 'depressing little engagements'.[23]

The final word goes to Major Watson, who went to inspect the remains of his tanks when the front line had moved further forward:

> Two of the tanks had been hit. A third was sinking into the mud. In the last was a heap of evil-smelling corpses. Either men who had been gassed had crawled into the tank to die, or more likely, men who had taken shelter had been gassed where they sat. The shell-holes near by contained half-decomposed bodies that had slipped into the stagnant water. The air was full of putrescence and the strong odour of foul mud. There was no one in sight except the dead. A shell came screaming over and plumped dully into the mud without exploding. Here and there was a little rusty wire, climbing in and out of the shell-holes like noisome weeds. A few yards away a block of mud-coloured concrete grew naturally out of the mud. An old entrenching tool, a decayed German pack, a battered tin of bully, and a broken rifle lay at our feet. We crept away hastily. The dead never stirred.[24]

CHAPTER 14

The Bogs of Passchendaele

Following this setback, there was a further hiatus in the British offensive in the Salient, and it would be more than three weeks before D Battalion saw more action. The delay was partly a result of the dreadful weather and ground conditions, but there was another, more fundamental reason: Sir Douglas Haig was making major changes to address the lack of progress in the first month of fighting.

Having consistently identified the crux of the battle as the Gheluvelt plateau, he was disappointed by the failure of Fifth Army to drive the Germans off this low ridge, which offered a natural vantage point over the battlefield. As a result he now transferred the responsibility for this sector, and the units fighting there, from General Gough to General Herbert Plumer's Second Army which had been attacking to the right. Gough later said this was done at his suggestion, but the claim does not seem particularly convincing. In fact, although the tank crews did not know it, by mid-August the commander of Fifth Army had lost faith in the offensive as completely as most of his men. In his memoirs he wrote:

> The state of the ground was by this time frightful. The labour of bringing up supplies and ammunition, of moving or firing the guns, which had often sunk up to their axles, was a fearful strain on the officers and men, even during the daily task of maintaining the battle front. When it came to the advance of infantry for an attack, across the water-logged shell-holes, movement was so slow and so fatiguing that only the shortest advances could be contemplated. In consequence I informed the Commander-in-Chief that tactical success was not possible, or would be too costly, under such conditions, and advised that the attack should now be abandoned.
>
> I had many talks with Haig during these days and repeated this opinion frequently, but he told me that the attack must be continued. His reasons were valid. He was looking at the broad picture of the whole theatre of war. He saw the possibilities of a German victory, a defeat of the whole Allied cause. There was only one Army in the field in a position to prevent this disaster, and that was the British Army in France. On it fell this heavy burden.[1]

To the men of D Battalion, who bore their share of the burden, it was probably not a major concern that the centre of gravity had shifted away from Fifth Army, whose headquarters were near their own at La Lovie; the square facade of the château remained as inscrutable as ever, and the staff officers strutted up and down its steps just as imperiously. All the crews could do was prepare for the next time they were called on to cross the dreaded Canal, and in the tankodrome at Oosthoek Wood, they began the task of repairing and refitting the few tanks that had returned in readiness for the next attack.

The losses also had to be made good, and this meant a welcome break for the crews who were now sent to pick up replacement vehicles, as described by Captain Edward

Glanville Smith: 'No. 12 Company, who had lost heavily in tanks in their first attack, were sent down to Erin to re-equip with new machines from England, which were brought up to the salient and parked in Oosthoek Wood.'[2] This meant an 80-mile round trip to the peaceful French countryside near St Pol-sur-Ternoise, where the Tank Corps had taken over a group of villages which now formed their rear support area. At the heart of this complex lay the Central Stores and Workshops at Erin, an 'engineer's paradise' covering seven acres of railway sidings and six acres of buildings, where the shortage of manpower was made up by thousands of imported workers from the Chinese Labour Corps. Here new tanks arrived by rail from factories in England, and here the damaged machines that had seen action were brought back to be repaired, and if possible returned to the front, or else cannibalised for spares.

Second Lieutenant Macintosh described the scene as he approached the railhead at Erin after collecting his new tank:

> They looked down upon the rows of huge sheds, green corrugated iron on steel girders, which comprised the actual shops. Flanking them could be seen two rows of big hangars – spare-part receiving and distributing shed [*sic*]. In the distance, close to the main line railway which ran up the valley, lay the salvage department, where old hulks reduced, apparently, to scrap-iron, were skilfully built up again into serviceable weapons of war; while above the salvage-shop was the huge square training-ground where new types, new methods, and new devices were constantly put on their trial … As they ran down the last hill, the tanks passed within a few yards of the barb-wire entanglements surrounding the Chinese compound. The placid Celestial [a common euphemism for the Chinese] was extensively used at Central Workshops, and under a N.C.O. who understood him was capable of surprisingly skilled work.[3]

* * *

The task of recovering the shattered hulks strewn across the Salient was entrusted to a small and specialized unit which had been growing in importance ever since the first tanks went into action. This dangerous work – often carried out under the guns of the enemy – seemed to attract characters even more colourful and *outré* than the rest of the Tank Corps.

At their head stood Major Robert Thomas Rowley Probyn Butler, the son of a baron whose early career had involved railway-building on the Indian North-West Frontier and ranching in Canada. He had already won the Military Cross for an underground battle with Turkish tunnellers at Gallipoli, and now led what were officially known as the Tank Salvage Companies. He was described as 'a big man in all ways – big frame, big hands and feet, big heart, big ideas, big courage. He loved a battle and his pale-blue eyes would sparkle with the idea of it, whether it was a battle of bullets and bayonets or of fists or of words, either written or spoken. And with it all he had a most kindly and entirely unselfish nature: altogether a most lovable man.'[4]

The same could not truthfully be said of his deputy, Lieutenant Ewen Cameron Bruce, though 'Bob' Butler charitably described him as 'a delightful person and unique in his ways'. The problem was that when Bruce disliked someone he made no secret of it, and Butler recounted how this got him into trouble back home when a passenger in the same railway carriage casually remarked that it was a terrible war, and should be stopped:

'Oh,' said Bruce … 'you are one of those pacifists, are you? Then get out of this carriage.' …the civilian didn't quite know what to make of him, but he soon found himself kicked through the door on to the platform. As a result of this episode Bruce was summoned, and when called upon by the magistrate to explain his action, he said, 'Well, you see, this person seemed to me such a nasty piece of work that I could not resist having five bob's worth.' 'All right,' said the magistrate, 'five shillings.' And that was that.[5]

Lieutenant Bruce's arm was amputated after being shattered by a shell at the start of the Battle of Passchendaele,[6] and although he returned to active service, Major Butler observed that 'his peculiarities were more marked, and in all that he said and did he seemed to make a point of defying convention more than ever'.[7] Fortunately neither his injury nor his idiosyncrasies hindered his performance on the battlefield, and he was awarded the Military Cross after he 'repaired and brought in two tanks which had been abandoned in full view of the enemy. By his energy, resource and courage he has salved many other apparently hopeless tanks, to the value of many thousands of pounds, and his personal example under shell fire and under most difficult conditions has raised the standard of salvage to a very high pitch.'[8]

After the war Bruce joined a small armoured detachment supporting the White Russians in their battle against the Bolsheviks, who he successfully drove out of the city of Tsaritsin while in command of a single tank – a feat that won him the Distinguished Service Order, and one that notably eluded the Germans two decades later when the city was better known as Stalingrad.[9] Following this his career took a darker turn, and he joined the Auxiliary Division of the Royal Irish Constabulary, which was engaged in what we would now call a 'dirty war' against the IRA and any suspected sympathisers. Forced to resign for beating a prisoner, he was eventually imprisoned for robbing an Irish creamery and died in disgrace, having forfeited both his rank and his medals.[10]

But those are other stories for another time, and for now there were dozens of tanks abandoned all over the Salient, many engulfed in glutinous mud, which could potentially be recovered and returned to service. Major Butler recalled: 'We had a certain amount of success, but it was weary work … Every time we came in for more or less of a bombardment, and casualties were frequent. Sometimes, after we had been working on a tank for days, it was hit and became a total wreck, and all our efforts were wasted.'[11] This could also be a gruesome business, as he discovered on entering one abandoned machine:

> It had been struck by a shell in front and the officer's head had been blown off. His body was lying across the driver's seat. My correct course of action was to drag the body out and to try to start up the engine, but it is an awkward thing to drag a man out of the driver's seat, and if his head is scattered about the tank it becomes very unpleasant. I, at any rate, was too squeamish to tackle it, and easing my conscience with the thought that the tank would be no good for fighting purposes even if it could run, I went on, hoping to find something more useful to be done elsewhere.[12]

The salvage of the D Battalion tanks damaged by shellfire at Bellevue on 21 August, including the first D51, was presumably a more straightforward task, and we know that she was recovered and repaired before returning to action for the rest of the war, though there are no details of her later service.

Major Butler recalled another early recruit to the tank salvage units: 'One second-lieutenant, who was sent to us because his [commanding officer] wanted to be rid of him, became a lieutenant-colonel within two years, and I served under him myself for a short time in 1919.'[13] This was Theodore Lanternier Wenger, whose name reflected his Swiss ancestry, though he was born and brought up in Staffordshire where his father was a wealthy manufacturer of chemicals used in the ceramics industry. Second Lieutenant Wenger had worked as an electrical engineer before joining the Army Service Corps in 711th Mechanical Transport Company, and then transferring to the Tank Corps.[14] Two of his brothers were also in the forces, and his sister became a nurse, but this was not enough to avert hostility at home over their German-sounding name, and the family had to mount a local publicity campaign to explain their true origins.[15] It was less clear what Theodore had done to incur the disapproval of his commanding officer, but we have reason to be grateful that he wound up in tank salvage, as he would later be directly responsible for the preservation of the second tank called D51 *Deborah*.

* * *

Eventually the battle resumed, but there would be no more of the piecemeal operations to which D Battalion had devoted so much effort with so little success. Instead, the offensive would now follow the doctrine advocated by General Plumer known as 'bite and hold', under which the enemy would be driven back by a series of methodical advances along the entire British front, preceded by a devastating bombardment and followed by a protective barrage to wipe out the anticipated counter-attacks. The first of these operations was fixed for 20 September, and once again tank support was to be provided by No. 12 Company under Major R.O.C. Ward. After so many setbacks there was some prospect of success, since the tanks would no longer keep to the roads but, in the words of Captain Edward Glanville Smith, 'were again to experiment a cross-country attack over ground that was thought to be less pounded than usual'.[16] There were additional grounds for optimism, since they would be fighting alongside the 51st (Highland) Division, which was making its name as one of the finest units in the British army, due partly to the character and qualities of its commander, Major-General George Montague Harper.

Although seemingly the archetype of a crusty general, and an Englishman to boot, Harper was a progressive and dynamic leader and enjoyed a unique bond of trust with his men, who famously referred to him as 'Uncle'. He was also held in high esteem by his own senior officers, and the commander of XVIII Corps, Lieutenant-General Maxse, was unstinting in his praise: 'He has an intimate up-to-date knowledge of infantry tactics and is thorough in his training methods. His division is organised from top to bottom in all departments, and he handles it in a masterly manner in active operations. I knew the 51st Division before General Harper commanded it and then considered it ill-organised and unsoldierlike. It is now one of the two or three best divisions in France and its fighting record is well known. I attribute its success mainly to its present commander and recommend him for promotion to a Corps.'[17]

It is worth quoting this assessment in view of later claims that Major-General Harper was a stick-in-the-mud who had a deep-seated hostility to tanks. While many in the army might have observed that tanks themselves had an unfortunate tendency to stick in the mud, there is no evidence that he was opposed to their use; indeed, his published *Notes on Infantry Tactics & Training*, gave consideration to the most effective ways in which infantry and tanks could work together.[18] The criticism of Harper was fostered by Colonel Baker-Carr, commander of 1st Tank Brigade, an equally strong character who was obviously rubbed up the wrong way by Harper's brusque manner, and later used his memoirs to settle their differences. But it would be several months before this conflict came to a head, and in the meantime, Baker-Carr merely observed that 'General Harper was much in evidence at the Corps Conferences and, although he was inclined to belittle the value of the tanks, he did not fail to put in a claim for a far greater number of machines than that to which he was justly entitled'.[19]

As it turned out, anyone involved in the fighting on 20 September might reasonably have had some doubts about the future of armoured warfare. For D Battalion, the battle followed a familiar pattern: the foreboding as they crossed the Canal, the carefully planned approach to their lying-up positions, the mounting tension during the 24-hour bombardment before the attack, and then, as soon as they got under way, the slow-motion slide to disaster as their efforts were swallowed up by the swamp.

Of the twelve tanks that took part, one was knocked out by shellfire before it had even left St Julien, and most of the others became irretrievably ditched within a few hundred yards of their starting-point, or broke down with mechanical trouble. The crew of D16 *Derek*, commanded by Second Lieutenant James Macintosh, were incapacitated by fumes from the exhaust, while a number of other tanks suffered direct hits.[20]

The only bright spot was provided by D44 *Dracula*, commanded by Second Lieutenant Charles Symonds who had hardly distinguished himself in the previous attack on 22 August, but now, in the words of his section commander Captain Edward Glanville Smith, performed 'almost superhuman deeds'.[21] *Dracula* was ordered to advance along the road from St Julien towards Poelcappelle and attack an enemy position called Delta House. Symonds' citation for the Military Cross told how he 'brought his tank through almost insurmountable obstacles. In his journey he surmounted over thirty trees felled slantwise across the road before reaching his final objective, which until his arrival was holding up the infantry. His tank was ditched on four separate occasions; but under heavy shell fire, and showing a total disregard to danger he collected material to make ramps, thus enabling his tank to reach firm ground.'[22]

The commander of D Battalion, Lieutenant-Colonel Kyngdon, described how Symonds 'then advanced with the infantry to their objective ... doing great execution with his Lewis guns, on the enemy who retired before them. On reaching a point just short of Delta House his engine gave out altogether, and although his crew worked for 2½ hours to repair the trouble it was of no avail.'[23] The crew handed over their Lewis guns to the Gordon Highlanders and showed them how to use the tank's 6-pounder gun, before making their way to the rear.[24] Two of the crewmen, who had worked in the open under fire four times to free their tank, received the Military Medal.[25]

It was a textbook example of co-operation with the infantry, though on that occasion sadly a unique one, as none of the other tanks from D Battalion got anywhere near their objectives. The only other one that made any contribution at all was D43 *Delysia*, commanded as before by Lieutenant Alfred Enoch, which advanced behind *Dracula* until its way was blocked by another tank that had slipped on a fallen tree, and then provided overhead fire to disrupt an enemy counter-attack.[26]

It was an even more depressing story for E Battalion, which had arrived from the UK to join 1st Tank Brigade in June, and had been awaiting its first taste of action in Oosthoek Wood ever since. No fewer than nineteen of their tanks took part in the attack, with Schuler Farm among their objectives, but it turned out to be less a baptism of fire than a baptism of mire. One after another they were swallowed up by the mud, and their commanding officer described the outcome: 'Owing to a succession of ditchings in the majority of cases, and direct hits on stationary tanks, no tank was able to be of any material assistance to the infantry.'[27]

As always the chaplain was on hand to provide moral support, and this time Captain the Reverend Huxtable travelled to the starting point inside one of E Battalion's tanks. However, any hopes of divine protection were dashed when a metal shrapnel ball hit him in the leg at Janet Farm, near the spot where George Macdonald's progress had been halted a month before.[28] It was the end of the chaplain's war, but his citation for the Military Cross said that even when wounded 'he refused to go back ... until he was satisfied he could do no more to assist the men'. The citation recognized all the occasions when he had gone forward with the crews, 'remaining with them under heavy shell fire, holding services in the tanks, assisting the men with their meals, and doing all in his power to encourage them and make them comfortable'.[29] One of D Battalion's tank commanders, Lieutenant Gerald Edwards, summed up his departure: 'A great loss to us.'[30]

* * *

It was another gloomy return to Oosthoek Wood for the tank crews, who knew they could not have done any more, but it had still not been nearly enough. Most of their tanks were left behind, awaiting salvage as soon as the conditions allowed, though D44 *Dracula* soon found itself under new ownership following a German counter-attack. Photographs show soldiers in jackboots and coalscuttle helmets posing proudly beside their trophy, but despite their best efforts the Germans were unable to get her moving, and instead blew up the hulk, where it remained to play a fateful role in a further attack by D Battalion.

The good news was that the offensive, which was officially christened the Battle of Menin Road, was overwhelmingly successful and the British gained virtually all their objectives, pushing their front line forward and then clinging onto the captured ground. Even the bunkers at Schuler Farm, which had been D51's objective on 22 August, finally fell.[31] It had been the first trial of a 'step-by-step' approach, and the *Official History* described it as an almost complete success: 'The much vaunted new German defence tactics had failed to stop the new method. The change was not appreciated in England or in France, and the success was underrated by the public, but not by the troops themselves, or by their adversaries.'[32]

While the advance was a cause for celebration, it also highlighted how superfluous tanks were to the overall military effort. The 51st (Highland) Division had swept forward with little armoured support, and one journalist told how groups of men who had been trained to deal with the German blockhouses 'went like wolves about them, firing their machine-guns and rifles through the loopholes if the garrisons would not come out'.[33] If Major-General Harper had been implacably opposed to tanks, he might have been expected to make the most of this, but the report from his headquarters simply said: 'Of 12 Tanks ... allotted for work on the Divisional front, one only, which did excellent service in an advanced position, was able effectively to assist in the attack.'[34] If anything, this was rather more positive than the report by Tank Corps headquarters, which noted glumly: '1st Brigade Tanks of little use – only 1 out of 30 reaches its objective.'[35]

The attack on 20 September was yet another example of what Winston Churchill, a notable proponent of tanks, called their 'misuse by Sir Douglas Haig ... in the bogs of

Passchendaele'.[36] The question was how much longer that misuse could continue, and there was a growing awareness that the powers-that-be were running out of patience. In the words of Captain Glanville Smith: 'During this period it was apparent that the fate of the Tank Corps was hanging in the balance. Numerous tank battalions had been thrown into the attack and though small successes had been gained, it was strongly rumoured that GHQ had come to the conclusion that the results did not justify the large waste of material, and incidentally money.'[37] Or as another member of D Battalion, Lieutenant Jack Coghlan, put it: 'The High Command was naturally disappointed at the poor results, and one school of thought held that persistence in the use of these expensive toys was damaging to the self-reliance of the infantry. Gross tactical mismanagement was the true cause of the failure, held the opposite school.'[38]

It was the worst possible time for a keen young officer to join the Tank Corps; but a newly-commissioned second lieutenant called Frank Heap had just completed months of training in England, and was even now crossing the Channel by troopship to join D Battalion. Whatever the War Office might decide about the future of the Tank Corps, for him at least there could be no turning back.

PART III
GATHERING FORCES

CHAPTER 15

The Coming of Frank Heap

Frank Heap's service file shows he sailed from Folkestone to Boulogne on 9 August 1917, and probably spent the next few weeks at the Tank Corps base near St Pol-sur-Ternoise and the driving school near Wailly before making his way to La Lovie.[1] On 25 September – an otherwise uneventful day – D Battalion's War Diary notes: 'On this date 1 Officer and 3 O.R. [other ranks] arrived as Reinforcements from … Depôt.'[2]

We know exactly how Frank Heap looked at this time, because he posed for a photograph before he left home wearing his freshly-tailored officer's uniform. Proudly displaying the badge of the Tank Corps, and the single 'pip' denoting his promotion to second lieutenant (or 'subaltern'), he peers quizzically at the camera through his pince-nez, a diffident and unintimidating figure.[3]

We also know how he appeared in figurative terms, because Second Lieutenant James Macintosh, writing as his alter ego 'Tosh', described just such a new arrival:

> Hurrying through the gateway as if his life depended on it, came the most beautifully apparelled of young subalterns. He was hung round about with all manner of map-cases, haversacks, field-glasses, and other 'Blighty touches'; from his pink cheeks to his pink breeches, the colour-scheme was a delight to the eye; and he was followed by a diminutive batman, almost obliterated by a most capacious valise. Up dashed the young officer, perspiringly followed by his faithful, if overloaded henchman. It was then that Tosh noticed the new-comer's badges – the new Tank badge of which he had heard, but which had not yet percolated to France, and on his right sleeve a resplendent Tank in black and silver thread.[4]

One hopes that Heap's arrival was met with an introduction as upbeat as that from Tosh: '"Well, you're lucky; you've struck the best of the bunch." Forthwith he plunged into an eulogy of the old D Battalion, which in the earliest days, as D Company had done such outstanding work, and had continued doing all the best work down to the present time. Such bursts of eloquence are common enough from old hand to new; in the present case it was swallowed eagerly enough.'[5]

We also know how Heap's brother officers appeared, for the very next day the battalion had a more eminent visitor: an official photographer from the Ministry of Information called Ernest Brooks, who depicted a group of officers smoking and relaxing in deckchairs against a backdrop of tents and drying blankets. Casually clad in jackets and shorts, their hair trimmed and pomaded, they play cards or cluster round to peruse the *Daily Mail*. They are accompanied by their pet dogs, one of which is posed next to a gramophone in a parody of the 'His Master's Voice' record label. It is a carefully studied picture of relaxation, which might as easily show the members of a college rugger team unwinding after a match.[6]

Although created as propaganda, the images did not lie, for this was indeed an idyllic period. Major William Watson, commander of No. 11 Company whose officers featured in the photographs, recalled:

My company had returned from the Canal, as it was not likely that we should be wanted again in the near future, and were living in shameless comfort at La Lovie. The rain had stopped – we always had bright sunshine in the Salient, when we were not ready to attack. If it had not been for the growl of the guns, an occasional shell in Poperinghe while we were bargaining for greengages, or the perseverance of the enemy airmen, who dropped bombs somewhere in the neighbourhood each fine night, we might have forgotten the war completely. There were walks through the pine-woods, canters over the heath, thrilling football matches against our rivals, little expeditions to Bailleul for fish, or Cassel for a pleasant dinner in the cool of the evening.[7]

Captain Edward Glanville Smith also found much to enjoy:

In camp the battalion was kept physically fit by daily drill of different sorts, but it became increasingly difficult to fill up the entire day. Frequent leave was given to Poperinghe which place had by now developed into a miniature 'West End,' containing numerous restaurants and about half-a-dozen divisional concert parties, such as the 'Whizz-Bangs,' 'Bow Bells,' etc., where humour was plentiful though somewhat crude. 'House,' bridge, ping-pong and gramophones were popular pastimes. Some fortunate beings were able to indulge in short motor trips to Amiens, St. Omer, and Dunkirk ... But most welcome of all was the fact that leave to England had reopened after a cessation of nine months, and the frequent departure of large parties of all ranks served to brighten an otherwise gloomy prospect.[8]

It must have been bizarre for Frank Heap, having followed the progress of the great Flanders offensive in the papers, and trained for months to be at the cutting edge of the conflict, to find himself in what we would now characterize as a holiday camp, though one with an underlying deadly purpose. Having been through public school and university, he no doubt slotted easily into the jovial bonhomie of the officers' mess, and as a token of acceptance he soon acquired a nickname. In such well-read company, it was hardly surprising that someone called Heap should be known to his brother officers as 'Uriah'.[9]

* * *

Of course it was not all fun and frolics. For many at La Lovie, there was also a mounting sense of frustration, and Captain Smith told how they were becoming '"fed up to the teeth" at a more or less continuous life of inaction.'[10]

Frank Heap must have sensed this, but for the time being he had to overcome some major personal challenges. Of the three companies that made up D Battalion, he was assigned to No. 12 – probably to replace another second lieutenant called John Elwy Symond, who had been wounded by a shell splinter when his tank was hit on 20 September.[11] This meant Frank's company commander would be the formidable Major R.O.C. Ward.

His first meeting with the major was an ordeal yet to come, but Frank Heap faced a more immediate test of his powers of leadership when he met the tank crew he was to command. This must have been daunting, since at least some of them had been in battle together, whereas Frank – although he had been on the Western Front for nearly a year-and-a-half – had not really been in battle at all, having served as a motorcycle despatch-rider delivering messages behind the lines. It was true that at twenty-five he was older than most of his crew, and was better educated and more affluent; but they must have been aware that he had spent most of the war as a humble corporal, and had only received his commission as a 'temporary gentleman' at the beginning of the year.[12]

In fact for the last few months Frank had been at the Tank Corps depot in Bovington, Dorset, going through the training course developed to teach the skills needed in the new unit. These included tank driving, use of the compass and various types of machine gun, and target practice with the revolver which crewmen carried for personal protection. At the coastal range in Lulworth he was taught how to fire the 6-pounder gun which was the principal armament of a male tank. He would also have learned how to use and care for carrier pigeons, which were the most reliable means of reporting on progress when in action. After he arrived in France he had further training in handling a tank over more realistic terrain at Wailly, where a section of German trenches had been taken over by the Tank Corps as their driving school and practice area.[13]

All this gave a comprehensive set of technical skills, but there was no effort to teach the most fundamental skill of all, namely how to command men in battle. This reflected the fact that the army had traditionally drawn its officer corps from a small and select group, many of whom belonged to long-serving military families and absorbed officer qualities almost literally with their mothers' milk. Although the army had expanded beyond all recognition, the idea that leadership was something that should, or could, be taught was slow to catch on, which meant there was little guidance for the aspiring officer, other than the advice of his surviving colleagues and the case-studies of heroism from the mass media, later collected in books such as *Deeds That Thrill the Empire*. The day after Frank Heap's arrival, an even younger subaltern called Wilfred Bion went into action for the first time with E Battalion, a frustrating experience which prompted him to ask: 'Could anyone, outside a public-school culture, believe in the fitness of a boy of nineteen to officer troops in battle?'[14]

However, one of the few good things to be said about the war was that it rubbed the edges off people. Frank Heap may not have been taught what makes a good officer, but at least he would have learned how to establish a rapport with men from a range of social backgrounds. His family was wealthy but not grand, and his service as a despatch-rider had thrown him together with all conditions of men. The same could be said of his crew, and although Heap had been both a public schoolboy and student in Cambridge, he was no longer a member of an alien species for a townsman like Gunner Joseph Cheverton, who had shared barrack-rooms and dug-outs with plenty of varsity men while in the Cambridgeshire Regiment. Gunner Fred Tipping, who was more than a decade older than Frank Heap, was probably something of a father figure, while Gunner William Galway, who was exactly the same age as his new commander, was easy to get along with thanks to his uproarious sense of humour: Heap described him as 'the life and soul of my crew, doing two men's work and cheering us all up'.[15]

The biggest challenge, if he had been so minded, could have been Gunner George Foot, who had also started the war as a despatch-rider but transferred to the tanks at the start, acquiring a wealth of experience and, as we have seen, a gallantry medal; in fact his three-day vigil in No Man's Land could have come straight out of *Deeds That Thrill the Empire*. But Frank Heap was in luck and George Foot, probably mindful that he might well face a similar promotion in future, chose to make his commander's arrival as easy as possible. Heap recognized this, and singled him out for praise: 'As a young officer in charge of a tank for the first time, I was helped to do my job by his tactful experience.'[16]

While we can glean something of Heap's impressions of his crew, we can only surmise what they made of him. Their initial response was probably to wonder whether Bovington was turning its officers out of a mould, since Frank Heap looked incredibly similar to George Macdonald, the ill-fated commander of the first D51, right down to the glasses they both wore for short-sightedness. It was true that neither presented a particularly martial appearance, but the crew had probably learned that it was hard to tell a book by its cover, or to extend the metaphor, however bookish a man appeared, he might still turn out to have a spine. No-one could predict how Frank Heap would react when he went into action, including Heap himself, but one thing was certain: the decisions he made, and the orders he gave, and his keenness or otherwise to 'get on', would eventually determine all their fates.

* * *

Having met his crew, Frank Heap now faced another important introduction – to his tank. This might sound straightforward in comparison, but these were complex machines that could be as wayward and unpredictable as any crewman or commanding officer. The crew probably travelled back to Erin to pick up their new charge as part of a consignment sent to replace those lost on 20 September. Frank found he had been allocated a new Mark IV female tank with the manufacturer's number 2620, the crew number D51, and the name *Deborah*.[17]

No doubt he had learned about the fate of the first D51, and was determined this one would have better luck. Apart from that, we can be sure his main reaction was disappointment, as his fellow commander Second Lieutenant Horace Birks explained: 'Everybody wanted a male tank. I was a junior officer, I got a female … The male tank was the thing because it had a gun and it was a more formidable weapon altogether. You could get out of it easier because it had quite a biggish door on the back of the sponson, but the female tank had doors no more than [a few feet] off the ground, and it was very difficult to get out of. If there was a fire or anything like that, it was odds on that somebody would get hurt.'[18]

The task of taking over a tank was a major chore for the commander and crew, in view of the huge range of tools and spares that had to be checked and signed for. Captain Edward Glanville Smith told how '297 articles of equipment (exclusive of ammunition) had to be collected from apparently an equal number of sheds'.[19] The best account of the process was given by Second Lieutenant James Macintosh, writing under his usual alias as 'Tosh':

> The first driver, a most important personage, who is responsible for the mechanical efficiency of the tank, proceeds to inspect her interior … The inside of a tank is not remarkable for comfort or capaciousness. The centre is occupied by a large engine, the rear by a huge differential, the two sides by field guns [Macintosh imagined he had a male tank, though in reality his was female too], and the front by seats and driving controls; while the roof is not high enough to allow of standing upright. The fact that eight men frequently spend many crowded hours of glorious life in the remaining crevices does not prevent one man, if careless, from banging his head and both elbows at the same time; especially as the lighting arrangements are artificial and inadequate. But our friend is an old hand, rendered cautious by many a bump on projecting rivet-heads, and he sets about his business of examination without further ado. Meanwhile, the second driver … and the

third driver ... enter by the other door, open the tool-boxes in the floor, and throw tools and equipment into a large box outside.

The equipment list of a tank is a document well worthy of study, comprising as it does such a medley of timber, hardware, and ironmongery as only a salvage-dump could ever rival ... Slowly and methodically Tosh wades through the list of items useful and ornamental, decorative and deadly. Periscopes are there, and plugs sparking; spanners, scrapers, and shovels; gun spares, engine spares, track spares. There is included a fishing net, with green rags tied to it, as a camouflage; there are signalling discs and 'flappers' which no tank commander has ever been known to use, but which are still religiously issued and must be exhibited.[20] Gradually order develops out of chaos; the checking is complete, and Tosh writes out a duplicate list of his deficiencies. Meanwhile, the crew stow the various implements away where they fondly hope they will be able to find them in case of need ...

While the gunners have been inspecting the 6-pounders ... Tosh has been examining his seat and the various devices round it. The tank commander's seat, a horsehair cushion, is set well up in the forepeak or cab; as he sits in it, his feet rest on the upward slope where the belly runs up to the curve of the nose. In front, behind, and to the left, are various flaps and 'gadgets' for observation; immediately above is a periscope-hole; to the right is a mounting for a Lewis gun, while beside the commander's seat is that for the driver, with similar flaps and with controls for driving the tank. Tosh tests them methodically, finds them O.K., and ... reports himself to his skipper as ready to move off for lunch.[21]

Despite his initial disappointment, Frank must also have felt a mounting surge of pride and anticipation as he seated himself at the controls of *Deborah* for the first time. It would have been hard not to feel an overwhelming sense of responsibility, not just for himself and his crew, but also for the great machine which was the product of such enormous labour and expense.

By now significant resources were being devoted to the production of tanks, each of which cost around £5,000 (excluding transportation charges),[22] and *Deborah* was one of 1,015 Mark IV fighting tanks that were built, of which 595 were female.[23] Factories in Lincoln, Newcastle-upon-Tyne and Glasgow were all involved in tank assembly, using components supplied by many other contractors, but by far the largest number came from the Metropolitan Carriage, Wagon and Finance Co. Ltd. in the West Midlands.[24] Based on the available records, it seems that *Deborah* probably began life at their factory in the Black Country town of Oldbury.[25]

After completion the tanks were handed over to a unit called No. 20 Squadron, Royal Naval Armoured Cars, which was responsible for testing and delivering them to France. The involvement of the Navy was a throwback to the earliest days of development, when the Admiralty had promoted the concept of 'land battleships', but their role was now limited to the vital but not very glamorous work of tank supply. As production stepped up, Squadron 20 opened testing grounds near the assembly plants, and *Deborah* probably first went through her paces at their centre in Oldbury, before being loaded onto a flatbed railway wagon and transported to Portsmouth for the crossing to Le Havre. The machines then continued their railway journey to Erin where they were handed over to the Tank Corps for distribution to the front-line battalions. The process was generally smooth and rapid, as described in a history of the unit: 'Great dexterity in handling tanks was acquired by Squadron 20 and at Oldbury (where the bulk of them were produced) the usual rule was to deliver them to Tank Headquarters in France 3 days after they left [the Testing] Station. There was no occasion upon which any tanks were lost on the sea journey to France.'[26]

Despite the extensive inspection and testing it had undergone, each tank had its own peculiar characteristics, and once the crew had taken it over, they began investigating and correcting these mechanical foibles. To quote Second Lieutenant Macintosh: 'The tanks a month ago had all been certified ready for action by a body of experts; but the crews which had now taken them over expected shortly to entrust their lives to them, and it was remarkable how much work they found to do on them before they were satisfied.'[27]

This process completed, Second Lieutenant Heap and his crew were ready to load *Deborah* onto another train that would transport them to Oosthoek Wood, to the tankodrome formerly occupied by her predecessor, there to await the call for action as the great offensive in the Ypres Salient ground steadily on. Wartime railway journeys were normally long drawn-out affairs as the trains crawled along between frequent and unexplained halts. This was maddening for anyone going home on leave, but otherwise it was one of the minor inconveniences of military life that had to be accepted, and could even be enjoyed were it not for the discomfort of the rolling stock. It meant there was time to smoke and chat, and for Frank Heap to get to know his brother officers, and to tell them a little about his own progress through peace and war.

CHAPTER 16

Heap's Progress

As with many of his fellow 'temporary gentlemen', Frank Heap's family had built their own fortune, and had done so more successfully than most, though the source of their wealth would have provoked derision among the young blades who traditionally made up the army's officers corps. The Heaps' origins lay in the moorlands of Lancashire, where Frank's father Joseph was brought up as the son of a stonemason. While most of his siblings went to work in the quarries or cotton mills, Joseph had a more academic bent and trained as a schoolmaster, a move that took him away from his home village to work in the cities of Liverpool and Bradford.[1]

It was then that fate intervened in the person of Joseph's father-in-law William Clarke, who had spotted a business opportunity in the seaside town of Blackpool, which was booming in popularity as a holiday destination for workers from the industrial north. Mr Clarke thought the coffee palaces on South Beach 'might be made a very useful and a profitable concern', and proved this so successfully that in 1882 Joseph Heap joined him as a partner.[2]

The firm of Clarke & Heap made its name by dishing up wholesome fare to the trippers who flocked in for their brief dream of freedom by the sea. The family's empire included the Station Restaurant, the Central Dining Rooms and the British Workman's Restaurant, while the advertisements boasted: 'Best food, quickly served, separate tea-pots. Picnic, choir, workmen, and school parties specially catered for at reasonable prices in separate rooms … 1,000 can dine at once.'[3] The firm had hit on a winning formula, its prosperity sustained by the tide of up to four million visitors who swept in each summer as predictably as the waves washing the seafront. As business flourished, other members of the family became involved until the Heaps formed a dining dynasty, and could rightfully claim to be 'Blackpool's principal provision merchants'.[4]

Joseph Heap, who had originally moved there to improve his health,[5] found the town was an even better tonic for his financial well-being, eventually amassing a fortune of more than £65,000,[6] which would have been enough to buy a whole company of tanks if he had been so minded. As the coffee palaces overflowed he turned to a higher calling, and in 1889 was elected to the Town Council of which he remained a member for the rest of his life, chairing the finance committee and undertaking a ceaseless round of civic duties as magistrate, hospital trustee, school governor, poor law guardian and member of the water board. In 1898 Alderman Heap was elected Mayor, and a handsome portrait in the town hall shows him in fur-trimmed gown and gold chain, a shrewd figure but not a severe one, in keeping with the local paper's pen-portrait: 'the stress and storm of political warfare never hardened him. On the contrary, as years and responsibilities weighed upon him, the heart of the man remained that of a child, tender, impressionable, quick to pain or gladness.'[7]

While this administrative labour may seem dull and worthy, Blackpool's progressive approach to local government underpinned its success as a resort, with the streets and shops lit by electricity when most places were still fumbling with gas-lamps, and an electric tramway to transport visitors along the prom. There, private enterprise developed the myriad attractions that turned Blackpool into 'a city of palaces of pleasure by the sea',[8] crowned by the Tower, then the tallest building in Britain, with a programme of entertainments which was excelled only by London and Paris, and made it a kind of Las Vegas of its day.

Alderman Heap stood at the hub of all this activity, leading a journalist to describe him as 'a pioneer of Blackpool's greatness.'[9] As a self-made man, he might have been expected to espouse a rampant Toryism, but in fact he remained a staunch Radical throughout his life, as well as keeping faith with the Wesleyan Methodism which had sustained his forebears in their moorland home. Joseph is even said to have been offered a peerage by Lloyd George, but according to his family he declined this after consulting his son Frank, for reasons that are unclear.[10]

For somehow, in the midst of this civic and commercial whirlwind, Alderman Heap had also found time for family life, and his wife Emma bore no fewer than eight children, five of whom survived into adulthood. When Frank came into the world in 1892 he had three older sisters, and another sister followed three years later to complete the family. He therefore grew up in an almost exclusively feminine household, which also included his grandmother, a maiden aunt and a number of housemaids.[11] Fortunately there was no shortage of space, since the family had moved into a suitably impressive residence on the outskirts of town, with a drive leading up to the front door, a suite of handsome rooms for entertaining (including a library and billiard room), eight bedrooms, and extensive gardens complete with croquet lawn, tennis court and bowling green.[12]

At some point in this cosy upbringing, it must have dawned on Frank that he would one day take over responsibility for the family's catering empire, since William Clarke had died before Frank was born, and his uncle, who was his father's business partner, never married. Frank accordingly had a special status within the household, and if his father was king of the coffee palaces, he was the heir apparent.

As a former schoolmaster, Alderman Heap appreciated the importance of education and was keen to ensure that Frank would have the best one possible. After attending Blackpool High School, he was sent to The Leys School, which had been founded to educate the sons of Methodists and enjoyed close links with the nearby University of Cambridge. Accordingly Frank was sent to the other side of the country and plunged into the rigours of public-school life – an all-male environment in which he seems to have thrived, being sociable and easy-going, and exhibiting a happy combination of athletic and academic prowess. Despite his short sight, he appears in a succession of rugby, cricket and lacrosse team photographs, while another shows him in bow tie and tweed jacket, arm in arm with his fellow prefects.[13]

Frank had also discovered the pleasures of military life through the school's Officers' Training Corps, which was set up as part of a national programme to improve the country's readiness for war. He rose to the rank of Cadet Colour Sergeant, and received the ultimate accolade in 1911 when he commanded the contingent sent by The Leys School to the Coronation of King George V.[14] In July more than 17,000 OTC members from all over Britain gathered in Windsor Great Park to be reviewed by the new King, and *The Times* found it an inspiring sight: 'It was a force of young soldiers, led by seasoned soldiers, quitting themselves like men, like citizens of a great Empire. As the King gazed down those serried ranks of service-clad youths that swung past him in unbroken array for close upon an hour he never saw a face but it was strained in earnest endeavour to do duty as a soldier and stedfast [*sic*] determination to simulate the bearing of manly citizenship.'[15] The special correspondent added: 'This force practically represented the entire intellectual reinforcement that the Military Services controlling the Empire will receive five or six years hence.'[16] But in this he was mistaken, for the army would need many more officers than that before the next few years were out.

* * *

Besides his sporting and military attainments, Frank did not need any intellectual reinforcement of his own, and became secretary of the literary society at The Leys School, where he also won an essay prize.[17] Once again the year 1911 marked a high point, as he was awarded a scholarship to read history at King's College, Cambridge, and was welcomed into the halls and cloisters of one of the country's great educational institutions, not to mention its 'immense and glorious' Gothic chapel.[18] It must have been a time of enormous pride for his family, and for Frank himself there was now a prospect of intellectual and social advancement more far-reaching even than the view from Blackpool Tower, from where the hills of Wales and the Lake District could be seen on a fine day, as well as 'a vast expanse of shimmering sea'.[19]

With his usual energy, Frank threw himself into university life with its myriad activities, not to mention the Officers' Training Corps in which he continued to play an enthusiastic role. Photographs of the college relay team and university lacrosse team[20] show a sociable young man with an open, inquiring face, and sometimes the glimmer of a smile that gives a hint of his sense of humour and lively mind. The only setback came when he narrowly missed selection for the British athletics team at the 1912 Olympics, despite a strong performance in the Public Schools Championships. It was a bitter disappointment to Frank, though also revealing that he had set his sights so high.[21]

It is doubtful if he encountered the aspiring poet Rupert Brooke, who had graduated from King's College two years before and was now leading a life of bucolic bohemianism in the nearby village of Grantchester, but there were plenty of other young men with whom Frank could forge friendships, engage in debate and dream of the future. Another photograph shows him in his college rooms, lounging at the head of a dining table decorated with orchids and a large pineapple, and surrounded by young bloods in blazers. The picture was taken in early 1913 and a note on the back identifies this as 'Mr Heap's dinner'.[22]

Perhaps it is not surprising that amidst this whirl of social and sporting activity, Frank metaphorically dropped the ball. In June 1913 he took the examinations that constituted the first part of his degree, and soon afterwards the college Council met to decide the fate of a dozen students whose performances had been below par. In Frank's case, they agreed that 'F.G. Heap ..., who has failed in the Historical Tripos, Part I, be deprived of his Scholarship as from the end of the present quarter and be required to leave the College.'[23]

The dizzying dream had ended, and no doubt the news was greeted with consternation by Frank's family, although his father was a practical man and probably reflected that he had not needed a fancy degree to turn Clarke & Heap's into a pillar of the local economy, or himself into a pillar of the local community. At the age of twenty-one, Frank seems to have accepted that it was time to immerse himself in the family business, probably reflecting that at least the firm would bring prosperity as long as Blackpool Tower stood and people needed holidays, since it is doubtful if any of them had ever heard of Torremolinos, and if they had, it might as well have been on the moon.

* * *

With the future so clearly mapped out, the outbreak of war the following August must have seemed a heaven-sent opportunity for some excitement, though the timing was as inconvenient as could be, falling as it did in the midst of Blackpool's peak season. It was a fine summer and there was no shortage of visitors, determined to make the most of their holidays before plunging into a war that seemed set to drag on for many months.

The papers were full of the first clashes on the Continent, and Frank left it as long as he decently could before pleading patriotic duty and hot-footing it to the recruiting office. He knew exactly where to go, as the army was facing a shortage of motorcycle despatch-riders who provided a vital link between units while on campaign. The historian of the army's signal service explained the challenge: 'To ensure good service in this important branch during mobile warfare, men of exceptional intelligence, endurance and courage, and, especially, men possessing initiative of a high order, were required ... In the early days, ... when all was hurry and every department was working overtime on unfamiliar problems, the shortage could not be made good at once. Although the University Officers' Training Corps came to the rescue with a particularly good type of men for the purpose, the mobilization and equipment of civilians took time.'[24]

Frank was ideally qualified, but by the time he arrived in Chatham on 15 September to enlist in the Royal Engineers, which was responsible for signalling, he probably felt he had missed the boat. To some extent he was right: William Watson, now a company commander in D Battalion, had been a student at Oxford when he went to Chatham two days after war was declared, and was immediately sent off as a despatch-rider in Britain's small regular army. Within two weeks he was in France, and by the time Frank joined up, Watson had already been through the great battles of Mons, Le Cateau and the Aisne.

For Frank, the journey to war would be more protracted, since he was posted to one of the new divisions that were being created at the behest of Lord Kitchener, the Secretary of State for War, and currently existed on paper only. The form Frank signed shows he was twenty-two years and four months old, worked as a caterer, and followed the Wesleyan religion. He was five feet seven-and-a-half inches tall and weighed 134 lbs, and had a dark complexion, dark brown hair, blue eyes, and a scar on his right shin. He was pronounced fit, and agreed to serve for three years 'unless the War lasts longer than 3 years, in which case you will be retained until the War is over'. Another form asked if he had a degree, to which he replied: 'None. Left University after 2 years to enter business career.'[25] To the army, however, a degree was a scrap of paper, and Frank was immediately taken on as a despatch-rider with the rank of corporal. This was normal for the role, conferring as it did a slightly higher status without giving him any inflated ideas about his importance in the military pecking-order.

Despite his English ancestry, Frank found himself assigned to the signals company of 9th (Scottish) Division, whose battalions bore the names and tartans of regiments with a stirring history, such as the Royal Scots, Black Watch and Gordon Highlanders. However, the battalions themselves were being created from scratch, as were the artillery batteries, field ambulances, and engineer and supply companies that also made up the division. In fact, apart from a smattering of officers and non-commissioned officers, virtually every member of the division had been a civilian when war broke out, and the challenge of equipping them and turning them into a fighting force was formidable, especially since a total of eighteen new divisions were being raised at the same time, with many more to follow.

In his history of 9th Division, Brevet-Major John Ewing looked back on what had been achieved: 'The pick of the nation offered itself for service. Youth, which had hitherto satisfied in sport and athletics its craving for adventure, was attracted rather than repelled by the novelty and danger of war, and young men in thousands left workshops, offices, and universities to join the Colours. Others, not so numerous, were drawn from the class of casual labourers … After selection the "First Hundred Thousand," the salt of their race, were sent to the various battalion depots, and then on to the training camps near Salisbury Plain.'[26]

The trials of drilling and training raw recruits in one of these new battalions were described with unrelenting cheeriness by Lieutenant John Beith in a series of magazine articles appropriately called *The First Hundred Thousand*, soon republished as a best-selling book. But whereas the infantry had everything to learn, Frank Heap must have found the next seven months a trial of his patience. He could already march and ride a motorcycle, and although he received training in signalling, time probably dragged at the camp in Aldershot.[27] The only consolation was that the war was obviously not going to be such a quickfire affair as many believed, and was still in full flow when 9th Division was finally ready to go overseas in May 1915, though the fighting had already stultified into the trench warfare which was to be its defining characteristic for the next three years.

* * *

It was a source of special pride that the 9th was the first of Kitchener's New Army divisions to go to war, and received a rousing send-off from the King himself: 'Your prompt patriotic answer to the Nation's call to arms will never be forgotten … In bidding you farewell I pray God may bless you in all your undertakings.'[28]

And so the division crossed to France 'to face the tempest which is shaking the foundations of the world', in the words of Lieutenant Beith, or rather of the Prime Minister who he was echoing. As they headed towards the front, Beith could not believe the transformation in his men: 'Our divisional column, with its trim, sturdy, infantry battalions, its jingling cavalry and artillery, its real live staff, and its imposing transport train, sets us thinking, by sheer force of contrast, of that dim and distant time seven months ago, when we wrestled perspiringly all through long and hot September days, on a dusty barrack square, with squad upon squad of dazed and refractory barbarians, who only ceased shuffling their feet in order to expectorate. And these are the self-same men!'[29] As the columns tramped and sang along the tree-lined roads, they were headed by relays of despatch-riders, and Corporal Heap must have swelled with pride to find himself at the forefront of his division, and metaphorically of the whole vast army of Kitchener's volunteers who were now flooding across the Channel.

During the earliest months of the war, as the opposing powers grappled and feinted across Belgium and northern France, the despatch-riders had played a crucial role in connecting the scattered military units, never knowing when they roared into a village whether it would contain the headquarters they were seeking, or the Germans they were seeking to avoid. As the history of the Royal Corps of Signals put it: 'The main onus of providing communications fell on the despatch riders, who rose nobly to the occasion. Casualties were heavy to both men and machines: to the former owing to the open nature of rear-guard actions, and to the latter because of the rough and treacherous *pavé* roads.'[30]

By the time Frank arrived, however, the trench-lines had stagnated and the main function of despatch-riders was to ferry documents between the headquarters of corps, divisions and brigades that were far enough behind the lines to be accessible by road. The fighting units in forward positions relied for communication on a fragile network of cables that were fixed to the trench walls or buried under them, and carried either Morse code signals or telephone voice messages. When 9th Division first went into battle it had a single wireless set,[31] which sounds worse than useless, but despite its obvious advantages wireless technology was unwieldy, unreliable and insecure, and was regarded by the army with 'the gravest suspicion'.[32]

Despite this, the scale and complexity of warfare made communications more crucial than ever, since multiple infantry units had to co-ordinate their activities with each other, and with the artillery and other arms. But the real signalling heroes were now to be found in dug-outs, huddled over their Morse code buzzers and emerging only to repair the cables when the bombardment was at its fiercest, or among the runners who carried vital messages back through the storm of steel.

During this time, 9th Division headquarters was joined by a liaison officer from the French army called Sergeant Émile Herzog, who was both amused and intrigued by the British people he encountered, and captured their idiosyncrasies in a book which was translated as *The Silence of Colonel Bramble*. As a serving soldier he had to use a pen-name, and took this from a village near Cambrai; he is therefore known to the world as André Maurois. His role meant Maurois often encountered the signallers who were Frank Heap's comrades, and his accounts suggest that as well as being 'the salt of their race', they were also the salt of the earth. Sheltering from the rain with a group of chauffeurs and motorcyclists, Maurois told how 'he always liked to find himself among this class of Englishman with their strong language and simple minds. These, like the rest, were good fellows, careless, courageous and light-hearted. They hummed the latest music-hall airs from London, showed him photographs of their wives, sweethearts and babies, and asked him when the damned war would be over.'[33] He also described an engineer who carried out repairs and told him how he dealt with communication problems: 'Telephones are like women, sir. No one really knows anything about them. One fine day, something goes wrong; you try to find out why, no good, you swear, you shake them up a bit and all is well.'[34]

The 9th Division spent four months learning the routine of trench warfare in quiet sectors, before the New Army was ready to be blooded at the Battle of Loos in September 1915. André Maurois was in the signalling room at divisional headquarters when the attack began and described how messages were taken down by the telephonists, plotted, and passed on. 'An officer, standing before the huge map, carefully manoeuvred small coloured flags, and all this methodical agitation reminded [him] of a large banking house on the Stock Exchange.' To Maurois, it was consistent with one of the officers' favourite remarks: 'A gentleman is never in a hurry.'[35]

But beyond the château walls, the men of 9th Division had been hurled into a desperate, chaotic battle among mining spoilheaps and pit villages, in which everything seemed to go wrong that possibly could. The bombardment failed to cut the German barbed wire, the poison gas that the British were using for the first time blew back in their faces, and successive waves of men were sent to charge the enemy's machine guns over the corpses of their comrades.

As the fragile system of communication broke down, the commanding officer of 9th Division went forward in person, only to be killed by a shell. When André Maurois heard the news he 'thought of the grey, smooth hair and fine features of the general, the gold and scarlet of his facings all soiled by the ignoble mud of battles. So much easy dignity, he thought, so much courteous authority, and to-morrow carrion, which the soldiers will trample under foot without knowing. But already, all round him, they were anxiously discussing who would be his successor.'[36]

Major-General George Thesiger was one of more than 6,000 casualties suffered by 9th Division in its first shattering encounter with the Germans' professional military machine.[37] From Loos the division moved north to the Ypres Salient, where it remained until the end of the year – described as 'a time of almost unmitigated gloom and discomfort'.[38] Even their planned departure a few days before Christmas 1915 was disrupted by a massive bombardment, and the War Diary recorded that 'although the motor cyclists continued to carry out their usual runs, one motor cycle was severely damaged at Shrapnel Corner, and a second at Kruisstraat. Their riders were unhurt.'[39]

The division then held a quiet sector before being plunged into the great offensive on the Somme in mid-July 1916. A photograph of Frank taken during the battle (mysteriously inscribed 'To Dearest Little Muff') shows him looking self-assured in his steel helmet, casually dressed in battle-stained shorts and puttees, with a revolver on his belt and two corporal's stripes on his sleeve.[40] Frank's local paper noted that he 'had a stirring time as a motor cycle dispatch rider, and had many exciting adventures, seeing considerable hard fighting at the battles of Loos, Neuve Chapelle, Ypres, and on the Somme'.[41] But despite his relaxed demeanour, Frank was now champing at the bit. The role of despatch-rider had largely settled down to that of a glorified postman, which was not what he had signed up for, especially since there was little chance of any glory. In addition he was clearly officer material, and the authorities had approved his application for a commission in an infantry regiment as early as March 1916.[42]

Frank had to wait six months before being recalled to England, where his ambitions received an early setback when he was rejected by the Royal Flying Corps on familiar grounds: the medical form stated simply 'Deficient vision – unfit'.[43] Fortunately, just three days later the newspapers began to trumpet the achievements of 'the mysterious "tanks"',[44] and suddenly a new and exciting opportunity presented itself that played to his sense of adventure, and to his knowledge of motors and machinery. On 30 January 1917 he was granted a commission in the Heavy Branch of the Machine Gun Corps, and began four months of intensive training in readiness for his return to the Western Front.[45] At last, Frank must have felt his time had come, and now it was up to him to seize this opportunity with both hands, and to make his father proud after he had let him down in his truncated university career.

Such was the story that Frank Heap recounted to his brother officers, with whatever additions and subtractions he judged appropriate for his audience. But by now the train had pulled up to the ramp in Oosthoek Wood, and it was time for Frank and his crew to begin the delicate task of unloading *Deborah* from her railway wagon and steering her into the tankodrome, to prepare for whatever fate, and the General Staff, had in store for them.

CHAPTER 17

'The Best Company of the Best Battalion'

At some stage Frank Heap had to face the final, and most forbidding, stage of his initiation: namely meeting the commander of No. 12 Company, Major R.O.C. Ward.

Each tank battalion was divided into three companies which formed the principal administrative and fighting units, and each of these had its own distinctive character, as Second Lieutenant Horace Birks explained: 'There were 10, 11 and 12 Companies in D Battalion, and they were very close together but extraordinarily detached, to be thoroughly Irish. You had nothing to do with 10 Company except to pinch their tools when they weren't there ... And when you went into Poperinghe for a night out they'd give you a lift in their lorry, but it was their lorry not your own. But on the other hand you were all ... very much D Battalion.'[1]

The company commanders therefore bore the main responsibility for their men and tanks both in and out of battle, and in this respect Frank had landed on his feet, though it may not have felt that way. Robert Oscar Cyril Ward had been one of the pre-war stars of the Harlequins rugby team, and embodied the kind of muscular leadership that transferred easily from the sports field to the battlefield. He was known to sports fans by the acronym 'ROC', but when Frank Heap was ushered into the Major's presence in his makeshift headquarters at La Lovie, the reason for his other nickname would have become clear. With his thick-set features, brawny physique and powerful personality, he was known as 'The Bull'.[2]

R.O.C. Ward seems to have born to the role of commanding men in battle, but he was actually another New Army man who had joined up a fortnight after Frank. Before that he had trained as a lawyer and worked as an accountant, and his pre-war military experience was limited to the school Cadet Corps.[3] Since the outbreak of war, however, he had fought ferociously both as an infantry and tank officer, and had cheated death several times – most recently in a dreadful accident which left his body permanently peppered with splinters from British hand grenades, and can have done nothing to improve his outlook on life.

Ward seems to have inspired almost universal admiration, with one NCO describing him simply as a 'marvellous man'. Interestingly though, he was not regarded with affection by all his junior officers. His volcanic style of leadership may have been ideal in combat, but he was also a hard taskmaster and seems to have lacked what we would now call 'people skills'. Second Lieutenant James Macintosh recalled an incident at Wailly, the area of captured German trenches that was used for tank training, where an officer managed to submerge his tank in a large pond, leaving the crew to wade ashore from their stranded machine. The reaction of R.O.C.'s deputy, Captain Walter Smith, was typically derisive: 'Damn it, man, you ought to be in the Inland Water Transport!'[4] Ward's response was very different, and illustrated his approach to command:

> The Major, however, saw little occasion for mirth in the situation. He was proud of being in command of the best Company of the best Battalion in the Corps, and he foresaw endless chaffing if the story once got about. Further, he considered

this a splendid opportunity for exhibiting that cast-iron discipline for which he would fain be famous. Accordingly, he applied the standing order that crews of ditched tanks will in all cases remain with their tank until ordered to abandon it, thus dooming our friend to a cheerless night in some dug-out in the old Boche line. A special order was issued to all ranks forbidding mention of the occurrence, while, early next morning, two tanks sallied forth, and, pulling in tandem, dragged the unfortunate from its inglorious position.[5]

Another junior officer in No. 12 Company, Second Lieutenant Ralph Cooney, was even more forthright when asked about his memories of the war:

Cooney: Our company commander was a fellow called R.O.C. Ward who used to play for England [sic] in the Harlequins.
Interviewer: What was he like to work with?
Cooney: He wasn't very popular. He was a great big chap and he was inclined to be a bit hard, I think. He was streets better than we were at all sorts of things [laughs].[6]

* * *

We can therefore be fairly sure what Frank Heap made of R.O.C. Ward as he fidgeted uneasily in front of him. As for Ward, he had seen many young officers come and go from the units under his command, and all too often their departure had been both catastrophic and terminal. He was probably not much impressed by Heap's mild-mannered appearance, nor by his spectacles. On the other hand he would have appreciated his cheerfulness and keenness, though he had seen those often enough before, and had paid tribute to them in many a letter of condolence.

No doubt Ward expressed polite interest at the fact they were both Cambridge 'Blues', having represented the university in their chosen sports – though in Ward's case these were rugby and boxing, whereas Frank had played lacrosse, which did not have quite the same ring to it. Both of them had first seen action in the Battle of Loos, but Frank had been behind the lines on his motorbike, whereas Ward had been in the thick of the fighting. There was not much else to say for now, other than to wish Heap the best of luck, but at least the formalities were over and the Major could get back to more pressing matters, and Frank could get back to the mess.

In fact the social gulf between them was not great, since they were both the sons of men who became rich through their own enterprise. Ward's father acquired his wealth from an import and export business which took him to British Columbia in Canada, where his diary noted one day in 1881: 'Bright & showery & windy. Boy born.' This was R.O.C., and when the Wards returned home at the turn of the century they brought no fewer than seven children who had been born in Canada.[7] The family settled in a smart area of London, and R.O.C. went to the prestigious Trinity College, Cambridge.[8] However, like Frank his varsity career was chiefly distinguished for its sporting achievements and he became a 'Double Blue', winning the heavyweight title in both public schools and inter-university boxing;[9] he was said to be the only man who ever lasted more than one round in the ring with John Hopley,[10] one of the finest heavyweights in the British Empire.

The year of his graduation in 1904 was also memorable for his parents' move to Oak Lawn, a substantial estate in Surrey, where Robert Ward senior 'lived the quiet life of a country gentleman'.[11] But a quiet life was not what his sons had in mind, and both R.O.C.'s younger brothers had joined the armed forces, with Victor becoming one of the first officers in the Royal Navy's newly-formed submarine service,[12] and Horace seeing service

Deborah in German hands in April 1918. *Photograph from Jean Luc Caudron*

Two Germans and their dog inspect the wreckage of *Deborah* some time between March and September 1918. *Photograph from Philippe Gorczynski*

Willie Anthony and his friends visit Flesquières on 16 March 1919, with *Deborah* visible in the street behind. *Photograph from the Anthony family*

The same view today.

'Uriah's bus': the photograph of Deborah showing damage inflicted later in the war, taken on 3 March 1919 and given to Frank Heap, which enabled her to be identified decades later. *Photograph from the Heap family*

'Burying of a tank': *Deborah* goes into the ground in 1919, from the album of Lieutenant-Colonel Theodore Wenger. *Photograph from Tank Museum*

The first commander of D51, Second Lieutenant George Macdonald (top right), with brother officers during the Battle of Passchendaele. These are (clockwise from George): James Clark, David Lewis (captured on 22 August) and Harold Dobinson.
Photograph from Catherine Piper

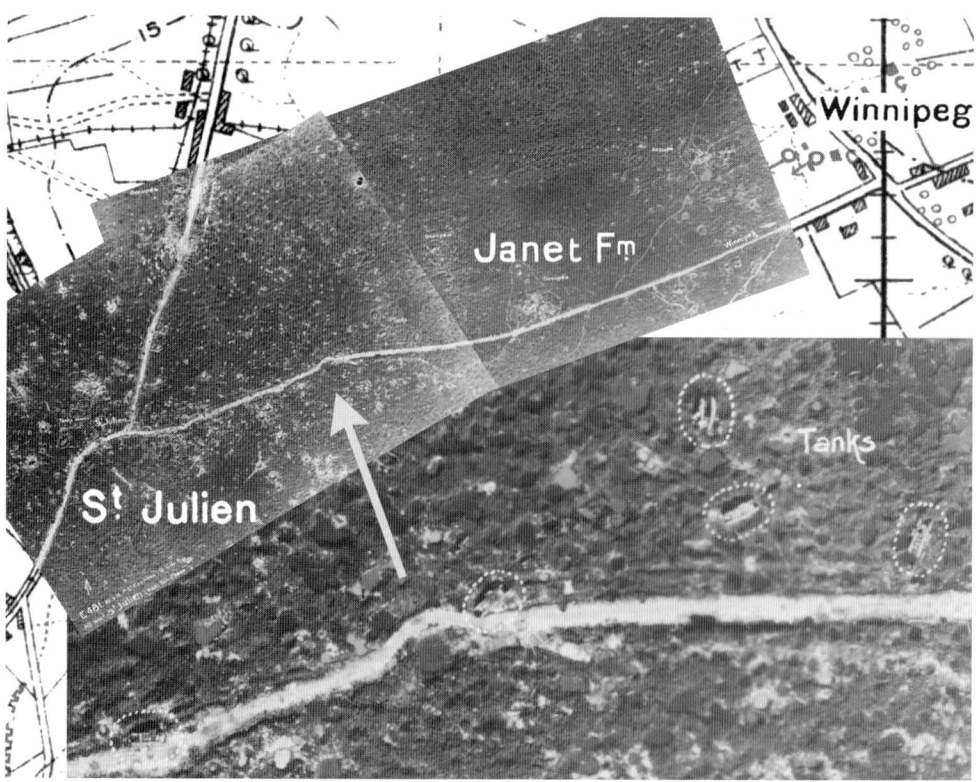

'An abomination of desolation': a group of abandoned tanks, including that used by George Macdonald and the crew of D51, beside the road out of St Julien following the attack on 22 August. *Photographs © Royal Museum of the Army and of Military History (Nr Inv KLM-MRA 201530003 & 20608-sint-juliaan)*

Second Lieutenant Frank Heap in his new Tank Corps officer's uniform. *Photograph from the Heap family*

Boy soldiers: Frank Heap (2nd from left) in camp with the Officers' Training Corps of The Leys School, Cambridge. *Photograph from the Heap family*

Gunner George Foot from *Deborah*'s crew, before he was awarded the Distinguished Conduct Medal for bravery. *Photograph from Charles Foot*

Gunner Fred Tipping, one of *Deborah*'s crewmen, in his Royal Artillery uniform. *Photograph from Mike Tipping*

Gunner William Galway, one of *Deborah*'s crewmen, in the uniform of the Royal Irish Rifles. *Photograph from the Galway family*

'Bit of a knave': Gunner Joseph Cheverton, one of *Deborah*'s crewmen. *Photograph from the Summers family*

Joseph Cheverton's fiancée Florrie Coote with rosemary plant – apparently wearing his Tank Corps badge on a necklace. *Photograph from Derek Leland*

Lance-Corporal David 'Bert' Marsden, a possible member of *Deborah*'s crew, in Tank Corps uniform with the light blue shoulder straps of D Battalion. *Photograph from David Melliar-Smith*

Colonel Christopher Baker-Carr (left), later in command of 1st Tank Brigade, with instructors at the Machine Gun School in St Omer, 1915. *Photograph from Sue Peck*

The future commander of D Battalion, Lieutenant-Colonel William Kyngdon (top left), with NCO and porters in East Africa, 1911. *Photograph from* Pemba, The Spice Island of Zanzibar, *by Captain John Craster*

'The Bull': *Deborah*'s company commander Major R.O.C. Ward with fellow officers of 6th Bn The Buffs in May 1915 before leaving England. *Photograph from Simon Ward*

as an infantry officer in the Boer War. R.O.C. chose a less dashing career in commerce and soon became secretary of a printing company,[13] but there were thrills aplenty on the rugby pitch, and with his brother Horace – known as 'Holly' – he became a mainstay of the Harlequins team forged by the legendary Adrian Stoop, whose inspired leadership turned it into one of the country's top clubs and established Twickenham as the home of English Rugby Union. R.O.C. was noted for strength rather than speed, and one writer observed that 'perhaps few forwards of his weight used their weight more than he'.[14]

R.O.C. also shared a special bond with his brother Victor, for in 1909 they married two sisters, the daughters of a wealthy landowner, at a joint ceremony in the south London suburb of Putney.[15] The local paper was almost overcome with excitement: 'The weddings were of a very picturesque description, as on one side it was a full naval wedding, the bridegroom, best man, and several others being in full naval uniform … Mr. R.O.C. Ward is well-known in Rugby football circles, having been for several seasons one of the most useful of the Harlequins' forwards and a county player.'[16]

With his new bride, R.O.C. settled in the respectable town of Watford where he became accountant to a firm of wholesale drapers. Despite their comfortable circumstances, married life did not begin easily and their first child died soon after he was born in 1912. The couple moved back to London where another son was born later that year, followed by a daughter in June 1914.[17] By now the family had moved to a spacious villa in Putney, close to his wife's childhood home, handy for the Harlequins' ground at Twickenham, and an easy train ride from the capital.

* * *

When war came, R.O.C. Ward must have envied his brothers who had already staked their places in the great adventure. Despite his lack of military experience, there was no chance he was going to stay on the sidelines, and fortunately the expansion of the army threw up plenty of opportunities. R.O.C.'s brother Holly was in the East Kent Regiment, known as The Buffs, and this now underwent rapid growth with the creation of new 'service' battalions manned by those who had answered Kitchener's call. In October 1914, R.O.C. travelled to Purfleet Camp in Essex to be commissioned as a lieutenant in the newly-formed 6th Battalion of the Buffs.[18] A month later, Holly was captured in a series of battles that became known as the 'race to the sea', and spent the rest of the war as a prisoner in Germany.[19] But R.O.C.'s army career was just beginning, and after training his battalion left England in June 1915, when, in the words of the regimental historian, 'yet another warlike body of Buffs made the great move and sailed for France to show of what stuff the old regiment was made'.[20]

Despite their keenness, it was some time before 6th Buffs got the chance to prove themselves. As with Frank Heap's division, they first had to learn the skills of trench warfare, and were sent to a quiet sector where the enemy could sometimes be heard but were seldom seen. Both sides were busy sniping and tunnelling under each other's positions to bury explosives, and R.O.C. did his best to liven things up by leading patrols, hurling grenades into the German trenches, and even setting off a mine when an attack seemed imminent.[21]

Their first taste of real fighting came in the Battle of Loos, a crushing encounter which left the citizen soldiers of the New Army in no doubt as to the power and professionalism of their opponents. On 13 October, in the closing stages of the battle, it was the turn of 6th Buffs to go over the top in an attack at Hulluch – an ugly name, and an ugly memory for those who survived. They were supposed to advance behind a smokescreen, but the War Diary described what happened: 'At 1 p.m. a smoke cloud was created along the line ... By about 2 p.m. all the smoke had cleared. At 2.15 p.m. the order was given to charge ... The men were met with a terrific fire, machine guns on three sides while the Germans were lying on their parapets giving rapid fire. The three [companies] were practically wiped out.'[22]

Around 190 men from 6th Battalion died that day, with as many more wounded or missing.[23] Ten of the thirteen officers who took part were killed,[24] among them Second Lieutenant Douglas Lambert, an England rugby star and R.O.C. Ward's team-mate in the Harlequins. His dazzling speed counted for nothing in this cruel game, and he was shot down along with his men. His body was lost for ever in the mud of Hulluch, and he never knew the son who was born two months later.[25]

Somehow R.O.C. emerged unscathed from this bloodbath, but he was a man of intelligence as well as action, and must have realized that sooner or later he would also end up throwing his life away for nothing. There had to be a better way of attacking heavily defended positions than simply hurling men and shells at them, and the same point had struck some members of the British General Staff. A wooden prototype had already been created of a mobile armoured fortress which could cross broken ground, crush barbed wire and support the infantry as they advanced. But it would be nearly a year before these machines were ready to go into action, and R.O.C. would have several more brushes with death before he was able to join his destiny with theirs.

In March 1916 he took part in another failed attack and was recommended for a gallantry award, though it was never given. A few days later he was wounded by a German trench mortar bomb, but was back on duty a week later.[26] When summer came the battalion moved south to join the huge offensive on the Somme, and it was here that fate delivered a final blow to R.O.C., by now a company commander. In the fighting near Ovillers, 6th Buffs determined to seize a position called Point 20, where a short section of trench known as a sap jutted out from the German front line. Boxes of hand grenades (or 'Mills bombs') were stockpiled in readiness, while a British trench mortar stood by to soften up the enemy position. What happened next teetered on the borderline between tragedy and farce: 'About 2.30 p.m. our [trench mortars] again bombarded Pt. 20 but unfortunately dropped one short into all the bombs. About 1,500 of our Mills exploded, one flying 60 yards and wounding Capt. R.O.C. Ward, Lieut. Sir R. Onslow Bart. and an orderly. As all the bombs were lost, the affair had to be given up.'[27]

The regimental historian described this as a 'somewhat curious accident',[28] but we can be sure this is not the language R.O.C. Ward himself would have used. He summarized the aftermath in a letter to the War Office applying for a payment known as a wound gratuity: 'I beg to state I was wounded ... by multiple bomb wounds in back & thigh ... I was operated upon [in Rouen] & had splinters removed from off my spine & from my left thigh. I was then transferred to King Edward VII Hospital ... London, where I was again operated on, but the operation was not successful in removing all the splinters.'[29]

The accident, though appalling, did at least have one positive aspect: it meant R.O.C. was back in England shortly after the birth of his son in August 1916.[30] The spell of enforced inactivity also gave him time to reflect on the frustration of trench warfare, and perhaps the mounting probability of his own demise. If so, the media fanfare that greeted the first tank action in September and the appeal for volunteers to join the Heavy Branch of the Machine Gun Corps would have fallen on fertile ground. Here, it appeared, was an opportunity to bring his courage to bear on the Germans more effectively than by simply charging at their machine guns.

So it was that in January 1917, R.O.C. Ward returned to France to join the HBMGC at its base near St Pol-sur-Ternoise, where the original companies that had conducted the first tank attacks were being expanded to battalion strength. This gave R.O.C., now promoted to major, the opportunity to stamp his considerable authority on his new command, No. 12 Company of D Battalion.[31] Major William Watson, who took over No. 11 Company at the same time, was impressed: he described Ward as 'the great athlete, the very embodiment of energy, the skilled leader of men, the best of good fellows', and recalled 'his enormous voice rolling out full-blooded instructions'.[32]

Four months later the tanks were back in action supporting the offensive at Arras, and the three companies of D Battalion were scattered along a twelve-mile front. If anyone imagined tanks would provide an easy solution to the challenges of trench warfare, the actions at Arras and Bullecourt were enough to disillusion them. R.O.C. Ward's company went into battle for the first time on 9 April 1917, supporting his former countrymen in the Canadian Corps, but the ground conditions were so bad that all eight tanks 'bellied' – in other words, the tracks sank so far into the mud that the tanks could not move and had to be dug out by their crews.

Despite this, the infantry reached their objectives and the Canadian commander was effusive in his praise of 12 Company:

> I have never seen a more gallant, efficient, capable or energetic lot in my life, their work was really marvellous and Ward himself was the centre of energy. The action of the members of one of the tanks who carried out repairs standing on the top of the tank while it was under concentrated fire from five guns, and carried out their work as intrepidly as though they had been 10 miles in rear of the line, is only characteristic of the whole work of the whole lot … At any other advance, I hope it may be my good fortune, to have Major Ward and his tanks with the Division for they are certainly the last word in efficiency.[33]

After this, his tanks were transported south to take part in an attack on Bullecourt on 3 May. According to Watson, their recent failure 'was naturally a keen disappointment to Ward, and he and his company … were spoiling for a fight'.[34] But the Germans had already beaten off another attack at Bullecourt on 11 April, when No. 11 Company had supported troops from Australia who were as dismissive of the tank crews' efforts as the Canadians were appreciative.

The second attack on Bullecourt, involving both Nos. 11 and 12 Companies, turned out to be no more successful than the first. The infantry were unable to penetrate the enemy lines, and the tanks suffered heavily from armour-piercing (A.P.) ammunition which was now widely available to the Germans. Slowly but surely the attack broke down, as 'furious messages came back from Ward'.[35] One of his officers summarized the outcome: 'The result of the attack was a tremendous disappointment to all, as we had fondly imagined exploiting "into the blue" … The casualties among the men were very heavy, and of the tank commanders seven out of eight were wounded … The following day was spent counting the number of holes in each tank, caused by A.P. bullets, one tank having between 20 and 30.'[36]

The failed attack left Ward 'wrathful but undismayed',[37] though there was nothing more he could do for the time being. The second battle of Bullecourt marked the end of this phase of action by D Battalion, and his men now withdrew for further training and refitting to prepare for whatever fate might hold in store, which turned out to be the even more disastrous Battle of Passchendaele.

CHAPTER 18

Redundant Oddments

As Frank Heap settled into his new role, there was one person he was unlikely to have much contact with, namely the commanding officer of D Battalion. This may seem strange, but the lieutenant-colonel in charge of a tank battalion was normally a distant figure, and William Frederick Robert Kyngdon seems to have been more distant than most.

In fact, Kyngdon remains so anonymous that one struggles to find any mention of him at all in the copious literature of the Tank Corps. Major William Watson, who was the battalion's most accomplished chronicler, wrote appreciatively about Kyngdon's predecessor, John Hardress-Lloyd – described as 'a man of big ideas' by none other than Lieutenant-Colonel John Fuller, himself a prominent military theorist.[1] When Kyngdon took over in May 1917, Watson commented simply that 'to our sorrow, Colonel Hardress Lloyd [sic] had left us to form a brigade, and a stranger from our particular rivals, "C" Battalion, had taken his place'.[2]

Lieutenant Jack Coghlan, one of D Battalion's junior officers, may have been thinking of Kyngdon when he wrote: 'The senior officers were not battlewise and had come mainly from those redundant oddments that a great army inevitably creates. Perhaps my criticism is harsh, but it did appear that they sought personal prestige rather than efficiency and never felt able to point out to the High Command that a suggested operation was unwise or impossible.'[3]

In defence of Kyngdon, it must be said that his role was not clearly defined, especially with a strong-minded brigade commander like Colonel Baker-Carr who was likely to dominate on questions of strategy. The fact was that the thirty-six fighting tanks, ninety officers and 825 or so 'other ranks' of D Battalion had never gone into battle as a single unit, and the primary responsibility for leadership therefore fell on the company commanders such as Watson and Ward. Even Tank Corps headquarters had not seen a battalion in its entirety before July 1917, when E Battalion arrived in France and the War Diary noted: 'This is the first occasion in the history of tanks that a complete battalion with tanks has paraded. It was a very imposing spectacle.'[4]

Nevertheless, it seems curious that someone so apparently lacking in charisma should have been appointed to such a key role, especially at this critical time. So who was the man who now led D Battalion, and was therefore responsible for the fate of Frank Heap and his crew? William Kyngdon had been born thirty-six years earlier in Sydney, Australia, the son and grandson of doctors who had emigrated to practice there. He first came to England at the age of twelve to attend public school, after which he went to a 'crammer' and gained a commission in the Royal Garrison Artillery.[5]

Initially Kyngdon joined the Militia, a volunteer force responsible for home defence, and therefore found himself defending the shores of South Wales against potential invaders, who in 1901 were few and far between. It was a slow start to his career, but he soon transferred to the regular army and a more exciting opportunity presented itself: service in West Africa with the Sierra Leone Artillery,[6] described as 'the only regular negro Royal Artillery unit', whose officers were sent from Britain on three-year postings.[7] When Kyngdon sailed from Liverpool to take up his new post in 1906, he could not have guessed that the next ten years of his life would be spent almost entirely in sub-Saharan Africa.

His experience in Sierra Leone stood him in good stead when the government of Zanzibar – a British protectorate off Africa's east coast – decided to conduct the first geographical survey of the neighbouring island of Pemba. In 1911 Kyngdon was seconded to work with Captain John Craster, who was disappointed to find his companion knew virtually nothing about surveying. 'But he had one more important qualification: he had spent four years on the West Coast of Africa without a day's illness. So far he had proved himself immune to all the diseases of Africa.'[8]

Sadly even this qualification proved illusory, and Craster recorded that 'the day after our arrival in Zanzibar Kyngdon had a sharp attack of fever. I confess his illness caused me a good deal of anxiety ... because it must inevitably reduce his strength and render him less able to endure the hard work, poor food, and exposure that would be our lot for the next eight months.'[9] Nevertheless, he soon recovered and the expedition members posed for a photograph before leaving Zanzibar: Kyngdon and Craster, scrubbed and moustachioed, clutching their solar topees, surrounded by native bearers and servants, the epitome of imperial pride and self-confidence.[10]

At that time map-making was a gruelling business, in which hilltops had to be cleared of foliage to erect survey points, and lines hacked through the undergrowth from one coral-fringed shore to the other. It was a constant struggle against exhaustion and disease, to which both men succumbed, on an island described by Craster as the haunt of witch-doctors, freed slaves and former cannibals. In the event the survey took ten months and the two men did not finally take leave of Pemba, and each other, until 1912.

Kyngdon had only just returned to England when he was sent back to Africa for another, even greater adventure.[11] Again this was a geographical expedition, but with added political sensitivities, for Germany was flexing its imperial muscles and had gained a foothold in West Africa by acquiring the Cameroons, a colony to the east of British-held Nigeria. In August 1912 an expedition was sent to fix the boundary between Nigeria and the Cameroons by building marker-posts along its length. Since the frontier traversed 360 miles (or 580 kilometres) of remote jungle and mountains, it promised to be a challenging trip, and there was an added complexity: the expedition consisted of two parties, one British and one German, each with its own bodyguard of native troops. The British team was headed by Captain Walter Nugent, assisted by Lieutenant Kyngdon, while the Germans were led by Oberleutnant Hermann Detzner.

The expedition was unusual enough to attract media interest, and Nugent apparently sold the cinematographic rights to a newsreel company for whom they filmed scenes of special interest. In one we see a British officer in shorts and topee – almost certainly Kyngdon – striding along a riverbank at the head of a column of porters, preceded by a party of native soldiers bearing a Union flag. In the next scene, the officer leads them into shot before planting the flag in the ground, and then directing the erection of a tent with imperious flapping gestures.[12]

Kyngdon may not have had natural screen presence, but Detzner clearly respected him, and the rest of the British party. Despite the growing tension between their countries, the teams established a good rapport, Nugent recording simply that they had 'worked together for more than six months without a single point of difference.'[13] Detzner generally shared this view, though he described an incident deep in the African bush when he was invited to lunch in the British camp despite warnings from Förstl, his faithful sergeant-major, who was convinced that war was about to be declared and the invitation was a trap.

Detzner insisted on going, arguing the British were 'men of honour', and found the party in full swing thanks to the cocktail-mixing skills of the expedition doctor and the sparkling wine brought by some visiting officers. 'The gramophone ... bawled out a constant succession of cake-walks, Scottish melodies and waltzes. The relaxed legs of the patrol officers became restless and two of them danced together, becoming more boisterous as the level of alcohol rose and made their blood run faster. Here Kyngdon took part in a wrestling-match with a younger colleague, there two more settled a dispute in a friendly fashion with their fists. It was the inevitable conclusion of any such drinking bout in British Nigeria.' That evening, Detzner was horrified to find that Förstl had secretly posted native troops all round the British camp, in case they turned out to be less honourable than Detzner had thought.[14]

Despite this the expedition came to a peaceful conclusion, and Kyngdon's next posting was to yet another topographical survey, this time to the Gold Coast which forms part of present-day Ghana.[15] He was there when Britain declared war on Germany, and immediately found himself at the heart of the action. East of the Gold Coast lay the minuscule German colony of Togoland, and Britain and France prepared to invade using the much stronger military forces in their neighbouring colonies. This was not simply a matter of settling imperial scores, as the Germans had built a powerful wireless station at Kamini which could transmit messages from their warships to Berlin. A small British invasion force accordingly landed on the coast of Togoland, and on 12 August 1914, a member of the Gold Coast Regiment became the first soldier in the British Army to fire a shot in anger during the Great War.[16] The equally tiny German force fell back, fighting as it went, and on 22 August Lieutenant George Thompson became the first British army officer to die as a result of enemy action.[17]

Other British and French troops entered Togoland at various points, and Kyngdon was sent in with forty armed police who joined up with a larger column of which he was made the intelligence officer. Shortly after this the Germans surrendered, having first demolished their prized wireless station. The campaign had been a success, though the newspapers acknowledged it was no more than a 'minor operation',[18] particularly with the British Expeditionary Force now in retreat across the Continent following its initial clash with the Germans at the Battle of Mons.

Though it was always a sideshow, the war in Africa grew in intensity, with protracted campaigns across the remaining German colonies. Fresh from their victory in Togoland, the British and French invaded the Cameroons to the east, but this proved a tougher nut to crack and it was fifteen months before the Germans were finally forced to surrender. The opposing armies, only a few thousand strong, were scattered across an area one-and-a-half times the size of Germany. It was a campaign of long marches through hostile terrain, ill-defined battle-lines and brief, often inconclusive skirmishes, in one of which Kyngdon was wounded in the arm while commanding a native gun battery in January 1915.[19]

After recovering he became a staff captain in the Cameroons Expeditionary Force,[20] and helped to plan the military operations that were gradually driving the Germans out of their former colony. Victory came in early 1916, though even the official historian had to admit that 'to a world whose thoughts were almost entirely filled, and its attention held, by the vast and more important events in the main theatres of war, the Allied operations in the Cameroons appeared at the time of minor interest'.[21] It has to be said that nothing much has happened since to change that view.

* * *

So where did this leave Kyngdon? The imperial struggle was still in full flow, and following victory in the Cameroons, the Gold Coast Regiment – to which he was attached[22] – sailed round the Cape to join in the battle for German East Africa (equivalent to modern-day Tanzania), where fighting would continue for the rest of the war. Kyngdon might reasonably have been expected to join them, but instead he headed north instead of south, and shook the dust of Africa from his uniform for ever.

By May 1916 he was back in England, a country he hardly knew, with a new unit called the Heavy Section of the Machine Gun Corps, about which hardly anyone knew anything,[23] for these were the men who were preparing to go into battle in a secret weapon, referred to simply as a 'tank' to disguise its true purpose. The Heavy Section, then based at Bisley in Surrey, consisted of six companies and Kyngdon was promoted to major and put in charge of one of them.[24]

Even for someone who been in many unfamiliar situations, the transition must have come as a shock. Kyngdon's service record lists his main qualifications as 'special knowledge of West Africa and its natives; knowledge of topographical survey'.[25] He had little experience of machinery or machine guns, and the men he now commanded, many from the industrial cities of Britain, must have seemed as outlandish to him as his barefoot native troops would have been to them. It is not clear who recommended him for the move, but Kyngdon had been in the army long enough not to question its ways, especially when they involved promotion and a step forward in his career.

While the new force was being trained on a secluded country estate near Thetford, Kyngdon was sent to France in August 1916 with one of its senior officers, Lieutenant-Colonel John Brough, 'to precede the Heavy Section and help to prepare for a continuation of its training'.[26] After this he took even greater responsibility as staff officer to Lieutenant-Colonel Robert Bradley, who had been given command of the Heavy Section in the field.[27]

However, both Brough and Bradley soon fell foul of GHQ: the former was felt to be 'difficult',[28] while the latter was reduced to 'a state of great perturbation'[29] when he was swamped with requests for information following the first tank attack. As a result Colonel Hugh Elles, who enjoyed the favour of GHQ as well as being 'a first-class officer',[30] was appointed to command the Heavy Section at the end of September, a post he held for the rest of the war.

The unpleasantness involving Bradley must have reflected poorly on his staff officer, who should presumably have fielded many of the requests that caused so much distress. At some point after Elles took over, Kyngdon was transferred from headquarters to C Company,[31] and was there when Lieutenant-Colonel Baker Carr became company commander in November 1916. Kyngdon clearly made a positive impression, and Baker-Carr noted that 'The officers, including one regular officer of the R.A. [i.e. Kyngdon], were a wonderful body of enthusiasts.'[32]

This endorsement may have been the key to Kyngdon's final, and greatest promotion, to Lieutenant-Colonel and commanding officer of D Battalion. Baker-Carr was an influential figure in the embryo Tank Corps – indeed, he claimed that Elles had twice recommended him to Sir Douglas Haig as the commander of the new force, but he was rejected on technical grounds because Baker-Carr was not a graduate of the Staff College, with the result that Elles took the post instead.[33] Baker-Carr's energy and enthusiasm were clearly valuable assets, though his memoir leaves the impression that if there was one thing he enjoyed more than being proved right, it was telling everyone he had been proved right. This was all the more satisfying when he first had to overcome ill-judged opposition, but the unfortunate result was that when he encountered someone equally strong-willed who persisted in taking a different approach, this could easily degenerate into a feud – the most notable of which, with Major-General George Harper who commanded 51st (Highland) Division, was to have important consequences for our understanding of D Battalion's war.

Be that as it may, in February 1917 a new layer of command was added to the HBMGC with the creation of tank brigades, one of which was headed by Baker-Carr. His 1st Tank Brigade initially consisted of C and D Battalions, but in May 1917 there was a further restructuring which meant that C Battalion was taken away and replaced with E and G Battalions. Having lost his old friends in C Battalion (a separation he admitted he 'much ... disliked'),[34] it was natural to choose someone he knew and trusted to lead D Battalion. All the better if that person had a solid track record as a professional soldier, and did not have the kind of big ideas that might challenge those of Baker-Carr, or it might uncharitably be said, many big ideas at all. Whether such an appointment would be in the best interests of the battalion remained to be seen.

There is another, even unkinder possibility: C Battalion may have supported Kyngdon's promotion in order to get rid of him, a practice that was far from uncommon. Second Lieutenant Wilfred Bion, who left a deliciously unguarded account of the politics within E Battalion, described the progress of one section commander (who was 'as wildly incompetent as any man I ever met'): 'He was so bad that, in order to get rid of him, our company were determined to promote him to second in command to a company – such promotion meant he would have to go to another company. In the end C Company got him. By August 1918 they had had enough of him, and he was promoted to O.C. Company [i.e. company commander] in order to get rid of him again. He was thus transferred to the 1st Battalion!'[35]

Although it is easy to dismiss Kyngdon as lacklustre, it is clear he had certain qualities which impressed his commanding officers and sustained his steady rise through the ranks. His years in Africa must have made him tough and resourceful, he had shown he could lead men from an entirely different race and culture, he had been involved in the Tank Corps almost from the start, and his travels with Hermann Detzner had given him an insight into the German military mind. Yet against all this, there is no evidence that he was likely to excel in the innovative field of mechanized warfare, or to provide an inspirational figurehead for his battalion. Although he had many years of experience, the officers he now commanded were mostly a very different breed from the regular army men with whom he was familiar. Drawn from a wide range of backgrounds, and in many cases from the ranks, the one thing most of them had in common was that they had not chosen a military career.

Prominent among these men was his company commander R.O.C. Ward, and one senses they must have had an uneasy relationship. By any token R.O.C. was a high achiever: he had a wealthier background and a better education than Kyngdon, was building a successful career and a loving family, and enjoyed the adulation of the sporting world. He had fought fearlessly, though fruitlessly, as both an infantry and tank officer. Against this Kyngdon, almost exactly the same age but unmarried, could point to some intrepid tropical adventures and a long army career, though his experience of actual warfare was limited to minor skirmishes in two countries hardly anyone had heard of. It must have taken Kyngdon's full powers of authority to keep Ward in his place, presumably buoyed by the support of Colonel Baker-Carr, and by the professional soldier's sense of superiority over a military outsider. But he clearly respected R.O.C.'s energy and aggression, and when there was a tough job to be done, No. 12 Company was always the one he would call on first.

CHAPTER 19

Out of the Salient

A week after Frank Heap's arrival at La Lovie, D Battalion was back in action again, but if he imagined he would be in the thick of it so soon, he was in for a disappointment. His company, No. 12, had more or less fought itself to a standstill on 22 August and 20 September, while No. 11 Company had also been badly mauled on 27 August. This time it was the turn of No. 10 Company, which had not yet seen action in the bogs of Passchendaele.

Major Watson's view was that '"No. 10" was a lucky company, and deserved its luck, until the end of the war'.[1] One manifestation of this was that it had not fired a shot in anger since the end of April 1917, when it took part in the ill-starred Battle of Arras. The reason for this inactivity may have been that the man appointed as company commander, Captain the Honourable John Dennis Yelverton Bingham, had been called away to play a key role in one of the most extraordinary operations of the war.[2]

This was the secret plan to land an amphibious invasion force behind enemy lines near the town of Ostend on the north Belgian coast. The so-called 'Operation Hush'

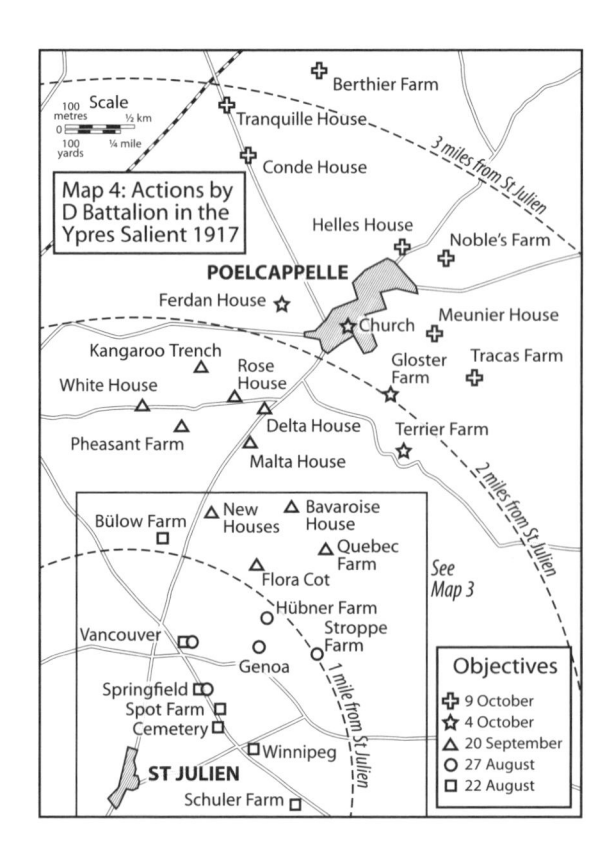

Map 4: Actions by D Battalion in the Ypres Salient 1917

Summary of D Battalion actions in the Ypres Salient 1917

✠ 9 October (No. 11 Company)
all 8 tanks lost
6 men killed, 14 wounded
no objectives taken; tanks halted before reaching centre of Poelcappelle

☆ 4 October (No. 10 Company)
2 out of 12 tanks lost
1 man killed, 3 wounded
all objectives taken with the help of tanks – 'the most successful tank operation in the Salient'

△ 20 September (No. 12 Company)
9 out of 12 tanks lost
3 men killed, 10 wounded
objectives taken by infantry; only 1-2 tanks able to provide support

○ 27 August (No. 11 Company)
all 4 tanks lost
2 men killed, 5 wounded
2 objectives taken (with tank support)

□ 22 August (No. 12 Company)
11 out of 16 tanks lost, including those hit at Bellevue during approach
7 men killed, 21 wounded, 8 captured
1 objective taken 'before tanks arrived'

Note: tanks are shown as 'lost' if they were ditched in bad ground, put out of action by shellfire, or broke down; some of these were subsequently salvaged. Casualty figures include both officers and 'other ranks'. The number killed includes those who later died of wounds.

formed an integral part of the British offensive in the Ypres Salient, and would begin as soon as the Germans had been driven back far enough back to allow their flank to be threatened by a coastal landing. With this in mind, three huge pontoons had been constructed, each 170 metres long, and at the appropriate time they were to be pushed across the Channel by warships and driven onto the beach.[3]

The flotilla would carry a formidable force including nearly 14,000 men, with nine tanks to lead the charge ashore. These had a crucial role, since the invasion beaches were lined by a sloping concrete sea-wall which could only be surmounted by tanks that were specially adapted for the purpose. Their tracks were spiked to climb the steep gradient, and they would push wooden frames which fitted the lip of the sea-wall and would – all being well – allow the invasion force to swarm over the obstacle and move inland. The beachhead would then be held until the main British armies attacking in the Salient were close enough to link up with them.

The plan was clearly beset with hazards, and total secrecy was essential if it was to have any chance of success. The enormous pontoons were moored up in the Thames Estuary, and the men who would take part were sealed off in a secure camp, awaiting the right combination of weather and tides as the British offensive ground forwards. Secret preparations were also under way for the tank crews involved, who were formed into a 'special detachment' headed by Captain Bingham. A replica of the sea-wall was built at the Tank Corps Central Workshops in Erin, and there they rehearsed with their modified machines in readiness for the moment when the plan would receive its ultimate test in action. Until his return, No. 10 Company was temporarily commanded by Captain Edgar Nisbet Marris, the son of a Lincolnshire solicitor whose thirst for adventure had taken him to the USA, where he enlisted in the army and served with the celebrated 7th Cavalry in the Philippines, before returning to join the British army after the outbreak of war.[4]

The attack on 4 October 1917, in which his men were to participate, had all the makings of a typical Salient tank disaster. Once again they had to advance along the shell-blasted road out of St Julien, but the approach route was now much longer since the front line had been pushed a mile further back towards the pulverized village of Poelcappelle, where the tanks were to support the infantry in attacking yet another series of concrete strongpoints.

Perhaps it was the luck of No. 10 Company, but for once everything went perfectly. The drivers had been honing their skills at the Wailly training area, and not one tank slipped off the road and ditched, while the German artillery fire was less intense than usual and none of the machines were knocked out, at least until the very end of the attack. Instead the tanks penetrated the village doing execution with anti-personnel 'case-shot' ammunition packed with shrapnel balls, which was used for the first time and was said to have had 'many opportunities of proving its value'.[5]

All the objectives were taken and the tanks withdrew with the loss of a single man. It was regarded as 'one of the most successful tank actions of the whole of the Flanders campaign in 1917',[6] but the luck ran out five days later when No. 11 Company followed up with another attack intended to push into and beyond Poelcappelle. After thirty hours of rainfall, any tank that left the road faced instant disaster, and the German gunners were back on devastating form – which could not be said of all the tank drivers.

The leading tank, D29 *Damon II* commanded by Lieutenant Jack Coghlan, reached the edge of the village where it was destroyed by a direct hit, and the same fate befell the next tank under Second Lieutenant Horace Birks. The rest of the column were unable to pass, and as they swung round on the slippery road, the machine bringing up the rear scraped against the hulk of D44 *Dracula*, abandoned after its heroic role on 20 September, and slithered across the road. The convoy was now caught in a trap, unable to go forward or back or to leave the road, and eventually all eight were destroyed or ditched.[7]

One of the section commanders disappeared after the tank he was travelling in was destroyed. This was Captain Frederick Talbot, who had fought as a cavalryman in the Boer War and begun the present war as a sergeant-major in 4th Dragoon Guards.[8] Major Watson, who called him 'the old dragoon', commented: 'I never had a better section-commander.' It had been a day of desperate tragedy: 'We had failed, and to me the sense of failure was inconceivably bitter. We began to feel that we were dogged by ill-fortune: the contrast between the magnificent achievement of Marris's company and the sudden overwhelming disaster that had swept down on my section was too glaring. And we mourned Talbot …'[9]

* * *

Whatever happened next, it was inevitable that No. 12 Company would be involved, and Frank Heap could not be far from his first trial by combat with the crew of *Deborah*. At the same time, the Third Battle of Ypres was clearly dragging to an end, and only a few more weeks of fighting were possible before the weather closed in and the war shut down for the winter. Some tank brigades had already been withdrawn from the Salient, and although D Battalion stayed behind, the heavy rain and poor ground conditions made it unlikely that they would be called on to support the offensive.

Amid the boredom and inactivity, the camp at La Lovie became a hotbed of speculation, with much talk of a 'grandiose scheme' for an all-out attack against the Passchendaele ridge. According to Major Watson: 'The whole Brigade, it was planned, would advance along the Poelcapelle and Langemarck Roads and deploy in the comparatively unshelled and theoretically passable country beyond. To us, perhaps prejudiced by disaster, the scheme appeared fantastic enough: the two roads could so easily be blocked by an accident or the enemy gunners …'[10]

Second Lieutenant Birks also recalled the wild stories that were circulating: 'The end of operations was obviously in sight, and as so often happens on these occasions rumour followed rumour: tanks were to be abandoned as an instrument of war and the recently formed Corps disbanded, all available machines were to be assembled in a last despairing attempt to reach Roulers, the whole Corps was to be withdrawn and transferred to Palestine. And then the final one, like a ray of sunshine through the early morning mist, we were to move south for a secret venture.'[11]

The last rumour, though vague, seemed to have some basis in fact, for on 27 October came a 'move order' from the adjutant, Captain Fred Cozens: '"D" Battalion, Tank Corps will move into the Wailly area commencing about 30th inst. Detailed times, dates and train arrangements will be notified later.'[12] This meant they were pulling back to the training area near Arras that served as a driving school and advanced base for the Tank Corps. It was a promising sign, and whatever lay behind it, one thing was certain: they were finally leaving the dreaded Salient. There would be no more sodden sojourns in the camp at La Lovie and the bleak tankodrome in Oosthoek Wood, no more time-wasting trips to the estaminets and concert-halls of Poperinghe, and no more doomed forays across the Canal into the dead zone beyond.

Birks recalled the impact of the announcement: 'Although the Corps had experienced more than a fair share of frustrations, setbacks and possibly casualties, morale had always been surprisingly high, and confirmation of orders to move out of the Ypres salient sent it rocketing sky-high; with almost indecent haste we withdrew across the canal, scarcely bothering to take a last look at Essex crossing, Ypres, Vlamertinghe, Oosthoek Wood, or any of the other spots which linger in the memory as accursed beyond belief.'[13]

There was known to be a shortage of accommodation at Wailly, and when D Battalion left they had to take along the huts and tents that had been used by G Battalion at La Lovie. After a few days of frantic preparation the trains drew into the sidings in Oosthoek Wood to be loaded up with tanks and stores. There was no need for secrecy now, and Captain Edward Glanville Smith recalled the unmilitary spectacle of their departure: 'A tank battalion on the move was always reminiscent of a tortoise in that it had to carry its home about with it. No rows of comfortable hutments were allotted it in the new area and tank trains carried not only the machines themselves, but tents, tarpaulins, duckboards, pit-props, floor-boarding, wire-beds, etc., etc., and anything that made for increased comfort. And so it was that on the evening of October 30th, when we bade our farewell to the Salient, our train resembled a timber-dump infinitely more than a mobile fighting unit. And at midnight we rumbled out of Belgium back to France.'[14]

* * *

Amid the excitement and uncertainty, there was little time to dwell on what they were leaving behind. D Battalion had arrived in the Ypres Salient nearly four months ago, and since then it had been in action for just six days. Out of fifty-four fighting tanks that had gone into action, only twenty had returned; of the remainder many had subsequently been salvaged and one or two captured, but the rest were abandoned or blown up where they lay. From its total strength of just over 900 men, D Battalion had lost twenty-one men killed, fifty-three wounded and eight captured,[15] which was a heavy enough price to pay, though negligible compared to the dreadful losses suffered by many other units.

To set against this, D Battalion could point to precious few positives – they had captured a few concrete strongpoints, led the successful action of 4 October, and given the infantry whatever support they could in terms of firepower and morale. While no-one doubted the courage and determination of the crews, it was clear the tanks had not justified their presence, or their existence. Even the commander of 1st Tank Brigade, Colonel Baker-Carr, conceded the Third Battle of Ypres had been a 'ghastly failure' for them, but underlined what had been obvious all along: 'The tanks failed through being employed in hopelessly unsuitable conditions. If the first submarine had been tested on Salisbury Plain, the results would not have been encouraging.'[16] Looking back over the past few months, Major Watson summarized the frustration they all felt: 'Why had tanks ever been sent to destruction at Ypres? There must be whole cemeteries of tanks in that damnable mud. And we had lost Talbot there.'[17]

For Frank Heap, there was no doubt a feeling of frustration that he had not yet taken part in an attack, but after all he had seen and heard of the Salient, probably also a guilty sense of relief. Wherever the next battle took place, it promised to be something entirely different, though whether that would be for better or worse remained to be seen. For the moment he faced the practical challenges of preparing D51 *Deborah* and his crew for the move, and coaxing her onto the railway truck that would transport them all south to meet whatever the future might hold.

CHAPTER 20

High Days and Highlanders

The training area at Wailly was already familiar to D Battalion, but when they arrived it was clear something big was afoot. After unloading his tank, Second Lieutenant James 'Tosh' Macintosh of No. 12 Company described the scene that greeted them:

> As they breasted a hill, they came in view of a little ruined village in the lap of the valley, where trees which had somehow escaped destruction lined the banks of a muddy stream. On the further slope of the valley was displayed an astonishing spectacle. By sections and by companies, by battalions and by brigades, in quarter column and in mass, lay serried rows of tanks, more tanks than Tosh had seen in his life before, while along the route ahead more tanks were moving to the assembly, and on the near horizon yet more tanks disported themselves on the old trench-system … Tosh's heart swelled as he looked at them, and filled with speechless emotion. 'Hell!' he ejaculated, and again 'Hell!'[1]

It was already obvious that the coming operation would be unlike anything they had seen before, but such was the level of secrecy that junior officers like James Macintosh and Frank Heap were told next to nothing. All they knew was they would spend the next two weeks at Wailly in intensive training, and would carry out a series of practice tank attacks in company and even battalion strength. After the previous piecemeal operations, this was a revelation in itself: 'Now we had our first inkling of attacks by tanks in mass with battalions as units, and to think that this was possible raised hopes all round.'[2]

The training at Wailly was necessary to refresh basic driving and tactical skills that had been forgotten in the Salient, where leaving the roads and moving across open country to attack a trench system was out of the question. For relatively new arrivals like Frank Heap, the next two weeks were a precious opportunity to get to know their machines, their crews, and their own capabilities in command.

Surprises came thick and fast, and the crews now learned they would go into action carrying an entirely new piece of equipment called a fascine. This was a massive bundle of brushwood weighing one-and-a-half tons, which was perched on the nose of the tank and secured by chains until released by pulling a lever, at which point it would roll forward into the enemy's trench to provide a kind of stepping-stone so the tank could get across. This was essential because the trenches they were to attack were known to be enormously wide, having been deliberately constructed by the Germans as anti-tank obstacles. There was a good deal of scepticism about this Heath Robinson device, but in the meantime there were many other concerns to occupy them.

The commanders and crews still had no idea where or when the attack would take place, but after a few days the veil of secrecy was lifted a little. Macintosh recalled the briefing given to No. 12 Company by their commander, Major R.O.C. Ward:

> An attack was shortly to be made on a certain sector; an attack in which tanks would play a very important part. Extreme secrecy was essential to success; given that secrecy, success of an unusual brilliance was, humanly speaking, inevitable

(we do not quote the Major's own words, which were more after this fashion: 'Damme, keep your mouths shut and it's an absolute sitter.') That very afternoon would be held the first of two practice attacks with the infantry who would co-operate with them in the real thing.

Now that the subject was no longer taboo, there was a lot of excited speculation as to where the attack would be made, and what it portended. That it was no minor show was clear from the number of battalions who would take part, also from the name of the division with whom [No. 12] Company was to co-operate. The prospect of an attack is not invariably a cause for congratulation, but, in this case, the battalion had so long been out of action, and their last show had been so full of difficulties and disappointments, that officers and men alike were delighted at the prospect of 'getting Jerry on the hop.'[3]

Like everyone else, Macintosh was impressed to discover which division they would be working with. Its identity was revealed in a suitably theatrical manner to Second Lieutenant Wilfred Bion of E Battalion as he waited at Wailly with his friend, Second Lieutenant Ernest Quainton, and their company commander, the bibulous and well-bred Major Christian de Falbe. Bion described the scene:

> This morning [de Falbe] was present, jolly, rubicund, at peace with himself and the world. The fresh November morning seemed an incongruous setting for him. Yet he had a Bacchus-like quality. He exuded an aroma of old port which civilized the rude rusticity of the scene, pervaded it rather than subdued it.
>
> 'Hullo Quainton dear boy', he said affectionately, like the Duchess when she met Alice ... 'Do I hear something?' His eyes twinkled.
>
> 'Sounds like bagpipes to me sir.'
>
> 'It *is* bagpipes', he said archly, putting his finger to his lips. 'Listen!'
>
> It was faint but clear, the skirl of pipes coming nearer. Over the crest there presently appeared the first files of marching men, battalion after battalion of kilted troops.
>
> We watched the rhythmical sway of the kilts as the battalions went by. Nothing was said, for we all knew who they were. In that war the 51st Division, Highland Territorials, had won a reputation second only to the Guards ...
>
> We had already learned in our very slight and brief experience that our lives depended on the stout hearts of the infantry who were in action with us ... We watched in silent relief ... The 51st Division? Someone meant business – at last![4]

Major William Watson of No. 11 Company, returning from leave in England to find the training in full swing, also described his 'great joy' at finding they would be fighting alongside the Highlanders. 'The apathy and bitter disappointment, caused by our misfortunes on the Poelcapelle Road, had disappeared completely, and the company, scenting a big mysterious battle, was as eager and energetic as if it had just disembarked in France. For once the secret was well kept. The air was full of rumours, but my officers knew nothing.'[5] Like R.O.C. Ward, Watson was allowed to visit the scene of the coming attack and the conclusion was summed by his reconnaissance officer, Second Lieutenant Frederick 'Jumbo' King: 'Unless the Boche catches on before the show, it's a gift!'[6]

The infantry had already carried out a number of practice attacks on their own training area, though these had the usual air of unreality. Trench-lines were marked out by coloured flags, and the orders said that: 'All three lines will be heavily wired (imaginary) ... Tanks will be represented by limbers.' However, there was also an important clue as to the conduct of the coming attack: 'The infantry will be preceded by a screen of tanks, which to the infantry will take the place of the artillery barrage.'[7]

This came as a bolt from the blue, because in the fighting on the Western Front a prolonged artillery bombardment was essential to blast a way through the enemy's barbed wire and destroy his machine guns before the infantry went in. There were many downsides to this approach, apart from the enormous cost of the shells. Firstly, a barrage lasting several days gave the enemy plenty of warning of an attack, and time to bring up reserves. Secondly, the ground was left so churned up that progress was difficult for the infantry, and impossible for cavalry or tanks. Thirdly, and most damningly, all the evidence was that it did not work, since the Germans had proved themselves adept at constructing underground defensive systems that enabled them to survive even the heaviest barrage, and were increasingly adopting a doctrine of 'defence in depth' which was less vulnerable to a bombardment of this kind. It was clear that another approach was needed, but much less clear whether tanks really were the answer. If not, it was the unprotected infantry, as well as the tank crews, who would pay the price.

Years later, Colonel Baker-Carr of 1st Tank Brigade claimed that the commander of 51st Division, Major-General George Harper, was never convinced by this approach: '"Uncle" Harper plainly demonstrated by his attitude that he thoroughly mistrusted the entire plan ... he took me on one side and described the whole conception as "a fantastic and most unmilitary scheme." Up to the very last moment he was completely lukewarm and, as I learned years later, had not hesitated to communicate his apprehensions to his brigade commanders.'[8]

Reflecting this scepticism, Harper was said to have devised his own attacking formations and tactics which were intended to protect the infantry by keeping them back from the tanks, with potentially disastrous results for the operation. This is a complex question which we will examine in due course, but for now we should note that tanks were notorious for drawing the enemy's fire, and if the infantry followed too close behind then they would be mown down and the attack would inevitably fail.

The optimal distance between tanks and the following infantry was the subject of ongoing debate. A training note from Third Army in late October merely said the leading infantry should be 'immediately behind' the tanks, and roughly 25–50 yards behind when they entered the wire.[9] However, on 11 November Lieutenant-Colonel John Fuller of the Tank Corps issued unequivocal guidance: 'When advancing behind tanks infantry should maintain 100 yards distance.'[10]

The headquarters of 51st Division gave more flexibility to those on the ground, but their overriding concern was that the infantry should stay in contact with the tanks at all times. Their instructions specified that infantry should cross No Man's Land in wave formation, in other words in extended lines at right-angles to the tanks' direction of advance, to minimize potential losses from enemy machine guns. They stated: 'The infantry following the tanks must not be involved [in] the hostile fire on the tanks. The distance at which they should follow the tanks cannot be laid down. It should not [be] less than 100 yards, and must be within signalling distance with the tanks.' The final point was stressed: 'The actual distance will be governed by the necessity for each platoon to keep touch with, and not lose sight of, its respective section of tanks.'[11] In case anyone was still in doubt, the instructions reiterated that 'in order to afford every chance of success to the operation, tank personnel and infantry must work constantly together and must understand thoroughly each other's methods.'[12]

When Colonel Baker-Carr issued his orders for the attack, these specified that the tanks 'will precede the infantry employed against 2nd objective by at least 100 yards'[13] – which was consistent with the instructions given by 51st Division. In other words, whatever initial misgivings Harper might have had, the orders from his headquarters gave no hint of any bad faith regarding tanks, and neither did the attitude of his men. On 6 November busloads of infantry arrived at Wailly for the first of a series of joint exercises, and the tank crews came face to face with the shaggy, kilted warriors of the Highland Division.[14]

The training sessions at Wailly gave a chance to rehearse their joint tactics, and no concerns were raised by either side. Indeed, the chance to train with the infantry was seen as a godsend by Tank Corps officers such as Captain Edward Glanville Smith: 'True that at Ypres we had sometimes met a few of the officers and sergeants with whom we were to co-operate, but now at Wailly tank company was allotted to infantry battalion and tank section to infantry company, which made it possible to practise and discuss the actual details of the show with the very officers and men we should later meet (we hoped) in the Hun second, third, etc., lines.'[15] Major William Watson was even more effusive:

> We trained with this splendid Division for ten days, working out the plans of our attack so closely that each platoon of Highlanders knew personally the crew of the tank which would lead it across No Man's Land. Tank officers and infantry officers attended each other's lectures and dined with each other. Our camp rang at night with strange Highland cries. As far as was humanly possible within the limits of time, we discussed and solved each other's difficulties, until it appeared that at least on one occasion a tank and infantry attack would in reality be 'a combined operation.'[16]

Another important aspect of the plan was also revealed at this time. The attack would consist of two phases, with a first wave of tanks and troops which was responsible for capturing the enemy's front-line trench system, and a second wave which would move through to capture the reserve trench system and the still-unnamed village behind. The tanks of No. 12 Company, including D51 *Deborah*, would make up the second wave, along with any surviving tanks from the first wave, and on 8 November they got the chance to rehearse this with the infantry battalions that would support them.[17]

One advantage of training at Wailly was that a section of the old German front line could be incorporated into the practice attacks, with the village of Ficheux standing in for the final objective, where buses were waiting to take the soldiers back to camp.

There was another, even more agreeable, aspect of these joint exercises. Captain Smith of No. 12 Company told how they soon became 'the best of friends' with their infantry colleagues, and this manifested itself in time-honoured fashion: 'Our liaison work off parade was, if anything, more successful than that on parade, and several hilarious nights were spent together. But it was almost asking the impossible to beat them at the game of "elbow lifting," and it was no disgrace to own defeat at the hands of the 51st Division.'[18] Second Lieutenant Horace Birks recalled a programme consisting of 'simple tactical exercises by day and the most colossal binges at night … Liaison … with our battalion of the Black Watch was very close, very intimate, very cordial, and both sides understood precisely what was required and expected.'[19]

Frank Heap, who had started his war with 9th (Scottish) Division, must have been in his element, and there were fond, though blurred, memories of one gathering from his colleague Second Lieutenant James Macintosh:

When they sat down to dinner each tank commander was next to the platoon commander who would be following him into action in a few days time. The circumstances, and the whisky, were propitious; fraternization proceeded at an unprecedented rate; and co-operation was so far ensured that in a short time many a platoon commander had his arm round the neck of his mate of the Tanks, while together they made completely successful attacks on bottle after bottle of 'the creature' [i.e. whisky] ... Parade next morning was called, not at eight, but at eleven, and ... before that hour there was much brewing of coffee in officers' tents.[20]

At last the time came for a parting of the ways, as the Highlanders returned to their own camps while the tank crews prepared for the move south to an unknown destination. For reasons of secrecy there were still few details to be had about the coming operation. Maps had been issued with the names blanked out, and even the conference held by Colonel Baker-Carr did not give much away, as Second Lieutenant Birks recalled: 'There was the usual rush of young officers for the back seats and I was successful in getting right at the back and as a result I was very little wiser at the end of half an hour's talking. As far as I can remember it was chiefly concerned with what a chance we were going to get, and so on and so on. After losing two tanks in the Ypres Salient I was a little sceptical about what was going to happen, and whether our view of a first class show coincided with that of our optimistic Brigadier.'[21] According to Captain Edward Glanville Smith, most of the officers and men still had no idea what was in store: 'Even when our intensive training was finished the future was shrouded in mystery, and none but the higher few knew the whys and wherefores of this latest development. Time alone could show.'[22]

But at least one thing was certain: the tanks crews and the infantry now knew each other, and knew they could count on each other. A bond had been created which spread throughout the ranks, as recalled by one officer from 51st Division: 'There is a story told of a party of men of, I think, the 6th Gordons, who had been induced to partake of refreshment by their opposite numbers of the Tank Corps. When the lorry with this party aboard was leaving Wailly, a Gordon, by way of farewell, shouted out at the top of his voice, "Guid auld forty-nine! We'll follow that auld . . onywhere," "49" evidently being a tank with which they were to work during the coming battle.'[23]

The next time they met it would be under very different circumstances, and for the time being they could only guess where the tanks would be called on to lead, and the infantry to follow.

PART IV
THE BATTLE OF CAMBRAI

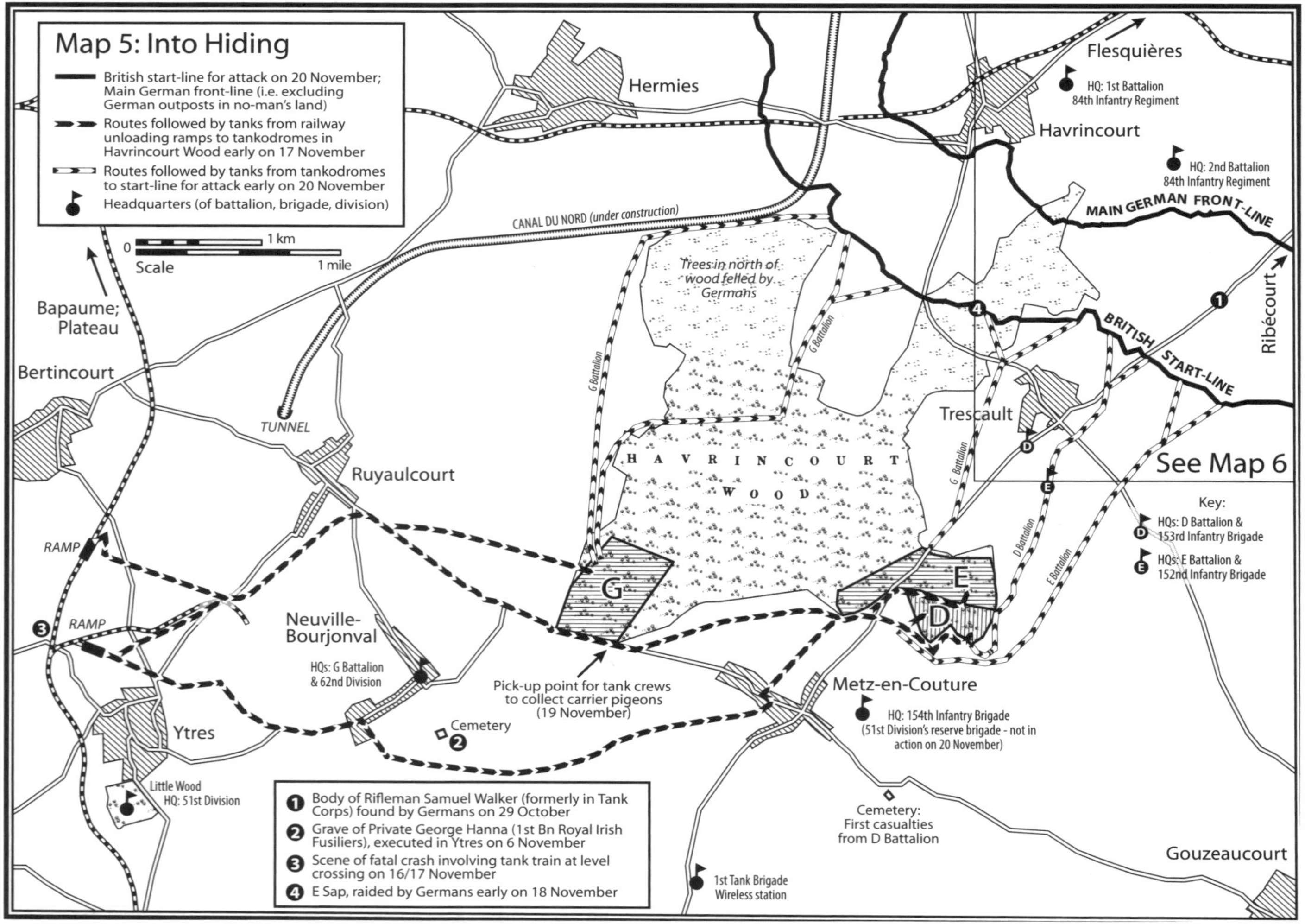

Map 5: Into Hiding
British start-line for attack on 20 November; Main German front-line (i.e. excluding German outposts in no-man's land)
Routes followed by tanks from railway unloading ramps to tankodromes in Havrincourt Wood early on 17 November
Routes followed by tanks from tankodromes to start-line for attack early on 20 November
Headquarters (of battalion, brigade, division)
0
1 km
1 mile
Scale
Bapaume; Plateau
Bertincourt
Hermies
CANAL DU NORD (under construction)
TUNNEL
Ruyaulcourt
Flesquières
HQ: 1st Battalion 84th Infantry Regiment
Havrincourt
HQ: 2nd Battalion 84th Infantry Regiment
MAIN GERMAN FRONT-LINE
BRITISH START-LINE
Ribécourt
Trees in north of wood felled by Germans
G Battalion
G Battalion
HAVRINCOURT WOOD
G Battalion
Trescault
See Map 6
D Battalion
E Battalion
Key:
HQs: D Battalion & 153rd Infantry Brigade
HQs: E Battalion & 152nd Infantry Brigade
G
E
D
RAMP
RAMP
Neuville-Bourjonval
HQs: G Battalion & 62nd Division
Pick-up point for tank crews to collect carrier pigeons (19 November)
Metz-en-Couture
HQ: 154th Infantry Brigade (51st Division's reserve brigade - not in action on 20 November)
Ytres
Cemetery
Little Wood
HQ: 51st Division
1 Body of Rifleman Samuel Walker (formerly in Tank Corps) found by Germans on 29 October
2 Grave of Private George Hanna (1st Bn Royal Irish Fusiliers), executed in Ytres on 6 November
3 Scene of fatal crash involving tank train at level crossing on 16/17 November
4 E Sap, raided by Germans early on 18 November
Cemetery: First casualties from D Battalion
1st Tank Brigade Wireless station
Gouzeaucourt

CHAPTER 21

Into Hiding

For the Highlanders, 13 November was a day of glorious inactivity. This was the anniversary of their greatest military triumph, the storming of the stronghold of Beaumont Hamel on the Somme, and was marked by a holiday for the troops, with sports and pipe concerts. The menu for one dinner has survived, with courses following the plan of attack from soup ('barrage de tomato') and 'first wave whiting' to 'café de l'objectif'. A message from Major-General Harper anticipated more victories to come: 'I am absolutely confident, and I feel that every man in the Division is confident, that, given a fair chance, the Highland Division can always defeat the enemy.'[1]

It was a different story for D Battalion, as this was the day set for their departure from Wailly. Major Watson told how 'at dawn on the 13th we arose and trekked a matter of five miles to Beaumetz Station, where, after an excellent and hilarious lunch at the local *estaminet*, we entrained successfully for an unknown destination'. Although he made light of it, the process was 'hideously complicated'.[2] Driving a tank up a ramp onto a flatbed railway truck, with only a few inches either side for clearance, was always a supreme test of driving skill, and this was also their first actual encounter with the fascines they had heard so much about. Each tank had to pick up its massive load, carry it onto the railway truck, and then deposit it carefully in front of the tank, otherwise the train would have been too tall to go through the tunnels.

Night had fallen when the trains finally pulled out, but they were not heading straight for the battlefront. Instead, at 3 o'clock the next morning they drew into an enormous railhead where the tanks were unloaded. Major Watson found this 'a vast confusing place, and even a major in the Tank Corps felt insignificant among the multitudinous rails, the slow dark trains, the sudden lights. Tanks, which had just detrained, came

---

Opposite: Map 5 illustrates the move into the forward area by D and E Battalions in preparation for the attack on 20 November.

On the left is the railway line used to bring in the tanks (including D51 *Deborah*) from the Plateau railhead, and the ramps where they were unloaded in the early hours of 17 November. Nearby is the level crossing where a tank train collided with a lorry, killing two men, as described in Chapter 21.

The routes followed by the tanks under cover of darkness are shown, along with the battalion tankodromes in Havrincourt Wood where they remained hidden for the next three days.

The main German front line is shown, but not the forward outposts scattered across No Man's Land.

The map also shows the move forward to the start-line in the early hours of 20 November by the tanks of 1st Tank Brigade (i.e. D, E and G Battalions), as described in Chapter 24. Note that the routes shown for G Battalion were also used by the tanks attached to this unit from D and E Battalions. The beginning of some routes has been omitted for clarity.

rumbling round the corners of odd huts. Lorries bumped through the mist with food and kit. Quiet railwaymen, mostly American, went steadily about their business.'[3] These were members of the US Army's 11th Engineers, who had been in France since August 1917 and whose skills were being employed in running the military rail network.[4]

The battalion had arrived at Plateau, where a sprawling complex of sidings and marshalling yards covered the uplands near Maricourt, a few miles south-east of Albert. This was familiar territory to some, since the first tanks had been unloaded near here just over a year before, on the way to their initial encounter in the Battle of Flers-Courcelette. Now the tanks were driven into nearby Billon Wood, which would be their hiding-place for the next couple of days, while as many men as possible were housed in the camp at Méaulte just outside Albert.

This was a vital opportunity for further preparation, as Second Lieutenant James Macintosh described: 'Busy the crews undoubtedly were that day. It was their last chance of free movement by day, and any further time for preparation was likely to be short. Furthermore, fascines were to be carried in position during the final move, and must now be adjusted so as to require the minimum of attention before action.'[5] Captain Edward Glanville Smith noted an additional complication: 'We were supposed to finally complete our equipment here in the matter of petrol, oil, grease, etc., and should have done so but for a great shortage of these materials, with the result that most battalions had to "scrounge" someone's else [sic], and this added a good deal of excitement to what might have been a very boring two days.'[6]

It was a clear, bitterly cold night when the crews, now exhausted from labour and lack of sleep, drove their machines out of Billon Wood on 15 November and back to the railhead for the final stage of the journey. The entire Tank Corps was slowly moving into position, and the rail schedules were under severe pressure with around forty trains loaded with hundreds of tanks leaving Plateau over a five-day period.[7]

As they stood by, the men of No. 12 Company learned their train had been delayed due to an accident and made the best of the situation, as described by Second Lieutenant Macintosh:

> Then some individual, one of our nameless heroes, had a heaven-sent inspiration. The countryside was littered with empty petrol-boxes. At his suggestion these were collected in the dip of a sunken road, a light was put to them, and in five minutes the entire company was dozing contentedly round a flaming bonfire, which, as Tosh sleepily murmured, was indeed *bon*. True, faces were scorched while backs were freezing, and there was not seating accommodation for all; but on such a night 'twas bliss to be even sectionally warm, and there is a stage of weariness at which standing ceases to be an effort. In fact, it was with profound regret that the company heard of the arrival of their train at 12.45 a.m., and, abandoning the glowing coals of the fire, started up their engines and drove on to the train.[8]

Captain Smith also fondly recalled the 'huge bonfire', and added a further detail: '"Mactosh" distinguished himself by going to sleep standing up – chiefly made possible by a small body and large feet.'[9]

Despite the pressure they were under, the American railway engineers found time to record the scene in a series of photographs showing the tanks, each with its huge fascine, manoeuvring delicately onto the rolling stock, and then lined up, a dozen or so tanks per train, ready for departure. At the front of one photograph can be seen D46

Dragon III, indicating that this is the train bearing No. 12 Company, and D51 *Deborah* is somewhere behind. The crew of *Dragon* are lounging in front of their tank, and they look remarkably cheerful, though they would have to get through another exhausting day and night before their journey came to an end.[10]

The trains drew out in the late afternoon for their final two-hour journey eastwards, reaching the detraining point at dusk. Major Watson was awaiting their arrival at a ramp near the village of Ytres when he heard some dreadful news: a train carrying tanks had collided with a lorry at a level crossing nearby, and there were reports of casualties.

> I hurried there. The train had collided with a lorry and pushed it a few hundred yards, when the last truck had been derailed and the tank on it had crushed the lorry against the slight embankment. Under the tank were two men. I was convinced that I had lost two of my men, until I discovered that the tanks belonged to Marris [of No. 10 Company] and the two unfortunate men had been on the lorry. The line was soon cleared. The derailed truck was uncoupled, and the tank, none the worse for its adventure, climbed up the embankment and joined its fellows at the ramp.[11]

Colonel Baker-Carr was even closer to the scene of the accident and arrived to find the lorry 'smashed to atoms'. He added: 'There was no sign whatever of the driver and we found him later, completely flattened out and crushed into the solid earth.'[12]

In fact, one of those who died was a train crewman, Sapper Frederick Bird of the Royal Engineers' Railway Operating Department. An inquiry found he had been riding on the front rail truck or 'bogie', piloting the train into position when a lorry pulled in front and collided, throwing the tank with its fascine onto him. Another railman who had tried to stop the accident told how after 'making a further search, I found the head of a man under a Caterpillar [i.e. tank] which had been thrown off a bogie'. A private in 1st Bn Royal Irish Fusiliers, who had presumably been in the lorry, also died (officially of 'traumatic asphyxia') and two of his comrades were injured, though the lorry driver was unhurt.[13] The accident, however tragic, could not be allowed to disrupt the timetable, and the wreckage was dragged clear using other tanks so the next trains could pull in with only a few minutes' delay.

It was in the early hours of 17 November when No. 12 Company finished detraining, and the tank commanders were ordered to gather at the ramp in the darkness to meet Major R.O.C. Ward, who had arrived by car. 'He explained that they were five miles from the line, and would be in view of the enemy most of the way forward; nor must they suppose that because he was silent he was not watchful. There lay before them a nine-mile run; the time was then 3.30, and they must be in the wood before day broke at seven. The going being mostly flat grass-land, they must make all possible speed.'[14]

Exhausted as they were, the last stage of that night's journey stood out in everyone's minds as an interminable ordeal; in fact Lieutenant Gerald Edwards called it 'the worst trek we ever did'.[15] The commanders, leading their tanks forward on foot, struggled to stay alert as they traversed mile after mile of 'absolutely featureless country',[16] following the white tape laid down to guide them through the gloom.

As the tanks trundled slowly forward, there was time to take in the fact that their surroundings were unlike anything they had previously encountered in war. Great battles, like the one they had left behind in the Ypres Salient, were normally preceded by a relentless build-up of men and material, and by a shattering artillery bombardment that could last a week. Instead, with only days to go before a major offensive, the countryside they were crossing looked deserted and deathly quiet. On closer inspection, however, Second Lieutenant Macintosh could see reassuring evidence of the scale of the preparations: 'The countryside was almost empty of man – there were no camps, there were no guns or dumps, the roads were almost empty. But in hollows and in sunken roads, in woods and among ruined houses, could be seen carefully hidden gun-pits; dug-outs empty of men; casualty clearing stations with their red crosses hidden – everywhere a secret but scrupulous preparation. Thrilled with the feeling that at last the old difficulties were to be overcome and a new method of war introduced, they clanked their slow way over untouched ground.'[17]

Towards the end of their trek, they reached the enormous wood where they were to stay hidden in the run-up to the attack. 'As they skirted the edge of the wood, which, though a mile from the line, was here almost untouched, they noticed more signs of a forthcoming attack. The wood itself was full of camps, all carefully camouflaged, while along the fringe were innumerable dumps, emplacements, and so forth ... No fewer than three light railways ran into the wood.'[18]

This 'strange fatiguing tramp' finally came to end as the tanks were manoeuvred into the shelter of the wood under cover of darkness. In some ways it was a reprise of their arrival in Oosthoek Wood five months earlier, except they were now just 3,000 yards (i.e. one-and-three-quarter miles, or two-and-three-quarter kilometres) from the German front line, with enemy outposts even closer in No Man's Land. Major Watson described how

> the tanks pushed boldly among the trees, and for the next two hours there was an ordered pandemonium. Each tank had to move an inch at a time for fear it should bring down a valuable tree or run over its commander, who probably had fallen backwards into the undergrowth. One tank would meet another in the darkness, and in swinging to avoid the other, would probably collide with a third. But by dawn – I do not know how it was done – every tank was safely in the wood; the men had fallen asleep anywhere, and the cooks with sly weary jests were trying to make a fire which would not smoke. Three thousand yards is a trifle near ...[19]

When Frank Heap and his fellow officers awoke a few hours later and gathered for lunch, they were finally issued with a map of the district and learned they were in Havrincourt Wood, three-quarters of a mile behind a village called Trescault, which lay just inside the British lines. They would remain there for the next three days, under the very noses of the enemy, while the rest of the attacking forces moved slowly and stealthily into position around them. Most of G Battalion's tanks were already hidden in another part of the wood, while E Battalion was arriving that night, with the rest of G Battalion to follow.[20] Similar moves were taking place to the south, so that a total of 476 machines from all nine battalions of the Tank Corps would soon be in position ready for the start of the attack.[21]

In the meantime, there was nothing to contradict Tosh's initial impressions: 'The peaceful atmosphere of this corner of the war was indescribable. By day hardly a "boom" broke the heavy silence; even by night machine-guns chattered quite perfunctorily, star-shells were few and far between, and the flash of a gun was a rare event. Meanwhile the tanks lay embowered in leafy growth, while high above them the trees met to screen them from prying eyes.'[22] It sounds almost idyllic, but in fact this was the start of a period of frantic, surreptitious activity and mounting tension for the tank crews, who were hidden well within range of the enemy's machine guns, not to mention artillery. The situation was made even worse because the men were not allowed to leave the wood, or to light fires for cooking. Major Watson shared in the general anxiety:

> For the next [few] days we had only one thought – would the Boche 'catch on'? The Ulster Division was still in the line, and, even if the enemy raided and took prisoners, the Ulstermen knew almost nothing. By day the occasional German aeroplane could see little, for there was little to see. Tanks, infantry, and guns were hidden in the woods. New gun-pits were camouflaged. There was no movement on the roads or in the villages. Our guns fired a few customary rounds every day and night, and the enemy replied. There was nothing unusual.
>
> But at night the roads were blocked with transport. Guns and more guns arrived, from field guns to enormous howitzers, that had rumbled down all the way from the Salient. Streams of lorries were bringing up ammunition, petrol, rations; and whole brigades of infantry, marching across the open country, had disappeared by dawn into the woods. Would the Boche 'catch on'?[23]

As the men of D Battalion slept off their exertions, they were awoken by a brief frenzy of artillery and small-arms fire in the early hours of the next morning. It was only a mile-and-a-quarter away from them, but that was far enough to pose no threat, and it died down soon afterwards. It turned out the Germans had indeed raided a British outpost in No Man's Land and captured some men from the Ulster Division, but the tank crews had plenty of other things to concern them, and no-one seems to have given it much thought.

CHAPTER 22

On the Silent Front

Just as *Deborah* and the rest of the great force of tanks were secretly moving into position, so were the infantry divisions that would support them in the attack in a few days' time. The sector had been held by 36th (Ulster) Division since August, when they were withdrawn from the Ypres Salient after suffering crushing losses there. They found themselves in an overwhelmingly peaceful area, though the commanders tried to keep up their men's fighting spirit by mounting sporadic raids on the German lines.

The 36th (Ulster) Division was now a very different formation from the one that had stormed the German lines at Thiepval on the first day of the Somme, when so many men were killed or wounded, including Gunner William Galway who was now in the crew of *Deborah*. Originally made up of members of the Ulster Volunteer Force, the demands of war meant the division's pure stock had been diluted by recruits from all over Britain and Ireland. Some battalions had been amalgamated after suffering heavy losses, including William Galway's old unit, 13th Bn Royal Irish Rifles. Others had joined the division, among them 1st Bn Royal Irish Fusiliers, whose Gaelic motto 'Faugh a Ballagh' ('Clear the way') had been their war-cry during a glorious episode in the Napoleonic Wars when they captured a French eagle at the Battle of Barrosa. The Ulster Division was taking part in the coming operation, but would be on the periphery of the British advance, which meant it was now being withdrawn from the line and replaced by the two fresh divisions that would lead the attack in this sector, namely 62nd (West Riding) Division and 51st (Highland) Division.

Like everything else, this great movement of men had to take place without the enemy noticing that anything was afoot – a huge challenge in such a quiet sector, when any abnormal activity would instantly attract attention. There was an additional sensitivity, because the mere presence of the crack 51st Division would ring alarm-bells if it was detected. During their early reconnaissance, its senior officers had worn ordinary uniforms instead of their distinctive Highland dress, just as visiting Tank Corps commanders had removed their badges and worn dark glasses to avoid being recognized.[1]

As night fell on 17 November, the relief got under way and the Yorkshiremen of 62nd Division filed into the trenches opposite the village of Havrincourt, replacing the Royal Irish Fusiliers who were moving back to billets in the village of Metz-en-Couture.[2] As a precaution, small squads of fusiliers were left behind to occupy a series of forward positions known as 'saps' dotted across No Man's Land. In the words of the divisional historian: 'To deceive the enemy as to the great concentration in front of him, a screen of the troops of [the Ulster Division] remained to hold the outpost line.'[3]

It was a depressing duty for the men who had to move out into No Man's Land and occupy a series of isolated posts several hundred yards in front of the main British lines, knowing their mates were heading back to warm billets in the rear area. They would have to hold these exposed outposts for the next two days, and they could only hope the time would pass quietly.

One of these posts was called 'E' Sap, and as the little garrison settled into their new home and peered into the darkness, they did not know that the Germans had been scanning their position for weeks, and even now, they were preparing to attack them in the dead of night.

* * *

The idea of mounting a raid on a British outpost was the brainchild of Hauptmann (i.e. Captain) Harro Soltau, commander of the 2nd Battalion of the 84th Infantry Regiment which was holding the line in front of Havrincourt. Like the Ulster Division opposite, the 84th was a regiment with a proud history, but it had also suffered heavy losses and was now rebuilding its strength in what the Germans called the 'stille (i.e. silent) Front', or the 'Sanatorium des Westens' – the sanatorium of the Western Front.

The raid was not triggered by any unusual activity on the British side, but Hauptmann Soltau faced a similar challenge of maintaining his men's fighting spirit in such a tranquil area, and encouraged patrolling and raiding as a means of probing the enemy's defences and gathering intelligence. In this case he had just the man for the job: one of his company commanders, Leutnant Bernhard Hegermann, had just completed a training course in stormtrooper tactics and was itching to put them into practice.

In early November, Leutnant Hegermann was told to prepare for a fighting patrol to capture prisoners from the position known as 'E' Sap, and immediately began the detailed planning and reconnaissance necessary to ensure success. He welcomed the chance of some excitement: 'It would liven up the never-ending monotony of trench duty, but the best thing about activities of this kind was that they put some vitality back into the men. Any soldier would be inwardly aroused, he would have something to occupy his mind again, as through his personal resolve he could create a worthwhile opportunity to distinguish himself.'[4] The men were just as keen, according to one of his senior NCOs, Fähnrich Hans Carstens: 'For a long time, many of us had been eager to put the Tommies on their guard once again, as they had recently become very cocky. It was therefore easy … to find enough volunteers from all four companies to mount a small surprise attack on the enemy trenches.'[5]

So it was that in the early hours of 18 November, Hegermann and his men crept out of the trenches to their jumping-off points in No Man's Land. They were lightly armed with pistols and hand grenades, and Fähnrich Carstens recalled their mood of grim determination: 'The most important thing was to get up and at them like Blücher, and on no count to hesitate. That went without saying for every one of us.'[6]

The raid went like clockwork, as described by Leutnant Hegermann:

> At precisely 6.30 a.m. [i.e. 5.30 a.m. UK time], artillery fire began on the foremost enemy position, and exactly three minutes later dropped back onto the enemy front line. It was perfectly positioned, and at the same moment – I was holding a watch and compass with luminous hands … – I fired a flare as a signal for the infantry to attack and for the pioneers to blow their charges [i.e. to clear a way through the barbed wire] … We threw some hand-grenades, and with cheers we broke into the English trenches … With the flashlights we had brought with us, we found the enemy sentries at their posts flattened against the sandbagged walls of the trench … Meanwhile the trench was searched, and with the first light of dawn breaking, I gave the order to withdraw.[7]

Fähnrich Carstens and his team also rushed forward on the signal:

> In a few bounds we were in the trench, right where an English double sentry-post stood. But instead of firing, both Tommies tried to escape to the left. That was a bad move, because in the meantime, the assault team from No. 8 Company had entered the trench there, so we had them in a trap. The other assault groups had also collared a few Tommies, and we then headed back on the signal from our leader. At the outpost our esteemed battalion commander, Hauptmann Soltau, was already waiting to congratulate us on our success. The raid had been worthwhile, we had brought six prisoners including a trainee officer and a lanky corporal … We were all delighted to have shown the Tommies that German soldiers would not let themselves be provoked with impunity, but still had the old fighting spirit in them, which our enemies have so often learned to fear.[8]

For the Germans, the raid was a triumph of co-ordination and courage, but for the British it was no more than a minor setback. The War Diary of 1st Bn Royal Irish Fusiliers gave a brief summary: 'At 5-30 a.m. the enemy, after a night in which persistent efforts had been made to cut our wire round "E" Sap, succeeded in rushing 1 post. 6 of our men are missing. The enemy's previous attempts had been driven off by our bombers but on this occasion he put down a box barrage of trench mortars etc. and succeeded in entering the Sap under cover of the noise and rushing the right hand post."[9]

The incident confirmed the wisdom of leaving a human screen in place to stop the enemy discovering that fresh divisions were moving into position. It was true that some men had been captured, but they knew very little about the forthcoming operation, and the secret should be safe as long as they kept their heads, and kept their mouths shut. Sir Douglas Haig himself was concerned until he received reassurance from the commander of Third Army: 'General Byng states that the prisoners taken by the enemy did not know of our intended operations. I was very anxious lest they might have given away information of these plans.'[10]

But when the Germans began interrogating the prisoners at their divisional headquarters in Cambrai, they could hardly believe what they heard.

* * *

For the men of D Battalion, 18 November was the day when they would finally learn the full details of the coming attack. The broad pattern of the operation was known by now, and they had already been given maps and aerial photographs, but the time had come for Frank Heap and his driver to get their first sight of the actual terrain, guided by 'Contours' – the company's reconnaissance officer (or R.O.), Second Lieutenant Horace Furminger. After a long approach walk along communication trenches, the tank commanders and drivers of No. 12 Company eventually reached the reserve line where troops were peacefully brewing tea, and after that they were in for a shock. All too often, the front line consisted of a muddy ditch manned by a few sentries, but as Second Lieutenant Macintosh described, this was something else:

> Instead, they came into a perfect example of the traversed trench, revetted and duck-boarded, with neat shelters and bomb-stores all carefully labelled, furnished with a broad and convenient fire-step and inhabited by a number of imperturbable and immaculate Jocks, who greeted them with polite smiles and went on cleaning their rifles.

The visitors were by this time filled with amazed hilarity. But more was to come. The R.O. wished to show them the lie of the country. Instead of cautiously erecting a periscope and offering each in turn a peep he climbed on the fire-step, unconcernedly popped his head above the parapet, and invited them to come and have a look. Picture the scene, ye who have known front lines which were unsafe on hands and knees – two bays full of young officers, each with a map, gazing cheerfully across direct into the Boche line![11]

They stared out over a No Man's Land that was around 1,200 yards wide, though with various saps running into it from both sides, and almost completely unmarked by shellfire. No. 11 Company was carrying out a similar reconnaissance, and Second Lieutenant Horace Birks described the prospect before them: 'It was possible to see that the going was firm and unbroken, carpeted with long dank grass which had been uncut for years. The outline of the Hindenburg line could just be seen here and there, but it was mostly invisible, being skilfully placed just behind the reverse side of a gentle ridge, its position defined by a most monstrous belt of wire unbelievably deep which ran across the whole front like a rusty grey river.'[12]

Beyond the concealed front line, the ground dipped further down to a valley lined by trees, of which only the tops were visible. This was the Grand Ravine, and its name was enough to trigger a surge of anxiety, since it would have to be crossed before they could approach their final objective. Maps and aerial photographs suggested that despite its name, it was nothing more than a narrow stream in the bed of an open valley, but they still had to prepare for any eventuality – no doubt recalling that the Steenbeek at St Julien looked just as innocuous on the map, but had been blasted into an impenetrable swamp. Major Clough Williams-Ellis commented that some people 'apparently coupled it in their minds with the Grand Cañon of Colorado',[13] while Brigadier-General Hugh Elles recalled: 'We spent many weeks trying to find out exactly how wide this imposingly named trench was and we never got reliable information.'[14] The infantry were also much exercised about the possible problems, and one officer recalled 'the rumours of planks and ladders that were to be carried to bridge the ravine, and of ropes to pull men through the water!'[15] Even if it did not turn out to be as much of a physical obstacle as they feared, it seemed likely the Germans would put up fierce resistance here, and if the valley was as broad and open as it looked, it could easily turn into a killing-field.

Beyond the unknown gulf of the Grand Ravine, the ground rose to a well-defined ridge on which stood the village of Flesquières, screened by woodland, with the trenches of the support system visible on the slopes in front of it. This would be the final objective for D Battalion, and in particular for *Deborah* and the other tanks of No. 12 Company. The surviving tanks of the first wave would also join in the second phase of the attack, though Second Lieutenant Birks of No. 11 Company commented: 'It was strange how little attention was directed to this feature.'[16]

All in all, the visit to the front line had given a further boost to their confidence, according to Macintosh: 'The condition of the ground was all that could be desired; landmarks were plentiful; trenches might be wide, but were not impassable; and it was with a very definite and justifiable optimism that [No. 12] Company looked forward to the day so nearly approaching.'[17] They might have been less confident if they had known that all this activity had attracted the attention of the enemy. Hauptmann Otto Fürsen, commander of 3rd Battalion, 84th Infantry Regiment, told how 'on the afternoon of 17 November, which was bright and sunny for a few hours, my adjutant … and I watched through periscope binoculars as two English officers from a sap held a map spread out on the edge of their trench, while one or the other apparently reconnoitred our position.'[18] It looked as if the British were planning something, but there was no clue what it might be.

* * *

On the evening of 18 November, after 'a hearty meal',[19] it was time for Major R.O.C. Ward to issue his orders, and the full details of the attack were finally revealed to Frank Heap and his brother officers. It was less than three weeks since they had left the Salient, and in that time they had been briefed about certain aspects of the operation, viewed the ground they were to attack, and heard innumerable rumours, so it was with a sense of relief that they finally learned the full picture. By this time their expectations were sky-high, and they were not to be disappointed, for it was no exaggeration to say this was a battle in which the Tank Corps would either make history, or become history.

The major's orders began with an overview: 'The general plan of operations is to break through the enemy's Hindenburg Line between Gonnelieu and Havrincourt on a front of two Corps with the assistance of tanks, and to open a way through his defensive system by which cavalry can pass to exploit the success gained by the infantry.'[20]

The Hindenburg Line was the British name for one of the most formidable defensive positions on the entire Western Front, known as the 'Siegfriedstellung' to the Germans who had prepared it far in the rear while the Battle of the Somme was raging to the west. It had therefore been designed and constructed away from the eyes of the enemy, and the Germans were able to build an extensive network of trenches and bunkers, protected by a barricade of barbed wire and occupying the best possible ground from a strategic point of view. In spring 1917 they had abandoned the former Somme battlefield and withdrawn to this new position, freeing up thousands of men by reducing the length of their front line, and leaving the British to advance across a region devastated by a ruthless scorched-earth policy.

There had been various Allied proposals for attacking this seemingly impregnable position, and the idea was taken up by senior officers of the Tank Corps as a more fruitful alternative to the doomed offensive in the Salient, following their meeting in August 1917 to discuss the 'advisability from a tank point of view of switching off the present operations and initiating a tank attack on some other part of the line'.[21]

Despite the strength of the enemy's trench system, they realized it could be vulnerable to an entirely new form of attack, occupying as it did well-drained downland which would be perfect tank country as long as it was not churned up by a long preparatory bombardment. The line was relatively thinly manned since the Germans were confident of their engineering skills, and knew the barbed wire would take days to blast aside by artillery fire, giving them plenty of time to bring up reserves at the slightest hint of a threat. The operation would therefore rely on secrecy, with tanks suddenly emerging from hiding to crush a way through the wire for the infantry and cavalry, while the artillery would launch a hurricane bombardment using guns that had not been registered in advance – in other words, they had not fired the usual ranging shots and observed where they fell, in order to ensure the guns were on target. This was also a major innovation which was only made possible thanks to major technical advances in ranging techniques, and to extraordinarily detailed planning.

Using these methods, the aim was to break through the German positions along a six-mile front between two canals – the St Quentin Canal to the east, and the Canal du

Nord to the west. Once this first phase was complete, the cavalry would advance through the gap to seize the high ground of Bourlon Wood, which dominated the area under attack and therefore had to be taken on the very first day. As soon as the bridges over the St Quentin Canal had been captured, other cavalry units would flood across them to encircle the town of Cambrai – an important German railhead and communication centre. They would then wheel round in a great sweeping manoeuvre to seize the crossings over the Sensée River to the north, preventing the Germans from bringing up reinforcements. This would leave a substantial area ringed by various waterways, within which the enemy's forces would be caught and crushed by the British advance.

The implications of all this were summarized in the orders from 1st Tank Brigade: 'The first phase of the operations is dependent on surprise, so that the enemy may have had no warning to strengthen his garrison and to bring up extra artillery. The measure of further success is entirely dependent on the speed with which the operation is carried out. The Bourlon position will be seized as rapidly as possible and advanced guards of all arms will be pushed forward for this purpose. It is very important that it should be captured the first day.'[22]

The tanks of D and E Battalions would be involved in the first phase of the operation only, with the first wave advancing as far as the so-called Blue Line which ran along the valley known as the Grand Ravine, and the second wave passing through the village of Flesquières to the Brown Line beyond. To their left, the first wave tanks of G Battalion would take the village of Havrincourt and then pass to the west of Flesquières, moving much further ahead to take the crossings on the Canal du Nord and the distant village of Graincourt. For this purpose their normal strength was supplemented by sixteen tanks attached from D and E Battalions.[23]

Major Ward's orders explained all this and covered the details of objectives, approach routes, boundaries, location of headquarters, and the timetable for the barrage. This was the first battle in which sections of tanks would operate as fighting units, so the section commanders also issued their own orders. This meant Captain Graeme Nixon was able to brief the crews of the three tanks under his command, namely D49 *Dollar Princess* under Second Lieutenant John McNiven, D50 *Dandy Dinmont* under Lieutenant Hugo Armitage, and D51 *Deborah*.[24] As the only male tank, D50 would play a crucial role in tackling any bunkers and other strongpoints once they reached their objective in the village of Flesquières.

We can get a sense of what he might have said from a surviving set of orders, jotted in pencil on pages torn from a field notebook, that were issued by Captain David Morris of No. 11 Company. Since his tanks were in the first wave, the orders are mostly concerned with how they would drop their fascines and work together to cross the front-line trench system. There was a disturbing vagueness about what would come next: 'After this, operations will be more or less "into the blue" & all tanks will follow me & support me in flag tank.' The one place that was likely to cause trouble was the Grand Ravine: 'Big opposition expected … Rush it with one "line abreast" & fight it hard.' After this the tanks of the second wave would take the lead: 'On reaching final objective … we will be relieved by fresh tanks of No 12 Company. Survivors will be prepared to accompany me to further action immediately.'[25]

The orders include a rallying-cry to his men: 'I leave the good name of the section in your hands … – do as usual & I will "thank you". Good luck to all ranks. Remember <u>we must</u> take Flesquiere [*sic*].'[26]

Finally, he threw down a challenge, referring to the fact that the Tank Corps commander, Brigadier-General Hugh Elles, was personally leading the attack inside one of H Battalion's tanks away to their right: 'General Ellis [*sic*] goes over with the 1st wave i.e. with us. <u>Race him</u>.'[27]

Frank Heap and the other commanders now had time to digest these various instructions. In Tosh's words: 'There was very little comment on the orders. The major's operation orders were masterpieces of their kind, and left nothing to be explained. Each tank commander took his map and his aeroplane-photographs, retired to his bivvy, and set about making himself perfectly sure of what he had to do. Then, with hearts beating high with hope and excitement, they lay down to enjoy what might well be their last sleep for some time.'[28]

CHAPTER 23

'Things Fall Apart'[1]

The Germans had also been busy since the trench raid in which they had captured six members of the Royal Irish Fusiliers. On 19 November, the intelligence officer of Second Army High Command completed his report on their interrogation, a copy of which has recently come to light in German archives. The revelations in it came as a bombshell:

> Among the troops there is general talk of a forthcoming attack which should provide better positions for the winter, and they also say Havrincourt is to be taken … In the past week a number of officers have been seen in the lines from different arms of the service, including artillery and engineer officers, who inspected the trenches and the ground in front. All the prisoners stated unanimously that large quantities of ammunition and engineering supplies had recently been stockpiled in Havrincourt Wood, and that new gun-pits were also being dug. The artillery in the sector is being greatly increased. One prisoner has personally seen newly arrived heavy guns in Metz-en-Couture. Furthermore, a stationary camouflaged tank was seen in Metz-en-Couture; two more tanks in Havrincourt Wood. One of the prisoners says the attack has been fixed for early on the 20th. Artillery fire will start at 2 a.m. and the infantry attack will take place at dawn.[2]

The prisoners also told their captors that fresh troops were in the area, including the elite 51st (Highland) Division:

> The anticipated attack will not be carried out by the 36th Division, but rather by the 51st Division. For this purpose, the relief should already have been under way on 17 November. This information was confirmed by a statement from one of the prisoners, who went back from the saphead to the front line to collect water on the evening of 17 November and found the 1st Royal Irish Fusiliers had already been relieved; by whom, he could not find out in the dark. Before the 1st RIF went into the line on 13 November, the prisoners saw pioneers from 51st Division (8th Royal Scots) in Metz-en-Couture, as well as various men from other battalions of 51st Division (Gordon Highlanders, Seaforth Highlanders and Royal Highlanders) … Besides the Highlanders referred to above, on 17 November one of the prisoners saw officers and NCOs from a West Yorkshire battalion getting their bearings in the front line.[3]

The intelligence officer correctly surmised these were from 62nd Division, and were also probably involved in the attack.

It was fortunate for the British that the prisoners had no idea of the full scale of the offensive – and were unaware that instead of the three tanks they had seen, it would involve more than a hundred times as many. But they had still given away crucial information, and the Germans now began their own frenzied preparations to foil the enemy's plans.

A century later, and far from the fears and horrors of the battlefield, it is hard to comprehend what could have driven the men to commit this act of betrayal, which completely overshadowed the earlier revelations of Sergeant Sam Phillips in terms of its military significance. Part of the reason no doubt lay in the men's feeling that they had been abandoned in No Man's Land. They told their captors about the sequence of events leading up to the raid:

> On the morning of 17 November the sergeant, together with ten men from his company, was ordered to hold a sap about 400 metres in front of the fire-trench until the morning of the 19th. They were given provisions for two days, but on the other hand to their amazement no Lewis gun and crew were assigned to them, although this sap ... was normally always held with one and sometimes even two Lewis guns. In addition, it was usual until then for around 30 men to hold these saps. The prisoners could only conclude from the strange circumstances surrounding their mission that the supposed imminent relief of their division was to remain concealed from the enemy in the event of a forcible German reconnaissance. The prisoners had the feeling they were being sacrificed, and were very bitter about this.[4]

However, the German report also reveals a darker side to the story. Of the six men captured, four were Irish, including two Catholics – one from Londonderry and the other from southern Ireland. It was a time of turmoil in Ireland, and some of the prisoners were motivated by hostility to British rule. The interrogation report noted:

> The political situation in Ireland seems to have strongly affected the morale of the Irishmen who are still present in the division in large numbers. A great animosity prevails towards England, with no interest whatsoever in her war aims ... The Irishmen among the prisoners are thoroughly war-weary and speak badly of the English. They say if an uprising takes place in Ireland, they would take up arms against England without more ado. Such an uprising was only a matter of time. It now had a much greater chance of success, as a great deal had been learned from the mistakes of the last rebellion in Easter 1916.[5]

It might be claimed that the information was extracted under duress, though this was expressly denied by an officer of the 84th Infantry Regiment who was himself captured a few days later: 'I would like to briefly comment here, how much the treatment of the prisoners [from the raid] contrasted with the way the English later dealt with us. Nothing was taken from them, although their handsome equipment aroused a good deal of envy, particularly their long rubber boots. They were not mistreated in any way, but rather people regarded them with respect.'[6]

This is borne out by a singular piece of evidence. Some time after their capture, the Germans took a photograph showing four of the prisoners posing with their guards. The men, wearing greatcoats and one with a bandaged hand, appear sombre but calm. A gaunt, lanky man wearing a cloth cap must be the corporal who was said to be 'as tall as a tree', while the other three are presumably some of the private soldiers. Behind them are two of their captors, one of whom is smiling, and it is hard not to notice the relaxed, companionable way in which his hand rests on the shoulder of the prisoner in front.[7]

* * *

The men who were captured have never been named, and in doing so we should be careful not to accuse any individual over what happened. The interrogation report is an aggregate of statements from all six prisoners, and in most cases there is nothing to identify the source. There is a clear focus on the grievances of the Irish, and attention must therefore focus on the four private soldiers, though two were from the Ulster Protestant community which has traditionally been loyal to Britain. The fact is we do not know who said what, and none of us should point the finger of blame unless we have experienced a similar desperate situation for ourselves.

The main prize for the Germans was the sergeant in charge of the squad, who was described as an 'Offizierstellvertreter', or 'trainee officer'. The interrogation report gives a detailed account of his military career, but despite this it would be impossible to identify him were it not for the records compiled by the International Committee of the Red Cross in Switzerland, and now available online.[8] A search through several thousand pages reveals the names of six men who were captured in the Trescault area on 18 November, and among them is Sergeant William Harold Whitaker.

By a stroke of fate, Sergeant Whitaker's service record has survived, and this precisely matches the account of his career given in the German report. The records also show he put up a fight, having been shot and bayoneted in the shoulder and hand during the raid.[9] In fact, examining Sergeant Whitaker's military record, it is hard to believe he could have committed any act of disloyalty. He had been born in North London and was just twenty years old at the time of the raid,[10] though he told his captors he was twenty-two.[11] He had joined the Territorial Army in 1913, and a month after the outbreak of war he was posted to Malta with 3rd Bn London Regiment to free up regular soldiers guarding the island. The battalion moved to France at the start of 1915,[12] and Private Whitaker soon excelled himself and was mentioned in dispatches for gallantry.[13]

He suffered a sprained knee in early 1916, but this proved an unexpected boost to his military career, for on recovery he was posted to GHQ at Rouen to work as a clerk in the so-called Third Echelon.[14] As he explained to the Germans: 'This department handles personnel issues and maintains lists of every single member of the British Expeditionary Force in France from the moment they are posted from the reinforcement depot at home. Well over 1,000 people work in the department.' Asked about relations between the British military and the French authorities and local residents, he said these were 'completely harmonious'.[15] By now he had been promoted to acting sergeant and was in line for a commission, but first he had to serve with a front-line battalion and was therefore attached to 1st Bn Royal Irish Fusiliers.[16]

Although Sergeant Whitaker gave the Germans a detailed account of his career, there was nothing in it that could have been of military value to them. They were not so interested in the other prisoners, commenting merely that 'with one exception they were born in Ireland, and were manual labourers by trade. Two of them belonged to the Special Reserve before the war, the others joined up as Kitchener men in 1915.'[17] Again it is necessary to scour the Red Cross records to find out more, and these enable us to identify five members of D Company, 1st Bn Royal Irish Fusiliers, whose details match the relevant date and place of capture.[18]

One of them was Lance-Corporal Frederick Charles Rowe, and photographs suggest he may have been the corporal who the Germans said was 'as tall as a tree'.[19] Lance-Corporal Rowe was also an Englishman, having been born in Hertfordshire, where his father was the foreman of a sewage farm. Frederick worked as a council labourer before joining the Bedfordshire Regiment and going to France with them in January 1915.[20]

Of the four Irishmen, one was actually English by birth, namely George Reginald Ball, listed variously as a private and corporal, who had been born in the garrison town of Aldershot nineteen years before. However, he was raised in Belfast where his father was a printer and a member of the Salvation Army. Private James Cope was slightly older at twenty-five, and a Belfast Protestant born and bred. He seems to have had unimpeachable Loyalist credentials, and the records suggest his father had joined the Royal Irish Rifles in 1886, and later signed the Ulster Covenant pledging support to the British crown. James himself had been in France since December 1914, while Rifleman George Cope, believed to be his brother, had been killed fighting with the Royal Irish Rifles in early 1917.[21]

The other two prisoners were Roman Catholics, and may therefore have had a more contentious relationship with the British state and its institutions. Private Neil McCauley was the twenty-eight year-old son of a council labourer from Londonderry, though his family roots were in County Donegal. The records are hard to interpret, but it appears his cousin Private Cornelius McCauley joined the Royal Munster Fusiliers before the war and died of wounds in Gallipoli in 1915. If so, this could easily have fed any sense of anger and disillusionment that Neil may have felt. Finally, Private Laurence O'Brien was a twenty-six year-old from County Wicklow in southern Ireland, who joined the Royal Irish Fusiliers in October 1914 and had been in France since August 1915. He was wounded in the hand and thigh during the raid, showing he also put up a fight to avoid being taken prisoner.[22]

* * *

However angry some of the men were about the situation in Ireland, and about their thankless posting to 'E' Sap, it still seems extraordinary that they could have passed on such sensitive information to the enemy, knowing it would endanger the lives of their own friends and fellow countrymen, apart from anyone else. It seems all the harder to believe that this betrayal emanated from 36th Division, whose heroism on 1 July 1916 has made it an enduring symbol of loyalty and sacrifice. However, the interrogation report claimed the division had changed beyond all recognition, and only half its members were even Irish. According to the German report:

> The division does not seem to have been brought back to its full fighting strength following heavy losses in Flanders. The good reputation the division has enjoyed up to now can no longer be sustained with the inferior reinforcements now arriving. Firstly, for months the reinforcements have not been completely made up of Irishmen. They now mostly consist of people from all parts of England together, including many convalescents who have been wounded two or three times before, and in the view of the prisoners are not physically up to the demands of war. Also an increasing number of conscripts are arriving who lack any front-line experience ... In view of these conditions, the current military value of the 36th Division cannot be rated highly.[23]

The poor quality of reinforcements was tragically underlined a few weeks before the raid, when a twenty-six year-old soldier in 1st Bn Royal Irish Fusiliers was court-martialled for desertion. Private George Hanna from Belfast had previously been sentenced to death not once, but twice for deserting or attempting to desert, first at Gallipoli in 1915 and then in Salonika the following year. Each time the sentence was commuted to imprisonment and then suspended so he could return to service, but with such a chaotic record it was unlikely he would ever make an effective soldier.[24]

A court martial on 19 October heard he had gone missing shortly after being ordered into the trenches for the first time with 1st Battalion, and gave himself up three days later in Amiens. His defence was pitiful but unconvincing: 'I had absolutely no intention of deserting. If I had not been detained I should have returned to camp. I have been three years on service; two of my brothers have been killed in France, and one at sea. I was refused leave to go and see my people. My last leave was in December 1914. I absented myself because I was upset at not being able to get leave, & I had heard from my sister to say that she had been expecting me home & when I did not come, it upset her & she was not well.'[25]

Private Hanna had been given enough chances, and the verdict was formally announced on 5 November: 'The death sentence on No. 12609 Pte. G. Hanna was promulgated at Barrosa Hall Metz ... This was the first death sentence ordered to be carried out in this Battn. since its arrival in France. Pte. Hanna was only about 5 hours with the Battn. He having joined with a draft but when warned for the trenches, disappeared. Firing Party, under Lieut. G. Reeve, M.C. proceeded to [Divisional Headquarters].'[26] Private Hanna was shot at 6.43 the next morning in the village of Ytres. Along with other men who suffered a similar punishment, he was pardoned in 2006 'as recognition that he was one of the many victims of the First World War and that execution was not a fate he deserved'.[27]

Of course this was an isolated incident, and after three years of war perhaps the most surprising thing is that there were not more of them. Whatever the Germans wanted to believe, 1st Bn Royal Irish Fusiliers, along with the rest of 36th (Ulster) Division, remained a potent force which would go on to fight gallantly in the Battle of Cambrai, and for the rest of the war.

At the same time, the political situation in Ireland was clearly having an effect, as demonstrated a few weeks later when four men from the Royal Dublin Fusiliers slipped away from their trenches south of Cambrai and gave themselves up to the enemy. This was a more deliberate form of desertion than the aimless drifting that had cost Private Hanna his life, and the German interrogation report provides a lengthy exposition of Irish hostility to British rule and support for Sinn Fein. It concludes with an extraordinary message, which they asked to be sent to their former comrades and signed with their own names:

To all good Irishmen of the 16th Division.

Dear Chums
  You are all a lot of fools to be staying there in these God dam dirty trenches. There is no such thing as shooting you. They Germans is nicest people I ever met we are getting plenty of bread and no such thing as bullybeef for your dinner. 2 blankets and a fine straw bed to lie on if I could only get back to tell you the life we have here is better than Blity [sic]. Take my advice and come over and not be fighting for England any longer.[28]

* * *

Whatever the combination of desperation, discontent and devil-may-care that led the captured Royal Irish Fusiliers to give away details of the coming operation, the Germans only had a few hours in which to react, and there was considerable uncertainty at the highest levels about whether the prisoners' revelations were accurate, and how best to respond.

The mention of tanks brought to mind a mystery that had exercised the Germans for some weeks. At the end of October, they had found the corpse of a British soldier in No Man's Land between Trescault and Ribécourt. He had obviously been killed while on patrol, and on examining his body, they found a Tank Corps badge in his wallet. It was a perplexing discovery in such a quiet sector, and suggested the dead man might have belonged to a tank crew, or at least come into contact with one that was visiting the area to prepare for an attack.[29]

In fact, a meticulous search of British and German records has revealed that the mystery had an innocent explanation. The body was that of Rifleman Samuel Walker, who was in 12th Bn Rifle Brigade and was killed during a night patrol on 20/21 October. He had previously spent several months as a gunner in D Battalion of the Tank Corps, and the badge which aroused so much suspicion was therefore a souvenir of his own service in the tanks. Although he had inadvertently set alarm-bells ringing, the Germans could draw no firm conclusions from their find, and Rifleman Walker's memento did not expose his former comrades to any additional danger. However, it was to have tragic consequences for his own family, since the Germans notified the Red Cross that they had found his body, but incorrectly reported him as belonging to the Tank Corps. As a result the news failed to reach his parents in Lincolnshire, who were told it was 'quite possible' that he had been captured. Samuel was eventually presumed dead in August 1918, and his grave was finally identified in the 1920s.[30]

However, the prisoners had now given more definite evidence of the threat facing the Germans. They could draw some comfort from the knowledge that any attack on Havrincourt would run into a determined defence, with the village itself occupied by 1st Battalion, 84th Infantry Regiment and the 2nd Battalion manning the line to their left (from the German viewpoint), and their supporting artillery dug in behind the Flesquières ridge. The position was already a strong one, but to be on the safe side the Germans now rushed both infantry and artillery reinforcements into the area to resist any possible advance.

This was helped by the arrival of thousands of men who were returning from the Eastern Front following the collapse of Russia. By coincidence, units from 107th Division had already begun arriving in Cambrai on the morning of 19 November, the plan being to let them find their feet on the 'silent front' before they plunged into any real fighting.

There should have been plenty of time to gather themselves and their equipment after the five-day rail journey, and then to familiarize themselves with the terrain and the other units around them. On 25 November they were due to replace a unit of the Landwehr, older reservists who were holding a section of the front line in front of the village of Ribécourt, south-east of Flesquières. The Germans were well aware that the Landwehr were a weak link, but they were only holding the line temporarily while 27th Reserve Infantry Regiment was withdrawn for training.

Artillery support for the incoming 107th Division was provided by 213th Field Artillery Regiment (FAR), and on the day of arrival its officers attended a briefing given by Generalleutnant (i.e. Major-General) Oskar Freiherr (i.e. Baron) von Watter, commander of 54th Division which held the entire sector including Havrincourt and Flesquières. With his white hair and moustache, von Watter bore a certain resemblance to 'Uncle' Harper, his opposite number in 51st (Highland) Division, and they also shared a nickname: his men referred to him fondly as 'Onkel Oskar'. Von Watter's own officers often stressed how vigorously he had responded to the warning of an attack, but one of the newly-arrived artillery officers told a different story, recalling the words of his briefing: 'Gentlemen, you have arrived in a completely quiet sector. The English are not planning anything. It may be they'll try to capture this outpost here, they have done something like it before, but I think even that is unlikely.'[31]

It was a reassuring message, and afterwards the battery commanders set off on horseback to inspect the area. When they returned to their billets a few hours later, the place was in turmoil. The information given by the prisoners had been flashed across the front and a heightened state of alert was ordered for the night ahead. The travel-weary men of 213th FAR had been ordered to deploy immediately to reinforce Flesquières, even though the sector was unknown to them.

Six batteries, each of three guns, were positioned in an arc behind the ridge of Flesquières and in front of the neighbouring village of Graincourt. The disused gun positions they took over varied greatly in strength – some were well built with protective shelters for the guns and interconnecting bunkers, while others had little cover for the guns and the dugouts had only one entrance, making them a death-trap under bombardment. Most worryingly of all, some of the positions were surrounded by old shell craters, showing their location was already well known to the enemy.

As they dragged their guns into position that night and the horse-drawn limbers jingled off into the darkness, the only consolation was that they were not alone: the area was also dotted with the batteries of 108th FAR, which formed part of the resident 54th Division and had been in the area since the summer, while the Landwehr also had support from 282nd FAR and a number of batteries of Landwehr foot artillery. The main problem was a chronic lack of ammunition, and the arrival of reinforcements placed an even greater strain on the limited supplies.

Infantry reinforcements were also pushed forward in case of attack. As an immediate measure, the 3rd Battalion, 84th Infantry Regiment was moved forward from its rest quarters in Noyelles to occupy the trenches in and around Flesquières. The seasoned troops of 27th Reserve Infantry Regiment, who had been temporarily replaced by the Landwehr, also began moving forward during the evening.[32] One of the officers described their departure for Flesquières from Fontaine, near Cambrai, at 10 p.m. (i.e. 9 p.m. UK time): 'The company moved off in the best of spirits ... As we marched through the headlight beams of the rumbling vehicles, our shadows marched alongside and ahead of us, magnified to enormous size against the bare gables of the houses – an impressive spectacle. During the approach march we witnessed the build-up of artillery from 107th Infantry Division behind Flesquières.'[33]

Amid this frenzy of activity, Major Fritz Hofmeister, the commander of 84th Infantry Regiment, felt fully in control. The epitome of a Prussian officer, he was described as 'a giant in stature, like a mighty cannon, overcoming everything through the iron rule of military discipline which knows nothing but giving and obeying orders, who understood better than anyone how to exercise this skill'.[34] When an officer of 27th Reserve Infantry Regiment reported to him with reinforcements, his response was dismissive: 'You men of the 27th Reserve are always a bit jumpy, to be sure. If there is an attack, we can take care of things for ourselves.'[35]

Many of his officers in the front line shared this confidence. Hauptmann (i.e. Captain) Wilhelm Wille was the commander of 1st Battalion, 84th Infantry Regiment, which held the village of Havrincourt – the main objective of the British raid if the prisoners were to be believed. However, it was obvious to him that the way to take such a strong position was not by assaulting it head-on, but rather by attacking the flanks to encircle the village and ridge from behind: 'I envisaged not so much a frontal attack ... as a thrust by the English on either side to cut off Havrincourt. On the map it was easy to establish that that was the probability.'[36] His assessment may have been reinforced by the knowledge that on either side of the 84th the line was held by units of the Landwehr, made up of older men who had been recalled to the colours and whose fighting capabilities were dubious.

Fortunately for them, the British knew nothing of this vulnerability, having refrained from raiding or other aggressive activity in the run-up to the offensive. In any case, the idea of a flanking attack had already been dismissed, according to the Tank Corps staff officer Lieutenant-Colonel John Fuller, who had advocated this approach but was over-ruled in favour of an unbroken line of men and machines: 'The truth is, that the plan as devised by the Third Army was not a work of art but a work of force – not the thrust of a rapier but the blow of a battering-ram.'[37]

To the left of Hauptmann Wille's 1st Battalion (from a German viewpoint), the line directly in front of Flesquières was held by 2nd Battalion, 84th Infantry Regiment, whose officers were also sceptical about the threat. They had been through similar fire-drills in the past, and were well aware that the British would not attack without a long preliminary bombardment. Despite this they now had to look lively, as described by their ordnance officer Leutnant Johannes Langfeldt:

> The order came in to supply the men with five days' rations and to distribute ammunition. That task kept me busy all afternoon on the 19th. The company commanders were called together for a conference. None of them took the matter completely seriously either. Towards evening the orders mounted up ... There were comings and goings from the battalion dayroom: runners went to and fro, from the regiment, to the companies and back again. Closer contact was established with the Landwehr battalion next to us [i.e. the 387th to their left], and inquiries came in from the machine-gun company and trench mortars, with messages from them. Late in the evening several machine gunners from the 27th Regiment reported to us, having been put at the battalion's disposal; they had to be allocated to their positions. Above all we tried to get hold of armour-piercing ammunition, but there were no supplies to be had.[38]

The 2nd Battalion was commanded by Hauptmann Harro Soltau, who attracted even greater adulation from his men than Major R.O.C. Ward did from his. Only two years separated the two in terms of age, but there were few other similarities, for whereas Ward had been an accountant until the outbreak of war and was married with children, Soltau had spent his entire career in the army, which was in a sense his family. Ward's greatest passion was sport in all its forms, but if Soltau had ever kicked a ball in his life, no-one saw fit to record the fact. At the same time, Ward's reputation as a cast-iron disciplinarian was strangely at odds with that of Soltau, a pastor's son who had a quicksilver quality we do not generally associate with the German army. He had been a strong-willed youngster with an outrageous gift for mimicry, and the decision to join up caused consternation to his parents, who joked that he should be on the stage but really wanted him to go into forestry. Major Hofmeister may represent our stereotypical view of the Prussian military machine, but it was also capable of fostering men such as Soltau, who was widely known as 'tolle Harro' ('good old Harro') and was renowned for exploits such as turning a winter training exercise into a huge snowball fight, and appropriating a horse-drawn carriage with a group of drunken colleagues for a breakneck cross-country drive on the Kaiser's birthday.[39]

Antics aside, he also had a solid professional reputation, and just as R.O.C. Ward was revered by his fellow company commander Major Watson, so Harro Soltau was praised by the other battalion commanders. Hauptmann Wille described Soltau as 'the image of a dashing, agile officer, like a razor-sharp damascened blade, of daredevil audacity, unshaken by every danger thrown at him which he overcame with unsurpassed energy, sweeping everything before him – the idol of his battalion'.[40]

However, there was one shadow hanging over Soltau: during the fighting at Verdun a year before he had been the most senior officer inside Fort Douaumont, which was captured from the French at the start of the battle and was now subjected by them to relentless bombardment, filling its shattered corridors with poison gas and threatening to detonate stockpiles of explosives. Cut off from the outside world and badly gassed himself, Soltau eventually ordered the depleted garrison to abandon the fort – a decision which handed the French a major symbolic victory, and for which he was held responsible by his own high command. Soltau avoided demotion thanks to the support of his divisional commander, Generalleutnant Freiherr von Watter, but he was still scarred by the events at Verdun and their aftermath.[41]

As evening fell on 19 November, Hauptmann Soltau and his men could at least relax in the knowledge that they had done as much as they could to prepare. As things quietened down, 'good old Harro' gathered half-a-dozen officers around him to unwind in the battalion dayroom in the Stollenweg, a sunken road lined with dugouts which contained his command post and headquarters. As always his dog Thyra was by his side, her collar labelled '2nd Battalion Messenger Dog' as a ploy by Soltau to get round the official ban on keeping pets at the front. Among the group was Leutnant Bernhard Hegermann, who had triggered the whole commotion by leading the raid in which the prisoners had been captured. Leutnant Langfeldt recalled: 'I believe it was either his or his wife's birthday, so the captain invited him to have a bottle of wine. This quiet, convivial hour on the eve of the fateful day shows, as in a mirror, the lack of concern we all felt despite every warning.' After that Leutnant Langfeldt had to go round to check his sentries, and when he got back he found the battalion headquarters in a state of deep repose.[42]

CHAPTER 24

To Shake Mightily the Earth

When the tank crews awoke on 19 November they were filled with a mixture of excitement and dread, knowing the attack would take place early the next morning, and they would have little if any sleep before then.

In the morning, Major R.O.C. Ward called a parade and addressed the members of his company. His words were recorded by Second Lieutenant Macintosh:

> He reminded them of their last attack and the many obstacles they had encountered – bad ground, bad weather, bad luck. Now was their chance to show that as in difficult circumstances they could stolidly fight against their difficulties, so when fortune at last turned they could make the most of a good opportunity. Once again [No. 12] Company had been chosen for the task which demanded enterprise and staying power; for, whereas the other companies had definite objectives, they who formed the second wave were first to overcome a series of definite obstacles, and were then to push on with an unlimited objective. He had often before spoken of 'pooping off into the blue'; at last there was nothing to prevent their doing so. The whole responsibility of the attack had been deliberately thrown on the Tank

Opposite and overleaf: Map 6 shows the sector attacked by 51st (Highland) Division, with D and E Battalions of the Tank Corps, on 20 November 1917.

On the left-hand side, the starting positions of D Battalion and the units of 153rd Infantry Brigade are shown, based on a detailed map in the brigade's War Diary. This includes the six wire-crushing tanks which led the advance, followed by the first-wave tanks of Nos. 10 and 11 Companies. Further back are the second-wave tanks of No. 12 Company, including D51 *Deborah*.

No similar map has been found for E Battalion and 152nd Infantry Brigade on the right-hand side, so their general presumed locations are shown.

The map shows how the leading troops and tanks formed up in front of the British front line before moving across No Man's Land to take the German outposts located there, and then attacking the first main system of trenches. Here a number of tanks broke down or became ditched, while two from E Battalion were knocked out by artillery early in the battle (approximate positions only are given for E Battalion tanks).

Ahead lay the broad valley known as the Grand Ravine, beyond which the ridge rises gradually towards Flesquières. The second wave of tanks and infantry advanced up this slope, crossing the railway embankment before attacking the second system of trenches skirting the village.

The German artillery batteries massed on the reverse slope of the Flesquières ridge are shown, though the available maps are sketchy and must be treated with caution. Map 6b shows the disposition of German forces, while Map 6c shows the plan for the British artillery bombardment which effectively laid down the timetable for the attack.

Contour lines have been omitted from the map for clarity, but these are shown on Map 6a, while Map 6d gives an overview of the full offensive mounted on 20 November. See Map 7 for a detailed view of the next phase of the attack on Flesquières. A full order of battle is given in Appendices B and C.

To Shake Mightily the Earth 155

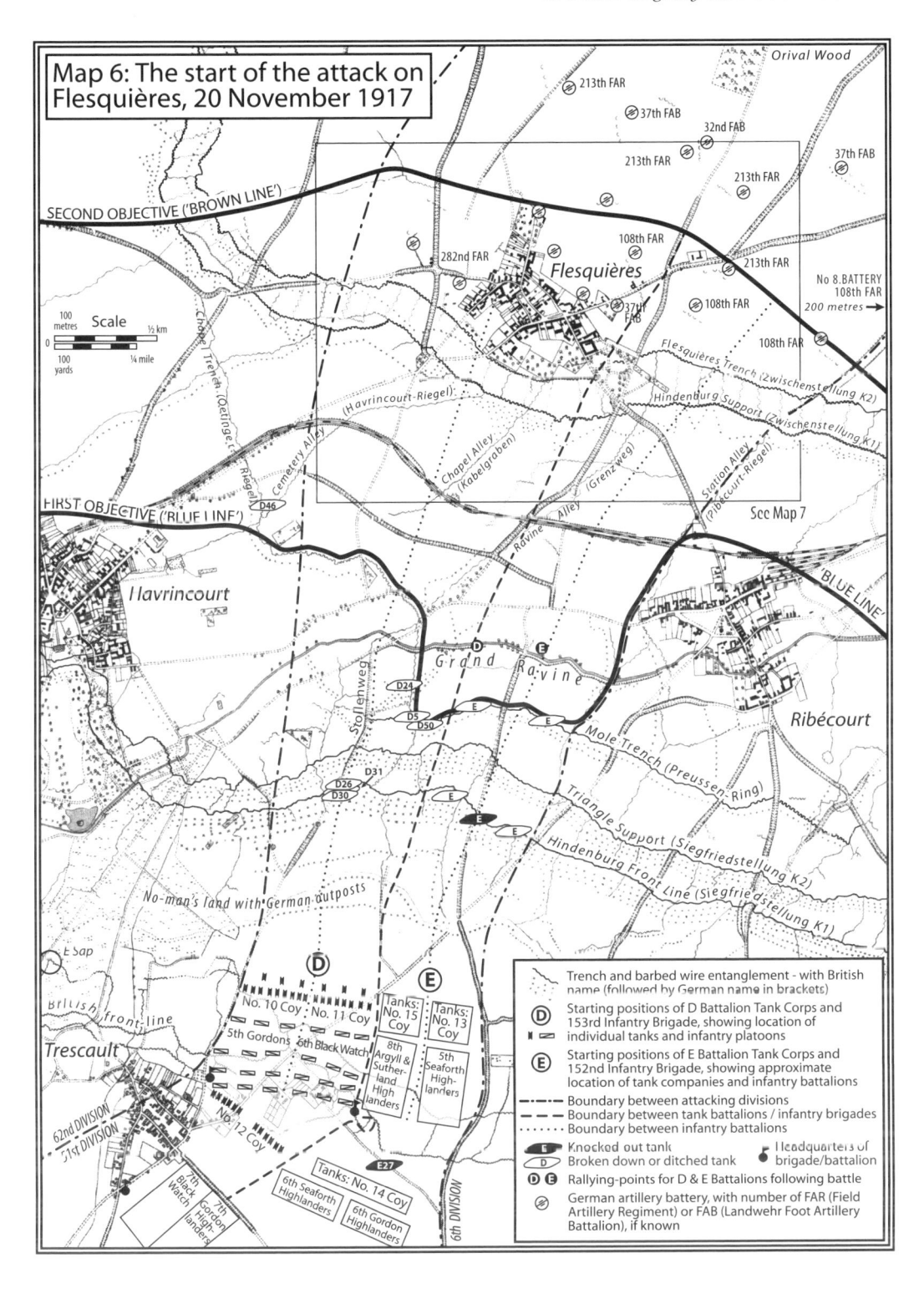

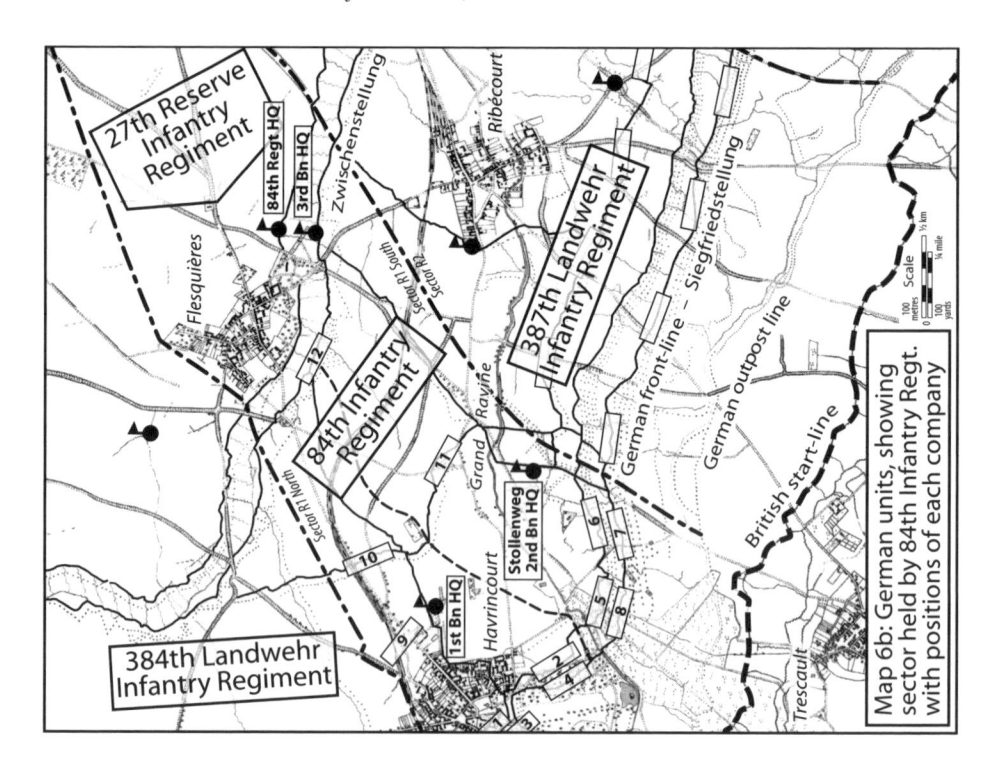

156 Deborah *and the War of the Tanks, 1917*

Map 6b: German units, showing sector held by 84th Infantry Regt. with positions of each company

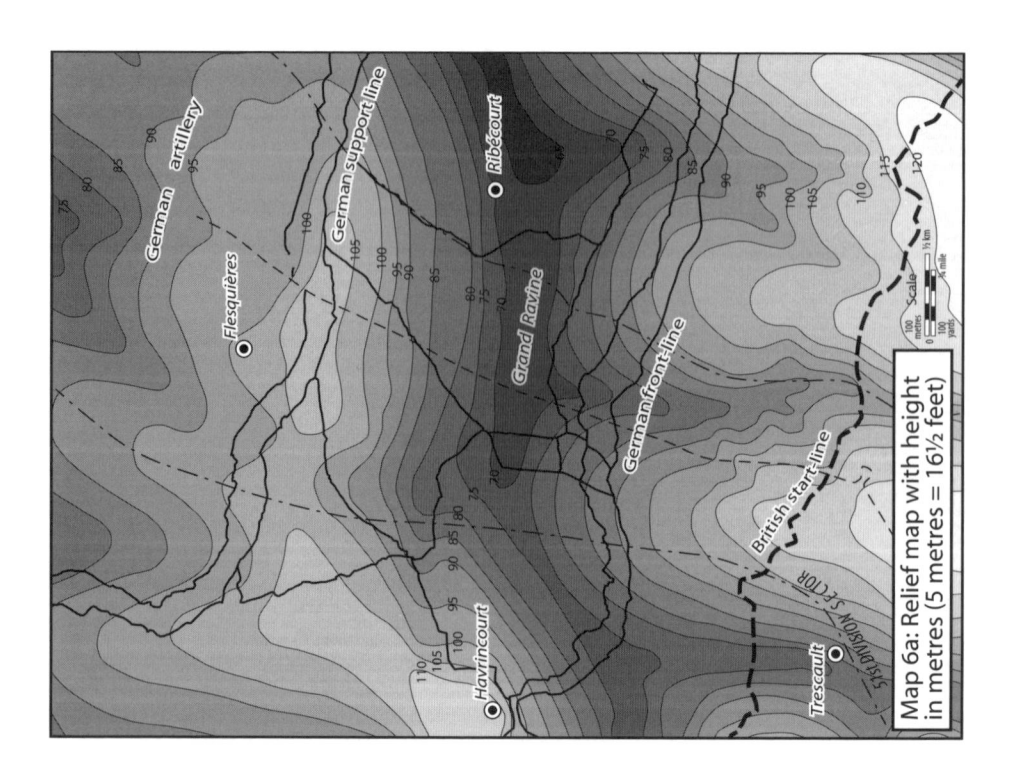

Map 6a: Relief map with height in metres (5 metres = 16½ feet)

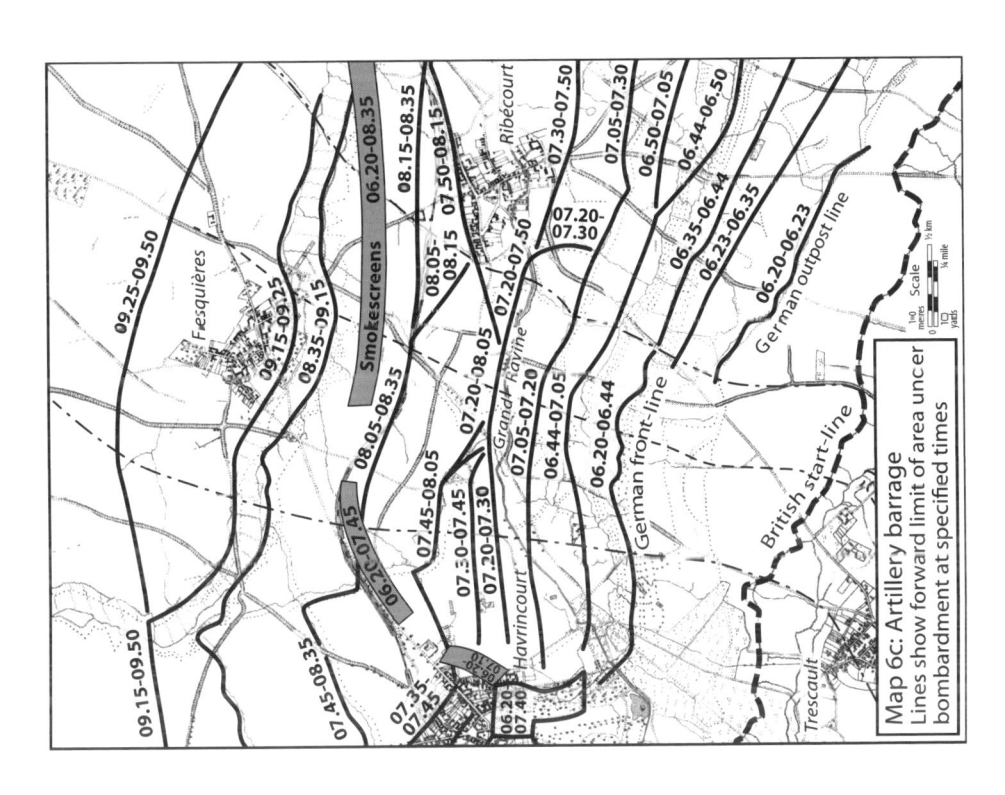

To Shake Mightily the Earth 157

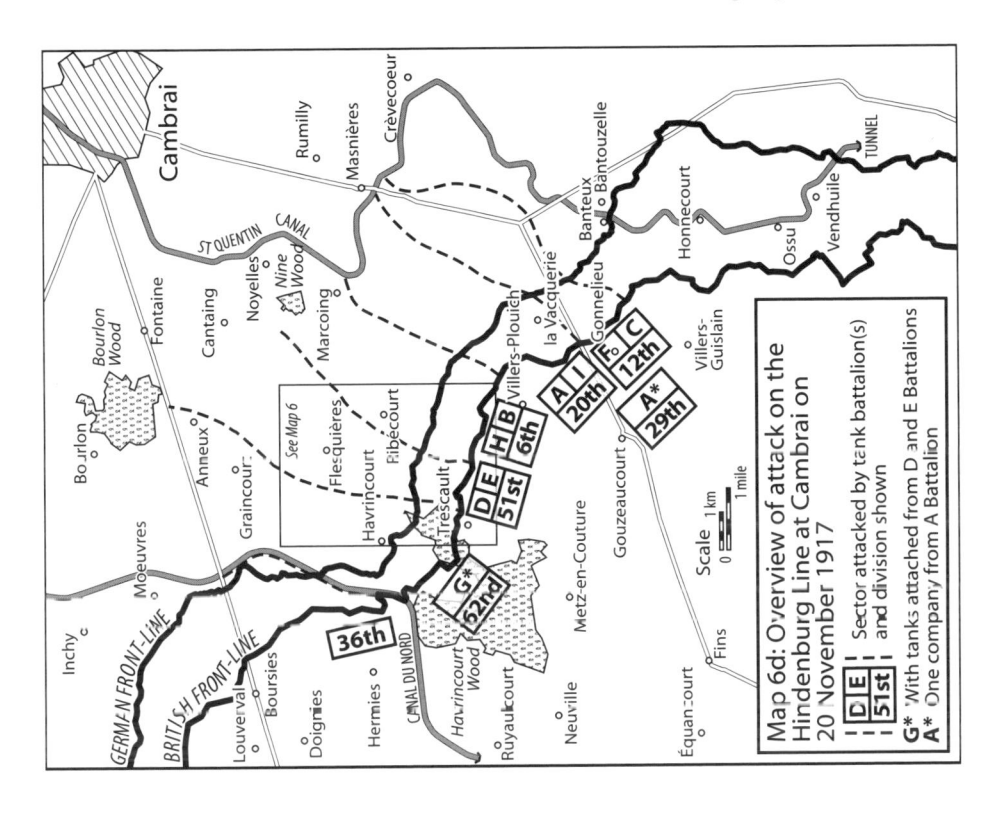

Map 6d: Overview of attack on the Hindenburg Line at Cambrai on 20 November 1917

Map 6c: Artillery barrage
Lines show forward limit of area under bombardment at specified times

Corps; it was their supreme opportunity. England expected that every tank would do its damndest.[1]

The last sentence was almost certainly not uttered by Major Ward, as it was a widely reported but inaccurate summary of the special order issued by Brigadier-General Elles to the Tank Corps before the battle.[2] But 'Tosh' probably felt that even if R.O.C. Ward had not said it, he would have wanted to.

After they had been dismissed, Frank Heap and his brother officers began preparing themselves for action, along the lines noted by 'Tosh': 'Following his invariable rule, he destroyed all unnecessary papers, and packed his valise ready to go down the line in case of need. Having written a couple of field postcards and a letter, he cleaned and loaded his revolver, arranged his maps, packed his haversack with shaving-kit and money in case he should be wounded, filled his flask and cigarette-case, inspected his field-dressing, gave his servant instructions, and went into lunch.'[3]

For everyone in Havrincourt Wood, 19 November was a day of 'almost unbearable suspense'. They were aware that some men had been captured the night before, but could only hope they knew nothing, or had revealed nothing. Major Watson was caught up in the tension: 'We did not know what the Germans had discovered from their prisoners. We could not believe that the attack could be really a surprise. Perhaps the enemy, unknown to us, had concentrated sufficient guns to blow us to pieces. We looked up for the German aeroplanes, which surely would fly low over the wood and discover its contents. Incredibly, nothing happened. The morning passed and the afternoon – a day was never so long ...'[4]

But for the crew of *Deborah*, the time passed in a blur as they made their final preparations, ready to leave the shelter of the wood and begin the slow move forward to their starting positions as soon as dusk fell. Before then they had to go over their tank methodically inspecting every tiny detail, checking the controls were working smoothly, stripping and cleaning the six Lewis guns, searching through the drums of ammunition looking for any speck of grit which might cause a blockage, and loading up supplies of petrol and water.

At 3 p.m. they had to pick up their carrier pigeons from a drop-off point at the edge of the wood. Once the tanks had gone into action, these fragile creatures were the most reliable means of communicating with the staff who were directing operations, though it was strictly a one-way traffic. The tank crew would write a message on a tiny scrap of paper and attach it to the pigeon's leg, hoping it would fly more than ten miles (or nearly twenty kilometres) back to its loft in Bapaume, from where the message would be telephoned to the headquarters of IV Corps. This was considerably more effective than the 'makeshift and exceedingly clumsy' wireless station which was to be carried forward in one of E Battalion's tanks and then set up in the Grand Ravine, if all went well.[5]

When all the preparations were completed, Frank Heap would have addressed his crew, running through the details of the operation with them once again, and doing his best to inspire them as he had done so often when his team was about to run onto the rugby or hockey pitch. There was a special occasion to be marked, since it was Gunner Joseph Cheverton's twentieth birthday the next day, but as Frank probably remarked, the celebrations would have to wait until they had given a hell of a birthday present to the Boche. In the meantime no doubt Joe received greetings from his family in Cambridge, and one scented card which he kept to read in private, and about which he would have received much teasing from the others. After that, Frank dismissed the crew to their final meal before action, and everyone settled down to wait for the dusk.

Earlier in the day, Second Lieutenant Horace Birks had noticed some unusual activity in the wood: 'A table was set up quite near us. [We] wondered what on earth was happening, and it was the brigade padre, Talbot … he started communion.' No gathering of more than ten men was permitted (the major's parade presumably being an exception), so the Reverend Neville Talbot, who was the Fifth Army's Assistant Chaplain-General, held one small service after another: 'The people took communion throughout the day, and he ran the whole day with [ten] people. It was quite astonishing.'[6]

Perhaps the Reverend Talbot used as his text a Biblical prophecy which he quoted in his book on religion at the Front, and which with God's help would come to pass for the Germans the next morning. Its subject was the day of reckoning: 'And the loftiness of man shall be bowed down, and the haughtiness of men shall be brought low; and the Lord alone shall be exalted in that day … And men shall go … into the holes of the earth, from before the terror of the Lord and from the glory of His majesty, when He ariseth to shake mightily the earth.'[7]

* * *

At 9.30 that evening the men paraded by sections, and a few minutes were spent giving them last-minute instructions. It was the final opportunity for Captain Graeme Nixon to address the crews of his three tanks, and after he had wished them luck they climbed aboard their machines, and fifteen minutes later they began crawling out of the wood.[8]

They were moving at last, but it was a painfully slow process. There were still eight-and-a-half hours to go before zero, and they had less than two miles (or three kilometres) to go to their jumping-off point, but the tanks had to clear the wood as soon as possible so that batteries of field guns could move into their pre-prepared positions. It was also vital to avoid making any noise that might alert the enemy, and the orders issued by Lieutenant Gerald Edwards to his crew in D34 *Diallance* stressed: 'Tanks to go at minimum pace. Throttle down as slowly as possible. Absolutely no talking in the tanks. No steering by brakes.'[9] The final point was vital to avoid revving the engine, but according to his grandson Brigadier Ben Edwards (a modern-day tank commander), it meant that steering would be a laborious process and the journey would be 'tedious in the extreme'.

The tanks of No. 11 Company led the way, followed by No. 10 Company,[10] and Major Watson described how 'At 8.45 P.M. my tanks began to move cautiously out of the wood and formed into column. At 9.30 P.M., with engines barely turning over, they glided imperceptibly and almost without noise towards the trenches. Standing in front of my own tanks, I could not hear them at two hundred yards.'[11]

As *Deborah* and the other tanks of No. 12 Company swung into line behind, Second Lieutenant Macintosh looked back the way they had come:

In this supreme hour of secrecy, not the glimmer of a torch might be shown, and tank commanders must strain their eyes in the dark and see as best they might. But in front of every tank was a glowing point of light – every pilot was smoking, and with his cigarette could signal to his crew. The irresistibly animal appearance of the tanks was greatly heightened as they loomed ghostly out of the darkness …

After half an hour's slow running, the tanks swung across a road. Like every other road on that fateful night, it was a solid mass of slow-moving traffic. The thousands of empty gun-emplacements would not still be empty at zero! As they went forward the night was stealthily alive with chinks of harness and rumble of wheels, and everywhere they passed groups of men busy with mysterious activities. Occasionally a star-shell floated in the distant air, its light revealing that the country was full of men and horses; then darkness closed down again, and only their stealthy noises betrayed their presence.[12]

The infantry were also moving up, as the Tank Corps staff officer Captain Evan Charteris discovered when he drove to the 1st Tank Brigade wireless station near Metz-en-Couture, a few miles behind the front line.

> When we got back to the motor, we could hear the tramp of men descending the road we had just passed over. Presently a section of the night seemed to be advancing slowly towards us, an indistinguishable mass of the darkness; they came at a pace which just on the active side of standing still. As they passed us we learned that they were a Highland battalion, part of the 51st Division … None of them spoke, and their silence, the weight and slowness of their tread, and the solemnity of their passing by, bore such an implication of fate, and were shrouded with so much mystery by the night, that one felt as if one were hailing men no longer of this world.[13]

* * *

Meanwhile, *Deborah* and the other tanks of D Battalion continued their laborious progress, following white tapes laid by the reconnaissance officers to guide them towards the front line. The occasional chatter of machine guns now sounded very close in the darkness as they picked their way across the British support trenches, with infantry advancing in the open around them.

Some time after midnight, Major William Watson met up with D Battalion's commander, Lieutenant-Colonel William Kyngdon, and together they paid a final visit to the headquarters of the infantry battalions they were working with. Watson observed that 'the trenches were packed with Highlanders, and it was with difficulty that we made our way through them'.[14] After this Kyngdon went off to the infantry brigade headquarters in Trescault, where he would await the start of the attack.[15]

Some time between 4.30 and 5.30 am, the silence was shattered by a sudden bombardment away to their left, in the direction of Havrincourt.[16] Second Lieutenant Macintosh described how 'trench-mortars barked viciously, machine-guns took up the affray, and five-nines might be heard whining across, to crump methodically in the little village away to the left. What did it mean? Had the Boche heard? Did he suspect, or was it merely a case of nerves?'[17] The shelling nearly caused disaster for 5th Bn Gordon Highlanders, one of the units attacking with D Battalion. Their commander told how the bombardment 'caught many of our fellows as they were waiting in the open at the starting-point. I feared … this might seriously affect the whole scheme, as we had a number killed and wounded. Luckily the bombardment stopped as quickly as it had begun, and the situation – as far we were concerned – was saved. Whether this little attention had been due to suspicions which their captures of the night before had aroused, or whether it was merely an ordinary "strafe" may never be explained.'[18] In fact the Germans were very much on the alert after the warning of an impending attack, and the bombardment was their response to a report that barbed wire was being cut in preparation for the expected raid on Havrincourt. They now assumed that any threat had been dealt with, and the attackers were able to resume their vigil and await the coming of dawn.

Also waiting anxiously were the crews of D Battalion, who had now reached their starting positions in No Man's Land. Out in front were the six wire-crushing tanks from No. 11 Company which would lead the advance, while 150 yards behind them the remaining eighteen or so tanks of Nos. 10 and 11 Companies were drawn up in a long line abreast, each with their accompanying groups of infantry. Further back, just behind the British front line, were the twelve tanks of No. 12 Company including *Deborah*, ready to go forward in the second wave half-an-hour after zero.[19]

Unseen on either side of them in the mist and darkness, a continuous wall of men and machines extended for six miles (or ten kilometres) along the entire British front – a total of 378 fighting tanks, with tens of thousands of infantrymen behind them and cavalrymen moving into position further back, and 1,000 guns hidden in the woods and valleys, and the aircraft of the Royal Flying Corps preparing to take off from their airfields at the first glimmer of dawn. Incredible though it seems, this whole vast army had been brought into position without the enemy having the slightest warning, beyond what they had gleaned from their prisoners.

In the sector to be attacked by D Battalion, Major Watson described the scene ten minutes before zero hour: 'At 6.10 A.M. the tanks were in their allotted positions, clearly marked out by tapes which Jumbo had laid earlier in the night … I was standing on the parados of a trench. The movement at my feet had ceased. The Highlanders were ready with fixed bayonets. Not a gun was firing, but there was a curious murmur in the air. To right of me and to left of me, in the dim light were tanks – tanks lined up in front of the wire, tanks swinging into position, and one or two belated tanks climbing over the trenches.'[20] For once the weather was on their side, and a thin mist concealed the attackers from view as night began to fade to the palest grey.

For some of the tank crews, exhaustion now overcame the tension as the minutes ticked past. This was the case with Lieutenant Gerald Edwards in one of the wire-crushing tanks, D34 *Diallance*: 'I sat in the tank with my feet on the engine to keep them warm and had a nap.'[21] It was the same for Second Lieutenant Fred Dawson in E45 *Elles II*, named after the Tank Corps commander: '"Wake up, sir" – my sergeant gave me a vigorous shake, and as consciousness slowly returned, I realised that I had been sleeping on the metal floor of the tank, that we were ten yards behind our front line, and due to attack in about 15 minutes … With the help of a generous "tot" of rum, we crossed our front line to take up position with "tails up." Everything was dead quiet.'[22]

One of the infantry units supporting them, the 8th Bn Argyll and Sutherland Highlanders, also found solace in army rum, or more likely their own native whisky, as they prepared to leave the sandbagged safety of their trenches: 'Just about six o'clock, we of company headquarters finished the last of our "iron ration" in a mutual toast to "Over the bags, and the best of luck." That done, we earnestly scanned our watches.'[23]

Further back, Frank Heap and the officers of No. 12 Company gathered round their commander, Major R.O.C. Ward, to await zero hour, as described by Second Lieutenant Macintosh:

> It is a truism that the best way to overcome nervousness is to make a joke of it … every one there, from long experience, knew that his companions were experiencing the same symptoms, and was much too sure of himself to suppose that they indicated fear. But set the least imaginative of men in their position, a few yards from an enemy with whom in five minutes he will be engaged in a

desperate struggle for life, and whether he be brave man or coward … he must feel some warning of overstrung nerves. Consequently as the officers sat round the rim of a shell-hole, they busied themselves with humorous descriptions of their own feelings, interspersed with gleeful pictures of the state of unpreparedness of the enemy, and the awful surprise which awaited him.

So passed ten minutes. It was now Z-10, and rising with one accord, they went forward beyond the tanks and peered into No Man's Land. Somewhere ahead in battle array, [No. 10 and 11] Company awaited the signal which for them would be the beginning of the attack. In the grey dawn, the further ridge was just visible, but no tanks or infantry could be distinguished. Slowly, in ticks which might have been heart-beats, the seconds passed; five minutes to go, four minutes, three minutes, two minutes – a long breath.

'Now for it,' cried the Major.

With the words, as at some dread command, the silence was rent with stupendous clamour, as up and down the line for miles thousands of guns belched flame.[24]

CHAPTER 25

'Now For It!'

After so many failed hopes, so many months of preparation, the moment of truth had finally arrived. Whatever happened next would determine whether tanks were truly viable as a weapon of war, and whether their crewmen would live or die.

Waiting by his tank as the barrage began, Second Lieutenant Wilfred Bion heard 'a moaning in the air'[1] as the first torrent of shells passed overhead, and then 'all the enemy trenches were outlined in low-bursting shrapnel. It looked like clouds of white with golden rain in the bursts. It was very beautiful – and very deadly.'[2]

The 4th Bn Seaforth Highlanders were in reserve at Metz-en-Couture, and from nearly three miles (or nearly four kilometres) behind the line, Lance-Corporal Willie Pennie was stunned by the scale of the bombardment:

> The roar of … guns of all calibres seemed to rend the very skies. It was simply one continuous roar, punctuated every now and then by a still louder crash which seemed to deafen the sense of hearing. It was dark for over an hour after the commencement of the bombardment, so that from horizon to horizon the sky was illuminated by the lurid glare of the gun flashes, and bursting enemy shells, intermingled with red signal lights and greenish white star shells, combined to create a spectacle which has never before been presented to mortal vision, a spectacle at which one gazed amazed, fascinated, spellbound.[3]

The sight was even more awe-inspiring for the tank commanders in the first wave like Second Lieutenant Horace Birks, watching from a few hundred yards away as the unregistered guns blasted the enemy trenches with astonishing accuracy, before they moved forward to the attack:

> With a terrific crash the guns all opened at once; there was an infinitesimal pause filled by the whine of passing shells, and then came the most beautiful sight I have ever seen; the whole of the enemy's lines were lit up in a tossing bubbling torrent of multi-coloured flame, and – most beautiful of all – nothing came back in reply. We lurched off in the growing light, I for one expecting the most frightful crash to come any minute. It seemed too good to be true, this steady rumbling forward over marvellous going, no holes, no shelling, and infantry following steadily behind.[4]

Slightly further back, Second Lieutenant Macintosh and his fellow officers in No. 12 Company could no longer contain themselves:

> With a cataclysmic crash the Boche line erupted in spouting volcanoes of smoke and earth, illumined in the flickering light of the incessant bursts. A second or two, and right, left and centre, up went flares of all colours – red, green, yellow, singly and in clusters – as the terrified front-line troops called upon their artillery to save them from annihilation. Meanwhile the officers, released at last from the intolerable strain of silence, cried out in delighted profanity at the hellish din of

the barrage. No one could hear his neighbour's voice – the field guns were seeing to that – all were perfectly happy to shout their comments to the air.

As the excitement gradually died down, they strained their eyes to see how their friends had been faring. Dawn was breaking, but the dust of the barrage and a thin ground-mist hid all sight of the enemy lines. Returning to their buses, the crews awaited, amid the crashing thunder, the signal to take their part in the fray.[5]

The wire-crushers and first-wave tanks moved off as soon as the barrage fell, the full-throated roar of their engines now mingling with the thunder of the guns.[6] Major William Watson of No. 11 Company saw his men going into action:

> In front of the wire tanks in a ragged line were surging forward inexorably over the short down grass. Above and around them hung the blue-grey smoke of their exhausts. Each tank was followed by a bunch of Highlanders, some running forward from cover to cover, but most of them tramping steadily behind their tanks. They disappeared into the valley. To the right the tanks were moving over the crest of the shoulder of the hill. To the left there were no tanks in sight. They were already in among the enemy.
>
> Beyond the enemy trenches the slopes [of Flesquières ridge], from which the German gunners might have observed the advancing tanks, were already enveloped in thick white smoke. The smoke-shells burst with a sheet of vivid red flame, pouring out blinding, suffocating clouds. It was as if flaring bonfires were burning behind a bank of white fog. Over all, innumerable aeroplanes were flying steadily to and fro.
>
> The enemy made little reply. A solitary field gun was endeavouring pathetically to put down a barrage. A shell would burst every few minutes on the same bay of the same trench. There were no other enemy shells that we could see. A machine-gun or two were still trained on our trenches, and an occasional vicious burst would bring the venturesome spectator scrambling down into the trench.[7]

This machine-gun fire was described by 51st Division headquarters as 'heavy, but wild and harmless',[8] though that was not always the case. Apart from that there was virtually no response from the enemy.

In the hilltop village of Flesquières, Hauptmann Otto Fürsen, the commander of 3rd Battalion, 84th Regiment, had just got back to his headquarters after visiting the forward positions to check all was well. Later he recalled: 'Then I drank some coffee and began to write home. That letter, with the time of 7 a.m. [i.e. 6 a.m. UK time], is lying before me. On the third page you can clearly see from the sudden shaky handwriting when the stupendous bombardment began, with shells of all calibres … The explosions could not be counted, but I would estimate around five or six a second.'[9] Or as the German official history put it: 'The ground shuddered and quaked under the weight of the onslaught.'[10] The prophecy had come true, and they were shaking mightily the earth.

A little later, Major Watson observed the second wave of tanks heading into action. 'On our left another column of tanks had already disappeared into the valley on their way to Flesquieres. It was Ward's company …'[11] Frank Heap and the crew of *Deborah* were on their way to war.

* * *

As the first wave of tanks and infantry made their way across No Man's Land, the most common impression was one of orderliness, as if this was an exercise or parade-ground manoeuvre, rather than an attack against one of the strongest enemy positions on the entire Western Front. Despite that, no-one knew for sure what would happen when they got to the other side.

The first great unknown was the barbed wire, which was an intimidating prospect for tank commanders like Second Lieutenant Horace Birks as they approached the enemy trenches:

> Emerging out of the gloom a dark mass came steadily towards us, the German wire. It appeared absolutely impenetrable. It was certainly the thickest and deepest I have ever seen, it stretched in front of us in three belts, each about 50 yards deep, and it came up to the bottom of our sponsons. It neither stopped the tank nor broke up and wound round and round with the tracks as we at first feared, but squashed flat and remained flat, leaving a broad carpet of wire as wide as the tank, over which the following infantry were able to pick their way without great difficulty. We were working with the [6th] Black Watch and they were well up and following quickly behind us. It was a relief to get through the wire and come out on to the main German position. All this time there had been no firing and very little shell fire, and the tanks on the right and left could be seen keeping station with us.[12]

For obvious reasons the infantry had been just as anxious about this aspect of the plan, but an officer of 8th Bn Argyll and Sutherland Highlanders paid tribute to the work of the tanks: 'It must be acknowledged that the paths so crushed were passed over with the greatest ease. In most places the wire was absolutely down, and flat; even at the worst, one could pass over in comfort with a little judicious exercise of the "heather step."'[13]

Ironically, the Germans' thoroughness had proved their undoing, since the solidly constructed wall of wire was easily crushed by a tank weighing almost thirty tons with its fascine. Colonel Baker-Carr explained: 'The worst sort of wire is … the loose concertina stuff. We go over it and it springs up behind. The best sort of wire from our point of view is well put up wire, good strong stakes, wire fairly taut, and the tank will flatten it out.'[14]

Once safely through the wire, the next question was whether the tanks would be able to cross the enormously wide front-line trenches, and everything now depended on what had been dubbed 'the wily fascine'.[15] Despite all the preparations, this did not go quite so smoothly for Second Lieutenant Birks: 'A red flag stuck in the parapet of the trench ahead of us showed where the leading tank had dropped its fascine, we ran up to it and approached slowly to make quite certain of dropping on it, and crossed over. It was an enormous trench, and there was one horrid moment when the tail dropped onto the fascine when it seemed to be touch and go if we could get over. Actually we did so without difficulty and moved forward to the next line.'[16] But he was luckier than others, including a couple of tanks which were victims of their own enthusiasm, according to Major Watson: 'Two of these unfortunates in their eagerness to kill had collided and slipped together inextricably into a trench.'[17]

After this another D Battalion tank became ditched, the hulks providing a useful landmark for Captain Robert Tennant Bruce of the Royal Army Medical Corps, who was in charge of 51st Division's stretcher-bearers, as he headed towards the 'immensely wide and deep' front-line trench. 'Stuck on the parapet of it, inextricably jammed though not much knocked about, were three abandoned tanks … One glance at the trench made us realise the wisdom and forethought of the bundles on the tanks. Even with their help I marvelled that they could cross at all.'[18]

Soon yet another machine became stuck fast, and Lieutenant Gerald Edwards had to take desperate measures to avoid the same fate in his wire-crushing tank D34 *Diallance*: 'I just missed being ditched too, in a dug out. Had to use a dead Jock under the right track to get a purchase on the ground to swing.'[19] The attack was too important to fail, and by helping another tank to get across, the dead man had increased his comrades' chances of survival, in keeping with the motto of the 51st Division: 'Là á Bhlàir's math na Càirdean', or in English, 'Friends are good on the day of battle'.

To the right, the tanks of E Battalion were also tackling the 'truly formidable obstacle' of the Hindenburg line, leading to 'a few exciting moments' for Second Lieutenant Fred Dawson in E45 *Elles II*. 'First, poised over the deep and wide excavation; then, releasing the fascine – would it drop all right? – we saw it lumber beautifully into the bottom. But could we get over? One can imagine our doubts, as we had witnessed a few ghastly failures at Wailly. Anyhow, down we dropped and up, up, up – no one thought of the "balance point" – until at last we crashed upon the other side, splitting open my section commander's head, and petrol cans, oil cans and ammunition boxes scattered all over the place.'[20]

This accident meant the battle was over before it had begun for his section commander, Captain Ernest Gregory. The wound was a 'Blighty one', although the medical board that examined him heard a different version of events, and recorded that he was 'hit by fragments of shell causing superficial gutter wounds ... followed by unconsciousness for a short time'.[21] Officers could claim a gratuity if they were wounded in action, and surely none of us would begrudge him this payment, even if the cause was not exactly as stated.

E Battalion faced an even more tragic setback when one of their machines suffered a direct hit almost on the start-line – a specially cruel stroke of fate considering the feebleness of the German counter-barrage. A note in the logbook of E27 *Ella* states: 'Tank blown up, direct hit on cab, not more than 5 minutes after the show commenced.' The commander, Second Lieutenant William Stobo Haining and his driver, Gunner Leslie Halkes Wray, were killed, and the rest of the crew wounded.[22] In one of his poems, Gunner Wray had contemplated death in terms reminiscent of Rupert Brooke: 'If I should fall grieve not that one so weak and poor as I should die ... Think only this; ... He died for England's sake.' His fellow crewmen wrote to his parents expressing their grief, but did not lose sight of the practicalities on which their own lives depended: 'We are very sorry to have lost such a faithful friend ... We cannot speak too highly of his good nature and the way he kept his engine.'[23] No tank driver could wish for a finer epitaph.

* * *

One British officer later wrote: 'How often one has wondered what were the thoughts of the immediate enemy at precisely 6.21 on the morning of the 20th November, 1917!'[24] Fortunately some did record their impressions, among them Leutnant Adolf Mestwarb of No. 7 Company, 84th Infantry Regiment, which found itself directly in the path of D Battalion's tanks:

> During the night of 19–20 November the English artillery remained relatively quiet, even towards morning it was remarkably silent – the calm before the storm! I stayed in the outpost line for almost the entire night, sending out patrols to insure

against any surprises, but there was nothing unusual to be seen. When dawn broke I decided it was time to fortify myself with a bite of breakfast, and for that purpose I went back to the sentry post into the dugout. But hardly had I got things ready when the storm broke. Soon after 7 a.m. [i.e. 6 a.m. UK time] English drum-fire erupted at once along the whole of our front line. I jumped up, grabbed the flare pistol, filled my pockets with red and green cartridges, and dashed back up above. There I immediately realized the barrage was falling on the front-line trenches behind us, which were presently engulfed in smoke and flames. The sentries in front instinctively pulled back to the outpost, whose defensive positions were manned in the meantime. Meanwhile we kept a sharp lookout.

The sentry beside me suddenly noticed something extraordinary; his words were: 'Sir, something square is coming.' I took a close look and realized straight away that it was a tank, which really did have a square appearance because of the gigantic bundle [i.e. fascine] lying on top of it. Now, we were all ready for one or two tanks – we had no idea about a large number of them – and immediately opened fire, but unfortunately without making the slightest impression on the brute. It moved further forward, firing as it went, then veered to the left to make room for those behind, which were now appearing one after another from behind the corner of the wood in front of us. What a splendid target that corner would have made for our artillery! But they did nothing to make themselves known, not a single shot fell. I sent up flares as soon as the first tanks appeared. All the cartridges I had I fired off, but nothing happened. Runners were sent to the battalion – the telephone was destroyed right at the start – but we heard nothing from them, so we were now completely cut off.

Meanwhile the tanks came rapidly further forward, across the trenches away to the left and right, firing all the time. Some stayed in place to cover the trenches, some went further across the second line [known as K2]. What could we do? The fact that we were completely powerless to stand up to these monsters, and the silence of our artillery had a depressing effect. In addition, numerous aircraft flew low over the trenches and vigorously poured down fire. This was no longer a battle, it was a one-sided massacre. Leutnant Mory [the company commander] had completely lost his head right at the start, when he was told about the tanks, but something had to be done. I ordered the neighbouring outpost by runner to pull back to the front line as well, taking everyone who could still go with them. The communication trench was under fire from both sides, and you could only negotiate it bent double, and had to run along in this way under a hail of bullets. That was a dreadful scramble, and we didn't bring many men with us.[25]

They reached the front-line trench to find it had already been evacuated, so headed straight for the second line where they found the men of No. 6 Company were already pulling back, led by their commander Leutnant Adolf Saucke. The survivors of No. 7 Company went with them, led by Leutnant Herbert Mory, but Leutnant Mestwarb was exhausted and stopped for a rest, only to find his escape route cut off by tanks: 'Our fate was sealed. Shortly afterwards masses of English [*sic* – they were actually Scottish] appeared from all sides and harassed us with hand grenades. Badly wounded by two splinters, I was unable to fight on and was taken prisoner … That was the end of No. 7 Company, with which I had stuck through so many fierce battles with hardly a break from the Vosges on to Champagne, Russia, Verdun and Flanders. It was grim!'[26]

* * *

Although a number of D Battalion tanks were ditched, they had still enabled the infantry to get through the wall of wire into the enemy's trenches. Working with them on the left were 5th Bn Gordon Highlanders, who described what happened: 'On reaching the Hindenburg Line, it proved to be so wide and deep that very few tanks succeeded in crossing it and at least three were completely ditched. Their presence was, however, sufficient to enable the front wave to capture the trench, which contained two machine guns.'[27]

Once the Gordons had broken into the front line the enemy were powerless to resist the Highlanders, as described by their battalion commander, Lieutenant-Colonel Maxwell McTaggart:

> With a yell of excitement our infantry were in the trench pursuing them down the track as hard as they could, inflicting terrible losses on them with bayonet, bullet and bomb. On close examination this front trench of the Hindenburg line was seen to be a wonderful piece of workmanship. Fully ten feet deep, and twelve to fifteen feet wide, it was indeed a serious obstacle for any tank to cross, and a great many were temporarily ditched. But they had effected their principal task. They had enabled the infantry to set foot in the German trench system, and if no tank was available to crush the wire above the ground, the men could get under the wire by running down the communication trenches.[28]

With only one tank still supporting them, the attack by 5th Bn Gordon Highlanders hung in the balance, but their report boasted how 'the situation was tackled with great dash and determination' as the infantry swarmed through the trench system, hurling phosphorus bombs into the deep dug-outs and killing or capturing anyone they encountered.[29] The accounts do not mention it, but this fearsome onslaught would have been accompanied by the skirl of bagpipes.

As they rushed through the first and second line trenches, they soon came upon a deep sunken road running at right angles to the main trench system and down towards the Grand Ravine. The Germans called this the Stollenweg, or 'Bunker Way', and it formed the heart of their defences in this sector. Its elaborate dug-outs housed the headquarters of the 2nd Battalion, 84th Infantry Regiment, and as the defenders were driven back, they now prepared to mount a last desperate stand.

CHAPTER 26

Till the Last Man

The hurricane bombardment had left the officers of 2nd Battalion, 84th Infantry Regiment, in no doubt that a full-scale attack was under way. Leutnant Johannes Langfeldt, who had spent the previous evening relaxing over a glass of wine in the Stollenweg, was now confronted there by a 'breathless and rather panicky' Leutnant Herbert Mory, who told how almost his entire company had been captured, and talked of 'a vast number of tanks'. It was a rude awakening for Leutnant Langfeldt, who did not think an attack was possible: 'I still recall how the scales fell from my eyes when I heard the word "tanks".'[1] Leutnant Adolf Saucke, commander of No. 6 Company, described Leutnant Mory as 'slightly wounded, completely out of breath and psychologically shattered', while even the battalion commander Hauptmann Harro Soltau was 'highly agitated' and could not take in that they had vacated the front line, and were not even in a position to hold the second. 'He ordered K2 [the second line] to be held, whatever the cost.'[2]

By now more and more men were flooding back into the Stollenweg, as described by Leutnant Langfeldt: 'First of all, disorganized parties who had lost their heads and were in headlong flight surged back along the sunken road. We had to use all the power we could summon to bring the men to reason and make them stop. The personal example of Hauptmann Soltau had a further effect on the majority and brought them to their senses.' A few slipped away across the Grand Ravine, but members of four companies were soon gathered in the Stollenweg until it was 'crammed full'.[3]

Unable to make contact with the headquarters of 84th Infantry Regiment, Hauptmann Soltau called together his officers, who recommended withdrawing until they had artillery support and could mount a counter-attack. Instead, his response showed he was still haunted by events at Fort Douaumont, and this was to seal their fate: 'A Prussian officer does not retreat.'[4]

Although they were cut off, a runner did get through to Flesquières with a message from Hauptmann Soltau, and this suggested the drama had reached its final act: 'We are keeping K2 [i.e. the support trench] so far still manned. K3 [i.e. the third-line trench] will be held under all circumstances. Tanks level with us and beyond. Six to eight tanks advancing on K1 North. Artillery must fire on K1 and K2. Reinforcements to the Stollenweg immediately. We will hold on till the last man.'[5] Soon afterwards another message reached Flesquières: 'Am holding on with brave members of my battalion. On both sides of the Stollenweg ... Artillery are not firing at the numerous tanks. Support – bring guns up to Flesquières.'[6] With that, the curtain fell.

The Stollenweg was now under sustained attack from tanks which patrolled the rim, pouring down fire on the defenders as the number of dead and wounded rose. Leutnant Saucke was standing with Unteroffizier (i.e. Corporal) Hans Glindemann when a shell splinter ripped open the NCO's arm from wrist to elbow. Saucke told how 'blood shot from the torn artery and my tunic was soaked in an instant. I managed to bind Glindemann's upper arm with a tourniquet, while he remained astonishingly calm.' As the losses mounted it was obvious that, in Saucke's words, 'the game was up'. Even Hauptmann Soltau had become strangely quiet: 'There was a peculiar expression in his eyes, as if he knew death was close at hand.'[7]

Despite his determination to stand firm, Hauptmann Soltau now joined the survivors as they dashed back towards a narrow trench called the Kabelgraben (known to the British as Chapel Alley), which was their only hope of getting back to Flesquières. In the words of Leutnant Saucke:

> We have hardly gone back a hundred metres when we bump into some Englishmen [*sic*] at a bend in the trench, who are coming down the trench towards us. The escape route is now completely blocked. Hauptmann Soltau leaps out of the trench, the leading NCO behind him. A couple of machine guns open up. The next moment the NCO falls back into the trench, bleeding from an arm wound, with the cry: 'Hauptmann Soltau has fallen!' I watch as our adjutant, Leutnant Elson, neatly dressed with black breeches and gleaming boots, half-raises himself out of the trench. I see a sudden blow strike his body. A shot through the heart has brought him a fine soldier's death. His body blocks the trench ... I myself peer cautiously over the rim of the trench. Half-left from me, no more than fifty metres away, stand two tanks. To their right in the sunken road are around a dozen of our men, disarmed. Quite automatically I raise my rifle and fire two or three shots. My lead finds its lodging in one of the short-skirted men.[8]

His shots were almost the last act of resistance by 2nd Battalion, and it is hard to avoid the conclusion that Hauptmann Soltau would have done better to order withdrawal when his officers suggested, rather than waiting until it was too late. But he had met a proud end, and at least he was spared the ignominy of capture, unlike many of his men. Years later Leutnant Saucke was still seething with anger:

> A young Scotsman fell on me, with his first grasp he tore the Iron Cross from my chest, and with his second ripped open my tunic to remove my watch with a satisfied smirk. The bandit didn't find much more on me. I had already thrown my Browning, map-case, binoculars, and little double-edged dagger into a muddy shell-hole. My wallet, which was thrust into my hip pocket, evaded the scoundrel, and the fact that I was wearing gloves saved my gold-coloured ring, the gift of a fellow student from Heidelberg. All my comrades had the same experience. They were plundered one after another using every trick in the book. Even wedding-rings were taken from the married men. Everything came under the heading of 'souvenirs', or military mementoes, whereby English officers later sought to excuse the outrageous conduct of their men.
>
> I must also here relate the sad fate of Leutnant Hinkeldeyn of 2nd Machine Gun Company, who lost his young life through an act of barbarism which mocks all humanity. Hinkeldeyn had already been taken prisoner and was standing there unarmed. An Englishman snatched his wallet, at which a photo or letter fell to the ground. When Hinkeldeyn grabbed for it, the Englishman took a step back, raised his rifle with arms braced, placed it on Hinkeldeyn's chest and pulled the trigger. A dastardly, cowardly murder which alas, like so many English outrages, will surely never be atoned.[9]

Sadly there were other similar stories that day. Leutnant Carl Beuck awaited the enemy's arrival squeezed into the narrow entrance of a dugout near the Stollenweg with two Vizefeldwebel (i.e. company sergeant-majors), Frahm and Jacobsen, their weapons leaning against the trench wall beside them.

> Not a minute has passed before a lanky Canadian [sic] appears on the opposite lip of the sunken road, perhaps eight to ten metres away. When he sees the three Germans he put his rifle to his cheek, aims and fires. With a scream, Frahm falls backwards. My left arm supports him; he has been shot in the middle of the chest. The 'hero' raises his rifle towards us a second time and again his shot finds its mark: Jacobsen's right arm is shattered, he is seared with dreadful pain. When will my turn come? Calmly the foe raises his rifle a third time and takes aim. I wait for his shot, my left arm still supporting one wounded comrade and my right arm the other; all three of us, standing upright, are staring the enemy in the eye. Then he lets his rifle drop, reaches his arm out towards us, and says 'Come on!'[10]

Leutnant Beuck was spared, but everything he had of value was taken, and Vizefeldwebel August Jacobsen later had his arm amputated in captivity. Another company commander said the behaviour of their captors was not '"gentlemanlike", as the English liked to put it', and also told of a man who was shot after being disarmed, while everyone was robbed of their valuables: 'My own shoulder-straps were cut off by an English officer, in whose presence an NCO took my watch.'[11] One soldier recorded the English phrases he picked up during his capture: 'Come on, Gerry!', 'Straight on, this way', and 'fokking watch' [sic].[12]

The trench mortar officer of 2nd Battalion, Leutnant Claus Rickert, said they thought 'souvenir' must be the enemy's battle-cry because the soldiers were shouting it as they took them prisoner, and asked: 'Were these soldiers or robbers before us?' To make matters worse, he was nearly bayoneted by a Scotsman 'who stank of schnapps', until his fellow captives convinced him that Rickert was responsible for mortars rather than machine guns. While being escorted back they were fired at by another soldier who was lying in wait behind a tank fascine, resulting in a set-to between the two groups of British. During this the prisoners were plundered again, while 'the officers calmly watched the looting'.[13]

Not surprisingly, there are few British accounts of prisoners being killed, though Captain Evan Charteris heard from two colleagues in the Tank Corps, one of whom saw 'a number of Germans being shot by our men after they had given sufficient indication of their inability to resist any further'. Another officer 'told me that he had seen a Tommy drive a pick through the head of a German as he emerged from a dug-out, and that when he had criticised this as a rather cold blooded proceeding, the Tommy said: "This morning when I was taking in a prisoner he made a bolt for it, and I've 'ad enough of that sort of thing."'[14]

On the other hand, there seems to have been a cheerful acceptance that the troops were entitled to enjoy the spoils of war. One officer of 5th Bn Seaforth Highlanders recalled: 'So sure were some of our own men of success that one of them went across with a canvas water bucket hung round his neck to collect souvenirs from the Boche prisoners and dug-outs; and I understand the bucket was well filled before the morning was far advanced.'[15]

A number of Tank Corps officers did condemn the looting, but mainly on the grounds that it disrupted and delayed the advance. One anonymous officer, almost certainly Major Alexander Gatehouse of E Battalion, recalled meeting 'a sergeant of the Argyll and Sutherland Highlanders who had collected 18 watches and 24 gold rings by the time he had got as far as the Grand Ravin [*sic*]'. He added: 'There is no doubt that looting, which went on all through the battle, slowed the infantry up seriously.'[16]

Any sympathy for the Germans over the loss of their possessions may be tempered by the knowledge that in withdrawing to the Hindenburg Line, they had devastated a large swathe of French farmland, systematically destroying farms and villages, felling orchards and poisoning wells. Nevertheless, they clearly felt that the behaviour of their captors had transgressed the rules of war, and they were probably right: the Hague Convention, which all the major powers had signed, stated that prisoners of war must be humanely treated and their personal belongings remained their own property.[17]

Leutnant Rickert was so aggrieved by the theft of his wallet containing 300 marks that he subsequently tried to claim compensation from the British War Ministry, but was told this was impossible unless he could produce a receipt. He noted darkly that this sum should be added to the reparations bill following the next war, though it was then only 1924.[18]

* * *

The German accounts speak of several tanks joining in the assault on the Stollenweg, but the Gordon Highlanders reported that they were supported by a single tank: 'In the Sunken Road, heavy casualties were inflicted on the enemy. The tank's 6-pounder did great execution and the dug-outs were effectively bombed by "B" Company, who killed and captured a great number of the enemy here. Among the prisoners was a commanding officer with his whole staff. This party was not captured without a sharp fight, as the Germans had mounted a machine gun firing along the Sunken Road and inflicted several casualties on our men.'[19]

The tank that played such a key role was almost certainly D47 *Demon II*, commanded by Second Lieutenant James Vose. Colonel Baker-Carr told how it 'cleared out many troublesome [machine guns] from a sunken road where our infantry could hardly advance. When the tank commander was satisfied that our infantry could advance he signalled them and they came up to take a bag of 100 or more prisoners without any trouble.'[20] The divisional historian praised the tank for doing 'magnificent execution' with 'shell after shell bursting in the midst of panic-stricken Germans'.[21]

By 10 a.m., the battle for the Stollenweg was over. As around 400 prisoners streamed back towards the rear, 5th Bn Gordon Highlanders settled into the quarters recently vacated by 84th Infantry Regiment and found them 'an amazing example of ingenuity and labour'. The battalion commander, Lieutenant-Colonel Maxwell McTaggart, described the headquarters and nearby medical aid post as 'underground palaces':

> Room after room had been laboriously excavated, and the walls and ceilings lined with expensive timber. Well-made chairs, tables, bedsteads, cupboards and shelves were to be found everywhere. The medical arrangements left nothing to be desired. So numerous were the shelters that there was no difficulty in housing the whole battalion, no matter where they might be. The dug-out I occupied was a gorgeous chamber, and its recent occupant must have been something of a 'knut' [i.e. a dandy or swell] as it smelt strongly of hair-oil and scent and numerous bottles of 'elixir' were found on his washing-stand. The fire trenches were equally well prepared – boarded and lined and drained in such a way that mud did not exist. The Germans are truly a wonderful people.[22]

Major William Watson came down the same sunken road in the wake of his tanks, and was similarly impressed:

On either side were dug-outs, stores, and cook-houses. Cauldrons of coffee and soup were still on the fire. This regimental headquarters the enemy had defended desperately. The trench-boards were slippery with blood, and fifteen to twenty corpses, all Germans and all bayoneted, lay strewn about the road like drunken men.

A Highland sergeant who, with a handful of men, was now in charge of the place, came out to greet us, puffing at a long cigar. All his men were smoking cigars, and it was indeed difficult that morning to find a Highlander without a cigar. He invited us into a large chamber cut out of the rock, from which a wide staircase descended into an enormous dug-out. The chamber was panelled deliciously with coloured woods and decorated with choice prints. Our host produced a bottle of good claret, and we drank to the health of the Fifty-first Division.[23]

One of his tank commanders, Lieutenant Gerald Edwards, added: 'In this sunken road were the most luxurious dug-outs I have ever seen. One was papered with plate glass mirrors reaching from floor to ceiling, like a Lyon's Café.'[24] Brigadier-General Henry Burn, commander of 152nd Infantry Brigade which attacked to their right, occupied another underground headquarters, built of concrete 'with panelled walls in which was carved at foot of steps (in German of course), "We fear nought except God & our own Artillery"', which at least gave the lie to the claim that the enemy had no sense of humour.[25]

In the words of the Gordon Highlanders' official history, it had been 'a great day' for them, having seized the enemy's stronghold in this sector with the loss of six men killed and fifty-six wounded.[26] Lieutenant-Colonel McTaggart – described as 'a most gallant little man; all blood and thunder'[27] – summed up the situation in a telegram: 'The men are in capital fettle especially as they have suffered so few casualties. Rations & water have arrived and every man has a dugout ... They will all therefore be fit for anything tomorrow.'[28]

For now the 5th Gordons could enjoy the spoils of war, but they would not have long to do so. The 7th Black Watch had already passed through their positions to conduct the next phase of the operation, and even now the attack was rolling steadily on towards the ridge of Flesquières.

* * *

To the right of 5th Gordons, the other leading battalions of 51st (Highland) Division encountered far less resistance – probably because they were facing not the battle-hardened warriors of 84th Infantry Regiment, but the maturer members of 387th Landwehr Infantry Regiment who took a more pragmatic view of their duty to the Fatherland. The German high command were well aware of this weak link in their defences and planned to replace the regiment a few days later. But that was no help now as the storm broke over the Landwehr men, who had encountered neither tanks nor Highlanders until waves of both burst out of the mist on that terrible morning.

Unlike the 84th, there is no detailed record of their actions, but we can draw our own conclusions from the ease with which their positions were overrun, and from their casualty figures which amounted to five dead, nine wounded and 1,582 missing (i.e. mostly taken prisoner).[29] They were, in the words of one German account, simply 'swept aside'.[30]

The clearest portrait of them comes from Captain Douglas Wimberley of 232nd Machine Gun Company, which formed part of 51st Division. As he advanced he saw 'a few disconsolate prisoners looking for someone to surrender to',[31] and later 'quite a number of Germans running about trying to escape from the tanks. They'd left the trenches and they'd left their dugouts – probably rightly – because had they stayed there no doubt they would have got the Mills bombs of the Jocks. They were a very poor type of German.'[32]

Wimberley and his men came across a group of prisoners walking towards them, 'all alone and without escort but as harmless as sucking doves, their morale being at zero'. They were set to work clearing a way through the barbed wire, and cut their hands to ribbons in their willingness to help. 'They were a miserable lot of men, unshaven of course, but so were we, but dirty, consumptive and small, or grossly fat, some of them very young, but most of them middle-aged men … quite a lot of them were wearing spectacles, rather like the cartoons of the time of what Germans were supposed to look like. They were a Landsturm [this should be Landwehr] division of "duds", poor devils … What a shock they must have had to see lines of great armoured tanks followed by the bayonets of the Jocks.'[33] As they swept forward, 8th Bn Argyll and Sutherland Highlanders also encountered 'parties of Germans too dazed and frightened to offer much resistance. Every now and then batches of prisoners were despatched to the rear, some without escort, while others were shepherded by the recipients of "blighty yins"' [i.e. wounds serious enough to require evacuation to Britain].[34]

On reaching their objective, the Argyll and Sutherlands dropped a grenade into one deep dug-out and heard a voice and footsteps below. According to their company commander: 'We fully expected to see a number of Germans appear, but to our surprise only one came up, an elderly man – he must have been at least fifty years of age – holding a huge piece of black bread which he carried on eating quite unconcernedly. He was left to his bread, with an added cigarette or two, until the next lot of prisoners was sent back.'[35] The officer added: 'Unlike this old man, many of the Germans seemed to be terror-stricken – probably the effect of their first real encounter with tanks.'[36]

To their right, 5th Bn Seaforth Highlanders also advanced virtually unopposed, although Lance-Corporal Robert McBeath won the Victoria Cross after he dealt with five machine guns which were holding up their advance from the village of Ribécourt, in the neighbouring divisional sector. The battalion also seized four field guns, 'the gunners scuttling for dear life before the kilted advance'. Even more satisfying was the capture of a horse-drawn field kitchen: 'The first wave pounced upon the waggon with the horses yoked and the Boche dinner cooking away merrily, but the driver elected to run away, much to his own detriment, for he did not run far. The morning air had created a keen appetite among the members of this Company, and right heartily did they tackle that hot meal of beef and vegetables which the cooker contained.'[37]

Despite the levity, the prisoners flooding back to the rear brought news that the attackers did not want to hear. At 10.20 a.m. the headquarters of IV Corps flashed a warning to its infantry divisions, along with 1st Tank Brigade and 1st Cavalry Division: 'Prisoners report that warning of our attack was conveyed to the Germans as the result of a raid by them. It is therefore possible that opposition may be encountered.'[38]

* * *

As they struggled to make sense of the chaos before them, the German commanders in Flesquières desperately sought to regain the initiative. Hauptmann Wille and the survivors from 1st Battalion, 84th Infantry Regiment, were still clinging on behind Havrincourt as the attackers flowed around them, while the 2nd Battalion under

Hauptmann Soltau had, in the words of one of his officers, 'shattered without flexing, like a pane of glass'.[39]

Reinforcements were available from 27th Reserve Infantry Regiment, which had been rushed towards Flesquières in response to the prisoners' warning of an impending attack, and two companies were now thrown forward to relieve the defenders and meet the British advance head-on.

As the counter-attack got under way, the men of No. 7 Company headed down the communication trench known as Havrincourt-Riegel (or Cemetery Alley to the British) in a bid to reach Havrincourt. Gefreiter (i.e. Lance-Corporal) Wilhelm Bär described what happened when they paused at the railway embankment:

> The company's officers seemed unsure whether they should stay and hold [the embankment] under the circumstances, or press on, but the order from battalion was: 'Forward at all costs'. Without further ado, our brave and beloved company commander Leutnant Hermann gave the order: 'Fix bayonets and charge over the embankment by sections,' as English machine guns were sweeping the railway tracks. We got over and away with few casualties, and then No. 7 Company deployed into extended line as calmly as on the parade ground and moved forward up the fire-spitting ridge ahead, towards the enemy. Here and there a man fell dead or wounded as we advanced fearlessly under the heaviest machine-gun fire, the English yielding everywhere at our onslaught.
>
> We were about 500-600 metres beyond the railway embankment when suddenly masses of English infantry and numerous tanks bore down on our company from all sides, while we were given hell by very low-flying English aircraft, two of which I saw crash.
>
> 'Into the shell-holes and rapid fire,' rang out the command, as appalling, almost volcanic fire erupted from all sides; we defended ourselves like demons. 'Fire at the infantry,' I screamed in the terrible uproar of battle. They were advancing behind the tanks, and the Englishmen fell in heaps. Without artillery, we were powerless against the tanks. They literally showered us with bullets, and our losses were heavy ... The firefight raged on, the ammunition giving out bit by bit as General Haig hurled more fresh forces against us. Faced with this superiority and surrounded on almost every side, the company went under and were taken prisoner.[40]

A few men managed to escape, but many including Gefreiter Bär were captured. Meanwhile, No. 6 Company set off down a parallel communication trench (the Grenzweg, known to the British as Ravine Alley) making for the Stollenweg. They soon ran into the same overwhelming force of tanks, infantry and aircraft, as described by Unteroffizier (i.e. Corporal) Senftleben:

> Our feet hurry over collapsed sections of trench. There on the right beside the trench stands a small barn or shed, its roof still resting on a few posts. Here all hell breaks loose. Then we abandon the trench, dash across the open road, and come closer to our objective. A sudden hold-up, shouts from ahead: 'Go back!' Schleswigers [i.e. from 84th Infantry Regiment] hurry past us: 'Turn round, comrades, Tommy's in the trenches!' They have already gone past; we stay where we are, though shells are falling close at hand. A question from behind: 'Who gave the order to go back?' ... Now that's what I call a real Prussian, German sense of duty!'[41]

However, they did turn round after an officer of the 84th explained the situation, and their own company commander had been killed:

> We make our way back up the trench, across the road again at a bound. At the barn, the trench is almost buried. Again our feet fall still: in the trench, blasted by a direct hit in the base, five comrades are lying in their blood. Over there lies a leg, a chunk of blood and brains is stuck to the trench wall, his head is missing and fixes us once more with a broken stare ... Slowly we steal past. No-one pays any attention to the bursting shells, concerned only with doing no further harm to the fallen.[42]

When he heard about the failure of the mission, their battalion commander decided to take things into his own hands. At the age of forty-six, and with one leg stiff and shortened from a previous war wound, Major Günther Stubenrauch led his two remaining companies forward in a final attempt to halt the British advance.

* * *

For all their determination, there is no specific mention of any counter-attacks in the British accounts. It seems the German efforts simply did not register as the unstoppable tide of men and machines swept forward. With little enemy artillery fire to trouble them, the tanks could operate more or less with impunity, hindered only by the broad trenches and the withering hail of small-arms fire.

In a letter home, Second Lieutenant George Koe of No. 10 Company called it 'a topping day's show' and 'the finest scrap I have had the pleasure of being in'. As reconnaissance officer he would not normally have taken part in the fighting, but his company commander, Major Edgar Marris, had other ideas:

> At dawn ... we heard and saw the beginning of the attack just as breakfast was ready. My C.O. [i.e. Marris] got his first, and then before I had time to drink more than a few mouthfuls of tea he was up and wanted to get away, so off we started, I with a kipper between two slices of bread in my left hand. However, we were too quick, and we got sniped going over No Man's Land. We stopped in a shell hole, and I got time to finish my breakfast. Well, we soon got into the Boche trenches and waited there for some time. Then along came one of our 'buses [i.e. tanks] which had had some slight trouble and had two men slightly wounded. My C.O. promptly got in and told me to come too. In we went and off we went. I had a machine gun to myself, and had some fine shooting at the Huns, as they ran in large numbers ... I guess I fired at least a thousand rounds that morning ... It was really 'Our Day,' I can assure you.[43]

The tank they climbed aboard was D11 *Dominie*, and Colonel Baker-Carr told how it 'led the infantry across the Hindenburg Line, clearing or killing the enemy with machine-gun fire without a hitch. The complete understanding which existed between infantry and tank crews made for a successful advance until a Hun bombing party was encountered, holding up our infantry. These bombers were annihilated.'[44]

In his somewhat breathless report, Baker-Carr described other 'outstanding instances' involving the tanks of D and E Battalions as they steamrollered their way through the German positions. Among them was D4 *Dryad II*:

> During the 8 hours this tank was in action, 8,000 rounds of [small arms ammunition] was poured into the enemy trenches and emplacements, sweeping a

Deborah's section commander Captain Graeme Nixon (left) and Lieutenant Alfred Enoch in August 1917. *Photograph from Russell Enoch*

Spoils of war: this may look like a German soldier, but in fact it is Lieutenant Enoch of D Battalion with trophies found in a captured dugout, probably after Cambrai – including a cigar, bottle of wine, and what looks like a sausage or cucumber. *Photograph from Russell Enoch*

Officers from No. 12 Company holding rabbits, no doubt destined for the pot. Seated in the middle row are Alfred Enoch (far left) and Edward Glanville Smith (far right). Seated on the ground are John McNiven (left) and Frank Heap (centre). *Photograph from Russell Enoch*

James Macintosh, author of *Men and Tanks*, back home in South Africa around 1930. *Photograph from John Macintosh*

Major William Watson, author of *A Company of Tanks*, in his previous role as an officer in the Army Cyclist Corps.
Photograph from William Watson

Official photograph of Major Watson's officers at La Lovie on 26 September 1917. They include Richard Cooper (4th from left, standing with dog); Gerald Edwards (seated with terrier); David Morris (seated at far end of card table, with dark hair) and Horace Birks (second from right, partly hidden by foliage).
Photograph from Imperial War Museum (Q 2898)

Aerial photo of Flesquières issued to British troops before the attack on 20 November. The direction of advance was from the bottom left-hand corner towards the top right. *Photograph from National Archives*

Four of the men from 1st Bn Royal Irish Fusiliers who were taken prisoner in a raid on 18 November, with their German captors (behind).

Trains carrying tanks from D Battalion (left) and C Battalion (right) preparing to leave the Plateau railhead a few days before Cambrai. The D Battalion train is headed by D46 Dragon III followed by D47 Demon II, with D51 Deborah somewhere behind. *Photograph from Imperial War Museum (detail from Q 46940)*

A tank from D Battalion moves forward, in one of the long-hidden paintings by Sergeant Claude Rowberry.
Photograph from Royal Tank Regiment

A German soldier's view of the fighting at Flesquières, from the history of 27th Reserve Infantry Regiment.

The legendary lone gunner becomes a nationalist icon: this postcard marks the dedication of the artillery memorial in Cologne in 1936.

A German artist's impression of the desperate battle between tanks and artillery at Flesquières.

Deborah emerges from the ground in November 1998, as Philippe Gorczynski describes events to a TV crew (front left). *Photograph from Philippe Gorczynski*

Descendants of *Deborah*'s crew meet for the first time in 2009. *Photograph from Press Association ©PA*

Deborah today. *Photograph from Nord Tourisme ©Nord Tourisme*

way for our infantry. In an eventful passage D3 [*Drone*] answered many calls from the infantry and annihilated hostile machine gun teams. Before reaching its final objective this crew cleared large numbers of the enemy from strong trenches in front of Chapel Wood, driving them in flight towards Flesquieres. [D2 *Duke of Cornwall II*] registered several direct hits with its 6 pounders on enemy machine guns, so smashing the most formidable means of defence offered by the enemy in that section of the Hindenburg Line.[45]

As so often, Baker-Carr focused on the positives, and concluded optimistically: 'Many more particulars will be obtainable as soon as the tank commanders can be interviewed and outside information obtained from the infantry commanders.'[46] But by then, a very different picture had begun to emerge.

Meanwhile the tanks of No. 12 Company – including *Deborah* – had moved off 200 yards behind the first wave and followed in their tracks, though that was not always easy, as Second Lieutenant James Macintosh found.

At last the front line came into view, a huge trench whose difficulties had not been over-estimated. Captured obviously, and in our hands; but where were the flags which were to have marked the presence of the first wave's fascines? Anxiously Tosh peered right and left. No sign of a flag; but away to the right he saw the explanation. Three tanks were ditched there, close together. Either their fascines had fallen off or they had proved useless, and the attempt to cross without had failed. Tosh determined to drop his own fascine. Lifting his hand to the lever he pulled it to one side; with a crackle the great bundle lurched forward, and dropped accurately into the trench. Tosh signalled his driver to go forward; the tank's nose dropped true on to the fascine, and in a second they were across. A glance behind showed that the nearest tank was preparing to follow him across.[47]

By 7.30 a.m., just over an hour after zero, the first tanks had already reached the Grand Ravine,[48] though some fighting was still going on in the trenches behind them. There would now be time for the tanks and infantry to regroup ready for the second phase of the attack.

PART V
BEYOND THE GRAND RAVINE

CHAPTER 27

A Mountain to Climb

When the tank crews began pulling into the Grand Ravine, their overriding response was relief. As they had hoped, its dramatic name belied a broad, flat valley containing an innocent stream, and although the Germans were still fighting a desperate rearguard action and counter-attacking where they could, there was no sign of the tremendous opposition or physical obstacles that were predicted here.

The so-called 'Blue Line' which formed the first objective ran along one side or other of this valley, and the operation had therefore reached a crucial stage. At this point the second wave of tanks from No. 12 Company (in D Battalion) and No. 14 Company (in E Battalion) would move to the forefront of the attack, supported by the surviving tanks from the first wave. Here they would also link up with the fresh infantry battalions which had passed through the first-wave battalions, now settling into the captured trenches behind them.

If one man had been made for this moment, it was Major R.O.C. Ward. The task of reorganizing his tanks and their supporting infantry, and inspiring them for the challenge ahead, was a fitting one for the heavyweight hero of the Harlequins, who was easily the most forceful and dynamic leader in D Battalion.

But when the crews clambered out of their machines to gasp in the fresh air of the Grand Ravine, they were greeted by shocking news: R.O.C. Ward was dead.

Unlike Hauptmann Soltau, who fell at the height of the battle, Major Ward was killed before it had really begun. As soon as the bombardment started, the Germans reacted by spraying the British lines with 'wild machine-gun fire which appeared to come from the Outpost Line, and overhead fire directed from rear systems'.[1] The headquarters of 51st Division called it 'harmless',[2] but one of these random bullets had struck and felled the major just as his tanks were about to move off – a few minutes after he had uttered the words that seemed to unleash the barrage: 'Now for it'.[3]

The death of this larger-than-life figure was met with horror by his counterpart in No. 11 Company, Major William Watson: 'It was almost impossible to believe that we should never see again "Roc" Ward, the great athlete, the very embodiment of energy, the skilled leader of men, the best of good fellows – and never hear again his enormous voice rolling out full-blooded instructions … When we heard of his death later, the joy of victory died away …'[4]

The response of his men was rather less impassioned, with Captain Edward Glanville Smith describing his death as 'most unfortunate', resulting as it did in 'a most disheartening start'.[5] Private Jason Addy's view was that 'he got killed because he persisted in getting out of the tank',[6] which was unfair since company commanders rarely went to battle inside their tanks; in fact brigade headquarters advised them not to, because 'they are unable to see the general trend of a battle and are out of touch'.[7]

Whatever the men's reactions, the death of R.O.C. Ward left a vital missing link in the chain of command. His deputy, Captain Walter Smith, now took charge, and although he seems to have been perfectly competent, he could hardly emulate the volcanic energy of the man they called 'The Bull'. R.O.C. Ward had been such a key player that the Tank Corps staff officer Captain Frederick Hotblack saw his death as one of the factors affecting the outcome of the battle.[8] But what was done could not be undone, and the game had to be played to its final whistle, even though R.O.C. Ward would not be on hand to cheer his team to victory or console them in defeat.

* * *

Even without this setback, the British forces gathering in the Grand Ravine – including the crew of D51 *Deborah* – could no longer have any doubts about the metaphorical mountain they had to climb. The low wooded ridge of Flesquières, which looked so innocuous from their own lines, now seemed to loom threateningly above them.

The survivors of 84th Infantry Regiment were fleeing back along communication trenches towards the village, which had been substantially reinforced at the last minute as a result of the prisoners' revelations. The British knew nothing of this, but they were aware that enemy field guns were dug in along the reverse slope of the ridge, and could only hope these had been obliterated by the artillery barrage.

Whatever the state of the enemy's forces, it was obvious that the second phase of the attack would be much harder than the first. During the long run-up to zero hour, there had been plenty of time for the tanks to form up with their infantry units in No Man's Land before moving off against pre-assigned objectives, in what many had likened to a field exercise. They also had the advantage of almost total surprise.

The words of R.O.C. Ward's pre-battle briefing now echoed in their ears: 'Once again [No. 12] Company had been chosen for the task which demanded enterprise and staying power; for, whereas the other companies had definite objectives, they who formed the second wave were first to overcome a series of definite obstacles, and were then to push on with an unlimited objective …'[9] Not only that, but D Battalion was already depleted by the loss of seven of its thirty-five fighting tanks, now lying ditched or broken down among the enemy's front-line trenches. Five of these were male tanks, so the firepower of the attacking force was dangerously eroded.[10]

The ditched tanks were mostly from the first wave, but there was one exception: D50 *Dandy Dinmont* was in No. 12 Company, and belonged to the same section as *Deborah*. As the only male tank in the section, *Dandy Dinmont*'s 6-pounders would have been a vital asset when they reached Flesquières. Its commander, Lieutenant Hugo Armitage, was popular with the men and generally praised by his superiors – one called him 'a sound officer of the right type' – though some felt his painstaking approach made him too slow in action.[11] For all this thoroughness, his tank now lay ditched and disabled by problems with its autovac, a notoriously temperamental device that fed petrol into the engine. *Dandy Dinmont* had not fired a single shot in anger, and the section commander, Captain Graeme Nixon, could only prepare to plough on with his two remaining female tanks.

The timetable for the attack on Flesquières was driven by the schedule of the artillery barrage, which had been calculated beforehand and plotted on maps distributed to the attackers. Bearing in mind the multiple uncertainties of the operation, it was clearly impossible to predict the exact speed of the advance. At the same time, communications on the battlefield were so rudimentary that it would be impossible to make changes to the barrage plan once the attack was under way. Many lives therefore depended on the decisions made at the planning stage, since it was crucial that the attackers could move forward protected by the barrage, without themselves becoming caught up in it.

According to the plan, the slopes in front of Flesquières would be plastered with high explosive from 8.05 to 8.35 a.m., supplementing the smokescreen which had been maintained on the ridge since zero. At precisely 8.35 a.m. the smokescreen would lift and the barrage would drop back to the main trench line in front of the village, known as Hindenburg Support, followed at 9.15 a.m. by a further move back to the second-line trenches and Flesquières itself. The village and the slopes behind would be pounded for the next ten minutes, after which the barrage would move even further back to hinder any attempt to retreat or bring up reinforcements. Heavy artillery would also bombard specific strongpoints, and in particular the known locations of enemy gun batteries.[12]

The schedule allowed some time for the attackers to gather their forces in the Grand Ravine, as explained in a IV Corps report: 'A pause was made on the Blue line till …8.35 a.m. to reorganize and allow the troops and tanks for the second objective to pass through.'[13] But inevitably, the timetable proved too quick for some crews and too slow for others.

Second Lieutenant Horace Birks was especially critical of the delay, and since he left several accounts of the battle and went on to become a major-general, his experiences carry considerable weight. Far from racing to beat Brigadier-General Elles as exhorted by his section commander, Captain David Morris, he found himself waiting for fifty minutes in the Grand Ravine while the barrage moved forward. There the spoils in the enemy's dug-outs proved a dangerous distraction.

After getting out to inspect the captured trenches, Birks returned to his tank to find only the driver still aboard: 'I searched frantically right and left, and in a few minutes the crew trickled back in ones and twos, laden with the most amazing collection of loot I have ever seen, chiefly consisting of field glasses, greatcoats, pickelhauben and such like. A particularly tough little Scotch Lance-Corporal came back with a frying pan of sausages, which he said he had got from an officer's dug-out …[14] I was furious with rage so they presented the best pair [of binoculars] to me and off we went again.'[15]

Looking back, he felt the pause led to a disastrous loss of momentum: 'It was a pity that this halt, organized for the best of reasons, jeopardized the whole of the attack in that particular area. The victorious, invincible sweep forward was arrested voluntarily; élan was discarded; that irresistible urge to venture farther was lost; the first flush of unexpected and complete success was succeeded by sober reflection of what was to be done as soon as the barrage lifted.'[16]

However, his experiences were far from universal and other tanks that had encountered heavier resistance in the first phase now found themselves racing to keep up with the covering artillery fire. Second Lieutenant James Macintosh recorded that 'unfortunately … time had been lost, and they were a good half-hour behind the barrage'.[17] Second Lieutenant Wilfred Bion from E Battalion pressed on after 'a pause' at the Grand Ravine: 'I reached Flesquières at about 9.10. This was rather too early. We were greeted with tremendous machine-gun fire.'[18]

* * *

Whether they had been rushing to keep up with the barrage or killing time until it moved forward, the second great wave of men and machines was soon making its steady way up the slopes towards Flesquières. The objective or 'Brown Line' lay on the far side of the village, but the woods which screened the houses were clearly impassable for tanks, so the tree-covered brow of the hill tended to act like a giant breakwater with the tanks working their way round on either side. As they began to come under more intense fire, D Battalion therefore became split up, with most of their tanks drawn towards the left-hand side of the village, while others (including D51 *Deborah*) moved to the right alongside those from E Battalion which were attacking there.

The advance began well for D Battalion, supported by fresh troops from 7th Bn Black Watch and 7th Bn Gordon Highlanders who drove the Germans back up their communication trenches towards the reserve system of trenches skirting the village. Shocking though it may seem, the main emotion recorded by the tank crews at this time was elation. Having swept through the German forward positions, and with the enemy now fleeing before them, there was a growing sense of impregnability inside their steel fortresses.

Second Lieutenant James Macintosh described what happened when D45 *Destroyer II* reached the communication trench known, with grim aptness, as Cemetery Alley. The Germans called this trench Havrincourt-Riegel, and were using it as an escape route back to Flesquières. As Macintosh swung his tank to patrol along the trench, he suddenly saw grey-clad figures leap from shelter and run across his front:

> Then for the crew of [his tank] began the rabbit-shooting of their fondest dreams. Streams and streams of the enemy, their retreat cut off by Tosh and their front menaced by the approaching wave, broke wildly from cover. As fast as the gunners could reload, they poured in a hail of bullets, Tosh himself firing and yelling like a maniac. At last the panic subsided, the remainder of the enemy apparently realizing the futility of an attempt to escape; but it left Tosh and his crew hoarse with joy and almost beside themselves with excitement. To those who have never experienced it, the lust of battle must always appear unnatural and terrible; but ever after Tosh would look back to those few minutes of slaughter as among the most joyful moments of his life.
>
> With the cessation of the panic bolt, all appeared to be over, and Tosh proceeded slowly parallel with the trench. Suddenly, in a shell-hole dead ahead, he noticed three living figures – Boche – in grey uniforms and big black helmets, kamerading [i.e. surrendering]. He drew closer to within a few yards. His approach threw them into the last extremity of terror; faces mottled with sickly green, eyes starting, mouths agape, their bodies racked with trembling, they knew not whether to bolt and be shot or stay and be run over.
>
> Tosh too was faced with a problem. If he left them they would infallibly get away to the enemy lines, but to shoot them in cold blood did not appeal to his instincts. Finally he swung left and blotted them from his mind.
>
> He was now approaching another section of the trench he had crossed. To his astonishment he found it still full of Boches, about 150 with two officers, all kamerading in approved style, and throwing equipment, bombs and rifles on to the parapet. This was too much for a man in Tosh's state of excitement. In defiance of orders, armed only with a revolver, he climbed out of his tank and strolled up and down the parados, yelling at the dumb-founded enemy in a marvellous mixture of bad French and worse Dutch, until finally the infantry arrived at the double, and he handed over the prisoners, climbed into the bus and carried on with the war.[19]

David Morris was also gripped by euphoria in his determination to beat the commander of the Tank Corps to their objective, and he was lucky to survive. Second Lieutenant Birks, now back in action after the halt in the Grand Ravine, witnessed an extraordinary spectacle: 'I then saw my next door neighbour tank come into view; it was carrying the section commander, who for some reason was riding on the top of the tank. He was hit in the shoulder almost at once, and grasping his arm he rolled down the back of the tank and disappeared inside.'[20] Captain Morris had lost his race, though not his life, and a few days later he was in an English hospital being treated for a septic 'through and through wound' of the shoulder. Not surprisingly his letter to the War Office requesting a gratuity did not go into too much detail, referring simply to 'a … severe … wound inflicted by a sniper outside the village of Flesqueres [sic]'.[21] The tank Morris had been riding on, D21 *Dreadnought III*, was still carrying its fascine which was now seen to be smoking. The only way for Birks to alert the crew was to fire a machine gun at their tank, after which they managed to dump the burning fascine in a shell-hole.[22]

Captain Edward Glanville Smith from No. 12 Company – another section commander, though a more level-headed one – described the scene after they left the Grand Ravine: 'Up the slope from there to Flesquieres the attack advanced with tanks in a perfect line from Havrincourt Village to Ribécourt, and the infantry following in high spirits. The crest of the ridge was reached after some of the best possible shooting practice with M.G.'s – and then the fun really began.'[23]

On the west side of the village there promised to be a repeat of the first phase of the attack as the tanks crushed paths through the barbed wire, and soon after 10 a.m. the Highlanders had taken possession of the main trench, known as Hindenburg Support. D Battalion's tanks now headed for the next trench-line, known as Flesquières Trench, which marked the final barrier separating the attackers from the village itself.

But when they advanced towards it, all hell broke loose.

CHAPTER 28

The Crack of Doom

As D45 *Destroyer II* approached the enemy front line, it passed the little cemetery on the outskirts of the village. Second Lieutenant James Macintosh described what happened next:

As Tosh crawled over the crest of the rise and crossed the trench, he noticed several Jocks pointing ahead and waving their arms wildly. He peered out, but could see no reason for their warning. As he was following the safe procedure of peppering all the surrounding country with his machine-gun, his attention was caught and held by an appalling sight. A tank to the right had suddenly burst into a bright sheet of flame, while such of the crew as were able could be seen scuttling like rabbits to shelter. A premonition passed through his mind – field guns! He turned back to try and spot them, when suddenly, at his very ear, there came a bang like unto the crack of doom, and all round him was flame and choking vapour, and the awful screaming of stricken men.

In subsequent recollection only two impressions remained of the next few seconds. He could remember crying 'Get out of it' at the top of his voice, and he could remember a terrible second while scrambling, scrabbling men tried to open the side door. When next his mind could record impressions he was lying flat in a shallow trench twenty yards away, his first driver by his side.

Tosh himself and the first driver were uninjured. Close by, in the trench, Tosh saw his N.C.O., who proved to be unhurt save for a generous lump of metal in the right cheek. He reported that the third driver, apparently demented, had fled wildly to the cemetery, fifty yards away. Of the eight, therefore, four were almost untouched.

The air was now fairly alive with bullets, but Tosh and his men, bent almost double, gained the partial shelter of the burning tank. Here they found a gunner, his face yellow with lyddite and distorted with shock. On examination, he had nothing worse than a broken leg and a slight arm-wound, but at present he was too dazed to help himself. They carried him to the comparative safety of the trench and returned to the tank. They then discovered a second gunner, evidently too far gone for help. He showed small signs of any wound, but even as Tosh bent over him he straightened slowly, spread his arms, and with a half-sigh he was dead.

'Poor old Jimmie,' said the first driver, 'he never knew what hit him.'

Tosh turned his head away towards the tank, started, and clutched his driver's arm. From the open door of what was now a smoking ruin crawled a terrible figure. One arm was smashed to pulp, one leg dragged; the body was soaked in blood. But the face – one whole cheek had been blown away, and through the gaping hole the tongue could be seen working feverishly over the shattered jaw. Worse still, the light in the eyes left no room for merciful doubt but that the wreck of a man was still sane. There was no shadow of pain – Tosh seized that crumb of comfort – only a strained perplexity at the unwieldiness of the crippled body.

Fighting with the deadly nausea which almost choked him, Tosh went to the man – his best gunner and firmest friend – and took him in his arms. After a moment's inspection he reached for his revolver, and for twenty seconds tried to nerve himself to the merciful deed. But the decision was too hard for him. Ghastly as the man's wounds were, he might not be beyond hope, and for the moment he could not – his eyes showed that he could not be suffering. With a sob Tosh laid him down and turned away.

The tank was burning fiercely, and the exploding ammunition made a continuous rattle. One man was still unaccounted for; but to enter her was impossible, and nothing could still be alive in that inferno. Beyond his revolver Tosh had no weapon. His first duty, therefore, was towards his wounded.

With many a stumble and many a rest in shell-holes, the three unwounded men carried off the gunner with the broken leg. The air was still full of the clack and whine of bullets, while the field gun which had knocked Tosh out was sending shells so low as apparently to skim the ground. Making for the cemetery they kept behind the shelter of its little quickset hedge, in which birds still twittered, and so, stumbling among the tombstones, came at last to the sunken cross-road behind it, where they deposited their burden.[1]

It was now obvious that the British barrage had failed to wipe out all the enemy's field guns, and that the German gunners were determined to stand and fight. They claimed another victim in D28 *Drake's Drum III* under Second Lieutenant John Henry de Burgh Shaw, described as 'a stout tank commander' by Major Watson, who told how he 'engaged in a duel with a field gun'.[2] Shaw had been in one of the first wire-crushing tanks and fought his way through to Flesquières:

There was a field battery near that village which had accounted for a number of tanks and one gun still remained in action. I advanced on this gun keeping machine guns continually firing on it, and got within 400 yards of it when I was hailed by a message from the infantry which called my attention to another gun quite close on my right and in a concealed position. As the field gun on which I had been advancing appeared to have been silenced I decided to try and knock out this other gun. I turned in the direction indicated by the message and crossing a slight rise perceived this gun, which was an anti-tank gun in a ground emplacement. The enemy were now on either side of us and this gun in front. I advanced straight towards this gun my idea being to ride over it and crush the emplacement.

I kept a continual fire on the aperture through which the gun protruded and when within 40 yards of it, it put a small shell through the front of the tank killing one of my crew. The shock caused the driver to stop the tank but we started again and when within 20 yards of the gun, still keeping a heavy machine-gun fire on it, it fired a second shell through the front of the cab very badly wounding one of the crew and slightly wounding another. The tank engine stopped immediately but did not catch fire. I got the remainder of the crew out as quickly as possible as the tank in that position and unable to move was a death trap.

I remained to assist the man who was so badly wounded and was in the act of dressing a wound preparatory to carrying him out when my tank was surrounded [by] enemy and rifles were pointed through the doors of the tank. I was surrounded within 3 or 4 minutes after the second shell was fired. One other of the crew was captured after evacuating the tank. I attribute my failure to demolish this gun emplacement to not having had a male tank.[3]

Shaw and his crewman were not the only members of D Battalion to end the day in German hands. D11 *Dominie* actually reached the second line of trenches and was only 200 yards from an enemy battery when it was hit, killing two men and wounding most of the others. The reconnaissance officer of No. 10 Company, Second Lieutenant George Koe, was on board with his company commander, having taken the place of two wounded gunners:

> After some time, when I was potting at a Hun machine gun that was holding out, I got hit by a splinter in the wrist and side, but it was only a surface wound and nothing to worry about. I had just got this tied up and had started firing again when – crash! and I saw sparks and flames all around. I guessed at once the 'bus was on fire, and I started to get the door open. I guess that was the worst half-minute I ever had in my life. I was last out of my 'bus and lay quiet on the grass.
>
> My C.O. [i.e. Major Marris] was wounded, so were most of the rest; the only unwounded people were a brother officer and myself, and we neither of us had our revolvers or ammunition. In addition, we were nearly half a mile in front of the infantry, and the enemy were mighty close to us. I tried to move the C.O., but I couldn't, and then C. [the tank commander, Lieutenant Thomas Cook] and I started to get back for assistance. It was a nasty trip, as I was sniped all the way – in fact, I had to do a lot of it on my tummy – crawling, in fact. However, I got back to a trench and found our fellows in it, and after making arrangements with the infantry to get the others in, we set off and went back to our wood again.[4]

Evidence suggests D11 *Dominie* was nothing like as far ahead of the infantry as Koe claimed, though it must have felt like it. However, it still proved impossible to bring back the wounded commander of No. 10 Company, Major Edgar Marris, who gave his own version of events:

> At about 11 am I was in one of my tanks and was approaching the village of Flesquieres … Just outside of the village the tank was hit by a light field gun at about 70 yards range. The tank immediately burst into flames. I was in the front seat. I fell over backwards and tried to reach the door. I got part of the way but remember no more, until I woke up to find 5 or 6 Germans dragging me to my feet, I was then lying just outside the tank. I was wounded in the face and badly burnt.[5]

That night, Hauptmann Otto Fürsen, the commander of 3rd Battalion, 84th Infantry Regiment, who had also been injured in the battle, went to a dressing station in Cambrai for a tetanus injection. He noted that 'a major from an English tank squadron, who had been wounded and captured, was also lying there'. It was Major Marris, who eventually recovered from his injuries and spent the rest of the war in captivity.[6]

Meanwhile, crews of the tanks that had been hit tried to warn their comrades of the danger. Private Thomas Fortune won a Military Medal for his efforts following the destruction of his tank, probably D6 *Devil-May-Care*, as described in the citation: 'A volunteer was called for to proceed to other tanks and to the infantry, who by this time were well in the rear, and warn them of the position of an active enemy battery. Although wounded, Pte Fortune immediately came forward, and in spite of very heavy machine-gun and snipers' fire gallantly carried out his instructions.'[7]

But it was to no avail, and the advance of D Battalion on the west side of Flesquières ground to a halt in the teeth of the ferocious artillery fire. Captain Edward Glanville Smith described the impasse:

> As 12 Company topped the ridge the first thing to be seen was a number of derelict tanks (survivors of 10 and 11 Companies) apparently knocked out by direct hits and most of them burning; and it was only a matter of a few seconds to discover the German battery on the western outskirts of Flesquieres which was doing the damage. The two tank sections on this flank of the village endeavoured to push round it, but within five minutes four out of the five had been knocked out, Lieut. [*sic*] R. A. Jones unfortunately being killed; and the fifth car had no option but to withdraw behind the crest, after the accompanying infantry had been seen safely into their objective, which was found to be unoccupied.[8]

In all, eight tanks were destroyed on the western outskirts of the village. Second Lieutenant Richard Alun Jones died in D41 *Devil II*, alongside his driver, Lance-Corporal Henry Monks. In a letter to the driver's family, Captain Smith described what happened in anodyne terms: 'It was while waiting for our infantry to come forward to take the trench that his tank was hit and he and the officer in charge were killed by a shell, splinters of the shell striking them on the head.'[9]

But Second Lieutenant James Macintosh, who helped to bury their bodies the next day, gave a more frank account: 'Arrived at the tank the men were faced with a particularly horrible work. A shell had landed on the cab, killing instantaneously both officer and first driver, and a fire subsequently starting, the bodies had been roasted where they lay. The officer had been a particular friend of Tosh's – still a boy at heart, with a boy's gaiety and untainted outlook on life. The death of a friend he had grown used to, but this was no ordinary death. Sick at heart, he thanked God that he directed [the burial] but need bear no actual hand.'[10]

Another of the tanks to be destroyed was D47 *Demon II*, which had done 'magnificent execution' a few hours before in the Stollenweg, though in this case the commander, Second Lieutenant James Vose, escaped unhurt, along with his section commander, Captain Harold Head, who had been on board.[11] However, one of the gunners, Private Walter Robinson, was killed, and in a letter to his father, Second Lieutenant Vose told how they 'had got right up to the final objective after driving the Boche out, when a shell from a concealed battery hit us. Your son was killed instantly & therefore suffered no pain whatever. 4 others were wounded by the same shell.' Referring to the earlier fighting, he added: 'It may give you some satisfaction to know that we must have got a few dozen Boche in revenge for your son's life.'[12]

Alongside the tragedy, there were many displays of bravery following the wholesale destruction of the tanks. After D32 *Dop Doctor II* was hit, Lance-Corporal John Tolson distinguished himself by organizing parties to bring in the wounded from several tanks that had been hit. His citation for the Military Medal said: 'On three separate occasions he went back under extremely heavy and practically point-blank machine-gun fire to dress and carry in the wounded. With utter disregard for personal safety, and entirely on his own initiative, he undoubtedly saved several lives.'[13]

One of the section commanders called Captain Christopher Field – inevitably known as 'Happy Fanny'[14] in reference to the comedian 'Happy' Fanny Fields – went forward to Flesquières on foot after the tank he was travelling in ran out of petrol. His citation for the Military Cross told how 'under very heavy machine-gun fire [he] rallied his crews of the tanks that had been hit, and supervised the collection of the wounded. His cheerfulness and contempt of danger had a most encouraging effect on all ranks.'[15]

One of his men, Sergeant George Taylor, did what he could to help the infantry after his tank had become ditched, mounting a Lewis gun on a trench parapet and silencing the enemy who were holding up the advance. His medal citation added: 'Later, though heavily sniped, he ran out to another tank and directed it so that the infantry could advance behind it without being exposed to fire. Again he gave valuable assistance in carrying back wounded under fire.'[16]

* * *

As soon as the fighting subsided, Second Lieutenant James Macintosh returned to collect his injured crewmen from D45 *Destroyer II*. The walking wounded were sent back to the dressing station, and he went in search of the seriously injured man who he had considered shooting to end his suffering:

> Stretcher-bearers were few and far between, but he succeeded in finding two. These he conducted through the cemetery, which still hummed with bullets, and between them they brought the pitiful wreck of a man to the cross-road. Tosh noted with a sigh of relief that he was now delirious.
>
> The next requisite was a stretcher. Prospecting along the road, Tosh found a Boche officer with a shattered leg lying on one waiting to be carried down. This was no time for niceties of behaviour. Lifting off the protesting man, they seized the stretcher, and in a minute Tosh was supporting his driver while the stretcher-bearers raised the load on to their shoulders.
>
> The way to the dressing-station lay along a road, but it was long and very tiring for the bearers. To Tosh it was endless, for the delirious man kept making determined efforts to get off the stretcher, groaning and crying the while with pain and mumbling and mowing with his shattered jaws. At last they reached the dressing-station, where the doctor pronounced the case very serious, but not altogether hopeless.[17]

The havoc had been wrought by a small number of field guns, probably from 282nd Field Artillery Regiment which had a battery sited immediately to the west of the village. A brief account appears in the German official history: 'Until early afternoon the battery defended itself successfully against the tanks, and so provided valuable flanking protection for the soldiers of Krebs' regiment [i.e. 27th Reserve Infantry Regiment]. Feldwebelleutnant Reinsch reports that the guns knocked out five tanks in a very short space of time ... Teams of pioneers ... helped the artillerymen to defend their fire-position. They skilfully removed the still serviceable machine guns from one destroyed tank and used them until the ammunition was used up.'[18]

Despite the courage and sacrifice of the tank crews, it was obvious that the attack to the west of Flesquières had failed, and although they had helped the Highlanders to take the first line of trenches (or Hindenburg Support), they were now unable to provide any further assistance. It was a grim prospect for the men of 7th Bn Black Watch, who summed up their dilemma: 'Following the tanks Hindenburg Support was taken about 10:35 a.m. All the tanks that reached Hindenburg Support were immediately knocked out by the anti-tank battery at [the crossroads on the west side of the village]. The wire between Hindenburg Support and Flesquieres Trench was uncut; there were no tanks on our front; the village of Flesquieres was still in enemy hands; there was no artillery barrage; consequently further advance at this time was impossible.'[19]

CHAPTER 29

Into the Hurricane

Although the attack to the west of Flesquières had failed, an equally substantial force – mostly made up of E Battalion's tanks with some elements of D Battalion, including D51 *Deborah* – was simultaneously approaching the village from its eastern side, supporting two further infantry units, the 6th Bn Seaforth Highlanders and 6th Bn Gordon Highlanders.

E Battalion had also suffered considerable attrition in the first phase of the operation, beginning with the stroke of fate that swept away E27 *Ella* and her crew. After this at least five more machines were lost crossing the Hindenburg Line, one receiving a direct hit and the rest suffering from mechanical trouble – including the unfortunate E24 *Ernest*, whose radiator escape pipe was torn off by the clutching barbed wire, leading to the loss of all its cooling water.[1]

Nevertheless, as they began the long climb out of the Grand Ravine, Second Lieutenant Wilfred Bion in E40 *Edward II* felt very much in control:

> The ease and orderliness of the operation after the chaos of Ypres induced a sense of unreality. The battlefield was set out like a diagram; the functions of infantry, gunners and tanks slotted together with such perfection that it seemed as if we were more pieces of a Staff Officer's dream than soldiers at war. Small pockets of German prisoners were being marched back, filled more with curiosity than fear as the spectacle unrolled before them ... They seemed awfully decent about it and indeed quite keen to watch what we were doing.
>
> I raced my tank – in those days four miles an hour – towards my objective, the village of Flesquieres. The firm ground made it easy and exhilarating. The ground sloped upwards to an enemy strong point. As we came nearer I could see how formidable was the barbed wire – at least six feet high and ten yards thick surrounding the fortification proper. As a routine I closed my flaps and plunged into the wire; for a moment I felt a slight tug as it gripped us. Then we broke through ...[2]

One of the men advancing behind him, Captain Alastair Macdonald of 6th Bn Seaforth Highlanders, described the scene in almost lyrical terms: 'The tanks glided along, bowing their way over the uneven ground, and the ardent waves of men followed over the dry dead grass ... Hindenburg support trench was the objective, and the guns were still pommelling it, as the advance approached.'[3]

As on the west side of the village, the tanks supporting the 6th Seaforths successfully crushed paths through the wire and the attackers were soon flooding into the first-line trenches. The left-hand company gratefully recorded the names of the tanks that made this possible with only three infantry casualties: *Edinburgh, Egypt, Eileen, Emperor, Endurance, Euryalus* and *Exquisite*. The right-hand company complained that the tanks had not come up, but they still found a way through the wire and reached the Hindenburg Support trench with only slightly heavier losses.[4]

But as they crested the ridge, it was as though the tanks of E Battalion – like those of D Battalion on the other side of the village – had strayed into the path of a hurricane.

* * *

Ever since zero hour, the German gunners of 108th and 213th Field Artillery Regiments (FAR) had been standing by, desperately seeking news from the infantrymen who streamed past their positions in full-scale retreat. A number of guns had been destroyed by the British barrage, and the batteries that remained were short of ammunition, but they were still capable of putting up resistance. Leutnant (i.e. Second Lieutenant) Erwin Zindler of 108th FAR – referring to himself as 'Lindemann' – described the anxious wait at No. 1 Battery, on the extreme right of E Battalion's advance, as the sounds of battle drew closer:

> Around 10 a.m. [i.e. 9 a.m. UK time] two wounded infantrymen from the 84th come back. They are agitated, half-crazy. We bombard them with questions. What's going on, what's going on?
>
> 'The English are attacking in a solid mass. One tank right beside another, in two or three lines one behind the next. Tanks, as far as the eye can see!'
>
> Their eyes grow wider. They are 'barrage eyes'. Lindemann recognizes once again the 'Douaumont stare' [i.e. from the fighting at Verdun]. Could it be true, what these people are saying? Is it fear of battle, exaggeration due to a temporary nervous breakdown? A solid mass of tanks? Impossible! Or could it be possible?
>
> And the noise of battle draws nearer.
>
> 'The first [gun] on the left and the first on the right – out of cover!' The gunners jump to. The gun-coverings are torn away.
>
> 'Gunners to the wheels!' With the first on the right, Oberleutnant [i.e. Lieutenant] von Köller joins in with his bare hands. Two guns stand free on the clayey turf. The wheels sink in. Officers and men haul ammunition at a trot.
>
> Nothing can be seen, though the fog is getting thinner all the time.
>
> In front of the battery there are scarcely 100 paces to the crest of the flat, extended ridge, behind which the guns are positioned …
>
> And the noise of battle draws nearer.
>
> Then two men from the battery run forward over the ridge, the last scouts. From far off, they are already shouting: 'English tanks! The tanks are almost here!'
>
> Lindemann jumps to the first on the left, Köller to the other gun. In their faces is an unearthly tension. Lindemann feels the pulse racing in his neck and head and fingertips. He aims the gun himself. His hands clutch the elevation and traverse controls. His eyes check the panoramic telescope, gunsight, spirit-level and regulator.
>
> The shell-case is in the barrel. The gunner stands ready. The others wait as if spellbound.
>
> In front there's a rumbling, as when heavy lorries start their engines. The racket is getting closer. The little group of men are shuddering with tension. When will the tanks come over the hill? Will they come together? Will they come one at a time?
>
> Then the superstructure of the first one appears over the ridge ahead. Rumbling, it slowly pushes its way higher. A tricky target, even at close range …
>
> If Lindemann aims a fraction of a millimetre too high, the shot will fall far away to the rear. If he aims too low by the same amount, it will be a rebound and will tear holes in the sky. He knows this.

Bang ... The shot's away.

Nothing? Their eyes strain forwards. Too high. Their pulses race.

The second ... crack! But where? There it goes, high in the air! A rebound! Too low!

And the tank rumbles higher up onto the ridge. Its machine gun housings are already completely visible. Two machine guns are ripping up the turf towards the gunshield. The spokes splinter, turf is flying. And the machine guns clatter like riveting hammers on a hollow ship's hull. A hundred paces separate the adversaries.

The third shot ... gone!

In front the sparks are flying. Knocked out.

There to the right, another tank! The range is longer. Turn the gun. The first is off target. The second is on.

A huge explosion. Spurts of flame. Knocked out.

More are appearing. Köller's gun joins in heartily, the lieutenant and staff officer-to-be has turned into a gunner.

The lads were as if transformed. They stood eye to eye with the enemy and his wall of tanks. But what a spirit possessed them! How intoxicatingly wonderful it was to be their leader. They tore into their work. No-one thought of taking cover. Standing free on the open ground, that was their place.

'Gun forward!' Exploit the momentary weakness of the enemy. Lindemann braced himself under the rear of the gun carriage, the others on the wheels. Many were hauling ammunition. Lindemann wanted to be up on the ridge, in the teeth of the enemy.

He still wasn't quite up there. There ... two tanks in motion! Fifty paces! The carriage is in position. In a matter of seconds both tanks are knocked out.[5]

Silhouetted against the skyline, the lumbering tanks were easy prey for the field guns and their crews waiting in the dead ground beyond.

In charge of E17 *Edinburgh II* was Second Lieutenant Miles Linzee Atkinson, with his section commander Captain Shirley Spreat beside him. Like R.O.C. Ward, Atkinson had played rugby for Cambridge, though he was seven years younger, and Captain Spreat called him 'the best type of a sporting British officer'. The captain described what happened in a letter to Atkinson's father, who was Mayor of Leamington in Warwickshire:

> We reached the village, and came under the fire of a German field battery at point-blank range. Your son continued to fight his tank until we were put out of action; he consulted with me, and we decided to evacuate the tank. Just as he got out a shell burst almost on top of him. Although at the time we were under hostile machine-gun fire, I think it was this shell which killed him ... I chose your son's tank to go over in, having the greatest faith in him, and knowing that while he lived nothing would stop him.[6]

Photographs taken shortly afterwards show the shattered hulk of *Edinburgh* poised above a German trench, proving they had at least gained their objective. A few yards away, frozen in motion by the shells that struck them at almost the same moment, stand E18 *Emperor II* and the wire-crusher *Euryalus*, with other wrecks visible beyond. Of the seven tanks that had given such vital support to 6th Bn Seaforth Highlanders, all but one were destroyed, with four of the commanders and many of their crew dead or wounded.[7]

When the other wire-crusher *Exquisite* was knocked out, the battalion history told how 'the crew evacuated their useless bus and bravely rushed forward to attack a German gun. Unfortunately the officer was killed and the surviving members of the crew were captured in this thrilling but forlorn effort.'[8] The tank commander was Second Lieutenant Thomas Wilson, and this seems to be the same incident described by Major Alexander Gatehouse, who told how an officer, 'wounded and dazed from the concussion' after his tank was knocked out, nevertheless 'advanced single-handed upon the German gunner with a large track-spanner in his hand. He fell after going about 15 yards shot by [the] gunner's revolver.'[9]

Not all the tanks headed towards the ridge. Second Lieutenant Wilfred Bion and the crew of E40 *Edward II* had crossed the front-line trench and were approaching the woodland in front of the village when machine-gun fire hammered into them with an 'appalling din':

> Taking control I drove the tank so that the bullets struck in front of me; they could do no harm against our armour, and I argued that so long as the bullets were striking on the armour in front of me we must be heading straight for the machine gun. As each bullet struck off a red-hot splinter from the armour, we had an improvised direction finder provided by the bullets themselves. Feeling my face pouring with a greasy sweat I put up my hand to wipe it away. Allen [the driver] looked white-faced and scared as I saw him looking at me. I noticed that my hands were covered with blood.[10]

This was the phenomenon known as 'splash', in which bullets striking the steel walls caused a hail of tiny metal fragments to fly off into the faces, hands, and sometimes eyes of the crew. The machine-gun fire was followed by a roar on the left side of the tank:

> 'Put it in reverse! Fire the left 6-pounder' – at anything, anywhere, to make them think we're fighting someone, I thought to myself.
>
> The moment the breech was opened to load, such a storm of bullets came up the barrel that gunner Allen [who had the same surname as the driver] left it in panic. At once the inside of the tank was an inferno. Richardson managed to close the breech and thanks to him we had nothing but a couple of flesh wounds amongst us.
>
> 'God damn your soul Allen you bastard!' I yelled at the cowering boy. I was blubbing with rage and fear myself.
>
> No sooner had the gun causing us such havoc been silenced, or had silenced itself, than an explosion from the rear of the tank rocked us all. The tank stopped.
>
> 'What's up?'
>
> 'Won't go', yelled Allen [the driver].
>
> What on earth had happened? I had no idea and couldn't think.
>
> 'I think it's catching fire by the petrol tank', reported O'Toole.
>
> 'Every man with a Lewis gun and as much ammo as you can carry. Now out you go! Richardson first – we've only one door – the left one. Fall out, firing your gun as you go. Into the trench!'
>
> Richardson tumbled out with only one bullet through his thigh. The enemy must have been as surprised as we were; all eight of us arrived safe in a bay of the enemy's trench system.

> When I could look back I saw that the tank had a shell hole where the right rear driving mechanism had been; it was effectually [sic] out of action, but the destruction of the gears had saved the petrol tank and ninety gallons of petrol from exploding in flames.[11]

What happened next led to Bion being recommended for the highest gallantry award, the Victoria Cross, though in the end he received the Distinguished Service Order. Taking a Lewis gun and four drums of ammunition, he climbed on top of the tank and opened fire on the enemy from the shelter of his fascine. Before them was a long brick wall, lined with German machine-gun posts, beyond which lay the wooded grounds of the château farm. From his vantage point, Bion was able to pour fire over this wall onto the enemy behind:

> By this time my escapade had stirred up a veritable hornets' nest in the copse. I do not know what I expected would happen – probably nothing – but I was surprised to find German troops, led by an officer, pouring out of a gap in the left distant corner of the wall. An officer pointed his swagger stick to direct his troops to me. I swung round and opened fire on them as they were coming through the gap. At the same moment my gun jammed.[12]

It was time to go, and Bion fled with his crew back to the nearest trench where he reported to the officer in charge, Captain George Edwards of 6th Bn Seaforth Highlanders, who had himself won the DSO a year before during the capture of Beaumont-Hamel. 'While I was talking to him in the trench there was the loud crack of a near bullet. He fell forward and I saw blood and brains bulge out at the back of his skull.' Captain Edwards had apparently been shot by a sniper hiding in a tree, who was himself brought down by Lewis gun fire. After this Bion, who was the only officer present, took charge of the infantry for a time until the Seaforths' commanding officer told him: 'Since you have no tanks you and your bloody Lance Corporal are no good to me. Get back to your HQ.'[13]

The newspaper correspondent Philip Gibbs described Bion's bravery in an article – without naming him – and concluded: 'That episode reveals the high quality of courage of the young men who take our tanks into action.'[14]

* * *

For the Germans manning the second-line trenches in front of Flesquières, the arrival of the tanks caused as much consternation as in the first line, but with two major differences: the defenders now knew what to expect, and they were supported by field guns which engaged the tanks at close-range. The contest therefore felt less unequal to Unteroffizier Senftleben of 27th Reserve Infantry Regiment (RIR), now manning a trench after returning from a failed counter-attack:

> The cry is already ringing in our ears: Tanks! Tanks! – Where, where? – There, out of the fog, which the English have artificially thickened with smoke shells, the clumsy leviathans are sliding towards us; the road is just right for their advance. Rifles and machine guns large and small direct their fire against the tanks. To our right the 2nd Machine Gun Company set up their weapons to provide cover. And though many a brave man falls, they continue firing to good effect. A tank is set on fire. Six or seven brown figures pour out of the opening at the rear. Those who are still standing surrender to our men …

> Help is on its way. Not far from the trench, almost directly behind us, a battery sets up its guns and points the barrels towards the tanks. In our sector alone we can count five, with three beside them to the left. Now they are coming close. Where a hole or trench blocks their way, they go down deep into it. Then the front part rears up high and the obstacle is overcome. Now the battery opens up. Already the second shot hits home. Rending metal, a pillar of fire. There the monster lies. And with cheers and waving of helmets we greet every shot as it strikes.[15]

A lance-corporal in 27th RIR, Gefreiter Zimmers, told how they had driven the attackers back down a communication trench when a tank moved round behind them:

> At first a paralysing fear grips us, since it's scarcely fifty metres away and we have no armour-piercing ammunition with us. Its machine guns hammer away unsettlingly, the dirt is thrown high in the air, the bullets whistle past our ears, and here and there a comrade sinks down silently. The same goes for us. Just wait, Tommy, you'll pay for this. And if we can't do any damage with our rifles, that's why we've got hand grenades … I pull out one grenade after another, they fly in an arc through the air, and explode in front, beside and on top of it. 'Good, very good,' shouts the section commander, 'Let's make it as hot as hell for them.'
>
> I had to use about twenty of them, and the sweat was pouring from my brow, but success was obvious: soon the rat-a-tat-ing stopped and spurts of flame shot up, so the petrol tanks were hit. A few Tommies hurriedly baled out but were shot down by accurate fire. The monster now lay silent and still, with plumes of fire pouring from its innards. A smoking wreck with a few partially decapitated Tommies hanging out, such are the pitiful remnants of Albion's invincible tanks.
>
> I was able to take out a second tank in this way during the attack, as a result of which four prisoners were brought in, and for this I was promoted to Vizefeldwebel [i.e. Company Sergeant-Major]. Eleven tanks, all destroyed, lay before our company's sector and won tremendous praise for our amazing artillery, who consistently knocked out the creeping monsters with their third shot.[16]

No doubt the tanks that Gefreiter Zimmers claimed to have knocked out with hand grenades were actually hit by field guns, but either way, the outcome was the same.

* * *

For the British infantry, the destruction of so many tanks turned what had been an orderly advance into a struggle for survival. Those supporting 6th Bn Seaforth Highlanders had been virtually wiped out before their eyes, and to their right, the 6th Gordons were also making their way uphill when they had, in the words of their regimental historian, 'a perfect view of one of the most dramatic episodes of the war'. It was the same story: 'As the six tanks moving in front of the battalion reached the wire in a straggling line, one after the other was knocked out by a 77 mm. battery firing at a range of about 500 yards. It was pretty cool shooting, and other tanks coming up later were treated in the same way.'[17]

E Battalion were less fastidious about their record-keeping than D Battalion, which makes it hard to establish exactly where the tanks met their fate, but it is clear that a total of sixteen machines were destroyed by direct hits at this stage of the battle. Second Lieutenant Fred Dawson found himself in the thick of the fighting in his tank E45 *Elles II*:

On gaining the crest of the ridge, we seemed to walk 'right into it.' Tanks were all over the place; some with noses up, some afire, but all motionless. At the time we hardly realised what had happened. However, we spotted the offending trench packed with Huns, fully exposed, and all their fire seemed concentrated on our tank. The trench was protected by a belt of wire about 50 yards deep. My gunners, in spite of the enemy's fire, were getting well on to their targets, and I could observe the 6-pounders bursting on the parapet. About twenty yards in the German wire, we received a direct hit, which left a gaping wound in the side of the tank, and which wounded every one except the driver and myself, but fortunately, left the engine still running.

As my gunners were out of action, and another shell had landed amongst the sprockets, I ordered my driver to reverse out of the wire. We just reached the fringe when my engine petered out. A hasty examination showed the carburettor pierced by a splinter. Meanwhile, a fire started on the top of the tank, amongst some spare ammunition we were carrying. There was nothing left but to evacuate, which we did one by one, carrying the badly wounded back to our infantry.[18]

Second Lieutenant Stanley Cohen, who suffered appalling burns to his face and hands in a later attack, also had a narrow escape in his tank *Ewen*:

When within sight of my objective, the second line, I realised that I was ahead of my companions and rather isolated, an undesirable condition. So as all seemed quiet I turned round to seek the others. Almost at once we were hit in the right side, by the driver. Some plates were buckled and he could not drive. In [fact] the tank came to a halt. Then another shell hit the roof immediately behind my head. I had a mighty clout, turned and saw a gaping hole only one inch from my head. The shell had struck where two plates met at an angle and where they were riveted by an angle piece, so making it specially strong ... There was nothing for it but to evacuate, take what we could and seek the shelter of the sunken road. There they found I was wounded in the back and I was sent back to a dressing station and eventually to Manchester.[19]

The section commander of both Cohen and Dawson, Captain Charles Homfray, was also caught up in the carnage: 'The tank that I was in then also got a direct hit, it did not set on fire but made a big hole in the six pounder casing and German machine gun bullets ricocheted round the inside of the tank and two of the crew were wounded. As our tank was now useless I gave orders for it to reverse into a nearby sunken road, out of the sight of the field gun which was obviously firing over direct sights.'[20]

Even the tanks that escaped destruction were now running short of petrol. Second Lieutenant Bion described an extraordinary escape by one of his closest friends, Second Lieutenant Ernest Quainton in *Ethel II*: 'His tank ran out of petrol in front of the German guns, and he lost four of his men from a direct hit. He was just in front of a sunk road, and by pouring whisky into the carburettor and throwing in his clutch the engine started, and he just toppled the tank into the road safe from direct fire! It sounds rather funny, but I wouldn't have been in his place for any amount.'[21] (However, Bion later fell out disastrously with Quainton and dismissed the story as 'probably a fabrication'.)[22]

The 6th Bn Gordon Highlanders who were following now found themselves in a terrible quandary. They could see the 'tank tragedy'[23] unfolding before them, but could not tell whether the tanks had managed to crush the wire all the way through to Hindenburg Support, the German front-line trench. In the words of their report: 'Owing to the formation of the enemy wire the officers commanding "B" and "D" Companies did not realise that the tanks had not got through, and continued the advance. On reaching the wire, however, it became apparent that all had been knocked out before penetrating it. The infantry came under a very intense machine-gun fire from [the] eastern edge of Flesquieres, and began to suffer casualties. ("B" Company lost 20 men and "D" Company 40 from this fire in a very few minutes).'[24]

The infantry gave what help they could to the tanks by picking off the German artillerymen with their Lewis guns across the barbed wire: 'One corporal of "D" Company did particularly good work, pouring a hail of bullets on the battery while it was loading, and time and again flinging himself down under cover just before it fired. The battery was silenced and the gun-crews destroyed'.[25] To their right, an officer from H Battalion whose tank had been hit by one of the same batteries crept forward through the long grass, taking a Lewis gun with which he 'scattered the crew'.[26] However, even with the field guns out of action, no more tanks were available to continue the advance and the infantry were forced to pull back. One small group managed to enter Hindenburg Support, but it was so shallow that they were pinned down by machine-gun fire from Flesquières. In this sector, the attack had ground to a halt before most of the men had got anywhere near the enemy trenches.

CHAPTER 30

Green Fields Beyond

We have mentioned that a small number of D Battalion's tanks joined the attack on the eastern side of the village, and their fortunes were varied. Among them was D43 *Delysia*, still with the crew's signed pin-up photo of the singer Alice Delysia beside the driver's seat, but now commanded by Second Lieutenant Harold Dobinson. Unlike so many others, *Delysia* was spared destruction when it broke down on the German front line with a faulty magneto – the electrical device which fired the spark plugs. Private Jason Addy described the consequences: 'Our tank got crippled and put out of action. Our officer now decided to wait until the shelling had ceased and the enemy had got well out of the way. After a while, and a drink of refreshing tea which we made, we began to look and see what had happened to our tank … After this, and borrowing parts from other tanks that had been worse hit than us, we got our own tank going again and took it back to Havrincourt Wood.'[1]

But most of the crews had more to contend with than breakdowns and boredom. D49 *Dollar Princess* had crossed the main Hindenburg Support line and was heading for the support trench in front of Flesquières when it became ditched and suffered a direct hit, near the spot where Second Lieutenant Wilfred Bion defied the enemy from the roof of his wrecked tank. *Dollar Princess*'s commander, Second Lieutenant John McNiven, escaped unhurt, though his section commander Captain Graeme Nixon, who was probably on board, was slightly wounded. It was a frustrating end to the battle for McNiven, who liked to grab life with both hands and whose favourite saying was: 'If a little is good, a lot is better.' He later recalled: 'One of my men received a nasty wound in the upper thigh and groin. I poured an entire bottle of iodine into the wound, while the boy cursed me. Later I saw him in the field hospital and he said I had saved his life.'[2] The destruction of *Dollar Princess* gives a vital clue to the whereabouts of *Deborah*, since they were both in the same section and the tanks were still operating together wherever possible.

As they went forward, Second Lieutenant Frank Heap and his crew must have glimpsed the devastation around them, the tanks engulfed in flames along the skyline to their right, and the crewmen struggling to drag themselves and their wounded comrades clear from the withering fire. They would have heard the machine-gun bullets that struck *Deborah*'s flanks like sledgehammer blows,[3] leaving the pitted marks that can be seen there to this day. And somehow, in the midst of all this, Heap and his driver spotted the only way that would lead directly to their objective, an entrance they could slip through that would take them into the heart of the enemy's stronghold, sheltered from the field guns that were exacting a dreadful toll from those who tried to pass the village on either side.

The route they had spotted took them along the road leading from Ribécourt into Flesquières, past the long brick wall over which Second Lieutenant Bion had directed his fire, and past the gap in the wall where the Germans had swarmed like angry hornets. It led straight into the centre of the village, which was still thick with enemy troops, though there were no field guns to worry about there, and the infantry had no weapons that were truly effective against tanks.

At some point, did Frank Heap pause to question the course he was about to take? Was he aware there were no other tanks or infantry following, and did he ask himself what they could hope to achieve by pressing on, alone and unsupported? Did he wonder how they – eight men and a monstrous machine – could hope to subdue the village single-handed, when so many other tanks had been destroyed or driven back?

Perhaps a more experienced commander might have decided it was pointless to proceed. For example, Captain Harold Head, who had commanded tanks on the Somme in 1916 and then at Arras and Passchendaele, and had just survived the bloodbath on the western side of Flesquières, later recalled his guiding principle: 'I never took my tank in anywhere I couldn't get it out of again.'[4]

But Frank Heap was determined to carry out his mission, and he and his crew would press on until they reached the Brown Line which marked their final objective, now less than half-a-mile ahead, and nothing on earth would stop them. There was no time for doubt, or any other emotion, as *Deborah* ground slowly forwards into the eye of the storm. Instead Frank must have concentrated on checking the map which marked the route to their final destination, and hammering messages to the gearsmen crouching in the noise and darkness behind, and wiping the sweat from his eyes to squint through the tiny peepholes in search of a flash of field-grey which would betray the presence of the enemy. The sensation was described by another soldier as he attacked in his armoured vehicle in a later conflict: 'Your heart is banging away, your body does not feel like you own it. It's like your whole life has been sharpened to a point, and that point is that one single minute. Everything that's gone before is like nothing.'[5]

* * *

By 10 a.m., it was obvious to Major Fritz Hofmeister, commander of 84th Infantry Regiment, that the defence of Flesquières was hanging in the balance. His soldiers were struggling to hold onto their positions, while the artillery were locked in a fight to the death with the tanks that were threatening the village on both sides. His 1st and 2nd Battalions had clearly been overwhelmed in the front line, and the counter-attacks by units of 27th Reserve Infantry Regiment had made no headway. The last of these forays had been led by Major Günther Stubenrauch, whose men were now trapped somewhere in front of the village, and Major Hofmeister was determined to send help.

The man he turned to was Leutnant S. Osenbrück, ordnance officer of his 3rd Battalion, who was ordered to muster everyone he could and launch a counter-attack down Havrincourt-Riegel (the communication trench known to the British as Cemetery Alley). As he set out on his mission, Osenbrück was lucky to bump into a company of 27th Reserve Infantry Regiment who were coming out of Flesquières. They were even luckier to bump into him, because they were about to run straight into two of D Battalion's tanks near the crossroads west of the village. Osenbrück described what happened next:

> 'Stop! Tanks! Go right, into the Pioneer Park!' I'm already over there. Two officers from the other company introduce themselves. 'No time – counter-attack in this direction! Spread out to the right. Further forward on the right! Get out of cover on the left!'
>
> 'Herr Leutnant, it's coming this way!'
>
> 'Where? Open fire, men! Machine gun here! Let's go, look lively!'

'It's jammed!'

'Then take hand grenades. Now over the top, and cheer! You'll be fine – I've only got a stick! Leutnant Brockers, take over the right flank, get them into the open. Leutnant Höfer, further forward with your platoon.'

Tacca-tacca-tacca-tack! The tank at the crossroads rattles away with its machine gun into the treetops. 'Off we go, men, forward! Can't you see he's firing into the trees?'[6]

At this critical moment, *Deborah* suddenly appeared on the road behind them:

'Herr Leutnant, a tank is driving through the village behind us.'

'Just let it go, man. The artillery will knock it out for sure when it comes out the other side. We're staying here whatever happens, and now it's going forward. March, march! Hurrah!'

'Herr Leutnant, the tank is moving even further ahead.'

'For God's sake, let it go! Forward march!'

Tacca-tacca-tacca-tack! Boom! Crash! A stink of phosphorus. The tank in the village is really letting us have it. Just keep calm. 'Everyone stay down. The enemy must not come any further. Set up the machine guns in front of the sandheap. Leutnant Haufmann, you stay with the machine gun.'

Tack! Tack! Tacca-tacca-tacca-tack! Leutnant Haufmann is shot in the stomach. 'Two volunteers, here!' Leutnant Höfer gets hit in the stomach as well. 'Leutnant Bielenberg, you take charge. This line must be held. I'm going for reinforcements!'[7]

In another account, Leutnant Osenbrück told how 'a tank travelling through Flesquières fired at us vigorously during this counter-attack, which made it extremely difficult for me to hold back the frightened men',[8] while Leutnant Bielenberg described their efforts to calm down the soldiers who were gripped by a 'tank panic'.[9]

* * *

Deborah was doing exactly what she was designed for, moving in behind the enemy to demoralize and destroy them. Her Lewis guns inflicted a number of casualties, probably including Leutnant Höfer who died soon afterwards from his stomach wound. The German counter-attack still went ahead and apparently succeeded in driving the attackers back – but not in reaching Major Stubenrauch, who was captured before getting anywhere near the survivors of 1st Battalion, 84th Infantry Regiment in Havrincourt. Their commander, Hauptmann Wilhelm Wille, saw Stubenrauch after they had both been taken prisoner: 'I called to him, he shrugged his shoulders and said: "There was nothing to be done."'[10] Meanwhile the commander of 84th Regiment, the 'giant' Major Hofmeister, was fatally wounded by a tank and Major Erich Krebs, commander of 27th Reserve Infantry Regiment, took charge of the forces holding Flesquières.

Frank Heap estimated they expended a total of 4,000 rounds during the battle,[11] and since a Lewis gun fired at least 500 rounds a minute, this means all five guns could have fired continuously for more than one-and-a-half minutes. This, in itself, shows they found no shortage of targets.

Following this clash, *Deborah* moved forward to the crossroads at the centre of Flesquières and swung slowly right onto the road leading out of the village towards Anneux and Cantaing – and towards the Brown Line. Only 250 yards later she reached the edge of the village, and for the first time Frank Heap had a heart-stopping glimpse of the fabled green fields beyond. Here *Deborah* halted in the lee of a battered farm building, and perhaps – as his family speculate – he climbed out to take a compass bearing and check they were on course. If so he was certainly fearless, since the village was still swarming with enemy soldiers and he could easily have been shot the moment he climbed out of his tank.

But as it turned out, the danger came from another direction altogether, and it was safer to be outside the tank than in.

* * *

Leutnant Osenbrück had promised his men that the artillery would destroy *Deborah* as she emerged from the village, and luckily for them a number of gun batteries were still standing by ready for action. Among them were men of 213th Field Artillery Regiment, who had been rushed into position in response to the prisoners' revelations of an imminent attack. The details are sketchy, so it is impossible to be certain, but No. 9 Battery was near the road that *Deborah* took out of Flesquières towards Anneux. Leutnant Richter from this battery described what happened:

> For some time the first infantrymen had been coming back through our position and told the worst horror stories. Eventually I succeeding in stopping a Feldwebelleutnant [i.e. warrant officer], who was slightly wounded in the head, as he passed through our position with five infantrymen and a machine gun with three boxes of ammunition. He took up a position with his men on a steep slope right behind the battery and supported us very effectively during the following period. The guns were dragged out of their pits to give better manoeuvrability. We ceased firing altogether …
>
> Retiring infantrymen described the hordes of tanks, and shortly afterwards just such a monster appeared at the village exit of Flesquieres and was knocked out by me with the third shot at 275 metres. A column of flames showed a hit in the petrol tank. Two of our men ran over, and told on their return of the half-charred corpses of the tank crew. They also brought with them a rubber coat, in whose pocket we found an order for the attack. An NCO took it back to the divisional position, along with an urgent request for ammunition or limbers.[12]

One of the infantrymen who stood guard over the battery was Ersatz Reservist Schäfer of 27th Reserve Infantry Regiment: 'We then had to pull back behind Flesquières to an artillery position. Under the command of Feldwebelleutnant Reinsch we there dragged the guns out of their pits; they had hit and put out of action a tank that emerged at the left (eastern) exit from Flesquières.'[13]

No. 8 Battery was also nearby, and Leutnant Neymeyr described a similar encounter, though his estimate of the time was improbably early: 'Already at around 9 o'clock [i.e. 8 a.m. UK time] infantrymen and gunners came back from the front, half-an-hour later whole squads of field and foot artillerymen who had blown up their guns or let them fall into the hands of the enemy as the case may be. At the same time we caught sight of a tank at the eastern exit of Flesquieres and knocked it out with a few shots. We were badly under pressure, as we only had around twenty more shells which we now saved for the direst emergency.'[14]

Leutnant Möhring of 108th Pioneer Company also witnessed the final moments of a tank which may have been *Deborah*: 'One tank drove through the village and came up the road towards Noyelles. It was rendered harmless by the battery (around 200 metres east of the village) with its third shot.'[15]

A few days later, Leutnant Osenbrück of 84th Infantry Regiment was discussing the battle with his men: '"Does anyone know what became of the tank that rolled behind us through Flesquières?" "Yes, Herr Leutnant! We took care of it. It got a broadside from a gun that was standing in a barn at the exit of the village. A 15cm [i.e. a howitzer, known to the British as a '5.9']. Only a couple of the gunners were still there – they aimed the gun, and we dragged the ammunition to it. We did a good job on them!"'[16]

* * *

Whichever battery it was that fired on *Deborah*, the effects were devastating. A volley of shells punched neat holes through the armour on the left side of the tank, but photographs taken a few months later show no visible damage to the right side[17] – which means the catastrophic blasts that tore her apart, leaving the front a tangled mass of steel, were inflicted later on.

But the detonation of the shells inside the confined space, followed by the fire which engulfed the interior, meant there was no chance for the crewmen inside. The side door beneath the sponson had been pushed open, and Frank Heap must have been sickened by what he saw spilling out of it. But for now there was no time to take in the horror, and it was enough to know that four of his crewmen had been killed outright.

The official account indicates that *Deborah* opened fire on the field guns before they knocked her out, describing how Frank Heap 'fought his tank with great gallantry and skill, leading the infantry on to five objectives. He proceeded through the village and engaged a battery of enemy field guns from which his tank received five direct hits, killing four of his crew.'[18] Their achievement was also recorded in the battalion's history: 'Only one tank succeeded in going through the village, and this tank was knocked out at the eastern edge immediately it emerged from the shelter of the houses.'[19]

Captain Edward Glanville Smith's version differed only in detail: 'Tanks pushed on, but were unsupported and could do nothing. Lieut. [*sic*] Heap ... courageously made his way to the far end of the village, but, on showing the nose of his tank beyond the last house, received two direct hits from a gun laid on to this spot and had four of his crew killed outright.'[20]

The dead men were Gunner Joseph Cheverton, killed on the day he turned twenty, along with Gunner Fred Tipping, the father of three young children, and Gunner George Foot who had endured the vigil in No Man's Land with his wounded officer a year before. The other victim was Gunner William Galway, the 'true Irish gentleman' who had survived the first day of the Somme, and Frank Heap's tribute shows he never lost his sense of humour: 'He kept us in shrieks of laughter right up to the moment of his death, and died with a laugh on his lips.'[21]

Frank Heap could do nothing for his comrades, or for the fifth crewman – still unidentified – who had been killed during the attack. But somehow two crewmen survived along with Heap, and they now found themselves in the worst possible situation: cut off inside a German-held village, armed with nothing more than revolvers, and facing the oncoming Highlanders who might well mistake them for the enemy, even if they could reach them across No Man's Land.

Meanwhile German soldiers were retreating down the road past the blazing tank; so whatever they did, they had better do it quickly.

* * *

At around this time, Major Watson arrived at the Grand Ravine and discovered the full scale of the setback:

> We found ourselves in the open with a tank a hundred yards away. We walked to it and discovered my section-commander, Wyatt, with Morris, who had been hit in the shoulder. They told me that we were held up outside Flesquieres, which was being cleverly defended by field guns. Several tanks had already been knocked out and others had nearly finished their petrol. And there was an unpleasant rumour that Marris was killed.
>
> We took to a narrow half-completed communication trench and pushed on up the hill towards the village, meeting the survivors of two crews of [E Battalion], whose tanks had been knocked out in endeavouring to enter Flesquieres from the east along the crest of the ridge. The trench was being shelled. From the sound of the guns it appeared that they were only a few hundred yards away. We walked steadily up the trench until we came to the railway embankment, five or six hundred yards from the outskirts of the village, and we could go no farther, for on the other side of the embankment were the enemy and some of my tanks.[22]

With Ward and Marris both out of action, Watson was the most senior officer on the scene. It was obvious the attack had broken down, but far less obvious to him – or anyone else – what to do about it. Perhaps R.O.C. Ward would have reacted differently, but for Watson the priorities were to let the other units know what was happening, and to find out more about the situation.

These were both sensible steps, but with hindsight it does seem he might have delegated them to others. Watson was accompanied by his second-in-command, the seasoned regular Major Richard Cooper, and his reconnaissance officer, Lieutenant Frederick 'Jumbo' King, who would appear to be obvious candidates for the two roles. Instead Watson left them *in situ*, and set off on a long trek across the battlefield which took him out of contact for much of the day. This is not to suggest that he could have done anything had he stayed; but at least he would have been there if the situation changed.

First he went back two miles (or three kilometres) to the nearest infantry battalion headquarters to inform them that Flesquières had not, as they believed, been taken, sending messages at the same time to inform Lieutenant-Colonel Kyngdon, who he believed to be at the infantry brigade headquarters in Trescault. The infantry commander did not believe the report, so Watson set off on a hazardous reconnaissance with his scout officer, who was finally convinced when they had to crawl on their hands and knees to avoid machine gun fire from the village, one bullet striking the heel of Watson's boot.

By his own account, it was 'a few hours'[23] before Major Watson met up with anyone else from D Battalion; and a great deal had happened in the meantime.

* * *

By late morning, the lead battalions of the 51st Division had therefore seized the main trench in front of Flesquières, known as Hindenburg Support, and in some places they had fought their way through to the next line, known as Flesquières Trench, but all their efforts to advance further had been beaten back by small-arms fire from the village. In most cases the tanks had succeeded in crushing paths through the wire, but many had been destroyed by close-range artillery fire, and those that survived were now dangerously low on petrol. Without their support to tackle the enemy's machine guns, the infantry had little chance of moving into the village while the Germans were defending it so tenaciously. In addition, the British field guns had begun their scheduled move forward to keep up with the advance, so there was no chance of a further bombardment, even if this could be arranged. There was no obvious solution to this impasse.

While all this was going on, the great force of cavalry had also begun its planned move forward to take over the next stage of the operation. Sir Douglas Haig was convinced the success of the battle would hinge on their ability to capture Bourlon Ridge – a low hill with its sinister crest of dark woodland, from which anyone who held it could overlook and ultimately dominate the entire region west of Cambrai. Since the ridge lay some five miles (or eight kilometres) behind the German lines, it was beyond the reach of most infantry and tanks, and the only realistic hope of taking it on the first day lay with the cavalry, who were still unsurpassed on the battlefield for speed and mobility.[24]

The entire Cavalry Corps was standing by to take part in the battle, just as the entire Tank Corps had done, and one might say they had just as much riding on it. Both arms had struggled to demonstrate their value in the prevailing military conditions, though the events of the last few hours suggested this assessment would have to be revised in the case of tanks. Now the time was coming for the cavalry to sweep forward, but before that the tanks had to give them one final push.

At the planning stage, much thought had been given to the preparation of routes suitable for horses, which could not negotiate the narrow paths crushed by tanks through the barbed wire. The solution was to provide a special force of wire-pulling tanks carrying huge grapnels like a ship's anchor attached to a cable, with which they would drag the wire aside to clear a way for the cavalry.

This force was commanded by Captain the Honourable John Bingham, who had spent a frustrating summer awaiting the order to charge his specially adapted tanks up the sea-wall near Ostend to spearhead the aborted coastal landing known as 'Operation Hush'. This time his efforts met with greater success, as described by Captain Stuart Hastie from D Battalion, who commanded a party of wire-pullers:

> The tank passed into the belt of wire dropping the grapnel as it proceeded, passed through the wire and turned to the right and proceeded up parallel to the belt of wire. The effect of this was to roll the grapnel and roll up the wire, pulling up stakes and everything until we had a mound of wire as high as a cottage, at which point the tank could go no further on account of the ... tremendous weight of this wire, and the cable was cut and the tank left to join the other fighting tanks in the battle, leaving behind it a gap of at least sixty yards from which every strand of wire and every post had been torn up and rolled up.[25]

Once again, the Germans' thoroughness counted against them, and the thickly matted belts of wire and stakes were easily dragged aside leaving a number of routes clear for the cavalry, including one from Trescault to Ribécourt and beyond.

No fewer than five cavalry divisions were to take part in the attack, consisting of 27,500 men plus horses,[26] with 1st Cavalry Division positioned directly behind the sector being attacked by D and E Battalions. Their planned approach route to Bourlon would take them through Ribécourt and then on a long, curving sweep to the east past Bois des Neufs, or Nine Wood, near the village of Marcoing. But if the situation permitted, they were to take a more direct route to Bourlon by going over the Flesquières ridge.

In the village of Metz-en-Couture behind the lines, Lance-Corporal Willie Pennie of 4th Bn Seaforth Highlanders witnessed the astonishing sight as 1st Cavalry Division moved forward to take part in the attack: 'The British cavalry began to make their appearance on the horizon about 8 o'clock passing through Metz on the road leading toward the lines. They came on in an endless line as far as the eye could reach till after 12 o'clock, a never to be forgotten spectacle as they passed within a [hundred yards] of our camp – Scots Greys, Lancers, Royal Horse Artillery, and last but by no means least the Bengal Lancers.'[27]

At 11.07, the headquarters of IV Corps – which was more than eight miles (or nearly thirteen kilometres) behind the front line, in the village of Villers-au-Flos – finally received the news it had been hoping for from 51st Division: 'Our men seen on Flesquieres line on both [brigade] fronts.'[28]

Eight minutes later, IV Corps headquarters flashed the news to 1st Cavalry Division, which was under its command: 'Road from Trescault … to Flesquieres reported fit for cavalry. Flesquieres now taken. Push forward through Brown Line.'[29] The next phase of the attack had begun.

Three minutes later, 1st Cavalry Division passed on the order to its 2nd Cavalry Brigade: 'Flesquieres reported taken. Push on via Trescault to Flesquieres.'[30] From 2nd Cavalry Brigade, the message was passed to their leading unit, the 4th Dragoon Guards, who had already moved up as far as Ribécourt. Fortunately this did not – as one might expect – trigger a doomed cavalry charge into a hail of machine-gun fire. In fact, the effect was rather the opposite.

The 4th Dragoon Guards could see perfectly well what was happening ahead, and it was obvious Flesquières had not been taken, while even Ribécourt itself was not entirely secure. Lieutenant David Williams recalled: 'We could see tanks alight and burning on the crest of the ridge, and the Scottish division who were supposed to be advancing with the tanks were pinned down on the slope and there was no possibility of advancing.'[31]

The Dragoon Guards were sent to investigate, but like Major Watson they only got as far as the railway embankment in front of the village.[32] Their arrival was witnessed by an officer of 8th Bn Argyll and Sutherland Highlanders who were holding the position: 'I can remember looking back over the valley and seeing what appeared to be tens of thousands of horsemen, and it was one of the most magnificent and inspiring sights one could imagine … One regiment rode up behind the embankment and the C.O. asked many questions which I answered to the best of my ability. However, after a short stay they about turned and rode back down the valley.'[33]

The commander of 2nd Cavalry Brigade then went to the Grand Ravine in person to see if they could move through Flesquières, and 'realised the impossibility of executing this order … I therefore returned to the advance regiment, ordered them to leave Flesquieres alone, to turn Ribécourt from the South and proceed as quickly as possible to Bois des Neuf.'[34]

An immediate bloodbath had been averted, but several hours had been wasted in the confusion. In the words of Lieutenant David Williams: 'The mistake was ever directing us to Flesquières … Regimental commanders should be given a free hand and merely told their objectives and told to get on as fast as they could, and not given detailed orders which turned out to be entirely wrong.'[35]

A subsequent report sent to Sir Douglas Haig said that ordering the Dragoon Guards into Flesquières had 'sounded the first note of the death knell of the cavalry operations, and the officer who carried it out or prepared to do so, completed the funeral ceremony. Three hours were wasted here of precious daylight, and nothing accomplished except the extinguishing of the possibility of any further valuable cavalry operations on Z day [i.e. 20 November].'[36]

Later there was much buck-passing between IV Corps and 1st Cavalry Division about who was to blame, but for now the race was on to overcome the delay. As the long columns of horsemen clattered away to the east, they knew time was running out and there was now little chance of taking Bourlon Wood before the end of that short November day.

During the afternoon small groups of cavalry did approach Flesquières to probe its defences, and the outcome demonstrates their appalling vulnerability on the modern battlefield. They belonged to King Edward's Horse, a unit made up of volunteers from the colonies and attached to the attacking divisions. Their commanding officer told how one patrol, led by Lieutenant Arthur Tutt, 'made a determined effort to find a line through the enemy trenches to the north-east. It carried out its task with great courage and dash but only succeeded in establishing the fact that the enemy still occupied a strong and continuous line on the further edge of the slope.' Lieutenant Tutt and his second-in-command were both severely wounded.[37]

Leutnant Möhring of 108th Pioneer Company described the same encounter: 'Towards 3 p.m. [i.e. 2 p.m. UK time] around two squadrons of English cavalry came riding towards us north-east of Flesquières, all on beautiful black horses with white blazes. We let them come to within 150 metres and then opened up with machine-gun fire. They immediately turned tail and rushed away in a wild flight with heavy losses, even through the barbed wire entanglement where many more horses fell.'[38]

* * *

Although Frank Heap and two of his crew had survived *Deborah*'s final journey, the danger was far from over, and they now had to somehow slip back to their own lines, avoiding capture or worse at the hands of the Germans who were still occupying the village.

It was vital to get away from their burning tank as quickly as possible, and the route they chose took them due south, behind the backs of the buildings lining the street up which they had come. But this also led them straight into a key enemy stronghold, the wooded grounds of the château farm, where they could see machine-gunners firing at the advancing British from behind the massive brick wall.

Second Lieutenant James Macintosh must have heard what happened directly from Frank Heap, his brother officer in No. 12 Company: 'On the right of Flesquières, one tank had succeeded in penetrating to the farther edge of the village; here it was blasted, four of the crew were killed outright, and the survivors crept back through the empty streets. The commander observed a machine gun in full operation from behind the shelter of the château wall, and was compelled to pass it by …'[39]

Soon after this, their worst fears were realized, as recounted by Second Lieutenant Macintosh: '… round the next corner he met a party of the enemy face to face, and for a moment neither could decide whether to surrender or to claim surrender, but in the nick of time a Jock scout appeared with bombs, and the Boches fled – eleven from two.'[40]

Decades later, Frank Heap's grandson Will Heap came across an old service revolver inside a trunk at the family home. 'It was massively heavy, a fearsome thing. I told my father about it, and he said "that probably saved your grandfather's life". The story was that Frank had gone round a corner and there were lots of Germans there, and he thought "they're going to kill me", so he pointed his revolver at them and they all stuck their hands up. And he ordered them in German to stay there, and carried on.'[41]

The revolver was handed in to the police by Frank's son, but one item from *Deborah* has survived – a red and yellow flag, now creased and faded, but still bearing burn-marks which must have been made by metal splinters inside the tank. The flag was carried by tank crews as a signal to tell the infantry 'All Clear – come on',[42] and Frank's family believe he took it with him so he could identify himself and his men to the British troops when they got close to their own lines.[43] As it turned out, the chance encounter with the 'Jock scout' had saved the day, and Frank Heap and his companions were escorted back to safety by the men of 51st Division.

Captain Edward Glanville Smith was impressed by Frank's achievement: 'He himself and the two other survivors somehow succeeded in fighting their way back to our lines.'[44] Heap was awarded the Military Cross for gallantry, and the citation summarized what happened after *Deborah* was destroyed: 'Although then behind the German lines he collected the remainder of his crew, and conducted them in good order back to our own lines in spite of heavy machine-gun and snipers' fire.'[45]

It was an epic escape, but it could not disguise the fact that not a single tank had managed to get past the German artillery, and although *Deborah* had come closest to reaching the objective, Flesquières still remained firmly in the hands of the enemy.

CHAPTER 31

Like a Boar at Bay

Some time in the early afternoon, while Frank Heap and his crew were making their way back through the German lines, the tank crews waiting in the Grand Ravine jumped up to salute the arrival of none other than the commanding officer of D Battalion, Lieutenant-Colonel William Kyngdon. He had left the infantry headquarters in Trescault to come forward and take charge of the situation in person.[1]

With all three of his three company commanders dead, captured or incommunicado, it was the appropriate course of action, but the challenge he now faced was enormous, perhaps insurmountable. Major R.O.C. Ward was the one man who might have been able to galvanize the few remaining tanks, formulate a rapid plan of action with the infantry on the ground, and lead an *ad hoc* assault on the village. But R.O.C. Ward was dead, and it was doubtful whether Kyngdon, the artilleryman and old colonial hand, would have either the capability or the charisma to pull it off.

His initial response was to call on one of his most experienced section commanders, Captain Alfred Enoch, who had taken part in the very first tank action in September 1916 and later commanded D43 *Delysia* in the attack on 22 August. The records show that Enoch went into the battle with only one fighting tank,[2] so he was probably also in charge of the supply tanks which dragged sledges laden with petrol and other essential materials.

The battalion history says 'the Section under Capt. A.J. Enoch was despatched through Flesquieres',[3] but they probably did not enter the village at this time and their mission was more limited, as described by Lieutenant-Colonel Kyngdon: 'I ... ordered 3 male tanks to approach the edge of the village and fire heavily into the wood in front of it.'[4] If it had taken enormous courage to approach Flesquières when no-one knew what was there, it must have been a truly terrifying prospect now the village was, in Major Watson's memorable phrase, 'surrounded with derelict tanks, like a boar at bay with dead hounds'.[5]

Captain Enoch must have gone forward fearing the worst, but this did not happen. Perhaps the tanks did not stray into the artillery's field of fire, or else the German gunners were simply too short of ammunition. The commander of 6th Bn Seaforth Highlanders, Lieutenant-Colonel Samuel McDonald, seized the opportunity offered by the tanks, but the necessary co-ordination was lacking: 'I ordered an advance under this covering fire. I got the men forward on right and left but the tanks had ceased firing and again there was a tremendous fusillade of machine-gun fire from the village.'[6] They gained a foothold in the second-line Flesquières Trench, but efforts to rush the village were driven back by fire from the wall fronting the château farm, behind which the survivors of *Deborah* had passed, and from houses in the village.

The Germans were unimpressed: 'Around 3 p.m. [i.e. 2 p.m. UK time] the English attacked again – tanks also attacked, but most of their shots went into the tree-tops so that numerous branches dropped down on us. The Tommies, who appeared at the edge of the park, came under fierce fire. With the help of the 27th [Reserve Infantry

Regiment] the attack was completely beaten off.'[7] Lieutenant-Colonel Kyngdon had to concede that nothing had been achieved by the tanks' foray: 'This had the effect of silencing the enemy's fire, but as soon as the tanks withdrew German machine guns again opened on our infantry.'[8]

However, later in the afternoon a more substantial opportunity presented itself when a group of wire-pulling tanks, having cleared the way for the cavalry to advance, arrived in the Grand Ravine to await further orders. Lieutenant-Colonel Kyngdon suddenly found himself with reinforcements: 'After they had filled with petrol [I] ordered 7 of them to work round the edge of the village and enter the village itself.'[9]

This was the best chance yet of seizing Flesquières and getting the operation back on track, and six of the tanks successfully entered the village from the north unhindered by enemy field guns.[10] But even if the infantry had been told what was going on, there was again a glaring lack of co-ordination. Lieutenant-Colonel McDonald sent one group of Seaforth Highlanders through the wood in front of the village and another into the village itself, supported by trench mortars and rifle grenades. This time he did not mince his words: 'The first party was driven back but the second entered the village and were pushing through when the tanks went away back, without rendering the required assistance.'[11]

One of his officers described the tanks' effort as 'distinctly disappointing on this occasion', and told how 'One small Seaforth section, who in the trail of these tanks, managed to effect an entry to the village, were left in their exposed posts until ordered to withdraw.'[12]

It had been the last throw of the dice for D Battalion, and Lieutenant-Colonel Kyngdon gave only the briefest summary: 'On reaching the village the tank commanders could see no signs of its being occupied, and after manoeuvring about until the light failed, withdrew. Again the enemy opened fire on our infantry as soon as the tanks had withdrawn.'[13] Although it was no consolation, Major Watson's original assessment had been proved correct: 'It was impossible ..., at this stage, to secure the necessary co-operation with the infantry, and an attack made by tanks alone would obviously fail.'[14]

The commander of 51st Division, Major-General George Harper, may have been thinking of this episode when he came to write the section on attacking villages in his infantry training manual: 'The only chance of success lies in close co-operation between the tanks and the infantry ... It will be of no avail for tanks to go independently down the streets of the village in no conformity with the movements of the infantry.'[15]

* * *

Although the frontal assault on Flesquières had failed, the solution was obvious – not just to the modern armchair strategist, but also to those on the ground at the time, and especially to the Germans, who were baffled as to why the British ignored such an outstanding opportunity.

By early afternoon, 62nd Division, attacking on the left, had occupied the village of Graincourt one-and-a-half miles (or two-and-a-half kilometres) north of Flesquières, and 6th Division had advanced so far on the right towards Nine Wood, Noyelles and Marcoing that its men were 'looking into the backs of the Germans in Flesquières at a distance of a mile'.[16] While 51st Division was, to quote one regimental historian, 'hanging back in an extraordinary way' and effectively 'lay in a sack',[17] the 62nd and 6th Divisions on either side had only to link up behind Flesquières and the enemy would find themselves in a sack, and one from which they were unlikely to escape.

210 Deborah *and the War of the Tanks, 1917*

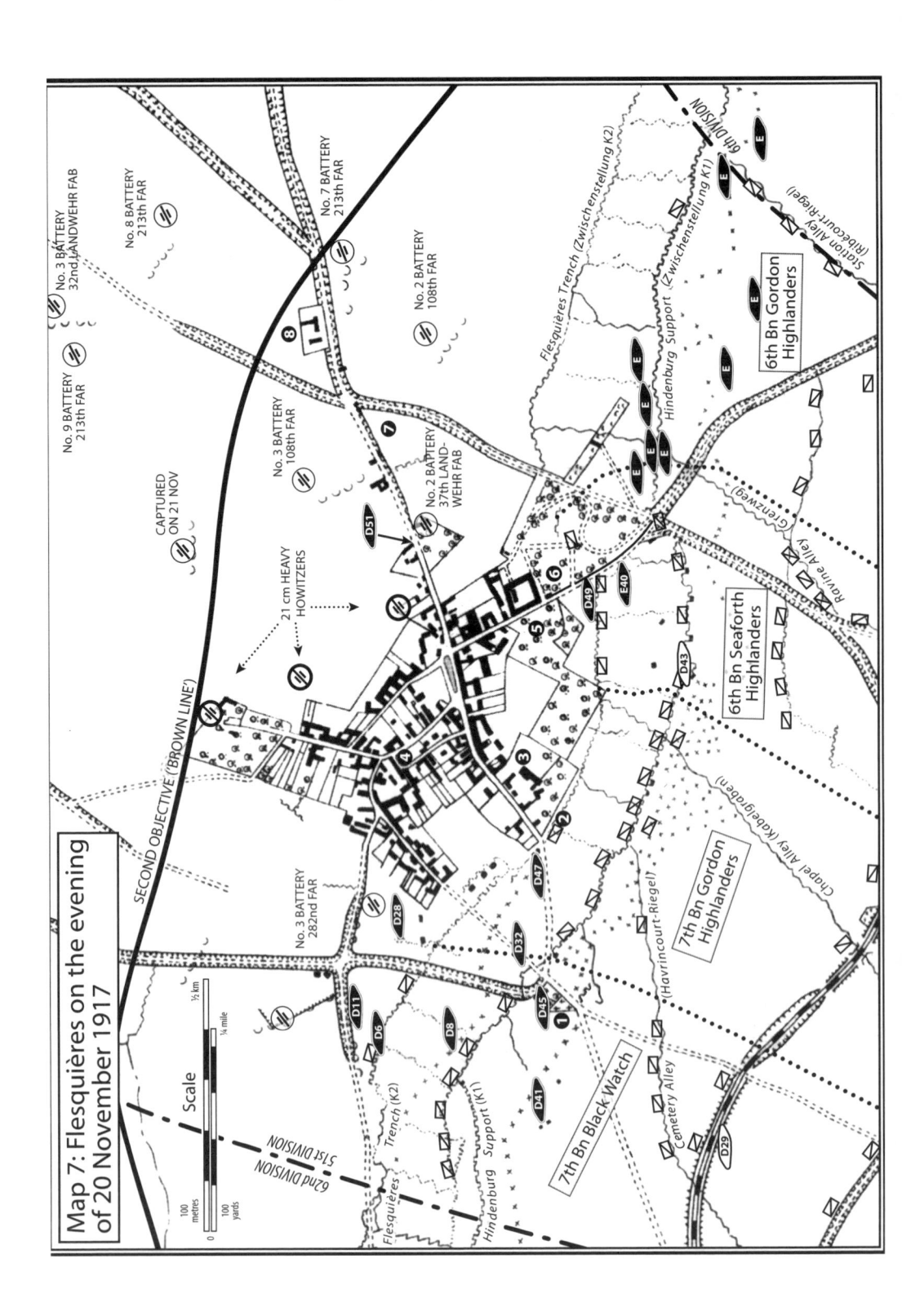

Map 7: Flesquières on the evening of 20 November 1917

Key to Map 7 (opposite)

- 〜〜 Trench
  with British name (followed by German name in brackets)
- ⋯⋯ Trench under construction
- ‧ ‧ ‧ ‧ Barbed wire entanglement
- ᴗ ᴗ ᴗ ᴗ Gun emplacements
- 🬛 Knocked-out tank
- ⬭ Broken down or ditched tank
  with battalion name, and crew number if known
- ▨ ▧ Infantry platoons
  (16 per battalion - each around 50 men)
- ▬▬ Objective line for attackers
- ▬ ▪ ▬ Boundary between divisions
- ‧‧‧‧‧ Boundary between positions held by attacking battalions
- ⊘ German artillery battery
  (each containing 3-4 field guns)
  FAR = Field Artillery Regiment
  FAB = Foot Artillery Battalion
- ⊘ German heavy howitzer
- ❶ French civilian cemetery, also used as German military cemetery
- ❷ Post-war burial site of D51 *Deborah*
- ❸ Flesquières Château
- ❹ Church, and entrance to catacombs (used as shelter)
- ❺ German pioneer park (i.e. engineers' depot)
- ❻ Grounds of Château Farm, with strong brick wall on south-west side
- ❼ Site of Flesquières Hill British Cemetery
- ❽ Sugar-beet factory

Map 7a: Situation on the evening of 20 November 1917, showing positions reached by attacking divisions

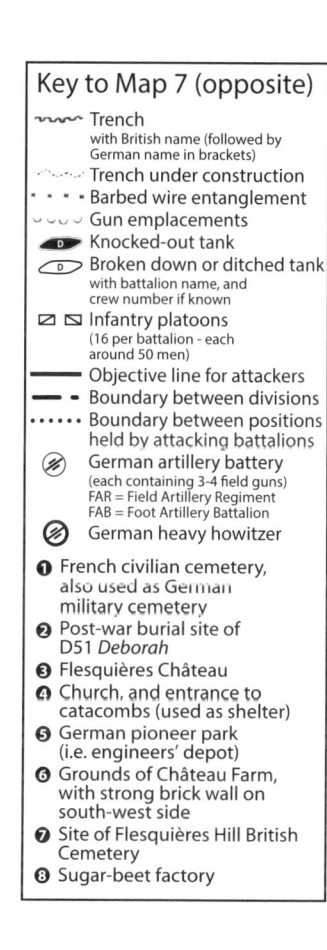

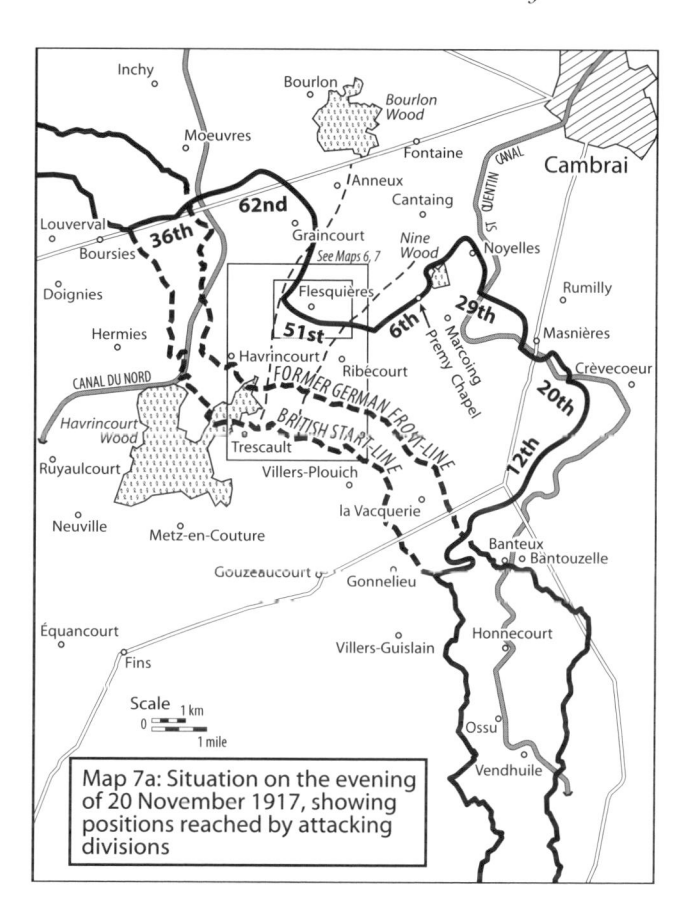

Map 7 shows the situation at Flesquières on the late afternoon of 20 November, with the locations of destroyed and ditched tanks, and the positions reached by attacking infantry from the second wave, as described in Chapters 28–31.

The infantry positions are taken from a map showing the situation at 7 p.m. in the War Diary of 51st Division headquarters. This illustrates how the Highlanders had taken most of the first line of trenches in front of the village, except on the right flank. However, they had largely failed to penetrate through to the second line.

Information on D Battalion's tanks is taken from Battlegraphs in the War Diaries of the battalion and 1st Tank Brigade. The exceptions are D28 *Drake's Drum III*, whose final position is not recorded, and D51 *Deborah*, which can be precisely located on photographs.

The position of E Battalion's tanks is more speculative, as details are not given in the Battlegraph, and the map is based on analysis of photographic evidence by Philippe Gorczynski. The approximate location of Second Lieutenant Bion's tank E40 *Edward II* is based on a sketch map in his *War Memoirs*.

German records do not show the exact disposition of forces holding the village at the time, consisting of survivors from 84th Infantry Regiment, 27th Reserve Infantry Regiment, and other assorted units. Positions of artillery batteries are based on the best available information, though by this stage many guns had been destroyed, moved or withdrawn.

Contour lines have been omitted for the sake of clarity, but reference should be made to the relief map 6a on p. 156, which shows how the artillery was hidden on the reverse slope of Flesquières ridge and destroyed the tanks as they appeared over the skyline.

Map 7a shows the wider situation, and illustrates how the attacking forces on either side of Flesquières could have joined up to encircle the village, as described in Chapter 31.

The Germans recognized their perilous position, according to Hauptmann Otto Fürsen, commander of 3rd Battalion, 84th Infantry Regiment: 'The distance between Nine Wood and Graincourt amounted to 3.5 kilometres, the terrain was visible in itself, and was becoming somewhat clearer at the time. It would have been easy for the English to establish a connection, and thus completely encircle and cut off the defenders of Flesquières – all the more so because they were not lacking in any means of reconnaissance.'[18]

Despite the primitive state of battlefield communications, the British commanders miles behind the front line were clear what had to be done. The situation was complicated because 51st and 62nd Divisions came under a different army corps to the neighbouring 6th Division, but this was obviously resolved. At 2.35 p.m., 51st Division was told to renew its attack from the south while 18th Brigade from 6th Division attacked Flesquières from the east, and 1st Cavalry Division worked round the north-east side of the village.[19]

The orders seemed clear, but the attack never went ahead, even though 18th Brigade felt confident of success: 'The enemy's resistance in Flesquieres was slackening, and there is little doubt that the village could have been entered with small loss.' Their report laid the blame on the neighbouring 152nd Brigade, which formed part of 51st Division: 'A message was ... received by telephone ... from [the commander of] 152nd Bde., asking that the projected attack should not be carried out, as the northern portion of the village was believed to be already in the hands of the 51st Division.'[20]

This was strange, since 152nd Brigade's commander also claimed to have been all in favour of the scheme: 'I consider that if an encircling movement had been ordered from the vicinity of Premy Chapel on the right, and Graincourt on the left, to be carried out by the Divisions on the flanks ..., many German guns and a considerable number of prisoners would have been captured who, in fact, made good their escape.'[21]

The 6th Bn Gordon Highlanders, who formed part of 152nd Brigade, told how they established contact with 18th Brigade with a view to supporting a flanking assault, though they were apparently concerned about the lack of liaison with 62nd Division on the left. According to the Gordons: 'It was evident that co-operation from the direction of the Flesquieres-Graincourt road would be required, and owing to the difficulty of communication the suggestion could not be got back in time for action before dark.'[22]

A regimental historian commented that 'the famous 51st Division machinery was not working at its best that day',[23] and the upshot was that despite being obvious to everyone what should be done, no-one actually did it. Clearly there had been a failure of command or communication, or both, but it is less clear who was to blame. In fact the fundamental problem may have been that after years of trench warfare in which advances were limited to the seizure of clearly defined objectives, the army had simply lost the ability to 'think on its feet' when the opportunity arose.

This was the view of Hauptmann Fürsen a decade later, as he endlessly pondered the question of why the British had not joined up their two flanks to encircle them: 'That which an ordinary German company commander would have observed and tried to execute if the tables were turned, was not realized in time, much less put into practice straight away, by the brigade commanders responsible to General Byng. Tactical expertise from a long peacetime training could simply not be learned in a few years of war, despite the declared organizational ability of the English.'[24]

It would be easy to see this as an outburst of arrogance from a defeated enemy, but a similar explanation was later put forward by Horace Birks, who had commanded a tank in the attack on Flesquières before helping to defeat the Germans in a second war. Looking back in 1949, he wrote: 'Relatively junior commanders had little or no experience in the use of manoeuvre, their knowledge of the functions of the supporting arms was negligible, their outlook was parochial with great reliance on the strong right arm and personal gallantry. The switch-over from this type of trench warfare to an attack which envisaged deep penetration in country selected for its opportunities for open warfare involved considerable readjustments which could scarcely be achieved with success in two or three weeks' elementary and somewhat ad hoc tactical exercises.'[25]

The outcome was that the advance remained checked at Flesquières throughout the afternoon and evening of 20 November, and the crack 51st Division remained, for the time being at least, 'in a sack'.

* * *

The tanks were in no position to help them out, and after completing his reconnaissance of the battlefield, Major William Watson of D Battalion met up with the survivors of his company near the railway embankment south-west of Flesquières. It was clear they could do no more, so the remaining machines were left under a skeleton guard in the Grand Ravine and they began the dispiriting tramp back to Havrincourt Wood as rain set in.

The tanks that were no longer capable of action were also withdrawn to Havrincourt Wood, among them D27 *Double Dee III* commanded by Second Lieutenant Horace Birks. During the attack he had maintained his position in front of the château and village, avoiding being drawn off to either flank but unable to penetrate the woods or help the infantry to advance under the intense machine-gun fire. His crew endured this close-range fire for an hour-and-a-half, until forced to withdraw with all but one of them wounded, several Lewis guns out of action, and petrol running low.

Birks told how 'about half-way back ... I ran into Colonel Kyngdon – the first time I'd seen the commanding officer for some time. I thought I should get a rocket, [but] he looked at my tank and told me that I'd better go back to the lying-up place.'[26] On the way they gave a lift to some wounded infantrymen inside and on top of the tank. 'They were all very grateful; they were all from the Highlands and did not speak readily understandable English.'[27]

On returning to Trescault, Birks discovered their tank had been almost literally shot to pieces by concentrated machine-gun fire:

> The barrel of the front gun was bent downwards and the casing torn and flattened, both the unditching rails were cut through and clanging together and the beam was see-sawing unevenly on the exhaust pipe, the hinges of one of the front flaps had been cut through and hung at an angle across the aperture, both the port guns were in a condition very little better than the front gun, and the port louvre was almost shot away. The hull itself was badly pitted in innumerable places, which was one of the reasons for the intensive splash which had been experienced inside the tank.[28]

When they reached Trescault at 2.15 p.m. another surprise awaited them in the form of a huge force of cavalry, still standing by ready to advance: 'It was the most extraordinary sight, the first time I'd ever seen a horsed cavalry brigade ready for action, and they were waiting for orders which unfortunately they never got.'[29] Either the battered tank or the immaculate cavalry would have to give way, and what happened next turned out to be symbolic: 'The brigade major tried to persuade us to drive past them on the side of the road, but the driver went slowly but firmly right through the middle of them all.'[30]

Later that evening, Birks' company commander, Major William Watson, was also in for a surprise when he got back to Havrincourt Wood and met up with the adjutant of D Battalion, Captain Fred Cozens. As usual, Major Watson exercised a dignified restraint, but there was no mistaking his disdain for the way Lieutenant-Colonel Kyngdon had handled the situation:

> The adjutant was much distressed, for he had had no news of the Colonel, who apparently had left the infantry brigade headquarters early in the day. A pile of messages were waiting for him, including, to my chagrin, those which I had sent him in such haste when I had discovered that the Highlanders were held up at the railway embankment. It was after nine, and I was wondering whether or not to inform the brigade, when the Colonel came in with Cooper [i.e. Watson's deputy, Major Richard Cooper].
>
> The Colonel, who had gone forward early in the battle, had found Cooper in the communication trench by the embankment, where I had left him with Jumbo to keep in touch with the situation. In the afternoon they had collected a few tanks and sent them into Flesquieres. The tanks had paraded through the outskirts of the village, and not a shot was fired at them; but later, when the infantry attacked again, the enemy came up from their hiding-places and let fly with machine-guns. At dusk Flesquieres was still inviolate.
>
> We cared little about anything, except sleep. The Colonel told us that we should not be required on the next day. So after a meal and a pipe we turned in for the night.[31]

For the men of the 51st Division, clinging to their hard-won positions before Flesquières, sleep was a rare commodity as they wrapped themselves in their rain-sodden kilts and prepared to renew their attack on the village. With the coming of nightfall the infantry were effectively on their own, and they removed Lewis guns from some of the derelict tanks to reinforce their positions.

Patrols sent into the village found the west side was lightly held by a few machine-gunners and snipers, and the battalions began preparing to mount a flanking attack, but 51st Division headquarters reported: 'Before it could be carried out information was received that a general attack, supported by artillery, was to take place at dawn.'[32]

* * *

It was scant consolation for the men of D and E Battalions, but 20 November 1917 had been one of the most stunningly successful days of the war for the British Army. In the space of a few hours they had punched their way through the most formidable German positions on the Western Front. In a war when advances were often measured in hundreds of yards and tens of thousands of casualties, they had driven the enemy back for a distance of three to four miles (or four to six-and-a-half kilometres) at a cost of around 4,000 men dead, wounded or missing. They had inflicted severe losses on the enemy, taken well over 4,000 prisoners, and destroyed or captured 100 field guns.[33] Incredible though it seems, in one day they had captured an area roughly equal to the entire gains in the Third Battle of Ypres.

All arms had contributed to this extraordinary achievement, but it was the massed use of tanks that had enabled the infantry to break through the German positions without prolonged artillery preparation, and thus preserve the surprise and provide the fire support that were essential to success.

But for all that, victory had not been total. The Tank Corps had paid a heavy price for its heroism, with 179 of its 378 fighting tanks out of action from a combination of direct hits, ditching and mechanical breakdowns.[34] The losses had been especially heavy in D and E Battalions, which had lost forty-three tanks out of the seventy that went into action, including *Deborah*. The great force of cavalry, hobbled by confusion and indecision, had not gone forward in any substantial numbers, and the strategically important Bourlon Ridge remained in the hands of the enemy, who began reinforcing it as quickly as possible.

On the other hand, it was clear that the German defenders of Flesquières had also suffered heavily, with 84th Infantry Regiment losing eight of its officers dead, two wounded and thirty-three captured. The regimental historian was unable to give a precise figure for NCOs and men, but estimated the casualties at around 1,500.[35] The 27th Reserve Infantry Regiment gave its total losses in the battle as twenty-seven officers and 983 NCOs and men killed, wounded and missing.[36]

However, one German officer claimed it was obvious from the moment of surrender that the attack would soon run out of steam. Hauptmann Wilhelm Wille, commander of 1st Battalion, 84th Infantry Regiment, who had led the defence of Havrincourt, watched the attacking forces with professional disdain: 'Anyone who closely followed the movements of the English artillery and cavalry soon observed the extraordinary aimlessness of their manoeuvres, and an almost incredible clumsiness in their execution. The batteries drove continuously to and fro, forwards, backwards and sideways, ending up in confusion, none of the batteries came into action. The English themselves appeared not to know what they wanted, and to be unable to come to any decision. Our initial fear that the English push would go through as far as Cambrai diminished more and more, the longer we observed this display of indecisiveness.'[37]

As they trudged back through Havrincourt Wood and Trescault towards Metz-en-Couture, Hauptmann Wille and his men witnessed the preparations for the continuing advance. They were impressed by the enemy's equipment, but not by their ability:

> On the roads were numerous columns of vehicles, all brand new with immaculate rubber tyres, the same picture as us in 1914 on the advance from Aachen to Liège [i.e. from Germany into Belgium], and yet quite different. The aimless driving about of the English batteries on the adjacent heights, and the mounted drills of the cavalry, seemed almost ludicrous. It was soon clear to us that 'the greatest advance in the world' [as a British general had described it to them] lacked any depth and strength, and would very soon be parried. This realization made us more confident again, and relieved us in our cruel fate.[38]

One might dismiss this as sour grapes from a loser, except there were also those on the British side who felt their senior commanders had not done enough to plan for success. This was the view of a number of men in the Tank Corps, including Lieutenant Jack Coghlan who escaped unhurt after his tank D29 *Damon III* broke down while attacking to the west of Flesquières: 'So unexpected was the victory that there were no supporting troops to exploit the success or even to consolidate the ground won.'[39] Or as another tank officer put it: 'Although there was nothing to stop us, there was no plan and no troops. Haig was caught, like the Germans later on, surprised at his own success!'[40]

The situation was especially pressing in the case of the Tank Corps, whose entire strength had been thrown into the battle on the first day. Lieutenant-Colonel John

Fuller later claimed to have foreseen this problem, and to have warned Brigadier-General Hugh Elles that 'to fight without a reserve is similar to playing cards without capital – it is sheer gambling. To trust to the cast of the dice is not generalship.'[41]

But whatever happened next, further progress was impossible until Flesquières had been taken, and as night fell, the village remained firmly in the hands of the Germans.

* * *

Unknown to the British, at 2 a.m. (all timings here are one hour ahead of UK time) Major Erich Krebs called an officer from 84th Infantry Regiment into his makeshift headquarters in the village:

> Keep what I'm saying now close to your chest, and discuss it with the officers of your regiment. We're sitting here almost completely surrounded by the English ... Leutnant Brockes ... has just come back [from divisional headquarters] with the order for us to withdraw. We are going to gradually disengage from the enemy and pull back to Cantaing ... You will take point position, and will try to accompany the seriously wounded. Your men from the 84th will take over the transport ... You will march off at 3 a.m., the remaining companies will follow as appropriate. The last company, the battalion and regimental staff, will march at 5 a.m. under the command of Leutnant Osenbrück.[42]

The decision was greeted with relief by Osenbrück himself: 'Thank God! So we weren't completely lost, and had escaped from captivity – but not quite! By then, the enemy might already have completely closed the noose.' It was therefore vital to keep up a semblance of normality as they prepared for departure: 'Here and there a flare was sent up into the pitch-black night. A few rifle shots, a salvo crackling across to deceive the enemy, which we could hear hammering against one of their ditched tanks.'

A few more flares were fired off as the final detachment slipped out of the trenches, up the sunken road and past the grounds of the château farm which they had defended so tenaciously the day before. As many field guns as possible were also withdrawn, though some had to be abandoned to the British. Soon afterwards Leutnant Osenbrück's men reached Cantaing and were on their way back to barracks in Cambrai. 'Over from Flesquières we hear a dull rumbling. The English are bombarding the positions we have just left. They'll be truly amazed when they find the birds have flown!'[43]

CHAPTER 32

A Bitter Evening

During the night, 51st Division received orders to renew its assault on Flesquières early the next day supported by an artillery barrage, though no tanks would be available. But patrols soon discovered that the enemy had already pulled back, and the Highlanders moved through the village to reach the Brown Line – their original objective – at around 6 a.m.[1]

After this, fresh battalions passed through them to continue the advance, and it seemed as though the offensive was back on track – much to the relief of the units that had struggled to take the village the day before, such as 6th Bn Gordon Highlanders: 'The men were tired but very keen and pleased that the advance which had been held up the previous day had eventually been accomplished.'[2] One of their officers described them as 'flushed with success' and added: 'As they lay down to rest they saw Cambrai a mile or two distant, and almost fancied they could strike the spires with a stone.'[3]

Nearby, 6th Bn Seaforth Highlanders were also relieved that the advance was back in full flow:

> The sights which we witnessed as we lay in our new positions brought fresh hopes. There were enthralling scenes – the cavalry cantering into action in perfect formation (not, unhappily, to be maintained for long); the 4th Gordon Highlanders, with pipes and drums, marching as at a review in column of route; the sight of a real live battery galloping forward and coming into action at our ears; and the constant coveys of aeroplanes low-flying and intrepid. We were all out on the common task, and the sight of others in their might, enthusiasm, and strength, had an inspiring effect upon our portion of the British Army.[4]

And so the fighting flowed on past Flesquières as suddenly as it had arrived, and the attackers swept forward towards their next objectives, in a determined drive to capture the key Bourlon ridge which had eluded them the day before.

* * *

Though it now lay in the rear, the area round Flesquières remained a scene of ceaseless activity, and the village swarmed with troops sheltering in the cellars and catacombs formerly occupied by the Germans. The newspaper correspondent Philip Gibbs described the 'fantastic and unimaginable scene' as he crossed the former battlefield from Havrincourt to Flesquières two days later:

> Every yard of it across the Hindenburg line – those great, wide trenches now empty of all life – was strewn with evidences of the enemy's panic-stricken flight in the beginning of the battle … the slope where the Scots had to fight their way to the strong high wall of red brick surrounding the château grounds was littered with things the enemy had left behind him – his field-grey overcoats, his shrapnel helmets, innumerable pairs of boots, his goatskin pouches, his rifles, bayonets, bandoliers, tunics and gas-masks …

> I followed the track of the tanks, and went through great gaps they had made in the barbed wire – acres of barbed wire – and went along the route of the Scots when they surged after the tanks on that great morning of surprise. Some of them had left their kilts behind, caught on barbed wire, and with no time to mind rents in the tartan of the Seaforths, they had gone on in their steel hats and very little else.
>
> And all this way to the battle was littered with letters in German and English, as though there had been a paper-chase instead of the hunting of men. They were the intimate letters which men wear close to their hearts until war snatches them away and tosses them to the breeze. 'Mein lieber bruder' I read, as I picked up one of them, and 'My darling hubby,' began a letter to a London boy who was now away by Bourlon Wood …
>
> Everywhere tanks were crawling over the ground, some of them moving forward into action, some of them out of action, mortally wounded, some of them like battle cruisers of the land, going forward in reconnaissance.
>
> Across, the field guns were moving up and drivers of gun limbers were urging their horses forward over the muddy slopes with new supplies of ammunition for the forward batteries. Small bodies of cavalry rode about, and put their horses to the gallop when black shrapnel burst overhead with a high snarling menace.[5]

The tanks of H Battalion, which had attacked to the right on 20 November, also crossed the Flesquières ridge the next day to support the advance. One of their section commanders, Captain Daniel Hickey, told how they passed the wrecked tanks of E Battalion:

> They lay there in the form of a crescent – I did not count them; but I believe there were anything up to eighteen of them – some with enormous holes blown in their sides and fronts. One or two were a shapeless mass of metal. There is no doubt that there were at least three, and probably four, batteries of German artillery, which between them did this damage … Then I caught sight of a grey object slightly ahead. It was the body of a German who had been terribly wounded in the abdomen. His hands were clasped in an agonised attempt to hold the rent together. I quickly averted my eyes, and thought: 'There but for the grace of God lies Dan Hickey.'[6]

There were other terrible reminders of the battle, none more so than on the road leading out of Flesquières to the east. Here, moving forward on the day after the attack, Captain Douglas Wimberley of 232nd Machine Gun Company stumbled upon the wreckage of *Deborah*. The full horror of her crew's fate – and the scene that had confronted Frank Heap and the other survivors as they fled – was revealed:

> I rode through the village and turned sharp right to the sugar refinery. Here there was a nasty sight. A half burnt tank straddled half across the road and outside the door were two dead members of the crew, blackened and half burnt, one had an appalling wound in the body as he had tried to get out at the door, and his entrails were out of his body in the road. It nearly made me sick – though after Ypres I didn't think a corpse could affect me, and I determined at once to change the rallying place – a half hour wait here would be bad for the men's morale, as to be reminded of death, so vividly, is not good for troops going into action. Later on in the day the mess was cleared up, but for days afterwards it was interesting to see how every horse that passed shied violently at the place, smelling the blood and burnt flesh.[7]

Captain Robert Tennant Bruce of the Royal Army Medical Corps also passed this way with the Catholic chaplain of 51st Division, Reverend Andrew Grant, who no doubt said a prayer over the dead men. They were on a tour of forward first aid posts, but this ended in disaster when they strayed into the German lines and were captured – an act of 'gross carelessness' and 'the most astounding stupidity', according to comments in their service files.[8] On the way they also passed the remains of *Deborah* and her dead crew: 'So far there had been little in the way of shelling to trouble us and the walk had not been unpleasant. On the outskirts of Flesquieres we had passed a derelict tank, with two headless bodies lying beside it.'[9]

The task of burying the bodies fell to a party led by Captain Harold Head and Second Lieutenant James Macintosh, who retraced the route taken by their tanks the previous morning. This took them past Cemetery Alley, which had been the scene of his terrible killing-spree: 'They … came to the trench which had provided Tosh with so much sport. The evidences of that sport were lying about, and he realized with something of a shock that these had been fellow-men he had so delighted to shoot.'[10]

Climbing the ridge, Second Lieutenant Macintosh came to the spot where his own tank, D45 *Destroyer II*, had been knocked out:

> As they drew near they came first upon the dead gunner. Arms outstretched, eyes staring at the sky, on his face a complete negation of expression, he seemed to Tosh a poignant reminder of the vanity of the flesh, and a potent indication of the spirit's immortality. These men with him – they had known the dead so much better than he – did they not feel the impossibility of this clay being all that was left of their friend and companion?
>
> Leaving his men to dig the grave and compose the body, Tosh passed to the farther side of the tank. From this side had come the shells. As he looked at that battered, broken wreck, he marvelled that anyone had come out of it alive. Seven shells in all had entered, and the shape was almost unrecognisable. Drawing nearer, Tosh peered in, and was left in no further doubt of the fate of his seventh man.
>
> Stepping back from the stench, he called for four men and a blanket.
>
> 'My God,' said one, 'burnt to death.'
>
> 'No, you fool,' exclaimed Tosh, with a queer irritability, 'can't you see he was killed before he was burnt? Come on, let's get it over.'
>
> In the pitiful blanket shroud the body was carried to the grave. Setting up the cross they had brought, the men covered it in; Tosh nailed on the two nameplates; together they saluted the dead and passed on.'[11]

After burying the dead from D41 *Devil II* nearby, they moved on towards Flesquières to find the remains of *Deborah*:

> Together they then marched through the village which the day before had formed their final objective. Only one tank had penetrated the village; towards her their steps were now bent.
>
> It was on the very extremity of the village that they came upon her. In the field beyond three field guns still lay. Having been warned of her approach, they had evidently watched for her appearance, and no sooner had she cleared the last house than they had reduced her to a flaming hulk.
>
> Of her crew of eight, four had escaped and had crept back through the enemy lines to safety. The other four were known by name, but their bodies were quite unrecognisable.

On the way home that night, Tosh marvelled at his insensibility. He and his men had seen sights that day which might have haunted them for life. Yet here they were, within an hour, joking with one another, looking forward to a hearty supper and a dreamless night's sleep. Yet they were not hardened or callous – at heart he knew them to be sympathetic almost to a fault.[12]

An artillery officer who later photographed the hulk of *Deborah* noted on the back 'crew buried on other side of road',[13] and there, for the next two years, the dead men and their tank would remain.

* * *

Back home, the newspapers on 21 November carried a brief report saying operations had been carried out near Cambrai 'with satisfactory results'.[14] The full story broke the next day: 'Great British Victory. Five-Mile Advance. Hindenburg Line Broken. A Battle of Tanks.'[15] The news of a sudden breakthrough after months of stagnation in the Ypres Salient was greeted with rejoicing, symbolized by the ringing of church-bells across the country: in the words of *The Times*, 'there was a continuous wave of cheerful sound carried from St. Paul's to the far north, through all the little villages with their modest belfries, through the bigger cathedral towns to the west of England and to Wales.'[16]

But the celebrations were tinged with foreboding for anyone with a relative in the Tank Corps, since it was clear that tanks had led the advance, and although there was no news of casualties yet, some losses were inevitable.

A week after R.O.C. Ward's death, a telegram arrived in London addressed to his wife. It said: 'Deeply regret to inform you Major R.O.C. Ward Tank Corps was killed in action November twentieth. The Army Council express their sympathy.' He was a well-known figure, and tributes soon appeared in the social and sporting journals, but that brought little comfort to his wife Florence, who now found herself alone with his three children, aged one, three and four, to bring up.[17]

In the case of twenty-year-old Second Lieutenant Richard Alun Jones, commander of D41 *Devil II*, whose burial had been supervised by his friend 'Tosh', there was a tragic twist: the local paper reported that his father, who was a Congregational minister in Wales, 'received the official telegram almost the same time as a postcard from their son, which stated he was then "quite well"'.[18]

Meanwhile the families of so-called 'other ranks', whose deaths did not merit the urgency of a telegram, could only wait for the postman to deliver either the message they prayed for from their loved one, or the one they dreaded from his commanding officer.

And so it was that Mr Charles Foot opened with trepidation the letter from a Field Post Office that arrived at his home, The Roses in Great Missenden, Bucks. It was dated 25 November, and it read:

Dear Mr. Foote,
It is my very painful duty to write and inform you of the death of your son Pte. G. Foote D.C.M. of this Company.

He was killed in action on the 20th Nov. the car receiving a direct hit from hostile artillery when well within the enemy lines.

Knowing your son as I did, it was a great shock to me when I heard of his death; and I cannot say enough in support of the very excellent work your boy did out here.

His crew officer will write and give you full details as soon as possible.

Again expressing my deepest sympathy,

I am, Sir,
Yours respectfully,
A. J. Enoch, Capt.[19]

The letter from Frank Heap followed the next day, and he made no attempt to disguise his pain:

> Dear Mr. Foote,
>
> It is with the deepest sympathy that I write to tell you of the death in action of your son George. He was in my tank in action on the 20th of this month, when it was struck by a shell. He was killed instantly and painlessly, I am glad to say.
>
> We buried him two days later where he had fallen. It may be some consolation that we had avenged him in advance.
>
> We all feel his loss very deeply, for his cheery spirits and unfailing good nature had endeared him to all.
>
> Of his courage, it would be impertinent on my part to speak, but his D.C.M. attested that. As a young officer in charge of a tank for the first time, I was helped to do my job by his tactful experience, and had he been spared, he would have made a splendid officer.
>
> We have had sad losses in the Company, but none will be missed like George. The whole company regrets him bitterly. It strengthens one's religious beliefs to suffer a loss like this. It is impossible that a soul like George's should not go on living. I feel convinced I shall meet him again.
>
> I am having a bitter evening now, as four more of my crew have also gone, all finer fellows than I shall ever be.
>
> Please excuse these halting words, which utterly fail to express my sorrow and sympathy.
>
> I envy you the honour of having given such a son to your country.
>
> May God help and comfort you in this hour of need.
>
> Yours in deepest sorrow.
> Frank G Heap
> 2nd Lieut.[20]

The letter makes it clear that one other member of his crew had died that day, in addition to the four who were killed when *Deborah* was knocked out, and who were buried together opposite their tank. This remains a mystery, though it could sometimes happen that crewmen lost their lives even if their tank survived – for instance from stray bullets entering through gaps in the armour. The normal procedure in this case was simply to roll the body out of the tank with a view to later burial. The fifth man could therefore have died earlier in the battle, or perhaps during their journey back to the British lines, though the accounts do not mention any casualties at that time.

The other letters that Frank Heap wrote on that day have been lost, though bereaved families would sometimes share messages of condolence with their local newspaper, and this happened with two of *Deborah*'s crew.

In the case of Joseph Cheverton, an obituary appeared in the *Cambridge Chronicle* in early December, along with a photograph – the same jaunty one on which he had written: 'What do you think of it – bit of a knave'. The article said:

Letters to deceased's father and to Miss Coote …, from his superior officer, pay a great tribute to Gunner Cheverton's work with the Tanks, and tell of the high esteem in which he was held by officers and comrades alike, especially by the writer. One letter describes him as a splendid fellow, a willing worker and a cheerful comrade. Gunner Cheverton was killed instantaneously by a shell during the big battle on November 20th and buried two days later with other of his comrades who were killed. The writer adds that a cross to his memory will be erected shortly.[21]

The letter to Florrie Coote has not survived, though her descendants kept the Tank Corps badge that was sent with it as a keepsake. However, Joseph Cheverton's family have preserved a battered 'In Memoriam' card: 'In loving memory of our only dear son Gnr. J. W. Cheverton Tank Corps. Killed in action Nov. 20th, 1917 on his 20th birthday. Sadly missed by his sorrowing father, mother and sisters.' The verse inside was no doubt much-used in those dark days, but nonetheless heartfelt:

> Far away in a distant land,
> Suddenly struck by death's strong hand,
> A son so dear a brother brave,
> Lies buried in a soldiers [sic] grave,
> His King and Country called him,
> That call was not in vain,
> On England's roll of Honour,
> You will find our dear boy's name.[22]

The *Belfast Evening Telegraph* carried an excerpt from Frank Heap's letter paying tribute to Gunner William Galway: 'In the course of a sympathetic communication to Mrs Galway, an officer says: "Your son was the life and soul of my crew, doing two men's work and cheering us all up. He kept us in shrieks of laughter right up to the moment of his death, and died with a laugh on his lips, like the true Irish gentlemen he was".'[23]

Other local papers devoted even less space to the lengthening casualty lists. Three days before Christmas, the *Nottinghamshire Guardian* carried the briefest of items: 'Killed in action, November 20th, Gunner Fred Tipping (late of Thomas Adams), beloved husband of Florrie Tipping.'[24]

He was one of thirty-two names in the newspaper's Roll of Honour that week.

CHAPTER 33

The Chance Was Gone

For the families of those who died, 20 November would remain forever frozen in time. For the British army, however, and for the survivors of D Battalion, it merely marked the opening of a battle that had to be fought to the finish. The advance continued for several days, but the character of the operation had changed: the surprise was gone, along with the euphoria of the first day, when the British army felt invincible and nothing could stand in its way. Although the sense of glorious adventure had faded, the General Staff could not bring themselves to halt the offensive, especially since the Bourlon ridge was so tantalisingly close, and unless that was taken all their gains would count for nothing.

The Tank Corps had done everything asked of it on the first day by smashing a way through the forward German defences, but the Cavalry Corps, for a range of reasons, had failed to flood through the gaps as planned. There had been two significant hold-ups on the first day, and both proved fatal to the dreams of a full-scale charge towards Cambrai. At Flesquières, as we have seen, the delay in taking the ridge led to a crucial hesitation on the part of the cavalry, while on the right, the strategically-important crossings over the St Quentin Canal at Masnières were blocked or destroyed, limiting the opportunity for an encircling thrust to the east. Even if the cavalry had gone forward, it is debatable how far they would have got, however, bearing in mind the Germans' strategy of defence in depth and the appalling vulnerability of horses to machine guns.

Despite the grievous blow they had suffered on the first day, the Germans were able to mount a desperate rearguard action while reinforcements were rushed towards the front. The British had thrown every fighting tank into the battle on the first day, so only the survivors were available to support the subsequent advance. Having suffered so much at the outset, D and E Battalions went into action just once more, leading an attack on the wood and village of Bourlon on 23 November.

D Battalion could muster a total of thirteen tanks which were assembled into two composite companies, and in marked contrast to the first day, there was little time for preparation, no time for reconnaissance, and no advance contact with the infantry units involved. The tanks were thrown straight into action in mid-morning, but despite this they helped the infantry to seize Bourlon Wood, though only seven of them reached the final objective.[1] It was a fierce battle in which D Battalion's tanks expended virtually all their ammunition, and in return were subjected to a relentless storm of machine-gun fire which put two of them out of action, including D34 *Diallance* whose commander Lieutenant Gerald Edwards described the action tersely as 'hell with the lid on'.[2]

The men whose tanks had previously been destroyed – including James Macintosh, and presumably Frank Heap – were able to watch the attack from a safe distance. The spectacle helped them appreciate what they had been through, as 'Tosh' described:

> To men who three days before had been in the thick of a similar affair, the panorama-view of that day's attack was an unforgettable experience. The first

thing to strike them was the noise. To the men actually engaged, the noise of modern war is an incidental hardly worthy of note; but in the position they were now in the crews were astonished at the din even of so ragged a barrage as was put up that day. Yet through all the thunder of the guns, the wicked chattering of innumerable machine-guns beat upon the ear in a vast wave of sound. 'My God,' said Tosh's first driver, 'what a hell of a hot shop it must be!'[3]

One of the companies was commanded by Major William Watson, with his former deputy Major Richard Cooper leading the other. The fighting was so fierce that both Cooper and his own deputy, Captain Walter Smith – who had taken charge of No. 12 Company after R.O.C. Ward's death – were wounded by stray bullets.[4] To their left, the last eleven tanks from E Battalion attacked with troops from 36th (Ulster) Division and were exposed to devastating artillery fire, no less than six of them suffering direct hits and 55 per cent of the crewmen becoming casualties.[5] Major Watson had a grandstand view of their advance:

> We watched one tank hesitate before it crossed the skyline and our hearts went out to the driver in sympathy. He made his decision, and the tank, brown against the sky, was instantly encircled by little puffs of white smoke, shells from the guns on the reverse slope. The man was brave, for he followed the course of a trench along the crest of the hill. My companion uttered a low exclamation of horror. Flames were coming from the rear of the tank, but its guns continued to fire and the tank continued to move. Suddenly the driver must have realised what was happening. The tank swung towards home. It was too late. Flames burst from the roof and the tank stopped, but the sponson doors never opened and the crew never came out ... When I left my post half an hour later the tank was still burning ...[6]

Following these additional losses there was no question of either battalion taking any further part in the offensive, and the surviving tanks and crews returned to Havrincourt Wood to carry out what repairs they could, and to prepare for withdrawal.

* * *

As the British advance pressed ahead, Sir Douglas Haig arrived in Trescault on 22 November to review the progress of operations being conducted by his Third Army. The commander-in-chief rode to a point overlooking the Flesquières ridge with Major-General Richard Mullens, commander of 1st Cavalry Division, known as 'Gobby Chops' on account of his pendulous cheeks. He now put those cheeks to good use by talking up the part played by the cavalry, as recorded in Haig's diary: 'Mullens explained all that his cavalry division had done, and said that this experience had been worth very much to them, and they were all as pleased as possible.'[7]

The visit confirmed Haig's view that events here had been pivotal to the entire battle: 'The holding up of the 51st Division at Flesquières on the 20th had far reaching consequences, because the cavalry were also held up and failed in consequence to get through!'[8]

The evidence of what had occurred was clearly visible in the form of 'a dozen or more' destroyed tanks on the ridgeline ahead. Here Haig first heard a story which caught and held his imagination: 'An eyewitness stated that on the appearance of the first tank all the personnel of a German battery (which was in a kind of chalk pit) fled. One officer, however, was able to collect a few men and with them worked a gun and from his concealed position knocked out tank after tank to the number of 8 or 9. The officer was then killed.'[9]

As the story was passed around, it gained an extraordinary twist: whereas Haig was told the officer had been accompanied by a skeleton crew, others maintained that he had manned his gun and fought to the death entirely alone. This was the version which appeared in the memoirs of Haig's intelligence chief, Brigadier-General John Charteris: 'One very gallant German gunner officer served his gun single-handed until killed, and knocked out several of the tanks.' Unfortunately this is less authoritative than it sounds, since his memoirs came out fourteen years later and unlike Haig, Charteris did not keep a diary.[10] However, the same story is repeated by almost everyone who fought at Flesquières, and by many who did not, and soon took on a life of its own, so it is worth examining in detail.

Among the multifarious versions of the story based on hearsay, only one person recorded actually seeing the dead officer beside his gun. This was Captain Geoffrey Dugdale, who viewed the captured trenches after lunch on 20 November: 'The first thing we came to was a German field battery, every gun out of action with the exception of one. By this was lying a single German officer, quite dead. In front of him were five tanks, which he had evidently succeeded in knocking out himself, single-handed, with his gun. A brave man.'[11]

It is not clear how Dugdale could tell the officer had been handling the gun alone, rather than with a crew whose other members had fled, as Haig was told. However, it is important to note that Dugdale was in 6th Bn King's (Shropshire Light Infantry), which formed part of 20th Division, and was based in the village of Villers-Plouich nearly two miles (or more than three kilometres) south-east of Trescault. So whatever Dugdale saw, it was some way from Flesquières.

Nevertheless, the story of the lone hero was everywhere, and since the destruction of tanks was most catastrophic round Flesquières, this is where it became rooted. Four days after the attack, 1st Bn Welsh Guards moved up to the west of the village and saw the wrecked machines from D Battalion: 'On the crest of the rise lay seven battered tanks, the work, it was said, of a German artillery major, who alone had remained with his guns ... The brigadier gave orders that his body should be found and buried with honour, but although search was made all round the gun emplacements no trace of such a person could be discovered.'[12]

That search continued, in metaphorical terms, for two decades, and was taken up by the Germans with results that we will consider in due course. Suffice to say for now that everyone in both D and E Battalions seems to have believed their tanks had been destroyed by the same German officer, despite the fact that they attacked on different sides of the village, and the same gun could not have hit both groups, unless it was firing from impossibly long range. In a strange way the crews seem to have derived some pride from this, and some comfort from having an almost recognizable adversary. No doubt Frank Heap and the survivors from *Deborah* believed they were among the victims, and no doubt they were as surprised as anyone else by the eventual outcome.

Meanwhile, the story was set in stone when Sir Douglas Haig issued his dispatch about the battle, which appeared in the newspapers in March 1918. The check at Flesquières was described as 'the obstacle which more than anything else had limited the results of the 20th November', and the dispatch told how a number of tanks were knocked out by German gun batteries beyond the crest of the hill. But one paragraph stood out in everyone's minds: 'Many of the hits upon our Tanks at Flesquières were obtained by a German artillery officer who, remaining alone at his battery, served a field gun single-handed until killed at his gun. The great bravery of this officer aroused the admiration of all ranks.'[13]

It was unprecedented to single out an enemy combatant for praise of this kind, and Haig presumably included it as a mitigating factor to explain the setback at Flesquières: any plan, after all, might founder in the face of such exceptional and suicidal courage. If so, he and his staff had not thought it through properly.

Firstly, some of the tank crews resented the fact that their own courage had not been singled out in the same way – though the dispatch did praise their 'utmost gallantry, enterprise and resolution'. Typically, it was left to Second Lieutenant Wilfred Bion to express a contrary view, though in a typically back-handed way: 'For my part I am glad that, even if one cannot oneself be capable of such courage, our C.-in-C. had the courage to acknowledge courage in our enemies.'[14]

Even worse, the dispatch seemed certain to raise German morale, and to foster doubts about the viability of tanks. Frederick Hotblack, the Tank Corps intelligence officer, summarized the key concern raised by the story: 'It leads ..., among those whose faith in tanks is small, to the inevitable question, "Since one man and one gun knocked out 16 tanks, what can a brigade of artillery do?"'[15] That question would only be answered after many years, and many further inquiries.

The figure of sixteen tanks destroyed by the lone officer came from the pen of none other than Sir Arthur Conan Doyle, in his history of the battle published shortly after the war.[16] It would be uncharitable to note that 1917 was also the year when the first patently bogus photographs of the 'Cottingley fairies' were taken, in which the great man also believed implicitly.

The story had not appeared in the newspapers before Haig's dispatch, but the normally trustworthy Philip Gibbs made up for this later, when he unexpectedly came up with an eyewitness account: 'The chief losses of the tanks were due to a German major of artillery, who served his own guns and knocked out a baker's dozen of these monsters as they crawled over the Flesquières Ridge. I saw them lying there with the blood and bones of their pilots and crews within their steel walls. It was a Highland soldier who checked the German major. "You're a brave man," he said, "but you've got to dee," and ran him through the stomach with his bayonet.'[17]

* * *

As soon as they had time to draw breath, the various units involved in the attack on 20 November prepared reports summarizing their part in the operation and the lessons to be learned. Whatever Haig's view of events at Flesquières, there was a sense that things had generally gone well, and above all that the tanks and infantry had worked excellently together.

For D Battalion, Lieutenant-Colonel William Kyngdon concluded that 'the attack was itself highly successful, and the co-operation between tanks and infantry left nothing to be desired. The only place at which the attack was held up was in Flesquieres village ...' Since their aim had been to capture the village, this was less than convincing, but he sidestepped the issue by describing the attempts to take the objective during the afternoon and evening, and left an overwhelming impression of a job well done. The training meant each tank and infantry platoon knew what was expected of them: 'In fact the battle was reduced to a state of drill before it commenced and on the day that drill was successfully carried out.'[18]

His counterpart in E Battalion, Lieutenant-Colonel John Burnett, presented a similar view: 'The infantry supported the tanks all through to the second enemy system in the most admirable manner ... I consider that the greatest factor of success in the operations under review was the preliminary work done at Wailly between the infantry and tanks.'[19]

True to form, Colonel Baker-Carr, commander of 1st Tank Brigade, was even more upbeat: 'The cases of assistance rendered to the infantry are too numerous to mention. The tanks invariably operated in front of the infantry, virtually leading them the whole way, enabling them to seize and consolidate positions with comparatively little loss and destroying numerous enemy machine guns.'[20] He noted some minor differences in the tactics used by 51st and 62nd Divisions, but had nothing but praise for them: 'The formations adopted by the infantry of the 2 Divisions with which this Brigade was operating differed slightly, but in principle were the same. Both were highly successful.'[21] This is significant, because a decade later he completely changed his tune. But that, also, we will consider in due course.

The infantry with whom they worked were also appreciative, including those in the second wave who had seen so many tanks destroyed before their eyes. The 7th Bn Gordon Highlanders had been pinned down in the trenches before Flesquières, but commented that 'the 6 tanks specially allotted to the battalion did everything possible to assist the advance and did not lose their formation until disabled by gun-fire'.[22]

The commander of 6th Bn Black Watch singled out one man for praise: 'I wish to place on record my indebtedness to and appreciation of the services rendered by Major Watson of D Tank Battalion. During the period of training he co-operated with me in a most hearty manner to the one end, and the smooth and successful way in which his company's tanks assembled on my front was directly due to the great efforts he expended on Y/Z night [i.e. the night of 19-20 November].'[23]

The 8th Bn Argyll and Sutherland Highlanders were just as positive about E Battalion: 'The action of the tanks was beyond all praise, and all my officers report that it is impossible to pick out any special tanks which distinguished themselves – as all did so well.'[24] The commander of E Battalion received recognition from the infantry brigade working with them: 'I would here mention that Lieut. Colonel Burnett, D.S.O. and his battalion staff and company commanders spared no effort in their endeavours to ensure the success of the operations.'[25]

Despite this, following the battle Second Lieutenant Wilfred Bion asserted, without giving any reasons, that Lieutenant-Colonel Burnett 'had been very strongly condemned by the [General Officer Commanding] 51st Div. for his behaviour at Cambrai and was almost certain to be recalled, although he fought hard against it'.[26] He may have been right, as Burnett was replaced as commander of E Battalion in January 1918, when he went away to hospital and never returned.[27] Lieutenant-Colonel Kyngdon retained his position as commander of D Battalion, but there must have been speculation about how long he would last in view of the fallout from the battle.

* * *

There was plenty of time for the commanders of D and E Battalions to work on their reports, since it was obvious they would play no further part in the fighting. Their final contribution had been helping to take Bourlon Wood, where British troops maintained a tenuous foothold for the next few days, though they were unable to make further progress to the far side of the wood or into the village beyond, and remained under relentless pressure from German bombardment and counter-attacks.

As the fighting raged, the appalling conditions there could not have been more different from those back in Havrincourt Wood, where the tank crews were now building proper shelters and, in the words of Major Watson, making themselves 'thoroughly comfortable'. He added: 'We felt a trifle guilty in our luxury as we watched the grim infantry going forward to the dark terrors of Bourlon, and my men in their kindness would give them part of their rations ... But war is war, and, putting Bourlon out of our minds, we made an expedition to Bapaume, had tea at the officers' club, a haircut and a shampoo, bought potatoes and eggs and dined sumptuously.'[28]

Finally, after another failed attempt to take Bourlon village, the commander of Third Army, General Sir Julian Byng, ordered a halt to the offensive on 27 November. The wooded crest of the hill had been captured, but the enemy still controlled the shoulders of the ridge, and it was clear there were insufficient resources to dislodge them. The British now settled down to consolidate their gains, but it was a dispiriting end to a campaign that had started so brilliantly. In the words of the official historian, 'None could view with satisfaction the events of the past seven days: so many attacks had failed, so many casualties had been suffered and so much hardship endured by the troops, in attempting to force a definite issue and to break a resistance of which the strength appeared to have been consistently under-estimated.'[29]

The Tank Corps was no longer required, and the crews of D Battalion were told to prepare for withdrawal to the camp at Méaulte, south of Albert, where they had stopped over briefly on their way to Cambrai and now expected to spend the winter. The tanks would be moved there by rail within a week, and early on 30 November Lieutenant-Colonel Kyngdon and his battalion headquarters left Havrincourt Wood taking their motor transport with them. Major Watson was sitting down to breakfast a few hours later when he noticed 'strange things' were happening:

> We walked out of the wood into the open to investigate. We could hear distinctly bursts of machine-gun fire, although the line should have been six miles away at least. German field gun shells – we could not be mistaken – were falling on the crest of a hill not three-quarters of a mile from the camp. On our left, that is to the north, there was heavy gun fire. On our right, in the direction of Gouzeaucourt, shells were falling, and there were continuous bursts of machine-gun fire.
>
> We had not fully realised what was happening, when a number of wounded infantrymen came straggling past. I questioned them. They told me that the enemy was attacking everywhere, that he had broken through near Gouzeaucourt, capturing many guns, and was, to the best of their belief, still advancing.[30]

The Germans had indeed rallied their forces, secretly brought up reserves and launched a massive counter-attack which caught the British as unawares as the original advance had caught them out ten days before.

In the words of D Battalion's history: 'This attack was a complete surprise and great disorganization ensued. The enemy were within a mile of Havrincourt Wood before any intimation of the attack was received. All fit tanks were at once deployed on the ridge S.E. of the Wood in readiness to hold up any further advance ... Co-operation was arranged with the Guards Division to retake Gouzeaucourt on the morning of the 1st December. Only two tanks were of any service owing to great lack of supplies.'[31]

The German assault took the form of a pincer movement designed to drive the British out of the ground they had taken. It was eventually halted through determined resistance on both axes of the advance, though not before the Germans had made substantial gains to the south, equivalent to the area captured by the British and resulting in a similar number of prisoners, so both sides could declare the honours were more or less even when the German advance ground to a halt. The British position in Bourlon Wood now formed an exposed and untenable salient, and on the night of 4/5 December they pulled back to a new 'line of resistance', mainly following the old Hindenburg support system along Flesquières ridge. The village now formed a much smaller salient, but the Germans had already shown this to be a naturally defensible position, and the British settled down there for the winter.

D Battalion finally pulled out of Havrincourt Wood on 5 December and moved back to Ytres, to the spot where Major R.O.C. Ward had met them as they unloaded their tanks in such high hopes less than three weeks before. Now the major lay buried in the cemetery at Metz-en-Couture, two dozen of his men were dead, and many of their tanks, including *Deborah*, lay wrecked and scattered across the battlefield, so it was a sadly depleted force that waited at the ramps ready for the train journey back to Plateau and Méaulte.

However, their duty was still not entirely done, as explained by Captain Edward Glanville Smith: 'Owing to the doubtful and somewhat unsafe conditions in the Cambrai Salient, it was decided that complete withdrawal of the Tank Corps was temporarily impossible, and, for a fortnight, sections of the various battalions were sent to the forward area in alternation, taking over the tanks there and acting as a defensive patrol behind the line.'[32] It was an unwelcome assignment, and when Second Lieutenant Bion took over a tank from D Battalion he recalled they 'looked in pretty poor spirits and didn't cheer us much.'[33] Fortunately there was no sign of hostile activity, and the men of D and E Battalions were able to celebrate Christmas in their bleak camp near Albert, and to await whatever the New Year might bring.

Inevitably, there were comings and goings within the battalion. Second Lieutenant Horace Furminger, or 'Contours', the reconnaissance officer of No. 12 Company, departed to his new posting in the Indian Army, while new company commanders arrived to replace Majors Ward and Marris who had been killed and captured respectively.[34]

Major William Watson had slightly longer to wait, but he returned to the UK at the beginning of 1918 for reasons that are unclear, though a document in his service record says he was 'sent back to England … as a "tired officer"'.[35] Tired or not, his new job was to set up the 4th Tank Carrier Company, whose task was to haul supplies for the fighting tanks – a vital and hazardous role, though hardly a glamorous one. He did not relish the move: 'One gloomy day I was ordered home with other company commanders to help form new battalions at the celebrated Bovington Camp. The orders came suddenly, although they had not been unexpected. On the 31st January I handed over the command of the company to B. [i.e. Major Hugh Baird], and the parting was the less bitter because I knew that the company would be safe and happy under him.'[36]

His departure was history's loss, for it meant that D Battalion – or 4th Tank Battalion, as it was now renamed – was deprived of its most erudite and informed chronicler.

* * *

The battle may have ended in chaos and recriminations for the British, but no-one could dispute that tanks were now a force to be reckoned with. Second Lieutenant Horace Birks described morale after Cambrai as 'tremendous throughout the Corps. We thought we had established ourselves, which was something, and of course we held everybody else in wholesome contempt.'[37]

On the other hand, contempt was too strong a word, but the cavalry had hardly covered themselves in glory. In this sense Cambrai could be seen as the death of the cavalry, though fortunately in metaphorical terms only, since there was no need to prove the point with a massacre of splendid horses and splendid men.

A report on 1st Cavalry Division, which had been in the Flesquières sector, was sent to Sir Douglas Haig to establish why they had failed to 'justify their traditions'.[38] The document was anonymous, but a note identifies the author as Major-General Sir Henry Macandrew, commander of 5th Cavalry Division – described as 'one of the best and most dashing of our cavalry leaders in the war'.[39] He concluded: 'It was the one chance the Cavalry has had in this war from start, to date, of carrying out its legitimate offensive role, and it failed from lack of offensive spirit, amongst the leaders … it failed from the lack of the spirit of enterprise and resolution – it failed as a result of three years in back areas, in trenches, in "intensive training" usually of the wrong … description, it failed because the offensive has entirely given way to the defensive spirit and because failure is not visited with the drastic penalty it deserves.'[40]

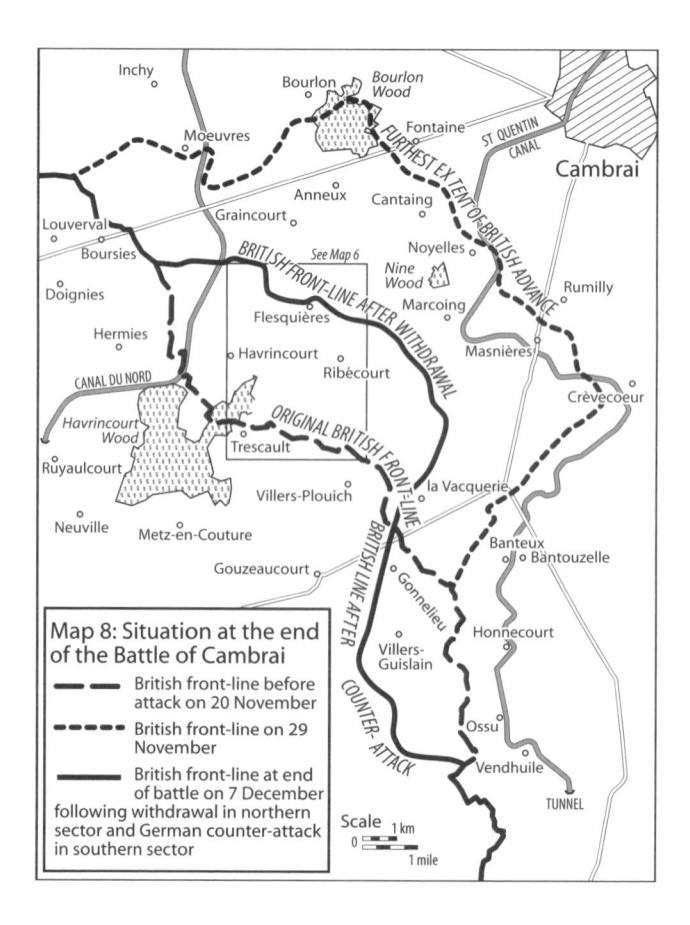

However, the idea that massed horsemen might ever have pursued the enemy through the streets of Cambrai and the drives of Bourlon Wood with the *arme blanche* was almost certainly a fanciful one. Although the German forward positions had been shattered, they still had subsidiary lines of defence, and if the cavalry had gone forward even a small number of machine guns would have sufficed to stop them in their tracks. In his authoritative history of the British cavalry, the Marquess of Anglesey concluded: 'There can be little point in stressing the number of "mistakes" made on 20 November by the cavalry commanders ... since they all, in effect, contributed to the saving of the arm from virtual annihilation.'[41]

For all that, the cavalry now had to live with the consequences, which were clear to the Australian journalist and historian Charles Bean when he encountered a group of horsemen a fortnight after the battle:

> The comment of the day and hour here is that the cavalry missed one of the chances of the war after waiting for it for four years. We met a brigade of cavalry trotting down the road through the long long [sic] desolate moorland which was last year the Somme battlefield. The Somme is all grey and brown with a very little yellow green tobacco stain in the grass, this time of year; one twelvemonth has been enough to transform it from a brown mud wilderness into a great moorland. And the cavalry trotting down the road seemed as stern and sad as the scenery. Their faces were rather set and I thought they looked self-conscious and were feeling that they had missed the Allies' chance for them.
>
> They blame themselves poor chaps. 'You know, we have come to think of limited objectives, of the next hill and the next mound of earth instead of the horizon and the wide plain.' ... And so on Nov. 20th when the infantry and tanks passed Flesquières on either side, as the cavalry was standing in masses just a mile or two away from it, waiting to go through ... – just because there were still a German Major in Flesquières with three or four machine guns and four field guns, still unreduced, the cavalry was held back by order from some Cavalry General ...
>
> The British cavalry – the famous regiments with glorious names like the Greys whom we met trotting with their horses half covered in yellow mud down the straight Roman road across that brown moorland – they were held hesitating for two or three all important hours – and the chance was gone.[42]

PART VI
ACROSS THE THRESHOLD

'At Cambrai we stood upon the threshold which separates the past from the future'

Tank Corps Journal, November 1922[1]

CHAPTER 34

Sticking to their Guns

Cambrai had changed everything, yet in a sense it had changed nothing. On 20 November it felt as if the British Army had awoken from a three-year nightmare in which it was struggling through an endless labyrinth of mud and machine guns. A few days later, it felt as if this brief awakening had itself been a dream.

Looking back over the battle, the Germans saw it as having two distinct phases: first the 'Tankschlacht' or tank battle, in which they had been driven back through a combination of guile, careful planning and mechanical ingenuity, and then the 'Angriffschlacht' or offensive battle, in which the gallant underdogs, their backs to the wall, had rallied to triumph against overwhelming odds. It is interesting that these two phases run exactly counter to our stereotyped view of the two armies and nations.

In a sense, therefore, both sides could draw some reassurance from the outcome of the battle; the British felt the use of tanks in combination with other arms meant that no defensive position could now be considered impregnable, especially once the more manoeuvrable Mark V model became available in early 1918. The Germans were acutely aware of this, and the Bavarian Crown Prince Rupprecht, commander of the army group which fought at Cambrai, summed up the situation: 'The enemy will be able to repeat such hit-and-run attacks wherever the terrain permits the use of tanks. So here we can no longer talk about "quiet fronts".'[2] On the other hand, the Germans felt their greater adaptability and more sophisticated infantry tactics gave them an advantage in the counter-attack and in any subsequent war of movement, especially with reinforcements flowing back after their victory on the Eastern Front.

Both these conclusions would be tested in the final year of the war, and one of them would be tested to destruction. It goes without saying that *Deborah* would take no active part in the further fighting, but she was a mute witness to two more battles, and suffered extensive damage in one of them.

The first of these came in March 1918, when the Germans swept forward in the great offensive known as the 'Kaiserschlacht', or Kaiser's battle, in which their stormtrooper tactics succeeded in driving the British far back towards the Somme. The Germans were once again left in possession of Flesquières, and for the first time they were able to inspect the tanks they had destroyed in the attack on 20 November. Many photographs were taken by soldiers who came to inspect the broken hulks strewn along the ridge, and one shows a German soldier standing proudly beside a wrecked tank in the village street, his terrier perched on its broken track. Another snapshot shows the same tank from the rear, and the number D51 can be made out on its hull. Together, they provide our first glimpse of *Deborah* since the moment of her destruction.[3]

These photographs show that *Deborah* had not yet suffered the massive damage to her front which is evident today, and this was probably inflicted six months later when the tide of war had turned again and the British were pushing forward on what would be their final advance to victory. In September 1918 a second great battle was fought at Flesquières, with improved Mark V tanks once again used to drive the Germans from their stronghold, which then remained in British hands until the end of the war. It seems likely that *Deborah* was hit again in the course of this battle, perhaps after being mistaken for a fighting tank, or perhaps during the British barrage, as her roof was penetrated at some point by a large-calibre shell. Whatever the cause, her mangled frame was now an even sorrier sight than before.

* * *

Although the war came to an end a few months after this, the battle over what happened at Cambrai, and particularly at Flesquières, continued to rage long afterwards, and is to some extent still being fought. Both sides struggled to make sense of what had taken place on 20 November, when the world war had been suddenly and temporarily thrown off its axis. Hanging over these post-war deliberations was the growing sense that Europe's conflicts had not been fully resolved and were likely to erupt again, and the lessons to be learned therefore took on a special significance for the future.

The first mystery to be solved was the identity of the German artillery officer who had apparently brought the combined forces of D and E Battalions to a standstill through his single-handed and suicidal act of defiance. In theory this should have been easy now the Germans were also involved in the search, but in reality they were just as mystified as the British.

The Germans were keen to celebrate a hero who had been so publicly praised by the enemy's commander in chief, but their problem (if it can be so called) was that very few artillerymen, and even fewer officers, had been killed on the first day of the battle, and none of them seemed to fit the bill. The losses in 108th Field Artillery Regiment (FAR), for example, amounted to two officers and seven other ranks killed along the entire divisional front, plus fifty-three wounded and eighty-three missing,[4] while 213th FAR lost one officer and two other ranks killed (plus one who later died of wounds),[5] and 282nd FAR did not lose any officers at all in this area. There was also a theoretical problem: if a single officer was responsible for knocking out so many tanks with a single gun, this would inevitably diminish the gallant efforts made by all the other batteries and regiments in halting the British advance.

Haig's dispatch had identified Flesquières as the location, so attention naturally focused on 108th FAR which had been holding the line there. Interestingly, when Leutnant Erwin Zindler came to write the regimental history just after the war, he made no mention of the incident. But Germany badly needed heroes, and Leutnant Zindler was a fervent nationalist who was keen to toe the party – and later more particularly the Nazi Party – line. In 1929, ten years after the history was published, he produced a more personal memoir which belatedly recalled an extraordinary act of heroism and identified the man responsible as Unteroffizier Johannes Joachim Theodor Krüger of 108th FAR, who was a member of No. 8 Battery which had been located near Flesquières.

Zindler wrote: 'In No. 8 Battery, which stood in a particularly threatening spot – it was surrounded on all sides by the enemy, the battery commander had already given the order to withdraw – a single corporal, Krüger by name, did not follow this order. He remained alone at his gun, hurriedly gave his documents with his paybook to his comrades, and fired. He accounted for many more tanks and so opened an escape route for his retreating companions. Despite the requests of the English he would not let himself be captured, firing until he fell, fatally wounded.'[6] Even though Krüger was an NCO, Zindler thought he must be the person referred to by Haig: 'He admittedly writes "officer", but 108th FAR has established through the commander of No. 8 Battery, Leutnant Behrmann ..., that only Unteroffizier Krüger could tally with the officer in Haig's report.'[7]

However, there was one important point the British could not really have been mistaken about. All their accounts said the lone hero was killed beside his gun, whereas in fact Unteroffizier Krüger had survived the battle, although he was badly wounded. Red Cross records show he was taken prisoner on 20 November, and after treatment for a gunshot wound in his side at the British No. 3 General Hospital in Le Tréport near Dieppe, he died there three weeks later on 10 December at the age of thirty.[8] He was buried in the nearby Mont Huon Military Cemetery, where he lies to this day.[9]

By coincidence, another member of the same No. 8 Battery had been captured and interrogated by the British, although the report says he 'did not display any high standard of intelligence'. The prisoner told how the guns had been dragged from their pits and opened fire on the advancing tanks at 700 yards range. 'All the tanks were hit and two were seen to be on fire. [British] infantry then came into view, and the battery personnel retired. They were, however, surrounded by another party of infantry and captured. This statement is confirmed by the fact that there are four derelict tanks, two at least of which are burnt out, about 300 or 400 yards in front of [their position].'[10] There was no mention of anyone refusing to surrender and staying behind to destroy even more tanks, but according to the later accounts, that is exactly what happened.

The regiment's casualty list confirms Krüger's date of death as 10 December,[11] so Zindler must have known he could not be the man identified in Haig's dispatch, but this became the widely accepted version, and remains so to this day. The old comrades' association of 108th FAR were so concerned that in 1931 they wrote to their former commander, Generalleutnant Freiherr von Watter, pointing out that Unteroffizier Krüger had not died in the battle, and supporting an alternative candidate, Leutnant Karl Müller of No. 9 Battery, who really was an officer and really had been killed on 20 November. Their letter ended with a quotation from the Bible: 'Honour to whom honour is due.'[12] The problem was that No. 9 Battery was situated south-east of Marcoing and was nowhere near Flesquières,[13] but he still continued to enjoy considerable support.[14]

In the previous century it was a German archaeologist who had uncovered the truth underlying the legend of Troy, but this more recent mystery proved a much tougher nut to crack – though like Achilles, the lone hero of Flesquières remained an inspiring figure whether real or not. In 1937 the military magazine *Der Frontsoldat Erzählt* (literally 'The Front-line Soldier Recounts') featured an article by a member of No. 8 Battery, repeating Zindler's version of the Krüger story.[15] Confusingly, the very next edition ran a poem of dubious merit extolling Müller:

> While hell erupts, there quietly lies in wait
> The Field Artillery Regiment 108.
>
> Lieutenant Müller, battery number nine,
> Directs his fire towards the battle line.
>
> Now airmen spy him, swooping overhead
> O'er man and gun erupts a storm of lead.
>
> Just one gun left! Now tank on tank must die:
> Twelve – thirteen – fourteen burned and broken lie.

> A fifteenth slowly lumbers close at hand
> Lieutenant Müller now must make his final stand.
>
> 'For Germany,' he cries, and tests once more his aim
> The fifteenth also is destroyed 'mid smoke and flame.
>
> Just one shot left, and when it blasts away
> The sixteenth too must meet its judgement day.
>
> 'The end', he cries, 'and now my work is done!'
> A pistol shot – he falls, eternal freedom won.
>
> And when in English hands the village lies
> They praise the fallen hero to the skies.
>
> Lieutenant Müller, battery nine, will stand
> As victor, hailed for evermore throughout the land.[16]

In contrast to the sombre memorial to the Royal Artillery at Hyde Park Corner in London, the Germans erected a monument to their own field artillery which was both startling and sensational. It showed a lone gunner behind his shattered cannon, preparing to hurl a stick grenade in a final act of defiance. The original model showed a tousle-haired warrior in an army greatcoat, but in the final version he wore a smart coat similar to those worn by Nazi party officials, and his features now bore a remarkable resemblance to those of the Führer himself. The statue was dedicated in 1936 on the riverbank in Cologne, the occasion coinciding with a reunion of artillery veterans. Germany was rearming, and their earlier sacrifice now served to inspire a new generation for the coming struggle.

At the same time, the former defenders of Flesquières were stung by criticisms that they had been caught unawares by the British, and Erwin Zindler of 108th FAR tried to correct this with an article in a leading journal of military theory called *Wissen und Wehr* (literally 'Knowledge and the Army'). This told how the regiment had practised anti-tank gunnery using horse-drawn targets under the far-sighted guidance of its divisional commander, Generalleutnant Freiherr von Watter, and was therefore ideally placed to repel an attack.[17] While this may well have been true, it ignored the fact that most of D Battalion's tank losses to the west of the village were probably caused by 282nd FAR, while the men of 213th FAR, who had never seen a tank before in their lives, still claimed to have knocked out at least twenty-three at Flesquières. In the words of the historian of 213th FAR: 'At first sight [the tanks] were naturally something out of the ordinary for the gunners, but firing over open sights is like a long-lost pleasure for them, especially when the first tank is knocked out with a few shots at around 950 metres.'[18] Despite this, Zindler's claims were reported in the British counterpart, *The Army Quarterly*,[19] and have now become part of the accepted orthodoxy surrounding the battle.

When von Watter died in 1939, the bishop who gave his funeral oration paid tribute to 'that unforgettable Unteroffizier Krüger, standing by his field gun and hurling shot after shot into the enemy's tanks'. It was exactly one week before the invasion of Poland, and a new generation would soon be called on to follow the example of Theodor Krüger, not to mention 'Onkel Oskar' who 'had implanted this spirit in the hearts of his soldiers'.[20]

* * *

While the Germans were busy building up the story of the lone hero, the British were just as busy knocking it down. No-one seems to have realized that Unteroffizier Krüger, far from being killed at his post, had died in captivity three weeks later and was buried in a cemetery on the Channel coast. Instead, British efforts were directed towards showing that the setback at Flesquières was caused not by one man and one gun, but by concentrated fire from multiple batteries.

Leading the investigation was Major Frederick Hotblack, who was sceptical, although he had not been at Flesquières on 20 November: 'I did pass by, early the next day, while the knocked-out tanks and most of the dead were still unmoved. From the positions of the tanks and the lie of the ground it appeared to me to be quite impossible for one gun, or even one battery, to have done the damage ... Wheelmarks, visible on the morning of November 21st, tended to confirm the statement that several batteries were concerned.'[21]

However, Major Hotblack had talked to several people who had seen a gun with a single German officer lying nearby, and he suggested that this might have been the body of Major Fritz Hofmeister, commander of 84th Infantry Regiment, who was badly injured in the fighting and whose body was lost as he was being carried away.[22] This seems unlikely as he was taken as far as the village of Noyelles, but it was true that the body found could have been that of an infantry officer even though it was found near a field gun.

With the discussion on rearmament in full flow, it was crucial to counter the suggestion that tanks were excessively vulnerable to artillery fire, and his findings were summed up in the headline of a letter to the *Royal Tank Corps Journal*: 'A Cambrai Myth?'[23] Another tank officer ridiculed 'the hoary old legend' of the artillery officer 'whose name I always thought was Munchausen, but which, in default of any German evidence of his existence, appears in reality to have been the Teutonic equivalent of Harris'.[24]

But despite their efforts to kill off the lone hero, he kept rising from the grave. In 1935 the War Office organized an instructional visit to pass on the lessons of Cambrai to a new generation of tank commanders. As well as Major Hotblack, lectures were given by Captain Horace Birks, formerly of D Battalion, and Major Alexander Gatehouse who had been in E Battalion.[25] Following the visit, Gatehouse fuelled the story of the 'gallant German gunner' by claiming he and Birks had discovered 'what we imagined was the exact position of the German battery, one of whose guns did such deadly destruction on 20th November'.[26] This was at the south-eastern corner of the village, and although it might have knocked out some of E Battalion's tanks, it could not possibly have seen those from D Battalion on the other side of the village.

After this the *Royal Tank Corps Journal* carried an even firmer putdown, and this time there was no ambiguous question-mark in the title, which was 'The Legend of Flesquieres'. This repeated the conclusion that 'the legend of the single gunner cannot be sustained', and whatever Theodore Krüger might have done, 'it was the combined effect of great masses of artillery that told'.[27]

There it should have rested, except that in 1941 the story was resurrected by Major Archibald Becke, a seventy-year-old ex-officer who published an extensive study in *The Journal of the Royal Artillery*. Perhaps surprisingly in view of the prevailing circumstances, he inclined towards the German version of events, possibly because it cast the gunners as heroes, and told how Unteroffizier Krüger had destroyed six tanks single-handed.[28] Becke also believed the gun had been sited to the east of Flesquières,

though he chose a different location to Gatehouse – who was now otherwise occupied commanding 4th Armoured Brigade in the Western Desert, and 'establish[ing] his reputation as a skilful and resourceful commander of armour'.[29]

It so happened that the volume on Cambrai was the last of the Official Histories to be published, and did not appear until 1948. The question of the lone gunner was a thorny one for the army's historian, and he tried to resolve it by contacting as many of the former commanders as possible. The results will be familiar to anyone who has tried to pin down a myth: plenty of people were sure it was true, and remembered exactly when they had heard about it, but no-one had any real evidence.

Brigadier-General Sir Standish Craufurd had commanded 18th Infantry Brigade, which attacked to the right of 51st Division. He wrote: 'I doubt if it is fair to a very gallant German officer to treat the story as a "legend". I was told the story by the 51st Division that same afternoon when occupying Premy Chapel Ridge and was shown the gun next day when Flesquières Village was captured. It was certainly very firmly believed in by the troops who actually took part.'[30]

Major Richard Purey-Cust, who had been with the artillery of 6th Division, was sure he could locate the battery that had knocked out seven tanks: 'I did go and have a look at it later in the day and I could probably find the place if I could borrow a Trench Map of that area.' But he was never sent quite the right map, and could never work out the exact spot.[31]

Major-General Sir John Davidson, who had been on the General Staff and was now chairman of the Bank of Australia, also clung to the story: 'I rode over the battle field [sic] with Haig, I think it was on the 3rd or 4th day, and it seemed to me at the time, and to him, and to all of us, that one German gun had in fact knocked out several tanks on the Flesquieres Ridge, and it surprised me to see it stated that that was not the case.'[32]

However, Lieutenant-General Sir Hugh Elles – the former commander of the Tank Corps, now responsible for organizing resistance to a possible German invasion of south-west England – was not having any of it. 'My then [staff officer] Hotblack, our military attaché in Berlin for four years, made exhaustive enquiries about this supposed incident and was never able to substantiate any of it. I met the German official historian in February 1939 and he was unable to throw any light at all.'[33]

This seems to have been decisive, and when the *Official History* came out it consigned the heroic gunner to a footnote, dismissing him as a 'legend' and adding: 'It seems certain ... that the losses suffered could never have been inflicted by one gun or even by one battery.' Zindler is credited with providing 'the only reliable evidence from either side', and his story about Krüger is mentioned,[34] but as we have seen, Zindler was not really very reliable at all.

The hero of Flesquières had finally met his match, and once again he had gone down fighting. There was no-one now to champion his cause in a Germany devastated by another war and racked with guilt over the military prowess that had once been its pride. The statue of the lone gunner, badly damaged in an Allied air raid, was removed from the riverbank at Cologne by British engineers, along with other reminders of the Nazi past, and now only the surrounding steps remain. His final memorial was the Unteroffizier-Krüger-Kaserne, a barracks in the German town of Kusel, but this has now closed and at the time of writing, it was being used to house refugees from the world's current conflicts.

In the end, all we can be reasonably sure about is that the body of a dead German officer was found near a field gun on the first day of the Battle of Cambrai, and the field gun was found near some destroyed tanks, but who he was, or where he was, or what he had been doing, no-one can say. He was unlikely to have been an artillery officer, since extensive searches have failed to find a suitable candidate. Even if he was, there is no evidence that he manned the gun alone, since the rest of his crew might simply have run away, as Haig was originally told. Even if they did knock out some tanks, there is no reason to think this was decisive, since there were many other gun batteries in action that day. The only thing we can say for certain is that the body was *not* that of Unteroffizier Theodor Krüger, since he was not an officer, and more importantly, not dead.

Despite overwhelming evidence to the contrary, the story – and the name of Theodor Krüger – still continue to surface from time to time in accounts of the battle, and perhaps that is no bad thing. There is something in it that appeals to us deep down, to our sense that even when we are overwhelmed by a tide of catastrophe, we can still make a difference as ordinary individuals, as long as we are prepared to defy impossible odds, to stand alone, and above all to stick to our guns.

CHAPTER 35

'The Fates Fought Against Us'

The legend of the lone gunner was not the only controversy that dominated the discussion of events at Flesquières in the decades that followed. There was another issue, more complex and contentious, that will probably never be fully resolved, though this time the battle was fought entirely between the British with the Germans standing on the sidelines.

To understand what happened, we must renew our acquaintance with Brigadier Christopher D'Arcy Bloomfield Saltern Baker-Carr, the energetic and colourful commander of 1st Tank Brigade, which included both D and E Battalions. This will be no hardship since he was, in the words of Major-General John Fuller, 'a most cheery companion', whose boundless enthusiasm and optimism had been important assets during those dark days.[1] However, although he could be said to have had a good war, peace often had a habit of treating him less kindly.

The pattern for this was set early on, following his initial military career which took him to the Sudan for the expedition to recapture Khartoum in 1898, then to Crete for the international occupation, then to South Africa for the Boer War where he was wounded, and finally to Egypt.[2] While all this was going on he found time to marry Sara Quinan, whose wealthy family had interests in the USA and South Africa,[3] where they moved after he retired from the army in 1906. However, his descendants recall that all did not go well there: 'His business supplying pit props to De Beers failed (he was sold a non-existent forest). He then went to Canada ... He suffered from severe financial problems and had borrowed £5,500 from one of his brothers.' According to his family: 'The First World War was therefore an opportunity for him to demonstrate, with success this time, his risk-taking capabilities.'[4]

Having distinguished himself once again in the army, the coming of peace in 1918 gave him another chance to prove his business acumen. He initially helped to develop a farm in Kenya, before returning to England[5] and becoming involved in the film industry, which seemed ideal for someone with his undoubted panache. In 1927 he became joint managing director of a new production company called Carr-Gloria Dupont, which announced ambitious plans to put out nine big-budget movies. Curiously enough considering the recent past, this was an Anglo-German enterprise built around the talents of the leading Berlin director Ewald Dupont.[6]

But alas, Baker-Carr enjoyed less success working with the Germans than he had working against them, and the studio folded without making a single film. The following year he was called before the Bankruptcy Court: 'He attributed his insolvency to his having lived beyond his means, and to recent unemployment, in consequence of which he had been unable to retrieve his financial position. The liabilities were roughly estimated at £800, the only asset disclosed being a gold watch worth £3.'[7]

His sorrows, to echo Shakespeare's words in *Hamlet*, came not single spies but in battalions. The following year he was named in a divorce case involving a Kenyan colonial official called Sydney La Fontaine, who alleged his wife had lived with Baker-

Carr and committed adultery with him in England and Corfu.[8] Unsurprisingly, after that his own wife Sara, who was the mother of his three sons and was then living in Shanghai, also filed for divorce.[9]

Thus it was that a volume of memoirs, providing they were sufficiently racy and controversial, was a valuable means of restoring his battered self-respect, and helping his battered finances. As an author Baker-Carr was well blessed, for he had a lively style and was closely involved with two weapons that had come to define the war, namely the machine gun and the tank. *From Chauffeur to Brigadier* appeared in 1930, and told how he fought his way back into uniform by volunteering as a general's driver, before setting up the army's Machine Gun School and then playing a key role in the formation of the Tank Corps.

A constant theme is the author's unerring gift for being proved right, normally against determined but ill-informed opposition, and it is clear the book was also a way to settle old scores. It must have been galling for Baker-Carr to have been in charge at one of the few places where tanks had been held up in the initial advance at Cambrai, and he now put forward an explanation that was appealing in its simplicity and could not easily be contradicted: it was all General Harper's fault.

The commander of 51st (Highland) Division was not an obvious target for vilification, having created one of the most effective and feared fighting units of the war before being promoted to the command of an army corps. In contrast to the widely held view of staff officers as distant and callous, Lieutenant-General Sir George Montague Harper loved and cared about his men, and they mostly reciprocated; indeed, the view of *The Times* was that 'there cannot have been many more popular officers in the Army than Harper'.[10] Despite his age and crusty manner, he had a progressive outlook and was described as having 'a sparkling brain, alive to all the changing conditions, unperturbed by events[11] – a description that could equally well apply to Baker-Carr. In Harper's case this was reflected in his *Notes on Infantry Tactics & Training*, originally issued to units under his command and later published in book form, which included a chapter on the most effective way for infantry to co-operate with tanks.[12] At the same time, Harper was not scared of upsetting people, and this seems to have included the equally strong-willed Baker-Carr, who recalled the 'wordy warfare' that went on between them.[13]

Baker-Carr alleged that at Cambrai, his adversary 'laid down a system of co-operation with tanks which was, essentially, based on disbelief. If all went well with the tanks, "my little fellers," as he affectionately called his division, could take advantage of the situation; if things, however, fared badly, then his men would not be implicated in any disaster and would suffer no heavy losses.' Thus far, the prosecution case against Harper sounds like a defence, since there was no point in sacrificing his men's lives unnecessarily. However, Baker-Carr criticized this approach by invoking the spectre of the lone artillery officer: 'The result of this method of "co-operation" was that the tanks outdistanced the laggard infantry and were massacred by the action of a single man whom one well-directed bullet would have settled.'[14]

The case against Harper was unanswerable, at least by the general himself, for the most tragic of reasons. In 1922 his car – which was found to have bald tyres – skidded and overturned on a muddy road while he was driving to his new home in Dorset. General Harper, who was then heading the army's Southern Command, died instantly from a fractured skull, and was buried with full military honours in Salisbury Cathedral.[15] His wife survived the accident, but they had no children and there was no-one to defend his posthumous reputation.

Although Baker-Carr's attack on Harper was the most compelling, it was not the first or the only one. Public criticism had come as early as 1920, when Brevet-Colonel John Fuller mentioned in a book how 51st Division was held up at Flesquières after having 'devised an attack formation of its own', adding 'it appears that the tanks out-distanced the infantry or that the tactics adopted did not permit of the infantry keeping close enough up to the tanks'.[16] After Harper's death he launched a more outspoken attack on the general's 'blundering tactics', claiming the tanks were 400 yards ahead of the infantry when they approached the ridge.[17] Major Frederick Hotblack also considered the 51st Division's attack formation to be among the factors that had contributed to failure,[18] and the criticisms were echoed by the prominent military theorist Captain Basil Liddell Hart.[19]

The one thing all these officers had in common was that none of them had actually witnessed the attack on Flesquières, though they obviously knew many who had. Only one of Harper's critics had seen what happened, and his views must carry some weight since this was none other than the commander of the Tank Corps, who famously joined the attack in an H Battalion tank to the right of E Battalion. In 1944, Lieutenant-General Sir Hugh Elles wrote to the official historian that Harper's system of advancing in 'waves' (i.e. lines of men extending at right-angles to the tank's direction of advance, designed to minimize losses from enemy fire) rather than 'worms' (i.e. lines of men following the tank along its direction of advance) had proved 'very faulty' and was responsible 'in some degree' for the disaster: 'The "waves" took a long time to get through the gaps in the wire and as a result the tanks going up the hill were 150-200 yards ahead of their supporting infantry. I know this because I saw it. If the infantry had been in "worms" on the tail of their tanks I am quite sure we should not have had all our losses on the reverse slope and Flesquières must have fallen very much more rapidly than it did.'[20] Reflecting this, the *Official History* concluded that the failure to take Flesquières was 'mainly' due to Harper's refusal to accept the battle drill that had been laid down.[21]

If Harper had been in a position to defend himself then knowing what we do of him, he may well have responded with a single word, and not a polite one at that. If he had gone further, he might have pointed out that no-one in the Tank Corps had raised any objections at the time, either in training or directly after the battle, and that the tactics worked perfectly well in the first phase of the attack, and throughout the operations conducted by 62nd Division to the left. He might have produced a series of exhibits for the defence, starting with Baker-Carr's own battle report which concluded: 'The formations adopted by the infantry of the 2 Divisions with which this Brigade was operating differed slightly, but in principle were the same. Both were highly successful.'[22]

Harper might have pointed out that his own instructions stressed the vital importance of the infantry keeping in contact with their tanks at all times.[23] He could have countered Elles' claim that his men should have been 'on the tail of their tanks' by referring to Baker-Carr's own instructions at the time, which said tanks should precede the infantry 'by at least 100 yards',[24] or Fuller's, which gave 100 yards as the optimum distance between them.[25] Going further, he might have produced a report prepared for Third Army, headed *Lessons from Recent Operations – Tank Corps*, which said: 'The general tendency of the infantry is to get too close to the tank. It was found that a suitable distance for the infantry to be maintained behind tanks was about 200 yards.'[26] He could also have pointed to Birks' description of his own tank after the battle, virtually shot to pieces by concentrated machine-gun fire, as evidence that no infantryman who was on its tail could possibly have survived.[27]

Harper might have highlighted the fact that only one of his units, the 6th Bn Gordon Highlanders, had reported losing the tracks made by their tanks through the enemy's wire, and this was also the only one that had reported killing German gunners with small-arms fire, so the argument was not as simple as his detractors made out.[28] The tank apologists argued that it would have been easy for the infantry to shoot the enemy artillerymen if they had been closer to the tanks, but one tank commander on the western side of the village told how the infantry had warned him about a field gun that was 'quite close', but neither he nor they could put it out of action before his tank was hit.[29]

Finally, Harper might have pointed out that once so many tanks had been destroyed, the infantry assault was almost bound to fail. This was because the first phase of the attack showed that the role of tanks was not simply to crush a way through the wire, vital though that was. Afterwards the infantry still relied on them for mobile fire support to neutralize enemy strongpoints, and in particular machine guns. In other words, with the tanks out of action there was very little chance of 51st Division taking Flesquières, however close behind they were. Of course, Baker-Carr and others believed there was only one German gunner, and if he had been shot then no more tanks would have been destroyed, but it is hard to resist Harper's supposed one-word response to that argument.

General Harper was not in a position to make any of these points himself, even had he been minded to, but a more balanced view has since been put forward by a number of historians. The first was Robert Woollcombe, grandson of the IV Corps commander at Cambrai, who substantially absolved Harper from blame (though not from all criticism) in his book about the battle in 1967.[30] Bryn Hammond took a similar view in a study published in 1995,[31] and two years later, John Hussey's detailed analysis in *British Army Review* concluded that much of Baker-Carr's critique was 'a red herring'.[32] Despite this it still continues to surface in discussions of the battle, and like the story of the lone gunner, General Harper's supposed antipathy to tanks is an idea that simply will not lie down.

* * *

We have explored two popular explanations for what went wrong at Flesquières, resulting in the destruction of many tanks – including *Deborah* – and a crucial delay in capturing the village. Both are appealing in their simplicity, but neither is particularly convincing.

The story of the lone artillery officer seems to have started as a 'trench myth' based on the flimsiest of evidence. It was then seized on by the British General Staff as an excuse for failure, and sustained by German nationalists as a beacon for hero-worship, before being ultimately discredited. The story of 51st Division's flawed tactics cannot be dismissed entirely, due to the eyewitness evidence of Hugh Elles, but it is hard to escape the feeling that General Harper was being made a scapegoat by some senior tank commanders. Baker-Carr may have had his own motives for this, but one should bear in mind that a debate about rearmament was raging at the time, and defending the reputation of tanks was vital for Britain's future military capability, even if Harper's reputation suffered in the process.

The long-running debate over these two issues has deflected attention from a number of factors which probably played a far greater role in holding up the British advance at Flesquières. In the words of Frederick Hotblack, who was wise and brave in equal measure, there is probably no single explanation for the setback: 'The Fates seem to have fought against the tanks at Flesquières. Everything was against them.'[33]

The Germans were already at an advantage, because the village on its low ridge formed a naturally defensible feature which was guarded on both sides by well-sited batteries of field guns, though these were thinly stretched and short of ammunition. It is now clear that the defence was significantly strengthened because some prisoners, partly motivated by hostility to British rule in Ireland, had warned the Germans that the area was about to come under attack. The British became aware of this security breach immediately afterwards from captured men and documents, but despite this, most accounts of the battle have played down the impact of the prisoners' revelations. Strangely, the betrayal seems to have barely registered with the Tank Corps – in contrast to the earlier disclosures of Sergeant Phillips, which aroused widespread condemnation despite having far less military significance.

Major Watson, for example, commented that the men captured before Cambrai 'fortunately knew little,' adding that the enemy 'gathered from them that we were ourselves preparing a substantial raid, and he brought into the line additional companies of machine-gunners and a few extra field guns'.[34] The results were also minimised in the official history of the Tank Corps: 'At the last moment a higher enemy authority seems to have again examined the prisoners, and, too late, an urgent warning was sent down to all units in the line to maintain a sharp look-out and to issue armour-piercing bullets immediately.'[35]

Both these accounts were published soon after the war, and drew on the snippets of information contained in the daily intelligence summaries issued by Tank Corps headquarters. These were generally accurate, though a few were wide of the mark: one quoted a letter from a German soldier which told how '6 prisoners had been taken and said that Havrincourt was to be taken in the course of the next day or so, because it was wanted as a birthday present for a British Princess'.[36]

However, the true scale of the enemy's response to news of the forthcoming attack was revealed when German accounts began to appear in the 1920s and 1930s. This was spelled out by Major Frederick Hotblack in a briefing to fellow officers of the Royal Tank Corps in 1935, with one eye on the threat of further conflict:

> It is only since the publication of the German History that we have known how much Flesquieres was reinforced as the result of the information given by prisoners ... The problems of preventing the leakage of information through troops in contact with the enemy persisted throughout the war and it is one which is likely to occur again. Officers should ensure that all soldiers realise that the danger, to their comrades, of giving away information is a very real one and that by the Hague Convention a prisoner is not required to give any information except his name and number ... This giving away of information was not one-sided; a very great deal was obtained from talkative German prisoners.[37]

In contrast to the British version of events, the Germans tended to emphasize their vigorous and rapid response to the prisoners' warning, desperate as they were to avoid the charge of being caught unawares. Even allowing for this, there is no doubt that substantial reinforcements from 84th Infantry Regiment, 27th Reserve Infantry

Regiment (RIR) and 213th Field Artillery Regiment (FAR) were moved into Flesquières to meet the anticipated threat, and that these made a crucial contribution to the defence of the village – indeed, the commander of 27th RIR, Major Erich Krebs, took charge when his counterpart in 84th Infantry Regiment was fatally wounded. The Germans frequently stressed the narrowness of the margin by which they had held Flesquières on 20 November, and it seems these last-minute reinforcements almost certainly swung the balance – while 213th FAR claimed to be responsible for the destruction of a number of tanks, possibly including *Deborah* herself.

As we have seen, once the initial attack had been beaten off, the only realistic chance of taking Flesquières occurred in the afternoon when a reserve of wire-pulling tanks became available. It is just possible these might have proved decisive if a further attack had been mounted in conjunction with the infantry. Clearly this would have been an enormous challenge, but if all had gone to plan it would have been in the hands of Major R.O.C. Ward, who had a better chance of pulling it off than anyone else. As it was, the burden of responsibility fell onto the commander of D Battalion; it was unfortunate that Lieutenant-Colonel Kyngdon had little experience of directing joint combat operations in the field, and this was neither the time nor the place to learn.

Even if R.O.C. Ward had survived, success was far from guaranteed, but it seems a much greater opportunity was missed after 6th and 62nd Divisions had gained their objectives to the right and left of Flesquières. There was now nothing to stop them sweeping round behind the village in a pincer movement, leaving its garrison clinging desperately to the high ground as the tide rose around them. This was obvious to both British and Germans at the time, and the failure to act seems to reflect a lack of experience and initiative on the part of the attacking commanders in the unfamiliar world of open warfare. Whoever was to blame, they allowed the best chance of keeping the attack on track to slip through their fingers, just as the last defenders were able to slip away to safety that night.

Of course, no-one can say what might have happened if Flesquières had fallen on the first day as planned. This was not the only setback to the British advance, for on the right flank the crossings over the St Quentin Canal had resisted capture, preventing the cavalry from thrusting forward to threaten Cambrai itself. Nevertheless, the questions are tantalising: if the cavalry had advanced over the Flesquières ridge, would the British have been able to occupy Bourlon Wood before nightfall? If they had seized that crucial position on 20 November, would the course of the battle, and perhaps even the war, have been fundamentally altered? We will never know, but some of the speculation stretches the bounds of credibility, bearing in mind the distances involved, the British unfamiliarity with open warfare and their lack of available reserves, and the Germans' ability to defend in depth and then counter-attack, as they did a few days later with devastating effect.

Whatever the reasons for the setback at Flesquières, and whatever might have been, the Tank Corps had achieved a powerful symbolic victory at Cambrai. It is no exaggeration to say that the British army stood on the threshold which separates the past from the future;[38] though no-one could be certain what lay beyond.

CHAPTER 36

A Peaceful, Unexceptional Place

The Western Front in the years after the war was a scene of unparalleled devastation, and also of relentless activity. Salvage and recovery teams were busy rebuilding the shattered infrastructure, as well as clearing away the debris of war and locating and burying the numberless corpses. As the wasteland slowly came back to life, the inhabitants returned to rebuild their homes and refill the trenches and shell-holes so they could start tilling the fields once more. Groups of German prisoners assisted in the work, while drifting across the countryside came parties of pilgrims – black-clad families of the fallen, and old soldiers in search of their dead comrades and the dead part of themselves.

The area round Cambrai was no exception, and among the soldiers posted to the town was Lance-Corporal Willie Anthony, who was in the Royal Anglesey Royal Engineers even though he came from Broxburn, near Edinburgh. This part of France had a special significance for him, because his younger brother Angus had been killed in a nearby village called Flesquières during the fighting on 27 September 1918, just six weeks before the end of the war.

Private Angus Anthony had been in 15th Tank Battalion and died when O56 *Orestes* was hit by a volley of shells near the ruined sugar-beet factory on the eastern side of the village. In a tragic twist, an officer called Captain Thomas Gibson was passing the next day and found a birthday card lying in the mud beside the wrecked tank, addressed simply to 'Angus' and mentioning Broxburn. Captain Gibson sent it back to his father in Glasgow, who sent it to the headmaster in Broxburn, who recognized the name and returned it to the original owner. This was Angus Anthony's mother, and the card bore the verses she had composed for his twenty-ninth birthday:

> Though out of sight
> Not out of mind
> My love for you is
> Still true and kind
>
> God loves you too
> May you love Him
> He'll give you strength
> This war to win
>
> I'll pray to Him
> To spare your life
> And bring you back
> To your own dear wife.[1]

But Private Angus Anthony was killed three days after his birthday, and now lay buried in the cemetery nearby. When Willie arrived in Cambrai he was determined to visit the village as soon as possible, to tend his brother's grave and describe the scene to their mother. It was New Year's Day 1919 when he finally made the eight-mile walk:

The road took me over a bleak, bare countryside, with widely scattered villages, all in tumble-down ruins as a result of the heavy fighting in this region ... I reached Flesquieres at last, a melancholy group of battered houses, all in ruin, and tenantless, not a soul to be seen or a sound to be heard.

Just before I entered the village, I reached the little military cemetery where Captain Gibson told us, so accurately, that Angus was buried. It was with bated breath that I ascended the few steps, between two tall trees, at the entrance. The cemetery is beautifully situated, facing the sun, and is divided into two parts – one for British soldiers, and one for German. There are about 100 German graves, and perhaps 60 British. There are a number of crosses over the British graves, but there is none over the men of the Tank Corps yet. So I had just to presume that the unnamed mounds must be those of Angus and his comrades.'[2]

Leaving the cemetery, Willie Anthony inspected the tanks surrounding the village – which he believed had been destroyed in September 1918, though the later Mark V models had already been salvaged, and the ones he saw dated back to the first attack of November 1917:

They are all still there – derelicts, just as they fell in action. I peeped inside in the hope of finding a name scribbled on the plates, but there was nothing. Those which had received direct hits were in a terrible mess, and indeed, the whole village showed it must have been a tight corner ...

Well mother, I fear this story will sadden you once again, but I think also that you will be pleased too that I have been able to make this visit and see the actual place. I know I felt pleased & satisfied myself. Angus is sleeping there peacefully beside his chums.[3]

Later he returned, bringing a wooden cross he had had made bearing his brother's name, and in February made a further fruitless search for O56 *Orestes*:

I took a walk through the village. There are a few Tommies stationed in it now, also a lot of the Chinese Labour Corps who are gathering up the wreckage of the battlefields. I went round the whole place in search of the tank with the number that [one of his crewmates] gave us, but could not find it. I examined nearly 20 derelict tanks, but none of the numbers were anything like the number he gave. Several tanks, of course, were reduced to a scrap heap, & it was impossible to find an identification mark so I had just to give up the search, but I was satisfied in having gone over all the ground, and seen the whole of the battlefield ...

I noticed today that some of the French farmers have got back to some of their fields with the plough, so you can see that no time is being lost in raising valuable crops for a needy people.[4]

Willie mentioned that the derelict tanks were 'all of the "D" and "E" Class', so these were indeed the ones knocked out on 20 November.[5]

On 16 March 1919 he borrowed a lorry and drove out with a local photographer to capture the scene. Willie hoped they would make 'a very interesting set of photos', and he was correct, for in one of them he and his mates are lying on a grassy bank next to the village street, and behind them can be seen a familiar shape beside the broken walls and rafters of a shelled farmhouse. It is D51 *Deborah*, her front now blasted open, and the picture provides the clearest evidence of the spot where she was destroyed.

Somewhere across the road were the graves of her crew, though the crosses are hidden by the scrubby undergrowth.[6]

There were many other visitors to Flesquières, and they took many photographs showing the group of wrecked tanks from E Battalion to the east of the village, scattered over the hummocky ground like ships on a stormy sea. *Deborah*, all alone in the village street, also provided a noteworthy spectacle, and on 3 March 1919 someone took a close-up snap of the tank beside the shell-ravaged farmhouse. He must have been a former member of D Battalion, and a friend of Frank Heap, since he knew his nickname and sent him a copy of the photograph captioned: 'Uriahs Bus. Knocked out Flesquires [*sic*] Nov. 20th 1917.'[7] It was a proud keepsake for Frank, who had the picture copied and framed, and this became a vital piece of evidence which would enable *Deborah* to be identified decades later.

Finally, in June 1920 at the age of seventy-two, Mrs Mary Anthony was able to make the journey she both dreaded and dreamed of, and visited her son's grave. An album entitled 'Memories of France' shows her, a frail bird-like figure in widow's weeds, in the cemetery at Flesquières.[8] Afterwards she sent some of the photographs to Captain Gibson: 'Although the journey had its mournful side, we found a great measure of satisfaction in being able to see the actual place where our dear one is laid, besides witnessing terrible havoc of war in the French villages ... I send you these photographs therefore as an indication that I have never forgotten your kindness at a time when you must have been much distracted yourself.'[9]

Such was the speed of the clear-up, that by the time of her visit the bodies of *Deborah*'s crew had been moved into the same cemetery, and their tank had been swallowed up in the ground – as it seemed – for ever.

* * *

A tank weighing the best part of 30 tonnes is not an easy thing to dispose of, and the salvage companies that had worked so gallantly during the war, recovering damaged machines and returning them to service, now put their specialized skills to use in clearing away the rusting hulks that littered the landscape.

The usual approach involved using a charge of gun-cotton to blow the tank apart into more manageable sections which could be buried or removed for scrap, and this was doubtless the fate of most of the tanks around Flesquières. In the case of *Deborah*, her position in the village street may have ensured her survival, since the buildings nearby – though already damaged – would have been completely demolished by the blast.

There was also a ready-made solution since the village was ringed by excavations prepared by the Germans to house underground bunkers, but never completed. Some still contained a lattice-work of steel struts ready for the concrete to be poured, but the one nearest to *Deborah* was probably just a huge hole in the ground. We cannot be sure when *Deborah* was removed and buried, but we know who was in charge of the operation. The Tank Museum contains a handsome photograph album donated by Lieutenant-Colonel Theodore Wenger, who commanded the Tank Field Battalion which was responsible for salvage.[10] Inside is a tiny photograph, no more than a few centimetres square, captioned 'Burying of a Tank'. Despite its small size, it is impressively detailed and shows two soldiers in workmen's clothes and service caps looking down on the tank that has just been dragged into a hole. From the damage to her side, it can only be *Deborah*.

She must have been pulled across the village for a third of a mile (or more than half a kilometre) by one or two other tanks, the forces involved being so great that the towing hawsers bent some of her massive steel plates almost back on themselves. Corrugated iron sheets were piled around the shattered front to keep the earth out and make the job easier, and other debris including poison-gas shells was dumped in the hole before it was filled in.

As the clear-up continued, the other tanks around the village were blown up, and in some cases perhaps buried. A former officer who toured the area a decade after the battle found no trace of them: 'Flesquières Wood still shows some signs of the fighting, dead, poisoned trees and shattered trunks standing above the new growth; but the village is a peaceful, unexceptional place.'[11]

A few years later, in 1931, another group of visitors arrived in the village in search of the past. These were German veterans of 54th Division revisiting the scenes of their battles, including the desperate rearguard action south of Flesquières.

> The members of the 84th [Infantry Regiment] who were present, with old trench maps in hand, struggled eagerly to find the landmarks of the former positions in the fields, now under full cultivation once again, and to reconstruct the combat operations of 20 November 1917. The 'kitchen gully' [i.e. Stollenweg] where Hauptmann Soltau had his command post on 20 November was identified without difficulty, and old, partly collapsed dugouts could still be found here. On the other hand, the Kabelgraben [i.e. Chapel Alley] where Hauptmann Soltau fell could no longer be located with certainty. The former members of the 84th who were present, particularly those who had taken part in the ordeal of 2nd Battalion on 20 November and had seen their heroic leader fall, stood in deep distress at this place of most mournful memory, and many eyes were damp in solemn remembrance of Hauptmann Soltau.[12]

These were not the only old soldiers moving across the battlefield, for the combatants continued their manoeuvres around the village for many years after the war, though these were now the armies of the dead. The Germans, who had created the military cemetery and still occupied part of it at the time of Willie Anthony's visit, had to give ground and their bodies were removed to another cemetery in Flesquières. This made space to bring in more of the British dead from smaller outlying cemeteries, as well as the men who had been buried where they fell, including Gunners Cheverton, Foot, Galway and Tipping whose graves had been across the road from *Deborah*.

Beside them was interred Private Walter Robinson, who had previously been buried elsewhere on the battlefield. For a time it was thought he might have been a member of *Deborah*'s crew, though the burial party responsible for collecting and reburying the bodies in December 1919 could not have known which tank he had fought in. Documents have since come to light showing he was in the crew of *Demon II*, so although he was not buried alongside his old crewmates, at least he was back with his comrades from No. 12 Company.

The dead men's relatives could pay to have an inscription on their headstones, and they used these to express their pride and sorrow. William Galway's mother chose 'Father in thy gracious keeping Leave we now our dear one sleeping'. George Foot's father opted for one of the most popular epitaphs: 'Greater love hath no man'. The headstone shows his rank as lance-corporal, so in death at least, George had achieved the promotion he deserved.[13]

A few years later the Germans were in retreat once again, this time to a great cemetery outside the town of Cambrai which holds the remains of more than 10,000 men. Among them were Major Fritz Hofmeister and Hauptmann Harro Soltau, who now lie with more than 2,700 of their comrades in a mass grave, beneath a dark canopy of trees and smothered by clutching ivy.[14] After that it was still not over: in 1930 two burial grounds established after the attack of 20 November – Flesquières Château Cemetery and 51st Divisional Cemetery – were closed down and hundreds of bodies, including some men from D Battalion, were moved to the larger cemetery at Orival Wood.[15] A letter from the Imperial War Graves Commission to one bereaved family explained that 'the position of the [Château] Cemetery conflicts with the French sanitary laws, and consequently the Commission have been unable to acquire the site, and have decided that the only course open to them is to exhume the remains for reburial ... The general policy of the Commission is against any exhumation of the British dead, but, as the result of negotiations lasting for some considerable time, the Commission are forced to the conclusion that no other course is open to them.'[16] Whatever this may say about the attitude of the local residents to the dead men in their midst, at least the soldiers on both sides could finally rest in peace.

* * *

Strangely enough, as the tanks disappeared from the battlefields they became an increasingly familiar sight on the streets of post-war Britain – or rather in parks and outside public buildings, where the obsolete machines were put on display in towns and cities across the country. This originated from a wartime programme of fundraising tours by so called 'tank banks', which offered an eye catching way of encouraging people to invest in War Bonds at a time when few civilians had seen a tank other than on cinema screens.

In Nottingham, for instance, Tank 119 *Ole Bill* arrived in January 1918 and for a week it was the focus of frenzied activity as the great and good exhorted the public to lend money – which they did, to the tune of more than £2½ million.[17] It was also an effective way of countering war weariness, a message driven home in a speech by the Duchess of Portland: 'She begged the people at home, the women, especially, not to grouse and grumble. They must keep up a cheerful spirit, and so support the brave men at the front.'[18]

It was only a matter of weeks since Florrie Tipping had learned of the death of her husband Fred in D51 *Deborah*, and perhaps she was among the crowds who went to see the tank in the Market Place, swarming with schoolchildren and civic dignitaries. If so she must have felt a certain pride, but perhaps she also wondered what on earth Fred had been doing getting mixed up in something like that, and how she was going to manage now bringing up his three young children, and whether the Duchess of Portland would have been more inclined to grouse and grumble if she lived in their little house in Sneinton instead of Welbeck Abbey, her enormous stately home.

After the war, in an echo of the 'patriotic pilgrimage' by the tank banks, more than 260 machines were presented to those towns and cities that had been especially active in fundraising. Once again these were greeted with outpourings of civic and military pride, and were placed on permanent display as a reminder of the local sacrifice and contribution to victory.

Thus it was that D46 *Dragon III*, which had broken down with engine trouble on 20 November 1917 while under the command of Second Lieutenant James Clark, now found a resting place beside the boating lake at Ryde on the Isle of Wight, sandwiched between a flower-bed and an ice-cream kiosk. There it provided a backdrop to many a holidaymaker's sunny snaps, though no doubt it cast a shadow over some of the men who drifted by with their families, and remembered seeing the same dark outline in a very different time and place.[19]

One of the D Battalion tanks that was knocked out by German artillery at Bellevue, shortly before the attack on 22 August 1917, also survived the war and went on display in the park at Gloucester. This was D42, probably named *Daphne*, which later became an exhibit at the Tank Museum in Bovington, and finally at the Museum of Lincolnshire Life in Lincoln, the town where the first tanks were designed and produced. During its travels the tank was renamed *Flirt II*, until its true identity was established recently through careful research.[20]

Similarly, visitors to the park at Cheshunt in Hertfordshire between the wars were greeted by a tank with the serial number 2740, mounted on a plinth beside the entrance. Various snapshots show it was a popular attraction: an elderly gentleman poses beside it in a boater, and a moustachioed man holds the hand of a little girl who has clambered onto the back and smiles proudly in her best hat and coat. The serial number shows this was the first D51, the tank which George Macdonald and his crew steered out of Oosthoek Wood in August 1917, only for it to be damaged at Bellevue, forcing them to transfer to another tank for their doomed mission against Schuler Farm.[21]

After their encounters with the enemy the tanks were repaired in the workshops at Erin, and the first D51 spent the rest of the war as a workhorse, hauling supplies for the Mark V fighting tanks before returning to Britain. What happened to the others is unknown, but they must have remained on the Western Front as their front horns bear the vertical white and red stripes added in 1918 to distinguish British tanks from the increasing number of captured ones being used by the Germans.

But the tanks that had been such a novelty in the flush of victory soon became a white elephant for their new owners, who resented the cost of upkeep and increasingly saw them as reminders of something most people would prefer to forget. The coming of another world war provided an excuse to remove the remaining presentation tanks, which were melted down to forge a new generation of fighting vehicles. D42 *Daphne* survived and became a museum piece, but D46 *Dragon*, the first D51 and hundreds more were swept away, leaving only the one at Ashford in Kent which had been turned into an electricity sub-station and remains there to this day.

Though the tanks were disappearing from the former battlefields, one that survived in Belgium became the centrepiece of the little community of Poelkapelle. This was D29 *Damon II*, which had reached the outskirts of the village in the final tank attack in the Ypres Salient on 9 October 1917, before being knocked out by artillery. Its commander, Lieutenant Jack Coghlan, escaped, but three of his crew were killed and the tank itself was swallowed up in the ground. After the war it was dug out and put on display at the village crossroads, becoming a popular attraction for the tourists and pilgrims who were visiting the area in increasing numbers. It was also a source of revenue for local youngsters, who would pose for photographs in return for small change and became known as the 'penny children'.[22] But a few years later the Salient had visitors of a different kind, and the German invaders had no use for souvenirs, particularly ones that reminded them of their previous defeat, and needed scrap metal as badly as the British. In 1941 *Damon II* was taken away, and although the villagers had many more pressing concerns, it still left a hole in their lives.

The inexorable advance of the German armoured divisions across Europe showed they had truly learned the lessons of Cambrai. Some time after the fall of France, a convoy of military vehicles pulled into the village of Havrincourt and an officer stepped out to revisit a place that was etched in his memory. It was Erwin Zindler, whose writings had celebrated the heroic resistance of 108th Field Artillery Regiment and identified Unteroffizier Krüger as the lone hero of Haig's dispatch. Now he was working on a new book called *Und Abermals Soldat ...* ('A Soldier Once Again ...'), describing his experiences as an artillery captain in the present conflict.

Zindler's visit took him through Flesquières and past the spot ('somewhere near that small silver poplar') where Unteroffizier Krüger had faced sixteen tanks and sacrificed himself for his country. Looking back, he felt a sense of pride: 'Fields of cabbages, turnips and chicory stood green and luscious. Acres of corn waved in the wind. It was a farmer's field like a thousand others, but celebrated in history for the first tank battle with a novel doctrine of warfare, and at the same time reflecting glory on the small handful of defenders ...'. Flesquières had remained impregnable for a simple reason: 'Because they were guardians of their homeland, aware of the women and children behind them, because without knowing the phrase "Germany must live, even if we must die", its sense had long ago become the soldier's law. They were warriors, not war-makers.'[23]

Zindler was again doing his best to boost morale, but when the book came out in 1943 the tide of war was already turning. The following September, American armoured vehicles swept into the village and drove the Germans out, this time for good. Flesquières was once again a peaceful, unexceptional place.

CHAPTER 37

Varied Fortunes

We have seen what happened to *Deborah* and the other tanks of D and E Battalions in the years after the war, and now it is time to examine the varied fortunes of those who fought inside them.

On 17 December 1920, a group of men gathered at one of London's most opulent venues, the Restaurant Frascati in Oxford Street, to work their way through a menu including oysters, fillets of sole, lamb cutlets, roast pheasant, and 'souffle glace Frascati'. This was the second reunion dinner for the officers of No. 12 Company, presided over by Major Edward Glanville Smith, who proposed the loyal toast, after which came the silent toast in which each man paid tribute to his comrades, both living and dead. At the end Major Smith passed round his menu to be signed, and the nickname 'Uriah' shows that Frank Heap was there, along with James Macintosh and around twenty of their brother officers.[1]

Major Smith also kept a list of names and addresses on the notepaper of Clarke & Heap, Frank's family firm, showing he had a hand in its preparation.[2] Perhaps there were other reunions after that, but if so Smith did not keep the menus, and after a while the list of names and addresses was no longer updated. The process of drifting apart had begun, familiar to anyone who grew up in the era before social media. As they swayed out of the warm restaurant into the chill of the West End, past the street musicians playing carols in their shabby greatcoats, there was a sense that the suffering and dangers of war had passed, but so had the spirit of comradeship that had made it tolerable, and even at times strangely enjoyable.

Of course, this was not true for everyone, and some men were left so physically or mentally scarred that they never recovered. This was the case with Lieutenant Stanley Cohen of E Battalion, who had returned to the front after being wounded in the attack on 20 November, only to suffer horrific burns to his face and hands, as well as the loss of an eye and a leg, when his tank was blown up in August 1918. After a year of treatment, the pioneering plastic surgeon Sir Harold Gillies performed surgery on him at Queen Mary's Hospital, Sidcup, grafting on skin to replace his badly damaged eyelids and nose.[3] Fortunately disfigurement and disability did not stop him having a successful career, and in 1921 he began a long association with *The Times*, initially helping to run their motor insurance scheme before transferring to the pension fund, of which he became secretary until retiring in 1959. The newspaper reported: 'He was in more ways than one well-equipped to face the problems involved in the administration of welfare schemes for, having been fearfully injured in the war of 1914-18, he was not unacquainted with illness and suffering.'[4]

But at a deeper level, he was terribly affected. His godson Paul Russell recalls that 'Stanley's fiancée deserted him because she was too horrified by his appearance to live with him', and although he married in 1945, it lasted less than a year. Though kindly, he could be severe, and he was haunted by the conviction that God had inflicted his injuries on him as a punishment for his actions in the war – in particular an episode in which he had to drive his tank over a German gun position. It was a war in which many people had done dreadful things, but he carried this burden of guilt alone until his death in 1972.[5]

Despite Stanley Cohen's suffering, at least he survived. Many other lives were shortened by military service, like that of Sergeant Owen Rowe from D Battalion, who died in 1923 at the age of twenty-five. After the war he ran a taxi firm in Bovington with another tank pioneer, Gunner Roy Reiffer, who wrote: 'His last action in France was at Cambrai where, on the first day of the offensive, he lost his leg while taking shelter outside his tank after it had caught fire. He … was discharged in 1919 … He contracted consumption, and after an illness of six months he died. No doubt the loss of his leg at Cambrai, in 1917, weakened his constitution to such an extent that he would be prone to catch disease quicker than an able-bodied man.'[6] Sergeant Rowe was buried in Devon, near the land his parents farmed, his coffin draped in the Union flag.[7]

However, some men were able to build on their wartime experiences as a basis for future careers. This obviously applied to those who stayed in the army, like Horace Birks, who had started the war as a rifleman and ended up as a second lieutenant, eventually retiring in 1946 as a major-general. During the Second World War he commanded an armoured brigade in the Western Desert, and it was said that 'his handling of the tanks and his design of the minefields in the rear had a major part in checking Rommel's successive efforts to capture Tobruk …'[8] Having survived two wars, he had a further brush with death in late 1945 when he parachuted from a crippled aircraft over the Austrian Alps, and was found by rescuers twenty-four hours later lying on a mountainside with a broken leg. This ended his military career, but he went on to become secretary of a London medical school, as well as an important source of reminiscences about the early years of the Tank Corps, until his death in 1985 at the age of eighty-seven.[9]

In a less tangible way, wartime experiences also influenced the later career of Wilfred Bion from E Battalion, who had won the Distinguished Service Order after keeping the enemy at bay with a Lewis gun from the roof of his tank. Bion was a unique combination of action man and intellectual, and after the war he studied first history and then medicine before moving into psychoanalysis, the field in which he established an enduring reputation. Bion developed a theory of group behaviour inspired by what he had witnessed in the army, and put his experiences to good use in the Second World War by developing a more effective approach to the selection of officers.[10]

Bion could not bring himself to write home to his parents during the First World War, apart from a single letter after Cambrai, which must have been agonizing for them but is of tremendous benefit to us, since he wrote a detailed account for them immediately after the war which was subsequently published as *War Memoirs*.[11] He supplemented this decades later with an autobiography which remained unfinished at his death in 1979,[12] and taken together these provide an honest and unguarded perspective on his time in the Tank Corps.

There are several other men to whom we owe a debt of gratitude for recording their wartime experiences. Second Lieutenant James Macintosh returned to South Africa after the war to begin a successful legal career, and in 1921 he published *Men and Tanks*, which gives the most detailed account of life in No. 12 Company, to which *Deborah* belonged.[13] The book is informative and entertaining, though a straitlaced reviewer in the *Tank Corps Journal* found some of it far-fetched: 'To those of you who joined the Corps since the Armistice we would say:– Read this book. You will like it. But you must not swallow quite all of it.'[14] One hopes the same could not be said of his later published works, which were sober legal textbooks with titles like *Negligence in Delict*.[15]

'Jim' Macintosh was a powerful figure, which made it all the more shocking when he collapsed and died from heart disease in 1943 at the age of just forty-five, leaving behind a widow and young son. The *South African Law Journal* paid tribute to him: 'Of unassuming and, on first acquaintance, somewhat reserved disposition, Jim Macintosh, with all his profound learning, was of a modest and gentle nature. When one got to know him he proved an amiable and companionable friend ... Moderate in all his tastes and habits, he was in every sense of the simple words "a good fellow".' The writer referred to his 'enthusiastic and cheerful presence',[16] and this comes across in *Men and Tanks*, although he pulls no punches in describing the horrors of war.

The other member of No. 12 Company to record his experiences in print was Major Edward Glanville Smith. His series of articles called 'The Wanderings of "D" in France' was published anonymously in the *Tank Corps Journal* in 1921,[17] and its author has only now been identified through careful detective work. So secretive was he that even his own relatives were unaware he had written it. Many of those involved in the war never spoke about their experiences, and Smith does not seem a likely communicator in the way that Macintosh does. In photographs he often appears sombre, and later suffered from depression as a result of his wartime experiences, but he also seems to have had a sense of the absurd, and one photograph in his album shows a group of officers – including Frank Heap – sitting in a field wearing their pyjamas. The rationale for this is lost, but it may relate to a family story about the time Smith went to war and found his mother had packed his pyjamas, which seemed somewhat incongruous in an army hut.[18] 'Glan' was also clearly an effective officer, and became commander of C (formerly No. 12) Company, as well as presiding over its post-war reunions. He started a family and worked as an export manager in the iron and steel industry, gaining a new lease of life with a further spell of military service in the Second World War, when he became a sergeant in the Home Guard. He died in 1970 at the age of seventy-seven.[19]

The third, and most celebrated, of D Battalion's authors was Major William Watson, who was demobilized in early 1919. He had already published an account of his early wartime experiences, called *Adventures of a Despatch Rider*,[20] but a further series of articles in the leading literary magazine *Blackwood's* ended abruptly in 1917[21] when the authorities clamped down on works by serving personnel.[22] It therefore came as no surprise when a further series began to appear in *Blackwood's* in May 1919, and this was republished in book form as *A Company of Tanks* – now regarded as a classic of Great War literature.[23]

During the war Watson had married the strikingly attractive Barbara Wake-Walker, a solicitor's daughter whose upbringing had been disrupted by her family's financial difficulties. William's daughter-in-law described him as having 'a very high intelligence, courage, and flair and natural charisma. It's no surprise that Barbara fell in love with him. She had not had much love in her young life, and now she was swept up in it.'[24] With three young children to support, Watson embarked on a career as a civil servant at the Ministry of Labour, focusing on issues of industry and education and becoming private secretary to a succession of ministers.[25] The contrast with his previous life could not have been more marked: 'Now I travel daily to St. James's Park station by the 9.31, and when a "file" returns to me after many days, I sometimes wonder how I ever managed, without writing a single "minute," to command a Company of Tanks.'[26] The war had been his literary inspiration, and although he continued to write, his efforts were now limited to a history book and anthology for children.

The Times commented that 'with his zeal, marked ability, and personal charm, Mr. Watson would undoubtedly have risen high in the Civil Service,' but alas, he died in 1932 at the age of just forty-one.[27] His daughter-in-law recalled: 'William died suddenly of pneumonia, no doubt as a result of trench fever in France, leaving Barbara with very little money. She was completely desolated by his loss and ill for a year after, during which period the children ... were sent away to school or to friends, until such time as she had ... bought a cottage where she was able to gather her family together again.'[28] It was a tragic end to a promising life, and to their dreams of happiness together after the hardship of war.

* * *

In 1962, the death of a veteran in a Surrey hospital resulted in another extraordinary record of D Battalion's war coming to light. Claude Rowberry had joined the Tank Corps after transferring from a cavalry regiment, being promoted to sergeant and winning the Military Medal for bravery in 1918. He was a complex, enigmatic character, and it turned out he also had a secret life: while serving in the Ypres Salient he had been struck by the 'terrible beauty' of the blasted landscape, and on his next leave he bought artist's materials so he could capture the scene in paint. Although Rowberry had no artistic background or training, he turned out to have a remarkable aptitude, and his paintings depicted the tanks and battlefields with a vivid, spontaneous energy.[29]

But whatever inner compulsion this activity fulfilled, there was no corresponding desire to display his work, which he kept hidden with obsessive secrecy. A journalist later recorded that 'back in civilian life, he carried on with his art in a locked studio. If his son was ever admitted ..., a newspaper or a piece of cloth was thrown over the current picture. When the picture was finished it went into [a] steel trunk without anyone having seen it.'

Rowberry worked as a senior salesman for a textile firm, returning to military service in 1939 when he rose to the rank of lieutenant-colonel, and painted his way through another war. Again the results were kept hidden in a way that even his son Donald found baffling: 'There was something almost feverish about the way he painted; something seemed to be driving him. And everything went into that steel trunk as soon as it was finished.'

When Claude died his widow could not bear to open the trunk, so it was only after her death in 1965 that his vision was finally shared with the world. An exhibition was held, and a sale eventually brought his work to a wider audience. The paintings he did while in D Battalion were bought by the Royal Tank Regiment, and now adorn the walls of their mess at Bovington where his work can at last enjoy the appreciation it deserves.

At this stage we should also pay tribute to another remarkable man who had no such urge to hide his light under a bushel. This was Brigadier-General Christopher Baker-Carr, whose memoirs may not have provided a solution to his own financial problems, but have given us a lively account of his time as commander of 1st Tank Brigade, as well as bringing him hands-down victory in his feud with Major-General Harper.[30]

As we have noted, Baker-Carr tended to prosper in uniform but not in a civilian suit, and this pattern was repeated when he joined the army for a third time in 1940 at the age of sixty-two. Initially based in Egypt, he was attached to the Spears Mission which attempted to resolve the future of Syria and the Lebanon to the satisfaction of de Gaulle and the local French community, but ended up antagonizing most of the parties instead. Anyone familiar with Baker-Carr's turbulent financial affairs would be astonished to learn that he was made the mission's Economic Adviser.[31]

His eventful life came to an end in 1949, and he would have been delighted that *The Times* saw him as representing 'that unconventional type of soldier which disturbs the equanimity of General Staffs but which, if it succeeds in overcoming their opposition, often contributes greatly to the winning of wars'.[32] Despite his personal troubles, an even more telling tribute appeared in the same newspaper for many years on the anniversary of his death, from his second wife: 'In treasured and unfading memory of my beloved husband, and in deep gratitude for the profound love and happiness he gave me.'[33]

The only member of D Battalion who might have competed with Baker-Carr for raffish glamour was Major Richard Cooper, who had been second-in-command of No. 11 Company and later won the Military Cross twice for bravery. Cooper's father was a landowner from the East Midlands who made his fortune in the Wild West, having acquired a ranch in Wyoming and become a prominent 'cattle baron'.[34] Even greater wealth flowed when oil was discovered on the land, and 'Dick' Cooper inherited a share of this along with his father's love of hunting, which took him round the world on expeditions to shoot game.

He also bought a coffee plantation in what is now Tanzania, but the real attractions of Africa were the wild animals that lived there, the dazzling people who came to shoot them, and the beautiful women who came with them. In this way 'Dick' Cooper became a confederate of Ernest Hemingway and the professional hunter Baron Bror Blixen, who recalled a visit to Kenya in 1929 by the German air ace Ernst Udet. Over dinner, Cooper apparently recorded how their trenches had been strafed by low-flying enemy aircraft in 1917, until he produced his hunting rifle: 'I ... thought I'd try it out on those buggers! Nothing to lose. The first one came straight for us, the pilot clearly visible hunched behind his machine gun. I fired some way in front and to my surprise he plummeted down like a pheasant behind me. The second the same. Hardly believing my luck and cheered on by the men, I quickly reloaded and got a shot off at the third just as he passed over. He also went down.' According to Blixen, this somewhat marred the evening because the three pilots were from Udet's unit and he had never found out what became of them, though having heard the story, one might feel he still lacked a credible explanation.[35] Cooper also served his country again in the Second World War, working as a military adviser in the Pacific and then at various headquarters after D-Day.[36] It would have been a travesty for such an eventful life to end quietly, and sure enough he died after falling from his boat while shooting birds on a lake on his African estate in 1952, having apparently suffered a heart attack. There were claims that he had been drinking, but whether or not this was the case, he had certainly lived life to the full.[37]

Many other men from D Battalion sought their fortune in Britain's far-flung colonies after the war. John McNiven, who had been in the same section as *Deborah*, moved to what is now Suriname where his family owned a sugar plantation, and also died by drowning, having suffered a black-out in his swimming pool on the island of Montserrat, though he reached the age of seventy-eight.[38] Major Edgar Marris, the commander of No. 10 Company who was wounded and taken prisoner at the Battle of Cambrai, settled in Tobago as a planter and died in what is now Guyana in 1944 at the age of fifty-seven.[39] James Vose, who had been a mechanical engineer before joining the Tank Corps, moved to Australia as the local representative for a munitions company, but the aircraft he was travelling on went missing on its way from what is now Sri Lanka to Australia in 1946, and his body was never found.[40]

* * *

The Second World War gave many of D Battalion's men a fresh taste of active service, but this time they found themselves confronting an enemy who was just as effective, but was now motivated by a merciless ideology.

R.O.C. Ward's stirring example of courage and sacrifice was carried on to the next generation, and his elder son Robert, who had been a civil servant in Singapore before the war, was killed in 1942 while fighting the Japanese invaders.[41] R.O.C.'s other son Patrick – who had already won the Military Cross twice – served in the Royal Tank Regiment and was killed in Normandy two years later.[42] His obituary in *The Times* shows he also inherited his father's sporting prowess: 'Major Patrick V. Ward, M.C., fought his battles with as much zest and good humour as he had displayed in the ring against a heavier opponent or in swiping the fastest bowler or stopping a rush in rugger … He is buried at Tourneval, and the French peasants still heap flowers on his grave.'[43]

Captain Walter Smith, who had taken command of No. 12 Company at Cambrai after R.O.C.'s death, joined up again, but this time in a strange twist he joined an antitank unit, and was sent to France at the end of 1939. In an even stranger twist, he met his son Stephen, who was in the Royal Army Medical Corps, on the same troopship, though neither had any idea the other was there. When the Germans swept through Belgium in May 1940, Walter hurried to the town where his son's field hospital was based but was told it had already left, so he made his way to Dunkirk where he was one of those evacuated on the famous flotilla of little ships, as was Major Patrick Ward.[44]

Walter's daughter Joan recalls that as soon as he arrived back, his first words were 'Has Stephen come home?', but his son had not made it to the coast and was posted 'missing, believed killed'. Later she learned what had happened: 'When their field hospital was evacuated, Stephen and his major … volunteered to remain behind to look after the wounded who were unable to travel. When located by the advancing German army, these unarmed medical staff and their helpless patients were taken outside, summarily shot, then buried in a communal grave … During his short life, his concern was for the good of mankind and he was faithful to the end.'[45]

Walter dealt with this tragedy as many others did at the time, by simply not referring to it, or his son, again. He served throughout the war but his health was affected by disease contracted in the Middle East, and in 1949 he moved with his family to Australia. As he grew older he found peace through painting, like Claude Rowberry, and died in 1968, never having fully recovered from his wartime illness.[46]

The Second World War claimed another victim in Fred Dawson from E Battalion, who had survived when his tank *Elles II* was knocked out near Flesquières, only to fall victim to German gunnery several decades later. Captain Dawson, who ran a food company in Yorkshire, rejoined the army at the age of forty-nine and was posted to the Dover area, where he was killed in 1940 by long-range artillery fire across the English Channel.[47]

Captain Harold Head, who had been the section commander of Macintosh and Vose at Cambrai, also became a victim, though not in such a literal sense. During the Second World War he served in the RAF and was involved in training the Czech agents who assassinated the notorious Nazi Reinhard Heydrich in Prague. The terrible reprisals launched by Hitler, including the destruction of the village of Lidice, caused him so much distress that he was unable to continue, and was transferred to the Bahamas where he trained RAF aircrew to fly American planes. Harold Head died in 1989, the last of the tank commanders who had taken part in the original attack at Flers, and was given a military funeral by the Royal Tank Regiment in recognition of his place in history.[48]

CHAPTER 38

Rosemary for Remembrance

These dramas aside, most of D Battalion's men sought their rewards and challenges closer to home, slowly building careers and families as they drifted through what a poet famously called 'the long littleness of life'.[1]

Lieutenant-Colonel William Kyngdon was eventually replaced as commander of 4th (formerly D) Battalion in August 1918 and returned to his former regiment, the Royal Artillery. He spent the rest of the war at various training camps in England, and four years later his military career ended with a peremptory letter saying he was being given compulsory retirement due to the reduction in size of the army.[2]

Kyngdon was only forty-one, had been in the army all his working life, and abroad for most of it, so it was not obvious where he would go from there. The colonies might have seemed an obvious choice, but instead he found a perfect niche closer to home, and in 1929 became secretary of Burnham and Berrow Golf Club in Somerset, having got married the year before. He seems to have slotted comfortably into this milieu, acting as judge for a comic dog show at the local carnival in 1931 where the prizes were presented by another club member, the playwright Ben Travers whose Aldwych farces gently satirized this cosy world.[3] A history of the golf club says: 'Lt. Colonel Kyngdon was the ideal man for Burnham and was respected by all members. He left in 1947 after almost twenty years service.'[4] The Colonel and his wife moved to Perthshire, where he died in 1961 at the age of eighty.[5] They had no children, and no personal records or photographs appear to have survived relating to his military service.

Captain Alfred Enoch, who had written the first letters of condolence to the families of *Deborah*'s crew, remained with 4th Tank Battalion throughout the war, eventually becoming adjutant. The coming of peace meant he could put his mechanical skills and love of machinery to good use, and he became a salesman before working his way up to become director and general manager of an engineering company in Wolverhampton. Unlike many survivors of the Great War he would sometimes reminisce about his experiences, and his son Russell recalls his excitement about the advance at Cambrai, his pride in the tanks, and his respect for the Germans' military prowess.[6] When the next war came he tried to return to the Royal Tank Regiment, but the authorities decided he was better employed continuing to run munitions factories at home.[7]

Like a number of others in this story, Alfred's final years were overshadowed by depression, a delayed response to the traumas of war. He was a practical man, and was taken aback when his son decided to become an actor, using his first names William Russell, though this attitude softened when he got his first film contract and he realized the money that could be made. Alfred died in 1959, when Russell's long career in stage, television and film was already under way, though before the proud moment when he became one of the first cast members in an experimental TV series called *Doctor Who*.[8]

Major Graeme Nixon, who had been *Deborah*'s section commander, later transferred to 5th (formerly E) Battalion, and in 1919 he was posted to the Tank Corps contingent seeking to bolster British rule in Ireland. He received the Military Cross as a reward for his years of service, as did Alfred Enoch, and his commanding officer gave a glowing testimonial: 'He ... has proved himself a capable leader of men. On the battlefield he was extraordinarily brave and always gained the confidence of all around him ... I consider that he is an officer who should do well in any walk of life.'[9]

This turned out to be teaching, and after the war Nixon returned to Liverpool and followed in his father's footsteps by becoming a schoolmaster. Like many others, he rejoined the army in the Second World War, becoming assistant commandant of a Military Detention Barracks in Yorkshire – an austere environment where wayward soldiers were reminded of the virtues of discipline.[10] After this he resumed his educational career and taught maths and physics at Quarry Bank School in Liverpool, where one pupil was often on the receiving end of a well-aimed stick of chalk. His family recall: 'He always hit him on the head – he was a good shot'.[11] A register from 1955 shows the same boy was given detention by Graeme Nixon for not doing his homework – one of a series of misdemeanours for which he was punished, including 'impudent answer to a question', 'silly noises in an examination', and, bizarrely, 'sabotage'.[12] Sadly, Graeme Nixon died in 1966 without witnessing the full rise to fame of this pupil, whose name was John Lennon.

* * *

Finally, what became of those most closely associated with *Deborah*? George Macdonald, the first commander of D51, who we left in a seaside convalescent hospital after he was wounded on 22 August 1917, eventually recovered and returned to the Western Front in a tank supply company, which sounds less glamorous than his former role but could be just as dangerous. In August 1918 he won the Military Cross for reconnoitring a route forward under heavy machine-gun fire, ensuring vital supplies got through to the fighting tanks, despite being wounded once again.[13] At the end of the war he was demobilized as no longer fit for service and returned home to New Zealand.

Unsettled by the war, he had no desire to pursue a legal career and instead became a sheep farmer, running the family's estate where he devoted his energies to improving the land, planting trees, breeding racehorses and raising his four sons. This brought stability and prosperity but not contentment, and towards the end of the Second World War he gave up the farm and other business interests while suffering from severe depression. Fortunately he was able to resolve his inner turmoil, and after this he rekindled an early passion for history and devoted the rest of his life to researching and recording the lives of the pioneering settlers of New Zealand.[14]

His own military career, which had begun with such enthusiasm, became anathema to him, according to his son:

> When we as children asked him about the war it was very difficult to get him to say anything ... Later on when I grew up he said he hated the war and the only thing that kept him sane was reading – poetry and books ... He refused to join the [Returned Soldiers' Association] – he said they glorified war and he was not in [the New Zealand Expeditionary Force] anyway. The only ANZAC Day parade [he] attended [was] when he was in the Home Guard during the next war. He annoyed his local commander because though he had better medals than the others he did not wear them ... So much for the war – he wanted to forget it.[15]

George Macdonald died in 1967, and his son summed up his life: 'He wished no ill to any man – he was in the literal and the accepted sense a gentleman.'[16]

Frank Heap, the second commander of D51, also served for the rest of the war in the Tank Corps, though he remained with 4th Tank Battalion and saw further action before returning home in April 1919. He brought a glowing reference from his commanding officer, who described him as 'a highly efficient officer, capable and indefatigable in the performance of his duties. Has done valuable service in action. Is an excellent all-round athlete.'[17]

There was no soul-searching about Frank's future, as his father was now in his sixties and the family's catering and hotel business would clearly benefit from his youthful energies. Less than two years later he married Ruth Griffiths, who came from another prosperous local family and was described in the newspaper as 'quite a young and very charming girl'.[18] They moved into the Blackpool house that Frank's parents had bought them as a wedding present, and two years later Ruth gave birth to a son. It appeared that after the storms of war, Frank could look forward to a stable and serene future.

Yet despite everything, he still had a craving for the kind of adrenalin surge he had experienced when his tank was crawling through a German-held village, or when he came face-to-face with a group of enemy soldiers armed only with his revolver. Such excitement was not to be found in an office, and instead he turned to the great outdoors and began spending as much spare time as possible in the mountains of the Lake District.

Frank became a keen member of the Fell & Rock Climbing Club, and his young wife also entered with enthusiasm into this hearty and male-dominated world. Photographs show their climbing and skiing trips as far afield as Skye and the Alps, Frank looking cheery and tweedy with his pipe, his wife winsome and gamine as they do battle with sheer cliffs armed only with hobnail boots and a hemp rope. The photographs also show their climbing companions, some of whom look as craggy as the mountains themselves, and this was to prove Frank's downfall.[19]

Although an enthusiastic climber, Frank was not a particularly agile one, and his wife soon began to climb harder routes, and to lead where he preferred to follow. It was hardly surprising that she fell under the spell of one of the young 'tigers' called A. T. Hargreaves, who had only to look at a rock face to find a new and harder route up it. In 1934 Frank, who was understandably devastated, divorced her on the grounds of adultery,[20] though they all remained members of the same climbing club and social circle. Surprisingly, a photograph shows them all together at the opening of the club's new hut just three years later – Frank and Ruth staring uncomfortably into the middle distance, and A. T. Hargreaves standing between them looking lean and relaxed.[21]

Frank served in the Home Guard during the Second World War, and as his once athletic frame drifted into portliness, he seemed to become the embodiment of the prosperous local businessman, being also a leading Freemason and a staunch Tory. But he carried on dreaming of mountain adventure and exploration, and he never lost his boundless energy, his curiosity about the world, or his sense of humour. He was also a kindly man, and supported his ex-wife financially after A. T. Hargreaves died in a skiing accident in 1952, though there was no reconciliation between them. His own death came four years later, and his ashes were scattered on the summit of his beloved Scafell.[22] The climbing club journal described him as 'a very good companion ... a wise, knowledgeable man, always happy to help and advise', and paid tribute again to his 'wise outlook on life', though it did not mention that as so often, his wisdom had been hard won.[23]

As for the crewmen who died when *Deborah* was destroyed, their names were added to local war memorials, while their photographs, medals and memorial plaques were treasured by their families and eventually passed on to the next generations. Those who came after were aware that an ancestor had been killed in a tank, but had no idea of the details, or that they would one day be able to see it for themselves, and even climb into its rusting, wrecked interior.

Back in Cambridge, Florence Coote never forgot Joseph Cheverton, the cheeky young lad who had been her fiancé and who died inside *Deborah*. His family placed a message in their local newspaper on the second anniversary of his death:

> In loving memory of our only dear son, Gunner J. Cheverton, of the Tank Corps, killed in action, November 20th, 1917, on his 20th birthday.
>
> Two years have passed our hearts still sore,
> As time goes on we miss him more,
> His loving smile, his cheerful face,
> There's none can fill that vacant place.
> From his broken-hearted mother, father and sisters, also Florrie.[24]

She eventually married in 1924 and they had a son, Derek Leland, who remembers seeing the letter sent to Florrie informing her of Joe's death and enclosing a Tank Corps cap badge. The letter was destroyed after her death in 1955, but the badge was kept and has now been passed to the descendants of Joseph Cheverton.[25]

Some years after Joe was killed, Florrie posed for a studio photograph wearing a pretty white outfit that might have been her wedding dress, apparently with the Tank Corps badge on a chain round her neck. She is alone, but beside her is a pot of rosemary. The significance of the photograph is clear, for this is a plant whose symbolism was known to Shakespeare: 'There's rosemary, that's for remembrance; pray you, love, remember.'[26]

* * *

At the end of the war, the men who had been taken prisoner began to return home, bringing stories of the hardships they had endured in captivity. The tank crews captured on 22 August came home, including Lieutenant David Lewis and the crew of D46 *Dragon*, as well as Captain Arthur Arnold from F Battalion, though he had developed tuberculosis as a result of poor medical treatment after being shot through the chest, and finally settled in South Africa, where he worked as a farmer until his death in 1969.[27]

There were also a small number of former prisoners-of-war who had been less tight-lipped under German interrogation, and who might have been expected to face questioning on their return, since the British were well aware of the breaches of security that had occurred. Among them were the men of 1st Bn Royal Irish Fusiliers who had been captured in the trench raid on 18 November, and whose information had been so crucial in helping the Germans to repel the attack on Flesquières. As we have seen, a group of six men were captured, and the interrogation report did not specify how many, or who, had given away vital information – though it did state that Irish bitterness at British rule was their primary motivation. In fact, there is no sign of official retribution against any of them, English or Irish, once the war was over. Perhaps an inquiry did take place and proved inconclusive, or more likely, the authorities were so busy managing the flood of repatriated prisoners and demobilized soldiers that they had neither the energy nor the appetite to reopen old wounds.

Sergeant William Whitaker, who had been in charge of the group, returned home to North London at the end of 1918 and left the army a few months later, but when he married in 1920 he was working as a clerk at the War Office, which indicates that no blame was attached to him for what happened. They had two children and he was working as a clerk at an engineering company in Surrey when he died in 1960, aged sixty-three.[28]

Lance-Corporal Frederick Rowe also came home in late 1918 but stayed in the army, returning to his original unit which was now renamed the Bedfordshire and Hertfordshire Regiment, and he was serving with them in India when his first child was born in 1922. A photograph shows him with sergeant's stripes and medal ribbons, every inch the proud old soldier, and again it is impossible to believe he would have done anything to harm his country. Fred later became a postman and factory worker before dying in 1959. His grandson could shed no further light on his military past: 'I knew nothing of Fred's war life, I was 17 when he died and he never spoke about the war to me.'[29]

Of the prisoners from Northern and Southern Ireland, none seems to have attracted any special attention after the war. All were sent the appropriate campaign medals in recognition of their military service, and James Cope also applied for a prisoner of war helper's medal, though this was reserved for French and Belgian civilians who had given support to captured soldiers.[30]

Like a number of them, Private Cope married soon after the war, but died in 1938 aged just forty-five from pneumonia and heart failure. He was treated in Craigavon House in Belfast, a hospital set up for members of the Ulster Volunteer Force, and his profession was given as 'ex-soldier', so again there is no sign of any concern about his wartime record.[31]

The others have proved more elusive, apart from Laurence O'Brien, who was the only Southern Irishman among the prisoners, and one of only two Catholics. After returning from captivity he went back into the armed forces in 1920, when he enlisted in the RAF as an Aircraftman 2nd Class and worked as a stoker at various air bases in England. His character was initially described as 'good', but this did not last, and two years later he was dismissed for misconduct, the cause being given as 'violence to superiors'. A month later, in October 1922, he volunteered to fight in Ireland's new National Army and after that he disappears from view. His war medals were returned unclaimed, but by then Ireland had become a Free State, and there were few who wanted to advertise the fact that they had fought for England's glory.[32]

Another prisoner who made his way home at the end of the war was Sergeant Sam Phillips of the Royal Welsh Fusiliers, and despite the anger felt by some in the Tank Corps, there is no evidence of any action being taken against him. He was demobilized in August 1919, and seems to have simply returned to his little terraced house in Wales, and resumed his work and family life. Like many other soldiers he was awarded the campaign medals that were commonly known as 'Pip, Squeak and Wilfred' after the popular cartoon characters, including the 1915 Star which he had earned by virtue of his service overseas in December 1915.[33]

But if there was such a thing as retribution, perhaps it came twenty-five years later, when another Sergeant Phillips was killed fighting the Germans during the Allies' victorious advance across Europe at the end of the Second World War. He was the eldest son of Sergeant Sam Phillips, and whatever his father may have done in the previous war, no-one could deny that he had fully repaid the debt of honour.[34] According to his family, Sam Phillips – who worked as a timber loader – was 'profoundly affected' by the tragedy, and died of heart disease two years later. His descendants had no knowledge of his actions in the First World War, could not believe that he might have been involved in any wrongdoing, and were distressed by the suggestion. Some personal details have been withheld from this account to avoid identifying them.[35]

As for Second Lieutenant Brommage, who led the disastrous trench raid in which Sergeant Phillips was captured, he spent the rest of the war in the Indian Army, eventually being promoted to captain. The coming of peace meant his services were no longer required and he left the army in 1921, but the colonial civil service provided an alternative career.[36] In 1972 *The Times* noted the death of 'Mr Joseph Charles Brommage, CIE, OBE, who was Additional Financial Adviser, Military Finance, India, from 1944 to 1947 … He became Military Accountant General, India, in 1947.' It is unlikely that he ever heard of Sergeant Phillips again, or would have wished to.[37]

Did a deputation of tankmen ever visit Sergeant Phillips after the war to express their opinions, as some of them had proposed? Again this seems highly doubtful, though it would have been easy enough for Sir Clough Williams-Ellis to call in person, since the renowned architect was a fellow Welshman who wrote the official history of the Tank Corps at a country house near his most celebrated creation, the Italianate village of Portmeirion. But Sir Clough's own son had been killed in action in 1944,[38] and if he ever made the journey, one hopes it might have concluded in mutual comfort rather than recrimination.

CHAPTER 39

Weapon of Friendship

Deborah had gone into the ground, and might have remained there for ever, were it not for a small plastic model of a First World War tank. As he assembled the Airfix construction kit, an interest was fired in the mind of a young Cambrai schoolboy called Philippe Gorczynski, and out of this grew a lifelong passion which ultimately led to his quest to find a real-life tank.[1] This youthful inquisitiveness may not seem surprising in a place renowned as the setting of the first great tank battle, but in the 1960s there was little awareness of what had happened there half a century before, and few ways of finding out.

Philippe – who was born and brought up in Cambrai, though his surname derives from the grandparents who left Poland in search of a better life in the 1930s – grew up surrounded by the legacy of war, but his early attention was focused on the better-known battlefields of the Somme away to the west where he went hunting for relics, a fascination that proved fatal to a number of his friends who showed insufficient respect for the rusting ordnance still littering the fields.

This hobby triggered a curiosity about the military cemeteries surrounding his hometown, and his attempts to find out more led to a local shopkeeper called Michel Bacquet, widely known as the 'Homme de Fer' (or 'Ironman'). His nickname came from the sign above his hardware store, but was also appropriate for someone with a long-standing interest in the armoured clashes that had taken place around Cambrai.

Sitting in the lounge of the Beatus, the thriving hotel he owns and runs with his wife Sandrine, Philippe recalls an event in 1977 that was to prove a turning-point: 'Michel Bacquet did something which was absolutely fantastic at that time – because of his passion, and his interest in the human side, he decided to contact all those men who wrote history not with a pen, but with their blood.'

Almost single-handed, the Ironman began lobbying British service organizations and French civic authorities to organize a visit commemorating the 60th anniversary of the battle. It was the final reunion for the ageing veterans of Cambrai, and more than sixty men took part, with an average age of eighty-two. Among them were some of the last survivors of D and E Battalions of the Tank Corps: William Levy, Ernest Hayward, Charles Homfray, and Jason Addy – the gunner who had gone to war in *Delysia* on 22 August 1917, and sat out the attack on 20 November after his tank broke down in the German lines.

The veterans were given an ecstatic welcome, not least by pupils from local schools who lined the streets, as described by one newspaper reporter: 'The children came and gave them presents and pinned little flags in their buttonholes and cheered them and many of the old men blessed the cold wind that bit into their faces and gave their eyes an excuse to water. At one stop the children waved a Union Jack with the motto stitched across it in English: "Our children understand how their fate was changed and by whose hand." Some of the old men cried unashamedly.'[2]

The visit was inspiring for Philippe, though also frustrating as he was unable to question the elderly visitors about their experiences. 'It was not easy for me as a teenager. My English was not so good and I was not able really to establish contact. It was a friendly time for them to share with one another rather than to collect information. It's a shame, but for me it was really a missed opportunity.' Nevertheless, the gathering had further fired his imagination, and Monsieur Bacquet published a book containing some of the men's reminiscences which provided further information and an all-important map.[3]

This was followed by another crucial meeting for Philippe, this time with a local schoolteacher called Jean-Luc Gibot who had extensive knowledge of the battle, and in the 1980s they began to collaborate on research. This culminated in the publication of a history of the battle called *En Suivant les Tanks*, or *Following the Tanks*.[4]

Their inquiries took them to libraries and archives across Britain and France, while Philippe also began scouring collectors' fairs for books and documents, including many photographs taken by German soldiers. 'It became like a drug to find them, and they were fantastic because no-one really was using the German documents, including British historians.' Sometimes it was possible to work out from photographs where a tank had been destroyed, and as Philippe explored he began to uncover rusting fragments of the tanks themselves.

Other people had tried to find a complete tank, including the Ironman himself, who had once hired divers to search the Canal du Nord to investigate rumours that a tank had fallen in during the war. All they found was a lorry engine, and when the remains of a tank called *Abou-Ben-Adam II* were unearthed by workmen building the A26 motorway near Cambrai, it was scrapped before the historians arrived, and all they recovered was the unditching beam and some fragments of the engine and track.

As Philippe scoured the battlefield, he would also visit nursing homes and seek out the oldest inhabitants to gather their wartime memories. When he arrived in the village of Ribécourt in 1992 he met a lady in her nineties called Marthe Bouleux who had previously lived in nearby Flesquières. What she told him on that first visit made his hair stand on end.

'She said, "Yes, my family was running a cafe in Flesquières and in front of the cafe there were some soldiers who buried a tank." Now I understand she was confused because she said they were German soldiers, but maybe her memories were a little misty. But in any case she remembered seeing some soldiers pushing a tank into a hole. I said: "Do you think it's still there?" and she said: "Yes, maybe!"'

Mme Bouleux was housebound, and although she did her best to describe the spot, Philippe was unable to identify it in a field of around ten acres. Other residents had also heard the story, among them a retired farmworker called Jean Lavallée: 'He said the man who owned the field always asked him to put in some earth because there was a little dip in the ground.' Another clue came from the letters preserved by the widow of Michel Bacquet, the Ironman, who had died in 1986. 'One day I found a note from a man who stayed in Flesquières during the Second World War, and he said at the exit of the village there was a place where the grass didn't grow, and some people said it was possible that a tank was buried there.' The final piece of evidence came in the form of an aerial photograph taken in 1948 and discovered by Jean-Luc Gibot, which showed a mysterious square area in the same field south of the château.

The time had come for action if Philippe was to achieve his dream of finding a tank – not as a mere souvenir, but as a unique way of commemorating the battle that had taken place on his doorstep. 'For me the tank was important because it could be a way to establish a monument to explain the story of the Battle of Cambrai. It would show that a big battle took place here, and nobody could forget that.'

Once he had gained the backing of the landowners, it was necessary to locate the spot precisely, and the local military helped out using aerial infrared photography and powerful metal-detectors. This confirmed there was something substantial buried in the field, but Philippe still had to contain his excitement: 'I was always suspicious, because it could be a heap of corrugated iron.' Official permission was needed to investigate further before an excavation could take place, and this was obtained with the support of Yves Desfossés, head of the Regional Archaeological Service, assisted by Alain Jacques from the Arras Archaeological Service.

Following further negotiations, an excavator finally moved onto the site on 5 November 1998, and less than three hours later it struck metal. The tank's roof hatch was exposed two metres below ground, and once it had been forced open, the interior was examined to make sure there were no bodies within. Then Philippe lowered himself inside: 'It was completely wet, it was dark, it was just like going down into a cellar. The first thing I could see by torchlight was the radiator, and I said, "My God!" Then I saw the engine, and a large pile of blue and white powder where the aluminium from the engine had disintegrated. It was possible to see the wooden floor, still with its grey paint, but completely rotten.' He also realized there were large holes in the tank's superstructure that had been covered with sheets of corrugated iron before the hole was filled in, suggesting it had been used as a shelter. The discovery of the buried tank had changed Philippe's life for ever, and he now dedicated himself to excavating and preserving her for posterity.

The first step was to refill the hole so a proper excavation could begin ten days later. Security was now a major concern as news of the discovery had spread far and wide, fuelled by worldwide media interest, and souvenir hunters had already stolen some items even though the site was fenced off. Volunteers remained round the clock during the dig, which lasted five days as earth and debris were removed, including a large number of poison-gas shells which had been dumped in the hole.

Finally, on 20 November 1998 – the 81st anniversary of the battle – the rusting, battered hulk of a female tank stood fully exposed, and three days later the twenty-three tonne load was hoisted from its grave by a contractor's crane. It was six years since Philippe's first meeting with Madame Bouleux, and sadly she had died months before her youthful memories were proved so accurate.

A few relics were found in the soft mud inside the tank: hand grenades, both British and German, the remains of an army service cap, some tools, a pair of signalling discs, and part of a machine gun. But apart from a number '1' faintly visible on the petrol tank, there was no evidence of her identity, and the red triangle painted on her side – apparently the emblem of 29th Division – has never been explained, since this unit attacked some way to the south.

The tank was buried in the area where D Battalion had suffered heavy losses to the west of Flesquières, and Philippe investigated various possible identities for the tank using military records and aerial photographs, until the mystery was solved a few weeks later thanks to an incredible stroke of fortune. Far away in the north of England, a civilian defence contractor called Will Heap was working with an officer from the Royal Tank Regiment, Major Charles Hunt, who mentioned that he would be attending the annual Cambrai Day dinner at Bovington. Will recalls what happened next: 'I said, my grandfather won the Military Cross at Cambrai, could you dig out a copy of the citation for me? And by the way, I have a photograph of his tank – you could take that down and see what they make of it.'⁵ The photograph, marked simply 'Mr Heap's bus', was passed to the Tank Museum's historian David Fletcher, who immediately made a crucial connection. The damage shown in the photograph exactly matched that on the tank recently excavated at Flesquières, which must therefore be D51 *Deborah* commanded by Second Lieutenant Frank Heap.

It was an unexpected discovery that was challenged by some, since the buried tank was found a third of a mile (or more than half a kilometre) from the spot where *Deborah* was knocked out. However, subsequent evidence has proved the identification correct beyond all doubt. Below the photograph was written 'Flequiers [*sic*] Nov 1917', which was slightly misleading as later evidence showed it was not taken until March 1919. However, it was assumed that the tank had been buried by the Germans after they captured the village in March 1918, probably to use as an underground shelter.

Following the excavation, no building was available in the village large enough to house *Deborah*, so for the next two years she remained under a tarpaulin in the farmyard belonging to the Mayor of Flesquières. Later Philippe was able to buy a large, empty barn in the centre of the village, and in 2000 the British army lent its support as 118th Recovery Company of the Royal Electrical and Mechanical Engineers moved the tank into her new home, where she has remained ever since. The same year *Deborah*'s future was assured when she was officially classified as a French historic monument. A group of friends and supporters was formed, called the Association of the Tank of Flesquières, to maintain the tank and to organize commemorative events including an annual ceremony on Cambrai Day. Philippe's dream of establishing a memorial to the battle also came to fruition with the creation of a monument south-east of the village, overlooking the ground attacked by *Deborah* and the other tanks of D and E Battalions.

Although *Deborah* is regularly sprayed with oil to keep rust at bay, the remains have never been washed or even brushed clean, a fact of great symbolic importance for Philippe. 'Five men were killed in *Deborah* and three others were inside, and their DNA is everywhere, so the tank is like a human thing. The earth on the tank is important, what is inside is important, and it must stay exactly like it is.'

The sepulchral gloom of *Deborah*'s barn provides an atmospheric setting for such a powerful relic of war, and every year thousands of people come to see her, each visit privately arranged with Philippe and normally introduced by him in person. In 2008, the visitors included a group of friends and former colleagues from the UK with a long-standing interest in the First World War, who determined then and there to help Philippe by uncovering the human story of *Deborah*. Three of them were current or former journalists and therefore experts in tracking down and interviewing people, while another member of the team contributed his formidable skills as a genealogist. The twentieth-century tools that had been used to excavate and investigate *Deborah* were now supplemented by the sophisticated research methods of the twenty-first century, including the internet, online databases and digital records. A new chapter in the history of *Deborah* was about to begin.

* * *

The challenge was that although Philippe was already in contact with the descendants of Frank Heap, and some other officers' families including those of D51's first commander, George Macdonald, and her company commander, R.O.C. Ward, he had no way of positively identifying the other crewmen or contacting their relatives. The citation for Frank Heap's Military Cross indicated that four men had died when the tank was destroyed, and though there was no direct evidence, it seemed there might well be a connection with five D Battalion men who were buried side-by-side in Flesquières Hill British Cemetery.

The team were able to confirm this using the records of the Commonwealth War Graves Commission, which showed that four of the men – Joseph Cheverton, George Foot, Frederick Tipping and William Galway – had originally been buried in the same map square where *Deborah* was knocked out.[6] Another photograph of *Deborah* had since come to light, provided by Jim Christie whose uncle was in Flesquières some time after the battle and noted that the crew were buried across the road from their tank.[7] So at least the four dead crewmen had been positively identified, and the task of tracing their relatives began.

The initial approach by Rob Kirk was to appeal for help through the local newspapers in their respective hometowns. The story was a compelling one, and with the help of journalists in Belfast, Nottingham and Cambridge, the team were soon in contact with the families of Gunners Galway, Tipping and Cheverton.[8] With each breakthrough came the excitement of forging another human link with *Deborah*, of putting a face to a name on a headstone, and piecing together the personal stories that lay behind her fateful mission. Like so many other families at home and abroad, the relatives were aware that a forebear had died in the Great War, and had preserved a few poignant relics: the medals they had won but mostly never worn, the bronze plaques issued to the families of the fallen and known with grim humour as 'death pennies', and the faded photographs which were a last treasured link with their loved ones. But unlike most families, they now had a tangible, visible record of their ancestors' war in the form of *Deborah* herself, and all have since become enthusiastic supporters of the research project. Frustratingly, however, in every case the letters, diaries or other documents which might have revealed more about the men's experiences had been lost over the decades, along with their official service records, which were destroyed when a London warehouse was bombed in the Blitz.

The final challenge was to trace the family of George Foot, and in this case there was no prospect of appealing for relatives through a local newspaper. The surname was not distinctive enough, and the family came from a North London suburb which lacked the clear geographical identity of the other men's hometowns. Instead, the team developed a tried and tested approach which involved gathering whatever evidence they could from military records and identifying the men's families in the censuses, before using birth, marriage and death records to prepare a family tree, concentrating on siblings and their descendants. This work was led by Alan Hawkins, an expert genealogist, and the last stage was usually to find the will of a close relative which would point forwards to the next generation. After this the traditional journalistic techniques of 'phone-bashing' and 'door-stepping' came into play.

In this way Vince McGarry, a retired journalist blessed with boundless enthusiasm and irresistible charm, called at the London home of George Foot's nephew Charles Foot, and struck gold. As well as his medals – including the Distinguished Conduct Medal awarded for his courage in an early tank attack on the Somme – Charles had preserved a tiny, hand-coloured photograph showing the angelic face of his uncle, and two even more precious documents, namely the letters sent to George's parents by his commanding officers to break the news of his death. One was written by Frank Heap, and so the four men's connection to *Deborah* was proved beyond all doubt.

The letter also revealed a mystery, because Frank wrote 'four more of my crew have also gone', showing that another of his crewmen had been killed during the battle. For a time it was thought Walter Robinson might have been a member of the crew, since he now lies buried alongside the others, and the Commonwealth War Graves Commission records show his original gravesite was closer to *Deborah* than to any other tank. However, when Vince McGarry tracked down his relatives in the USA, it turned out they had kept a number of vital documents, including the letter of condolence written by Walter's tank commander, who turned out to be James Vose. This showed that Walter had been in *Demon II* rather than *Deborah*, and at the time of writing, the identity of the fifth dead crewman remains a mystery.[9]

The Robinson family had also kept a letter written by Walter's father Fred to break the news to another of his sons. Fred had been widowed a few years previously, and now his son's death left him 'utterly heartbroken'. Forwarding the message sent by Second Lieutenant Vose, he wrote to his son: 'I must ask you to return the letter to me when you have finished with it, as I intend to keep it, I expect it will be found in some drawer after I have joined Mother & Wal.' The letter has been lovingly preserved by his family, along with a number of photographs of Walter, the last one with its jaunty message: 'Cheer up Dad!!!! For all's well that ends well.'[10]

Meanwhile there was another equally baffling question: who were the two crewmen who had survived the attack and escaped from *Deborah* along with Frank Heap? One was almost certainly the driver, and therefore probably an NCO, but there was no obvious way to identify them. Perhaps it was clutching at straws, but one approach was to compare the casualty lists for 22 August and 20 November – the two dates when D51 went into action alongside other tanks from No. 12 Company.[11] Apart from Walter Robinson, only one man appeared on both casualty lists, namely Lance-Corporal David 'Bert' Marsden, whose service record gave his occupation at the end of the war as 'tank driver'. Bert survived the war and resumed his career as a butcher before dying in 1969.[12]

Bert Marsden's family were easy to track down and eager to help, though sadly they had no evidence linking him to a specific tank, nor was this information given in his surviving service record. Like many other veterans of the Great War, he had rarely spoken of his experiences, apart from a few brief but vivid recollections from his grandson, David Melliar-Smith: 'He told me that the only reason he survived was because at the moment the shells hit [his tank], he had moved back to get more ammunition for his machine gun. He also told me that for years after the war, they were still taking metal out of him. At some time in the 1950s I recall him telling me about the piece of shrapnel that was lodged underneath his diaphragm. He was X-rayed at Guy's Hospital where they found the piece of shrapnel, but decided that it would be too dangerous to remove.'[13]

All we can say for certain is that Bert Marsden was in the same company as *Deborah*, and was wounded on 20 November. In fact, this may reduce the chances that he was in *Deborah*'s crew, since the survivors escaped on foot and there is no mention of any of them being wounded. However, there is one final enigma: when Bert's granddaughter was born in 1951 she was christened Deborah. Was this a coincidence, or a tribute to the tank in which he had so nearly died? We will probably never know, but his descendants have been welcomed as members of the extended 'Deborah family'.

Meanwhile, the project continued at full tilt. As the focus for many battlefield visits to Cambrai, Philippe often met the relatives of former combatants and these provided a rich vein for further investigation, along with his ever expanding collection of books and photographs. My own focus was on historical research, hunting down and analysing the records and documents preserved in libraries and archives across Britain, France and Germany. In this way a number of previously unknown descriptions of the battle were brought to light, while the authors of some anonymous accounts were identified for the first time – notably Edward Glanville Smith, whose series of articles appeared in the *Tank Corps Journal* in the 1920s.

Another vivid account by George Koe was discovered in his long-defunct company journal, and most precious of all were the specific references to *Deborah* found in the writings of James Macintosh, Douglas Wimberley and Robert Tennant Bruce, as well as in various German accounts. Despite every effort, however, the most crucial document of all – the Battle History Sheet prepared by Frank Heap following the battle – has not come to light, and we have to accept that it probably never will.

During the research it also emerged that vital information about two tank actions had been given away to the Germans by captured British soldiers, the second time with direct and disastrous consequences for *Deborah*'s crew. These cases, though isolated and distressing, were investigated by the team and the full circumstances now stand revealed for the first time.

By 2009 the team had contacted the descendants of everyone closely connected with *Deborah*, including the families of all her known crewmen, and the scene was set for a historic gathering.

* * *

In Flesquières, on the 92nd anniversary of the day *Deborah* was destroyed, the descendants of her crew met up for the first time for a weekend of commemoration and celebration.

The grandsons and great-grandsons of Frank Heap were there, along with those of George Macdonald who had flown in from New Zealand and Bulgaria. The families of Joseph Cheverton, George Foot, Fred Tipping and David Marsden were present, as was the great-nephew of Theodore Wenger, the man responsible for burying *Deborah*, who had come over from South Africa. The man who identified her, David Fletcher of the Tank Museum, was there, as were Johan and Luc Vanbeselaere from Poelkapelle – now involved in a remarkable project to build their own full-size working replica of a tank to replace the lost *Damon II*.

In the packed Salle des Fêtes (or village hall), a review of the team's research was presented by Philippe Gorczynski, Rob Kirk and myself. The cemetery was the setting for a moving night-time ceremony in which the poetry of Wilfred Owen was read by Russell Enoch, the son of Captain Alfred Enoch and a professional actor. Across the gravestones, John Heap read the letter of condolence that his great-grandfather, Frank Heap, had written to the family of George Foot, while the dead man's nephew Charles Foot looked on. The evening ended with the 'Flame of Memory', a cascade of fireworks and flares which turned the sky red and evoked the sight and sound of battle, and a bagpipe lament in memory of the Highlanders who had fought and died there.

Doris Summers, the elderly niece of Joseph Cheverton, was unable to attend in person but was fascinated to hear about the ceremony, and proud that her family was represented. When told about the achingly beautiful song of the skylarks that can sometimes be heard in the battlefields and cemeteries of the Western Front, she replied: 'I expect it's the souls of the men, singing.'

Since that unforgettable weekend, the research has continued apace and new information continues to emerge. Important insights were provided by Iona Murray, an archaeologist who contacted Philippe with a rich archive of material from her great-grandfather, who visited Flesquières after the war in search of his brother's grave. One photograph showed the exact spot where *Deborah* was knocked out, and confirmed that the hulk had remained in the village street until at least March 1919, rather than being buried during the war as previously supposed.

Another breakthrough came with the discovery of two photographs of *Deborah*, taken by German soldiers after they occupied the village in March 1918. In these pictures the tank appears relatively intact, proving that the extensive damage to her front and right side was inflicted later in the war, probably during the fighting in September 1918.[14]

Finally, during routine maintenance and inspection work on the tank it was noticed that a painted number was faintly visible inside her cab, just above the driver's and commander's seats.[15] This was 2620, listed in battalion records as the manufacturer's number of D51 *Deborah*. It was the final proof, if any were needed, that this was indeed 'Mr Heap's bus'.

Now, as we near the centenary of the battle in which D51 *Deborah* was destroyed, there are hopes that she will be given a new and permanent home. Plans are well advanced to create a special, purpose-built museum in which she will be properly displayed for the first time, on a site adjacent to the cemetery in which her crewmen lie buried and almost within sight of the spot where she was knocked out by German artillery.

For *Deborah*, it will mark the end of a journey that has lasted 100 years and has seen her become a static, but moving, memorial to all those who fought and died in the Battle of Cambrai. For Philippe Gorczynski, it will mean the fulfilment of a dream.

* * *

Setting out from the sleepy village of Trescault, it takes an hour or so of pleasant country walking to reach Flesquières, perched on its low wooded ridge just over two-and-a-half miles (or four kilometres) away.

Near the starting point is a little civilian cemetery with a handful of Commonwealth war graves, mostly dating from early 1917 when this was a 'silent front' and each side generally allowed the other to go about their business in peace. Near this spot, the crews of *Deborah* and the rest of No. 12 Company assembled on that misty November morning and waited for the bombardment to come crashing down, signalling that it was time for them to go forward into the unknown.

From here a muddy track leads gently downhill between fields of crops, and one soon passes over the British front line, crosses No Man's Land with its thick belt of German wire, and reaches the yawning chasm of the Hindenburg Line – though in the imagination only, for the scars have long since healed, the forest of wire has been uprooted, and the landscape lies once again bland and blameless.

Only when the path becomes narrow and sunken between high banks is there a sense of some darker purpose, for this is the start of the Stollenweg, and one soon passes shattered slabs of concrete and a steel girder showing this was once the heart of the German defences in this sector. Further on, the deepest part of the gully – where Hauptmann Soltau and his men mounted their last desperate stand – has been filled in and planted with trees, and the path descends gently to the flat floor of a broad, open valley.

This is the so-called Grand Ravine, and from here the track rises gently towards the east side of Flesquières, passing the squat bulk of a concrete bunker and the curving hedgerow which marks the line of the disused railway where the attackers sheltered. As height is gained the flagpoles of the memorial come into view on the ridge ahead, and then the strongly-built brick wall which was such a formidable obstacle for the Highlanders. Hidden away in nooks and corners of the landscape are bunkers and machine-gun posts, each with its carefully calculated field of fire, some so perfectly preserved that they look as if the defenders had abandoned them a few hours ago, rather than nearly a century.

On gaining the road one turns left, following *Deborah*'s route along the quiet village street, and then turns right at the crossroads to reach the spot where her short journey, and the lives of half her crew, came to an end. It is rare to meet anyone on the walk, and Flesquières remains 'a peaceful, unexceptional place' with nothing to show that it was once the setting for one of the most epoch-making events in history.

Nothing, that is, apart from the cemetery with its rows of headstones, and *Deborah* herself, a mute witness to tragedy that has re-emerged from the grave to bring so many people together, and to bring the past so vividly to life. It is appropriate to end this story with the words of Philippe Gorczynski:

> *Deborah* was for a time a terrible war machine, but now she is an amazing 'weapon' of friendship. You can understand why I am eternally indebted to her for what she has given to me, and what she continues to give to all of us.

APPENDIX A

Order of Battle of D Battalion Tank Corps, and associated infantry and tank units, at Battle of Passchendaele (22 August 1917)

DIRECTION OF ATTACK →

CORPS	DIVISION	INFANTRY BRIGADE	INFANTRY BATTALION (BN)	TANK BN & COMPANY	GROUP	TANK SECTION	TANK CREW NUMBER AND NAME (FORMER TANK IN BRACKETS)*	TANK COMMANDER	TANK OBJECTIVE
XVIII	11th	33rd	6th Bn Border Regt				No tank support		
			6th Bn Lincs Regt	D Bn: No. 12 Company Major Robert (R.O.C.) Ward	Northern	No. 9 Section Captain Edward Glanville Smith	G24 *Gridiron* (D41 *Devil*)	Lieut Andrew Lawrie	BÜLOW FARM
							D44 *Dracula*	2nd Lieut Charles Symonds	
		144th	6th Bn Gloucs Regt				G21 *Geyser* (D42 *Daphne?*)	2nd Lieut Henry Sherwood	VANCOUVER
							D43 *Delysia*	Lieut Alfred Enoch	
	48th	143rd	7th Bn Royal Warks Regt			No. 10 Section Lieut David Lewis	G30 *Gazeka* (D45 *Destroyer?*)	2nd Lieut John Symond	SPRINGFIELD
							D46 *Dragon*	Lieut David Lewis	
							D47 *Demon*	2nd Lieut James Vose	SPOT FARM
					Southern		D48 *Diablo*	2nd Lieut James Clark	CEMETERY
			5th Bn Royal Warks Regt			No. 12 Section Captain Graeme Nixon	D49 *Dollar Princess*	Lieut Percy Paulet King	WINNIPEG
							D50 *Dandy Dinmont*	2nd Lieut Harold Dobinson	
							G22 *Grasshopper* (D51 *Deborah?*)	2nd Lieut George Macdonald	SCHULER FARM (see note†)
							D52 *Despot*	2nd Lieut Harry Shaw	
XIX	61st	184th	2/4th Bn Ox & Bucks Light Infantry (L.I.)	F Bn: No. 18 Company (Major Philip Hammond)	No. 1 route	1st wave: No. 9 Section Captain Donald Richardson	F42 *Faun*	2nd Lieut Albert Peters	POND FARM; HINDU COTTAGE; SCHULER FARM
			2"5th Bn Gloucs Regt			2nd wave: No. 10 Section Captain Arthur Arnold	F46 *Fay*	2nd Lieut Gerald Brooks	
			2/1st Bucks Bn Ox & Bucks L.I.				6 other tanks		(OTHER OBJECTIVES)
	15th	44th & 45th		C Bn No. 8 Coy			10 tanks		

Order of battle shown roughly north-west (top of table) to south-east (bottom of table)

Grey highlights: More details about unit / individual / tank given in text

* The tanks shown in brackets are those put out of action at Bellevue on 21 August, with the names and numbers of the G Bn tanks taken over their crews. In most cases the names of the original D Bn tanks are not known for certain, including D51.

† Schuler Farm is shown as a tank objective for D Bn, but it was not an objective for infantry of 5th Bn Royal Warwickshire Regiment. Instead, on passing Winnipeg and approaching Schuler Farm, the crews of tanks G22 (formerly D51) and D52 would cross over into the sector being attacked by infantry units of XIX Corps and tanks from F Bn.

APPENDIX B

Order of Battle of British and German units at Flesquières in Battle of Cambrai (20 November 1917)

			SECTOR	HAVRINCOURT GRAINCOURT	FLESQUIÈRES				RIBÉCOURT
GERMAN	REINFORCEMENTS 19-20 NOVEMBER	ARTILLERY					2nd & 3rd Abteilung 213th Field Artillery Regiment (107th Inf. Div.)		
		INFANTRY					1st &2nd Bns 27th Reserve Infantry Regiment (54th Inf. Div.)		
	2ND LINE	ARTILLERY			108th Field Artillery Regiment (54th Inf. Div.)	282nd Field Artillery Regiment (20th Landwehr Div.)	Landwehr Foot Artillery Batteries 32, 37		
		INFANTRY		384th Landwehr Infantry Regiment (20th Landwehr Div.)		REINFORCE-MENTS 19 NOVEMBER	3rd Bn 84th Infantry Regiment (54th Inf. Div.)		
	1ST LINE	INFANTRY		1st Bn 84th Infantry Regiment (54th Inf. Div.)	2nd Bn 84th Infantry Regiment (54th Inf. Div.)		387th Landwehr Infantry Regiment (20th Landwehr Div.)		
BRITISH DIRECTION OF ATTACK	1ST WAVE	TANK BN & COMPANY		G Bn Tank Corps, plus at least 5 tanks from D Bn and 7 from E Bn	D Bn No. 10 Coy	D Bn No. 11 Coy	E Bn No. 15 Coy	E Bn No. 13 Coy	B and H Bns Tank Corps
		INFANTRY BN			5th Bn Gordon Highlanders	6th Bn Black Watch	8th Bn Argyll & Sutherland Highlanders	5th Bn Seaforth Highlanders	
	2ND WAVE	TANK BN & COMPANY			D Bn No. 12 Coy		E Bn No. 14 Coy		
		INFANTRY BN			7th Bn Black Watch	7th Bn Gordon Highlanders	6th Bn Seaforth Highlanders	6th Bn Gordon Highlanders	
	INFANTRY BRIGADE(S)			185th, 186th, 187th	153rd		152nd		16th, 18th, 71st
	DIVISION			62nd (2nd West Riding)	51st (Highland)				6th
	TANK BRIGADE				1st				2nd
	CORPS				IV				III

Order of battle shown roughly north-west (top of table) to south-east (bottom of table)

Grey highlights: More details about unit / individual / tank given in text

APPENDIX C

Order of Battle of D Battalion Tank Corps at Battle of Cambrai (20 November 1917)

BRIGADE	BATTALION	ROLE	COMPANY	SECTION	TANK CREW NUMBER AND NAME	TANK COMMANDER
1st Tank Brigade: Commander Colonel Christopher Baker-Carr Reconnaissance officer Captain Clough Williams-Ellis	D Battalion: Commander Lieut-Colonel William Kyngdon Adjutant Captain Frederick Cozens	Wire-crushers & First wave	No. 10 Company Commander Major Edgar Marris 2 i/c Captain Herbert Pearsall Reconnaissance officer 2nd Lieut George Koe	No. 1 Section Captain John Martin	D2 *Duke of Cornwall II*	2nd Lieut William Wallace
					D3 *Drone*	2nd Lieut Alexander Heffill
					D14 *Darius*	Lieut Clifford Salmon
				No. 2 Section Captain Cecil Nicholls	D4 *Dryad II*	2nd Lieut Stanley Knox
					D6 *Devil-May-Care*	Lieut Sydney Glasscock
					D8 *Diogenes*	2nd Lieut Lionel Short
				No. 3 Section Captain Robin Boucher	D9 *Damocles*	2nd Lieut Reginald Baker
					D10 *Diana*	2nd Lieut Walter Miller
					D11 *Dominie*	Lieut Thomas Cook
				No. 4 Section Captain Norman MacKeown	D18 *Don*	Lieut Henry Smith
					D1 *Druid II*	Lieut Eric Dawe
					D5 *Dakoit II*	Lieut Robert Heptonstall
			No. 11 Company Commander Major William Watson 2 i/c Major Richard Cooper Reconnaissance officer 2nd Lieut Frederick King	No. 5 Section Captain David Morris	D21 *Dreadnought III*	2nd Lieut Horace Richards
					D23 *Dashing Dragoon III*	2nd Lieut Ernest Hemmings
					D27 *Double Dee III*	2nd Lieut Horace Birks
				No. 6 Section Captain Wilfred Wyatt (wire-crushers)	D26 *Don Quixote II*	2nd Lieut Reginald Frank
					D28 *Drake's Drum III*	2nd Lieut John Shaw
					D34 *Diallance*	Lieut Gerald Edwards
				No. 7 Section Captain Christopher Field	D29 *Damon III*	Lieut John Coghlan
					D30 *Dusky Dis II*	2nd Lieut Wilfred Head
					D31 *Dolly II*	2nd Lieut Daniel Stevens
				No. 8 Section Captain Frank Telfer	D24 *Deuce of Diamonds*	Lieut Ronald Grant
					D32 *Dop Doctor II*	2nd Lieut Gerald Butler
		Second wave	No. 12 Company Commander Major Robert (R.O.C.) Ward 2 i/c Captain Walter Smith Reconnaissance officer 2nd Lieut Horace Furminger	No. 9 Section Captain Edward Glanville Smith	D41 *Devil II*	2nd Lieut Richard Jones
					D42 *Daphne III*	2nd Lieut George Killey
					D43 *Delysia*	2nd Lieut Harold Dobinson
					D44 *Dracula II*	2nd Lieut Charles Symonds
				No. 10 Section Captain Harold Head	D45 *Destroyer II*	2nd Lieut James Macintosh
					D46 *Dragon III*	2nd Lieut James Clark
					D47 *Demon II*	2nd Lieut James Vose
					D48 *Diablo II*	2nd Lieut Frederick Tritton
				No. 11 Section Captain Alfred Enoch	D54 *Diadem II*	2nd Lieut Eric Owen
					(Two supply tanks?)	(Details not recorded)
				No. 12 Section Captain Graeme Nixon	D49 *Dollar Princess*	2nd Lieut John McNiven
					D50 *Dandy Dinmont*	Lieut Hugo Armitage
					D51 *Deborah*	2nd Lieut Frank Heap

Grey highlights: More details about individual / tank given in text

Notes

Foreword (pp. xii–xv)
1. Precis notes by H. L. Birks for War Office battlefield tour in March 1935, in Tank Museum (E2006.342). Published as 'The Tank in Action', in *Royal Tank Corps Journal* (November 1935). A number of minor edits have been made.
2. 'Tales of a Gaspipe Officer' by 'Despatch Rider' (W. H. L. Watson), *Blackwood's Magazine* (February 1916), p. 257. His service record in NA (WO 339/23425) shows he was evacuated home after being wounded in May 1915.
3. Steuben, pp. 31–2 – article by Leutnant B. Hegermann.
4. From Part Three in a series of articles entitled 'Return to Hell' by Henry Williamson in *Evening Standard*, 1 July 1964.

Chapter 1: A Vision of the World's End (pp. 3–11)
1. Modern Flemish spellings are used here, but the British referred to Poperinge as Poperinghe, De Lovie as La Lovie and Ieper as Ypres.
2. Harvey Cushing, *From a Surgeon's Journal 1915-1918*, London, 1936, p. 165.
3. Watson, *A Company of Tanks*, p. 104.
4. Bion, *War Memoirs*, pp. 26–8.
5. Bion, *The Long Week-end*, p. 124.
6. Gibbs, *From Bapaume to Passchendaele 1917*, p. 13.
7. Martel, pp. 20–1.
8. See *Official History – Passchendaele*, p. 138. This shows that 4,283,550 shells of all calibres were fired along the 15-mile front from 15 July to 2 August.
9. Baker-Carr, *From Chauffeur to Brigadier*, pp. 226–7.
10. War Diary of 184th Tunnelling Company, Royal Engineers in NA (WO 95/336).
11. Ibid.
12. Watson, *A Company of Tanks*, p. 118.
13. War Diary of 3rd Bn Tank Corps in NA (WO 95/106).
14. War Diary of 4th Bn Tank Corps in NA (WO 95/110). Note that the name *Deborah* is not recorded before November 1917.
15. Ibid.
16. Browne, pp. 105–6.
17. Watson, *A Company of Tanks*, p. 122.
18. Baker-Carr, *From Chauffeur to Brigadier*, pp. 238–9.
19. Anon., 'The Wanderings of "D" in France'. This series of articles was published anonymously, but extensive research has enabled the author to be identified.
20. *Official History – Passchendaele*, pp. 177–8.
21. *Report on Action of Tanks on 31st July 1917* in War Diary of Tank Corps HQ in NA (WO 95/92). A slightly different analysis of the figures is in *Official History – Passchendaele*, p. 179: 'Of 117 fighting tanks which had gone into action, 77 had been ditched, bellied or had broken down mechanically, and 42 of these, including those receiving direct hits by shell, had become a total loss.'
22. *Preliminary Report on Tank Operations on 31st July, 1917* in War Diary of Tank Corps HQ in NA (WO 95/91). This comment does not seem to have found its way into the final report.
23. *Report of Action of Tanks on 31st July 1917* in War Diary of Tank Corps HQ in NA (WO 95/92).
24. Ibid.
25. *Report upon the action of the Tanks in the battle of the 31st July*, dated 14 August 1917, in War Diary of Tank Corps HQ in NA (WO 95/92).
26. Ibid.
27. Ibid.
28. War Diary of Tank Corps HQ in NA (WO 95/92).

Chapter 2: Temporary Gentlemen (pp. 12–18)
1. Gough, p. 193.
2. *6th Tank Battalion War History* in War Diary in NA (WO 95/107).
3. Anon., 'The Wanderings of "D" in France'.
4. Browne, p. 191
5. Anon., *H.Q. Tanks 1917-1918*, privately printed 1920, pp. 4–5. Although anonymous, this has been identified as the work of Captain Evan Charteris.
6. Ibid., pp. 5–6.
7. Ibid., pp. 7–8.
8. Bion, *The Long Week-end*, p. 121; sentences from 'I heard' to 'one's heart' added from *Commentary* in Bion, *War Memoirs*, p. 206.
9. Macintosh, *Men and Tanks*, p. 13.
10. The Mark IV tank carried Lewis guns, whose ammunition was fed from a drum rather than a belt, and were therefore not machine guns in the strictest sense. However, this term was often used at the time, as it is in this book.
11. *Dictionary of New Zealand Biography*, entry by Graham M. Miller and Richard L. N. Greenaway, available online at *Te Ara – the Encyclopedia of New Zealand*.
12. Angus Macdonald, *George Macdonald, Gentleman – Sometime Farmer – Sometime Historian*, unpublished biography.
13. Ibid.
14. Ibid.
15. Service record in NA (WO 339/29568).
16. Ibid.
17. Ibid.
18. Ibid.
19. Letter dated 26 August 1915 in Christchurch City Libraries (Archive 825).
20. Ibid.
21. Service record in NA (WO 339/29568).

22. Ibid.
23. *The Press*, Christchurch, 6 November 1916.
24. Service record in NA (WO 339/29568).
25. Anon., 'The Wanderings of "D" in France'.
26. Service record in NA (WO 339/74665).
27. Macintosh, *Men and Tanks*, pp. 9–10.
28. Service record in NA (WO 339/80502).

Chapter 3: A Very Fine Lot Indeed (pp. 19–24)
1. Baker-Carr, *From Chauffeur to Brigadier*, p. 288.
2. Arthur Jenkin, *A Tank Driver's Experiences, or Incidents in a Soldier's Life*, London, 1922, p. 122.
3. *Organisation of the Heavy Section of the Machine Gun Corps later known as the Tank Corps* in NA (WO 158/804). The Heavy Branch was originally known as the Heavy Section.
4. Interview in Liddle Collection (278).
5. Watson, *A Company of Tanks*, p. 16.
6. Harold A. Littledale, 'With the Tanks', *The Atlantic Monthly* (December 1918), p. 836.
7. Details from service record in NA (WO 363); father's obituary in *The Cornishman and Cornish Telegraph*, 29 May 1930; US Censuses; immigration/emigration records; Elizabeth A. Brennan and Elizabeth C. Clarage, *Who's Who of Pulitzer Prize Winners*, Phoenix, Arizona, 1998.
8. Bion, *War Memoirs*, p. 8.
9. Bion, *Commentary* in *War Memoirs*, p. 201.
10. Birks, 'Cambrai – The Attack on Flésquières Ridge [*sic*]'.
11. Letter from Charles E. Foot in City of Westminster Archives Centre (991/15).
12. Family recollection from Charles Foot.
13. Details from birth certificate, census records and *The Bucks Herald*, 9 December 1916.
14. Gibbs, *Realities of War*, p. 316. In an earlier book (*The Battles of the Somme*, p. 256) Gibbs describes a more upbeat meeting with a tank 'skipper' who referred to his tank as 'my beauty' – he is said to be a 'young officer (who is about five feet high)', which makes it fairly certain this was George's tank commander.
15. Alan H. Maude (ed.), *The 47th (London) Division 1914–1919 – By Some Who Served with it in the Great War*, London, 1922, p. 64.
16. Letter in Tank Museum. In view of the critical comments I have elected not to identify the commander of Foot's tank, or the author of the letter.
17. Interview in IWM Sound Archive (870).
18. Pidgeon, p. 105.
19. *London Gazette*, 14 November 1916.
20. War Diary of 4th Bn Tank Corps in NA (WO 95/110).
21. Service records, held by Ministry of Defence; family recollections.
22. Notebook of Captain A. G. Woods in Tank Museum (E1963.38.1). Evidence of their friendship comes from a studio photograph showing them together in August 1917, now in the possession of Russell Enoch.
23. War Diary of 2nd New Zealand Infantry Brigade HQ in NA (WO 95/3693).
24. War Diary of 4th Bn Tank Corps in NA (WO 95/110).
25. See Pidgeon, p. 168 – original source not identified, but widely quoted in contemporary accounts such as Gibbs, *The Battles of the Somme*, p. 264, and Captain Basil Williams, *Raising and Training the New Armies*, London, 1918, p. 217.
26. *Official History – Somme*, p. 366.
27. War Diary of 4th Bn Tank Corps in NA (WO 95/110).
28. Ibid.

Chapter 4: *Dracula*'s Fate (pp. 25–28)
1. Notebook and Diary of Captain A. G. Woods in Tank Museum (E1963.38.1), This is one of a number of documents that use the alternative spelling 'Foote'.
2. War Diary of 4th Bn Tank Corps in NA (WO 95/110).
3. Service record in NA (WO 339/45302).
4. War Diary of 4th Bn Tank Corps in NA (WO 95/110).
5. Colonel H. Stewart, *The New Zealand Division 1916-1919 – A Popular History Based on Official Records*, Auckland, 1921, pp. 111–12.
6. *The Times*, 6 October 1916.
7. *Official History – Somme*, p. 430.
8. Service record in NA (WO 339/45302).
9. Letter from grandson of Second Lieutenant William Sampson in Tank Museum (E1972.81.2).
10. Citation in *Supplement to the Tank Corps Book of Honour*.
11. Service record in NA (WO 363). Glaister may have been one of those who stayed in the shell crater with Wakley and Foot, but the wording of his medal citation and the dates of his wound and treatment make it more likely that he mounted a rescue attempt from the British lines.
12. *Official History – Somme*, p. 432.
13. Gibbs, *The Battles of the Somme*, pp. 322–3.
14. Notebook and Diary of Captain A. G. Woods in Tank Museum (E1963.38.1).
15. *The Bucks Herald*, 9 December 1916.
16. *The Times*, 6 October 1916.
17. Citation in *Supplement to the Tank Corps Book of Honour*.
18. Service record in NA (WO 363).
19. Letter in Glaister's file in Tank Museum (E2003.36).
20. Information from Shaun Corkerry and Stuart Nicholson in Whitehaven.
21. Letter in Glaister's file in Tank Museum (E2003.36).
22. Service record in NA (WO 363).
23. Service record in NA (WO 339/45302).
24. Ibid.
25. Ibid.
26. Divorce file in NA (J 77/1702/2962).
27. *The Times*, 2 May 1921.
28. *The Times*, 8 May 1922.

Chapter 5: Of Knaves and Jokers (pp. 29–34)
Thanks to Cliff Brown and Ron Clifton for their assistance in Cambridge, and to Nigel Henderson, Lester Morrow and Robert Corbett in Belfast.
1. Photograph in possession of family.
2. Birth certificate, baptism register, census returns.
3. From Rupert Brooke, *The Old Vicarage, Grantchester*.
4. Census records; family recollections and photographs.
5. Riddell and Clayton, pp. 5 and 280–1.
6. *Cambridge Independent Press*, 23 April 1915.
7. Medal index cards.

8. CWGC records.
9. Riddell and Clayton, p. 29.
10. Adam, p. 195.
11. Riddell and Clayton, p. 30. He added: 'Subsequent events proved that this estimate of the value of the 1st Cambridgeshires was hopelessly inaccurate.'
12. Ibid., p. 34.
13. Ibid., p. 44.
14. Ibid., pp. 48–9.
15. Adam, pp. 242–3.
16. *Cambridge Chronicle*, 12 December 1917.
17. War Diary of 1/1st Bn Cambridgeshire Regiment in NA (WO 95/2590/1).
18. Riddell and Clayton, pp. 74–5.
19. See Adam, *Arthur Innes Adam 1894-1916* and *In a World I Never Made*, London, 1967, p. 46 by his sister Barbara Wootton.
20. Shown by consecutive entries in medal register in NA (WO 329/1775).
21. Census records.
22. *Belfast Evening Telegraph*, 15 December 1917.
23. Census records.
24. Service records in NA (WO 363); they had consecutive service numbers showing they joined up at the same time.
25. Medal index card.
26. War Diary of 13th Bn Royal Irish Rifles in NA (WO 95/2506/3).
27. Ibid.
28. Falls, *The History of the 36th (Ulster) Division*, p. 59.
29. War Diary of 13th Bn Royal Irish Rifles in NA (WO 95/2506/3).
30. CWGC records.
31. War Diary of 13th Bn Royal Irish Rifles in NA (WO 95/2506/3).
32. Date of transfer known from the single surviving page of his service record in NA (WO 363).

Chapter 6: The Sword of Deborah (pp. 35–39)
1. Photographs in possession of family.
2. Census records.
3. He gave this as his occupation in the 1911 Census, though in 1916 *Wright's Directory* still listed him as a warehouseman.
4. Employer's name given in *Nottinghamshire Guardian*, 22 December 1917.
5. Photographs in possession of family.
6. War Diary of 1st Bn King's Own (Royal Lancaster Regiment) in NA (WO 95/1506/1).
7. Census records.
8. Family recollections.
9. Service record in NA (WO 363).
10. Medal index cards and service records for George and Charles Dimler in NA (WO 363 and WO 364).
11. War Diary of 9th Motor Machine Gun Battery in NA (WO 95/1038).
12. Ibid.
13. Watson, *A Company of Tanks*, p. 16.
14. Photographs in possession of family.
15. D Bn Battlegraph for 22 August 1917 in Tank Museum (E2006.1861).
16. Birth records for England and Wales.
17. Judges 5:31 in *Authorised King James Bible*.
18. *Henry VI Part I* Act I Scene 2. *The Sword of Deborah – First-Hand Impressions of the British Women's Army*

in France is the title of a book by F. Tennyson Jesse (London, 1918).
19. Names from War Diary of 4th Bn Tank Corps in NA (WO 95/110).
20. Service record in NA (WO 339/99800).
21. Names from War Diary of 4th Bn Tank Corps in NA (WO 95/110).
22. Macintosh, *Men and Tanks*, p. 13.
23. Coghlan, 'Cambrai Day'.
24. Letter in the possession of Mme Bacquet, Cambrai.

Chapter 7: In Honour Bound (pp. 40–46)
1. Tank Corps Summary of Information for 5 August 1917 in NA (WO 157/239).
2. Fifth Army Intelligence Summary in NA (WO 157/213).
3. War Diary of 113th Infantry Brigade HQ in NA (WO 95/2553).
4. Service record in NA (WO 339/64664).
5. War Diary of Fifth Army HQ General Staff in NA (WO 95/520).
6. Ibid.
7. Ibid.
8. Ibid.
9. War Diary of 14th Bn Royal Welsh Fusiliers in NA (WO 95/2555/2).
10. *Aussagen zweier englischer Gefangener vom XIV/R.W.Fus.* in Militärarchiv, Freiburg (PH3/584).
11. Ibid.
12. Ibid.
13. War Diary of 113th Infantry Brigade HQ in NA (WO 95/2553).
14. CWGC records.
15. War Diary of Fifth Army Adjutant and Quarter-Master General in NA (WO 95/525).
16. Ibid.
17. Williams-Ellis, p. 77.
18. Browne, pp. 107–8.
19. Baker-Carr, *From Chauffeur to Brigadier*, p. 239.
20. Mitchell, p. 101.
21. Service record in NA (WO 339/64664).
22. Letter in *The Daily Telegraph* on 6 July 1934, from 'George E. Mackenzie, Minister of Kirkhope, and late Lt., 153rd Bde., R.H.A., B.E.F.'
23. W. H. A. Groom, *Poor Bloody Infantry – A Memoir of the First World War*, London, 1976, p. 127.
24. Rorie, p. 147.
25. War Diary of 3rd Bn Tank Corps in NA (WO 95/106).
26. *Aussagen zweier englischer Gefangener vom XIV/R.W.Fus.* in Militärarchiv, Freiburg (PH3/584).
27. Browne, p. 107.
28. Watson, *A Company of Tanks*, p. 119.
29. Williams-Ellis, p. 77.
30. Brigadier-General J. Charteris, *Memorandum: Prevention of Espionage and Leakage of Information*, GHQ 27 December 1916. A copy is preserved in the papers of Sir John Monash in the Australian War Memorial (RCDIG0000617).
31. Watson, *A Company of Tanks*, p. 119.
32. *Nominal Roll of N.C.O.'s and Men of the 14th Bn. Royal Welsh Fusiliers who embarked with the Battalion on Dec. 1st, 1915*, in Bangor University Archives (BMSS/7060).
33. Medal index card.
34. International Committee of the Red Cross records.

35. *Y Seren*, 15 September 1917.
36. *Cambrian News*, 21 September 1917. The article says the letter was sent on 25 July, which must be a mistake as he was not captured until 26/27 July.
37. Marriage certificate, census records, birth/ marriage/death records.

Chapter 8: Ray of Sunshine (pp. 49–55)
1. This was the usual spelling used by the British during the war, though the village is now generally known by its Flemish name of Sint-Juliaan. Langemarck is now properly known as Langemark Poelkapelle.
2. Baker-Carr, *From Chauffeur to Brigadier*, p. 251.
3. Order No. 91 in War Diary of 33rd Infantry Brigade HQ in NA (WO 95/1811).
4. This is the scheme outlined in Order No. 13 dated 17 August 1917 in War Diary of 1st Brigade Tank Corps HQ in NA (WO 95/98). Browne, p. 197 says 'this plan was afterwards modified considerably, for what reason I do not know'.
5. War Diary of 7th Bn Tank Corps in NA (WO 95/100).
6. Undated report in papers of General Sir Ivor Maxse in IWM (PP/MCR/C42).
7. Fuller, *Memoirs of an Unconventional Soldier*, p. 154.
8. Ibid., p. 94; see also Fuller, *Tanks in the Great War 1914–1918*, p. xvi.
9. Lecture by Lt-Col. Baker-Carr on 'The Employment of Tanks' in Tank Museum (E2004.3211).
10. Baker-Carr, *From Chauffeur to Brigadier*, p. 252.
11. Letter from Ivor to Mary Maxse dated 20 August 1917 in West Sussex Record Office (WSRO), Chichester. Thanks to Tony Maxse for permission to quote from these papers, and to Rhodri Lewis at WSRO.
12. Letter from Leo to Ivor Maxse dated 11 September 1917 in WSRO.
13. *The Times*, 21 August 1917. The article appeared anonymously but the author is named as Beach Thomas in Browne, pp. 234–5. Douglas Browne says the story was based on interviews with men who had not taken part in the battle, since the actual participants were asleep, and says of the article, 'those of us who had been there were unable to recognise a single detail'.
14. Williams-Ellis, p. 93.
15. Browne, p. 236.
16. Williams-Ellis, p. 93.
17. *GHQ Summary of Information* dated 28 August 1917 in NA (WO 157/23).
18. Browne, p. 195.
19. Stühmke, pp. 178–9.
20. 125th Infantry Regiment Stab Kriegstagebuch (i.e. HQ War Diary) in Hauptstaatsarchiv Stuttgart (M411 Bd 1082).
21. 51st Infantry Brigade Kriegstagebuch in Hauptstaatsarchiv Stuttgart (M410 Bü 938). The report is timed at 10.35 a.m. on 19 August 1917.
22. German trench-maps show the bunker slightly north of Vancouver as marked on British maps, but the accounts of the action make it clear they must have been the same.
23. Stühmke, pp. 180–1.
24. Divisionsbefehl (i.e. divisional order) issued at 9.30 p.m. on 19 August 1917, in 26th Infantry Division Kriegstagebuch Anlagen (i.e. appendices) in Hauptstaatsarchiv Stuttgart (M410 Bd 177).
25. 125th Infantry Regiment Stab Kriegstagebuch in Hauptstaatsarchiv Stuttgart (M411 Bd 1082).
26. 51st Infantry Brigade Kriegstagebuch in Hauptstaatsarchiv Stuttgart (M410 Bü 938). Report at the end of 20 August 1917.
27. Divisionsbefehl at 11.30 p.m. on 20 August 1917 in 26th Infantry Division Kriegstagebuch Anlagen in Hauptstaatsarchiv Stuttgart (M410 Bd 177).

Chapter 9: Crossing the Canal (pp. 56–61)
1. This is the date given in Anon., 'The Wanderings of "D" in France', but the War Diaries of 1st Brigade Tank Corps HQ and 4th Bn Tank Corps show they set out on the following day (i.e. 20 August).
2. Anon., 'The Wanderings of "D" in France'.
3. Browne, p. 199. Elephant-iron shelters were built of heavy-gauge corrugated iron.
4. Anon., 'The Wanderings of "D" in France'.
5. Ibid.
6. Browne, pp. 204–5.
7. *Official History – Passchendaele*, p. 202.
8. War Diary of 1st Brigade Tank Corps HQ in NA (WO 95/98).
9. War Diary of 4th Bn Tank Corps in NA (WO 95/110).
10. War Diary of 143rd Infantry Brigade HQ in NA (WO 95/2754).
11. War Diary of 11th Division HQ in NA (WO 95/1788).
12. Watson, *A Company of Tanks*, p. 133.
13. Browne, p. 217.
14. H.L.B. (i.e. Horace Leslie Birks), 'The Brewery, Poelcapelle, October, 1917', *The Tank* (October 1955).
15. War Diary of 4th Bn Tank Corps in NA (WO 95/110).
16. Watson, *A Company of Tanks*, p. 140.
17. Anon., 'The Wanderings of "D" in France'.
18. War Diary of 4th Bn Tank Corps in NA (WO 95/110).
19. Anon., 'The Wanderings of "D" in France'.
20. This is presumed because infantry accounts of the battle refer to the new D Battalion names and numbers rather than the former G Battalion ones. For simplicity, the tanks are generally referred to here by their new D Battalion numbers, and by the names with which those numbers were associated. Apart from D51, the other changes were as follows:
    - Crew of D41 (name given in 33rd Infantry Brigade report as *Devil*) under Second Lieutenant Andrew Lawrie transferred to G24 *Gridiron*.
    - Crew of D42 (associated with name *Daphne*) under Second Lieutenant Henry Sherwood transferred to G21 *Geyser*.
    - Crew of D45 (associated with name *Destroyer*) under Second Lieutenant John Symond transferred to G30 *Gazeka*.

    These details are taken from 4th Bn War Diary and D Battalion Battlegraph for 22 August 1917 in Tank Museum (E2006.1861). They do not give names for the four D Bn tanks which did not go into action (including D51).
21. Judd, 'The Middle Years of the War'. Some changes have been made to punctuation, notably the omission of numerous exclamation marks.
22. Stühmke, p. 181.

Chapter 10: Into the Pillar of Fire (pp. 62–71)
1. Anon., 'The Wanderings of "D" in France'. Smith refers to 'twelve 125 h.p. Daimler engines' but they were actually 105 h.p.
2. War Diary of 184th Tunnelling Company, Royal Engineers in NA (WO 95/336).
3. Judd, 'The Middle Years of the War'.
4. War Diary of 48th Division HQ in NA (WO 95/2746).
5. Interview in IWM Sound Archive (7031). This recording was made when Jason Addy was on a visit to Cambrai in 1977 (see Chapter 39 below), and closely follows an account in Lyn Macdonald, *They Called it Passchendaele*, London, 1978, pp. 156–8. There are a number of inconsistencies in the account, hardly surprising so many decades after the battle. He names the tank commander who died as Lieutenant Knight, whereas the only officer to be killed on that date was Lieutenant Lawrie, whose name has therefore been substituted here for consistency. In addition, Addy gives their objective as Bülow Farm rather than Vancouver, and insists they evacuated two wounded men, whereas Jagger's medal citation only refers to one.
6. Interview in IWM Sound Archive (870). The order of sentences has been slightly changed.
7. Bion, *War Memoirs*, p. 30.
8. War Diary of 4th Bn Tank Corps in NA (WO 95/110).
9. Census records; Maurice, p. 242.
10. War Diary of 33rd Infantry Brigade HQ in NA (WO 95/1811).
11. War Diary of 48th Division HQ in NA (WO 95/2746).
12. War Diary of 1st Brigade Tank Corps HQ in NA (WO 95/98).
13. War Diary of 48th Division HQ in NA (WO 95/2746).
14. War Diary of 11th Division HQ in NA (WO 95/1788).
15. War Diary of Fifth Army HQ General Staff in NA (WO 95/520).
16. War Diary of 11th Division HQ in NA (WO 95/1788).
17. Anon., 'The Wanderings of "D" in France'.
18. War Diary of 11th Division HQ in NA (WO 95/1788).
19. War Diary of 6th Bn Gloucestershire Regiment in NA (WO 95/2758).
20. War Diary of 144th Infantry Brigade HQ in NA (WO 95/2757/1).
21. War Diary of 48th Division HQ in NA (WO 95/2746).
22. Ibid.
23. From Part Five in a series of articles entitled 'Return to Hell' by Henry Williamson in *Evening Standard*, 3 July 1964.
24. Stühmke, p. 182.
25. Anon., 'The Wanderings of "D" in France'.
26. D Bn Battlegraph for 22 August 1917 in Tank Museum (E2006.1861).
27. War Diary of 144th Infantry Brigade HQ in NA (WO 95/2757).
28. Interview in IWM Sound Archive (7031).
29. Mitchell, pp. 118–19.
30. Interview in IWM Sound Archive (7031).
31. Maurice, pp. 243, 255–6 and 283–4.
32. Service record in NA (WO 363); emigration records for SS *Kroonland*.
33. War Diary of 48th Division HQ in NA (WO 95/2746).
34. Service records in NA (WO 364 and WO 374/41936), census records.
35. War Diary of 4th Bn Tank Corps in NA (WO 95/110).
36. Anon., 'The Wanderings of "D" in France'.
37. D Bn Battlegraph for 22 August 1917 in Tank Museum (E2006.1861).
38. War Diary of 7th Bn Royal Warwickshire Regiment in NA (WO 95/2756/1).
39. War Diary of 48th Division HQ in NA (WO 95/2746).
40. Ibid.
41. Charles Carrington, *Soldier from the Wars Returning*, London, 1965, p. 101.
42. War Diary of 48th Division HQ in NA (WO 95/2746).
43. Ibid.
44. War Diary of 4th Bn Tank Corps in NA (WO 95/110).
45. War Diary of 1st Brigade Tank Corps HQ in NA (WO 95/98).
46. Watson, *A Company of Tanks*, pp. 140–1.
47. *Vernehmung von 1 Offizier und 7 Mann der 12. Komp. D.-Batl. Tank-Corps, ... 1 Offizier und 3 Mann der 18. Komp. F.-Batl. Tank-Corps, ...* dated 26 August 1917 in Militärarchiv, Freiburg im Breisgau (PH/3/585). The manufacturer's number of D46 *Dragon* was actually 2058.
48. Nachrichtenblatt (i.e. bulletin) Nr. 36 dated 25 August 1917 in 2nd Battalion, 125th Infantry Regiment Kriegstagebuch Anlagen in Hauptstaatsarchiv Stuttgart (M411 Bd 1151).

Chapter 11: *Deborah*, the Dead Man and the Drummer (pp. 72–79)
1. Anon., 'The Wanderings of "D" in France'.
2. See War Diary of Tank Corps HQ in NA (WO 95/92) and *XVIII Corps Report on Operations of August 22nd 1917* in papers of General Sir Ivor Maxse in IWM (PP/MCR/C42).
3. War Diary of 48th Division HQ in NA (WO 95/2746).
4. D Bn Battlegraph for 22 August 1917 in Tank Museum (E2006.1861).
5. Service record in NA (WO 339/80499).
6. War Diary of 4th Bn Tank Corps in NA (WO 95/110).
7. Photographs from Royal Museum of the Army and of Military History (Nr Inv KLM-MRA 201530003 & 20608-sint-juliaan).
8. War Diary of 5th Bn Royal Warwickshire Regiment in NA (WO 95/2755/1).
9. Lieutenant C. E. Carrington, *The War Record of the 1/5th Battalion, The Royal Warwickshire Regiment*, Birmingham, 1922, pp. 55–6. *A Subaltern's War* was originally published under his pen-name Charles Edmonds.
10. *Report on Operations 22nd Aug: 1917* in NA (WO 158/839).
11. Service record in NA (WO 339/29568).

12. Anon., 'The Wanderings of "D" in France'.
13. Service record in NA (WO 374/26074); Indian Army service record in British Library (L/MIL/9/485/135-46); nickname from Anon., 'The Wanderings of "D" in France'.
14. Judd, 'The Middle Years of the War'.
15. War Diary of 6th Bn Tank Corps in NA (WO 95/107).
16. Service record in NA (WO 339/53827).
17. War Diary of 6th Bn Tank Corps in NA (WO 95/107).
18. *Official History – Passchendaele*, p. 203.
19. War Diary of 61st Division HQ in NA (WO 95/3034).
20. War Diary of 6th Bn Tank Corps in NA (WO 95/107). For fuller accounts see John Foley, *The Boilerplate War*, London, 1963, and Tony Spagnoly and Ted Smith, *Cameos of the Western Front – Salient Points Two*, Barnsley, 1998.
21. *Vernehmung von 1 Offizier und 7 Mann der 12. Komp. D.-Batl. Tank-Corps, ... 1 Offizier und 3 Mann der 18. Komp. E.-Batl. Tank-Corps, ...* dated 26 August 1917 in Militärarchiv, Freiburg im Breisgau (PH/3/585).
22. Service record in NA (WO 339/53827).
23. *Vernehmung von 1 Offizier und 7 Mann der 12. Komp. D.-Batl. Tank-Corps, ... 1 Offizier und 3 Mann der 18. Komp. E.-Batl. Tank-Corps, ...* dated 26 August 1917 in Militärarchiv, Freiburg im Breisgau (PH/3/585).
24. Ibid.
25. Service record in NA (WO 339/53827).
26. *Vernehmung von 1 Offizier und 7 Mann der 12. Komp. D.-Batl. Tank-Corps, ... 1 Offizier und 3 Mann der 18. Komp. E.-Batl. Tank-Corps, ...* dated 26 August 1917 in Militärarchiv, Freiburg im Breisgau (PH/3/585).
27. Ibid.
28. Ibid.
29. Ibid.
30. Ibid.
31. Stühmke, p. 183.

Chapter 12 : Failure is an Orphan (pp. 80–84)
1. War Diary of Fifth Army HQ General Staff in NA (WO 95/520).
2. War Diary of Tank Corps HQ in NA (WO 95/92).
3. War Diary of 11th Division HQ in NA (WO 95/1788).
4. War Diary of XVIII Corps HQ in NA (WO 95/952) – letter dated 22 August 1917.
5. Report dated 27 September 1917 in papers of General Sir Ivor Maxse in IWM (PP/MCR/C42).
6. Browne, p. 236.
7. Martel, p. 21.
8. *XVIII Corps Report on Operations of August 22nd 1917* in papers of General Sir Ivor Maxse in IWM (PP/MCR/C42).
9. John Baynes, *Far From a Donkey – The Life of General Sir Ivor Maxse*, London & Washington, 1995.
10. CWGC records.
11. War Diary of 184th Infantry Brigade HQ in NA (WO 95/3063).

12. 125th Infantry Regiment Stab Kriegstagebuch (i.e. HQ War Diary) in Hauptstaatsarchiv Stuttgart (M411 Bd 1082).
13. *Kampferfahrungen eines Kampftruppen-Kommandeurs aus den letzten Tagen* (i.e. Battle experiences the commander of a combat unit in the last few days) dated 25 August 1917, in 26th Infantry Division Kriegstagebuch Anlagen in Hauptstaatsarchiv Stuttgart (M410 Bd 177).
14. Ibid.
15. Fernspruch Nr. 26 to Oberst Stühmke dated 24 August 1917, in 125th Infantry Regiment Stab Kriegstagebuch Anlagen in Hauptstaatsarchiv Stuttgart (M411 Bd 1102)
16. Watson, *A Company of Tanks*, p. 140.
17. *Official History – Passchendaele*, p. 202.
18. Williams-Ellis, pp. 92–4.
19. Major-General J. F. C. Fuller, 'Summary of Tank Operations 1916-1918', *Royal Tank Corps Journal* (March-June 1934).
20. From transcript of unpublished memoir dated 27 October 1933 by Private Frank Cunnington of 2/5th Nottinghamshire and Derbyshire Regiment (Sherwood Foresters), by courtesy of Julian Sykes.
21. Ibid.
22. Letter from Ivor to Mary Maxse dated 5 November 1917 in West Sussex Record Office. The original ends with a question-mark which has been omitted here.
23. Judd, 'The Middle Years of the War'.
24. For more on Pond Farm, see this website: http://depondfarm.be/en
25. From Part Four in a series of articles entitled 'Return to Hell' by Henry Williamson in *Evening Standard*, 2 July 1964.
26. For details see service record in NA (WO 363) and R. K. R. Thornton (ed.), *Ivor Gurney – Collected Letters*, Manchester, 1991.
27. Copyright The Ivor Gurney Estate. Extracts are from his poem *The Man* in Gloucestershire Archives (D10500/1/P/4/98/13), which appeared in Michael Hurd, *The Ordeal of Ivor Gurney*, Oxford, 1978, pp. 103–5. Thanks to the Ivor Gurney Trust for permission to reproduce these extracts, and to Tim Kendall's *War Poetry* blog for pointing out Ivor Gurney's connection with the battle.

Chapter 13: The Dead Never Stirred (pp. 85–89)
1. Service record in NA (WO 339/29568).
2. *The Times*, 23 August 1917.
3. Macintosh, *Men and Tanks*, p. 127.
4. Anon., 'The Wanderings of "D" in France'.
5. *Beckenham Journal, Penge and Sydenham Advertiser*, 15 September 1917.
6. Ibid.
7. Bion, *The Long Week-end*, p. 138.
8. Watson, *A Company of Tanks*, pp. 143–4. Watson refers to him as 'the padre' without giving his name.
9. War Diary of 4th Bn Tank Corps in NA (WO 95/110).
10. War Diary of 144th Infantry Brigade HQ in NA (WO 95/2757).
11. War Diary of Fifth Army General Staff in NA (WO 95/520).
12. War Diary of XVIII Corps HQ in NA (WO 95/951).

13. Vaughan, pp. 221–9.
14. Ibid., pp. 224–5.
15. Ibid., pp. 225–8.
16. War Diary of 4th Bn Tank Corps in NA (WO 95/110).
17. War Diary of Fifth Army General Staff in NA (WO 95/520).
18. Harry Vaughan is not believed to be related to Edwin Campion Vaughan.
19. War Diary of 4th Bn Tank Corps in NA (WO 95/110).
20. Vaughan, p. 228.
21. Ibid., p. 229.
22. *Official History – Passchendaele*, p. 207.
23. Williams-Ellis, pp. 94–5.
24. Watson, *A Company of Tanks*, pp. 146–7.

Chapter 14: The Bogs of Passchendaele (pp. 90–96)
1. Gough, p. 205.
2. Anon., 'The Wanderings of "D" in France'.
3. Macintosh, *Men and Tanks*, p. 33.
4. *The Times*, 22 December 1938.
5. Butler, 'Reminiscences of Salvage Work'.
6. Service record in NA (WO 374/10210).
7. Butler, 'Reminiscences of Salvage Work'.
8. Supplement to *London Gazette*, 17 September 1917.
9. For a more detailed account, see Liddell Hart, *The Tanks Volume One*, pp. 211–13.
10. Service record in NA (WO 374/10210).
11. Butler, 'Reminiscences of Salvage Work'.
12. Ibid.
13. Ibid.
14. Census records; service record in NA (WO 339/61434).
15. Family recollections.
16. Anon., 'The Wanderings of "D" in France'.
17. Report dated 27 September 1917 in papers of General Sir Ivor Maxse in IWM (PP/MCR/C42).
18. Lieutenant-General Sir G. M. Harper, *Notes on Infantry Tactics & Training*, London, 1919.
19. Baker-Carr, *From Chauffeur to Brigadier*, p. 235.
20. War Diary of 1st Brigade Tank Corps HQ in NA (WO 95/98).
21. Anon., 'The Wanderings of "D" in France'.
22. Maurice, p. 100.
23. War Diary of 4th Bn Tank Corps in NA (WO 95/110).
24. War Diary of 1st Brigade Tank Corps HQ in NA (WO 95/98).
25. Maurice, p. 259.
26. War Diary of 4th Bn Tank Corps in NA (WO 95/110).
27. War Diary of 5th Bn Tank Corps in NA (WO 95/111).
28. Service record in NA (WO 374/36122).
29. Maurice, pp. 96–7.
30. Handwritten note by Lieutenant Gerald Edwards in Watson, *A Company of Tanks*, p. 143.
31. War Diary of Fifth Army General Staff in NA (WO 95/520).
32. *Official History – Passchendaele*, p. 278.
33. Gibbs, *From Bapaume to Passchendaele 1917*, p. 292.
34. War Diary of 51st Division HQ in NA (WO 95/2846).
35. War Diary of Tank Corps HQ in NA (WO 95/92).
36. It appears Winston Churchill did not invent this memorable phrase, but he used it in a letter to Brigadier-General Sir James Edmonds dated 26 January 1938 in NA (CAB 45/200).
37. Anon., 'The Wanderings of "D" in France'.
38. Coghlan, 'Cambrai Day'.

Chapter 15: The Coming of Frank Heap (pp. 98–103)
1. Service record, held by Ministry of Defence.
2. War Diary of 4th Bn Tank Corps in NA (WO 95/110). This is presumed to refer to Frank Heap as no other arrivals are recorded over this period.
3. Photograph in possession of family.
4. Macintosh, *Men and Tanks*, p. 2. He wrote 'X Battalion' and 'X Company' but the correct names have been inserted here.
5. Ibid, p. 3.
6. The photos are captioned 'Tank officers in camp at Poperinghe, 26th September 1917' (IWM refs. Q 2897, Q 2898 and Q 2899). A letter in *The Tank* (January 1956) identifies the officers as (left to right) unknown (seated far left), Lieut. William Struthers (standing), 2nd Lieut. Frederick King (seated), Major Richard Cooper, Capt. Wilfred Wyatt, Lieut. Gerald Edwards and 2nd Lieut. Gerald Butler. Round table (left to right): Lieut Edward Sartin, Capt. David Morris, Capt. Hugh Skinner, 2nd Lieut. Harold Puttock, Capt. Christopher Field, 2nd Lieut. Daniel Stevens seated on ground, and 2nd Lieut. Horace Birks second from right.
7. Watson, *A Company of Tanks*, pp. 148–9.
8. Anon., 'The Wanderings of "D" in France'.
9. See photograph of *Deborah* sent to Frank Heap captioned 'Uriah's bus'; also dinner menu in possession of Edward Glanville Smith's family signed 'Uriah (F. G. Heap)'.
10. Anon., 'The Wanderings of "D" in France'.
11. War Diary of 4th Bn Tank Corps in NA (WO 95/110).
12. The *Army List* shows date of commission as 31 January 1917.
13. Service record, held by Ministry of Defence.
14. Bion, *The Long Week-end*, p. 133.
15. *Belfast Evening Telegraph*, 15 December 1917.
16. Letter from Frank Heap dated 26 November 1917.
17. War Diary of 4th Bn Tank Corps in NA (WO 95/110).
18. Interview in IWM Sound Archive (870).
19. Anon., 'The Wanderings of "D" in France'.
20. The 'flapper' was an impractical device called the Ayrton fan, intended to dispel poison gas.
21. Macintosh, *Men and Tanks*, pp. 14–19.
22. Elles, A paper entitled *Man power in construction of tanks* in NA (WO 158/819) says: 'The cost of a large fighting Tank is taken at £5,000.'
23. *Organisation and supply of tanks, etc, 1915 to 1918* in NA (MUN 5/391/1940/7) Chapter 5.
24. Elles.
25. Gwyn Evans, 'De-coding Mark IV Serial Numbers – Part One', *Tankette: Magazine of the Miniature Armoured Fighting Vehicle Association* Vol. 49 No. 6 (2014). Thanks to Gwyn Evans for his help.
26. *History of No 20 Squadron, Royal Naval Armoured Cars 1915-19* in NA (MUN 5/391/1940/5).
27. Macintosh, *Men and Tanks*, pp. 19–20.

Notes 285

Chapter 16: Heap's Progress (pp. 104–110)
1. Census records; *Yorkshire Post*, 30 January 1925.
2. *Burnley Gazette*, 15 January 1890.
3. *Burnley Express*, 4 July 1908, and George E. Martin, *Breezy Blackpool*, Mate's Illustrated Guides, 1899.
4. *American Register*, 17 May 1914.
5. *Manchester Evening News*, 13 September 1899.
6. *National Probate Calendar* (1925) shows his estate at death was £66,094-3s.
7. *Blackpool Gazette*, 31 January 1925.
8. George E. Martin, *Breezy Blackpool*, Mate's Illustrated Guides, 1899.
9. *Blackpool Gazette*, 31 January 1925.
10. Family recollections.
11. Census and birth/marriage/death records.
12. Sale particulars in *Yorkshire Post*, 4 April 1925.
13. Photographs in possession of family.
14. Service record, held by Ministry of Defence.
15. *The Times*, 4 July 1911.
16. Ibid.
17. Archives of The Leys School.
18. From *Inside of King's College Chapel, Cambridge* by William Wordsworth.
19. George E. Martin, *Breezy Blackpool*, Mate's Illustrated Guides, 1899.
20. Photographs in possession of family.
21. Family recollections.
22. Photographs in possession of family.
23. Council minutes in King's College Archives Centre (KCGB/5/1/4/7), p. 179. Thanks to Dr Patricia McGuire, archivist of King's College, Cambridge.
24. Priestley, p 16
25. Service record, held by Ministry of Defence.
26. Ewing, pp. 5–6.
27. Service record, held by Ministry of Defence.
28. Ewing, p. 11.
29. Ian Hay, *The First Hundred Thousand*, Edinburgh & London, 1915, pp. 170–80. This was the pen-name of Lieutenant, later Major, John Hay Beith of 10th Bn Argyll and Sutherland Highlanders. The Prime Minister Herbert Asquith referred to 'a tempest which is shaking the foundations of the world' in the House of Commons on 1 March 1915 – see *Hansard*.
30. Major-General R. F. H. Nalder, *The Royal Corps of Signals – A History of its Antecedents and Development (circa 1800-1955)*, London, 1958, p. 92.
31. Ewing, p. 31.
32. Priestley, pp. 9 and 29.
33. Maurois, p. 122. The US edition credits the translation to Thurfrida Wake.
34. Ibid., p. 115.
35. Ibid., pp. 124–6.
36. Ibid., p. 131. CWGC records show Major-General George Thesiger, commanding 9th Division, died on 26 September 1915, aged forty-seven, and is commemorated on the Loos Memorial.
37. Ewing, p. 409.
38. Ibid., pp. 64–5.
39. War Diary of 9th Division Signals Company in NA (WO 95/1756/2).
40. Photograph in possession of family.
41. *Blackpool Times & Herald*, 12 January 1918.
42. Service record, held by Ministry of Defence.
43. Ibid.
44. See headline in *The Times*, 16 September 1916.
45. Service record, held by Ministry of Defence.

Chapter 17: 'The Best Company of the Best Battalion' (pp. 111–115).
1. Interview in IWM Sound Archive (870). The order of some sentences has been changed.
2. Letter from Horace Birks dated 3 December 1954 in Liddell Hart Centre for Military Archives (LIDDELL 9/28/64).
3. Service record in NA (WO 339/12569).
4. Macintosh, *Men and Tanks*, p. 64. He does not name Captain Walter Smith, but refers to him as 'the second in command'.
5. Ibid., pp. 64–5.
6. Interview in IWM Sound Archive (494).
7. Diary and family tree in possession of family.
8. *Cambridge University Alumni 1261-1900*
9. *The Times*, 1 December 1917.
10. *The Times*, 12 September 1958.
11. *Dorking & Leatherhead Advertiser*, 10 November 1928.
12. Marriage certificate.
13. Ibid.
14. Unidentified newspaper article in possession of family.
15. Marriage certificate.
16. *Wandsworth Borough News*, 24 April 1909.
17. Census and birth/marriage/death records.
18. Service record in NA (WO 339/12569).
19. International Committee of the Red Cross records.
20. Moody, p 71
21. War Diary of 6th Bn Buffs (East Kent Regiment) in NA (WO 95/1860).
22. Ibid.
23. CWGC records.
24. Moody, p. 108.
25. Rugby History Society website.
26. War Diary of 6th Bn Buffs (East Kent Regiment) in NA (WO 95/1860).
27. Ibid.
28. Moody, p. 144.
29. Service record in NA (WO 339/12569).
30. Ibid.
31. War Diary of 4th Bn Tank Corps in NA (WO 95/110).
32. Watson, *A Company of Tanks*, p. 183.
33. Letter from Major-General Henry Burstall, commander of 2nd Canadian Division, dated 11 April 1917 in War Diary of 1st Brigade Tank Corps HQ in NA (WO 95/97).
34. Watson, *A Company of Tanks*, p. 75.
35. Ibid., p. 81.
36. Anon., 'The Wanderings of "D" in France'.
37. Watson, *A Company of Tanks*, p. 83.

Chapter 18: Redundant Oddments (pp. 116–121)
1. Fuller, *Tanks in the Great War 1914-1918*, p. xvi.
2. Watson, *A Company of Tanks*, p. 90.
3. Coghlan, 'Cambrai Day'.
4. War Diary of Tank Corps HQ in NA (WO 95/91) – this was at Wailly on 21 July.
5. Service record, held by Ministry of Defence.
6. Ibid.
7. Col. K. W. Maurice-Jones, *The History of Coast Artillery in the British Army*, London, 1959, p. 161.

8. Captain J. E. E. Craster, *Pemba, The Spice Island of Zanzibar*, London & Leipsic, 1913, p. 15.
9. Ibid., p. 22.
10. Ibid., frontispiece.
11. Service record, held by Ministry of Defence.
12. *With the Anglo-German Boundary Commission in West Africa 1912-1913* by Warwick Trading Co. in IWM Film Archive (MGH 2248),
13. Captain W. V. Nugent, 'The Geographical Results of the Nigeria-Kamerun Boundary Demarcation Commission of 1912-13', *Geographical Journal* (June 1914).
14. Hermann Detzner, *Im Lande des Dju-Dju – Reiseerlebnisse im Östlichen Stromgebiet des Niger*, Berlin, 1923, p. 350.
15. Service record, held by Ministry of Defence.
16. *Official History – Togoland and Cameroons*, p. 8 pic.
17. CWGC records.
18. *The Times*, 28 August 1914.
19. *Sydney Morning Herald*, 18 March 1915.
20. Service record, held by Ministry of Defence.
21. *Official History – Togoland and Cameroons*, p. 423.
22. Medical index card.
23. Service record, held by Ministry of Defence.
24. Swinton, pp. 220–1. This shows Major W. F. R. Kyngdon (Royal Artillery) commanded F Company.
25. Service record, held by Ministry of Defence.
26. Swinton, p. 274.
27. Major A. F. Becke, *Order of Battle Part 4 – The Army Council, G.H.Q.s, Armies, and Corps 1914-1918*, London, 1945, p. 267.
28. Swinton, p. 280.
29. Ibid., p. 286.
30. Ibid., p. 288.
31. See Movement Orders dated 22 October 1916 issued on behalf of the officer commanding the Heavy Section of the MGC and signed by Kyngdon, in War Diary of C Company Heavy Section in NA (WO 95/96/6).
32. Baker-Carr, *From Chauffeur to Brigadier*, p. 206.
33. Ibid., pp. 202–3.
34. Ibid., p. 232.
35. Bion, *War Memoirs*, p. 67.

Chapter 19: Out of the Salient (pp. 122–125)
1. Watson, *A Company of Tanks*, p. 75.
2. War Diary of 4th Bn Tank Corps in NA (WO 95/110).
3. For more on 'Operation Hush', see Admiral Sir Reginald Bacon, *The Dover Patrol 1915–1917 Vol. 1*, London, 1919, pp. 223–60.
4. Census records; US Army enlistment records; service record, held by Ministry of Defence.
5. C. D Baker-Carr, *General Account of the Attack on and Capture of Poelcappelle* in National Army Museum (2006-09-5-4-8-1).
6. Anon., 'The Wanderings of "D" in France'.
7. See War Diaries of 1st Brigade Tank Corps HQ in NA (WO 95/98) and 4th Bn Tank Corps in NA (WO 95/110); Watson, *A Company of Tanks*, pp. 154–60; H.L.B. (i.e. Horace Leslie Birks), 'The Brewery, Poelcapelle, October, 1917', *The Tank* (October 1955); Coghlan, 'Cambrai Day'.
8. Service record in NA (WO 339/99800).
9. Watson, *A Company of Tanks*, pp. 159–61.
10. Ibid., pp. 160–1.
11. Birks, 'Cambrai – The Attack on Flésquières Ridge [*sic*]'.
12. War Diary of 4th Bn Tank Corps in NA (WO 95/110).
13. Birks, 'Cambrai – The Attack on Flésquières Ridge [*sic*]'.
14. Anon., 'The Wanderings of "D" in France'.
15. CWGC records; War Diary of 4th Bn Tank Corps in NA (WO 95/110).
16. Baker-Carr, *From Chauffeur to Brigadier*, p. 255.
17. Watson, *A Company of Tanks*, p. 222.

Chapter 20: High Days and Highlanders (pp. 126–130)
1. Macintosh, *Men and Tanks*, pp. 54–5.
2. Anon., 'The Wanderings of "D" in France'.
3. Macintosh, *Men and Tanks*, pp. 72–3. He refers to 'C' Company, which was the later name of No. 12 Company.
4. Bion, *The Long Week-end*, pp. 151–2.
5. Watson, *A Company of Tanks*, p. 162.
6. Ibid., p. 166.
7. War Diary of 153rd Infantry Brigade HQ in NA (WO 95/2873).
8. Baker-Carr, *From Chauffeur to Brigadier*, pp. 260–1.
9. *Training Note. Tank and infantry operations without methodical artillery preparation*, from Third Army dated 30 October 1917, in *Official History – Cambrai*, pp. 348–54 and various War Diaries. The note says 'Infantry should keep from 25 to 50 paces behind the Tank as it enters the wire, so as not to get entangled in any trailing strands.'
10. *Notes on Tank and Infantry Training* in War Diary of Tank Corps HQ in NA (WO 95/92).
11. *Instructions No. 1* dated 7 November 1917 in War Diary of 51st Division HQ in NA (WO 95/2846).
12. Ibid.
13. *Order No. 21* dated 15 November 1917 in War Diary of 1st Brigade Tank Corps HQ in NA (WO 95/98).
14. War Diary of 4th Bn Tank Corps in NA (WO 95/110).
15. Anon., 'The Wanderings of "D" in France'.
16. Watson, *A Company of Tanks*, p. 163.
17. War Diary of 4th Bn Tank Corps in NA (WO 95/110).
18. Anon., 'The Wanderings of "D" in France'.
19. Birks, 'Cambrai – The Attack on Flésquières Ridge [*sic*]'.
20. Macintosh, *Men and Tanks*, pp. 82–3.
21. Account from *History of Cambrai* compiled by Major-General Sir Percy Hobart in Tank Museum (E2006.381). The account is anonymous, but clearly by Birks as the details are similar to his other descriptions of the battle.
22. Anon., 'The Wanderings of "D" in France'.
23. 'L.I.', 'Cambrai, 1917 – The Impressions of an Infantryman'.

Chapter 21: Into Hiding (pp. 133–137)
1. War Diary of 5th Bn Seaforth Highlanders in NA (WO 95/2866).
2. Watson, *A Company of Tanks*, pp. 167–8.
3. Ibid.
4. See V. T. Boughton, *History of the Eleventh Engineers, United States Army*, New York, 1926.
5. Macintosh, *Men and Tanks*, pp. 90–1.
6. Anon., 'The Wanderings of "D" in France'.

7. Details in War Diary of Tank Corps HQ in NA (WO 95/92).
8. Macintosh, *Men and Tanks*, pp. 90–1.
9. Anon., 'The Wanderings of "D" in France'.
10. Photograph from Railway Construction Engineers Collection in IWM (Q 46939).
11. Watson, *A Company of Tanks*, p. 169.
12. Baker-Carr, *From Chauffeur to Brigadier*, p. 265.
13. *Proceedings of a Court of Enquiry* in service record of Sapper Frederick Bird in NA (WO 363). The soldier who died was Private John McNally.
14. Macintosh, *Men and Tanks*, pp. 93–4.
15. Handwritten note by Lieutenant Gerald Edwards in Watson, *A Company of Tanks*, p. 169.
16. Macintosh, *Men and Tanks*, pp. 93–4.
17. Macintosh, 'The Tanks at Cambrai', p. 183.
18. Macintosh, *Men and Tanks*, pp. 95–6.
19. Watson, *A Company of Tanks*, pp. 169–71.
20. War Diary of 7th Bn Tank Corps in NA (WO 95/100) shows two companies arrived on 15 November and one company on 18 November. War Diary of 5th Bn Tank Corps in NA (WO 95/111) shows their tanks arrived on 17 November.
21. *Official History Cambrai*, pp. 27–8. This total was made up 378 fighting tanks, fifty-four supply tanks, thirty-two wire-pulling tanks, and twelve others carrying bridging and communications equipment.
22. Macintosh, *Men and Tanks*, pp. 97–8.
23. Watson, *A Company of Tanks*, pp. 169–71.

Chapter 22: On the Silent Front (pp. 138–144)

1. See letter from Elles in NA (CAB 45/118): 'Fuller and I, for instance, never visited the area except in trench coats and black goggles.'
2. War Diary of 1st Bn Royal Irish Fusiliers in NA (WO 95/2502/2).
3. Falls, *The History of the 36th (Ulster) Division*, p. 141.
4. Steuben, p. 41.
5. Hülsemann, p. 57.
6. Ibid., p. 58.
7. Ibid., p. 64.
8. Ibid., p. 58. The corporal is described as 'baumlang' – literally 'as tall as a tree'.
9. War Diary of 1st Bn Royal Irish Fusiliers in NA (WO 95/2502/2).
10. Diary of Field Marshal Sir Douglas Haig – copy in NA (WO 256/24). Entry for 18 November 1917.
11. Macintosh, *Men and Tanks*, p. 99.
12. Birks, 'Cambrai – The Attack on Flesquières Ridge [*sic*]'.
13. Williams-Ellis, p. 102.
14. Letter from Elles in NA (CAB 45/118).
15. 'L.I.', 'Some Reminiscences of a War-time Soldier III. – A Tank to the Rescue'.
16. Birks, 'Cambrai – The Attack on Flesquières Ridge [*sic*]'.
17. Macintosh, *Men and Tanks*, pp. 99–101.
18. Hülsemann, p. 238.
19. Macintosh, *Men and Tanks*, p. 99.
20. Major Ward's orders have not survived, but would probably have included this overview from the orders to D Bn dated 18 November 1917, in War Diary of 4th Bn Tank Corps in NA (WO 95/110).
21. War Diary of Tank Corps HQ in NA (WO 95/92).
22. War Diary of 1st Brigade Tank Corps HQ in NA (WO 95/98).
23. War Diary of 7th Bn Tank Corps, including History of 7th Tank Bn, in NA (WO 95/100).
24. D Bn Battlegraph in NA (MFQ 1/1384).
25. *Operation Order No 5 Section* by Captain D. A. Morris in Tank Museum (E1992.68.3). The order of some sentences has been some changed, punctuation added and capital letters removed.
26. Ibid.
27. Ibid.
28. Macintosh, *Men and Tanks*, p. 102.

Chapter 23: 'Things Fall Apart' (pp. 145–153)

1. The chapter title is a quote from *The Second Coming* by Ireland's greatest poet, W. B Yeats: 'Things fall apart; the centre cannot hold'.
2. *Vernehmung eines Sergeanten und 5 Mann vom I/R. Ir.Fus …* in Militärarchiv, Freiburg im Breisgau (PH3/558).
3. Ibid.
4. Ibid.
5. Ibid.
6. Hülsemann, pp. 65 6. This comment comes from Leutnant Johannes Langfeldt, ordnance officer of 2nd Battalion, 84th Infantry Regiment (see also below).
7. Steuben, p. 104.
8. International Committee of the Red Cross (ICRC) records.
9. Service record in NA (WO 364).
10. Census and birth/marriage/death records.
11. *Vernehmung eines Sergeanten und 5 Mann vom I/R. Ir.Fus …* in Militärarchiv, Freiburg im Breisgau (PH3/558).
12. Ibid., and service record in NA (WO 364).
13. Supplement to *London Gazette*, 1 January 1916, p. 57.
14. Service record in NA (WO 364).
15. *Vernehmung eines Sergeanten und 5 Mann vom I/R. Ir.Fus …* in Militärarchiv, Freiburg im Breisgau (PH3/558).
16. Ibid., and service record in NA (WO 364).
17. *Vernehmung eines Sergeanten und 5 Mann vom I/R. Ir.Fus …* in Militärarchiv, Freiburg im Breisgau (PH3/558).
18. ICRC records.
19. ICRC records show his rank as lance-corporal, though his medal index card (MIC) describes him as a private. The corporal in question could also be George Ball, who is shown as a private in ICRC records at the time of capture, though his MIC describes him as an acting corporal.
20. Census records, medal index card.
21. Census records, medal records, ICRC records, CWGC records.
22. Ibid.
23. *Vernehmung eines Sergeanten und 5 Mann vom I/R. Ir.Fus …* in Militärarchiv, Freiburg im Breisgau (PH3/558).
24. The court martial took place on 19 October 1917 – see record in NA (WO 71/611). Age from CWGC records, which show he is buried in Neuville-Bourjonval British Cemetery.
25. Ibid.

26. War Diary of 1st Bn Royal Irish Fusiliers in NA (WO 95/2502/2).
27. See record in NA (WO 71/611).
28. *Vernehmung von 4 irischen Überläufern ... der I./R. Dub. Fus ... eingebracht am 18.12.17, westlich Ossus* in Hauptstaatsarchiv Stuttgart (M33/2 Bü 583). The report includes the original text in English and says the spelling is unaltered from the original.
29. See Dahlmann, p. 348.
30. The dead man's unit is given in a document entitled *Bericht ueber die Wache vom 25.X. – 1.XI.1917* in Hauptstaatsarchiv Stuttgart (M 33/2 Bü 241). Rifleman Walker is named in the War Diary of 12th Bn Rifle Brigade in NA (WO 95/2121), and his service record in NA (WO 363) shows he was previously in the HBMGC. Further details come from ICRC records, and from documents and newspaper cuttings in the possession of his family. Thanks are due to Pat and Martin Tebbs, Carroll and Amanda Rushby, and Emma Gowshall for information about Rifleman Walker and his two brothers, who also died in the war.
31. Wedel, p. 158.
32. Two companies of 27th Reserve Infantry Regiment (RIR), plus the machine-gun company, were sent to Flesquières on 19 November, and transport was arranged to bring in the rest of 1st Battalion the next morning. The 2nd Battalion moved to Marcoing to be ready for deployment, and moved to Flesquières early on 20 November, adding substantially to the forces holding the village.
33. Dahlmann, pp. 353–4.
34. Hülsemann, p. 95. The description is by Hauptmann Wille.
35. Dahlmann, pp. 354.
36. Hülsemann, p. 89.
37. Fuller, *Memoirs of an Unconventional Soldier*, pp. 187–9.
38. Hülsemann, pp. 66.
39. Steuben, pp. 14–19.
40. Hülsemann, p. 95.
41. Steuben, pp. 36–7 and 88–92.
42. Hülsemann, p. 66. Leutnant Hegermann confirms in Steuben, p. 31, that his birthday was on 19 November. The anecdote about Thyra also comes from Leutnant Langfeldt, in Steuben, p. 71.

Chapter 24: To Shake Mightily the Earth (pp. 154–62)
1. Macintosh, *Men and Tanks*, pp. 102–3. He refers to 'C' Company, which was the later name of No. 12 Company.
2. See Williams-Ellis, p. 108 on Elles' Special Order No. 6: 'It was not the incitement to "do their damnedest" which the contemporary Press fathered upon him. That spurious fosterling he hated the worse, the more he perceived its popularity.'
3. Macintosh, *Men and Tanks*, p. 103.
4. Watson, *A Company of Tanks*, p. 172.
5. *Communications 1st Bde Tank Corps* in War Diary of 1st Brigade Tank Corps HQ in NA (WO 95/98).
6. Interview in IWM Sound Archive (870). The order of some sentences has been changed.
7. Isaiah 2:19, quoted in Rev. Neville S. Talbot, *Thoughts on Religion at the Front*, London, 1917. He was a co-founder of Talbot House, the celebrated rest and recreation centre in Poperinghe named after his brother who was killed in 1915.
8. Timings from Macintosh, *Men and Tanks*, p. 104.
9. Orders in possession of Brigadier Ben Edwards.
10. War Diary of 4th Bn Tank Corps in NA (WO 95/110).
11. Watson, *A Company of Tanks*, p. 172.
12. Macintosh, *Men and Tanks*, pp. 105–6.
13. Anon., *H.Q. Tanks 1917-1918*, 1920, p. 64. Although the book is anonymous, the same passage occurs in an article entitled 'My Recollections of Cambrai' by the Hon. Evan Charteris in *Tank Corps Journal* (November 1922).
14. Watson, *A Company of Tanks*, p. 172.
15. War Diary of 4th Bn Tank Corps in NA (WO 95/110).
16. Baker-Carr, *From Chauffeur to Brigadier*, p. 268 says this happened 'at about half-past four, an hour and a half before zero', but McTaggart (see Note 18 below) gives the time as 5.30 a.m.
17. Macintosh, *Men and Tanks*, p. 107.
18. McTaggart, 'The Great Battle of Cambrai'.
19. History of 4th Tank Bn in War Diary in NA (WO 95/110) says the wire-crushers were from No. 10 Company, but Orders in War Diary say they were from No. 11 Company. This is confirmed because accounts by Edwards and Shaw (who were both in No. 11 Company) state they were in wire-crushing tanks.
20. Watson, *A Company of Tanks*, p. 173.
21. Handwritten note by Lieutenant Gerald Edwards in Macintosh, *Men and Tanks*, p. 113.
22. Anon, 'Cambrai: A Tank Commander's Impression', *Tank Corps Journal* (November 1922). The article is anonymous but the identity of the author can be worked out from internal evidence. The E Bn Battlegraph (in Tank Museum) does not give a crew number for *Elles II*, and this is taken from the report of an action on 20 September 1917 in the War Diary of 5th Bn Tank Corps in NA (WO 95/111).
23. 'L.I.', 'Some Reminiscences of a War-time Soldier III. – A Tank to the Rescue'.
24. Macintosh, *Men and Tanks* pp. 108–10. The original refers to 'A' and 'B' Company.

Chapter 25: 'Now For It!' (pp. 163–168)
1. Bion, *The Long Week-end*, p. 161.
2. Bion, *War Memoirs*, p. 47.
3. *An Account of my Sojourn in France & Germany during the Great War 1917-1919* by Willie Pennie in IWM (11255). His account refers to 'ten thousand guns', which is what it must have seemed like, though the actual number was much smaller.
4. From *History of Cambrai* compiled by Major-General Sir Percy Hobart in Tank Museum (E2006.381). The account is anonymous, but clearly by Birks.
5. Macintosh, *Men and Tanks*, pp. 110–11.
6. This phrase is taken from 'L.I.', 'Cambrai, 1917 – The Impressions of an Infantryman'.
7. Watson, *A Company of Tanks*, pp. 173–4.
8. *51st Division Report on the Operations S.W. of Cambrai* in NA (WO 158/390).
9. Hülsemann, p. 243.
10. Strutz, p. 18.

11. Watson, *A Company of Tanks*, p. 174.
12. From *History of Cambrai* compiled by Major-General Sir Percy Hobart in Tank Museum (E2006.381). As in other accounts, Birks says they were working with '4th Black Watch' but this must be wrong as this battalion did not take part in the battle.
13. 'L.I.', 'Some Reminiscences of a War-time Soldier III. – A Tank to the Rescue'.
14. *Lecture by Lt-Col. Baker Carr on 'The Employment of Tanks'* in Tank Museum (E2004.3211).
15. Watson, *A Company of Tanks*, p. 166.
16. From *History of Cambrai* compiled by Major-General Sir Percy Hobart in Tank Museum (E2006.381).
17. Watson, *A Company of Tanks*, p. 179. These were probably D26 *Don Quixote II* and D31 *Dolly II*, which are shown on the D Bn Battlegraph in NA (MFQ 1/1384) in virtually the same location. The Battlegraph also shows D9 *Damocles* and D30 *Dusky Dis II* ditched nearby.
18. Rorie, chapter on Cambrai by Captain Robert Tennant Bruce, p. 165. The third tank was probably D30 *Dusky Dis II*.
19. Handwritten note by Lieutenant Gerald Edwards in Macintosh, *Men and Tanks* p. 113. His grandson Brigadier Ben Edwards, himself a tank commander, comments: 'It may seem callous today to have used the body of a comrade in such a manner, but things were different then. My grandfather had lost his previous tank, and a member of his crew, to enemy fire at the Third Battle of Ypres, and they had to fight their way back over No Man's Land on foot. No sane man would have wanted to repeat that. He well knew that to become static once committed to battle made the tank a magnet for bullets, usually resulting in the loss of the vehicle and members of the crew. It would have seemed acceptable to "ask" a comrade to make one final sacrifice when arguably he no longer needed his body, for the sake of eight crewmen, a tank, and the essential moral and fire support that each working vehicle gave to the infantry.'
20. Anon. 'Cambrai: A Tank Commander's Impression', *Tank Corps Journal* (November 1922). See previous notes on this source.
21. Service record in NA (WO 339/57980).
22. File of Captain Leonard Johnson in Tank Museum (E1978.212).
23. File of Private Leonard Wray in Tank Museum (E2006.4328).
24. 'L.I.', 'Some Reminiscences of a War-time Soldier III. – A Tank to the Rescue'.
25. Hülsemann, pp. 84–5.
26. Ibid., p. 85.
27. *Account of Operations of November 20th. 1917 near Havrincourt* in War Diary of 5th Bn Gordon Highlanders in NA (WO 95/2881).
28. McTaggart, 'The Great Battle of Cambrai'.
29. *Account of Operations of November 20th. 1917 near Havrincourt* in War Diary of 5th Bn Gordon Highlanders in NA (WO 95/2881).

Chapter 26: Till the Last Man (pp. 169–177)
1. Hülsemann, pp. 66–7.
2. Ibid., pp. 71–2. Leutnant Herbert Mory was also captured, and never returned home: he died in West Yorkshire in 1919 aged twenty-three, and is buried at Cannock Chase German Military Cemetery in Staffordshire.
3. Ibid., p. 67.
4. Ibid., p. 68.
5. Steuben, p. 93. The order of messages is reversed in some accounts, but this version from his biography is taken as definitive.
6. Ibid.
7. Hülsemann, pp. 73–4.
8. Ibid., p. 74.
9. Ibid., pp. 74–5.
10. Ibid., p. 77. The additional information about Vizefeldwebel Jacobsen, and first names, come from ICRC records.
11. Ibid., p. 98. This was Leutnant Johannes Andresen, commander of No. 4 Company. Shoulder-straps were often removed for intelligence-gathering purposes, as they carried a number identifying the prisoner's regiment.
12. Ibid., p. 104. This was Musketier Wilhelm Dose of No. 10 Company.
13. Ibid., pp. 82–3.
14. *H.Q. Tanks 1917-1918*, privately printed, 1920, pp. 77–8. Although anonymous, this has been identified as the work of Captain Evan Charteris. Both these reports relate to 20 November, but there is no indication where they took place, or which units were responsible. Charteris identifies the second informant as Lieutenant-Colonel John Brockbank, who was head of Tank Corps Central Workshops and Stores.
15. Captain D. Sutherland, *War Diary of the Fifth Seaforth Highlanders*, London, 1920, p. 138.
16. From *History of Cambrai* compiled by Major-General Sir Percy Hobart in Tank Museum (E2006.381). The account is anonymous, but from internal evidence the author can be identified as Gatehouse.
17. See Hague Conventions (1899 and 1907) on ICRC website.
18. Hülsemann, pp. 82–3.
19. *Account of Operations of November 20th. 1917 near Havrincourt* in War Diary of 5th Bn Gordon Highlanders in NA (WO 95/2881).
20. *Brief narratives of some of the outstanding instances during operation by tanks of 1 Bde, 20-23 Nov 17* by Colonel C. D. Baker-Carr dated 26 November, in Liddell Hart Centre for Military Archives (FULLER 1/3/7 1917).
21. Major F. W. Bewsher, *The History of the 51st (Highland) Division 1914-1918*, Edinburgh & London, 1921, p. 244.
22. McTaggart, 'The Great Battle of Cambrai'.
23. Watson, *A Company of Tanks*, p. 175.
24. Handwritten note by Lieutenant Gerald Edwards in Watson, *A Company of Tanks*, p. 175.
25. Letter to official historian dated 11 October 1944 in NA (CAB 45/118)
26. Falls, *The Life of a Regiment Volume IV*, p. 168.
27. Nicholson, p. 148.
28. Telegram in War Diary of 5th Bn Gordon Highlanders in NA (WO 95/2881).
29. Strutz, p. 27n.
30. *General Oskar Freiherr von Watter: Dem Gedenken eines großen Soldaten von den alten Kameraden der*

54. *Infanterie-Division des Weltkrieges*, Hansestadt Hamburg, 1940, p. 84.
31. Major-General D. N. Wimberley, *Scottish Soldier*, unpublished memoir in IWM (PP/MCR/182), p. 87. Thanks to Neil Wimberley for permission to quote from this document.
32. Interview in IWM Sound Archive (4266).
33. Wimberley, *Scottish Soldier*, unpublished memoir in IWM (PP/MCR/182), p. 88; the section from 'quite a lot ...' to ' ...look like' has been added from the IWM interview.
34. 'L.I.', 'Some Reminiscences of a War-time Soldier III. – A Tank to the Rescue'.
35. Ibid.
36. 'L.I.', 'Cambrai, 1917 – The Impressions of an Infantryman'.
37. Captain D. Sutherland, *War Diary of the Fifth Seaforth Highlanders*, London, 1920, pp. 138–9.
38. War Diary of IV Corps HQ in NA (WO 95/716).
39. Hülsemann, p. 130. This comment was made by Leutnant Johannes Langfeldt, 2nd Battalion ordnance officer.
40. Dahlmann, p. 364.
41. Ibid., p. 367.
42. Ibid.
43. Compiled from two letters published in *The I.O.B.* [i.e. Imperial Ottoman Bank] *Gazette* (January 1918). Koe does not say which tank he was in, but this can be worked from the evidence in his letters.
44. *Brief narratives of some of the outstanding instances during operation by tanks of 1 Bde, 20-23 Nov 17* by Colonel C. D. Baker-Carr dated 26 November, in Liddell Hart Centre for Military Archives (FULLER 1/3/7 1917).
45. Ibid. The report does not include tank names, which have been added from the D Bn Battlegraph in NA (MFQ 1/1384). In the case of D2, he gives the crew number as D16 but shows the commander as Second Lieutenant Wallace. The Battlegraph shows Wallace was actually in command of D2.
46. Ibid.
47. Macintosh, *Men and Tanks*, p. 113.
48. See message from 51st Division in War Diary of IV Corps HQ in NA (WO 95/716): 'Tanks seen travelling E to W at Grand Ravine K.29.Central (7.30 a.m.)'.

Chapter 27: A Mountain to Climb (pp. 180–184)
1. War Diary of 6th Bn Black Watch in NA (WO 95/2876).
2. *51st Division Report on the Operations S.W. of Cambrai* in NA (WO 158/390).
3. Macintosh, *Men and Tanks*, p. 110.
4. Watson, *A Company of Tanks*, pp. 183 and 174–5.
5. Anon., 'The Wanderings of "D" in France'.
6. Interview in Liddle Collection (278).
7. *Summary of Operations*, p. 10 in War Diary of 1st Brigade Tank Corps HQ in NA (WO 95/98).
8. See Hotblack, 'Recollections of Cambrai'.
9. Macintosh, *Men and Tanks*, p. 103.
10. D Bn Battlegraph in NA (MFQ 1/1384) shows D9 *Damocles*, D26 *Don Quixote II*, D30 *Dusky Dis II*, and D31 *Dolly II* were all ditched, in some cases with mechanical trouble, in the enemy front-line trench. D5 *Dakoit II* and D50 *Dandy Dinmont* were ditched in the third-line position known as Mole Trench, and D24 *Deuce of Diamonds* was ditched with mechanical trouble a little further on.
11. Service record in British Library (L/MIL/9/536/117-26) – this comment was made in 1924 when he was serving in the Indian Army.
12. Barrage map from *51st Division Report on the Operations S.W. of Cambrai* in NA (WO 158/390).
13. IV Corps report *Havrincourt – Bourlon Operations* in NA (WO 158/318).
14. From *History of Cambrai* compiled by Major-General Sir Percy Hobart in Tank Museum (E2006.381). The account is anonymous, but clearly by Birks.
15. Interview in IWM Sound Archive (4024).
16. Birks, 'Cambrai – The Attack on Flésquières Ridge [*sic*]'.
17. Macintosh, *Men and Tanks*, p. 115.
18. Bion, *War Memoirs*, p. 48.
19. Macintosh, *Men and Tanks*, pp. 117–19. He does not name the trench, but it can be identified from his description of the tank's route.
20. From *History of Cambrai* compiled by Major-General Sir Percy Hobart in Tank Museum (E2006.381). The account is anonymous but is clearly by Birks, and does not name Morris, who was Birks' section commander.
21. Service record in NA (WO 339/52089). The word 'severe' has been added from the following sentence.
22. From *History of Cambrai* compiled by Major-General Sir Percy Hobart in Tank Museum (E2006.381).
23. Anon., 'The Wanderings of "D" in France'.

Chapter 28: The Crack of Doom (pp. 185–189)
1. Macintosh, *Men and Tanks*, pp. 119–23. The dead and wounded men have not so far been identified.
2. Watson, *A Company of Tanks*, pp. 183 and 179. He uses the initial 'S.' but it is clear who is being referred to.
3. *Statement regarding circumstances which led to capture* in Shaw's service record, held by Ministry of Defence.
4. *The I.O.B.* [i.e. Imperial Ottoman Bank] *Gazette*, January 1918. Koe does not say which tank he was in, but this can be worked from the evidence in his letters.
5. *Statement regarding circumstances which led to capture* in Marris's service record, held by Ministry of Defence.
6. Hülsemann, p. 253.
7. Maurice, p. 264. His service record in NA (WO 363) indicates he was in No. 10 Company, from which only two tanks were knocked out at this stage in the battle. The circumstances seem to fit what we know of D6 *Devil-May-Care*, commanded by Lieutenant Sydney Glasscock, who was killed.
8. Anon., 'The Wanderings of "D" in France'. R. A. Jones was actually a second lieutenant (see service record in NA, WO 339/131917).
9. Letter to sister of Lance-Corporal Monks in possession of Richard Cousse. Thanks to him for permission to quote from this letter.
10. Macintosh, *Men and Tanks*, p. 131. Macintosh does not identify the tank or its commander, but his

description of the location and circumstances makes it clear this was D41 *Devil II*.
11. See ibid., pp. 123–4. He names the section commander as 'Captain Alphen, M.C.' but the D Bn Battlegraph gives his true identity.
12. Letter in possession of family.
13. Maurice, p. 261. This does not identify Lance-Corporal Tolson's tank, but he refers to 'Mr Butler my Crew Commander at Passendale & Cambri [*sic*]' in a letter in Liddell Hart Centre for Military Archives (LIDDELL 9/28/63 1916-1963). Second Lieutenant Gerald Butler was commander of D32 *Dop Doctor II*.
14. See Watson, *A Company of Tanks*, p. 21.
15. Maurice, p. 102.
16. Ibid., p. 264. The connection with Field is shown in Watson, *A Company of Tanks*, p. 179: 'F. and one of his sergeants had shown the utmost gallantry in collecting the wounded under fire and rallying the men.'
17. Macintosh, *Men and Tanks*, pp. 125–6.
18. Strutz, p. 46.
19. *Narrative of Operations* in War Diary of 7th Bn Black Watch in NA (WO 95/2879).

Chapter 29: Into the Hurricane (pp. 190–197)
1. Details from War Diary of 5th Bn Tank Corps in NA (WO 95/111) and E Bn Battlegraph (in Tank Museum). These do not give a crew number for *Ernest*, but this tank had the number E24 in previous engagements in September 1917.
2. Bion, *The Long Week-end*, p. 161.
3. Peel and Macdonald, p. 54. Macdonald wrote the second part of the book, which is quoted here.
4. War Diary of 6th Bn Seaforth Highlanders in NA (WO 95/2867).
5. Zindler, *Auf Biegen und Brechen*, pp. 236–8. In this translation a number of very short paragraphs have been run together, and some sentences now end with full stops where the original uses dots (...); some exclamation marks have also been omitted.
6. *De Ruvigny's Roll of Honour Vol. 3*, p. 11. The section commander is not named but can be identified from the Battlegraph.
7. Of the tanks named in the report, the E Bn Battlegraph shows that E17 *Edinburgh* (Second Lieutenant Miles Atkinson killed), *Egypt* (Second Lieutenant George Testi killed), E18 *Emperor II*, E10 *Endurance* (Second Lieutenant Ronald Barringer wounded), WC *Euryalus*, and WC *Exquisite* (Second Lieutenant Thomas Wilson killed) all suffered direct hits. Only *Eileen* survived the battle and returned to the rallying-point, though it was destroyed in further fighting two days later. The total number of dead and wounded 'other ranks' is known, but not which tanks they were in.
8. War History of 5th Tank Bn, in War Diary of 5th Bn Tank Corps in NA (WO 95/111).
9. This combines two accounts of the incident: firstly a letter from Major A. H. Gatehouse to the *Royal Tank Corps Journal* in October 1935, and secondly an anonymous account (also apparently by Gatehouse) in the *History of Cambrai* compiled by Major-General Sir Percy Hobart in Tank Museum (E2006.381). Both name the officer as Second Lieutenant Atkinson, but this is inconsistent with the account of Atkinson's death given by his section commander.
10. Bion, *The Long Week-end*.
11. Ibid., pp. 162–3. In the original, 'breech' is spelled 'breach'.
12. Ibid., p. 164.
13. Ibid., pp. 165–6.
14. *Daily Chronicle*, 11 December 1917. The same report appears in Gibbs, *Open Warfare*, p. 101.
15. Dahlmann, *Reserve-Infanterie-Rgt. Nr. 27 im Weltkriege*, pp. 376–7.
16. Ibid., p. 382.
17. Falls, *The Life of a Regiment Volume IV*, pp. 168–9.
18. 'Cambrai: A Tank Commander's Impression', *Tank Corps Journal* (November 1922). See previous notes on this source.
19. Unpublished autobiography in possession of family.
20. Letter in the possession of Mme Bacquet, Cambrai. As section commander, it seems likely that Homfray would have been in his only male tank – *Ewen*, commanded by Cohen. However, the events he describes seem more similar to the account of *Ethel II*, commanded by Quainton.
21. Bion, *War Memoirs*, p. 52.
22. *Commentary* in Bion, *War Memoirs*, p. 204. Bion gives a completely different account and says Quainton's tank broke down just after the Grand Ravine and was destroyed by a direct hit, though no-one was injured. This version is inconsistent with the E Bn Battlegraph which shows that *Ethel II* progressed to the final objective and suffered a direct hit, but returned to the rallying-point.
23. Falls, *The Life of a Regiment Volume IV*, p. 169.
24. War Diary of 6th Bn Gordon Highlanders in NA (WO 95/2868/1).
25. Mackenzie, p. 132.
26. Hickey, p. 107.

Chapter 30: Green Fields Beyond (pp. 198–207)
1. Interview in IWM Sound Archive (7031).
2. Biographical notes from his son Ian MacNiven. Note that this anecdote is not specifically linked to Cambrai. John changed the spelling of his surname to MacNiven during the war.
3. See Bion, *The Long Week-end*, p. 162.
4. Family recollections.
5. Comment by Corporal Dave Drew of the Staffordshire Regiment, from 'The Most Telling Hours of Young Lives', a pooled dispatch by Colin Wills of *The Sunday Mirror* sent from Kuwait on 2 March 1991 during the First Gulf War.
6. Hülsemann, p.109, though this does not give his full name; also in Dahlmann, p. 373.
7. Ibid.
8. Hülsemann, p. 61.
9. Ibid., p. 118.
10. Ibid., p. 92.
11. War Diary of 4th Bn Tank Corps in NA (WO 95/110).
12. Wedel, pp. 168–9.
13. Dahlmann, p. 375.
14. Wedel, pp. 167–8.
15. Dahlmann, pp. 374–5.
16. Hülsemann, p. 125.
17. Photographs in possession of Jean Luc Caudron and Philippe Gorczynski.

18. Maurice, p. 102.
19. History of 4th Tank Bn in War Diary in NA (WO 95/110).
20. Anon., 'The Wanderings of "D" in France'. Frank Heap was then a second lieutenant.
21. *Belfast Evening Telegraph*, 15 December 1917.
22. Watson, *A Company of Tanks*, pp. 176–7.
23. Ibid., p. 178.
24. This obviously ignores the Royal Flying Corps, which was above the battlefield.
25. Interview in IWM Sound Archives (4126). Hastie formerly commanded D17 *Dinnaken*, the tank that famously 'walked up the High Street of Flers' in the first attack on 15 September 1916.
26. Anglesey, p. 108.
27. Willie Pennie, *An Account of my Sojourn in France & Germany during the Great War 1917-1919* in IWM (11255). He writes 'a 100 yds'. I have added a dash after 'camp'.
28. War Diary of IV Corps HQ in NA (WO 95/716).
29. Ibid.
30. War Diary of 1st Cavalry Division HQ in NA (WO 95/1097).
31. Interview in Liddle Collection (590).
32. War Diary of 4th Dragoon Guards in NA (WO 95/1112).
33. 'L.I.', 'Cambrai, 1917 – The Impressions of an Infantryman'.
34. War Diary of 2nd Cavalry Brigade HQ in NA (WO 95/1110). The commander was Brigadier-General Desmond Beale-Browne.
35. Interview in Liddle Collection (590).
36. *1st Cavalry Division*, private report in *Diary of Sir Douglas Haig* – copy in NA (WO 256/24). A note identifies the author as Major-General Sir Henry Macandrew, commander of 5th Cavalry Division.
37. Lieut.-Colonel Lionel James (ed.), *The History of King Edward's Horse (The King's Oversea Dominions Regiment)*, London, 1921, p. 236.
38. Dahlmann, p. 375.
39. Macintosh, 'The Tanks at Cambrai', pp. 191–2.
40. Ibid., p. 192.
41. Recollection from Will Heap.
42. Orders dated 6 November 1917 in War Diary of 152nd Infantry Brigade HQ in NA (WO 95/2863).
43. Recollection from Will Heap.
44. Anon., 'The Wanderings of "D" in France'.
45. Maurice, p. 102.

Chapter 31: Like a Boar at Bay (pp. 208–216)
1. *Report on Operations* in War Diary of 4th Bn Tank Corps in NA (WO 95/110).
2. D Bn Battlegraph in NA (MFQ 1/1384).
3. History of 4th Tank Bn in War Diary in NA (WO 95/110).
4. *Report on Operations* in War Diary of 4th Bn Tank Corps in NA (WO 95/110).
5. Watson, *A Company of Tanks*, p. 179.
6. War Diary of 6th Bn Seaforth Highlanders in NA (WO 95/2867).
7. Hülsemann, p. 118, from an account by Leutnant Bielenberg.
8. *Report on Operations* in War Diary of 4th Bn Tank Corps in NA (WO 95/110).
9. Ibid.
10. War Diary of 1st Brigade Tank Corps HQ in NA (WO 95/98).
11. War Diary of 6th Bn Seaforth Highlanders in NA (WO 95/2867).
12. Peel and Macdonald, p. 55.
13. *Report on Operations* in War Diary of 4th Bn Tank Corps in NA (WO 95/110).
14. Watson, *A Company of Tanks*, p. 179.
15. Harper, pp. 72–3.
16. *Official History – Cambrai*, p. 82.
17. Falls, *The Life of a Regiment Volume IV*, p. 169.
18. Hülsemann, p. 249.
19. War Diary of IV Corps HQ in NA (WO 95/716).
20. War Diary of 18th Infantry Brigade HQ in NA (WO 95/1615).
21. War Diary of 152nd Infantry Brigade HQ in NA (WO 95/2863).
22. War Diary of 6th Bn Gordon Highlanders in NA (WO 95/2868/1).
23. Falls, *The Life of a Regiment Volume IV*, p. 169.
24. Hülsemann, pp. 249–50.
25. Birks, 'Cambrai – The Attack on Flésquières Ridge [sic]'.
26. Compiled from interviews in IWM Sound Archive (refs. 870 and 4024).
27. From account in the *History of Cambrai* compiled by Major-General Sir Percy Hobart in Tank Museum (E2006.381). The account is anonymous, but clearly by Birks.
28. Birks, 'Cambrai – The Attack on Flésquières Ridge [sic]'.
29. Interview in IWM Sound Archive (4024). The timing is taken from his account in Hobart's *History of Cambrai*, where he identifies them as the Ambala Cavalry Brigade, though this must be incorrect.
30. From account in the *History of Cambrai* compiled by Major-General Sir Percy Hobart in Tank Museum (E2006.381).
31. Watson, *A Company of Tanks*, pp. 180–1.
32. *51st Division Report on the Operations S.W. of Cambrai* in NA (WO 158/390).
33. *Official History – Cambrai*, p. 88.
34. Ibid., p. 90.
35. Hülsemann, p. 53. This is from a report by Oberleutnant Nissen, adjutant of 3rd Battalion.
36. Hauptmann Dahlmann, *Gefechtskalender des Res.- Inf. Regts. 27, 1914/1918*, Berlin, 1923, p. 33.
37. Hülsemann, p. 91.
38. Ibid., p. 92.
39. Coghlan, 'Cambrai Day'.
40. Unpublished memoirs of Colonel Norman Dillon, then in B Battalion, Tank Corps, in National Army Museum (1987-03-9).
41. Fuller, *Memoirs of an Unconventional Soldier*, p. 188.
42. Hülsemann, p. 122. The officer who met Major Krebs was Leutnant Schulz, trench mortar officer of No. 3 Battalion.
43. Ibid.

Chapter 32: A Bitter Evening (pp. 217–222)
1. *51st Division Report on the Operations S.W. of Cambrai* in NA (WO 158/390).
2. War Diary of 6th Bn Gordon Highlanders in NA (WO 95/2868/1).
3. Mackenzie, p. 133.
4. Peel and Macdonald, p. 66.

5. *Nottingham Evening Post*, 27 November 1917. The dispatch was sent on the previous day. A slightly revised version appeared in Philip Gibbs, *Open Warfare*, pp. 56–7.
6. Hickey, pp. 109–10.
7. From *Scottish Soldier*, an unpublished memoir by Major-General D. N. Wimberley in IWM (PP/MCR/182), p. 90. From the date and location given it is clear this refers to *Deborah*.
8. See Captain Bruce's service record in NA (WO 374/10263) and Rev. Grant's service record in NA (WO 374/28544). Despite the critical comments, in both cases an official investigation concluded: '… the [Army] Council considers that no blame attaches to him in the matter.'
9. Rorie, chapter on Cambrai by Captain R. T. Bruce, p. 170.
10. Macintosh, *Men and Tanks*, pp 128–9. He names the section commander as 'Captain Alphen, M.C.' but the D Bn Battlegraph gives his true identity.
11. Macintosh, *Men and Tanks*, pp. 129–30.
12. Ibid., pp. 131–2.
13. Photograph and note by Lieutenant Alexander Christie of Royal Garrison Artillery. Thanks to his nephew Jim Christie for this information.
14. *The Times*, 21 November 1917.
15. *The Times*, 22 November 1917.
16. *The Times*, 24 November 1917.
17. Service record in NA (WO 339/12569).
18. *Carmarthen Journal*, 7 December 1917.
19. Letter in possession of Charles Foot.
20. Ibid.
21. *Cambridge Chronicle*, 12 December 1917. His surname is misspelled 'Chiverton' in the article.
22. Card in possession of family. Some changes have been made to punctuation and capitalisation.
23. *Belfast Evening Telegraph*, 15 December 1917.
24. *Nottinghamshire Guardian*, 22 December 1917.

Chapter 33: The Chance Was Gone (pp. 223–231)
1. War Diary of 4th Bn Tank Corps in NA (WO 95/110) and D Bn Battlegraph in NA (MFQ 1/1384).
2. Handwritten note by Lieutenant Gerald Edwards in Watson, *A Company of Tanks*, p. 166.
3. Macintosh, *Men and Tanks*, pp. 137–8.
4. War Diary of 4th Bn Tank Corps in NA (WO 95/110) and D Bn Battlegraph in NA (MFQ 1/1384).
5. War Diary of 5th Bn Tank Corps in NA (WO 95/111).
6. Watson, *A Company of Tanks*, p. 190.
7. *Diary of Sir Douglas Haig* – copy in NA (WO 256/24).
8. Ibid.
9. Ibid.
10. Brigadier-General John Charteris, *At G.H.Q.*, London, 1931, p. 270.
11. Captain Geoffrey Dugdale, *"Langemarck" and "Cambrai" – A War Narrative 1914–1918*, Shrewsbury, 1932, p. 109.
12. C. H. Dudley Ward, *History of the Welsh Guards*, London, 1920, p. 172.
13. Sir Douglas Haig's Dispatch on the Battle of Cambrai in *The Times*, 5 March 1918.
14. Bion, *The Long Week-end*, p. 166. Bion says he was unaware of the story before reading about it in Haig's Dispatch.
15. Hotblack, 'A Cambrai Myth?'.
16. Arthur Conan Doyle, *The British Campaign in France and Flanders 1917*, London, 1919, p. 245.
17. Gibbs, *Realities of War*, p. 398.
18. Report on Operations in War Diary of 4th Bn Tank Corps in NA (WO 95/110).
19. *Report on Operations, 20th: November, 1917* dated 28 November 1917 in War Diary of 5th Bn Tank Corps in NA (WO 95/111).
20. *Summary of Operations* in War Diary of 1st Brigade Tank Corps HQ in NA (WO 95/98).
21. Ibid.
22. *Report on Operations* in War Diary of 7th Bn Gordon Highlanders in NA (WO 95/2882/1).
23. *Narrative of Events* in War Diary 6th Black Watch in NA (WO 95/2876).
24. *Appendices* in War Diary of 8th Bn Argyll and Sutherland Highlanders in NA (WO 95/2865/2).
25. *Account of Operations Before Cambrai* in War Diary of 152nd Infantry Brigade HQ in NA (WO 95/2863).
26. Bion, *War Memoirs*, p. 65.
27. War Diary of 5th Bn Tank Corps in NA (WO 95/111).
28. Watson, *A Company of Tanks* pp. 195–6.
29. *Official History – Cambrai*, pp. 158–9.
30. Watson, *A Company of Tanks*, pp. 196–7.
31. History of 4th Tank Bn in War Diary in NA (WO 95/110).
32. Anon., 'The Wanderings of "D" in France'.
33. Bion, *War Memoirs*, p. 58.
34. War Diary of 4th Bn Tank Corps in NA (WO 95/110).
35. Service record in NA (WO 339/23425). This gives the date as February 1917, which must be a mistake for February 1918.
36. Watson, *A Company of Tanks*, p. 221.
37. Interview in IWM Sound Archive (870).
38. *1st Cavalry Division*, private report in *Diary of Sir Douglas Haig* – copy in NA (WO 256/24).
39. *The Times*, 24 July 1919.
40. *1st Cavalry Division*, private report in *Diary of Sir Douglas Haig* – copy in NA (WO 256/24).
41. Anglesey, p. 158.
42. *Diary, November-December 1917* by C. E. W. Bean – entry for 9 December 1917 (pp. 80–4) in Australian War Memorial (AWM38 3DRL606/94/1). The original contains a number of abbreviations and some shorthand characters, which have been expanded here.

Chapter 34: Sticking to their Guns (pp. 234–240)
1. From 'The Meaning of Cambrai', anonymous article in *Tank Corps Journal* (November 1922).
2. *Der Englische Angriff bei Cambrai am 20.11.1917*, report by Heeresgruppe Kronprinz Rupprecht dated 4 December 1917, in Hauptstaatsarchiv Stuttgart (M 33/2 Bü 73). The underlining is in the original.
3. Photographs in possession of Jean Luc Caudron and Philippe Gorczynski.
4. Rockstroh and Zindler, p. 97.
5. Wedel, pp. 297–307.
6. Zindler, *Auf Biegen und Brechen*, p. 244.
7. Ibid., pp. 246–7.

8. International Committee of the Red Cross records.
9. Volksbund Deutsche Kriegsgräberfürsorge records.
10. *Third Army Intelligence Summary* dated 25 November 1917 in NA (WO 157/158).
11. *Auszug aus der Verlustliste des Feld-Artillerie-Regiments Nr. 108* in Militärarchiv, Freiburg im Breisgau (PH12/II/109).
12. Letter from Kameradschaftliche Vereinigung ehem. Angehöriger des F.A.R. 108 to Generalleutnant Freiherr von Watter dated 22 May 1932. A photocopy of this letter is in the papers of the late Gerhardt Remmel in the Historial de la Grande Guerre at Péronne. The original is apparently in the Hauptstaatsarchiv Stuttgart, but it has not been possible to locate this under the reference given. The final sentence is from Romans 13:7.
13. Letter from Reichsarchiv to Generalleutnant Freiherr von Watter dated 13 April 1928.
14. Wedel, p. 174 – this says Leutnant Müller was named by 'various sources'.
15. Kamerad Hoischen (former Gefreiter in No. 8 Battery, 108 FAR), 'Der Held von Cambrai', *Der Frontsoldat Erzählt* No. 7 (1937).
16. Ernst Kleuker, 'Vor Zwanzig Jahren: Der Leutnant von Cambrai', *Der Frontsoldat Erzählt* No. 8 (1937). This is a somewhat loose translation that attempts to capture the spirit of the original.
17. Erwin Zindler, 'Erziehungsarbeit an einer Infanterie-Division und ihr Erfolg in der Tankschlacht bei Cambrai', *Wissen und Wehr* (1937), pp. 327–43.
18. Wedel, p. 166.
19. Anonymous, 'More Light on Cambrai, 1917', *The Army Quarterly* (October 1937), pp. 142–4.
20. Oration by Feldbischof D. Dohrmann in *Trauerfeier für den ... Generalleutnant a.D. Oskar Frhr. von Watter* on 25 August 1939, in Hauptstaatsarchiv Stuttgart (M 430/2 Bü 2309).
21. Hotblack, 'A Cambrai Myth?'.
22. Ibid.
23. Ibid.
24. Captain E. W. Sheppard, 'Mrs. Partington Again', *The Army Quarterly* (April 1931).
25. The War Office (R.T.C.) Battlefield Tour took place on 25–29 March 1935. Notes from the visit are preserved at the Tank Museum, and were also incorporated into the *History of Cambrai* compiled by Major-General Sir Percy Hobart in Tank Museum (E2006.381).
26. Letter in *Royal Tank Corps Journal* (October 1935).
27. 'The Legend of Flesquieres', *Royal Tank Corps Journal* (November 1935). The article is anonymous but may well be by Hotblack.
28. Major A. F. Becke, 'Cambrai, 1917. The Tanks at Flesquières on the 20th November', *Journal of the Royal Artillery* (January 1947).
29. *The Times*, 4 September 1964.
30. Letter dated 3 August 1944 in NA (CAB 45/118).
31. Letters dated 4 July to 14 September 1935 (year given in covering note) in War Diary of Third Army HQ in NA (WO 95/367).
32. Letter dated 28 November 1944 in NA (CAB 45/118).
33. Letter dated 23 March 1944 in NA (CAB 45/118).
34. *Official History – Cambrai*, p. 59 (footnote).

Chapter 35: 'The Fates Fought Against Us' (pp. 241–246)
1. Fuller, *Memoirs of an Unconventional Soldier* p. 94; Fuller, *Tanks in the Great War 1914-1918*, p. xvi.
2. Service record, held by Ministry of Defence.
3. *Cheltenham Chronicle*, 16 August 1902.
4. Notes from Tony Rundell and Mary Baker-Carr.
5. *The Times*, 15 March 1928.
6. *The Times*, 13 April 1927.
7. *The Times*, 4 February 1928.
8. *The Times*, 14 December 1929.
9. Divorce files in NA (J 77/2651/2340 and J 77/2959/1442).
10. *The Times*, 16 December 1922.
11. Nicholson, p. 140.
12. Harper, *Notes on Infantry Tactics & Training*.
13. Baker-Carr, *From Chauffeur to Brigadier*, p. 73.
14. Ibid., pp. 269–70.
15. See *Western Morning News*, 16 December 1922; *The Times*, 16, 18 and 20 December 1922.
16. Fuller, *Tanks in the Great War 1914-1918*, p. 149.
17. Fuller, *Memoirs of an Unconventional Soldier*, p. 209.
18. Hotblack, 'Recollections of Cambrai, 1917'.
19. Liddell Hart, *The Real War*, pp. 376–7. See also Liddell Hart, *The Tanks, Vol One*, pp. 141–3.
20. Letter dated 23 March 1944 in NA (CAB 45/118).
21. *Official History – Cambrai*, p. 280.
22. *Summary of Operations* by Colonel C. D. Baker-Carr dated 9 December 1917 in War Diary of 1st Brigade Tank Corps HQ in NA (WO 95/98).
23. *Instructions No. 1* dated 7 November 1917 in War Diary of 51st Division HQ in NA (WO 95/2846).
24. *Order No. 21* dated 15 November 1917 in War Diary of 1st Brigade Tank Corps HQ in NA (WO 95/98).
25. *Notes on Tank and Infantry Training* in War Diary of Tank Corps HQ in NA (WO 95/92).
26. *Lessons from Recent Operations – Tank Corps*, unsigned and undated report in Third Army file *Cambrai: Narrative of Operations and Lessons Learnt* in NA (WO 158/316).
27. See account in the *History of Cambrai* compiled by Major-General Sir Percy Hobart in Tank Museum (E2006.381). The account is anonymous, but clearly by Birks.
28. War Diary of 6th Bn Gordon Highlanders in NA (WO 95/2868/1); Mackenzie, p. 132.
29. *Statement regarding circumstances which led to capture* in service record of Second Lieutenant John Shaw, held by Ministry of Defence.
30. Robert Woollcombe, *The First Tank Battle – Cambrai 1917*, London, 1967.
31. Bryn Hammond, 'General Harper and the failure of 51st (Highland) Division at Cambrai, 20 November 1917', *Imperial War Museum Review* No. 10 (1995).
32. John Hussey, 'Uncle Harper at Cambrai – A Reconsideration', *British Army Review* (December 1997).
33. Hotblack, 'Recollections of Cambrai, 1917'.
34. Watson, *A Company of Tanks*, p. 172.
35. Williams-Ellis, p. 109.
36. Tank Corps Summary of Information dated 27 November 1917 in NA (WO 157/240).
37. Preliminary lecture notes signed F.L.H. from RTR visit in March 1935, in Tank Museum (E2006.342).
38. From 'The Meaning of Cambrai', anonymous article in *Tank Corps Journal* (November 1922).

Chapter 36: A Peaceful, Unexceptional Place (pp. 247–253)

1. Birthday card in possession of Anthony family.
2. Letter dated 1 January 1919 in possession of Anthony family.
3. Ibid.
4. Letters dated 16 February 1919 in possession of Anthony family.
5. Ibid.
6. Photographs and letter dated 17 March 1919 in possession of Anthony family.
7. Photograph in possession of Heap family.
8. Album in possession of Anthony family.
9. Transcription of shorthand letter dated 10 April 1923 in possession of Anthony family.
10. Photograph in Tank Museum (2380-F3).
11. H. A. Taylor, *Good-bye to the Battlefields: To-day and Yesterday on the Western Front*, London, 1928, p. 165.
12. Steuben, p. 87 – account by Leutnant Ernst Albers.
13. CWGC records.
14. Cambrai East Military Cemetery contains the bodies of 10,685 German soldiers, as well as many from other countries including Britain, France and Russia. The mass grave contains 2,746 Germans, 2,307 of them unknown. The plaque listing known burials includes Major Fritz Hofmeister, but Hauptmann Soltau's name is missing although he appears in the cemetery register.
15. CWGC records.
16. Letter dated 23 April 1930 – thanks to Philippe Gorczynski for providing this.
17. *Nottingham Evening Post*, 29 January 1918.
18. *Nottingham Evening Post*, 25 January 1918.
19. Thanks to Gwyn Evans for pointing out this connection.
20. See Gwyn Evans, 'Rediscovery of the Gloucester Presentation Tank', *Transactions of the Bristol & Gloucestershire Archaeological Society* 132 (2014), pp. 229–35.
21. Information from Gwyn Evans; photographs from Great War Forum.
22. Information from Johan Vanbeselaere.
23. Zindler, *Und Abermals Soldat ...*, pp. 255–6.

Chapter 37: Varied Fortunes (pp. 254–259)

1. Documents in possession of family.
2. Ibid.
3. Service record in NA (WO 339/68648); notes and photographs from Gillies Archive (3900). Thanks to Dr Andrew Bamji for providing these materials.
4. *The Times*, 6 May 1972.
5. Unpublished biography by Paul Russell; information from Rev Ian Cohen.
6. Letter in *Tank Corps Journal*, September 1923.
7. *Western Times*, 14 August 1923.
8. *The Times*, 28 March 1985.
9. Service record (held by Ministry of Defence) and interviews in IWM Sound Archive.
10. *Oxford Dictionary of National Biography*.
11. Bion, *War Memoirs 1917-1919* – see Sources.
12. Bion, *The Long Week-end 1897-1919* – see Sources.
13. Macintosh, *Men and Tanks* – see Sources.
14. Review by 'W.T.S.' in *Tank Corps Journal* (February 1921).
15. J. C. Macintosh, *Negligence in Delict*, Capetown & Johannesburg, 1926.
16. *South African Law Journal* (1943), p. 307.
17. 'The Wanderings of "D" in France (More especially of 12 Company) By a P.B.I. (attached)', *Tank Corps Journal* (March–December 1921). P.B.I. stands for 'poor bloody infantry' and refers to the fact that Smith was previously in 17th Bn London Regiment.
18. Photographs in possession of family.
19. Recollections from family.
20. Watson, *Adventures of a Despatch Rider* – see Sources.
21. 'Tales of a Gaspipe Officer' by 'Despatch Rider', *Blackwood's Magazine* (December 1915 to March 1916, and January 1917).
22. Service record in NA (WO 339/23425).
23. Watson, *A Company of Tanks* – see Sources. Originally published in *Blackwood's Magazine* (May 1919 to February 1920).
24. Notes of interview by Dawn Lowe-Watson on 10 July 1976, in possession of family.
25. *The Times*, 21 December 1932.
26. Watson, *A Company of Tanks*, p. 296.
27. *The Times*, 21 December 1932.
28. Notes of interview on 10 July 1976, in possession of family.
29. Based on articles by Andrew Causey in *The Illustrated London News*, 4 September 1965, by David Cohen in *Stand To! – The Journal of the Western Front Association* No. 62 (September 2001), and in an unidentified local newspaper (in Tank Museum). Thanks to Lieutenant-Colonel Stephen May and Colonel John Longman of the Royal Tank Regiment.
30. Baker-Carr, *From Chauffeur to Brigadier* – see Sources. The book was republished by Leonaur in 2012 with a foreword by his great-niece Mary Baker-Carr.
31. Service record, held by Ministry of Defence.
32. *The Times*, 11 January 1949.
33. *The Times*, 10 January 1951, and various years to at least 1964.
34. Information on Cooper House, Laramie, Wyoming in US National Register of Historic Places Inventory.
35. Ulf Aschan, *The Man Whom Women Loved – The Life of Bror Blixen*, New York, 1987, pp. 135–6. The author, who was Blixen's godson, does not give a source for the story.
36. Service record, held by Ministry of Defence.
37. See Jeffrey Meyers, *Hemingway – A Biography*, New York, 1985, p. 247. The source is given as an interview with Hemingway's son Patrick.
38. Recollections from families.
39. Ibid.
40. Ibid.
41. CWGC records.
42. Ibid.
43. *The Times*, 16 October 1944.
44. Recollections from family, including unpublished biography by Walter's daughter Joan Bullock (née Smith). Her source for the account of his death is not known.
45. Ibid.
46. Ibid.

47. *Hull Daily Mail*, 30 September 1940.
48. Recollections from family.

Chapter 38: Rosemary for Remembrance (pp. 260–265)
1. From *Youth* by Frances Cornford, a tribute to Rupert Brooke.
2. Service record, held by Ministry of Defence.
3. *Taunton Courier & Western Advertiser*, 10 August 1932.
4. Philip Richards, *Between the Church & the Lighthouse – The History of Burnham and Berrow Golf Club*, Worcestershire, 2001, p. 87. Thanks to the club president, Nick Brown, for his assistance.
5. Death certificate.
6. Recollections from family.
7. Service record, held by Ministry of Defence.
8. Recollections from family.
9. Service record, held by Ministry of Defence; Maurice, pp. 76 and 81.
10. Service record, held by Ministry of Defence.
11. Recollections from family.
12. Press release about sale of detention sheets by TracksAuction.com on 22 November 2013.
13. Maurice, p. 158.
14. *George Macdonald, Gentleman, Sometime Farmer, Sometime Historian* – unpublished biography by his son Angus Macdonald.
15. Ibid.
16. Ibid.
17. Service record, held by Ministry of Defence.
18. *Blackpool Gazette & Herald*, 11 October 1921.
19. Photographs and recollections from family.
20. Divorce file in NA (J 77/3285/369).
21. Photograph in *Fell and Rock Journal* (1988), p. 410.
22. Photographs and recollections from family.
23. Obituary by S. H. Cross in *Journal of Fell and Rock Climbing Club* (1958), pp. 192–3.
24. *Cambridge Independent Press*, 21 November 1919. His surname is misspelled 'Chiverton'.
25. Photographs and recollections from family.
26. The quote is from *Hamlet*.
27. Service record in NA (WO 339/53827).
28. Marriage and death certificates, 1939 Register.
29. Photographs and recollections from family.
30. Medal index cards.
31. Death certificate.
32. Medal index card; RAF service record (AIR 79/2858); court martial register in NA (AIR 21/1A); Irish Army Census 1922.
33. Medal index card.
34. CWGC records.
35. Recollections from family.
36. Service record in NA (WO 339/64604).
37. *The Times*, 16 February 1972.
38. CWGC records.

Chapter 39: Weapon of Friendship (pp. 266–274)
1. From interview conducted at Hotel Beatus, Cambrai on 1 February 2015.
2. *Sunday Times*, 22 November 1977 – report by Ian Murray.
3. Michel Bacquet, *La Bataille de Cambrai*, Mallez Imprimeurs, 1977.
4. Jean-Luc Gibot and Philippe Gorczynski, *En Suivant les Tanks*, 1997; *Following the Tanks* translated by Wendy MacAdam, 1999.
5. From interview with Will Heap.
6. CWGC records.
7. Photograph in possession of Jim Christie.
8. See articles in *Belfast Telegraph*, 21 July 2008; *Nottingham Evening Post*, 29 December 2008; and *Cambridge News*, 26 January 2009.
9. Documents and photographs in possession of family.
10. Ibid.
11. War Diary of 4th Bn Tank Corps in NA (WO 95/110).
12. Service record in NA (WO 363).
13. Recollections from family.
14. Photographs in possession of Jean Luc Caudron and Philippe Gorczynski.
15. The number inside the cab was discovered by Ian Douglas.

Sources

Official Histories

Official History – Cambrai: Miles, Captain Wilfred, *History of the Great War: Military Operations France and Belgium 1917: The Battle of Cambrai*, London, 1948.

Official History – Passchendaele: Edmonds, Brigadier-General Sir James E., *History of the Great War: Military Operations France and Belgium 1917 Vol. II: 7th June-10th November Messines and Third Ypres (Passchendaele)*, London, 1948.

Official History – Somme: Miles, Captain Wilfred, *History of the Great War: Military Operations France and Belgium, 1916 Vol. II: 2nd July 1916 to the End of the Battles of the Somme*, London, 1938.

Official History – Togoland and Cameroons: Moberly, Brigadier-General F. J., *History of the Great War: Military Operations, Togoland and the Cameroons, 1914-1916*, London, 1931.

Published Sources

Adam, Adela Marion, *Arthur Innes Adam 1894 1916 A Record Founded on His Letters*, Cambridge, 1920.
Anglesey, The Marquess of, *A History of the British Cavalry 1816 to 1919 – Vol. 8 The Western Front, 1915-1918*, London, 1997.
Anon. [Captain Edward Glanville Smith], 'The Wanderings of "D" in France', *Tank Corps Journal* (March–December 1921).
Baker-Carr, Brigadier-General C. D., *From Chauffeur to Brigadier*, London, 1930.
Bion, Wilfred R., *The Long Week-end 1897-1919 – Part of a Life*, edited by Francesca Bion, London, 1986.
——, *War Memoirs 1917-1919*, edited by Francesca Bion, London, 1997.
Birks, Major-General H. L., 'Cambrai – The Attack on Flésquières Ridge [sic]', *Royal Armoured Corps Journal* (October 1949).
Browne, Captain D. G., *The Tank in Action*, Edinburgh & London, 1920.
Butler, Captain R. P., 'Reminiscences of Salvage Work', *Royal Tank Corps Journal* (June–July 1932).
Coghlan, Major J. A., 'Cambrai Day – The Early Days of the Royal Tank Corps', *Chambers's Journal* (November 1956).
Dahlmann, Reinhold, *Reserve-Infanterie-Rgt. Nr. 27 im Weltkriege 1914/1918 (Deutsche Tat im Weltkrieg 1914/1918 – Geschichten der Kämpfe Deutscher Truppen Band 40)*, Berlin, 1934.
Elles, Colonel Commandant Sir Hugh, 'Some Notes on Tank Development During the War', *The Army Quarterly* (July 1921).
Ewing, John, *The History of the 9th (Scottish) Division 1914-1919*, London, 1921.
Falls, Cyril, *The History of the 36th (Ulster) Division*, Belfast and London, 1922.
——, *The Life of a Regiment Volume IV – The Gordon Highlanders in the First World War 1914-1919*, Aberdeen, 1958.
Fuller, Major-General J. F. C., *Tanks in the Great War 1914-1918*, London, 1920.
——, *Memoirs of an Unconventional Soldier*, London, 1936.
Gibbs, Philip, *The Battles of the Somme*, London, 1917.
——, *From Bapaume to Passchendaele 1917*, London, 1918.
——, *Open Warfare – The Way to Victory*, London, 1919.
——, *Realities of War*, London, 1920.
Gough, General Sir Hubert, *The Fifth Army*, London, 1931.
Harper, Lieutenant-General Sir G. M., *Notes on Infantry Tactics & Training*, London, 1919.
Hickey, Captain D. E., *Rolling into Action – Memoirs of a Tank Corps Section Commander*, London, 1934.
Hotblack, F. E., 'Recollections of Cambrai, 1917', *Tank Corps Journal* (November 1923).
——, 'A Cambrai Myth?', *Royal Tank Corps Journal* (March 1933).
Hülsemann, Oberstleutnant, *Erinnerungsblätter der Ehemaligen Mansteiner – Geschichte des Infanterie-Regiments von Manstein (Schleswigsches) Nr. 84 1914-1918*, Hamburg, 1923-4.
Judd, A. C., 'The Middle Years of the War' in *Great War Adventures (18th Series)* – no date but published in the 1930s.
'L.I.', 'Some Reminiscences of a War-time Soldier III. – A Tank to the Rescue', *Royal Tank Corps Journal* (April 1926).

——, 'Cambrai, 1917 – The Impressions of an Infantryman', *Royal Tank Corps Journal* (December 1927).
Liddell Hart, B. H., *The Real War 1914-1918*, London, 1930.
——, *The Tanks – The History of the Royal Tank Regiment and its Predecessors ... Volume One 1914-1939*, London, 1959.
Macintosh, J. C., 'The Tanks at Cambrai' in John Buchan (ed.), *The Long Road to Victory*, London, 1920.
——, *Men and Tanks*, London, 1921.
Mackenzie, Captain D., *The Sixth Gordons in France and Flanders (with the 7th and 51st Divisions)*, Aberdeen, 1921.
McTaggart, M. F., 'The Great Battle of Cambrai', *The Nineteenth Century and After* (July 1920).
Martel, Lieutenant-Colonel G. Le Q., *In the Wake of the Tank – The First Fifteen Years of Mechanization in the British Army*, London, 1935.
Maurice, Major R. F. G., *The Tank Corps Book of Honour*, Ballantyne, 1919.
Maurois, André, *The Silence of Colonel Bramble*, translated from the French, London & New York, 1919.
Mitchell, F., *Tank Warfare – The Story of the Tanks in the Great War*, London, 1933.
Moody, Colonel R. S. H., *Historical Records of the Buffs East Kent Regiment ... 1914-1919*, London, 1922.
Nicholson, Colonel W. N., *Behind the Lines – An Account of Administrative Staffwork in the British Army 1914-18*, London, 1939.
Peel, Captain R. T. and Macdonald, Captain A. H., *Campaign Reminiscences: 6th Seaforth Highlanders*, Elgin, 1923.
Pidgeon, Trevor, *The Tanks at Flers*, Cobham, 1995.
Priestley, R. E., *The Signal Service in the European War of 1914 to 1918 (France)*, Chatham, 1921.
Riddell, Brigadier-General E., and Clayton, Colonel M. C., *The Cambridgeshires 1914 to 1919*, Cambridge, 1934.
Rockstroh, Oberleutnant, and Zindler, Leutnant, *Regimentsgeschichte des Feldartillerieregiments No. 108*, Hamburg, 1919.
Rorie, Colonel David, *A Medico's Luck in the War – Being Reminiscences of R.A.M.C. Work with the 51st (Highland) Division*, Aberdeen, 1929.
Steuben, Oberstleutnant Arndt von, *Harro Soltau, das Lebensbild eines Frontoffiziers*, Hamburg, 1936.
Strutz, Hauptm. a. D. Dr. Georg, *Schlachten des Weltkrieges ... im Auftrage des Reichsarchivs, Band 31 Die Tankschlacht bei Cambrai 20.-29. November 1917*, Oldenburg, 1929.
Stühmke, General, *Das Infanterie-Regiment 'Kaiser Friedrich, König von Preußen' (7. Württ.) Nr. 125 im Weltkrieg 1914-1918*, Stuttgart, 1923.
Swinton, Major-General Sir Ernest D., *Eyewitness – Being Personal Reminiscences of Certain Phases of the Great War, Including the Genesis of the Tank*, London, 1932.
Vaughan, Edwin Campion, *Some Desperate Glory – The Diary of a Young Officer, 1917*, London, 1981.
Watson, Major W. H. L., *Adventures of a Despatch Rider*, Edinburgh & London, 1915.
——, *A Company of Tanks*, Edinburgh & London, 1920.
Wedel, Oberstleutnant V., *Das Feldartillerie-Regiment 213 (Aus Deutschlands Großer Zeit 14. Band)*, Zeulenroda-Thür, undated c.1930.
Williams-Ellis, Major Clough, and Williams-Ellis, A., *The Tank Corps*, London, 1919.
Zindler, Erwin, *Auf Biegen und Brechen*, Leipzig, 1929.
——, *Und Abermals Soldat*, Leipzig, 1943.

Index

Adam, Capt Arthur ('Parson Snowy') 30, 31, 32
Addy, Pte Jason 20, 39, 63, 67–9, 79, 84, 180, 198, 266
Albert (France) 17, 134
Aldershot (Hants) 108, 148
Andresen, Lt Johannes 171
Anthony, Pte Angus and Lance-Corporal Willie 247–9, 250
Argyll and Sutherland Highlanders: 8th Bn 141, 161, 165, 171–2, 174, 205, 227, 276; 10th Bn 108
Armitage, Lt Hugo 143, 181, 277
Army Service Corps 9, 16, 17–18, 20, 23; 711th Mechanical Transport Company 93
Arnold, Lt Arthur 25, 27, 59, 76–8, 263, 275
Arras, Battle of 18, 53, 69, 81 2, 115, 122, 199
artillery *see under* Royal Artillery and German army: artillery
Ashford (Kent) 252
Atkinson, 2nd Lt Miles 192
Australia (inc. Australian army units) 5, 115, 116, 231, 239, 258, 259
Aylesbury (Bucks) 21

Bacquet, Michel 266–7
Baird, Maj Hugh 229
Baker-Carr, Col Christopher 6, 8–9, 19, 44, 50, 51, 54, 57, 64, 70, 81, 93–4, 116, 119–21, 125, 128, 130, 135, 165, 172, 176–7, 227, 241–4, 257–8, 277
Ball, Pte George 148
Bär, Gefreiter Wilhelm 175
Bean, Charles 231
Beaumetz (France) 133
Becke, Maj Archibald 238–9
Bedfordshire (and Hertfordshire) Regiment 147, 264
Beith, Lt John ('Ian Hay') 108
Belfast (Co. Down) 33, 148, 222, 264, 270
Bellevue (Belgium) 56–7, 59–60, 62, 74, 80, 87, 92, 252, 275
Beuck, Lt Carl 170–1
Bielenberg, Lt 200, 208–9
Billon Wood (France) 134
Bingham, Capt the Hon John 122–3, 204
Bion, 2nd Lt Wilfred 4, 13, 21, 63–4, 86, 100, 120, 127, 163, 182, 190, 193–4, 196, 198, 211, 226, 227, 229, 255
Bird, Spr Frederick 135
Birks, 2nd Lt Horace xii–xiii, 21, 23, 25, 58, 63, 101, 111, 123–5, 129, 130, 141, 159, 163, 165, 182, 183–4, 212–14, 229, 238, 243–4, 255, 277
Bisley (Surrey) 119
Blackpool (Lancs) 85, 104–7, 262
Black Watch (Royal Highlanders) 107, 145; 6th Bn 129, 165, 227, 276; 7th Bn 173, 183, 189, 276
Blixen, Baron Bror 258
Bouleux, Marthe 267, 268

Boulogne (France) 98
Bourlon, inc. Wood (France) 143, 204, 206, 215, 217–18, 223, 227–8, 229, 246
Bovington (Dorset) 17–18, 28, 100–1, 229, 252, 255, 257, 268
Bradley, Lt-Col Robert 119
Brielen Bridge (Belgium) 56
British Army *see also* cavalry, and individual regiments by name (e.g. Royal Artillery, Tank Corps)
  General Headquarters (GHQ) 6, 11, 44, 51, 85, 96, 119, 147 *see also* Haig, Sir Douglas
  armies: Second Army 12, 90, Third Army 30, 128, 140, 152, 224, 228, 243; Fifth Army 9, 10, 12, 13, 10, 12 3, 11, 51, 65, 80, 87, 88, 90, 159
  corps: III Corps 276; IV Corps 158, 174, 182, 205–6, 212, 244, 276; XVIII Corps 51, 58, 80, 82, 87, 93, 275; XIX Corps 58–9, 77, 275
  divisions: 6th Division 209, 212, 239, 246, 276; 9th (Scottish) Division 107 10, 129; 11th (Northern) Division 57–8, 65, 80, 275; 16th (Irish) Division 149; 20th (Light) Division 225; 29th Division 268; 36th (Ulster) Division 31, 32, 33–4, 137–8, 145, 148–9, 224; 38th (Welsh) Division 44; 47th (2nd London) Division 25–6; 48th (South Midland) Division 57, 58, 70, 72, 80, 275; 51st (Highland) Division 44, 93–4, 95, 120, 127, 128–30, 133, 145, 150, 160, 164, 165, 166, 173, 180, 203, 205, 207, 209, 212, 213, 214, 217, 219, 224, 227, 239, 242–4, 276; 61st (2nd South Midland) Division 58, 74, 77, 81, 275; 62nd (West Riding) Division 138, 145, 209, 212, 227, 243, 246, 276
  infantry brigades: 18th Brigade 212, 239, 33rd Brigade 64, 275; 113th Brigade 40, 44; 143rd Brigade 58, 66, 70, 275; 152nd Brigade 154, 173, 212, 227, 276; 153rd Brigade 154, 160, 203, 214, 276; 184th Brigade 58, 81, 275
Brommage, 2nd Lt Joseph 40–1, 44, 265
Brooks, Ernest 98
Brooks, 2nd Lt Gerald 76–7, 275
Brough, Lt-Col John 119
Browne, 2nd Lt Douglas 8, 12, 43, 45, 52, 56, 57, 58, 81
Bruce, Lt Ewen 91–2
Bruce, Capt Robert 165–6, 219, 272
Buffs (East Kent Regiment): 6th Bn 113–4
Bullecourt, Battle of 18, 64, 69, 115
Bülow Farm (Belgium) 63, 64, 65, 80, 275
Burn, Brig-Gen Henry 173
Burnett, Lt-Col John 227
Burnham and Berrow Golf Club (Somerset) 260
Butler, Lt-Col Charles (7th Earl of Carrick) 17
Butler, 2nd Lt Gerald 277
Butler, Maj Robert 91–3
Byng, Gen Sir Julian 140, 212, 228

Cambrai, Battle of: initial planning & preparations 11, 124–5; training 126–30; move into position 133–9; German raid 139–40; reconnaissance by tank commanders 140–2; plans for attack 142–4; German preparations 145, 150–3; move to starting positions (19 Nov) 154–62; first phase of attack (20 Nov) 163–81; second phase of attack (20 Nov) 181–207; further operations (20 Nov) 208–14; German withdrawal 216; overview of first day 214–6, 223, 226–7, 229–34, 245–6; aftermath of first day's fighting 218–22, 224–5, 235–45; advance continues (21 Nov) 217; attack on 23 Nov 223–4; subsequent operations to end of battle 227–9; German advance (Mar 1918) 234; 2nd Battle (Sep 1918) 234–5
Cambridge (Cambs) 29–30, 100, 192, 221–2, 263, 270; King's College 106; Leys School 105–6; Trinity College 112
Cambridgeshire Regiment 30–2, 34
Canada (inc. Canadian army units) 20, 50, 65, 83–4, 91, 112, 115, 241
carrier pigeons xii–xiii, 70, 72, 100, 158
Carrington, 2nd Lt Charles 73
Carstens, Fähnrich Hans 139–40
casualty figures: Battle of Somme – 36th Div 34; Third Battle of Ypres – opening 10; attack on 19 Aug 51, 55; attack on 22 Aug 81; total losses in D Bn 122, 125; Battle of Cambrai – opening 173, 214–5, 235
cavalry 11, 20, 108, 128, 143, 204–6, 213–14, 215, 217, 218, 223, 224, 230–1, 246, 257; 1st Cavalry Division 174, 204–6, 212, 224, 230; 2nd Cavalry Brigade 205; 2nd Dragoons (Royal Scots Greys) 205, 231; 4th Dragoon Guards 38, 124, 205–6; 5th Cavalry Division 205–6, 230; King Edward's Horse 206
Cemetery Alley, or Havrincourt-Riegel (France) 175, 183, 199, 219
Chapel Alley, or Kabelgraben (France) 170, 250
Charteris, Capt Evan 12–13, 160, 171
Charteris, Brig-Gen John 52, 225
Chatham (Kent) 107
Cheshunt (Herts) 252
Cheverton, Gnr Joseph 29–32, 36, 100, 158–9, 202, 221–2, 250, 263, 270, 272
Clark, 2nd Lt James 72, 251–2, 275, 277
Clarke, William 104–5
coastal landing *see under* 'Operation Hush'
Cockcroft (Belgium) 50, 55, 80–1
Coghlan, Lt John ('Jack') 39, 96, 116, 123, 215, 252, 277
Cohen, 2nd Lt Stanley 196, 254–5
Coke, Lt-Col Jacynth 17–18
Cologne (i.e. Köln, Germany) 237, 239
Cook, Lt Thomas 187, 277
Cooney, 2nd Lt Ralph 112
Cooper, Maj Richard 203, 214, 224, 258, 277
Coote, Florence and George 29–30, 32, 222, 263
Cope, Pte James 148, 264
Court, 2nd Lt Gordon 24
Cozens, Capt Frederick 8, 124, 214, 277
Craster, Capt John 117
Craufurd, Brig-Gen Sir Standish 239
Cunnington, Pte Frank 82–3

Davidson, Maj-Gen Sir John 239
Dawson, 2nd Lt Fred 161, 166, 195–6, 259

Deborah (D51) *see under* tanks
De Falbe, Maj Christian 127
De Lovie (Belgium) *see under* La Lovie
Delta House (Belgium) 94
Delysia, Alice 39, 63, 198
despatch-riders 22, 87, 99–100, 107–10, 256
Detzner, Oberlt Hermann 117–18, 120
Dimler, Frederick 36, 37
Dobinson, 2nd Lt Harold 72, 198, 275, 277
Docker, Sir Dudley 51 *see also* Metropolitan Carriage, Wagon & Finance Co. Ltd.
Dose, Musketier Wilhelm 171
Dozingham Military Cemetery (Belgium) 3, 4, 88–9
Dugdale, Capt Geoffrey 225
Dupont, Ewald 241
Dürr, Lt 67, 79

Eaucourt l'Abbaye (France) 25–7
Edwards, Capt George 194
Edwards, Lt Gerald 95, 135, 159, 161, 166, 173, 223, 277
Elles, Brig-Gen Hugh 6, 10, 11, 119–20, 141, 144, 158, 182, 216, 239, 243–4
Elson, Lt Werner 170
Enoch, Lt Alfred 23–4, 39, 63, 66, 67–9, 94, 208, 220–1, 260–1, 272, 275, 277
Erin (France) 91, 101–2, 123, 252
Ewing, Maj John 108

Fanshawe, Maj-Gen Sir Robert 70, 80
Farquharson, Maj Arthur 16
fascines 126, 134, 135, 165–6, 167, 171, 177, 184, 194
Field, Capt Christopher 188–9, 277
Flers-Courcelette, Battle of 6, 19, 22–5, 59, 134, 259 *see also* Somme, Battle of the
Flesquières (France) name xvi; plans for attack 129, 141, 143, German reinforcements 150–2, 245–6; bombardment 164, 181–2; during first phase of attack 169–70, 173, 174–5, 177; second phase of attack – western side of village xii–xiii, 182–9; eastern side of village 190–8; *Deborah*'s action in village 198–202, 206–7; further attempts to take village 208–9, 246; cavalry operations 204–6, 224, 230–1; failure to mount flanking attack 209–13, 246; withdrawal of tanks 213–14; German withdrawal 216; capture of village 217; aftermath of attack 217–20; story of 'lone gunner' 224–5, 235–40, 244, 253; controversy over 51st Division tactics 128–9, 241–4; assessments of attack 214–6, 223, 226–7, 245–6; British withdrawal to ridge (4/5 Dec 1917) 229; German recapture of village (Mar 1918) 234; British recapture of village (Sep 1918) 234–5, 247; post-war condition of village 247–9; disposal of tanks 249–50; burial of bodies 250–1, 270; post-war German visits to village 250, 253; discovery and excavation of Deborah 267–9; reunion in 2009 272–3; in present day 273–4
Flesquières Trench (France) 184, 189, 203, 208
Flixecourt (France) 30
Folkestone (Kent) 98
Foot, Gnr George 21–3, 24, 25–9, 100, 202, 220–1, 250, 270–1, 272
Fortune, Pte Thomas 187
Frahm, Vizefeldwebel 170–1
Fuller, Lt-Col John 11, 51, 82, 116, 128, 152, 215–6, 241, 243

Furminger, 2nd Lt Horace 74, 140, 229, 277
Fürsen, Hauptmann Otto 141–2, 164, 187, 212

Gallipoli (Turkey) 18, 23, 91, 148
Galway, Gnr William 32–4, 35–6, 100, 138, 202, 222, 250, 270
gas warfare 5, 31–2, 42, 50, 59, 61, 80, 81, 84, 89, 109, 153, 250, 268
Gatehouse, Maj Alexander 171–2, 193, 238–9
George V, King 105, 108
German army
  armies: Second Army 145
  infantry divisions: 26th Division 55; 54th Division 150–1, 216, 250, 276; 107th Division 150–1, 276
  infantry brigades: 51st Brigade 53–4, 55
  infantry regiments: 23rd Reserve Infantry Regiment 70–1, 81; 27th Reserve Infantry Regiment 150, 151, 152, 175, 189, 194–5, 199–200, 201, 208–9, 215, 245–6, 276; 84th Infantry Regiment 139–40, 141–2, 146, 150, 151–3, 164, 166–7, 168–71, 172, 173, 174–6, 181, 187, 191, 199–200, 202, 208–9, 212, 215, 216, 238, 245–6, 250, 276; 125th Infantry Regiment 52–5, 66–7, 81–2; 387th Landwehr Infantry Regiment 150, 151, 152, 173–4, 276
  artillery, general: 53–4, 55, 59, 123; 108th Field Artillery Regiment 151, 191–2, 235–7, 253, 276; 213th Field Artillery Regiment 150–1, 191, 201, 235, 237, 246, 276; 282nd Field Artillery Regiment 151, 189, 235, 237, 276
  pioneers: 108th Pioneer Company 201–2, 206
Gibbs, Philip 5, 22, 26–7, 194, 217–8, 226
Gibson, Capt Thomas 247–8, 249
Glaister, Gnr Jacob 25–8
Glasscock, Lt Sydney 277
Glindemann, Unteroffizier Hans 169–70
Gloucester (Gloucs) 252
Gloucestershire Regiment: 2/5th Bn 74, 84, 275; 6th Bn 65–6, 275
Gorczynski, Philippe 211, 266 74
Gordon Highlanders 94, 107, 145; 4th Bn 217; 5th Bn 160, 168, 172–3, 276; 6th Bn 130, 190, 195, 196–7, 212, 217, 244, 276; 7th Bn 183, 227, 276
Gough, Gen Sir Hubert 10, 12, 13, 42–3, 88, 90
Graincourt (France) 143, 151, 209, 212
Grand Ravine (France) 141, 143, 158, 168, 169, 172, 177, 180–2, 183–4, 190, 203, 205, 208–9, 213, 273–4
Grant, Rev Andrew 219
Great Missenden (Bucks) 21, 220–1
Gregory, Capt Ernest 166
Groom, Pte William 44
Gurney, Ivor 84

Hague Convention, the 172, 245
Haig, Gen Sir Douglas xiv, 5, 11, 22, 51, 52, 90, 95–6, 119, 140, 175, 204, 205, 215, 224–6, 230, 235–6, 239–40, 253
Haigh, Capt Richard 69
Haining, 2nd Lt William 166
Hanna, Pte George 148–9
Hardress-Lloyd, Col John 11, 116
Hargreaves, Albert (A.T.) 262
Harper, Maj-Gen George 93–4, 95, 120, 128–9, 133, 150, 209, 242–4, 257
Hastie, Lt Stuart 24, 204

Havrincourt, inc. Wood (France) 135–7, 138, 139, 142, 143, 145, 150, 151–2, 158, 159, 160, 174, 175, 184, 198, 200, 213, 214, 215, 217, 224, 228, 229, 245, 253
Hay, Ian *see under* Beith, Lt John
Head, Capt Harold 188, 199, 219, 259, 277
Heap, 2nd Lt Frank 96–112, 116, 122, 124–6, 129, 136, 140, 142, 144, 158–9, 161, 164, 198–9, 200–2, 206–7, 218, 221–2, 223, 225, 249, 254, 256, 262, 268–71, 272–3, 277
Heap, Alderman Joseph 104–5, 106
Heavy Section/Branch Machine Gun Corps (HBMGC) *see under* Tank Corps
Hegermann, Lt Bernhard xiv, 139, 153
Herzog, Sgt Émile *see under* Maurois, André
Hickey, Lt Daniel 197, 218
High Wood (France) 22, 25
Hindenburg Line, or Siegfriedstellung 141, 142, 165–8, 172, 176, 177, 217, 220, 273
Hindenburg Support trench (France) 182, 184, 189, 190, 197, 198, 203, 229
Hinkeldeyn, Lt Hermann 170
Höfer, Lt 200
Hofmeister, Maj Fritz 151, 152, 199, 200, 238, 251
Holywood (Co. Down) 33
Homfray, Capt Charles 196, 266
hospitals *see under* medical treatment and wounds
Hotblack, Capt Frederick 181, 226, 238–9, 243, 245
Howard, Lt-Col Henry 70
Huxtable, Capt the Rev Arthur 86, 87, 95

Ieper *see under* Ypres (Belgium)
India (inc. Indian army units) 20, 23, 28, 44, 74, 91, 213, 229, 264, 265
intelligence and interrogation of prisoners 8–9, 40–6, 52, 139–40, 145–8, 149–50, 174, 245–6, 263–5
Ireland and political situation 33–4, 92, 138, 146–7, 148–9, 245, 260, 263–4

Jacobsen, Vizefeldwebel August 170–1
Jagger, Lance-Cpl Ernest 67–9
Janet Farm (Belgium) 72, 95
Jenkin, Arthur 19
John, Cpl 41–3, 44, 45
Jones, 2nd Lt Richard 188, 220, 277
Judd, Pte Arthur 60–1, 62–3, 74–6, 83

Kiggell, Lt-Gen Launcelot 51
King, 2nd Lt Frederick ('Jumbo') 7, 127, 203, 277
King's (Liverpool) Regiment: 6th Bn 69
King's Own (Royal Lancaster Regiment): 1st Bn 36
King's (Shropshire Light Infantry): 6th Bn 225
Koe, 2nd Lt George 176, 187, 272, 277
Köller, Oberlt von 191–2
Koln (i.e. Cologne, Germany) 237, 239
Krebs, Maj Erich 189, 200, 216, 246
Krüger, Unteroffizier Johannes ('Theodor') 235–40, 253
Kyngdon, Lt-Col William 56, 57, 59, 70, 94, 116–21, 160, 203, 208–9, 213, 214, 226, 227, 228, 246, 260, 277

La Fontaine, Sydney 241–2
La Lovie / De Lovie (Belgium) 4, 9, 10, 11, 12–13, 40, 52, 69, 90, 98–9, 124–5

Lambert, 2nd Lt Douglas 114
Langfeldt, Lt Johannes 146, 152, 153, 169, 175
La Touche, Maj Cecil 28
Lawrie, Lt Andrew 64–5, 67–8, 73–4, 79, 275
Leamington (Warwickshire) 192
Le Havre (France) 28, 102
Lennon, John 261
Lewis, Lt David 69–71, 263, 275
Lewis gun xiii, 15, 41, 61, 68, 73, 75, 77, 94, 102, 146, 158, 189, 193–4, 197, 200, 213, 214
Lincoln and Lincolnshire 22, 102, 123, 150, 252
Lincolnshire Regiment: 6th Bn 64–5, 275
Littledale, Sgt Harold 20
Liverpool and Merseyside 36–7, 69, 104, 117, 261
London 15–16, 25–6, 39, 84, 109, 112, 114, 147, 218, 220, 237, 255, 256, 263, 270, 271; Camden 21; Knightsbridge 85; Mayfair 28; Restaurant Frascati, Oxford Street 254; Putney 113
London Regiment: 3rd Bn 147; 5th Bn 44
Londonderry (Co. Londonderry) 146, 148
'Lone hero' of Flesquières *see under* Flesquières, story of 'lone gunner'
Loos, Battle of 109–10, 112, 113–4
looting 37, 170–2, 173, 174, 182
Lytham St Anne's (Lancs) 85

Macandrew, Maj-Gen Sir Henry 205–6, 230
McBeath, Cpl Robert 174
McCauley, Pte Neil 148
Macdonald, Capt Alistair 190, 209, 217
Macdonald, 2nd Lt George 15–18, 20, 36, 56, 59, 72, 73, 84, 85, 95, 101, 252, 261, 269, 272, 275
McDonald, Lt-Col Samuel 208, 209
Macintosh, 2nd Lt James ('Tosh') 14, 18, 39, 85, 91, 94, 98, 101–2, 103, 111–12, 126–7, 129–30, 134, 136, 140–1, 144, 154–8, 159–60, 161–2, 163–4, 177, 182, 183, 185–6, 188, 189, 206, 219–20, 223–4, 254, 255–6, 259, 272, 277
Mackenzie, Lt George 44
McNiven (later MacNiven), 2nd Lt John 143, 198, 258, 277
McTaggart, Lt-Col Maxwell 160, 168, 172, 173
Machine Gun Corps (MGC) 20; 232nd Machine Gun Company 173–4, 218 *see under* Tank Corps for MGC Heavy Section/Branch; *see also* Motor Machine Gun Service
Marcoing (France) 204, 209, 236
Marris, Capt Edgar 123, 124, 135, 176, 187, 203, 229, 258, 277
Marsden, Lance-Cpl David ('Bert') 36–7, 74, 271, 272
Martel, Lt-Col Giffard 5, 81
Maurois, André (pen-name of Sgt Émile Herzog) 109–10
Maxse, Lt-Gen Sir Ivor 51, 58, 80, 81, 83, 93
Maxse, Leo 51–2
Méaulte (France) 134, 228, 229
medical treatment and wounds 16, 17, 26–8, 68–9, 73, 78, 79, 82–3, 84, 85, 88–9, 92, 95, 114, 135, 166, 169–70, 171, 176, 184, 185–6, 187, 189, 193, 198, 213, 218–19, 236, 254–5, 259, 261, 271
Messines, Battle of 5, 42
Mestwarb, Lt Adolf 166–7
Metropolitan Carriage, Wagon and Finance Co. Ltd. 51–2, 102

Metz-en-Couture (France) 138, 145, 149, 160, 163, 204–5, 215, 229
Mitchell, 2nd Lt Frank 44, 68
Möhring, Lt 201–2, 206
Monks, Lance-Cpl Henry 188
Morris, Lt David 143, 182, 183–4, 203, 277
Mory, Lt Herbert 167, 169
Motor Machine Gun Service (MMGS) 20, 36, 37
Mullens, Maj-Gen Richard 224
Müller, Lt Karl 236–7
Murat Farm (Belgium) 56–7, 59

naming of tanks 38–9
New Zealand (inc. New Zealand army units) 5, 15–16, 23, 25–6, 261, 272
Neymeyr, Lt 201
Nixon, Capt Graeme 23–4, 72, 85–6, 143, 159, 181, 198, 260–1, 275, 277
Nottingham (Notts) 35, 222, 251, 270
Nugent, Maj-Gen Oliver 34
Nugent, Capt Walter 117

O'Brien, Pte Laurence 148, 264
Öchsler, Unteroffizier Theodor 70–1
Officers Training Corps 41, 105–6, 107
Oldbury (West Midlands) 22, 102–3
Oosthoek Wood (Belgium) 4, 7–9, 13–15, 37–8, 40, 43, 44–5, 56, 59, 78, 91, 94, 125, 136, 252
'Operation Hush' 122–3, 204
Osenbrück, Lt S. 199–200, 201, 202, 216
Oxford (Oxfordshire) 15, 16, 60, 107
Oxfordshire & Buckinghamshire Light Infantry: 2/4th Bn 58, 60, 62–3, 74–6, 83, 275

Passchendaele, Battle of *see under* Ypres, Third Battle of
Pearsall, Lt Herbert 23, 277
Pennie, Lance-Cpl Willie 163, 204–5
Phillips, Sgt Samuel 40, 41–6, 77, 146, 245, 264–5
Philpotts, Cpl Frank 41
pigeons *see under* carrier pigeons
Plateau railhead (France) 133–4, 229
Plumer, Gen Hubert 90, 93
Poelcappelle / Poelkapelle (Belgium), inc. Poelcappelle road 54, 57, 58, 64–5, 87, 94, 123–4, 127, 252, 272
poison gas *see under* gas warfare
Pond Farm (Belgium) 60, 74, 76, 77, 83, 275
Poperinghe/Poperinge (Belgium) 3, 9, 13, 78, 99, 111
Portsmouth (Hants) 102
presentation tanks 251–2
Preston, Pte Alfred 85–6
prisoners-of-war *see under* intelligence and interrogation of prisoners
Purey-Cust, Maj Richard 239
Purfleet (Essex) 113
Puttock, 2nd Lt Harold 88

Quainton, 2nd Lt Ernest 127, 196
Queen Mary's Hospital, Sidcup (Kent) 254

railways 4, 7–8, 21, 22, 33, 91–2, 102–3, 113, 124, 125, 133–5, 136, 143, 150, 175, 203, 205, 213, 228, 229, 274

Dinmont (D50) 38, 72, 143, 181, 275, 277; *Daphne* (D42) 65, 252, 275, 277; *Dashing Dragoon* (D23) 38, 277; *Deborah* (D51) xiii–xiv, 8, 13–15, 19, 36, 38, 45, 52, 56, 57, 58, 59–60, 72, 73, 74, 83, 85, 92, 93, 101, 129, 135, 141, 143, 158–9, 160, 161, 164, 177, 181, 183, 190, 198–9, 200–2, 206–7, 208, 215, 218–19, 219–22, 225, 229, 234–5, 246, 248–50, 251, 255, 258, 260, 261–3, 266, 267–73, 274, 275, 277; *Demon* (D47) 72, 172, 188, 250, 271, 275, 277; *Delysia* (D43) 39, 63, 65–6, 67–9, 94, 198, 208, 266, 275, 277; *Derek* (D16) 94; *Despot* (D52) 58, 72, 275; *Destroyer* (D45) 69, 183, 185–6, 189, 219, 275, 277; *Deuce of Diamonds* (D24) 277; *Devil* (D41) 64, 65, 67–8, 79, 80, 188, 219, 220, 275, 277; *Devil-May-Care* (D6) 38, 187, 277; *Diablo* (D48) 72, 275, 277; *Diallance* (D34) 159, 161, 166, 223, 277; *Die Hard* (D11) 23; *Dinnaken* (D17) 24; *Dollar Princess* (D49) 38–9, 72, 143, 198, 275, 277; *Dolly* (D31) 277; *Dominie* (D11) 176, 187, 277; *Don Quixote* (D26) 88–9, 277; *Dop Doctor* (D32) 39, 188, 277; *Double Dee* (D27) 89, 213–14, 277; *Dracula* (D16) 25–7, 38, 59, 76; *Dracula* (D44) 64–5, 80, 94, 95, 124, 275, 277; *Dragon* (D46) 69–71, 74, 77, 88, 134–5, 251–2, 263, 275, 277; *Drake's Drum* (D28) 38, 186–7, 277; *Dreadnought* (D21) 38, 184, 277; *Drone* (D3) 177, 277; *Dryad* (D4) 176–7, 277; *Duke of Cornwall* (D2) 177, 277; *Dusky Dis* (D30) 38, 277; *Edinburgh* (E17) 190, 192; *Edward* (E40) 190, 193–4; *Egypt* 190; *Eileen* 190; *Ella* (E27) 166, 190; *Elles* (E45) 161, 166, 195–6, 259; *Emperor* (E18) 190, 192–3; *Endurance* (E10) 190; *Ernest* (E24) 190; *Ethel* 196; *Euryalus* 190, 192–3; *Ewen* 196; *Exquisite* 190, 193; *Faun* (F42) 76, 275; *Fay* (F46) 76–7, 275; *Flirt* 252; *Fray Bentos* (F41) 39, 77; *Fritz Phlattner* (F43) 39; *Gazeka* (G30) 275; *Geyser* (G21) 275; *Gorgonzola* (G29) 61; *Grasshopper* (G22) 59–60, 275; *Gridiron* (G24) 275; *Ole Bill* (119) 251; *Orestes* (O56) 247, 248
Taylor, Sgt George 189
Thesiger, Maj-Gen George 109–10
Thetford (Norfolk/Suffolk) 22, 119
Thiepval (France) 31, 33–4, 36, 138
Thomas, William Beach 52
Thompson, Lt George 118
Tipping, Gnr Frederick 35–6, 100, 202, 222, 250, 251, 270, 272
Tipping, Pte Harry 35, 36
Tolson, Lance-Cpl John 188
Travers, Ben 260
Trescault (France) 136, 147, 150, 160, 203, 204, 205, 208, 213–14, 215, 224, 273
Triangle Farm (Belgium) 50, 66, 84, 87
Tutt, Lt Arthur 206
Twigg, Pte Sydney 89
Tyne Cot Cemetery (Belgium) 79

Udet, Ernst 258
Uniacke, Lt-Col Evelyn 41
United States of America (inc. US army units) 16–17, 20, 42, 43, 69, 123, 241, 253, 259, 271; 7th Cavalry 123; 11th Engineers 134

Vanbeselaere, Johan 3–4, 272
Vancouver (Belgium) 50, 52, 54, 63, 65–7, 80, 83–4, 86, 87, 275; *see also* Staigerhaus

Vaughan, Lt Edwin 87–8, 89
Vaughan, Pte Harry 88–9
Verdun (France) 5, 153, 167, 169, 191
Vose, 2nd Lt James 18, 72, 172, 188, 258, 259, 271, 275, 277

Wailly (France) 18, 98, 100, 111–12, 123, 124, 125, 126–8, 129–30, 133, 166, 227
Wakley, 2nd Lt William 25–8
Walker, Rifleman Samuel 150
Ward, Capt Horace ('Holly') 113
Ward, Maj Robert (R.O.C.) 56, 59, 63, 65, 70, 87, 93, 99, 111–15, 116, 120–1, 126–7, 135, 142, 143, 144, 152–3, 154–8, 161–2, 164, 180–1, 192, 203, 208, 220, 224, 229, 246, 259, 269, 275, 277
Watford (Herts) 113
Watson, Maj William xiv, 4, 7, 8, 20, 37, 45, 58, 59, 69, 70, 82, 86–7, 89, 98–9, 107, 115, 116, 122, 124, 125, 127, 129, 133–4, 135, 136, 137, 158, 159, 160, 161, 164, 165, 172–3, 180, 186, 203, 205, 208, 209, 213, 214, 224, 227, 228, 229, 245, 256–7, 277
Watter, Generallt Oskar Freiherr von 150–1, 153, 236, 237
Weeks, Sgt Joshua 64–5, 79; *see also* Lawrie, Lt Andrew
Welsh Guards: 1st Bn 225
Welsh Regiment 21–2
Wenger, 2nd Lt Theodore 93, 249, 272
Wheldon, Maj Wynn 40
Whitaker, Sgt William 147, 263–4
Whitchaven (Cumbria) 27
Wille, Hauptmann Wilhelm 151–2, 153, 174, 200, 215
Williams, Lt David 205
Williams-Ellis, Capt Clough 43, 45, 52, 82, 86, 89, 141, 265, 277
Williamson, Henry xv, 67, 83–4
Wilson, 2nd Lt Thomas 193
Wimberley, Capt Douglas 173–4, 218, 272
Windsor (Berks) 105–6
Winnipeg (Belgium) 50, 52, 57, 58, 72–3, 80, 83, 87, 275
wireless communication 109, 118, 158, 160
Woods, Capt Arthur 19, 25, 27
wounded, care of *see under* medical treatment and wounds
Wray, Gnr Leslie 166
Wyatt, Capt Wilfred 203, 277

Ypres/Ieper (Belgium) 4, 5, 6, 83, 84, 125
Ypres, Third Battle of: planning and preparation 5–9; trench raid (26–27 Jul) 40–6; opening of battle (31 Jul) 9–11; attack on 16 Aug 49–50; 'Battle of the Cockcroft' (19 Aug) 50–5, 81–2, 85; attack on 22 Aug, inc. preparations and aftermath 56–86; attack on 27 Aug 86–9; reorganization 90, 93; 'Battle of Menin Road' (20 Sep) 93–6; attack on 4 Oct 122–3; attack on 9 Oct 123–4; withdrawal 124–5; summary of tank operations 122, 125
Ypres-Yser / Ieper-Ijzer Canal (Belgium) 4, 40, 41, 56
Ytres (France) 135, 149, 229

Zimmers, Gefreiter 195
Zindler, Lt Erwin 191–2, 235–7, 239, 253

Ravine Alley, or Grenzweg (France) 175
Reiffer, Gnr Roy 255
Reinsch, Feldwebel 189, 201
Ribécourt (France) 150, 174, 184, 204, 205, 267
Richter, Lt 201
Rickert, Lt Claus 171, 172
Riddell, Brig-Gen Edward 31, 32
Rifle Brigade: 12th Bn 150
Robinson, Lt Frederick 23
Robinson, Pte Walter 188, 250, 271
Rouen (France) 27, 114, 147
Rowberry, Sgt Claude 257, 259
Rowe, Lance-Cpl Frederick 147, 264
Rowe, Sgt Owen 255
Royal Army Medical Corps 165–6, 219, 259 *see also* medical treatment and wounds
Royal Artillery 5, 6, 10, 16–17, 20, 31, 36, 37, 42, 44, 53, 54, 55, 61, 62–3, 70, 74–5, 81, 108, 116–17, 128, 142, 145, 162–4, 181–2, 215, 217, 218, 220, 237, 238, 239, 260
Royal Berkshire Regiment: 2/4th Bn 74, 75, 275
Royal Dublin Fusiliers: 1st Bn 149
Royal Electrical and Mechanical Engineers: 118th Recovery Company 269
Royal Engineers 50, 56, 239: 9th Divisional Signals Company 107–10; 184th Tunnelling Company 7, 62; Railway Operating Department 135; Royal Anglesey Royal Engineers 247; *see also* despatch-riders
Royal Flying Corps 11, 17, 18, 20, 75, 110, 161, 164, 167, 175, 217
Royal Irish Fusiliers: 1st Bn 135, 138–9, 140, 145–9, 263–4
Royal Irish Rifles: 13th Bn 33–4, 138; 16th Bn 148
Royal Munster Fusiliers: 1st Bn 148
Royal Naval Armoured Cars: No. 20 Squadron 102–3
Royal Scots 107; 8th Bn 145
Royal Warwickshire Regiment: 5th Bn 58, 73, 275; 7th Bn 69–70, 275; 8th Bn 87–8, 89
Royal Welsh Fusiliers: 14th Bn 40–6, 264–5
Ryde (Isle of Wight) 251–2

St Julien/Sint-Juliaan (Belgium) 49–50, 57, 62, 65, 69, 83, 87, 94, 141
St Pol-sur-Ternoise (France) 91, 98, 115
Salonika (Greece) 30, 148
salvage and recovery of tanks 91–3, 95, 249–50, 252
Sandiford, Pte William 41
Saucke, Lt Adolf 167, 169–70
Savage, Col William 34
Schäfer, Ersatz Reservist 201
Schuler Farm and Schuler Galleries (Belgium) 58–9, 60, 72, 74, 76, 77, 82, 87, 94, 95, 275
Schwaben Redoubt (France) 31, 32, 34
Seaforth Highlanders 145, 218; 4th Bn 163, 204–5; 5th Bn 171, 174, 276; 6th Bn 190, 192, 194, 195, 208, 209, 217, 276
Second World War 53, 92, 237, 238–9, 252–3, 255, 256, 257, 258, 259, 261, 262, 264, 265, 267
Senftleben, Unteroffizier 175–6, 194–5
Shakespeare, William 38, 241, 263
Shaw, 2nd Lieut Harry 72, 275
Shaw, 2nd Lieut John 186–7, 244, 277
Sherwood, 2nd Lt Henry 67, 275

Siegfriedstellung *see under* Hindenburg Line
signalling *see under* carrier pigeons, despatch-riders, Royal Engineers, wireless communication
Sladen, Brig-Gen Gerald 70
Smith, Capt Edward Glanville 9, 12, 18, 56–7, 59, 62, 65, 67, 69, 72, 73, 85, 90–1, 93, 94, 96, 99, 101, 115, 125, 129, 130, 134, 180, 184, 188, 202, 207, 229, 254, 256, 272, 275, 277
Smith, Capt Walter 111, 180–1, 224, 259, 277
Soltau, Hauptmann Harro 139, 140, 152–3, 169–70, 174–5, 180, 250, 251, 273
Somme, Battle of the 6, 9, 10, 22–7, 31–2, 33–4, 37, 52–3, 60, 110, 114, 133, 138, 142, 199, 231, 234, 266; *see also* Flers-Courcelette, Battle of
Spreat, Capt Shirley 192
Springfield (Belgium) 50, 52, 57, 66, 69–71, 80, 86, 87–9, 275
Staiger, Lt 54, 61
Staigerhaus (Belgium) 54, 61, 65, 66–7, 69, 79 *see also* Vancouver
Stollenweg (France) 153, 168–9, 170–1, 172–3, 175, 188, 250, 273
Stubenrauch, Maj Günther 176, 199, 200
Stühmke, Oberst Reinhold 53, 67
Summers, Maj Frank 27
Symond, 2nd Lt John 99, 275
Symonds, 2nd Lt Charles 64, 65, 94, 275, 277

Talbot, Capt Frederick 38, 124, 125
Talbot, Rev Neville 159
Tank Corps 6–7, 17, 19–21, 32, 34, 43, 52, 96, 100, 122–3, 124, 136, 142–3, 161, 223, 228, 229, 245, 246; Headquarters 5, 6, 10–11, 12–13, 40, 80, 81, 82, 95, 116, 119–20, 144, 152, 171, 215–6, 226, 238–9, 243–5; 1st Tank Brigade 6, 7, 8–9, 19, 44, 51, 52, 57, 81, 86, 94, 95, 120, 125, 128–9, 130, 143, 174, 176–7, 227, 241–3, 257–8; A (1st) Tank Bn 44, 120; C (3rd) Tank Bn (originally C Company) 7, 22, 44, 57, 116, 119, 120; D (4th) Tank Bn (originally D Company) 7–8, 9, 11, 12, 18, 19, 20, 22–8, 38–9, 45, 52, 55–60, 62, 63, 64–6, 67–74, 77–80, 82–3, 85–6, 86–91, 92, 93–4, 95, 96, 98–9, 111–12, 115–16, 119–22, 123–7, 129–30, 133–7, 140–2, 143–4, 150, 154–66, 168, 172–3, 176–81, 182–9, 198–203, 206–9, 213–15, 218–22, 223–4, 225, 226–7, 228–9, 234–5, 246, 248–52, 254, 255–7, 258–63, 275–7; E (5th) Tank Bn 13, 20–1, 45, 63–4, 86, 94–5, 100, 116, 120, 127, 136, 143, 158, 161, 163, 166, 171–2, 180, 182, 183, 190–1, 192–4, 195–7, 203, 215, 218, 223–4, 225, 227, 229, 248–9, 254–5, 259, 260, 276; F (6th) Tank Bn 39, 57, 58–9, 60, 74, 76–9, 81, 263; G (7th) Tank Bn 7, 8, 12, 28, 43, 50–2, 56, 57, 58, 59, 61, 81, 120, 125, 136, 143, 276; H (8th) Tank Bn 144, 197, 218, 243, 276; 15th Tank Bn 247–8; 4th Tank Carrier Company 229; Tank Salvage (later Field) Companies *see under* salvage and recovery of tanks
tank costs 102
tank names 38–9
tank production 22, 102
tanks (NB the same names and crew numbers were sometimes used by a number of tanks in succession): *Abou-Ben-Adam* (A2) 267; *Britannia* 69; D7 23; D12 23–4; *Dakoit* (D5) 38, 277; *Damocles* (D9) 277; *Damon* (D29) 39, 123, 215, 252, 272, 277; *Dandy*